PRAISE FOR MAX I. DIMONT'S

## JEWS, GOD AND HISTORY

"Done with warmth and vitality. Written for laymen by a scholarly layman who has a passion for his theme."

—MAX LERNER

"By far the liveliest popular history of the Jewish people that I have ever read. In many ways, a strikingly original synthesis of Jewish history."

—RICHARD B. MORRIS,
author of *The Forging of the Union, 1781–1789*
and *Witnesses at the Creation*

MAX I. DIMONT, author of *The Indestructible Jews, The Jews in America, The Amazing Adventures of the Jewish People,* and *Appointment in Jerusalem,* was born in Helsinki, Finland, and came to the United States in 1930. He taught himself English by reading Shakespeare's plays, the Bible, and American plays translated into Finnish. After serving in intelligence with the U.S. Army during World War II, he worked in public relations and employee relations for Edison Brothers Stores in St. Louis. Following the first publication of the bestselling *Jews, God and History,* he lectured extensively on Jewish history throughout the United States, Canada, South Africa, Brazil, and Finland until his death in 1992.

OTHER BOOKS BY MAX I. DIMONT

*Appointment in Jerusalem*
*The Indestructible Jews*
*The Jews in America*
*The Amazing Adventures of the Jewish People*

# JEWS, GOD
## AND
# HISTORY

**2ND EDITION**

## MAX I. DIMONT

Edited and Revised by
Ethel Dimont

SIGNET CLASSICS

SIGNET CLASSICS
Published by New American Library, a division of
Penguin Group (USA) Inc., 375 Hudson Street,
New York, New York 10014, USA
Penguin Group (Canada), 90 Eglinton Avenue East, Suite 700, Toronto,
Ontario M4P 2Y3, Canada (a division of Pearson Penguin Canada Inc.)
Penguin Books Ltd., 80 Strand, London WC2R 0RL, England
Penguin Ireland, 25 St. Stephen's Green, Dublin 2,
Ireland (a division of Penguin Books Ltd.)
Penguin Group (Australia), 250 Camberwell Road, Camberwell, Victoria 3124,
Australia (a division of Pearson Australia Group Pty. Ltd.)
Penguin Books India Pvt. Ltd., 11 Community Centre, Panchsheel Park,
New Delhi - 110 017, India
Penguin Group (NZ), 67 Apollo Drive, Rosedale, North Shore 0632,
New Zealand (a division of Pearson New Zealand Ltd.)
Penguin Books (South Africa) (Pty.) Ltd., 24 Sturdee Avenue,
Rosebank, Johannesburg 2196, South Africa

Penguin Books Ltd., Registered Offices:
80 Strand, London WC2R 0RL, England

Published by Signet Classics, an imprint of New American Library, a division
of Penguin Group (USA) Inc. Second edition previously published in a Mentor mass market edition and a New American Library trade paperback
edition.

First Signet Classics Printing, June 2004
10  9  8  7

This book is respectfully dedicated to
my late father, Hyman Dimont,
a humanist in the great Talmudic tradition,
who early taught me to cherish the proverb
of Solomon: "To know wisdom and instruction;
to comprehend the words of understanding;
to receive the discipline of wisdom, justice,
and right, and equity."

# CONTENTS

PREFACE                                            xi

IT HAPPENED ONLY ONCE IN HISTORY!                   1

*A streamlined review of the four thou-
sand years and the six civilizations which
have cradled the Jewish people, examining some of the perverse factors in one of
history's most illogical survivals—that of
a nation which has proclaimed itself
God's Chosen People, and almost has the
world convinced of it.*

I: THE PORTABLE GOD                                13

*An in-depth survey of the Pagan Age,
which begins with a band of nomads
known as Hebrews, who elbow their way
into history, "invent" a monopoly God,
establish a kingdom, survive defeat, and
outlive their conquerors, only to run
headlong into the Greeks.*

   1: THE GRAND ILLUSION                      17
   2: THE RELUCTANT PROPHET                    24
   3: JUDGES, KINGS, AND USURPERS              37
   4: RELIGION IS PACKAGED                     52

II: THE AGE OF THE "APIKORSIM"                      67

*How the Jews defended themselves
against the "Apikorsim"—the Epicurean
Greeks—and their naked statues; and
how they survived military slaughter at
the hands of the Romans, who laid
Jerusalem waste and made much of Palestine off-limits to them.*

5: THE BAITED PIN-UP CULTURE   71
6: THE FIGHT THAT FAILED   81
7: ROME, CAESARISM, AND REBELLION   86
8: THE SEALED COFFIN   97
9: THE CONQUERING WORD   107
10: A NEW DEAL FOR DIASPORA   115

III: MOSES, CHRIST, AND CAESAR   123

*An unorthodox account of the establishment of the Christian "Son religion" in competition with the Jewish "Father religion," and how it challenged the might of Rome to become the creed of Europe.*

11: MESSIAH AND APOSTLE   127
12: THE CHURCH TRIUMPHANT   142

IV: THE INVISIBLE WORLD OF THE TALMUD   157

*The incredible tale of how a handful of Jews scattered among alien cultures in three continents grew into an influential "intellectual world" by virtue of the invisible power of Talmudic learning, and how that learning finally consumed itself in the ghettos of medieval Europe.*

13: THE "IVY LEAGUE" YESHIVAS   163
14: BIBLIOSCLEROSIS OF THE TALMUD   173

V: MUHAMMAD, ALLAH, AND JEHOVAH   185

*The improbable but true tale of a camel driver's establishment of a world empire in the name of Allah, wherein the Jews rose to their Golden Age of creativity, only to be plunged into a Dark Age with the eclipse of the Crescent and the ascent of the Cross.*

15: HISTORY TRAVELS TO MECCA   189

16: The Jewish Renaissance in Mufti     197
17: The Rise and Fall of the Jewish
    Protestant Revolt     204

## VI: THE PRINCE AND THE YELLOW STAR     211

*How the Jews with only a gesture—con-
version—could have saved themselves
from banishment in the ghetto, but instead
chose the yellow star of ignominy, yet became indispensable to the medieval prince
because they were the only ones who carried the torch of learning and the spirit of
enterprise in an age of darkness.*

18: Crusades, Renaissance, and
    Reformation     215
19: Concerto for Violence     239
20: The Yellow Badge of Courage     252
21: The Ghetto Capitalist     263
22: Kabala and Kinnanhorra     276

## VII: ON THE HORNS OF MODERN "ISMS"     295

*The second Jewish Exodus—from the
ghetto into a rapidly shrinking world of
freedom, where the Jews become prime
ministers, generals, merchant princes, and
the charter members in an intellectual
avant-garde that was to change the destiny
of the world and hurl new challenges to
Jewish survival reminiscent of Babylonian times.*

23: Anatomy of Emancipation     299
24: Rehearsal for Racism     323
25: Western Europe: The New
    Enlightenment     341
26: Eastern Europe: The New Humanism     356
27: United States: The New Babylon     369
28: The Brown-Shirted Christ Killers     391

29: THE WILL TO WIN: FROM ZIONISM TO THE
    STATE OF ISRAEL                                      410

VIII: CONCLUSION:
    A CULTURAL MOSAIC                                    451

*Concluding the odyssey of the Jewish
people through four thousand years of
history, venturing a historical explanation
of the remarkable survival of this people,
which is as modern and intellectually
alive today as it was four millennia ago.*

30: EXILED TO FREEDOM                                    453

APPENDIX: THE RECENT HISTORY OF
    PALESTINE/ISRAEL                                     461
BIBLIOGRAPHY                                             491
INDEX                                                    509

# PREFACE

*At the time of his death in 1992, Max Dimont was in the process of updating* Jews, God and History. *Having worked with him from the time he started thinking about writing this book in 1955, I feel he would have wanted the task finished. I have used as much of his material as possible and tried to keep faith with his ideas, concerns, and beliefs in Jews and Jewish history, but I ask the reader's understanding of what might be obvious differences in style. No one can write like Max Dimont; I certainly cannot.*

*I would also like to take this opportunity to thank Max's readers for having made* Jews, God and History *a classic in its own time, and to have done so while he was still alive to appreciate it.*

*Just as with all his other works, our daughter Gail Goldey was always there, with her sharp pencil and discerning mind, to come to my aid in completing this manuscript.*

—Ethel Dimont
1993

Most history books about Jews are written by Jews for Jews, or by scholars for scholars. But Jewish history is too fascinating, too interesting, too incredible to remain the private property of Jews and scholars. This book is a popular history of this amazing people, written without bowing to orthodoxy or pandering to anti-intellectualism. It will furnish the arguments, the data, the ideas, but the reader will have to furnish his intelligent understanding. The author is not seeking to convince anyone or change anyone's opinion. This book is designed to entertain, to inform, and to stimulate.

The real history of the Jews has not yet been written. It took Europe sixteen hundred years after the decline of Greece to realize that her literature, science, and architecture had their roots in Grecian civilization. It may take another few hundred years to establish that the spiritual, moral, ethical, and ideological roots of Western civilization are embedded in Judaism. To put it differently—the furniture in the Western world is Grecian, but the house in which Western man dwells is Jewish. This is a viewpoint which is beginning to appear more and more in the writings of both churchmen and secular scholars.

Jewish history cannot be told as the history of Jews only, because they have nearly always lived within the context of other civilizations. The destiny of the Jews has paralleled the destinies of those same civilizations, except in one important respect. Somehow the Jews managed to escape the cultural death of each of the civilizations within which they dwelled. Somehow the Jews managed to survive the death of one civilization and continue their cultural growth in another which was emerging at the time.

How did they survive?

To tell this four-thousand-year story of survival on four continents and in six major civilizations, this book makes use of a new method of viewing Jewish history. It presents the general history of each of these civilizations, analyzes Jewish events within the framework of these other cultures, and then examines those ideas, unique to the Jews, which enabled them to survive as a national group and which gave them the vitality to continue as a culture-producing society. Thus *Jewish* history becomes part of *world* history, and the reader will be able to correlate Jewish events with contemporary events.

This book attempts to portray the broad sweep of Jewish history, the grandeur and humor of the Jewish *comédie humaine*, and to present Jewish history through the eyes of a twentieth-century Western man rather than a sixteenth-century ghetto Talmudist.

Many dates in Jewish history are subject to controversy, but as long as the logic of Jewish history itself is not affected we have arbitrarily chosen one date without interrupting the flow of the narrative to debate the merits of other dates. So, for instance, we begin Jewish history with 2000 B.C., around which time Abraham is reputed to have left the city of Ur, though some scholars place this event several centuries later. We date the beginning of the Jewish sojourn and subsequent captivity in Egypt from 1600 to

1200 B.C., the beginning of the settlement of Canaan after 1200 B.C., and so on, again with the full awareness that these dates are still debated by some historians. As a rule, the dates favored are those used in *The Standard Jewish Encyclopedia*.

For the sake of clarity, we have also taken the liberty of Anglicizing the plural endings of several Hebrew, Yiddish, and German words. So, for instance, we have rendered the plural of the word *Hasid* not as *Hasidim* but as *Hasidists*, and the plural of *shtetl* not as *shtetlach* but as *shtetls*. Wherever suitable we have also presented biblical and secular interpretations of the same events to show that Jewish history remains unaffected and equally fascinating whichever viewpoint one adopts.

And now it is my pleasure to make several acknowledgments. First and foremost I wish to thank Mr. Gordon LeBert, a dedicated Episcopalian, an experienced editor, and a scholar in American and English literature, with whom I worked for many, many hours perfecting the manuscript. His fine ear for language permitted no discordant note in a sentence, his talent for organization ruled out any wrong sequence of events, and his insistence upon perfection often led me to rewrite a paragraph endlessly until the idea it contained was comprehensible on the first reading.

My next acknowledgments must go to two scholars. Dr. Julius J. Nodel, Rabbi, Shaare Emeth Temple, St. Louis, Missouri, read every chapter as it was completed, and to his impressive scholarship and unstinting help this book owes much of its strength. Dr. Jacob R. Marcus, Director of American Jewish Archives and Professor of American Jewish History, Hebrew Union College–Jewish Institute of Religion, Cincinnati, Ohio, meticulously read the manuscript through the Middle Ages and generously offered many valuable suggestions. The book gained strength not only from their many excellent suggestions, but also from their at times diametrically opposed opinions.

I wish to thank the following individuals: Professors Franklin Haimo and Laurence Iannaccone, of Washington University, St. Louis, the former for help in checking my scientific information and the latter for advice on medieval and modern history; Professor Henry G. Manne, of St. Louis University, St. Louis, for suggestions pertaining to economic theories; Professor George Kimball Plochmann, of Southern Illinois University, Carbondale, for clarifying many abstruse concepts in ancient and medieval philosophy; and the Reverend Donald Olland Fatchett, now minister of the Northmond Evangelical and Reformed Church, La Mesa, California, who read all sections pertaining to Christianity and saved me from many errors. I wish to stress, however, that the wording and views expressed in this book are mine.

I take this opportunity to show my appreciation to my wife, Ethel, for the many hours she spent reading each chapter aloud as a final test of its fluidity of language and coherence of thought, and to my daughter Gail whose history major at Radcliffe made her a valuable and perceptive critic of the manuscript. To both go my heartfelt thanks for their patient understanding of my total absorption in this book for the past five years.

I wish to express my profound respect to Joseph Gaer, Director, Jewish Heritage Foundation, a humanist and a scholar, for his and the Jewish Heritage Foundation's interest in this book, and for their sponsorship of its publication.

—M.I.D.
1962

# IT HAPPENED
# ONLY ONCE
# IN HISTORY!

*A streamlined review of the four thousand years and the six civilizations which have cradled the Jewish people, examining some of the perverse factors in one of history's most illogical survivals—that of a nation which has proclaimed itself God's Chosen People, and almost has the world convinced of it.*

There are nearly five and a half billion people on this earth, of whom less than eighteen million—less than one third of one percent—are classified as Jews. Statistically, they should hardly be heard of, like the Ainu tucked away in a corner of Asia, bystanders of history. But the Jews are heard of totally out of proportion to their small numbers. The Jewish contribution to the world's list of great names in religion, science, literature, music, finance, and philosophy is staggering.

The period of greatness of ancient Greece lasted five hundred years. Then that nation lapsed into a people of herdsmen, never again to regain its former glory. Not so with the Jews. Their creative period extends through their entire four-thousand-year history. Their contributions have been absorbed by both East and West, though neither is always aware of it or willing to admit the debt if made aware of it.

From this people sprang Jesus Christ, acclaimed Son of God by more than 850 million Christians, the largest religious body in the world. From this people came Paul, organizer of the Christian Church. The religion of the Jews influenced the Muhammadan faith, second-largest religious organization in the world, with over 400 million adherents claiming descent from Abraham and Ishmael. The Mormons say they are the descendants of the tribes of Israel.

Another Jew is venerated by more than one billion people. He is Karl Marx, whose book *Das Kapital* is the secular gospel of Communists the world over, with Marx himself enshrined in Russia and China. Albert Einstein, the Jewish mathematician, ushered in the atomic age and opened a path to the moon with his theoretical physics. A Jewish psychiatrist, Sigmund Freud, lifted the lid of man's mind. His discovery of psychoanalysis revolutionized

3

man's concept of himself and the relation of mind to matter. Three hundred years earlier, a Jewish philosopher, Baruch Spinoza, pried philosophy loose from mysticism, opening a path to rationalism and modern science.

Through the ages, the Jews successively introduced such concepts as prayer, church, redemption, universal education, charity—and did so hundreds of years before the rest of the world was ready to accept them. And yet, up until 1948, for close to three thousand years, the Jews did not even have a country of their own. They dwelt among the Babylonians, lived in the Hellenic world, stood at the bier of the Roman Empire, flourished in the Muhammadan civilization, emerged from a twelve-hundred-year darkness known as the Middle Ages, and rose to new intellectual heights in modern times.

Great nations of the pagan era which appeared at the same time the Jews did have totally disappeared. The Babylonians, the Persians, the Phoenicians, the Hittites, the Philistines—all have vanished from the face of the earth, after once having been great and mighty powers. The Chinese, Hindu, and Egyptian peoples are the only ones living today who are as old as the Jewish people. But these three civilizations had only *one* main cultural period, and their impact on succeeding civilizations has not been great. They contained neither the seeds for their own rebirth nor the seeds for the birth of other civilizations. Unlike the Jews, they were not driven out of their countries, nor did they face the problem of survival in alien lands. The Greeks and the Romans are the only other nations which have influenced the history of Western man as profoundly as the Jews. But the people who now dwell in Greece and Italy are not the same as those who dwelt in ancient Hellas and Rome.

Thus, there are three elements in Jewish survival which make the history of this people different from that of all other people. They have had a continuous living history for four thousand years and have been an intellectual and spiritual force for three thousand years. They survived three thousand years without a country of their own, yet preserved their ethnic identity among alien cultures. They have expressed their ideas not only in their own language, but in practically all the major languages of the world.

Little is generally known of the extent of Jewish writings in every field of human thought. The reason for this is not hard to find. To read French, German, or English literature or science one needs only to know French, German, or English. To read Jewish literature and science one has to know not only Hebrew and Yiddish, but also Aramaic, Arabic, Latin, Greek, and virtually every modern European language.

All civilizations we know about have left a record of their history in material things. We know them through tablets or ruins dug up by archaeologists. But we know of the Jews in ancient times mostly from the ideas they taught and the impact which these ideas had upon other people and other civilizations. There are few Jewish tablets to tell of battles and few Jewish ruins to tell of former splendor. The paradox is that those people who left only monuments behind as a record of their existence have vanished with time, whereas the Jews, who left ideas, have survived.

World history has hurled six challenges at the Jews, each a threat to their very survival. The Jews rose to each challenge and lived to meet the next.

The pagan world was the first challenge to Jewish survival. The Jews were a small band of nomads, stage extras among such mighty nations as Babylonia, Assyria, Phoenicia, Egypt, Persia. How did they manage to survive as a cultural group during this seventeen-hundred-year span of their history, when all these great nations clashed and annihilated one another? During this period the Jews came perilously close to disappearing. What saved them were the ideas with which they responded to each of the dangers encountered.

Having survived seventeen hundred years of wandering, enslavement, decimation in battle, and exile, the Jews returned to their homeland only to run into the Greco-Roman period of their history. This was their second challenge, and it was a miracle that the Jews emerged from it at all. Everything Hellas touched during those magic years of her greatness became Hellenized, including her conquerors, the Romans. Greek religion, art, and literature; Roman legions, law, and government—all left an indelible stamp on the entire civilized world. But when the Roman legions were defeated, this culture collapsed and died. The nations which were subjugated first by Greece and then by Rome disappeared. New nations took their place by force of arms. The Jews, however, remained, not by the might of their arms but by the might of their cohesive ideas.

The third challenge to the Jews came about through a phenomenon which is unique and unparalleled in history. Two Judaisms had been created, one in Palestine, the other in *Diaspora*, a word from the Greek meaning a "scattering," or "scatter about," and signifying that body of Jews scattered about in the gentile world outside Palestine. From the time of the expulsion of the Jews from Jerusalem by the Babylonians in the sixth century B.C. to the time of the liberation of the Jews from the ghettos in the nineteenth century A.D. was the era of the fragmentation of the Jewish people into small groupings, dispersed over tremendous land areas and among the most divergent cultures. How could the Jews be kept from assimilation and absorption into the sea of alien people around them?

The Jews met this challenge with the creation of a religious-legal code—the Talmud—which served as a unifying force and a spiritual rallying point. This was the "Talmudic Age" in Jewish history, when the Talmud almost invisibly ruled the Jews for close to fifteen hundred years.

In the seventh century, Judaism gave birth to yet another religion—Islam, founded by Muhammad—and this was its fourth challenge. Within a hundred years the Muhammadan Empire rose to challenge Western civilization. Yet, within this religion, whose adherents hated Christianity with an unrelenting hatred, the Jews not only survived but rose to one of their greatest literary, scientific, and intellectual peaks. The Jew in this age became statesman, philosopher, physician, scientist, tradesman, and cosmopolitan capitalist. Arabic became his mother tongue. This era also saw the philandering Jew. He not only wrote on religion and philosophy, but also rhapsodized about love. Seven hundred years passed and the pendulum swung. The Islamic world crumbled and the Jewish culture in the Islamic world crumbled with it.

The fifth challenge was the Middle Ages, and this period was a dark one for both Jew and Western man. It was a twelve-hundred-year fight by the Jews against extinction. All non-Christian nations which were defeated in the name of the Cross were converted to the Cross, except the Jews. Yet the Jews emerged from this twelve-hundred-year dark age spiritually and culturally alive. The ideas their great men had given them had been tested and found workable. When the walls of the ghetto fell, it did not take the Jews more than one generation to become part of the warp and woof of Western civilization. Within one generation, and within the shadow of the ghetto, they became prime ministers, captains of industry, military leaders, and charter members in an intellectual avant-garde which was to reshape the thinking of Europe.

The sixth challenge is the Modern Age itself. The appearance of nationalism, industrialism, communism, and fascism in the nineteenth and twentieth centuries has held special challenges for the Jews, in addition to a new, virulent disease of the Western mind—anti-Semitism. New responses for survival have had to be forged to meet these new challenges. Whether these responses will be adequate, only the future will tell.

We see, then, that Jewish history unfolds not within one but within six civilizations. This contradicts many schools of history, which hold that this is an impossibility since, like a human being, a civilization has only one life span, usually lasting five hundred years, but no longer than a thousand years. Yet, as we have seen, the Jews have lasted four thousand years, have had six cultures in six alien civilizations, and most likely will have a seventh. How can we reconcile fact and theory?

There are eight basic ways of viewing history, each from a different vantage point. Generally, a historian selects a face of history to his liking, thus stressing the viewpoint which seems best to him. We will make use of all of these faces of history except the first one, the "unhistoric" or "Henry Ford" way. It was Ford who once declared that "history is bunk," and that if he wanted to know anything he could always hire a professor who would tell him. This view sees all events as unrelated occurrences, a mishmash of dates, names, and battles, from which nothing can be learned or divined.

The second way of looking at history might be termed the "political interpretation." Here, history is looked upon as a succession of dynasties, laws, battles. Kings are strong or weak, wars won or lost, laws good or bad, and all events are presented in neat order from A to Z, from 2000 B.C. to 2000 A.D. This, as a rule, is the type of history taught in schools.

A third face is the geographic one. According to this school, climate and soil determine formation of character. This idea originated with the Greeks. Even today there are many who contend that the only scientific way to explain man's social institutions is to study his physical environment, such as topography, soil, climate. This is a rather difficult theory to apply to the Jews. They have lived in practically every climate, yet managed to retain a common ethnic identity and culture. This is evident in Israel today, where Jewish exiles from all over the world—Arabia, North Africa, Europe, America—within a short time were fused into one people. It cannot be denied, though, that geographic factors have changed or modified many traits and behavior patterns of the Jews.

The fourth way to interpret history is an economic one. This is the Marxian school. It says that history is determined by the way goods are produced. Let us suppose, says the Marxist, that the economy of a feudal system is being changed to capitalism. This new capitalistic mode of production, says the Marxist, will change that country's social institutions—its religion, ethics, morals, and values—in order to justify and sanctify and institutionalize the new way of economic life. In the same way, if a capitalist country were transformed into a communist society, it would automatically begin to change its cultural and social institutions to conform with the new way of producing things until the new way of life became part of everyday behavior.

The fifth is an even newer concept than the economic interpretation of history. Founded by Professor Sigmund Freud at the beginning of the twentieth century, this school holds that social institutions and human history are the result of a process of repressing unconscious hostilities. Civilization, says the psychoanalytic historian, can be obtained only at the price of giving up the lusts that lurk in our unconscious—unbridled sexual gratification, murder, incest, sadism, violence. Only when man has mastered his impulses can he turn his energies into creative, civilizing channels. Which impulses man represses, how severely he represses them, and what methods he uses for this repression will determine his culture and his art forms, says the psychoanalyst.

The sixth face is the philosophical one. Its three most famous followers are the German philosopher Georg Wilhelm Friedrich Hegel, the Prussian philosopher-historian Oswald Spengler, and the British historian Arnold Toynbee. Though these three philosophical interpreters of history differ widely, they have this in common: They see history not as a series of isolated happenings, but as a flow of events having continuity. Each civilization, they hold, follows a more or less predictable pattern. They think of each civilization as a living thing, which, like a human being, has an infancy, childhood, adolescence, maturity, old age, and finally death. How long a civilization lasts, they say, depends upon the ideas and ideals by which that civilization lives. The philosophical interpreters of history try to discover these forces within all civilizations in order to find their common element.

In Spengler's view, civilizations are foredoomed to death. Civilizations go through the spring of early origins, mature into the summer of their greatest physical achievement, grow into the autumn of great intellectual heights, decline into the winter of their civilization, and finally die. Writing in 1918, when England was at the height of her prestige, and Russia and China but fifth-rate powers, Spengler predicted in his book *The Decline of the West* that Western civilization was in the winter of its cycle and would die by the twenty-third century, to be superseded either by a Slavic civilization (Russia) or by a Sinic one (China), which were in the spring of their development. This way of viewing history is known as "cyclic," because each civilization has its own beginning, middle, and end.

In contrast to the cyclic view, we have Toynbee's "linear" concept, as expressed in his *Study of History*. Toynbee holds that a civilization is not an independent totality but a progression—an evolution—from lower to higher forms. So, for instance, in his view the Islamic civilization was derived from lower Iranic and Arabic cultures, which in turn were given birth by something he calls "Syriac society." Thus, the Islamic civilization need not have died, Toynbee holds, but could have evolved into an even higher culture had it responded properly to the challenges hurled at it in the thirteenth and fourteenth centuries. In the Toynbee philosophy, civilizations can go on eternally if they continue to meet new challenges with the right responses.

Since the history of the Jews did not fit into either Spengler's or Toynbee's system, Spengler ignored it and Toynbee reduced it to an occasional footnote, describing the Jews as fossils of history. Yet, if both Spengler and Toynbee had been less blinded by prejudice and misconceptions about Jewish history, they could well have fitted it within the framework of their philosophies. In this book, we shall use their theories to explain this seemingly "impossible" Jewish survival.

The "cult of personality" is the seventh face of history. Proponents of this school hold that events are motivated by the dynamic force of great men. If not for Washington, they say, there would have been no American Revolution; if not for Robespierre, there would have been no French Revolution; if not for Lenin, there would have been no Russian Revolution. Men create the events, claim these historians, in contrast to the economic interpreters who insist on the exact opposite, that events create the men.

The eighth face of history, the religious, is both the oldest and newest concept. The Bible is the best example of this type of historical writing in the past. This way of viewing history looks upon events as a struggle between good and evil, between morality and immorality. Most Jewish history, until recent times, has been written from this viewpoint.

The religious way of writing history has become discredited in modern times. But it has been resurrected by a new *genre* of writers known as "existential theologians," such as the Roman Catholic Jacques Maritain, the Russian Orthodox Catholic Nikolai Berdyaev, the Protestant Paul Tillich, and the Jewish Martin Buber. In essence, these existential theologians hold that though God may not interfere directly in the shaping of history, it is the relationship which man thinks exists between him and God that does shape history. We are so obsessed today by the notion that only "scientific facts" have validity, we are inclined to forget that people holding "unscientific," unprovable ideas may determine the course of history more often than do rational facts.

This is especially true in the case of the Jews. Martin Buber holds that the central theme running through their history is the relation between the Jew and his God, Jehovah. In the Jewish religious view of history, God has given man freedom of action. Man, as conceived by the Jewish existentialists, has the power to turn to God or away from God. He can act either for God or against God. What happens between God and man is history. In the Jewish way of looking at things, success in an undertaking, for instance, is not viewed as blessed by God. A man may arrive at power because he was unscrupulous, not because God aided him. This leaves God free to hold man accountable for his actions—both successes and failures.

This man-God relationship was responsible for the great gulf in thinking which began to separate the Jews from the rest of the pagan world four thousand years ago. The pagan idea of god tied man to his gods. The Jewish concept of man's relation to God freed the Jews for independent action. Western man, in fact, did not arrive at this idea of religious freedom until the Reformation, when Martin Luther rejected the Papacy and changed the man-God relationship to one approximating that of the Jews. Luther then invited the Jews to join Protestantism, because he believed there now was no gulf between Judaism and Christianity.* There is not a single "concrete fact" in this series of events, only men holding "unscientific ideas"; yet we can see how decisive were these unprovable ideas for the course of world history.

The circle is complete. Beginning with God as the Creator of history, man invented other explanations—an anarchic one viewing history as a series of blind events, a philosophic one looking at history as a series of purposive events, an economic one holding productive methods as a determinant force, a psychological one giving priority to unconscious drives, a "great man" theory hewing to the

---

*For an analysis of the meaning of man's freedom from God and self-accountability, the interested reader is referred to Erich Fromm's *Escape from Freedom.*

idea of man himself as the creator of his historic destiny, and, finally, back to God at the helm.

In this book we shall view Jewish history from all vantage points, without stopping to debate the merits or demerits of theological disputes. Whether true or not, men have always believed in "unscientific concepts," and these beliefs often are the real "facts" which shape their destiny. This author holds with the psychoanalytic, philosophical, and existentialist interpreters of history, that ideas motivate man and that it is these ideas which create history. A society without ideas has no history. It merely exists.

# 1

# THE PORTABLE GOD

*An in-depth survey of the Pagan Age, which begins with a band of nomads known as Hebrews, who elbow their way into history, "invent" a monopoly God, establish a kingdom, survive defeat, and outlive their conquerors, only to run headlong into the Greeks.*

# THE PAGAN PERIOD
## 2000 B.C. TO 300 B.C.

| PAGAN HISTORY | | JEWISH HISTORY |
| --- | --- | --- |
| Civilization of Susa and Kish. Pre-Dynastic period of Egypt. | 4500 B.C. | |
| Civilization in Sumeria. | 3600 | |
| First Dynasty in Egypt. | 3500 | |
| Sargon unites Sumeria and Akkadia. | 2800 | |
| Middle Kingdom in Egypt. | 2400 | |
| | | *The Period of Wanderings:* 2000 B.C. to 1200 B.C. |
| Hammurabi establishes Babylonian Empire (Chaldea). Egyptian Empire extended. Rise of Assyria. Hyksos invade Egypt. | 2000 to 1200 | Abraham and Sarah leave Ur in Chaldea (Babylonia). Age of the Patriarchs. Wandering in the land of Canaan. Joseph takes the Jews to Egypt. Pharaohs enslave them. |

| | | |
|---|---|---|
| Egyptian supremacy challenged. Internal revolts and civil wars in Egypt. | 1200 B.C. to 1100 | Moses leads the Jews out of Egypt. Wanderings in the Sinai Desert. Jews conquer Canaanites in Palestine. |
| | | *Independence Period:* 1200 B.C. to 900 B.C. |
| Tiglath-Pileser I extends Assyrian Empire. | 1100 to 1000 | Age of Judges. |
| Syria and Phoenicia become great powers. | 1000 to 900 | Saul becomes first king of Jews. Reign of King David. |
| Upheavals in Egypt. Reign of foreign dynasties. | 900 to 800 | Reign of King Solomon. Breakup of Palestine into the kingdoms of Judah and Israel. |
| | | *Assyrian and Babylonian Dominations:* 800 B.C. to 500 B.C. |
| Tiglath-Pileser III ascends throne of Assyria. Takes Damascus and Samaria, capital of Israel. | 800 to 700 | Israel conquered by Assyrians; its people taken captive and dispersed. End of Israelites. |
| Disintegration of Assyrian Empire. Conquest by resurgent Babylonia. | 700 to 600 | Josiah, King of Judah. Restoration of the "Law." |

| | | |
|---|---|---|
| Nebuchadrezzar, King of Babylonia, invades Judah. | 600 B.C. to 500 | The kingdom of Judah falls. Jews deported to Babylonia. Destruction of Jerusalem. |

(The sixth century B.C. heralded the end of Semitic empires and cultures. Now began the age of Indo-European civilizations.)

| | | *Persian Domination:* 500 B.C. to 300 B.C. |
|---|---|---|
| Cyrus, King of Persia, defeats the Babylonians, establishes Persian supremacy. | 500 to 400 | First return of Jews from Babylonia to Palestine. Temple rebuilt. |
| Cambyses, Emperor of Persia, defeats Egypt. | 400 to 334 | Second return of Jews from Babylon under Ezra. |
| Alexander the Great of Greece defeats Persians at Granicus; becomes master of Middle East. Annexes Palestine. | 334 to 322 | Jews come under Grecian influence. First contact with the West. Greco-Roman period begins. |

# THE GRAND ILLUSION

The Jews elbowed their way into history late and inconspicuously. They went through no Stone or Bronze Age.
They had no Iron Age. For the first eight hundred years of
their existence they wandered in and out of the great civilizations surrounding them. They had no buildings, no
cities, no armies, and possessed, in fact, no weapons. All
they carried with them were their ideas, which eventually
conquered the world without making them its masters.

Jewish history dates from the day, four thousand years
ago, when a man named Abraham had an encounter with
God, known to him as Jehovah. The dialogue between Jew
and God begins then. This continuing dialogue is the history of the Jews, with the rest of the world as interested
eavesdroppers.

But before we start the history of the Jews in the Pagan
Age—during which time they were passed like concubines
from the Egyptians to the Assyrians to the Babylonians to
the Persians to the Greeks to the Romans—let us briefly
review what happened in history prior to their entrance
upon the scene.

The first signs of civilization, with all the classical symptoms—cities, agriculture, the calendar, refinement of
weapons, armies, and taxes—began cropping up about
4500 B.C. History gave birth to two civilizations at the same
time, both Semitic, one to the northeast of Palestine, the
other to the southwest of it. It took twenty-five hundred
years before these civilizations—Mesopotamian and
Egyptian—found out about each other. After that, the
fight was on, with Palestine paying the price for being a
buffer state.

Civilization in Mesopotamia, now part of modern Iraq,
began with city-states. The oldest and most prominent
were Susa, Kish, and Ur. It was around these cities that the
first empires were formed. Just where they were located

can be more easily visualized if we draw an east-west line through the middle of Mesopotamia. The northern part became Assyria, and the southern part, Babylonia. Now, imagine Babylonia also divided in half. The upper part was the former kingdom of Akkad, and the lower part the kingdom of Sumeria, the first two empire civilizations.

In the third millennium B.C. there arose in Akkad a great Semitic king by the name of Sargon I, who conquered the Sumerians and formed the Sumerian-Akkadian kingdom. The people in this kingdom had a high standard of living and a highly developed culture. They also had a powerful tool which transformed this Asiatic civilization from an agricultural economy to one of commerce and industry. This tool was cuneiform writing (from the Latin *cuneus*, meaning "wedge," descriptive of the shape of the characters), a great improvement over the Egyptian hieroglyphics.

It remained for a king and lawgiver named Hammurabi to unite, around 2100 B.C., all city-states in this area into one vast Babylonian Empire. Hammurabi was the Moses of the Babylonians, giving them their code of law as a present from heaven, much as Moses was to give his code of law to the Israelites at Mount Sinai one thousand years later.

During these twenty-five hundred years, while the peoples in these civilizations built cities, enriched themselves with plunder, enjoyed their mistresses, wrote laws, drank wine, and dreamed of world conquest, the Jews were nonexistent. Then, about the year 2000 B.C., when a new and restless Semitic tribe, the Assyrians, lean and hungry, began to challenge the soft and rich life of the Babylonians, a man named Terah took his son Abraham, Abraham's wife, Sarah, and his grandson Lot, the nephew of Abraham, and emigrated from the cosmopolitan city of Ur in Babylonia.

Who were they—Terah, Abraham, Sarah, Lot? History does not know and the Bible does not identify them beyond tracing Terah's genealogy to Shem, one of the three sons of Noah. Was Terah a Babylonian? What language did he speak? What was his occupation? Certainly not a sheepherder, living as he did in one of the most sophisticated cities of that age.

All these are questions the Bible leaves unanswered.

But by the act of crossing the River Euphrates, Terah and his family group become the first people in the Bible identified as *Ivriim*, of which the English version is "Hebrews," the people "who crossed over," the people "from the other side of the river."

The wanderings of Terah and his small group took them six hundred miles northwest from Ur to the land of Haran, in the southern part of what is now Turkey. Here Terah, who had left Ur at no one's prompting, dies. Here Abraham has a strange experience. It is here that he meets the Lord God "Jehovah"* for the first time. It was a meeting comparable to the later famous encounter of Paul with the vision of Christ on the road to Damascus. Abraham's experience was as portentous to the Jews as Paul's was to the Christians.

At this encounter between Abraham and God, it is God who proposes a covenant to the patriarch, who is now seventy-five years old. If Abraham will follow the commandments of God, then He, in His turn, will make the descendants of Abraham His Chosen People and place them under His protection. We must note here that God does not say that they shall be better—merely that they shall exist as a separate and distinct entity and be His people. How this is to be brought about is not revealed. God at this time stipulates only one commandment, and makes only one promise. The commandment is that all males of His Chosen People must be circumcised on the eighth day after birth, or, if converted into the faith, then circumcised upon conversion. The promise is the land of Canaan.

Did this really happen? Views vary all the way from the

---

*In the Old Testament, God is referred to in three ways: as "Elohim," which is translated as "God"; as "JHVH," which is translated as "Lord"; and as "JHVH Elohim," which is translated as "Lord God." The Orthodox Jew never pronounces the name "JHVH" though it occurs nearly 7,000 times in the Bible. When he comes to that word, he pronounces it "Adonai," meaning "my Lord." Hence the translation of "JHVH" as "Lord." No one knows how the name was pronounced originally, as its utterance was already forbidden by the second century B.C. and the Hebrew vowel points were not invented until several centuries later. Purists make no attempt at reconstruction, and simply write "JHVH" or "YHVH," as j is pronounced like a y in Hebrew. Other scholars render it as "Jahveh" or "Yahveh," but the most popular transliteration still is "Jehovah."

fundamentalist position of a literal acceptance of every word to the rejection of every word by the skeptics. We say it could have happened, but in a slightly different way. If we view this encounter through the lens of modern psychoanalysis, it might become understandable in modern terms.

Psychiatrists are familiar with a psychological phenomenon known as "projection." Let us say that an individual is obsessed by a thought, which, because it is painful or forbidden, he does not want to acknowledge as his own. On the other hand, he can't give it up. He wants the thought, but doesn't want to be its owner. He longs for it unconsciously, but wants to reject it on a conscious level. His mind therefore resorts to an unconscious "trick." He "projects" the thought onto someone else, and then convinces himself that it is the other person who suggested the thought to him or accused him of it. These methods of hearing or perceiving such projected messages are known as auditory or visual hallucinations—that is, hearing voices, or seeing things, that are not there.

People who have such hallucinations are not necessarily neurotic or psychotic. They can be very intense or inspired people. From a psychoanalytic viewpoint, therefore, it could be that Abraham himself conceived the idea of a covenant with an Almighty Father figure, represented as Jehovah, and projected onto this father figure his own wish to safeguard his children and his children's children for future generations.

From a historical viewpoint, it makes no difference whether it was Abraham who projected this experience onto an imaginary Jehovah or a real Jehovah who proposed it to Abraham. The fact remains that after four thousand years the idea of a covenant between the Jews and Jehovah is still alive and mentioned daily in prayers in synagogues throughout the world. Though many aspects of Jews and Judaism have been changed or modified during their subsequent four-thousand-year history, this idea of a covenant with God has remained constant. This in turn gave rise to a *will to survive as Jews*, which has been the driving force in Judaism. Without it there can be no Judaism and no Jews. When this concept disappears, when the Jew, through a lack of this inner compulsion, no longer wishes to retain his identity as a Jew, then nothing will stand between him and assimilation, between him and his final disappearance. The methods whereby this wish has been perpetuated have changed through the ages, but the aim has not. Jewish history is a succession of ideas designed to perpetuate this aim.

"How goodly are your tents, O Jacob, and your dwellings, O Israel," exults a pagan priest in the Book of Numbers. This, of course, is poetic license, for nomadic life breeds neither art nor culture. For four hundred years Abraham and his descendants wandered about as nomads in the land of Canaan, without a country of their own or a stable form of government. They practiced their rite of circumcision and, though they were often esteemed by their neighbors, they were equally often regarded as a most strange people, perhaps even a little crazy, worshiping a God one could not see.

The Decalogue (the Ten Commandments of Moses) with its prohibition against other gods did not come into being until four hundred years after this nomadic period. The Book of Genesis abounds with examples of idols being part of the household goods of the patriarchs. Three things, however, kept the Jews together during the first four centuries of their existence: the ideas which Abraham had conceived (or, if one prefers, the ideas which had been vouchsafed to him—namely, that the Jews had the one and only exclusive God); the rite of circumcision; and the prohibition of human sacrifice (as so movingly told in the story of the binding of Isaac). Once the Jews accepted the idea of monotheism (the doctrine that there is only one God), they began to behave in a special way without consciously knowing they were doing so. This change in behavior was at first imperceptible, but became ever more noticeable, setting them farther and farther apart from others.

Because one has to treat an invisible god differently than a visible one, the Jews developed a ritual distinctly different from that of the surrounding pagans. Because Jehovah is immortal He never dies, and because He never dies He never has to be resurrected. Thus the Jews dispensed with the resurrection rites of the pagans. Because there is but one God, there can be no mythological wars between gods, and thus the Jews dispensed with the entire pagan hierarchy of gods and the wars between them. Because Jehovah is motivated by spirituality, He never indulges in sex life. Thus the Jews did away with all fertility rites.

The example set by Jehovah—that of being completely withdrawn from sexuality—led to a curbing of licentious impulses through an inner discipline by the Jews, rather than through fear of laws. Compare the path sexuality took in Jewish life with the path it took in Grecian civilization. The Greek gods themselves set the pattern for the unbridled lust and perversion which finally weakened the moral fiber of that people; whereas the Jews, even when they later came in contact with the Greeks, refused to indulge in the Grecian sexual excesses. The Jews also avoided the path of total sexual abstinence later taken by the early Christian Church. They steered a course between sexual excess and continence, following to the letter the Lord's commandment to have many children. In their zeal to follow this injunction literally, it is understandable if some erred a little on the side of liberality. Many a pagan mistress, disguised as a "handmaiden," dwelt in the tents of the lusty patriarchs who "begat" progeny in abundance at an age when modern man settles down to collect his Social Security.

The nomadic life agreed with the patriarchs, for all, according to the Bible, lived over a hundred years. By the time Abraham begat Isaac, and Isaac begat Jacob, and Jacob begat his twelve sons, including Joseph, four hundred years of Jewish history had slipped by. Then a famine swept the lands northeast of Egypt, and the hungry people of many lands, including the Hebrews, drifted toward the fertile Nile delta, toward Egypt, in search of food. History records that they were warmly welcomed by Egypt.

It was under the leadership of Joseph that the famine-stricken Hebrews emigrated from Canaan to Egypt. The Book of Genesis tells us the fascinating story of how Joseph was sold by his brothers into slavery in Egypt. Here he became a favorite of Pharaoh, rose to viceroy, and with Pharaoh's permission invited his brothers and fellow Hebrews to settle there. Here they tended their flocks peaceably until a new Pharaoh arose in the land who was not so kindly disposed to them and enslaved them. Except for the Bible, no source we know of makes any specific mention of this Jewish sojourn and subsequent captivity in Egypt, but the busy spade of the archaeologist has turned up convincing corollary evidence that these events did take place.

From the ingathering of the Jews into Egypt by Joseph in the sixteenth century B.C. until the outgathering of the Jews from Egypt under Moses, in the twelfth century, there is a four-hundred-year silence. The Bible compresses these fateful four centuries into a few sentences. This silence raises many perplexing questions. What portion of this period did the Jews in Egypt live in freedom and what portion in slavery? What religion did they practice? What language did they speak? Was there intermarriage? How did they maintain their Judaism as slaves? Who were their leaders until the advent of Moses? No one knows.

Not all the Jews left Canaan to go into Egypt with Joseph. Many remained behind, surviving the famine and keeping their covenant with Jehovah. This remnant of Jews, still known as Hebrews, remained free men, while their brothers were enslaved in Egypt. Is this enslavement of the Jews in Egypt the fulfillment of a prophecy made by Jehovah to Abraham four centuries earlier? For it is written in Genesis (15:13–14), "Know of a surety that thy seed shall be a stranger in a land that is not theirs, and shall serve them; and they shall afflict them four hundred years; and also that nation, whom they shall serve, will I judge; and afterward shall they come out with great substance." Or is this prophecy an interpolation by later authors, who write with the hindsight of history of the great fusion to take place in Canaan when Moses leads the Israelites, as they are now called, out of Egypt into the land of Canaan, to reunite them with the remnants of Hebrews who had stayed behind?

Meanwhile the Jews—Hebrews or Israelites—are slaves in Egypt. What will happen to Abraham's grand illusion that his seed will inherit the earth? Was it all a delusion? Or was it a prophecy to be taken up by other men appointed by God and fulfilled at a later date?

# THE RELUCTANT PROPHET

Who were the friendly Egyptians who extended to Joseph and his brothers and the members of his tribe such hospitality? The archaeologist's spade fortunately has told us much about this fascinating people and their early civilization. Historians have divided Egypt's early history into thirty dynasties and then grouped these dynasties into periods. These are the Pre-Dynastic Period (4500 to 3500), the Old Kingdom (3500 to 2400), the Middle Kingdom (2400 to 1600), and the Empire Period (1600 to 1100).

In the Pre-Dynastic days, the Lower and Upper Egyptian kingdoms were united, hieroglyphics were developed, the calendar was invented, and the first writing paper (papyrus) was manufactured. During the Old Kingdom, graphic art reached its highest forms and the building of the first pyramids was begun. This also was the era of navigation, and Egypt became a sea power. The time of the Middle Kingdom was the classical age of literature in Egypt. It saw the introduction of new architecture and new art forms. The Empire Period ushered in an era of great prosperity, and it was at this time that Egypt pushed her frontiers toward Palestine and beyond, beginning her power struggle with Assyria and Babylonia. This period was also of the greatest importance to the Jews. It was at the beginning of the Empire Period that they entered Egypt at the invitation of Joseph, the Egyptianized viceroy, and it was toward the end of this period that they left Egypt at the command of Moses, the Egyptianized prince.

Why had the Egyptians been so friendly toward them in one century and then enslaved them in another? Again the archaeologists may have uncovered the answer to the riddle. In the early sixteenth century B.C., unidentified Asiatic tribes known as Hyksos, probably Semitic, conquered Egypt. They established themselves as that country's rulers, founded a new dynasty, and built a new capital,

Avaris, near the Palestinian border. It was the Hyksos Pharaoh who had invited the Jews and other peoples hard hit by the famine to settle in Egypt. A century and a half later, the tide of history turned. The Egyptians overthrew their Hyksos masters and enslaved them as well as the peoples they had invited into the country. Ramses II, one of the new Egyptian Pharaohs, did indeed, as the Bible tells us, set about rebuilding Avaris into a new capital which, with due modesty, he named Ramses. The work was done by slave battalions consisting of Hyksos and the other non-Egyptians who lived in the country. There is little reason to doubt that the Jews were among them. Everything dug up thus far by archaeologists has substantiated biblical accounts, though historians are far from sure of the actual chronology.

How many years the Jews were slaves in Egypt is hard to tell. We know of no attempt on their part to fight for their own freedom or of any liberator appearing to free them, until the arrival of Moses, who is the greatest yet the most paradoxical figure in Jewish history. Though Moses is to Judaism what Jesus is to Christianity, the Jews have built no holidays around events in his life as the Christians have with the life of Jesus. The Gospels are based on the sayings of Jesus but there is not a single quotable "quote" in the Five Books of Moses which can be attributed to Moses. Though he was the liberator who led the Jews out of bondage in Egypt, his name is mentioned only once, *en passant*, in the Haggadah, the narrative recited by Jews every Passover in memory of this Exodus. The Ten Commandments of Moses are the pillars upon which Judaism rests, yet the only visual image the Jews have of him is a statue, not by a Jew, but by a Renaissance Christian, Michelangelo. This horned* statue of Moses has etched itself into the consciousness of man, giving Moses that magnificence to which his deeds entitle him, but which the Jews

---

*Many commentaries explain the horns on the Michelangelo statue of Moses as the result of a biblical mistranslation. The Bible states that when Moses came down Mount Sinai with the Ten Commandments, his face "shone." The word used in the Bible is *koran*, from the root word *keren*, meaning "to shine," or "a ray of light." But it also means "horn." The accepted translation today is "shone."

do not want to enshrine. He is the most ambivalent figure in Jewish history, revered but not commemorated.

Like the lives of all heroes in antiquity, that of Moses too is shrouded in legend. The Book of Exodus relates that the Pharaoh "who knew not Joseph" gave orders that all Jewish male children were to be killed at birth to prevent the Jews from multiplying too rapidly, though logic might lead us to believe that he would have welcomed such fecundity as a cheap source of future manpower. In these dangerous days, a man from the tribe of Levi took a wife from that same tribe, and they had a son, Moses, whom they hid from the Egyptians for three months. When the danger of keeping him in the house became too great, his parents placed him in a waterproof basket in the Nile, floating it down the river. A daughter of the Pharaoh came to the river to bathe, found Moses, took compassion on the child, and decided to adopt it. She took him to the palace, where he was brought up as an Egyptian prince.

Again, as with all legendary heroes, we know nothing of the early childhood and manhood of Moses. One day, when he was about thirty years old, he saw an Egyptian taskmaster beat a Jewish slave. His heart went out to his brethren, the Jews, and he slew the Egyptian. To escape the wrath of Pharaoh, Moses fled to Midian. Here he met Zipporah, the daughter of a Midianite priest named Jethro, and married her. One day, as he tended his father-in-law's flocks near the mountain of Horeb, Moses encountered Jehovah, Who identified Himself as the God of Abraham. God commanded Moses to return to Egypt and lead the Jews to freedom. It was a most reluctant Moses who finally accepted the commandment, after God had alternately cajoled and threatened him.

The reluctant Prophet now assumes his role of leadership, taking the Jews out of Egypt, through the Reed Sea (Red Sea), into the Sinai desert. The journey around the Sinai peninsula takes forty years, during which time the old generation dies out and a new generation grows up. It is here in the Sinai desert that Moses gives his people the Ten Commandments and the other Mosaic laws, which serve as a framework for the Jewish democracy and nationhood to follow. Having accomplished his mission, Moses dies without having set foot in the Promised Land. His death is a mystery and his burial place remains unknown.

This biblical version of the life of Moses raises many perplexing questions. Moses was brought up as an Egyptian prince. Where did he learn Hebrew, and why did he identify himself with the Jewish slaves instead of with Egyptian royalty? He did not have any difficulty conversing with the Midianites. What language did he speak to them? His encounter with Jehovah, reminiscent of Abraham's similar encounter, raises more perplexing questions. Jehovah makes the same covenant with Moses that He made with Abraham. Jehovah commands Moses to take the Jews to the land of Canaan, the very place where He had led Abraham, and imposes upon Moses and the people whom he is leading out of Egypt the same rite of circumcision. Had this rite been abandoned by the Jews in Egypt? Moses' son, as we shall discuss later, was not circumcised. Why had his parents not circumcised him when he was eight days old in accordance with the covenant of Abraham?

Let us pose a hypothetical question: Were the *Hebrews* who left Ur with Abraham in 2000 B.C. and the *Hebrews* who entered Egypt under Joseph in 1600 B.C., the same people as the Israelites who were led out of Egypt by Moses in 1200 B.C.? Were these Israelites who came out of Egypt the descendants of Abraham, Isaac, and Jacob, or were they a different people? In Genesis, the book dealing with their history before their entry into Egypt, the Jews are, with one exception, referred to as Hebrews, not as Israelites. After their exodus from Egypt and in the other Books of Moses, the Jews are referred to mostly as Israelites, very seldom as Hebrews. After the exodus, it is the pagans who usually refer to the Jews as Hebrews, whereas the Jews usually refer to themselves as Israelites.*

---

*There are two instances, which at first sight, might seem like other exceptions, but they are not. In the first, God changes the name of Jacob to *Israel*, meaning "man who fought God," from the Hebrew *Yisro-el*. Thereafter Jacob, and Jacob only, is referred to as Israel, with the noted exception (Genesis 47:27). In the second instance, the next-to-last chapter in Genesis (49:2), Jacob uses the word *Israel*, but only in reference to himself: ". . . and hear ye sons of Jacob; and hearken unto Israel, your father."

A challenging and perplexing duality runs through the Five Books of Moses in the Old Testament. There are not only two peoples, the Hebrews and the Israelites, but also two Moseses, the Levite Moses and the Midianite Moses. There are also two Gods, one referred to as "Jehovah" (translated as "Lord") and the other named "Elohim" (translated as "God"). Later in the Old Testament we read of two kingdoms, fused into one, then broken in two. There are two rival temples, one in the kingdom of Judah, in Jerusalem, the other in the kingdom of Israel, in Bethel. There are two versions of many, many other events, as the perceptive reader of the Old Testament may have noticed. Are we dealing with two versions of the same story, or with two different stories merged into one?

Scholars through the ages have speculated on what might be the real identity of Moses. Some have even questioned whether he existed at all. But most agree that it was Moses, or someone who went under the name of Moses, who led the Jews out of slavery in Egypt. This, however, does not solve the perplexing questions raised by biblical scholars.

Let us reject for a moment the theological explanation that it was God who chose the Jews as His people. Let us also reject the supposition that it was God who successively appointed Abraham and Moses as the instruments for carrying out His will. Let us instead pose these questions: Could it have been Abraham who originated the ideas of monotheism and the "Chosen People," and could it have been Moses who reintroduced them? Or, could it have been that Moses originated both ideas, which then were attributed retroactively to Abraham by later editors of the scriptures, to give continuity to the origins of the Israelites? Or was Moses perhaps even a non-Jew, as some scholars claim, who *chose* the Jews as the people to whom to give his religious ideas? This then might give a secular explanation to the origin of the term "Chosen People." Did a fusion take place in Canaan, between the Israelites whom Moses led out of Egypt and the Hebrews who did not enter Egypt with Joseph? If so, was this a fusion of two peoples, strangers to each other, with two different gods to be merged into one, or were they the same people, grown apart during the four-hundred-year captivity in Egypt?

Sigmund Freud, in his book *Moses and Monotheism*, has presented the interesting theory that Moses was a non-Jew who welded the Israelites of Egypt and the Hebrews of Canaan into one people. His main premise is that Moses was either an Egyptian prince or a priest who gave the Jews their monotheistic religion.* In vain, says Freud, did this Egyptian Moses try to give his new religion to the Egyptians, who refused to accept such a strange and heretical notion of an invisible God. In those days everyone knew that the earth was flat, that the sun rotated around the earth, and that all gods were visible. Like a true fanatic, Moses then deliberately chose the Israelite people, who at that time were living in slavery in Egypt, promising to free them from their bondage if they in turn would accept his special brand of religion. What historical evidence is there for such a theory?

At about the time of the Israelite slavery in Egypt, there ruled a king by the name of Amenhotep IV who attempted to change the people's polytheistic religion, or belief in many gods, to a monotheistic one. He made Aton, one of the Egyptian sun-gods, supreme. But the people were afraid of this invisible, all-powerful God. The priests also were opposed to a god who threatened to put them out of business. A palace revolution took place; Amenhotep was deposed and killed in the revolution that swept all of Egypt and lasted for close to a century. In the end the old order was reestablished.

In the chaos and ferment of the Egyptian revolution, Freud says, a little-noted incident may have taken place. Could it have been that a priest or prince named Moses was fired with the idea of perpetuating the dying sect of the Aton religion, just as Paul was fired with an ambition to establish Christianity? Could it have been that when the Egyptians would not accept the Aton religion, Moses de-

---

*This author cannot understand the outcry against the notion that Moses might have been an Egyptian prince, when Jews accept with equanimity the fact that Abraham, the founder of the Jewish people, was a Babylonian who did not become a Jew until his seventy-fifth year. The wonderful saga of the Jewish people lies in the ideas they have propounded, and if the Jews had the sense to follow Moses, whether Egyptian, Midianite, or Hebrew, so much more to their credit.

termined to give it to the Jews? This is no fanciful concept. Again the comparison can be made with Paul. When the Jews would not have the teachings of Christ, Paul took his gospel to the gentiles—an ironic twist of history.

Moses, then, according to this theory, decided that the Jews were the most likely people for him to *choose* for his new religion. They were in Egypt, they were slaves, they were chafing for freedom. A bargain was struck. As the price of liberty, the Jews would accept Moses as their leader and his religion as their own. We must remember that in its early days Christianity, too, was embraced mainly by slaves.

What evidence does there exist in the Bible for Freud's supposition that Moses may not have been a Jew, but was perhaps an Egyptian?* According to the Bible, Pharaoh's daughter gave him the name Moshe (or Mose), of which "Moses" is the Greek rendition, because, as she explained, "I drew him out of the water." This presupposes that she knew the finer points of esoteric Hebrew grammar. Language experts, however, have pointed out the word is not Hebrew at all, but Egyptian for *child*, found in such famed Egyptian names as Ramses (*Ra-mose*, "child of Ra"), or Thotmose (*Thot-mose*, "child of Thot"), names formed much the same way as some names are formed today, like Johnson, the "son of John."

Scholars still debate why Moses' son was not circumcised at birth. It is as if by an afterthought God realizes He has entrusted the exodus of the Jews from Egypt to someone who has not observed the Jewish rite of circumcision, and now He wants to kill Moses. Had Moses lapsed from Judaism, or was he himself an uncircumcised gentile? It is Zipporah, Moses' wife, who quickly performs the operation as if to appease God's wrath. Zipporah had also thought Moses was an Egyptian when she first met him, as did her father, the Midianite priest. The Bible states that Moses had a speech defect, stuttering, which he used as an excuse for not wanting to accept God's assignment, an announcement which comes as a surprise to the Bible reader because this is the first mention of such stuttering. God

---

*The interested reader is referred to Karl Abraham's monograph, "Amenhotep" in *Clinical Papers and Essays on Psychoanalysis*, in addition to Freud's *Moses and Monotheism*.

then informs Moses that he has a brother named Aaron, who will serve as an interpreter—another surprise, as the Bible has also failed to mention this brother previously. Could it be that Moses did indeed have an interpreter, but for different reasons? It was not for a speech defect that Moses needed an interpreter, suggests Freud, but because he did not speak the Hebrew language.

This, of course, is not conclusive evidence, but it gives some basis for such a speculation. Let us now use a little biblical exegesis, or critical scriptural interpretation, to explore the puzzle of the duality that runs through the early Jewish history.

Biblical scholars have conjectured that the Old Testament is composed essentially of four major narratives, the "J," "E," "JE," and "P" documents woven into one.* The "J" documents are so named because in them God is always referred to as "Jehovah." They are the oldest, written around the ninth century B.C. in the southern kingdom of Judah. The "E" documents, so called because in them God is referred to as "Elohim," were written about a hundred years after the "J" documents in the eighth century in the northern kingdom of Israel. Scholars assume the "P," or "Priestly," documents were composed some two hundred years or so after the "E," about 600 B.C. In the fifth century, Jewish priests combined portions of the "J" and "E" documents, adding a little handiwork of their own (known as pious fraud), which are referred to as the "JE" documents, since God in these passages is referred to as "Jehovah Elohim" (translated as "Lord God").

The final fusion of the Five Books of Moses, called the *Pentateuch*, occurred around 450 B.C.—in other words, not until eight to sixteen hundred years after some of the events narrated in them took place. Is it not reasonable to suppose that in that period of time, before there were any written records, many changes and alterations must have occurred as the stories and legends were handed down orally from generation to generation? Furthermore, as we have seen, priests, prophets, and policy makers were also busy during these centuries editing the manuscripts.

---

*A fifth major narrative, the Deuteronomic Code, or "D," is discussed in another chapter.

Let us now again assume that it was Moses who first conceived the idea of a covenant with a "chosen people." Could it be that the duality referred to actually deals with two peoples, one, the Hebrews of Abraham and the other, the Israelites of Moses, each having a different God, one called "Jehovah" by the Hebrews, the other called "Elohim" by the Israelites? Could it be that these two peoples were later fused into their first unity by Moses? We must remember that all the Hebrews did not go with Joseph into Egypt. Many remained behind in the land of Canaan, where they continued to practice the Jehovah cult as it had been taught by their ancestors Abraham, Isaac, and Jacob. When Moses brought the Israelites into the land of Canaan, the task of Judges, Kings, and Prophets became, as we shall see, one of welding these two peoples into one unified nation and these two cults into one religion. If we accept this viewpoint, we can explain the story of Abraham's encounter with Jehovah as a later addition by biblical editors. It can further be explained as a partially successful attempt by the rulers to unify two racially related but religiously different peoples by conferring upon them the same God through the simple device of having both Abraham and Moses receive the same revelation from Jehovah and Elohim, now called Jehovah Elohim, the Lord God.

Though we have discussed these theories on the identity of Moses and the origins of Hebrews and Israelites at length, we wish neither to discredit nor to affirm them, but merely to point out that in our way of viewing history, it makes no difference whether Moses was a Jew or not, whether the Hebrews and Israelites were the same or different people, or to whom God first revealed His covenant. What made Jewish history was the fact that the Jews accepted the ideas in the covenant no matter how or by whom they came about. The fact also remains that with Moses, whether Jew or Egyptian, the form and content of the previous Judaism changed. Moses was the first in a series of men of God—to be known as Prophets—who universalized the Jewish Godhead.

The central point in the Moses story, contained in the Books of Exodus, Leviticus, Numbers, and Deuteronomy, is the giving of the Law, the establishment of the Mosaic

Code. Everything before this has been a prelude. Everything after this is an anticlimax. This giving of the Law was the very act of bringing forth a new nation. Indeed, the grand design of the entire Book of Exodus resembles that of primitive tribal initiation rites, but on a high, ethical, symbolic plane. Before the young males in a primitive tribe can join adult society, they have to go through initiation rites which have these five elements in common: a symbolic death; a symbolic rebirth; a symbolic mutilation uniting them into a brotherhood; a new name given to each initiated member; and, finally, revelation of the tribal laws. The forty years of wandering in the Sinai desert by the Jews under the leadership of Moses, during which time the old generation died out and a new generation was born, represents the symbolic death and rebirth in the "initiation rite" of Exodus. All males are then circumcised. Next the Hebrews are given a new name, the People of Israel. Finally, the new law, the Torah, is revealed to them.

The Torah was a bold leap into the future, a giant stride ahead of anything existing at that time. Its concept of equality before the law, a law based on a *written code*, seems to be a Semitic innovation. The Sumerians, whose written code of laws dates back to 2500 B.C., were probably the first people on earth to have a written code, but it lacked the passion for justice of the Mosaic laws. Five hundred years later, the Sumerian code was augmented and incorporated by the Babylonians into the Code of Hammurabi, but again this body of laws did not have the democratic spirit of the Torah. A written judicial code applicable to all without favoritism was totally unknown to the Egyptians until 300 B.C. We know of no written Roman laws until the second century B.C.

The Mosaic Code, then, was the first truly judicial, written code and eclipsed previously known laws with its all-encompassing humanism, its passion for justice, its love of democracy. It also helped to establish a new Jewish character and directed Jewish thinking into new paths which tended to set the Jews further apart from their neighbors.

The ideological content of these Mosaic laws is of great interest. Here we find the Jewish concept of the state and philosophy of law. These laws were essentially divided into three categories: those dealing with man's relation to man, those dealing with man's relation to the state, and those dealing with man's relation to God.

The laws of Moses anticipate the statehood God promised the Israelites. Though at this juncture of their history the Jews are still nomads, the Code of Moses is not for a nomadic people. These laws of Moses are designed to safeguard a national entity, not merely the family unit, though individual rights are never subordinated to the needs of the state. The lofty framework of these laws permitted the emergence of a democratic form of government virile enough to last eight hundred years until the Prophets in turn renovated them. The American Constitution thus far has weathered just over two hundred years.

The Mosaic Code laid down the first principles for a separation of church and state, a concept not encountered again in world history until three thousand years later, during the Enlightenment in the eighteenth century of our era. In the Mosaic Code the civil authority was independent of the priesthood. Though it is true that the priesthood had the right to settle cases not specifically covered by Mosaic law (Deuteronomy 17:8–12), that did not place it above the civil government. The priesthood was charged with the responsibility of keeping this government within the framework of Mosaic law, just as the United States Supreme Court is not above the federal government but is, nevertheless, charged with the responsibility of keeping it within the framework of the Constitution. Moses also laid the foundation for another separation, which has since become indispensable to any democracy. He created an independent judiciary.

There is a curious resemblance between the philosophic outlook of American constitutional law and that of Mosaic law. The federal government has only the powers specifically granted to it by the Constitution. The individual states can do anything not specifically denied to them. In essence, the Mosaic law also established the principle that the Jews could do anything not specifically denied to them. Instead of saying "Do such and such a thing," the laws of Moses usually say "Don't do this or that." Even where the Mosaic law makes a positive statement, it is often either an amendment to a negative commandment or else hemmed in by a negative admonition, saying, in effect, "When you do this, then don't do that." The Ten Commandments, for instance, list only three *do's* but seven *don'ts*. The three positive Commandments are: "I am the Lord thy God"; observe the Sabbath; and honor your parents. The seven *don'ts* leave little doubt as to what one is not supposed to do. By fencing in only the negative, Moses left an open field for positive action. This allowed the Jews great flexibility. As long as they did not do anything specifically prohibited, they could, like the individual American states, do anything they wanted to do. This type of thinking led Jewish philosophers into stating their maxims in negations.

We can see this gulf in thinking interestingly illustrated in a maxim attributed by Christians to Jesus and by Jews to Hillel, one of the great teachers of Judaism. According to the Christians, Jesus said, "Do unto others what you want others *to do* unto you." According to the Jews, Hillel, who lived 100 years before Jesus, said, "*Do not do* unto others what you *don't want* others to do unto you." There is a world of philosophic difference between these two expressions, and the reader is invited to ponder on them and reason out why he would prefer one to the other as applied to himself.

In reading these laws, formulated some three thousand years ago, one is amazed at their humanitarianism. One cannot help but wonder if the world would not be better off today if these laws, in the main, had been universally adopted. Slaves were treated more humanely and leniently than they were treated in the United States in 1850. All laws applying to free men also applied to the slaves, who had to be set free after seven years of servitude. Divorce laws were more liberal in the time of Moses than in present-day England, and women were held in high esteem.

It might be of interest to outline briefly the views on sex held by Jews twelve hundred years before Christ. The Puritan idea of sex as a sin never gained a foothold in Judaism. Sexual desire was held to be normal. It also was felt that its fulfillment should be within the marriage institution only. Therefore, early marriages were encouraged. Cohabitation between man and wife should be joyous, but it also had to be voluntary. It was a crime for one partner—wife or husband—willfully to avoid sex relations, and such continued avoidance was grounds for divorce. Bachelorhood was frowned upon, and all males were strenuously encouraged to marry, whereas women were given greater freedom to remain unmarried, though they, too, were expected to marry early.

The Mosaic Code also realized that transgressions would occur and therefore provided for the safety of children born out of wedlock. Children born to partners who could not marry legally (such as one partner already married, or couples related by blood) were the only ones regarded as bastards. All other children born out of wedlock were legitimate and could not be disinherited. Chastity among the unmarried was held in high esteem, prostitution was looked upon as a degradation, and religious prostitution, so prevalent in pagan days, was viewed with abhorrence. Homosexual relations between men were grave criminal offenses, whereas such relations between women were regarded as scandalous but not criminal.

The Second Commandment, prohibiting the making of images of God, had a profound influence on the Jewish character. Freud makes a most interesting observation. If there were to be no images of God, he says, it would also follow that God would have neither a name nor a countenance, which would lead, as it did, to the compulsion to worship an invisible God. "If this prohibition was to be accepted," says Freud, "it was bound to exercise a profound influence. For it signified subordinating sense perception to an abstract idea; it was a triumph of spirituality over the senses."

By making God spiritual instead of material the Jews were left free to change the spirituality of God instead of merely altering his physical appearance. This was done successively by prophets, redeemers, and rabbis. Having a spiritual God rather than gods in stone gave the Jews a feeling of cultural superiority. Thus Moses succeeded in inculcating a feeling of pride in the Jews, not merely a veneer of uniqueness. The intellectualism of the Jews was a character trait which also followed as a direct result of making God abstract. Another result was the renunciation of brutality and sadism. Here we have an instance where a value judgment can be put to a statistical test. Though Jews presently constitute 3 percent of the total American population, the number of Jews imprisoned for crimes of violence is but one tenth of one percent of the prison population. For whatever else Jews are sent to prison, it is not, as a rule, for sadistic acts—murder, rape, beating, or bestiality—though exceptions do exist. This tremendous disproportion in the statistic continually amazes sociologists.

The Second Commandment also had an adverse effect. It helped to stultify the Jewish artistic spirit. Because the Jews were prohibited from making images of God, they turned away from painting, sculpture, and architecture, though, as will later be discussed, there were notable exceptions. Not until the nineteenth century A.D., when Jews began disregarding the Second Commandment the way the Christians had been doing for two thousand years, did they, too, begin to develop painters, sculptors, and architects. However, by the nineteenth century the Jewish character had already been formed, and their expansion into the fields of plastic arts does not seem to have affected this "Jewish character."

The Mosaic theophany—the giving of the divine law— had been accomplished. The mission of Moses had been fulfilled. Now he had to die. Younger men were ready to take over the destiny of this people to whom he had given a constitution. Abraham's grand illusion had not been a delusion. Moses, the reluctant Prophet, had made it a reality.

THREE

# Judges, Kings, and Usurpers

When, finally, in the twelfth century B.C. the Jews settled in a country they could call their own, they used the worst possible judgment. They selected a strip of land that was a corridor for the armies of warring empires. Over and over again the Jews were to pay for this error of judgment by being decimated in battle, sold into slavery, or deported to alien lands. Yet they showed up persistently at the same old place, building anew their little strip of real estate which has been alternately called Canaan, Palestine, Israel, Judah, Judea, and now again, Israel.

The exodus from Egypt had been led by Moses; the return to Canaan, the Promised Land, was led by his appointed successor, Joshua. In true hero fashion Joshua defeated all enemies because of his superior personal cunning and valor. The Canaanites, though formidable enemies with their war chariots and walled cities, were not a united nation but loosely federated city-states, each ruled by a petty king. In vain they tried to align themselves against the invading Jews, but under Joshua's leadership the Jewish armies struck before the opposition could unite. Joshua crossed the River Jordan, leading his small army against the Jebusites in the south, crushing an alliance headed by the Jebusite king. Then, swerving north, he defeated the Canaanite tribes led by the king of Hazor. The biblical account of the destruction by the Jews of the Canaanite culture which then followed may sound barbarous to readers unfamiliar with the history and practices of antiquity. Actually it was far less barbarous than the destruction of the Cretan culture by the invading Greeks in the eleventh century B.C. or the destruction of the Etruscan culture by the invading Romans in the same century. The Canaanite civilization fell because the Jews did away with the abominable Canaanite religious practices on which it was based—the human sacrifice to the god Moloch, the lewd rites demanded by the local Canaanite god known as Baal, and the unrestrained orgies and sacred prostitution in the name of a female goddess called Asherah, or Baala. As the Canaanite resistance died, the first rough boundaries of what eventually became Palestine were formed.

Dramatically speaking, Canaan was a perfect setting for the "return of the natives." The emigrant Israelites from Egypt were coming back to Canaan after a four-hundred-year absence to be reunited with their brethren, the Hebrews, those descendants of Abraham, Isaac, and Jacob who had not accepted Joseph's invitation four centuries earlier to come to Egypt. This integration of the Israelites from Egypt with the Hebrews in Canaan took close to two hundred years. But even then it was an imperfect fusion, a piece of political soldering that fell apart at the first signs of stress.

With the settlement of Canaan, the Jews ceased being a nomadic people, and a peculiar political institution, which has no counterpart in history, was born. It was the *Shoftim*, or Judges, who were thought of as divinely inspired men, accountable to God by God. They established the first democracy in the world, four hundred years before the Greeks. Roughly speaking, the era of the Judges corresponds to the Jeffersonian period in American history—a weak central government with "tribes' rights" instead of states' rights.

The new nation consisted of the biblical twelve tribes. The Elders dispensed justice within each tribe, just as municipal and state courts dispense justice within each state. However, above the authority of the Elder was that of the Judge, just as above the authority of the state is the federal Constitution. The Judge was the Commander in Chief in times of war and the Chief Executive in times of peace. His powers were limited by law, but he could delegate responsibility just as the President of the United States can delegate responsibility through his Cabinet ministers.

The Judge could summon the "Senate" and "Popular Assembly" and propose subjects for deliberation. The function of the "Senate" members was the same as that of our Senators today. Like the House of Lords in England, the "Senate" was not only the legislative but also the judicial arm of government. In Greco-Roman days, this "Senate," known as the Sanhedrin, lost most of its legislative functions and became primarily a judicial forum.

The Popular Assembly resembled the U.S. House of Representatives. Even in the days before the Judges, the Books of Moses are full of such references as "and all the congregation of Israel," or "and all Israel." As the Jews at the time of the giving of the Law at Mount Sinai numbered more than 600,000* according to the Bible, it is unlikely that Moses could speak to them all at the same time. In all likelihood he spoke to the elected representatives of each tribe.

---

*Many scholars believe that the actual figure was perhaps 600 or 6,000 families, as it is hardly likely that the Sinai and Negev deserts could have sustained 600,000 adult males, their families, and their servants— about three million people—for forty years of wandering.

It is not by accident that American democracy so closely resembles the first government by the Jews, for the founding fathers were brought up on the Bible, and many were conversant enough with Hebrew to be able to read the Old Testament in the original. Many scholars now hold that the Palestine government under the Judges, not the democracy of Greece, served as the blueprint for the American Constitution.

It was during this period also, between 1300 and 800 B.C., that the written alphabet, mankind's most useful tool, was invented by either the Phoenicians or the Hebrews. Until recent times, scholars have been wont to credit this invention to the Phoenicians, but late archaeological findings lend greater and greater credence to the theory that it may have been a Hebrew invention. In the Old Testament Hebrews refer to their language not as Hebrew or Israelite but as the language of Canaan. Here they found a highly developed language (Ugaritic), culture, and oral literature, especially poetry, which bears a remarkable resemblance to Hebrew Old Testament poetry. The genius of the Jews was not so much the form of the poetry—probably Canaanite or Ugaritic—as its content.

For two centuries government by Judges worked, but the system had one fatal weakness. It did not provide the basis for a strong centralized leadership. Each Judge was selected by his own tribe. In times of crisis, the tribes were convinced, God would unite them and send an "inspired leader" who, like Joan of Arc, would deliver them from evil. Indeed, the Jews did have their own Joan of Arc in Deborah, a female Judge. So firm were they in this conviction that no successor was ever provided. Each crisis, they felt, would itself create a Deliverer. In this "Deliverer" we see the roots of the messianic concepts to come.

This weakness in not providing for a head of state prevented the development of a stable government. Though the system of divine Judges served to instill the spirit of God in the people, it failed to bring domestic tranquillity. The period was one of strife. The economic interpreter of history can explain this as a transition period, during which a previously nomadic people changed its social system to one more suitable to an agricultural economy. There is no doubt the social and economic conditions did call for a more centralized government. The new mode of living in houses and towns, instead of on the backs of mules and in tents, finally did force a change in government structure.

The Jews met this challenge by establishing a constitutional monarchy, and the first Jewish dynasty came into existence. The constitutional monarchy formed by the Twelve Tribes of Israel about 1000 B.C. was the first of its kind in the world. It was a form of government used for a brief period by the Greeks and Romans, then fated to disappear until the signing of the Magna Carta, after which it was honored more in the breach than the observance for several hundred years.

Because of the free and direct contact between man and God in Jewish monotheism, however, the Jewish idea of kingship differed from that of the pagans. The pagans attributed divine descent to their king; he was the state, the state religion, and the center of their religious cult. Not so with the Jews, who never thought of any of their kings as descendants of God. The Jewish king was as accountable to the law for his judicial, moral, and religious conduct as any ordinary citizen. There were no special laws, no special exemptions, for the Jewish king.

Saul was the first anointed king of Palestine, though he was such in name only. The first actual king of Palestine was David, and the second his son Solomon. David extended the kingdom by war; Solomon preserved it by peace. Though David was a warrior king, his claim to fame among Jews rests on three achievements totally unconnected with war. He made Jerusalem a symbol, an ideal, and a holy place: first, by making Jerusalem the political capital of Palestine; second, by earmarking the Temple for that city; and third, by enshrining the Ark in Jerusalem. But because David was a warrior king, and the Temple was dedicated to peace, God did not permit David to build it. This task was entrusted to his son, Solomon. During King David's reign, the Ark was kept in a special tent. Solomon enshrined it in the Temple. However, David planned all too well. Jerusalem became not only the symbol of Judaism, but the symbol of two other religions—Christianity and Islam.

When David died, he left a kingdom which, to the Jews, looked like an empire. It was, however, beset by many enemies. The "empire" extended from the Euphrates River to the Gulf of Akaba, about five times the size of present-day Israel, but this expansion had been achieved at the expense of other nations. The Jebusites, who had given Jerusalem its name, were driven out, but not vanquished; the Philistines, who had given Palestine its name, were subdued, but not shattered. No sooner had David been buried than the Jebusites and Philistines joined other nations defeated by the Jews and rebelled against Palestine to regain their lost lands. Neither the Jebusites nor the Philistines succeeded in reconquering Jerusalem or Palestine, but the other formerly subdued nations were able to free their lands. King Solomon did not attempt to regain them. He set out to make peace by diplomacy, and having achieved external peace, he set about to industrialize the country.

It was no easier for Solomon to change the dynamics of an agricultural society to an urbanized way of life than it was for others to change feudal societies to capitalist states. To accomplish this, Solomon broke the political might of the individual tribes in the same way that the United States had to break the political strength of the individual states. He had to do this for very practical reasons.

In an essay entitled "Politics as a Vocation,"* the German sociologist Max Weber points out that a strong federal government cannot be established until it alone, and not the individual states which comprise it, has in its hands all major administrative functions and the sole power to wage war. When an individual state in a federation no longer can raise enough revenue to maintain its own armies, says Weber, and has to depend on the federal government for money, then that state has lost in actuality the sovereignty it may still maintain as a fiction. The parallel in American history is obvious.

Solomon had to assert "federal power" over "tribal power." He had to break the political might of the tribes because of their ability to maintain their own armies and their ability to tax themselves sufficiently to remain financially independent. To break their power and independence, Solomon divided the country into twelve taxable

---

*H. H. Gerth and C. Wright Mills, *From Max Weber: Essays in Sociology* (Oxford University Press, 1946).

units, deliberately cutting across tribal lines to weaken their influence. Then, through heavy taxation and enforced labor, he created a large landless class, forcing people to move to the cities so that workers would be available for the new commercial and industrial establishments. Under the system of the Judges (an agricultural economy) the family was the central economic unit. Under the system of Solomon (an industrial economy) the individual became the economic unit. This weakened family ties and parental authority in the same way that the "mobile families" of today, created by nationwide industries, are weakening family relationships and community ties.

But Solomon tried to accomplish the changeover from an agricultural to an industrial society too quickly. In breaking up the old order he set in motion a series of events he could not control. Though cities sprang up, though trade developed, though industry thrived, they did not grow quickly enough to absorb the great mass of landless people streaming into the cities looking for jobs. As time went on, the evils of too rapid an industrialization became all too evident. At the time of Solomon's death the nation was plagued with some of the same social and economic ills which plague nations today—landless farmers, forced labor, unemployment, absentee-landlordism, a small class of rich oppressing a large mass of poor. Excessive wealth, then as now, bred vice and corruption, and these, in turn, bred perverted justice.

Solomon had also laid the seeds for future religious discord, causing yet another serious schism in the social pattern. Idolatry had found its way into Palestine via his bedroom. At this time intermarriage and polygamy had not as yet been forbidden. Whatever religions Solomon's many foreign wives and mistresses professed, he allowed them to practice them openly. Solomon's attitude toward religion resembled that attributed to the Romans by historian Edward Gibbon, who said: "The various modes of worship which prevailed in the Roman world were all considered by the people as equally true, by the philosophers as equally false, and by the magistrate as equally useful. And thus toleration not only produced mutual indulgence, but even religious concord." This view was not shared by the people in Palestine. Solomon's tolerance produced neither indulgence nor concord. It produced civil war.

Palestine, even in the days of King David, had never had a strong centralized government. It was a weakly fused dual kingdom, Israel in the north and Judah in the south. The king of Judah could not govern in Israel without the consent of the Israelites. This consent was given David before he was crowned king. Such had not been the case with Solomon. To be sure Israel would accept his son Solomon as king, after his own death, David had to take him twice to Israel (probably to its capital Shechem) for a coronation under his supervision, for in II Chronicles (29:22–23) we read: "And they made Solomon the son of David king the second time . . . and all Israel hearkened to him." This dual coronation of Solomon underscores the dual structure and fragility of the kingdom.

When Solomon died in 931 B.C., his son Rehoboam succeeded him only to the throne of Judah. Like his father before him, he also had to proceed to Shechem to be crowned there. Here the Elders of Israel met him to ask redress for political and religious grievances. This scene was reminiscent of a page in American history when the colonists petitioned their English king for redress of grievances, only to be met with insolence instead of understanding. In a very dramatic sequence, the Bible (I Kings 12:1–15) tells of this historic meeting between the freemen of Israel, who asserted the principle that the ruler is the servant of the people he rules, and Rehoboam, who had discarded that principle.

The spokesman for the Elders was Jeroboam, an Israelite general who had returned from exile in Egypt, where he had fled after the failure of a rebellion against Solomon's tyrannical rule. Like other vain and arrogant kings, Rehoboam refused to listen to the voice of moderation and conciliation. Instead, he sent an army against Israel which was, however, decisively defeated. Within one year after Solomon's death, the kingdom of Palestine was no more. It was torn apart at the seams where Joshua, David, and Solomon had tried to stitch it. Jeroboam became king of Israel, which was comprised of ten of the twelve tribes, and Rehoboam remained ruler of Judah, composed of the remaining two tribes. This civil war between Israel and Judah, started by Rehoboam, lasted for one hundred years.

Not only Jewish history but the Jews themselves now assume a new mask. During his first thousand years, the mask of the Jew was that of a nomad and tiller of the soil, living by his wits, preferring peace, and taking to the sword only when forced to do so. In the second millennium of his history the nomadic mask was discarded. He became a man of war, intrepid in battle, unmatched in valor. Like the Greeks, the Jews had their Marathons—magnificent victories in the face of incredible odds. But, unlike the Greeks, who remained passive after their defeat at the hands of the Romans, the Jews rose time and again in armed rebellion against their oppressors, striking for their freedom and religious liberty. The stereotyped mask of meekness was later fitted on the Jew by Western civilization.

David and Solomon are the two most generally known Jewish kings, and little interest is shown in the many, many other kings who ruled Israel and Judah after the breakup of Palestine. Yet the history of these two kingdoms under these kings is far more interesting and adventurous than the history of Palestine ever was under David or Solomon. With a bravery bordering on effrontery, the Jews waged war against such mighty powers as Damascus, Phoenicia, Egypt. When other nations trembled at the approach of Assyrian and Babylonian armies, it was Israel and Judah who rallied the strength and courage of their bigger neighbors into alliances to stand up against the enemy. Their kings were not cautious, timid politicians but Renaissance men with a penchant for colorful action.

The history of the two independent kingdoms of Judah and Israel resembles that of Italy under the Medici in its incredible succession of intrigue, treachery, usurpation, assassination, and regicide. But though the period is interwoven with the macabre and the irrational, there is, nevertheless, a grand design in the pattern. Three variations on the same theme can be discerned as a common leitmotif during these three centuries—preventing the absorption of Jewish monotheism into pagan ritual, maintaining morality and justice as social goals, and preserving the Jewish people as an ethnic entity. As Israel was the first kingdom to fall, let us first follow the course of her history, then return to Judah.

The throne of Israel was a precarious post, offering the ruler an average occupancy of eleven years. Altogether, nine separate dynasties rose and fell during the 212-year period of its monarchy, one dynasty lasting as little as seven days. Few of the nineteen kings who occupied the throne died of natural causes.

Jeroboam began his reign by deepening the rift between the two countries. He added religious rancor to political acrimony by building a temple in Bethel to rival the one in Jerusalem. It was during this time that the first "J" documents were written in Judah. A few decades later the "E" documents were composed in Israel, perhaps in competition with the "J" documents, thus paralleling the rival temples in Jerusalem and Bethel.

A succession of inept rulers brought Israel to the brink of chaos from which she was saved by the strong hand of King Omri (866 B.C.), one of her most colorful and adventurous rulers. He was the Napoleon of his age, beset with similar problems and taking similar measures to solve them. Omri first ended the civil strife which had broken out in Israel itself. Then he smashed the invading armies of half a dozen hostile nations. Next he shifted the capital from Shechem to Samaria, reformed the laws of the country, and encouraged trade and commerce. With these reforms accomplished, Omri decided to expand his kingdom with conquests of his own and he was successful beyond his own expectations. His fame as a warrior king spread throughout the entire ancient world, and his name was feared and respected by such powers as Assyria and Moab. An Assyrian monument uncovered by archaeologists refers to Israel as "the land of Omri." The famous Moabite Stone, now in the Louvre in Paris, speaks of the conquest of the Moabites by Omri and the final freedom of Moab from the Israelites.

But, unwittingly, Omri also laid the foundation for future disaster by marrying his son Ahab to the archbitch of history, Jezebel, a Sidonite princess. Her father was a priest who assassinated the king of Sidon, usurped the throne, and taught his daughter the art of treachery and murder for personal aggrandizement. As consort queen of Israel, she set the political kettle boiling by ending the civil rights which the Israelites so stoutly had fought for. She then fanned the flame of religious hatred by introducing Baal worship, "sacred prostitution," and the sacrifice of children to Moloch, the fire god.

Though Jezebel led Ahab by the nose in domestic politics, he used his own head in foreign affairs. He smashed the armies of Phoenicia, Damascus, Sidon, and Tyre, but instead of treating their kings as enemies, he embraced them as brothers. Ahab needed peace in the west, because he saw the danger of a resurgent Assyria in the east.

The Assyrians, who facially resembled Nazi caricatures of Polish Jews, had begun to flex their conquest muscles about the time Abraham left Babylonia. But they soon ran into trouble. For a thousand years they dreamed of an empire, and in the eleventh century B.C. their dreams were realized. By the tenth century the Assyrians had subjugated Babylonia and adjacent territories, and in the ninth century they were ready to expand toward the west. Egypt was the prize, but the path led through Israel.

When Assyria was ready to strike, Ahab was prepared. The historic battle took place at Karkar (854 B.C.), where the might of Assyria clashed with the massed strength of the twelve buffer states organized by Ahab, with Jewish battalions in the vanguard. Over 20,000 men died in that battle, but when it was over, Ahab had dealt the Assyrians a stunning defeat that set their timetable for conquest back a hundred years.

The death of King Ahab was a signal for a breakthrough of the pent-up hatred against Jezebel. The conspirators, led by the Prophet Elisha, picked a general named Jehu to lead the crusade against the "harlot of Sidon." Elisha anointed Jehu for good luck. It was a successful anointment. Jehu not only assassinated Jezebel but also murdered every member of the house of Ahab, then ascended the vacant throne of Israel. He was a ruthless ruler and an able administrator. The worship of Baal was mercilessly extirpated. Commerce and industry were vigorously encouraged.

Fifty years of peace and prosperity followed. Israel again ventured on a little imperialism and found herself blessed with success. Soon she doubled her territory. Her neighbors, in awe of the powerful army of this small state, left her alone. Then a cloud appeared on the tranquil Israel horizon. Tiglath-Pileser III, the Bismarck of his time, the man of blood and thunder, had seized the throne of Nineveh, capital of Assyria. He was the man in the chariot destined to bring about the Assyrian Empire her rulers had dreamed about for a thousand years.

The Assyrian technique for conquest resembled that of Nazi Germany. She blackmailed the smaller nations into subjugation. Tiglath-Pileser threatened to march his armies against Israel unless the Israelites paid him a huge sum as tribute. This demand divided the people in Israel into pro- and anti-Assyrian factions; the former advocated paying the Assyrians the tribute demanded, while the latter exhorted the nation to spend "millions for defense but not one cent for tribute."

To pay or not to pay was the question, and it was a question of life or death as pro- and anti-Assyrian kings of Israel succeeded each other swiftly, the "outs" removing the "ins" by assassination. When the third pro-Assyrian Israelite king was assassinated, and payment of tribute stopped for a third time, Tiglath-Pileser felt it was time to take action and marched at the head of a huge army against Israel. Everyone expected the Israelites to capitulate and accept the inevitable, but this Israel did not choose to do. She decided to fight, and almost won.

Historians usually dismiss the Assyrian-Israeli war in a few sentences, as though it were one of history's small and unimportant skirmishes. Yet, if we look at this war objectively, comparing it to other battles of antiquity, we are forced to the conclusion that the battles in this war were not only momentous but incredible on the face of it. The Russo-Finnish encounter in 1939 was but a minor skirmish in the World War II drama. Yet Finland's stand against the Russian colossus for six months has been hailed as a monument to bravery. Assyria was mightier, larger, and more formidable in relation to Israel than Russia to Finland. Yet it took the Assyrians ten years and three kings to vanquish Israel.

The Israelites inflicted several bitter defeats on Tiglath-Pileser, who, for all his vaunted ferocity, was only able to wrest several minor provinces from Israel. His successor, Shalmaneser V, had no more luck. Finally, Sargon II, who succeeded Shalmaneser, captured Samaria, the capital of

Israel, in 722 B.C. If historians look upon this as a minor battle, Sargon, who was there, did not. To be sure that he never again would have to face so formidable a foe, which for ten years had humiliated the Assyrians by holding at bay the armies of her mighty empire, Sargon deported the entire population. The kingdom of Israel was over.

The history of Judah uncannily parallels that of Israel. Though the Davidic line was to rule Judah from the time of the split (933 B.C.) until her own defeat 347 years later, that country's throne was as precarious a post as Israel's. Twenty kings held it for an average of seventeen years each; all, however, were of the same dynasty.

Judah got off to a bad start. She was invaded by Egypt, but no sooner had she thrown off the Egyptian yoke than she embarked on an expansionist policy of her own. The Phoenicians, Arabians, Philistines, Moabites, Syrians—all were defeated at various times and sizable parts of their territories incorporated into Judah. These wars of conquest continued for a century, with occasional defeats mixed in with the victories. The Jehu rebellion in Israel, however, also weakened Judah to the extent that she was unable to hold on to the nations she had conquered. Each now seized the opportunity for freedom, and Judah found herself reduced to the size she had started with a hundred years earlier.

Since Israel had a Jezebel, Judah had to have one too. This was obligingly provided for Judah by Queen Jezebel herself in the shapely form of her daughter Athaliah, whom she married off to Jehoram, King of Judah. Jehoram died of a strange disease which caused his bowels to fall out, and as II Chronicles 21:20 states with commendable understatement, "he departed joyless." His youngest son, Ahaziah, was made king the same year that Jehu went on a murder spree in Israel, and in his zeal Jehu also murdered the young Ahaziah. Athaliah saw her opportunity. "Every daughter gets to be like her mother; that's her tragedy," reads an epigram by Oscar Wilde. Athaliah was no exception. She seized the throne of Judah and murdered everyone in the royal house of David with the exception of Jehoash, an infant prince who was spirited away by an aunt.

For six years Athaliah reigned as queen. A counterplot

put a gruesome end to her, and the Davidic line was restored in Judah with the coronation of the seven-year-old
Jehoash, who lived to reign for forty years. An era of good
will followed. The civil war between Judah and Israel came
to an end at last after a hundred years of bloodshed.

When Assyria had staged her comeback under Tiglath-
Pileser, Judah, acting under the advice of the Prophet Isaiah, stayed out of the fracas. Isaiah's political philosophy
was that of George Washington—no entangling alliances.
The kings of Judah paid heed to Isaiah's words and paid
the tribute demanded by Assyria. In silent terror they
watched Israel, which had stopped paying tribute, being
devastated. When the carnage was over, the great pro-
Assyrian-versus-anti-Assyrian debate which had torn Israel
apart now began to rip Judah to pieces. As in Israel, two
parties were formed in Judah, one pro-Assyrian, cautioning
the country to continue to pay the tribute demanded by the
Assyrians, and the other, a pro-Egyptian party, advocating
an alliance with Egypt and Syria to fight Assyria.

The pro-Egyptian faction finally won. A north-south
axis, with Judah as the fulcrum, was formed. Syria was to
rebel in the north, Egypt was to strike in the south, and
Judah was to keep things boiling in the middle. The Assyrians moved swiftly, and the north-south axis snapped. On
beholding Assyria's vast armies, both Syria and Egypt sued
for peace, and Judah was left to face the enraged Assyrians
by herself. Then a miracle happened. One morning the
Jews were surprised to see the besieging Assyrians outside
the gates of Jerusalem breaking up camp and departing in
haste. The Jews celebrated the event as a good sign from
heaven; the Greek historian Herodotus had another explanation. A plague of mice (typhus) had struck the Assyrian
camp. The reader is invited to take his choice, for,
whichever explanation he takes, the fact remains the
same—Judah was saved.

Realizing that continued favors from heaven cannot be
taken for granted, the king of Judah decided to resume the
payment of tribute. Who knows, he reasoned, maybe another miracle from heaven would later take place and
somebody else would destroy the Assyrians for him. That
is precisely what happened.

The Assyrians were the sad sacks of history. They had

the same bad luck as that ascribed by Abraham Lincoln to one of his generals—an uncanny ability to "wrest defeat from the jaws of victory." When at long last Assyria succeeded in pushing her frontiers from the Persian Gulf to the Libyan Desert, she was given no time to enjoy the fruits of her hard-won victories. The Babylonians, the first people defeated by Assyria, rebelled. They sacked Nineveh, the Assyrian capital (612 B.C.). An Assyrian general tried to save a remnant of the Empire, but at the historic Battle of Carchemish (605 B.C.), in alliance with the Egyptians, Babylonia annihilated the Assyrian forces. The Assyrian nation ceased to exist.

The former Assyrian Empire fell into the hands of Babylonia, and with it, Judah. But submission was no more in the make-up of the people of Judah than it had been in the people of Israel. The end of Judah was equally inevitable. It was a tragedy in three acts. After a few years of Babylonian rule, Judah staged its first rebellion in 600 B.C. King Nebuchadrezzar (also known as Nebuchadnezzar) sent an army of irregulars to quell the uprising. To his amazement, it was trounced by the Jews. This time Nebuchadrezzar himself came at the head of his combined forces, only to discover what the Assyrians before him had found—that the Jews were intrepid foes. Jerusalem was besieged and finally fell in 597 B.C. Nebuchadrezzar took the eighteen-year-old King Jehoiachin into captivity and deported 8,000 of the country's leading citizens—all who might possibly foment another uprising. He did not sack Jerusalem at this time, or devastate the country. Instead he appointed twenty-one-year-old Zedekiah, the last king of the house of David, to the throne of Judah as puppet ruler.

No sooner had Nebuchadrezzar, the Babylonian king, withdrawn his armies from Judah, than an anti-Babylonian intrigue got under way. Judah aligned herself with Egypt to strike for independence. An enraged Nebuchadrezzar again marched on his enemies. The Egyptians succumbed within a few weeks; the Jews held out for a year and a half. Finally, in the fateful year of 586 B.C., after a six-month siege, the Babylonians breached the walls of Jerusalem. Zedekiah was captured, his sons were slain before his sight, and then his eyes were torn out. The Temple was destroyed, the city was looted and reduced to rubble. Everybody was deported to Babylonia except the poor, the sick, and the crippled.

Those Babylonian soldiers who had survived the two previous wars with Judah were to learn the road to Jerusalem well. They had to make a third march to that city. Nebuchadrezzar had underestimated the "poor, the sick, and the crippled." The governor appointed by Nebuchadrezzar was slain. The Babylonian garrison at Mizpah was slaughtered. But this third rebellion was undertaken more in the spirit of defiance than in the hope of victory. After three wars and three defeats, the kingdom of Judah was finished—136 years after the fall of Israel.

The observations made on the three Israel-Assyrian wars apply with equal pertinency to the three Judah-Babylonian wars. It was again a case of a small nation holding out against insuperable odds, standing up against a tremendous empire embracing a land mass that stretched from the Persian Gulf to the Mediterranean. The wonder was not that Babylonia won. The wonder was that the Jews almost defeated her.

FOUR

# RELIGION IS PACKAGED

With the death of Israel and Judah, according to the Spenglerian concept of history, it was time for the Palestinian civilization to die. Moses, Joshua, and the Judges had ushered in the spring of her civilization; David and Solomon had represented her summer stage. Even though civil war had split the kingdom in two, each part had followed a parallel course leading to an autumn phase, with the winter periods for both setting in with militarism and ending in final annihilation. As history goes, Palestine had lived a full life. But was the Jewish state founded at Mount Sinai in 1200 B.C. really dead?

Indeed, it looked as if Jewish history were going to be no exception to Spengler's rule. The Ten Tribes of Israel never reappeared in the pages of history after their defeat at the hands of the Assyrians. When the Babylonians exiled the Jews of Judah, it looked as if this would be the end of them too. But it did not turn out that way. Something happened in the interim between the defeat of Israel in 722 B.C. and the defeat of Judah in 586 B.C. which made it possible for the latter to survive and to germinate a new phase of Jewish life.

In pagan days, captives marching into exile usually marched to extinction—not physically, but as a national entity. Because one set of idols was exchangeable for another, captive peoples usually embraced both the idols and the *Weltanschauung* (way of looking at things) of the conquerors. This was the starting point for assimilation, further hastened by the custom of embracing each other's women, an exchange of goodwill between victor and vanquished which added pleasure to a semblance of democracy. The captives did not particularly care whether or not they survived as Hittites, Phoenicians, Syrians, or Jebusites, as long as they had a chance to continue to live. The pagan was willing to lose both his religious and national identities. Such was the case with the kingdom of Israel. Such, however, was *not* the case with Judah.

Why did the Jews of Judah survive whereas the Jews of Israel did not? The political and economic interpreters of history give this answer: The Assyrian policy was to break up conquered nations into small segments, then to disperse the segments throughout the empire in order to destroy national and ethnic unity, in contrast to the Babylonian policy of keeping exiled peoples intact. But this rule did not hold true in every case. Many nations vanquished by Assyria lived in spite of this fragmentation policy, only to disintegrate later when conquered by some other power. Other nations defeated by Babylonia lost their national identities without being strewn all over the map.

There must be more to survival in exile than mere chance. There must be a continuous and conscious effort on the part of the exiles to retain their identities, both religious and national. The Israelites did not have such a conscious will to remain Jews, whereas the captives of Judah carried with them into captivity an implacable will to survive as Jews. What gave them the will to retain their Jewishness in the face of every obstacle and threat? Somewhere

between the fall of Israel and the fall of Judah a spiritual
reawakening of the people of Judah took place. A new
Jewish character and a new concept of Jewishness itself
was forged.

We have seen how Judah, after the fall of Israel, was divided into bitter factions. In addition to external threats,
she was beset with internal strife. Idolatry was gaining
greater strength, the rich were oppressing the poor, intermarriage was diluting the Jewish strain—again the triple
threat to Jewish identity, a threat to her religion, morality,
and racial purity. The former unity was all but gone. The
historic stage was set for the disappearance of Judah too.

This is a classic example of a Toynbeean challenge facing a civilization. Because Judah did not respond with solutions permitting her to continue as an independent
nation, Toynbee, like Spengler, felt that Jewish civilization
came to an end at this point. But the Jews persistently bob
up in subsequent history, refusing to fit into his framework.
Whereas Spengler just ignored the Jews after this date,
Toynbee swept them off his tidy pages into footnotes, char-
acterizing them as fossils. One is reminded of the perhaps
apocryphal story about the Swedish botanist Linnaeus
(1707–1778), who, after having classified all plants, began
the classification of animals. He implicitly believed in the
theory of special creation as opposed to the theory of evolution. One day, when walking in his garden, he saw a bug
which his expert eye immediately told him was a proof for
the theory of evolution as against the theory of special creation. Linnaeus stepped on the bug and buried it in the
sand. He missed the chance of being Darwin.

Toynbee notwithstanding, Judah met the challenge of
the times by responding with two ideas which not only
saved her from national extinction but are still influencing
the Western world today. The first idea was the canonization of part of Holy Scripture, making it the word of God.
This gave the world first the Old testament, then the New.
The second idea was the "packaging" of Jewish religion for
export. This gave the world first Christianity, then Is-
lamism.

In her hour of crisis, Judah had the good fortune to inherit King Josiah (638 B.C.), a ruler with a fertile mind and
a flexible conscience dedicated to a good cause. His father,

a pro-Assyrian king of Judah, had been assassinated by the pro-Egyptians. These assassins, in turn, were murdered by the pro-Assyrians, who placed Josiah on the throne. Josiah was aware of the social inequities corroding the fabric of his country, but he was astute enough to realize that he could institute no social legislation without also introducing religious reforms, inasmuch as justice and morality were tied in with the Mosaic Code. He therefore decided not only to aim for a more just distribution of wealth, but also to purge the temples of idols.

Josiah chose to gamble for high stakes. He conceived a grandiose plan, simple, yet daring. For this he needed what journalists call an "angle" and a "peg." An angle is a viewpoint from which a story is written to make it hang together, and a peg is a time element. Josiah's angle was to attribute to God the reforms which he wanted to institute; his peg was a dramatic way to introduce these reforms. He entrusted these highly secret plans to his High Priests who stood for the same reforms. The plan called for the editing and the fusing of parts of the "J" and "E" documents into "Holy Scripture." When finished, these revised documents were hidden in a secluded part of the main Temple. With great fanfare, King Josiah proclaimed throughout the land that a book written by Moses at the command of God had been found in the Temple and would be read aloud to the people. This Book is now known as Deuteronomy, or the "D" document.

Another version of this event is that the documents had actually been in the Temple since the days of Solomon, and that they were accidentally discovered when the Temple was renovated. Whichever explanation one accepts, the facts are that the effect was awe-inspiring and greater than Josiah had anticipated, if indeed he had authored the event. Jews came from every part of the kingdom to listen to the words of Moses being read to them. A wave of patriotism and religious reawakening swept the entire nation. Riding on this emotional crest, Josiah purged the temples of idols, forbade the Baal and Astarte cults, and rammed through a bill of social rights.

Josiah's sanctification of Deuteronomy also established something else, something sociologists call "charismatic power." Sociologists conceive of two kinds of power. One originates in an office which ultimately has the physical means of enforcing its will. The second, which does not have such physical means, relies on the sanctity of the office itself. This latter power is called "charismatic," to distinguish it from political and military power. Charismatic power is possible when people voluntarily submit themselves to the will of such an office. The President, for example, has political power because he has military power. The Pope, on the other hand, has charismatic power, because his office, no matter who holds it, commands the voluntary obedience of millions though he has no longer any physical means of enforcing his will. Stalin, when he wanted to give the impression that the Pope had no power, once pointedly asked, "How many divisions does the Pope have?" thus missing the essence of the Pope's source of power.

Until Josiah's time, the Jews had experienced little charismatic authority, only political. In the days of early monotheism, God Himself had to threaten that if His commandments were not obeyed, vengeance would be wreaked not only upon the culprit, but upon his descendants for several generations. Now the Jews, out of an inner discipline, imposed upon themselves the willingness to obey the authority of the Book.

This forging of an inner discipline, this adherence to the dictates of an inner voice, and this bowing to a higher ideal in the face of physical danger was begun by Josiah, but the work was perfected and finished by the Prophets.

Before answering the question, Who are the Prophets? we must ask, What is a Prophet? Though prophets have existed in many civilizations, the Prophet had a special and unique meaning in Jewish history. He was above the seer and above the priest because the Jewish people implicitly believed that their Prophets were men sent by God to show man the path to righteousness. The Prophet in Jewish history was concerned with preserving the purity of the Jewish religion. This led him into the field of man's moral corruption and to the idea that the Jews, who were the Chosen People of God, must set an example for the rest of mankind. By doing this, the Prophets set in motion a series of forces which transformed not only the Jewish religion and the Jews, but also their concept of Jehovah.

The voice of the first "rhapsodic" Prophet (as the Prophets in the Old Testament are generally referred to in Jewish theology) was Amos (769 B.C.). Though born in Judah, he preached in Israel until finally deported back to Judah as an undesirable alien. Hosea followed in his footsteps. The rest of the Prophets all preached in Judah, from Isaiah to Malachi, the last of the Prophets.

When Amos and Hosea first preached in Israel, the people laughed, the priests were infuriated, and the kings were uneasy. When the Assyrian cohorts, "gleaming with purple and gold," swooped down on Israel, the people went down to defeat with the words of these two Prophets ringing in their ears. But their words had not registered with the Israelites. That was their undoing, for they did not know what we now know, that to survive captivity they would need an "exportable Jehovah," a religion so resilient that it would be able to flourish on foreign soil. Not having it, they were assimilated and disappeared.

After the fall of Israel, when other Prophets, notably Isaiah and Jeremiah, carried on the new concept of Judaism, their words sank into the Jewish consciousness. By the time it was Judah's turn to be defeated and to have her people exiled, the Prophets had already developed and perfected an exportable religion. When the vanquished Jews of Judah trudged the captivity road to Babylon, the words of the Prophets had taken root in their racial memory.

What, in essence, was it that the Prophets taught and exhorted? What they said—and it is remarkable that they were not all put to death for saying it*—was, in effect, that *ritual* and *cult* in themselves were of no value to God. Humanity, justice, and morality, they contended, were superior to any cult. God, they said, did not want rituals; He wanted higher moral standards from men. God abhorred sacrifice, they contended; therefore, it was no sin if one did not offer sacrifices to God. The real sin, they held, was corruption and perversion of justice.

These were fantastic and daring notions in those days, when sacrifice and ritual were religion itself. Among the

---

*According to legend, Isaiah was executed, but there is no factual confirmation.

Jews this new doctrine of the Prophets began to undermine the influence of the priests. The Prophetic message changed the character of the Jewish priest from a performer of ritual to that of rabbi, a teacher of Judaism, just as Luther's religious concepts changed the role of the priest in the Catholic Church to that of a minister in the Protestant Church.

From the Prophetic teaching that the Jews must set an example for the rest of mankind grew the idea that the physical commandments of Judaism were for Jews only, but that the spiritual and moral message of Judaism was for all mankind. Now a progression in Jewish religious thought reveals itself. Judaism, which began its life as the exclusive property of a few Jewish families, enlarged by Moses to include all the tribes of Israel, expanded by Josiah to bind the Jewish nation, was now made universal by the Prophets.

With the ideas supplied by the Prophets, the Jews in Babylonian captivity set about renovating their religion and giving it a "new look." The Temple had been tied by law to Jerusalem, and sacrifice had to be offered in it according to rigid ritual and formula. By having undermined the value of sacrifice, by having made morality superior to ritual, the Prophets freed the Jewish religion from the confinement of time and place.

On the soil of Babylon the Jews created two new ideas which have since become the possessions of mankind. Instead of a temple for sacrifice, the Jews built synagogues for religious assembly; instead of rituals for God, the Jews offered prayers to God. The synagogue became the prototype for the church of the Christians and the mosque of the Muslims; prayer became the universal symbol of devotion to God.

Through synagogue and prayer, the Jew no longer was tied to any specific priesthood, temple, or country. He could set up shop in any land and be in direct communication with God—without intermediaries. The Jewish religion, which had been immobile and rigid, now became an exportable commodity, resilient and invisible. Survival of the Jews in captivity and in dispersion was assured.

Many Jewish history books draw a picture of sorrow and desolation when writing of the Jewish captivity in

Babylon. Fortunately, this is an inaccurate picture. In the sixth century Babylonia was ruled by a series of enlightened kings who treated their captives with tolerance. Those Jews who "wept by the rivers of Babylon" were but a handful of zealots; the rest of the Jews fell in love with the country, prospered, and became cultured.

Babylonian trade routes took the Jews to every corner of the known world, making them men of commerce and international trade. In the libraries of Babylon the Jews found a world treasure of manuscripts; they acquired a love for books and a taste for learning. They acquired manners, grace, and refinement. The unknown poet who in Psalm 137 sang, "If I forget thee, O Jerusalem, let my right hand forget her cunning. If I do not remember thee, let my tongue cleave to the roof of my mouth,"* may have expressed a sentiment current at the beginning of the exile, but certainly not a sentiment prevalent fifty years later. By then both words and tune had changed. When the sled of Jewish history made a complete turnabout, heading back to Jerusalem, few Babylonian Jews were on it. Again, Jewish fate had been caught up in world history, and to understand the direction it took, we must go back to the history of the dominant military powers.

After four millenniums of Semitic civilizations, Asia Minor fell under the rule of a new people, the Persians, and a new race, the Aryans, latecomers to the circle of culture bearers. In the sixth century B.C., when Babylonia stood at the height of her power, there was no Persia. Who in 1910 would have believed that England, then the undisputed ruler of the seas, in another fifty years would sink to the status of a third-class power, and that Russia, then a third-class power, in the same time would rise to be a dominant world force? Who in 600 B.C. would have believed that in another fifty years Babylonia, then the ruler of the world, would be wiped off the face of the earth by a people that did not as yet exist? Yet history had slated this unknown people to become the inheritors of the civilized world.

The origins of the Persians are uncertain. Historians

---

*The Psalm is attributed to King David, who died in 960 B.C., and, therefore, would be describing events three hundred years before they took place.

surmise they were the early Medes. The founding of the Persian Empire is the accomplishment of one man, Cyrus the Great. In 560 B.C. he became king of a petty city-state in the Middle East hinterland. Ten years later he was king of Media, a small kingdom south of the Caspian Sea. In 539 he defeated Babylonia, and by 530 B.C. he handed his son Cambyses the new Persian Empire extending from the Indus River to the Mediterranean and from the Caucasus to the Indian Ocean. Cambyses added Egypt to his inheritance. The Persians now stood at the summit, not knowing that the Greeks were around the corner with a challenge. Meanwhile, with the defeat of the Babylonians, the Jews were flung into the Persian orbit for two eventful centuries.

As the inheritor of a "Jewish problem," Cyrus took an action that literally stunned the Jews. He gave them permission to return to their homeland. True, it was not loving kindness which prompted him to give them their freedom. He felt that a tribute-paying nation would be more profitable than a devastated country. If he could induce the Jews to return to Jerusalem, he was sure they would rebuild the city and the country, and turn the desolation into a profitable source of revenue.

Whatever the motives of Cyrus, his act caught the Jews totally unprepared, and his graciousness was not greeted with unmitigated joy in every quarter. In fact, the decree created mixed emotions and loyalties. Why go back to Jerusalem where only desolation, poverty, and unremitting hard labor stared one in the face? This situation could be likened to a similar one today. Not many American Jews migrated to Israel when it became an independent state in 1948. Like the American Jew today, the Babylonian Jew said, "I'm a good Babylonian [American]. Why should I go?"

The Jews had not only prospered in Babylonian exile and become refined, they had also multiplied. Whereas at the beginning of the exile there had been hardly 125,000 Jews in the entire world, there were now 150,000 Jews in Babylonia itself. About a fourth decided to take advantage of Cyrus's edict and return to Jerusalem. Here they joined the small number of Jews who had managed to survive the debris and ruin of those devastating three wars which had led to exile in Babylonia fifty years earlier.

A wag once defined Zionism as a movement of one Jew sending a second Jew to Palestine on a third Jew's money. This remark could very well have originated in Babylonia, because wealthy Babylonian Jews began subsidizing the return to Jerusalem of less fortunate Jews, and in this way there was a continuous trickle of Jews back to the homeland after the first mass exodus. Jerusalem became prosperous again. The population grew, agriculture and commerce flourished, and the increased tribute Cyrus had foreseen flowed into his coffers.

But in Palestine, the Jewish leaders were worried. The country, for all intents and purposes, was still a satellite nation. Any day a ruler could ascend the throne of Persia who might not have the tolerant attitude of Cyrus. The threat of expulsion or abrogation of religious liberties might one day hang over their heads. What additional measures could Jewish leaders take to prevent the ethnic extinction of the Jews in such an eventuality? The problem, they felt, was no longer how to survive as individual Jews, but how to survive as a recognizable Jewish people. Could a feeling of Jewishness be embedded even deeper in the Jewish soul than the Prophets had thrust it? Could such a feeling be driven into the unconscious so deeply as to become a part of the total personality? These answers were provided by the leaders of a second mass exodus of Jews from Babylonia to Jerusalem.

The mass of Jews in the first Babylonian exodus had for the most part been drawn from the zealots and from the poor. In spite of this, they had a triumvirate of most distinguished leadership—two princes and a Zadokite* High Priest. Prince Sheshbazzar and Prince Zerubbabel were descendants of the royal house of David, and both hoped to become king of Judah. Jeshua, the Zadokite, hoped to be anointed High Priest. Only Jeshua's dream was realized. Sheshbazzar, who began the rebuilding of the Temple which the Babylonians had destroyed, mysteriously disappears from the pages of the Bible. Zerubbabel, who finished the Temple, vanishes equally mysteriously. A clue to

---

*Zadok was the first High Priest appointed by King David. Descendants of Zadok, known as Zadokites, were held in highest esteem and honor by Jews.

their sudden disappearance is furnished in the Old Testament (Ezra and Zechariah), which hints that the Jews tried to crown each of them king. It is entirely possible—and this is a conjecture—that the Persians, who would not tolerate the establishment of a royal house in Judah, unceremoniously beheaded both Sheshbazzar and Zerubbabel for high treason. On the other hand, the Persians did not oppose a Jewish High Priest. It is not surprising, therefore, that we read in the Old Testament (Zechariah 6:11) that a crown of silver and gold was placed on the head of Jeshua as he was anointed High Priest and ruler of Jerusalem.

The crowning of Jeshua as High Priest was of great significance to the Jews because it gave them a form of self-government in exile which was acceptable to their conquerors, without arousing suspicion that they would try to establish an independent kingdom. After having been successively ruled first by Judges, then by kings, Palestine was to be ruled, with but a brief interruption, for the next five hundred years by High Priests. Palestine, however, never became a theocracy* because of the balance of power in Jewish democracy. The power of the Sanhedrin and the Popular Assemblies always kept Jewish government under secular, not priestly, control, though the titular head, residing in the office of High Priest, gave it the outward semblance of a theocracy.

The leaders of the first exodus from Babylonia had set the political boundaries for their homeland; the leaders of the second exodus set the spiritual framework. Searching for the answers to the problem of ethnic survival were two high-born Jews, Nehemiah and Ezra, both influential in Persian court circles. Nehemiah, also a descendant of Zadok, was a "cupbearer to the king," and Ezra was a scribe at the court. Both became the Pauls of a new Judaism.

Nehemiah was appointed governor of Judah by the Persian king. As governor he enacted social-reform laws, stim-

---

*Theocracy—from two Greek words, *theos* meaning "god," and *kratein* meaning "to rule": hence a government by priests who claim divine permission from God to rule. The Jewish High Priest could no more claim divine permission to rule or descent from God than could the Jewish king.

ulated commerce and industry, and rebuilt the walls around Jerusalem. Ezra had heard of the low state of morale among the first settlers of Judah. He became obsessed with the mission to establish firmly for all time a Jewish consciousness in his people. This, he was convinced, could be done only by reinstituting Mosaic law as fundamental law. It was this accomplishment which earned him the title of "Second Moses."

In the year 458 B.C., with the permission of the Persian king, Ezra headed the second mass exodus of eighteen hundred Jews from Babylonia to Jerusalem. Here Ezra joined hands with Nehemiah. The first move of this alliance between priest and aristocrat was a ban on intermarriage between Jews and non-Jews, the first in Jewish history, and the first such ban on intermarriage in the world. This action did not sit well with many nations. Think of the gall of this small nation, just freed from captivity, saying in effect that no man or woman of any other nation was good enough for the children of Israel. It did not sit well with many Jews either, and the Book of Ruth is considered to have been written at this time as a protest against such discrimination. However, it must be stressed that this action was not motivated by a philosophy of superiority, or as a rejection of other people as inferior, but was strictly a defense against future religious dilution. The Chosen People should stay chosen. This Ezra-Nehemiah edict had a cumulatively greater and greater binding force on the Jews, and eventually was to help them survive the waves of assimilation which almost overwhelmed them during Greco-Roman, Islamic, and modern times.

As a second move toward forging a national religious and spiritual Jewish character, Ezra and Nehemiah decided not only to revise the Book of Deuteronomy but to add to it four other Books of Moses. Under their direction, priest and scholar labored diligently to fuse the most important of the divergent Mosaic documents, including the Deuteronomy of Josiah, into the five books of the Pentateuch, namely, Genesis, Exodus, Leviticus, Numbers, and Deuteronomy. All Five Books of Moses were now made divine. From here on, no deletions, changes or additions to the Pentateuch could be made, nor have any been made.

The dramatic "peg" used by Josiah to introduce his version of Deuteronomy was also used in the year 444 B.C. by Ezra and Nehemiah to introduce the Pentateuch. Heralds were sent into every corner of the Persian Empire to spread the news that on the Jewish New Year's Day the Five Books of Moses, written by Moses, would be read aloud to all the people. The news was on everyone's tongue, and on that eventful New Year's Day Jews from all over the empire thronged into Jerusalem. Because people had already begun to forget Hebrew, interpreters were on hand to explain in Aramaic all difficult passages. The Aramaic language, the Esperanto of the Middle Eastern melting pot of Semitic peoples, had become the everyday speech of the Jews as well as that of dozens of other Semitic nations.

The idea of having interpreters proved popular and became a permanent institution in Jewish life. Because it was decreed that no part of the Bible could remain obscure, a school known as *Midrash* (meaning "exposition") developed. These expositors of the Bible became highly respected members of every Jewish community and foreshadowed the academies, or yeshivas, to be founded by the Jews at the beginning of the Christian Era. So that the people would not forget the Law of Moses, Ezra and Nehemiah also decreed that the Pentateuch had to be read in every synagogue throughout each year on the Sabbath day and twice during the week. Right after every Jewish New Year, the reading was started over again with the first chapter of Genesis.

It must be pointed out that the above account of the origin of the Pentateuch is by no means universally accepted. We have given a secular explanation, to which many scholars subscribe, but not all. A considerable segment of people hold the view that the Pentateuch is divinely inspired and written by one person. In this book we have presented, and will continue to present, the secular viewpoint without claiming that this is the only interpretation, or that a religiously oriented answer is less accurate. The books in the New Testament, as we shall later see, were introduced much in the same manner by men who wanted them declared divine. The important thing is that irrespective of which explanation one accepts, the events took place, and these events shaped history.

Eight hundred years after the death of Moses the Jewishness of the Jew had been established as a result of the reforms of Josiah, the doctrines of the Prophets, and the innovations of Ezra and Nehemiah.

The Babylonian Jews who had returned to Jerusalem brought with them their love for books. They stimulated a new intellectual life in Palestine. Palestine and Babylonia rivaled each other in scholarship and intellectual ferment for many centuries until, three hundred years after the destruction of the Temple in Jerusalem by the Romans, Babylonia became the sanctuary and repository for Jewish learning for a thousand years.

The Babylonian Jews also introduced the concept of the synagogue into Palestine, where it existed side by side with the Temple. The synagogue, however, did not displace the Temple in importance until after the destruction of that Temple in 70 A.D. But in spite of the continued existence of the Temple cult in Jerusalem, the synagogue took on a new form in both Babylonia and Palestine. The new love for study brought Jews of all social and economic classes into closer communion. This common respect for knowledge rapidly changed the function of the synagogue. Because its use became threefold, the synagogue itself was known by three names, depending upon which service it performed— *Beth Tephila*, the "House of Prayer"; *Beth Hamidrash*, the "House of Study"; and *Beth Haknesseth*, the "House of Assembly." (The word *Knesseth* is the name for the parliament of Israel today.) This expansion of the Jewish religious framework to include prayer, learning, and government set the pattern for yet other concepts to come— namely, standard prayer books and liturgy, universal education, freedom of assembly, and self-government in exile, all instituted first by the Jews and later adopted by other nations.

The dream of Abraham and the vision of Moses for a unified Jewish people, obeying the commandments of the Lord God Jehovah out of an inner compulsion, had been fulfilled. They were now to be tested in the crucible of history. The center of civilization was shifting from the Near East to Europe. Alexander the Great of Macedonia was on the march in quest of empire, bringing with him a new way of life, a new civilization, and new challenges to the Jews.

# II

# THE AGE OF THE "APIKORSIM"

*How the Jews defended themselves against the "Apikorsim"—the Epicurean Greeks—and their naked statues; and how they survived military slaughter at the hands of the Romans, who laid Jerusalem waste and made much of Palestine off limits to them.*

# THE GRECO-ROMAN PERIOD
## 300 B.C. TO 300 A.D.

| GRECO-ROMAN HISTORY | | JEWISH HISTORY |
|---|---|---|
| Aryan tribes invade Greek peninsula from Asia Minor. | 1300 B.C. to 1200 | Jews are slaves in Egypt. |
| Age of Achilles; Siege of Troy. | 1200 to 1100 | Moses leads Jews out of bondage in Egypt. Jews settle in Palestine. |
| Aeolians. Ionians, Dorians filter into Greece from Northern Balkans. Cretan and Aegean civilizations destroyed. | 1100 to 800 | Age of Judges. David and Solomon kings. Division of Palestine into Judah and Israel. |
| Age of Homer. Greeks become known as Hellenes. Rome founded by barbaric invaders. | 800 to 700 | Century of Prophets. Kingdom of Israel destroyed by Assyrians. |
| First formation of Greek city-states. | 700 to 600 | Josiah king of Judah. Age of Jeremiah and Isaiah. |
| Romans destroy Etruscan culture. | 600 to 500 | Babylonians conquer Judah, deport Jews. Persians defeat Babylonians; set Jews free to return to Palestine. |

| | | |
|---|---|---|
| Greek-Persian wars begin. Battles of Marathon and Salamis. Roman Republic founded. | 500 B.C. to 400 | Second return of Jews from Babylonia. The reforms of Ezra and Nehemiah. |
| Rise of Macedonia. Alexander the Great defeats the Persians. Samnite wars make Romans masters of Italy. | 400 to 300 | Jews come under Grecian rule and Hellenic influence. First contact with West. |
| Breakup of Alexander's empire into Seleucid and Ptolemaic kingdoms. First and Second Punic and Macedonian wars establish Romans as dominant Mediterranean power. | 300 to 200 | Bible translated into Greek. Foundations for Christianity laid. |

a: *Ptolemaic Kingdom:* Centered in Egypt and Palestine. Ruled by house of Ptolemy until 30 B.C. when annexed by the Romans.

Palestine under Ptolemaic rule from 323 to 198 B.C. Has self-government under rule of High Priests.

b: *Seleucid Kingdom:* Centered in Asia Minor and Babylonia. Conquered by Rome in 67 B.C.

Palestine wrested from Ptolemies in 198 by Seleucids. Maccabean revolt.

| | | |
|---|---|---|
| Disintegration of Greek city-states. Romans defeat Hannibal. Third Macedonian War makes Romans masters of Greece. | 200 to 100 | Maccabees establish Hasmonean dynasty. Strife between Sadducees and Pharisees. |
| Rome conquers the East, invades Britain, becomes ruler of known world. Age of Caesar. End of Roman Republic. | 100 B.C. to 1 A.D. | Palestine conquered by Romans (63). Jesus Christ born. Herod King of the Jews. |
| Age of absolute dictatorships. Octavian, Vespasian, Titus, Nero. Height of Roman power. Christians persecuted. | 1 A.D. to 100 | Pontius Pilate procurator of Judea. Christ crucified by Romans. First Jewish uprising against Roman oppression. Titus destroys Jerusalem. |
| Century of uprisings and revolts. Persecution of Christians continues. | 100 to 200 | Second and third Jewish rebellions. Bar Kochba insurrection. Palestine devastated and made off-limits to Jews. |
| Collapse of constitutional government. Beginning of end for Romans. Army in control of state. | 200 to 300 | Jews dispersed throughout empire, become Roman citizens. Permitted to resettle in Palestine. |

# FIVE

# THE BAITED PIN-UP CULTURE

One thinks of the Hellenization of the Alexandrian empire as being all-pervasive. Actually it was like a hoop skirt; it covered much but touched little. The conquering Greeks tried to change the Near East by fitting her into this vast hoop skirt. Within it they placed their wares of art, science, and pleasure, which constituted their exportable Hellenism.* A succession of Jewish leaders exhorted the Jews to resist the lure of the Hellenized pin-up culture. They exposed the bait in Grecian hedonism, or philosophy of pleasure, and warned them against the folly of committing national suicide by exchanging their Jewish heritage for an "ersatz" Greek culture.

The introduction of Hellenism in the Near East during the third century B.C. resembled the introduction of the Renaissance into feudal Poland during the fifteenth century A.D. In Poland, the nobility wore powdered wigs and handkerchiefs doused with the finest French perfumes. But underneath the powdered wigs the lice crawled; behind the scent of perfume lurked the stench of unwashed bodies. In the Near East, Hellenism was for the city slickers. Behind the glittering façades of "Greek cities" were the baked-mud hovels of the Oriental peasants. Though a few pagan intellectuals read Greek poetry, the great majority of the people were illiterate. Though Greek thought dominated the Near East for six hundred years, no original native contribution to art, letters, or philosophy ever grew out of this fusion between Occident and Orient.

There was one exception—the Jews. Though most of them rejected Hellenism itself, Greek philosophy fell on fertile soil. Though the Jews in the main did resist the

---

*We must make a distinction between "Hellenistic" and "Hellenic." The first refers to the exportable phase of Greek culture; the second is the term applied to the civilization in Greece itself.

Greek philosophies, they mastered the Greek philosophers. The Jews absorbed everything intellectual which the Greeks had to offer. To everything intellectual they borrowed, they added a Jewish touch. The Greeks then took these retouched ideas back from the Jews. The result was something neither had foreseen. The Greeks emerged in a Jewish-made mantle known as Christianity; the Jews wore a Greek philosophic tunic labeled "Talmudism."* But in spite of this extensive borrowing from each other for six centuries, the Greeks regarded the Jews as barbarians without manners, and the Jews viewed the Greeks as heathens without morals.

Who were these Greeks, and how did they get mixed up with the Jews—or the Jews with them? Historians do not know much about their early origins except that, like the Persians, they were an Aryan people. At about the time that Moses led the Israelites out of Egypt, the Greeks invaded the Aegean Peninsula from the Anatolian Plain in Asia Minor. Greek history properly begins with the establishment of the key city-states of Athens, Sparta, and Corinth in the seventh century B.C., about the time Israel was defeated by the Assyrians. In the fifth and fourth centuries, Greece gave birth to a succession of great men in almost every field of learning except religion.

The fifth century, the height of Greek achievement, her Golden Age, was also her century of anxiety. The Greeks lived under the constant threat of domination by their fellow Aryans, the Persians. By the sixth century, Persia had extended her empire to the Aegean shores, and by the fifth century Greece was on Persia's timetable for conquest. There was no question as to who would annihilate whom. There was no logical reason for a supposition that the tiny Greek city-states would defeat the colossus from the East, but that is precisely what happened at the famed land battle at Marathon (490 B.C.) and the equally famed sea battle at Salamis (480 B.C.), where the Greeks shattered the vastly superior Persian forces. It was illogical, but as history never stops to apologize for her inconsistencies, she continued to

---

*The theme of this statement will be developed in Part IV, "The Invisible World of the Talmud," dealing with the origins and growth of Talmudism.

be illogical and permitted the Greek tribes to defeat the Persian armies over and over again.

Between defeating the Persians, the Greeks went back to their favorite pastime—fighting among themselves. It never occurred to them to pursue the defeated enemy into his homeland. The Greeks thought their civilization too good for the barbarians. Why invade and be burdened with the problem of governing and educating them? Alexander the Great was the first Greek on record who had different ideas on that point. He dreamed of a world empire. In 334 B.C. he crossed the Hellespont with 32,000 infantrymen and shattered the armies of an empire which had millions of soldiers at its command. The Persian armies were first defeated at the River Granicus, then annihilated at the Battle of Issus, where Alexander demanded the unconditional surrender of Darius III. The Persian Empire ceased to exist. By the law of "winner take all," the Jews passed under Greek rule.

For some unexplained reason, the hot-tempered Jews did not fight Alexander, though in the past, heedless of odds, they had not hesitated to take arms against enemies equally formidable. Instead, according to a persistent legend, the High Priest of Jerusalem headed a formal procession to welcome Alexander (332 B.C.). The Macedonian king took an instant liking to these "fierce barbarians" who, to his great astonishment, carried no visible gods with them to greet him. He granted them internal political and religious freedom, an act which made him the "patron saint" of the Jews, if one can speak of such a thing.

Alexander's ambition was not only to establish a Grecian empire, but to extend Hellenic culture the world over. He wanted the people in his domain to speak Greek, act Greek, be Greek. This he hoped to accomplish by Hellenizing all conquered provinces. His method of indoctrination was exceedingly simple, though highly effective. Instead of the sword, Alexander used sex. To establish Greek culture as a way of life in the conquered territories, Alexander ordered his officers and men to intermarry with the native populations and to beget many children. Within ten years he founded twenty-five Greek cities in the Middle East, chief among them Alexandria in Egypt. So effective was his method of acculturation by insemination that, but for his untimely death at the age of thirty-two, he would probably have succeeded. His successors, however, were more interested in military and political power than in propagation of the Hellenic ideal. No sooner had Alexander died than his great domain was ripped apart by the swords of his dissenting generals. Three of them contended for the empire, but none was strong enough to seize it, so each grabbed a part of it. Antigonus laid claim to Greece; Seleucus took possession of Asia Minor and Syria, founding the Seleucid Empire; Ptolemy grabbed Egypt and Palestine, founding the Ptolemaic Empire.

The Ptolemaic kings generally subscribed to the philosophy of "live and let live." As long as the Palestinian Jews paid taxes, they were left alone. They enjoyed a large measure of self-government and complete cultural and religious freedom. The chief administrator was the High Priest, whose power was held in check by the Sanhedrin so that there would be no chance for the High Priest to confuse his will with that of God. The Sanhedrin acted in the dual capacity of senate and supreme court, with its members chosen from the leading families, scholars, and intellectuals. When acting as a supreme court, this body had seventy-one members; when judging cases involving capital offense, it was composed of twenty-three judges; in civil cases and lesser criminal offenses, a minimum of three members was required.

The statement that the American system of law is based partly upon Roman concepts has been made so often that we take it for granted, without examining the source from which Roman laws might stem. The remarkable resemblances among Roman law, present-day American law, and Jewish jurisprudence in biblical days is more than mere coincidence. The Jews devised, four centuries before Christ, a legal system based on the dignity of man and individual equality before the law, while Europe still had trial by ordeal as late as the fifteenth century. The rabbis viewed law as a vehicle for justice; laws without justice were regarded as immoral. Even though the Jews in those days had no jury system,* the procedures for the indictment and trial of

---

*Many democracies today do not have a jury system; they hold that a jury is only another organized form of law, and that justice can flourish equally with or without a jury, just as injustice can exist with or without a jury system.

an accused person were similar to the procedures in American courts today. The accused was presumed to be innocent until proved guilty. He had a right to counsel and to a proper trial. He had a right to call witnesses, to confront his accusers, and to testify in his own behalf. He could not be compelled to testify against himself, and he could not be placed in double jeopardy. The accused individual was permitted to appeal, or have others appeal in his behalf, if new evidence should turn up.

Though the bulk of the population was still agricultural, many turned to commerce and industry, which took those so engaged to every outpost of the former Alexandrian empire. The Jews prospered and multiplied. "They have penetrated into every state so that it is difficult to find a single place in the world in which this tribe has not been received and become dominant," wrote the Greek geographer and philosopher Strabo in the first century B.C. Every Greek city in Asia Minor had a considerable Jewish population. But underneath the façade of tranquillity, two struggles were taking place. One was an internal struggle among the Jews themselves against Hellenization. The other was an external tug of war between the Ptolemies and Seleucids.

When the Jews came under Grecian rule, their real enemy was Hellenism. The subsequent fight between Greek and Jew was the fight between two ideas packaged for export—Alexander's Hellenic culture, and the Judaic religion of the Prophets. The Prophets won.

The Hellenization of the Jews began inconspicuously. First it infected their language, manners, and customs; then it encroached upon their morals, ethics, and religion. The first was a daytime breakthrough, between nine and five, when Jewish and Greek businessmen met in bazaars and coffee houses. The second took place after five, when Jewish and Greek youths met in gymnasiums, theaters, and cabarets.

Under the impact of daily business associations, the Jews assumed Greek names for the same reasons American Jews today Anglicize their names; they spoke Greek for the same reason educated Europeans spoke French in the later Baroque era; they abandoned their traditional Jewish dress for the Greek tunic for the same reason Chinese and Japanese today shed their traditional costumes for Westernized clothing. Greek words crept into Jewish religious writings. Even synagogues began to resemble Grecian temples. Jews throughout the world experienced a shock, and Christians a sad surprise, when archaeological excavations in a former Greco-Roman outpost brought to light a Jewish synagogue, which at first was mistaken for a Grecian temple.* Its walls were covered with beautiful, colorful paintings, portraying biblical scenes. They are so highly reminiscent of Byzantine painting that scholars now, to their great discomfiture, are forced to credit the Jews as the originators of an art form heretofore thought of as strictly Christian.

The after-five social encounters between Jewish and Greek youth had an even more corrosive effect on traditional Jewish ways than the nine-to-five business intermixing of their elders. Greek games were exceedingly popular, and soon nude wrestling was commonplace among Jewish males. In the theater the younger set came in contact with the urbane sophistication of the Greeks, and from here the door led to the cabaret and to the couch of the concubine. Soon pleasure was pursued as a policy, and "folly soared into philosophy." The road to apostasy ran from the front pew in the synagogue to a seat in the theater to the embrace of the *hetaera* to a front pew in a pagan temple.

Just as Jewish businessmen yielded to Greek manners and Jewish youth to Greek pleasure, so the Jewish intellectuals succumbed to the spell of the Greek philosophers, whom the orthodox Jews regarded with more alarm than they did the courtesans. The latter could corrupt only the body, whereas the former corrupted the mind. Of all the Greek philosophers, the Epicureans were singled out as special targets for condemnation. The Epicureans were the cynics who taught that the gods did not intervene in human affairs. They taught that it was man's duty to free himself from such superstitions as punishment and reward, and that there was no such thing as morality and immorality, only pleasure. The pursuit of pleasure, the Epicureans held, was man's only true goal. Under the impact of this distortion of the philosophy of Epicurus, immorality and licen-

---

*Carl H. Kraeling, *The Excavations of Dura-Europos*, Final Report VIII, Part I, *The Synagogue.*

tiousness replaced the traditional values of chastity and faithfulness. So threatening were the inroads made by the Epicureans on Jewish youth that their very name—"Apikoros" in Hebrew—became a dreaded curse so deeply embedded that it persists until this day among Jews.

Though the inroads of Hellenization were considerable, most Jews remained anti-Hellenistic. Two ideological strands bound the anti-Hellenizers together. One was the prestige and power of the Mosaic law, still considered divine by the people; the other was the firm belief that the Davidic line of kings would be restored. Slowly these sentiments forged the anti-Hellenizers into a political party, whose members became known as the Hasideans, or pietists, who must not be confused with the Hasidists, a Jewish religious sect which made its appearance in eighteenth-century Europe. The Hasidean party, which had originally been formed as a protest against drinking and carousing, now turned against the Epicureans in particular and against all things Grecian in general. As more and more members flocked to its banner, it gained political strength and came to play the dominant role in the events to follow.

For 125 years the Seleucids and Ptolemies fought over the control of Palestine. Finally, after more than a century of struggle, the Seleucid king, Antiochus III, known as "the Great," succeeded in wrestling Palestine from the Ptolemies. Antiochus continued the tolerant policies of its former rulers, permitting the Jews even greater internal freedom because of the remarkable aptitude they had shown for self-government.

Antiochus had the grandiose idea of unifying the entire former Alexandrian empire under his rule. He marched his troops to Egypt, where he ran headlong into the Romans. One look at the Roman legions, and Antiochus got out. In spite of his ignominious retreat, he felt he could defeat the Romans if he but had a unified empire behind him, and that an intense Hellenization program, which included erecting statues of the Greek gods and himself throughout his domain, would give him that unity. This nationalistic drive was a success in the greatest part of his empire, but it ran into a snag in Palestine. The Jews argued that by bearing arms and paying taxes to Antiochus they had proved their loyalty and good citizenship without having to prove it further by erecting statues of the king in their temples. Antiochus agreed, but his second son, Antiochus Epiphanes, who inherited the throne in 176 B.C., after the murder of his brother, did not. Antiochus Epiphanes felt that the Hellenization program begun by his father should also include the Jews, not because he had anything against them, but as a matter of principle. The Jews could not see it that way. The result was a tragic war with comic overtones and unexpected results.

It was the custom of the Seleucid kings to appoint the governors ruling the provinces in their realm. In the case of the Jews, who had self-government, the king usually appointed a High Priest recommended by the Jews themselves. The Hellenized Jewish aristocrats thought that it would be to their advantage if they helped Antiochus in his ambition to Hellenize Palestine. Through intrigue and bribery these aristocrats prevailed upon Antiochus to appoint to this office a Jewish priest named Jason, a leading Hellenizer in Palestine. What 125 years of Ptolemaic and Seleucid rule had not been able to bring about, Jason accomplished in twelve months. He opened the gates of the Temple to pagan rites. Grecian statues were introduced into the Holy Sanctuary; Jewish priests garbed in Grecian costumes officiated at Greek cultic rites. Greek games performed by naked Jewish boys became a common spectacle in the Temple courtyards. Jewish envoys were sent to pagan festivals to represent Jerusalem. Anger and resentment smoldered. Jews from all economic and social strata flocked to the ranks of the Hasideans, whose leaders, like the Prophets of five hundred years earlier, began to thunder against licentiousness and idolatry. The events which now took place were not planned. They just happened that way.

Antiochus Epiphanes has been so entrenched in Jewish history as a villain that few Jews can see the war which ensued for what it really was—not an uprising against tyrannical Seleucids, but a revolt by Jewish anti-Hellenizers against Jewish Hellenizers. Nothing anti-Jewish was imposed on the Jews by the Seleucids. The same laws, just or unjust, had been applied to everybody. All complied, except the Jews. Neither had any Seleucid king demanded the extremes imposed by Jason. The rebellion, sparked by an unforeseen event, was started by the Jews. It was this rebellion which invited the reprisals that followed, not Jewish noncompliance with the Seleucid Hellenization program.

With Hellenism triumphant in his realm, Antiochus Epiphanes felt it was time to implement ideas with deeds, and he marched against Egypt. A rumor reached the Jews that he had been slain in a battle with the Romans. Hasidean party leaders seized the opportunity and struck at the Jewish Hellenizers, permanently disposing of all the Jewish officials and priests appointed by Antiochus by the simple device of throwing them over the walls of the temple, a one-hundred-foot drop from which none recovered. The statues followed the officials over the wall. Then began a systematic massacre of all known Hellenizers. The Hasideans took over the rule of the country.

Alas, it had been a false rumor. Antiochus was very much alive and full of rage. He had only suffered the same humiliating rebuff at the hands of the Romans as had his illustrious father. Faced with an ultimatum by the Romans to get out of Egypt and with an uprising in Palestine, Antiochus thought it more prudent to vent his anger on the Jews. He marched his armies out of Egypt into Jerusalem, where he senselessly slaughtered 10,000 inhabitants without inquiring into their party affiliations. A new set of statues was installed in the Temple, and a new set of High Priests was appointed to tend to them. Just as Alexander the Great had invited the Jews to settle in his Greek cities, so Antiochus invited the pagans to come and settle in Jerusalem to dilute the Jewish population.

Had Antiochus stopped here, the breach might have been healed. But unfortunately his injured pride did not permit this. Out of sheer spite he outlawed the Sabbath day and forbade circumcision. The Hasidean party, whose members had been practically wiped out in the Seleucid reprisals, now found new adherents among those Jews who previously had stood for moderate Hellenization. A second uprising was inevitable, and again a totally unforeseen event sparked it.

In a little town outside Jerusalem, a Greek official attempted to force an aged Jewish priest to sacrifice to

Greek gods. The name of the priest was Mattathias, of the Hasmonean house. Rather than commit this sacrilege, Mattathias slew the official. Antiochus ordered new reprisals, and the Jewish population rose en masse to the defense of Mattathias, who, with his five sons, now took over the conduct of the war. They became known as the *Maccabees*—from the Hebrew word for "hammer"—because in battle after battle they dealt "hammer blows" to the Seleucid armies.* It was the beginning of a bitter war, a new kind of war, the world's first religious war, fought with grim determination, heedless of cost and sacrifice.

With amazement, the Seleucid Greeks watched how this people stoically and heroically died for ideas, not possessions. Their disdain for the "barbarian" Jews changed to respect and awe. They could not understand this kind of war. It stood to reason that when a country's armies were defeated, its capital occupied, its king captured, its temple and gods smashed, the people would submit as a matter of course. But these Jews did not submit. As each Jew carried his temple in his heart, the Seleucids ruefully realized they would have to kill all of them in order to kill their religious ideas. As each Jew resisted being killed, a bitter, protracted fight ensued. The legend of the Maccabees spread throughout the Hellenic world.

At first Antiochus had not thought much of this rebellion. He sent a small, crack expeditionary force against the Maccabees to teach them a lesson. The Jews annihilated it. Stung by this unexpected defeat, Antiochus assembled a huge, first-rate army and marched at the head of it against Jerusalem. So confident was he of victory that he brought with him a battalion of slave auctioneers and circulated posters throughout the empire quoting the latest prices for Jewish slaves. But his soothsayers had misread the stars. In 164 B.C. the Jews shattered his armies and recaptured Jerusalem. The Temple was purged of all idols and rededicated to God, giving birth to the feast of Hanukkah, which commemorates this victory.

The war with the Seleucids lasted twenty-five years.

---

*Another explanation is that "Maccabee" is a contraction of the first syllables of their war cry, "Mi ko-mocho ba-eilim, Adonoi?"—"Who is like unto Thee, O Lord?"

Jewish arms were blessed not only with valor but also with continued success. They won battle after battle, and slowly the Seleucids retreated from Palestinian soil. Antiochus Epiphanes died without realizing his dream of selling the Jews in the slave markets of the world. His successor offered the Jews full religious freedom, but, flushed with victory, the Jews held out for complete independence and carried the war to enemy territory. Uncertain of final victory, the Seleucids now offered them independence, and the Jews, worn out by a quarter century of fighting, accepted.

One by one, four of the five sons of Mattathias had been slain in the protracted war. Simon, the only survivor, signed the peace treaty in the year 143 B.C. After an incredible war, the impossible had been achieved—a new Jewish Kingdom of Judah had been established.


S I X
_____

# The Fight That Failed


In 143 B.C., with the second establishment of Judah, the Jewish people were 1,857 years old. By this time, according to the Spenglerian and Toynbeean philosophies, history should have buried them, mankind forgotten them, and archaeologists rediscovered them. But God, fate, or blind circumstance had willed it differently. The Jews were not only very much alive, but unwittingly they were busy formulating ways and means for destroying their newly established kingdom.

Though Simon, the only surviving son of Mattathias, was never anointed king, he is nevertheless regarded as the first of the Hasmonean dynasty. Officially he was High Priest of Jerusalem and governor of Judah. He was a wise and shrewd ruler. He realized that the Seleucids and Ptolemies were only biding their time for a propitious moment to strike back at Judah. Anticipating the rising star of the Roman Empire, he signed a mutual defense pact with the Romans to forestall a future invasion by the Seleucids and Ptolemies. A famous limerick parodies the consequences of this action:

> There was a young lady of Niger
> Who smiled as she rode on a tiger;
> They came back from the ride
> With the lady inside
> And the smile on the face of the tiger.

For almost eighty years the smile was on the face of the rider of the Roman tiger; after that, the smile was on the tiger which had swallowed the Jewish rider. It was not, however, Roman perfidy, but internal Hasmonean strife which brought about the downfall of the new kingdom.

A classic political rift fatally divided the Hasmonean house, setting brother against brother, father against son, people against ruler. At the bottom boiled the issue of Hellenism. At the top simmered three political parties, each one contributing to the destruction of Jerusalem, the dispersion of the Jews, and the creation of Christianity.

We have seen how the ill-advised repressive measures of Antiochus Epiphanes drove Jews of every religious gradation and economic class under the one banner of the Hasideans as a protest not against Hellenism, but against the denial of religious liberty. Many Jews, especially the rich and the aristocrats, had desired a measure of Hellenization without the disappearance of Judaism. Now that victory over the Seleucids was achieved and the threat of annihilation averted, there was nothing to hold these divergent groups together. Lacking counterpressure, the internal pressure of the Jewish Hellenizers exploded the Hasideans into three new, separate parties—the Essenes, the Pharisees, and the Sadducees.

The Essene membership came from the nucleus of the former Hasidean party. But the Essenes had no taste for politics and withdrew from secular activities to devote their entire lives to religious contemplation. As time went by, they formed their own religious communities, as did the Quakers and Amish in America. The Essene Jews developed a messianic religion, giving birth to the ideas which were to play a dominant role in the lives of John the Baptist and Jesus.

The anti-Hellenizers in the Hasidean party, who could not go along with the Essenes in their extreme views and withdrawal from life, separated themselves into a second party known as the "Pharisees," or "Separatists." The pro-Hellenizers, on the other hand, who had joined the Hasideans only to fight a common enemy, now formed their own party, the Sadducees. With time, the political tension between Sadducees and Pharisees increased in intensity until it finally broke out into open conflict. The paradox of the strife between Sadducee and Pharisee was that whereas the Sadducees were liberal in their political views and conservative in their religious thinking, the Pharisees were conservative in their politics and liberal in their religion. The Sadducees stood for Temple, Priest, and Sacrifice—the pre-Prophetic concept of Judaism. The Pharisees stood for Synagogue, Rabbi, and Prayer—the post-Prophetic concept of Judaism. The Sadducees were the party of the aristocrats and priestly class; the Pharisees were the party of the common men.

The Sadducees represented the liberal, enlightened political viewpoint. They felt that neither their country nor Judaism would be jeopardized by a reasonable amount of Hellenic cultural influence, in the same way that many American Jews today believe that they can safely embrace the best features of American life without having to give up their Jewishness. When Jesus preached in Galilee and Jerusalem, the Sadducees did not regard him as a radical, but as a zealot—in other words, as a Pharisee.

The Pharisees, again, looked upon the Sadducees as conservatives, upon the Essenes as zealots, and upon themselves as liberals. They were against Hellenization because it represented an alien culture, but they were not against developing a cultural and political liberalism of their own. They believed in the principle of religious evolution. The Pharisees stressed the new Oral Law, a series of reinterpretations of Mosaic law. They were responsible for introducing the elasticity into Judaism which made possible its survival in the times of stress ahead.

Trouble between the two parties started after Simon was murdered by his son-in-law. Simon's son, John Hyrcanus, was crowned king and anointed High Priest, merging the two offices into one. In this dual role of king and

High Priest, he managed to offend his own party, the Pharisees. He hired foreign mercenaries, struck coins bearing his name, and plundered the tomb of King David, taking from it three thousand talents of silver. The Pharisees were so enraged at his actions that they demanded he give up his office of High Priest. In a fit of anger, Hyrcanus switched his party affiliation to the Sadducees, and further infuriated the Pharisees by introducing several Hellenizing measures. The breach widened.

Hyrcanus extended the frontiers of Palestine by annexing the pagan territories of the Idumeans and Galileans, about 135 B.C., and then committed an act which was to bring his country untold grief. He converted the pagan Idumeans and Galileans to Judaism by the sword. From Idumea came one of the greatest scourges of the Jews, a king, hated by the Jews, but called "Herod the Great" by history. It was to the Galileans that Jesus Christ first preached his Essene doctrines about 150 years later, and it was in Galilee that he made his first converts.

Murder, fratricide, matricide, and regicide, marked the ascension of Aristobulus I, son of Hyrcanus, to the throne. Hyrcanus, realizing from his own experience the dangers of having king and High Priest rolled into one office, had made plans for his wife to succeed him to the throne and for Aristobulus to succeed him to the office of High Priest. Aristobulus felt differently. He murdered his mother and one brother, imprisoned his other brothers, and seized both the throne and the robes of the High Priest. He was an ardent Sadducee who carried his Hellenization ideas to offensive extremes. Fortunately, his rule lasted only one year, and he was succeeded by his brother, Alexander Janneus.

Janneus was a despotic, violent ruler who maintained an iron grip on the country with the aid of foreign mercenaries. He, too, extended the borders of Palestine until it equaled in size what it had been under King David's rule. During his reign the schism between Pharisees and Sadducees reached the breaking point. Civil war broke out. Perhaps the most ironic event in Jewish history now occurred. The Pharisees asked the Seleucids for help, and they obliged with an invading army. At the last minute the Pharisees realized the folly of aligning themselves with their archenemies, and joined Janneus in defeating them. Now that danger was averted, Janneus wreaked a terrible vengeance on the Pharisee conspirators, as bloody as any in history. Fortunately for Palestine, his reign came to a swift end in 78 B.C. He was succeeded by his wife, Alexandra, who proved to be the most capable of the Hasmonean rulers.

Queen Alexandra's reign, brief as it was (78–69), has been called a Golden Age. She instituted vast social reforms. Upon the advice of her brother, a rabbi, she founded free elementary schools and made primary education compulsory for boys and girls. In the first century before Christ, in a world full of illiteracy, illiteracy among the Jews in the tiny kingdom of Palestine was for all practical purposes banished. Illustrious though her record was in social thinking, she committed a grave political error. She was ardently pro-Pharisee, and when she became queen it was the turn of the Sadducees to feel the steel of vindictive vengeance. Disaster was not to be delayed much longer.

The theme of rivalry between two brothers plays an almost obsessive role in Jewish history. The Bible is full of such rivalry—Cain and Abel, Isaac and Ishmael, Jacob and Esau, Solomon and Adonijah, and now Hyrcanus II and Aristobulus II, sons of Alexandra. This rivalry was to have disastrous consequences. As no queen could become High Priest, Alexandra had appointed her eldest son, Hyrcanus, a Pharisee, to that office. When she died, Hyrcanus seized the throne also. His brother, Aristobulus, a Sadducee, led a rebellion against this usurpation and, with the help of the priesthood, Hyrcanus was deposed. Civil war broke out. With the aid of the neighboring Nabateans, Hyrcanus wrested his throne back from his brother. Seeking revenge, Aristobulus appealed to the Romans for help. Fate had so timed it that at the outbreak of civil war in Palestine, in 67 B.C., the Romans, under Pompey, had finished their conquest of Syria, placing their armies right at the border of Palestine. The Romans ordered Hyrcanus off the throne and out of the country. Such was the fear of Rome's military might that Hyrcanus did just that. Aristobulus was back in power.

Jewish history at this point resembles a Gilbert and Sullivan comedy, except for the disaster in the last act. Hyrcanus appealed to Pompey to be reinstated to the throne as the rightful heir; Aristobulus pleaded to keep his job as the rightful Pretender, and the Pharisees, sick of all kings, petitioned Pompey not to recognize either. Pompey listened to all three, heeded none. In the year 63 B.C. he marched into the Maccabean Kingdom of Judah, conquered it, and renamed it Judea.

After seventy-six years of independence of the second Kingdom of Judah, the grandsons of the first Maccabean king had destroyed what Simon Maccabeus had wrought. The fight for freedom begun by the aged priest and patriarch, Mattathias, had failed.

SEVEN

# ROME, CAESARISM, AND REBELLION

Who were these conquering Romans?

Again, as with the Greeks, historians do not know for certain. Legend has it that, at the time Isaiah was creating his immortal prose in Judah, a wolf of unknown parentage was nursing Romulus and Remus, the future founders of Rome (753 B.C.), into sturdy, barbaric manhood. For three hundred years the early Romans struggled to gain a toehold in history. They began their career by exterminating the Etruscans, a highly civilized race with an advanced culture, who had preceded them in Italy. This auspicious beginning almost came to an abrupt end when savage tribes known as the Gauls invaded the Italian plains from the forests of Germany. After a century of fighting, the Romans were able to drive them back. The second invasion, a thousand years later, was to be more successful.

A series of little and big wars made Rome the ruler of the world in the three centuries between 350 and 50 B.C. Three Samnite Wars made the Romans masters over Central Italy. Three Punic Wars made them masters of all Italy, Spain, and North Africa. Three Macedonian Wars brought all Greece under Roman rule. At the dawn of the first century B.C. the Romans stood at the periphery of Asia Minor. Ahead beckoned Alexander's former empire.

Meanwhile, in Rome itself, a fearful struggle for power was taking shape. She was about to scrap her republican form of government for an emperor and a dictatorship. Yet the change was not as great as many historians generally make it out to be. Rome had always been a contradiction in terms. She began life as a republic, but never was a democracy. She was a state governed by patricians—the rich—with a political morsel now and then thrown to the plebeians—the poor. Senate members and the ruling consuls came from the ranks of the patricians only. The successful wars did not benefit the plebeians, who grew poorer, but only the patricians, who grew richer.

Whatever law had prevailed in Rome in the past broke down in this century. The rapacity, corruption, and cruelty which had always characterized her rule reached a crescendo. Justice, as well as public office, was bought, and bribery became an honored public occupation. Bills of attainder, disguised as laws, cheated the people of their lands; moneylending at such usurious rates as 10 percent a month was a patrician privilege, and defaulting small debtors could be broken on the rack. Selling one's children into slavery to escape this cruel fate was so common that it no longer elicited compassion. Successful wars had flooded the country with slaves in such abundance that free labor and free enterprise practically disappeared. As class distinctions sharpened, the gulf between the landless and the propertied grew into an unbridgeable chasm. One demagogue after another succeeded to power by bribery and treachery. They butchered their opponents, graced the Senate with the severed heads of the slain, and lined the highways with the crucified bodies of the captives. This brew of Romanism and savagery bred a Caesarism via three great slave revolts and three social wars.

While this bloodshed was carried on in Rome itself in the name of law, another campaign of bloodshed was carried on outside Rome in the name of glory. Three Mithridatic Wars brought the former Alexandrian empire into the Roman orbit. During the third Mithridatic War (74–64

B.C.), a military campaign led by Gnaeus Pompey brought struggling Judah into the Roman web of captive nations.

After his successful war in the East, Pompey, enriched by plunder, returned to Rome to make a bid for supreme power. Two other Romans, Marcus Crassus and Julius Caesar, had anticipated him, and the resulting stalemate was ended by a merger of forces known as the First Triumvirate. Pompey, the soldier, represented the senators; Crassus, the financier, represented the patricians; and Caesar, the aristocrat claiming descent from Venus and Jupiter, represented the plebeians. But ambition proved stronger than friendship. The Triumvirate ended in war and died at the battle of Pharsalus (48 B.C.), in Thessaly, Greece, where Pompey was defeated. Caesar now became consul in name, but absolute dictator in reality. Rome shed all pretense of democracy.

After his defeat Pompey fled to Egypt, with Caesar in pursuit. Here Pompey met death at the hands of an assassin, and Caesar met love in the arms of the Queen of Egypt, Cleopatra, who was not an Egyptian as is so often claimed, but a Grecian princess, the last surviving ruler of the house of Ptolemy, named after the Greek general who had founded that dynasty. While Caesar made love to Cleopatra, his legions overran Egypt, and the momentum carried them across the borders of Judah. Jerusalem now passed from Pompey's rule to that of Rome. For the loss of her country, Caesar gave Cleopatra a son as a consolation prize. The Jews got taxes. The Caesar and Cleopatra idyl came to a tragic end when Octavian Augustus succeeded to the purple after Caesar's assassination at the hands of Brutus. Octavian stripped Cleopatra of country, title, and riches. Rather than end up in his triumphal procession in Rome (30 B.C.), she committed suicide. This was the end of the Ptolemaic empire.

The Romans were now the rulers of the world. Though they strode over the face of the earth with the rights of conquerors, there was an undercurrent of inferiority in their swagger. This inferiority complex was a gift given them by their next-door neighbors, the Greeks.

The unique relationship which existed between Greece, the conquered nation, and Rome, the conqueror, is brilliantly summed up in Edgar Allan Poe's expression "To the

glory that was Greece,/And the grandeur that was Rome."
This relationship could be compared to that of a mistress
and her lover—the mistress, Greece, beautiful, cultured,
haughty; the lover, Rome, strong, rich, uncouth. The Romans never could wash off their mark of inferiority, and
they keenly felt their lack of a culture and their inability to
produce one. Vainly they tried to make up for this lack by
an ever greater show of grandeur. But Rome remained the
"tradesman turned gentleman," always uneasy in the presence of the cultural aristocracy of vanquished Greece.

In spite of their successes in the field of war, the Romans continued to be utterly dependent on Greece for
their ideas. They were the "practical men," the anti-
intellectuals. Whatever art, literature, and science Rome
did produce were but second-rate copies of Greek origi-
nals. Rome knew only of force as a method for counteract-
ing the encroachment of new ideas. The moment history
severed Rome from Greece, Rome fell apart. When she no
longer had Greece to nourish her arts and sciences, Rome
succumbed culturally and politically to the barbarian invasions.

Some historians have drawn a parallel between the relationship of Rome and Greece on the one hand, and
America and Western Europe on the other. The West Europeans, like the Greeks, they say, are the intellectuals, the
pacesetters in literature, the innovators in art, and the theoreticians in science. The Americans, they contend, are, like
the Romans, anti-intellectual in their thinking, followers in
literature, copyists in art, and technicians in science. American intellectual, artistic, and scientific edifices are mere su-
perstructures resting on European trailblazing, and
though American culture may have its deviations from
that of Western Europe, it is basically a pale imitation of
the original European pattern. Should America ever be
severed from Europe, they conclude, the days of the United
States would be numbered, because America, having nothing intellectual to sustain her, would then stagnate for lack
of ideas, just as Rome did when she was severed from
Greece. ·

If the above theory is true, it would help explain why the
Romans never made a cultural impact on the Jews.
Throughout the Roman domination it was the Greeks who

continued to influence Jewish intellectual life. The Romans affected only the physical conditions of Jewish existence. Caught between the mind of Greece and the sword of Rome, the Jews executed a four-hundred-year balancing act under, over, and between the pitfalls they encountered in those four centuries. Of the defeated peoples who became part of the Roman Empire—all of them remnants of great and mighty kingdoms and dynasties—it was the Jews who were slated to be the first to break the streak of luck in Rome's course of conquest.

Roman rule of Judah (or Judea, as she was renamed by her conquerors) began under the worst possible circumstances, with civil wars raging in both nations. Pompey, who captured Judah, not in the name of Rome but in his own, was the military ruler of that country from 63 to 48 B.C., but he appointed a Jew and an Idumean to govern the country for him. Now that Judea was no longer independent, Aristobulus and Hyrcanus, the two sons of the Hasmonean Queen Alexandra, reversed their previous roles. Aristobulus, the Sadducee, resisted Pompey's rule. Hyrcanus, the Pharisee, submitted to it. Pompey therefore made Hyrcanus the High Priest and ethnarch (the Roman name for a ruler of a people) of Judea. But he also appointed an Idumean named Antipater as political adviser to Hyrcanus. This was the beginning of the Jewish tragedy under Roman rule.

Antipater is one of history's most unsavory characters. It was Antipater who had previously advised Hyrcanus to seek the help of the Nabateans in his power struggle with his brother Aristobulus. The successful outcome of that struggle gained Antipater great influence in Judea. He was also a sycophant, servile to any Roman he thought would win. By playing up to Pompey, he was appointed Governor of Idumea. After the defeat of Pompey at the battle of Pharsalus (48 B.C.) in Greece, Caesar took over the rule of Judea in the name of Rome. Antipater now played up to Caesar, who named him administrator of Judea. When Caesar was assassinated Antipater fawned on Cassius, one of the conspirators in Caesar's murder. After Antipater died in 43 B.C., poisoned by loving family members at a feast with his concubines, he was succeeded by his son Herod.

The son had learned from his father. Seeing the rising star of Octavian (Augustus), Herod made his way to Rome. He ingratiated himself into Octavian's favor and was appointed king of the Jews. Herod's first act was to execute Hyrcanus. Aristobulus had been captured by the Romans and sent to Rome, where he died of poisoning. The Hasmonean dynasty, established in a blaze of glory, had come to an inglorious end.

While Herod was in Rome, a fantastic interlude took place in Judea. There was still one Hasmonean descendant left, Antigonus, the son of Aristobulus. When his father was captured by the Romans, Antigonus fled to Parthia and talked the Parthians into marching under him against Jerusalem's Roman overlords. To his own surprise, Antigonus defeated the Romans and drove them out of Judea. He made Jerusalem once again the capital of an independent Palestine with himself as king and High Priest.

Herod, who had been proclaimed king of the Jews by the Romans, was beside himself with rage. For three years Antigonus was able to hold Herod and his lend-lease Roman legions at bay, but finally he was forced to surrender to the superior numbers of the Romans. In 37 B.C. Herod and the Romans captured Jerusalem, and Antigonus and forty-five Sanhedrin members suspected of conspiracy were put to death. At last Herod was able to sit on the throne of Judea. The final twist of irony had occurred. The Idumeans, who had been forcibly converted to Judaism eighty years previously by John Hyrcanus, the son of the founder of the Hasmonean dynasty, now ruled the people who had converted them.

It may be clear to others why Herod has been called "the Great," but to the Jews it has always remained a mystery. Herod was the archmurderer of his time. He murdered forty-five members of the Sanhedrin, reducing that formerly independent judicial body to the status of a rubber stamp. He intimidated the High Priests into subservience with threats of assassination. He murdered his rivals, his favorite wife, and several of his sons, and according to the Gospel of Matthew he imitated the biblical Pharaoh by ordering the execution of all male infants in Bethlehem because he feared a prophecy that a rival to his throne would be born there.

Though most Jews despised and hated Herod, they accepted him as king because one of his ten wives was Mariamne, a Maccabean princess. He had two sons by her and the Jews hoped that one of them would inherit the throne and bring back the Maccabean lineage to Judea. But Herod murdered them both. Upon Herod's death, Antipas and Archelaus, two sons of Herod by a Samaritan wife, were appointed by the Romans to rule the Jews. Antipas was given Galilee, and Archelaus was given Judea, Samaria, and Idumea.

Archelaus proved even more despotic than his father, without any of his father's abilities. In desperation the Jews petitioned the Roman emperor, Augustus, to depose him and to their surprise the emperor did so. The change was something none had been able to imagine—a change for the worse. Augustus appointed the first of a series of procurators (the Roman word for "governors") to rule the province. With but a brief exception, Judea was ruled by such procurators until the outbreak of war against Rome in 66 A.D.

Under the procurators, Roman rule reached an all-time low. In a sense, the Romans were the victims of circumstance. A new empire, Parthia, made up of the remnants of the former Babylonian, Assyrian, and Persian kingdoms, was shaping up in the East, from India to the frontiers of Judea. Though the Romans were the victors in battle after battle against the Parthians, they never were able to defeat them decisively. Thus the Parthians remained a constant threat on the eastern frontier, with Judea as the most logical place for a Parthian breakthrough into the Roman Empire. The Romans thought that if they could keep Judea strongly garrisoned and ruled by an iron hand they would be able to contain the enemy. This fear of the Parthians led the Romans to excesses which their good judgment normally would have kept them from committing. Their repressive measures led to defiance by the Jews, which, in turn, bred further retaliation.

The first procurator began his rule by imposing a census on the Jews for taxation purposes. Agitation swept the country, not because it affected religion but because it threatened pocketbooks. The Romans had a system of taxation which was especially susceptible to graft. The privilege of collecting taxes could be bought by the highest bidder, who was then free to collect as much tax as he wished and to keep for himself everything above the minimum required by the government.

The last taxable penny had already been wrung out of the Jews in Judea by Herod during his forty-six-year rule. Little more could be mined there. The story was different in Galilee, where the Roman census-taking and new tax laws also applied. Against all expectations, Antipas, in contrast to his brother Archelaus, turned out to be a good ruler. He was pro-Hellenistic; he built cities in the Greek image and introduced the Greek mode and manner of living into Galilee. The formerly pagan Galileans, so recently converted to Judaism by John Hyrcanus, were tolerant of this Hellenization for, not knowing better, they thought of it partly as Judaism itself. The stable government of Antipas brought the country unprecedented prosperity. Galilee was ripe for rape by avaricious tax collectors.

It was here in Galilee that the first of a series of minor rebellions against Roman rule broke out as a prelude to the great Jewish war to come. The political situation in Judea and Galilee in the first century A.D. greatly resembled the political situation back in the first kingdoms of Israel and Judah in the eighth and sixth centuries B.C., when Assyria and Babylonia were enemies of the Jews. Two parties had been formed in Israel when Assyria threatened Israel's independence—a war party and a peace party. Two parties had been formed in Judah when Babylonia rattled her saber—a party advocating war and a party advocating peace. Now history repeated itself. Two parties were formed in Judea and Galilee. One was the Zealot party, known as the War Party, urging a stand against Rome; the other was the Peace Party, cautioning against such folly.

Politically, the composition of the Zealot party was closely akin to the earlier Hasidean party which had been responsible for the Maccabean rebellion. As the Romans committed one atrocity after another, despair drove more and more of the Peace Party members into the ranks of the Zealots, in the same way that the extremes of Antiochus Epiphanes had forced the pro-Hellenist Jews to join the anti-Hellenist Hasideans. These new Zealot members came first from the ranks of the Pharisees, Sadducees, and

Essenes, and later from a new Jewish sect known as the Christians. In the first century A.D., the Pharisees were the most numerous, the Sadducees the most powerful, the Essenes the most devout, and the Christians the most intolerant. With the decline of the Hasmonean kingdom, the Pharisee, Sadducee, and Essene parties lost more and more of their political complexion. They developed along their own religious lines, hardening into religious sects and diverging from one another, until forced to reunite, as in the pre-Hasmonean times, in a desperate stand against Rome.

The Pharisees represented the middle ground of Jewish religious thinking. They were exceedingly tolerant in their religious views, totally different from the New Testament picture of them as narrow-minded bigots. The Pharisees believed in the resurrection of the dead, in the coming of a messiah, and in the immortality of the soul. Whenever two interpretations of the Torah—the Law—were possible, they always chose the more lenient view. They developed the tradition of Oral Law, a sort of portable "do-it-yourself" jurisprudence kit to keep up with the changing times.

To the extreme right of the Pharisees were the Sadducees. They did not believe in immortality or resurrection, and denied the existence of the hereafter. They were the political realists, the materialists, the protectors of the *status quo*, whose chief occupation was the preservation of the Temple cult. Their ritual was rigid and fixed, permitting little change, hewing to the letter of the law, not its spirit. As this was the sect of the rich, the aristocrats, and the priests, they wielded great political power in spite of their small numbers. They controlled the Temple and dominated the judicial body of the Sanhedrin.

Just as the Sadducees represented the right wing of the many Jewish religious sects, so the Essenes represented the extreme left. The Essenes, who had started their withdrawal from political life as early as the beginning of the Hasmonean dynasty, continued that withdrawal under Roman occupation. By the time the war against Rome broke out, they already had separated themselves into their own communities on the periphery of the smaller cities, just as the Amish and Quakers have done today in America. Like the Pharisees, the Essenes believed in the immortality of the soul, in resurrection, and in the concept of a messiah. They also believed in the punishment of the wicked in an everlasting hell, and reward for the good in heaven. They developed elaborate purification rites, one of which was baptism, that is, immersion in water for remission of sins, or a rebirth into a new life. The Essenes preferred celibacy, and in the words of the historian Josephus, "they reject pleasure as an evil, but esteem continence and the conquest of our passions to be virtue." In order to preserve their numbers, they held, like the Apostle Paul in later years, that it was "better to marry than to burn," and therefore permitted occasional marriages. Most new members, however, came through the adoption of children from other sects who then were trained in the ascetic ways of the Essenes.

To these three main sects, a fourth was added in the third decade of the first century A.D., namely, the Christian sect. Its founder, Jesus, was baptized in the Essene manner by another Jew, John the Baptist, in all probability also an Essene, since he preached and baptized in the vicinity where the Essenes had their largest and most influential community and monastery. When Jesus was crucified by the Romans, the Christians were threatened with oblivion, but through a vigorous proselytization program initiated by one of their former persecutors, Saul of Tarsus, later known as Paul, the movement rapidly gained new adherents, most of them non-Jews.

It was from the ranks of the first two of these sects that the Zealots gained most of their members. In the beginning the Zealots were strongest in Galilee, where, as pointed out, they were responsible for the first Jewish uprising against Rome which took place in 6 A.D. It was premature, as the people had not yet joined their ranks in any great numbers. Though the uprising was ruthlessly suppressed by the Romans, the cause was not. It smoldered. As it smoldered, the ranks of the Zealots swelled.

Inexorably, like a Greek tragedy, the Jewish-Roman conflict was approaching its climax. Between the years 7 and 41 A.D. seven different procurators ruled Judea. All of them were hack appointees—for the most part, crude soldiers who had risen from the ranks. They had no skill in diplomacy or feeling for social amenities. They com-

pounded mistakes with cruelty, and their vision of statesmanship ended with the conviction that there was no problem which could not be solved by bloodshed. Ideas, they
were convinced, died when a man's head was severed from
his shoulders. Slowly, inevitably, their stupid atrocities
forced more and more Pharisees, Sadducees, and Essenes
to join the ranks of the Zealots who were preaching total
war against the Romans.

A brief interlude, insignificant in its consequences, interrupted this avalanche of events with comic relief. An unwanted king was again bestowed on the Jews by the
Romans in the person of Herod's grandson, Agrippa I. He
had been brought up in Rome in luxury and extravagance.
He was adopted by Emperor Tiberius and became the intimate of Emperor Caligula, who brought an end to the
first series of procurators in order to make Agrippa king.
Under Agrippa, once again all the Jewish provinces were
united into one kingdom. His rule was a form of benevo-
lent misgovernment, which lasted three years, from 41 to
44 A.D. He died as he had lived—theatrically. At a state
function where he was being acclaimed as a god, he keeled
over and died as a mortal.

With Agrippa dead, Judea's appointment with destiny
became inevitable. The strange interlude was over. The Romans put all the old props back on the stage of Jewish history. A new series of procurators were trotted out, all as
incompetent and mendacious as their predecessors, and
Palestine again was divided as before. The stage was set for
a dramatic and momentous challenge. Each new procurator gave another turn to the screw. The breaking point was
approaching. Rome, sensing trouble, hastily changed the
grossly incompetent Procurator Albinus for what was to be
the last of the Roman procurators, Florus.

But it was too late. In the end it was not the atrocities
which provoked the war, but plain stupidity. During a
Passover celebration, thinking it great fun, Florus seized
the vestments of the High Priest and violated with obsceni-
ties the most sacred beliefs of the Jews, who now added
contempt to their hatred of the Romans.

In gangster style, Florus demanded that the Jews pay
him seventeen gold talents ($350,000) out of Temple funds
for protection. Pharisees, Sadducees, Essenes, even the

Jewish Christians still living in Judea, streamed to the ranks of the Zealots. In May, 66 A.D., the Zealots stormed the Roman garrison outside Jerusalem and routed the legions stationed there. The action electrified the country. Open rebellion broke out in every city, in every village, in every province. Judea, Idumea, Samaria, and Galilee united against their common enemy. A postage-stamp-size country had risen against Imperium Romanum, the giant oppressor of the world.

EIGHT

# THE SEALED COFFIN

The conquered nations comprising the Roman Empire watched with incredulity as the Jews, singlehanded, fought the Roman Goliath. The Jews came so close to winning the war that Rome was forced to use her full military weight against them to insure victory where normally only a small expeditionary force should have sufficed. The Romans knew the world was watching, knew the stakes were high. They knew that were they to falter, were the Jews to win their independence, the entire Roman world might be aflame with the spirit of revolt. So they proceeded with a ruthlessness demanded by the seriousness of the challenge. The bloody business of massacre and countermassacre succeeded one another with unrelenting horror.

The first year of the war was a shock to the Romans. From nearby Syria the Roman general Cestus Gallus came galloping with his legions to quell the uprising and was sent back reeling. The situation became so serious that Emperor Nero called for the services of his most able general, Vespasian, and gave him the command of Rome's finest legions. After a year of bitter fighting Vespasian was able to check the Galilean armies under the command of a general who later became world famous as a Jewish historian. His name was Joseph ben Mattathias, known as Flavius Josephus (38–100 A.D.), who gave to the world the only eyewitness account of these fateful years.

Josephus was a Palestinian Jew of a wealthy, priestly family. Educated in the best schools of Rome, he had returned to Judea to pursue a military career, rising to supreme commander of the Galilean forces. When the Galilean armies were shattered, Josephus was captured and brought before Vespasian. The future Roman emperor and the future Jewish historian became friends; and, from Vespasian, Josephus obtained permission to accompany the Roman forces during the siege of Jerusalem so he could write the history of that war. For this, Josephus has been labeled a traitor, and is still so regarded by most Jews today. However, his books, *History of the Jewish War* and *Antiquities of the Jews*, are the most valuable volumes in existence dealing with the two fateful centuries of Jewish history, 100 B.C. to 100 A.D.

Slowly, as the war continued into its third year, Vespasian gained ground. By the year 68 A.D. he had captured Judea, but not the prize, Jerusalem. Attack after attack against the city proved futile; his legionnaires were unable to dent the determined defense. As the only alternative to defeat, Vespasian settled down for a siege of the city, hoping that by starving the population he would be able to force the surrender of the Jews.

The war now ground to a standstill. From a military viewpoint the year 68 had no significance, but in Jewish spiritual history it was a momentous turning point. From Jerusalem emerged a philosopher-rabbi, Jochanan ben Zakkai, who gave Judaism a new life as its soul flickered in the besieged city. Like Josephus, Jochanan ben Zakkai belonged to the Peace Party. Like Josephus, he was convinced that the stand taken by the Zealots could lead only to tragedy. He deserted the war which he thought was hopeless and, like Josephus, had an encounter with Vespasian. But far from being dubbed a traitor, Jochanan ben Zakkai was acclaimed the savior of Judaism.

Jochanan ben Zakkai was a leading Pharisee intellectual. He foresaw the holocaust which would overtake the Jews, the dispersion the Romans would impose upon his people, and he feared that if Jewish leadership did not lay foundations for keeping Jewish learning alive Judaism would be doomed. He became obsessed with the idea that he must found a Jewish academy which would carry the torch of Jewish learning to the disenfranchised Jews who would be dispersed throughout the Hellenic-Roman world. He had to get out of doomed Jerusalem. He had to get to the ear of Vespasian.

Besieged Jerusalem was a hellhole. People were dying by the thousands of starvation and pestilence. Leaving the city was forbidden, on pain of death. Suspected Peace Party members were thrown over the wall by the Zealots, who held as tight a grip inside the city as the Romans did outside. To outwit the Zealots, Jochanan ben Zakkai resorted to a ruse. He took a few of his disciples into his confidence and outlined his plan to them. The disciples then went out into the street, tore their clothes according to the plan, and in mournful voices announced that their great rabbi, Jochanan ben Zakkai, had died of the plague. They asked and received permission from the Zealot authorities to bury the revered rabbi outside the gates of Jerusalem to check the spread of pestilence in the city. With a show of great grief, clad in sackcloth and ashes, the disciples carried a sealed coffin with the live Jochanan ben Zakkai in it out of Jerusalem and to the tent of Vespasian, where they opened the coffin and the rabbi stepped out.

What did General Vespasian, broadsword at side, legions at the ready, confident in the victory of his arms, think of this bearded Jew, dressed in the fringed tunic of his forebears, who looked him straight in the eye, unafraid? What did he want, this Jewish patriarch who had escaped the dying city in a coffin? Not to spare his life, Vespasian knew, for he had risked it coming to see him. The general waited, and the rabbi spoke. He had a prophecy and a request to make, said the rabbi. The general indicated he would listen. Boldly Jochanan ben Zakkai prophesied that Vespasian would soon be emperor, and in such an eventuality, would Emperor Vespasian grant him, Jochanan ben Zakkai, and a few of his disciples, permission to establish a small school of Jewish learning in some Palestinian town where they could continue to study ancient Jewish Scripture in peace. Stunned by the prophecy and surprised by the modesty of the request—which to a soldier like Vespasian made no sense—he promised the favor would be granted provided the prophecy came true.

It was not superstition on which Rabbi ben Zakkai had

based his prediction. He had made a shrewd and calculated guess. That same year Nero had committed suicide. As the Romans had no laws of succession, it stood to reason that eventually the throne would go to the strongest man, who, in ben Zakkai's mind, was Vespasian. In that same year, three political and military hacks held the throne of Rome in succession, each assassinated after a few months in office. Jochanan ben Zakkai had guessed right. In the year 69 the Roman Senate offered the throne to Vespasian. Unlettered and superstitious as Vespasian was, he could not help but be awed by the bearded rabbi's prophecy. He kept his promise to Zakkai, who now founded the first yeshiva—Jewish academy of learning—in the town of Jabneh, north of Jerusalem. It was destined to play a central role in Jewish survival.

Before leaving for Rome to assume the purple, Vespasian entrusted his son Titus with the responsibility of carrying on the war against the Jews. This war and the subsequent destruction of Jerusalem seldom receive their rightful place in history. Christians vaguely remember the destruction of Jerusalem as something come true according to prophecy in the Gospels,* written after the event took place; Jews react emotionally to the event. Both miss its grandeur as a clash of two formidable foes locked in one of the greatest battles in antiquity.

Alexander the Great had used 32,000 men to carve out his vast empire. Caesar had fewer than 25,000 legionnaires with which to conquer Gaul and to invade Britain. Hannibal had no more than 50,000 soldiers when he crossed the Alps to defeat the Romans. Titus was forced to use 80,000 soldiers to vanquish the beleaguered Jews in Jerusalem, which was defended by no more than 23,400 Jewish soldiers.** Even so, he was loath to risk the flower of the

---

*Actually only one of the Four Gospels, Mark, contains any "prophecy" of a destruction of Jerusalem. The other three Gospels were written even later, but they make no mention of such a "prophecy." Mark wrote his Gospel in Rome, about 70 A.D., the year the Romans destroyed the city. By this time Jerusalem had been under Roman siege for three years, and one needed no prophetic powers to predict the outcome.
**Josephus, in *The Jewish War* (Penguin Classics edition, page 274), gives the breakdown of Jewish troops as follows: 10,000 under command of Simon bar Giora, 6,000 led by John of Gisela, 5,000 Idumeans, and 2,400 Zealots.

Roman military in a direct attack, fearing great losses. Instead, he decided upon psychological warfare to frighten the Jews into surrender. He commanded his soldiers to dress in full battle uniform, then staged a military parade around the walls of Jerusalem in an awesome display of Roman might. Earth and heaven were swept together into one immense dust cloud and the blood-soaked ground shook as 70,000 foot soldiers marched, 10,000 cavalry rode, and thousands of battering rams were drawn by the gates of Jerusalem. The parade lasted three days. When the show was over, the performers got a loud Bronx cheer from the watching Jews on the ramparts.

Enraged, Titus ordered an attack. For two weeks siege guns hurled rocks as big as Volkswagens at the northern wall of Jerusalem, tearing a gaping hole in the fortifications. Through this hole streamed the legionnaires and to the defense ran the Jews. It was man-to-man combat, sword against sword, spear against spear, desperation against desperation. After two weeks of savage hand-to-hand fighting, the Jews drove the Romans out. Titus now realized he would never win in open combat, that he had to starve the Jews until they were so weakened that further resistance would be impossible. To make sure that no food or water supply would reach the city from the outside, Titus completely sealed off Jerusalem from the rest of the world with a wall of earth as high as the stone wall around Jerusalem itself. Anyone not a Roman soldier caught anywhere in this vast dry moat was crucified on the top of the earthen wall in sight of the Jews inside the city. It was not uncommon for as many as five hundred people a day to be so executed. The air was redolent with the stench of rotting flesh and rent by the cries of agony of the crucified. But the Jews held out for still another year, the fourth year of the war, to the discomfiture of Titus.

The end was inevitable. With battering rams and portable bridges, the Romans stormed the walls of Jerusalem. Like termites they spilled into the city, slaughtering a populace reduced to helplessness by starvation. Four years of bitter defeats at the hands of the Jews had made a mockery of the vaunted invincibility of the Roman legions, and only killing could now soothe their bruised vanity. The Temple was put to the torch, infants thrown into the flames, women raped, priests massacred, Zealots thrown from the wall. Survivors of the carnage were earmarked for the triumphal procession to be held in Rome, sold as slaves, held for the wild beasts in the arenas, or saved to be thrown off the Tarpeian Rock in Rome for amusement. At no time did the Romans more justly earn the grim words of their own historian, Tacitus, who said, "They make a desolation and call it peace." Altogether, Tacitus estimates 600,000 defenseless Jewish civilians were slain in the aftermath of the siege.

On the surface of it, the Jewish War should have been no more than a small ripple on the periphery of the Roman Empire which a legion or two could have suppressed. But such was not the case. It had been a devastating war. Though heavy casualties were inflicted by the Romans on the Jews, it had been a Pyrrhic victory, for the Romans too had suffered frightful losses. They had won, not because of greater valor or skill, but because of greater numbers. To hide the poverty of this victory, the Romans staged a spectacular triumphal parade. They struck special coins in remembrance of the war. They constructed the magnificent Triumphal Arch of Titus—an honor reserved for commemorating great victories over mighty nations against incredible odds. The Arch of Titus still stands in Rome—but as a symbol of what? Of the conquering Romans, who have vanished, or of the "conquered enemy," the Jews, who still live today as an unconquered people?

This Jewish war had yet another effect. Though the heartland of Europe remained docile, the eastern half of the Empire took heart. Jerusalem had held the legions of Rome at bay for four years. The Jews had shown the Romans were not invincible. The spirit of revolt now fanned the Near East. It smoldered again in the hearts of the Jews in Judea, though they had been reduced to destitution by Roman reprisals.

The impetus for a second Jewish revolt in 113 A.D. was given by a Parthian invasion into Roman territory. Emperor Trajan marched against the Parthians, but now the Jews rebelled in Egypt, in Antioch, in Cyrene, in Cyprus. Alarmed at what was happening, Trajan interrupted his campaign against the Parthians to take up the threat posed by the Jews. For three years the war raged and the outcome hung in the balance. The Jews finally had to capitulate for lack of arms and men.

Again it had been a costly victory for Rome. It had so sapped Roman strength that the war against the Parthians could not be renewed and had to be abandoned. This second uprising also marked a crucial turning point in Roman history. Whereas till then a triumphant Rome had been staking out her imperial eagles on ever-expanding frontiers, the tide now turned against her. With the ascension of Hadrian to the throne of Rome in 117, the frontiers of the Roman Empire began to shrink.

Emperor Hadrian, who had succeeded Trajan to the throne, was so relieved at the end of the costly Jewish War that he promised the Jews they could rebuild the temple in Jerusalem. But lulled by the calm that had settled over the land, he reneged on his promise and built a temple not for Jehovah but for Jupiter. He named it Aelia Capitolina and turned Jerusalem into a Roman city. If Hadrian thought that the defeat of the Jews in the second uprising had dissuaded them from trying a third time, he had completely miscalculated the situation.

A new hope was sweeping the ranks of the Jews. A military messiah had arisen among them. A great scholar was his apostle and armor-bearer. The messiah on horseback was Simon ben Cozeba, or bar Kochba ("Son of the Star"), and the scholar was Rabbi Akiba. This combination of an armored messiah and a revered rabbi was the catalytic agent that coalesced the dispirited Jews into a new fighting force.

Little is known of bar Kochba's early life. Letters discovered near the Dead Sea at Muruba'at picture him as an autocratic and irascible soldier of great physical strength and magnetic personality, capable of inspiring blind devotion and utter fearlessness. The Talmud adds another character trait, that of impiousness. It quotes him as once having exclaimed, "Lord, don't help us and don't spoil it for us." The Sanhedrin took an equally jaundiced view of bar Kochba's claim to messiahship. Only the faith and prestige of Rabbi Akiba saved him.

Rabbi Akiba was the most illustrious personality of his time, and one of the most honored scholars in Jewish history. He began life as a semi-illiterate shepherd. In true fairy-tale fashion he fell in love with the beautiful daughter of one of the richest leading citizens of Jerusalem and married her. At her insistence, Akiba went to school together with their small son and took up the study of the Torah. He acquired such immense learning and brought such illuminating new insights into the Torah and into man-God relationships that he became symbolically the spiritual as well as temporal ruler of the Jews. His interpretations of the Torah became the way of life for many Jews wherever they lived.

It was Rabbi Akiba who confirmed Simon bar Kochba's claim that he was a messiah and a descendant of King David. When the two issued a call to arms against the Romans, Jews of every sect by the tens of thousands flocked to their standards, but not the Christians, who were caught in a dilemma. The Christians were suffering as much as the Jews, if not more, under the Roman yoke and could under normal circumstances have joined the Jews in the rebellion. But, already having a messiah in Jesus, they could not accept another messiah in bar Kochba, and thus they could not join the Jews in the showdown with the Romans.

When the rebellion exploded in 132 A.D., it took the Romans by surprise. They had totally underestimated the Jewish will to resist and Jewish ability to fight a third war. To the horror of the Romans, the Jews repelled their armies in battle after battle. If others have tried to minimize the size and importance of this war, Hadrian did not. He fully realized the portentous consequences to the empire should Rome lose this war. Fearful of such a calamity, and taking no chances, he summoned his ablest general, Julius Severus, from the British front, where he had been sent to quell a revolt of the Celts. Hadrian felt that a lesser general and fewer men could subdue the British, who in his mind constituted less of a threat to the preservation of the empire than did the Jews. Severus entered the Holy Land at the head of 3,000 crack troops and gave battle to bar Kochba's numerically inferior army. The Imperial Eagles were dealt an ignominious defeat.

Severus too realized he could not win in open battle. He decided on tactics such as were later used by General Sherman in the American Civil War, those of total warfare—destroying and burning all that could not be used by his own armies. Severus, of course, added a Roman refinement, the systematic slaughter of every living thing, combatant and noncombatant in his path—men, women, children, cattle. It was a slow, graceless, bitter, unyielding fight, but the despairing Romans had no choice. They had to win this war. After two years of grinding, ruthless, merciless butchery, the Jewish lines wavered as the populace was reduced to the vanishing point. In the year 135 bar Kochba's forces surrendered. Bar Kochba had been killed in battle, and the Romans assuaged their fury by executing Akiba with refined torture. Those who could, fled to Parthia, where they were welcomed with open arms.

Jerusalem, and what had been Judean Palestine, was now made off-limits to the Jews. Those who had not perished in the war or managed to escape into Parthia were sold into slavery. Yet of the three Jewish wars, the third one had been the costliest to the Romans. When Hadrian reported its conclusion to the Senate, he omitted the customary ending, "I and my army are well," for neither was well. Hadrian had suffered a tremendous loss of face; his armies had been decimated; his victory, like that of Titus, had been a Pyrrhic one. The empire was buckling under the internal pressure of provinces beginning to strike for freedom. The frontier was no longer a fixed boundary. It was an undulating mass of armed men poised to cross it.

Some may argue that this account of the three Jewish wars is an imaginative heightening of history, that these three wars hardly made a dent in the monolithic Roman Empire. Such skepticism is understandable, since historians as a rule delve little into these three Jewish-Roman wars and there is little general knowledge about them. The true dimensions of these wars can be measured with a modern historical analogy. The Hungarian rebellion against Russia in 1956 lasted but a few months, yet the whole Russian Communist edifice was badly shaken, and all the satellite nations were poised for rebellion. Suppose that the Hungarians had not caved in after a few months, but had carried on an active war against the Russians for four years, as the Jews did against the Romans. Suppose that Russian casualties had not been a few hundred, but tens of thousands. Suppose that after the first Hungarian rebellion there had been two other such uprisings. And suppose that in each of these uprisings the Hungarians had been able to hold out for several years against Russian infantry and tanks, each time inflicting on them telling blows and heavy casualties. What historian would then say that Russia had not been weakened by such events, that her prestige had not suffered after such costly victories against so small a foe? Viewed in this light, the Jewish wars against Rome reveal a greater significance than has usually been accorded them.

The Roman phase of Jewish history came to an end with the reign of Hadrian. Though the greatest number of Jews continued to live under Roman rule to the very end of that empire, Rome had less effect on the Jews than ever before. Though the Romans accepted the Jews—in fact, conferred citizenship upon all Jews in 212 A.D.—it was the Jews who now rejected the Romans.

Something strange and unprecedented happened. The Jews had become a "marginal minority," with the inner, spiritual strength to reject the dominant majority. They had no doubt that their Jewish culture was superior to that of the Romans. From where had this new fortitude, this new spiritual strength, come?

The secret had been locked in that sealed coffin smuggled out of dying Jerusalem, secured in the mind and heart of Rabbi Jochanan ben Zakkai. The yeshiva for Jewish learning which he had founded in Jabneh had begun to operate. It had become a factory for the production of superego Mosaic dynamos to power the new-model inner-directed Jew. But though these Mosaic dynamos were certified "Made in Jabneh," many of the parts were stamped "Manufactured in Greece."

# NINE

# THE CONQUERING WORD

Most political historians seldom give more than a passing paragraph to the Jews during the Greco-Roman period. When they do refer to them, it is usually as "a small nomadic band," or "narrow-minded zealots," or "bigots fighting in defense of circumcision and pigless diet." Much of this attitude has been handed down by Greek and Roman writers of the time. But such judgments reflect ignorance of Jewish history, literature, and culture, rather than contempt for the Jews. This is not the only explanation, however. Many of these political historians are uncomfortable in the world of ideas. They grapple only with concrete things. It is easier to view history as a succession of battles and booty. The nations noted in their histories are those which acquired the most real estate, amassed the most gold, sculptured the nicest statues, and built the most magnificent buildings. As the Jews never possessed or created many of these things, it is only natural for this type of historian to regard them as unimportant appendages of history. One can count Greek statues, evaluate the cost of Roman marble baths, measure the length of roads, and it all adds up to an impressive figure. What other conclusion can be reached except that these were magnificent civilizations?

That the Greeks and Romans often referred to the Jews in contemptuous terms proves nothing. They held everybody except themselves in contempt. The Romans even looked with contempt on the Greeks although frequently imitating them. When one examines the reasons the Greeks and Romans gave for holding the Jews in such avowed contempt, the basis for such a value judgment disappears. The Romans, who nailed live people to wooden crosses and called it justice, expressed horror at the Jewish rite of circumcision. The Romans, who pitted defenseless slaves against wild beasts and called it amusement, viewed as "barbaric" the Jewish feast of Passover which celebrated man's freedom from slavery. The Greeks and Romans, who mercilessly worked man and beast seven days a week and called it industry, looked with scorn on the Jewish practice of a day of rest every seventh day for freeman, slave, and animal. The graceful Greeks laughed at the "graceless" Jews for recoiling in horror at the Greek custom of exposing an infant to death when the shape of its skull or nose did not please them. Because the Jews did not bring up their daughters to become prostitutes in temples, because they did not look upon pederasty as the noblest form of human love, because they placed duty to God above pleasure of man, the Greeks and Romans regarded them as barbarians.

Statues, paintings, buildings are an index to a culture, but so is literature. Literature is the truest mirror of the culture of a civilization. The Greeks had a great literature, and that entitles them to a place in the commonwealth of cultured nations; but so did the Jews. Could a "barbaric people" have produced the literature the Jewish people did, a literature which has endured well over two thousand years and has become the foundation of Western civilization? The works of the Greeks and Romans are studied today as intellectual exercises in special university courses, but the literary works of the Jews are the living principles of mankind. The Jewish achievement in literature stands alone and incomparable, not the work of "narrow-minded bigots" but the achievement of an inspired and highly civilized people.

Only recently have cultural historians and independent scholars begun to examine the great fusion which took place between Greek and Jewish ideas and the imprint each left on the other. They have uncovered strong Judaic currents in Greek philosophical works, and revealed the existence of major Hellenic thought in Jewish theological writings.

The intermingling of two streams in Greek civilization produced that cultural mixture known as "Hellenism." One stream was her art, architecture, science, and philosophy; the other was the Greek way of life itself, her manners, morals, and religion. We have seen how the Pharisees, who fought Hellenism, objected to Greek manners and morals, but accepted her art and philosophy; whereas the Sadducees, who accepted Grecian manners and morals, rejected her art and philosophy. When Jerusalem was made off-limits to the Jews, the Sadducees disappeared. Their religion had been tied to the Temple in Jerusalem. There was no longer any Temple. Their cult had been tied to sacrifice. There no longer existed any sacrifice. Their dogma had become inflexible; their thinking had not kept abreast of the times. No new streams of philosophy had been allowed to invigorate Sadducean institutions. Like the Oriental pagans, the Sadducees had borrowed only the outer trappings of Hellenism, not its substance; and thus, with the other pagans, they stagnated. It remained for the Pharisees to carry on the torch of Jewish ideology. The light which this torch shed was unmistakably Jewish, but the torch itself had been ignited by the Greek philosophers.

Before we examine the interaction of Jewish and Greek thought, let it first be stated, there was also a great philosophical gulf separating them. Someone once summed up that difference this way: The Jew asked, "What must I do?" The Greek asked, "Why must I do it?" Or, as a Jewish historian expressed it, "The Greeks believed in the holiness of beauty, the Jews believed in the beauty of holiness." True, many Jews who loved Hellenism saw Judaism as a crude way of life, aesthetically oppressive. But a greater number of Jews, who admired many facets of Hellenic culture, also saw much in it which repulsed them—naïve paganism, insensitivity to human suffering, adulation of beauty at the expense of spirituality, cheap sophistry, barbaric infanticide. Too often a performance in the amphitheater did not mean a play by Sophocles, but a lewd exhibition; too often the pursuit of beauty did not mean the admiration of *objets d'art*, but the pursuit of pretty boys and the favor of courtesans.

But, if thousands of Jews saw this, so did hundreds of thousands of Greeks and Romans. The Jewish way of life made a great impression on them. They liked the nonsexualized symbols of Judaism and respected the dignity of the Jewish God, who did not deign to sneak out at night into the beds of other men's wives, as did the Greek and Roman gods. They admired the Jews for not indulging in the bacchanalian revelry so common in those days among the pagans, and they envied the devotion of the Jewish people to spiritual, family, and scholastic ideals rather than materialistic goals. In the two-century span, 100 B.C. to 100 A.D., thousands of Sabbath candles flickered in Grecian and Roman homes—so many, in fact, that the Roman philosopher Seneca noted this phenomenon by remarking that Jewish customs were everywhere so prevalent that the Romans were in danger of being swallowed up by them.

This observation by Seneca was not just a figure of speech. The respect so many Greeks, Romans, and other pagans had for Jewish virtue and ideology did indeed threaten to undermine the pagan nations and might have done so if it had not been for the Christian sect, which began to proselytize more actively than did the Jews themselves. Not many people today realize that in the first century A.D. over 10 percent of the population of the Roman Empire was Jewish—seven million out of seventy million. Of these seven million professing the Jewish faith, only an estimated four million were Jewish by virtue of centuries of descent; the rest were converted pagans or of converted-pagan descent. This was one of the practical aspects of the intellectual fusion between pagan and Jew. The rate of conversion would have been even greater but for two factors: the rigorous dietary laws, and the necessity for circumcision. In Paul's time the early Christian sect dropped these two requirements, and the pagans flocked to the Christian religion, whose entrance specifications were less demanding than the Jewish.

These facts permit us to understand a series of uprisings during Greek and Roman times against the Jews in Alexandria, Antioch, Cyprus, and other cities with large Jewish populations. Many pagans resented both those who converted to Judaism and the Jews who did the converting. This resentment later shifted to the Christians, who, with their more aggressive proselytization program, were gaining even more converts than the Jews. Another source of pagan resentment toward the Jews was the attitude of the Jews. Whereas the entire world tried to imitate the ways of the Greeks and Romans, the larger segment of the Jewish population looked upon them with scorn. Both the Greeks and Romans resented this Jewish attitude of superiority.

This resentment was given added fuel by the refusal of the Jews to intermarry with the dominant majorities.

The biggest source of irritation, however, was the practical matter of who got the good jobs in the bureaucracy of the Roman Empire. The Jews held influential positions and seats of learning totally out of proportion to their numbers. In Egypt, in Syria, in Damascus, in Greece, Jews were ensconced in high legislative, judicial, executive, and scholastic places. It was not favoritism or bribery which had lofted them to these high positions, but intelligence and industry. These they had not acquired by accident but by the series of innovations which Jewish leaders had instituted centuries earlier.

Because of their compulsory universal education, the Jews were literate. Because of their monotheism and their invisible God, their intellectual powers had been heightened. Because their "portable tabernacle" did not tie them down to any specific place, they could move with opportunity without giving up their unity. Whereas the Greek intellectual, the Roman patrician, and other pagan nobles looked upon work as something ignoble, the Jews invested work with dignity. Given advantages in education, upbringing, and outlook, it was no wonder that the Jews outstripped their pagan competitors in the scramble for the better jobs. Five centuries later, when the Christians came to power, they had to enact laws prohibiting Jews from holding policy-making posts in order to avert the possibility of all important jobs going to Jews by virtue of ability. It was only natural that success should earn its merited envy. When the Jews in Palestine rebelled against their Roman masters, what could be more righteous than for the pagans in Alexandria, Antioch, and Cyprus to come to the aid of the Romans by pillaging the Jews?

But the most important single reason for the extent of the great fusion of Jewish and Greek ideas which took place during this period was the effect that Jewish theology began to have on Greek philosophy and literature. A book written by Jews was destined to make a great impact on the Greco-Roman world. This book was the translation of the Old Testament into Greek, known as the Septuagint, which turned out to be a great piece of Greek literature. It was a bestseller which found its way into more pagan than Jewish homes. It was the conquering word that spread Jewish humanism and philosophy to the Greeks and Romans. When Paul came to preach to the Greeks and Romans, he did not preach a totally strange creed. The people were already familiar with the Old Testament.

As previously pointed out, the Five Books of Moses had been canonized in the year 444 B.C. During the subsequent five hundred years, under Persian, Greek, and Roman domination, the Jews wrote, revised, admitted, and canonized all the books now comprising the Jewish Old Testament. All of these biblical books were written in Hebrew, with the exception of a few chapters in Ezra and Daniel, which are in Aramaic. During the Hasmonean dynasty, the present Hebrew names were given to the different books, and their order determined. Nothing has been changed since.

There is an interesting legend telling how the Greek translation of the Old Testament came to be called the Septuagint. About 250 B.C., word of a famous and beautifully written book possessed by the Jews had reached the ear of the Ptolemaic King Philadelphus. He suggested that seventy Jewish scholars translate the work into Greek. According to this pious legend, each of the seventy scholars worked independently, yet all seventy translations, when completed, were identical, word for word, thus proving God's guiding hand. And so the work became known as the book of the "Seventy," or *Septuagint* in Greek.

The secular account for this translation differs shamelessly from the legend. The cruel fact was that in cities like Alexandria and Antioch, Damascus and Athens, Jews forgot Hebrew and began to speak Greek in the same way American Jews today speak English instead of Yiddish. Jewish leaders felt that the contents of the Old Testament were more important than the language, and that a Bible in Greek would have a greater binding force on the Jews than no Bible at all. A translation of the Bible was therefore ordered. The Jewish leaders had guessed right. The Septuagint was greatly instrumental in pulling many half-assimilated Jews back into the orbit of Judaism.

Great as the influence of the Septuagint was on the Jews, however, it exerted an even greater influence on the Greeks. Conversion to Judaism was now spread by the written word.

But even more significantly, many of those who did not convert gained a deeper understanding of Judaism and a greater respect for the Jews and their culture.

A great intellectual interaction took place. Jewish theology became so all-pervasive that it affected not only Greek thinking but also future Christian dogma. Some scholars even maintain that Christian dogma was not derived completely from the teachings of Paul, as previously supposed, but influenced by the writings of a Jewish philosopher named Philo, who, about 35 to 40 A.D., synthesized the Old Testament with the works of the Greek philosopher Plato. Though little is known of Philo today, by either Jews or Christians, he probably played a more crucial role in shaping both Judaism and Christianity than either Rabbi Akiba or Paul. Philo shaped Judaism around a Grecian metaphysical framework so thoroughly that it influenced both Jews and Christians in the creation of their new theologies.

Philo was the son of the wealthiest and most Hellenized Jewish family in Alexandria. He was educated in the finest private schools, spoke fluent Greek and Latin, but very little Hebrew. An ardent disciple of Plato, he was imbued with the idea of synthesizing the best in Jewish religion with the best in Greek philosophy. His life is hidden in obscurity, but we do know of one dramatic event. The mad Emperor Caligula had demanded veneration as a god. The Alexandrians, envious of the positions of eminence and wealth the Jews had attained in that city, saw a wonderful opportunity for revenge under the guise of patriotism. They insisted that the Jews also obey this edict, knowing full well that this would be against their religion. When the Jews refused, as they had anticipated, the Alexandrians declared them traitors, thus giving themselves an excuse to plunder Jewish wealth with justified indignation. Upon the shoulders of Philo fell the task of going to Rome to reason with the mad emperor.

The situation was not only hopeless, but absurd. Caligula was murdering thousands of Roman patricians at whim or as a cure for heartburn. To ask such a madman to give up part of his delusion that he was a god for the sake of a few Jewish rebels who refused to do him homage was madness itself. Yet Philo accomplished the absurd by treating Caligula the way a modern psychiatrist would treat a paranoid. By keeping his head and his dignity, by answering questions frankly, by treating the emperor as though he were sane and fully responsible for his deeds, Philo was almost able to convince Caligula that the Jews could be loyal citizens without having to erect statues of him in their temples. We don't know what Caligula's final decision might have been, for in the year 41 this incestuous and epileptic emperor was murdered and was succeeded by Claudius, who, though regarded as a driveling imbecile by the Romans, nevertheless ordered the chagrined and amazed Alexandrians to quit their plunderings and make restitution to the Jews.

Philo, who was familiar with the Old Testament only in its Greek translation, decided to make it even more acceptable to Greek intellectuals by putting Greek clothing on Jewish revelation. This he did with the aid of allegory and the philosophy of Plato. Though God created the world, argued Philo, God did not influence the world directly, but indirectly through *Logos*, that is, through "the Word."* Because the human soul stems from the "Divine Source," continued Philo, it is capable of conceiving of the nature of divinity itself. This human ability to conceive of divinity, said Philo, could be done in two ways: through the spirit of prophecy, or through inner mystic meditation. Judaism, in Philo's opinion, was the instrument which enabled man to achieve moral perfection, and the Torah was the path to union with God. It was on the allegorical concepts of Philo's Logos and the inner mystic contemplation of God that Paul built his Christology. The Jews used the opposite pole of Philo's philosophy—the spirit of prophecy. They built their Judaism by searching the Torah for new meanings.

This search into the Torah for new meanings kept the

---

*We can see how this idea was taken directly by the Christians, for instance, in the Gospel According to Saint John, which begins: "In the beginning was the Word, and the Word was with God, and the Word was God." Ironically, this opening sentence in John is now more of a Jewish doctrine than a Christian one. The Christians made the "Son of Man" equal to God, whereas it was the Jews who followed John's injunction and made "the Word," that is, the Torah, equal to God. It is to the Jews that "the Word is God."

Jewish religion modern and up-to-date, in spite of en-
croaching centuries. The contact with the Greeks had introduced the Jews to science and philosophy. They used
this science as a tool with which to extract further meanings from the Torah by applying to it ever subtler forms of
Greek logic. Greek philosophy enabled them to expand
their universe of thought. But the Jews were practical men
as well as theoreticians. One cannot promote Judaism
without Jews, so Jewish leaders proceeded to read into the
Torah the sensible maxim that it was the obligation of the
Jews to preserve themselves in order to preserve Judaism.
It behooved Jewish leaders to think up new ways and
means for survival. It was time to preserve ideology with
bread and butter.

TEN

# A NEW DEAL FOR DIASPORA

The third Jewish war against Rome had brought Jewish political fortunes to the brink of economic and social disaster.
In the second century A.D., the majority of Jews were stateless and dispersed into every corner of the Roman world,
from India to the Atlantic Ocean, over three continents,
two empires, and dozens of nations. They had already defied two thousand years of history. Logically and historically the Jews were overdue to lose their ethnic unity and
disappear. But they did not disappear. They responded to
this new challenge with another formula for survival—
"Diaspora Judaism."

We have already defined the word *Diaspora* as coming
from the Greek, meaning "a scattering" or "to scatter
about," and today the word has come to signify that body
of Jews not living in Israel itself but scattered outside the
boundaries of that country. Actually, Diaspora means far
more than this. Diaspora is both a way of life and an intellectual concept, a state of being and a state of mind. To understand its complexity, let us retrace its history.

Some historians date the Diaspora from the time of the

destruction of the first kingdom of Judah and the subsequent Babylonian captivity. If that were so, there would be no difference between the words "exile" and "Diaspora," because the Jews were exiled to Babylonia and lived there in exile. Actually, the true Diaspora for the Jews began with the Persian conquest of Babylonia. When the Persians permitted the Jews to return to their homeland, most of them chose to remain where they were instead of going back to Palestine. The Jewish sojourn in Babylonia before the Persian victory had been *involuntary* and maintained by force. The Jewish stay in Babylonia after their liberation was *voluntary*. Before they had lived in "exile"; now they lived in "Diaspora."

There is one other, more fundamental, difference between the concepts of "exile" and "Diaspora," however. A people in exile, banished from its homeland, produces no culture, but gradually either dies out through assimilation, or stagnates by reverting to a nomadic existence. This has been the history of all other exiled peoples. The Jews were the only exception. The Diaspora produced new Jewish cultures. Though the inner core of each Diaspora culture always remained distinctly Jewish, each took on the dominant traits of the host civilization. It was always Jehovah and monotheism, no matter how each such Diaspora culture was packaged—in Greek tunic, in Arab mufti, or in American ivy-league. When a civilization was philosophic, like that of the Greeks, the Jews became philosophers. When it was composed predominantly of poets and mathematicians, like that of the Arabs, the Jews became poets and mathematicians. When it was scientific and abstract, like that of the modern Europeans, the Jews became scientists and theoreticians. When it was pragmatic and suburban, like the American, the Jews became pragmatists and suburbanites. Only when a culture or civilization contradicted the basic ethical monotheism of the Jews were they unable to adapt or be adapted to it. The Jews were part of, yet distinct from, the civilization in which they lived.

The Jewish intellectuals who had stayed on in Babylonia after the exile created the first Jewish cultural Diaspora capital in Babylon, and soon began to influence the art and culture of Jerusalem. The Jews, for instance, added a touch of their own to the Persian art forms, and many scholars now believe that it was this Jewish touch which created the Byzantine school of painting of which the Dura-Europos paintings are so reminiscent. When the Greeks conquered the Persians, bringing the Jews under their influence, it could have been predicted that Jewish culture would assume the coloration of Grecian civilization as it did.

With Greek domination, two new Jewish cultural centers developed, one in Jerusalem, the other in Alexandria, giving the Jews three intellectual centers—one native and two Diaspora cultures. For about three hundred years, from 200 B.C. to 100 A.D., the Alexandrian Jews gained intellectual ascendancy, but after that they steadily declined until the spark was finally extinguished three hundred years after the destruction of the Temple. The Jewish community in Babylon was destined to inherit the Diaspora intellectual scepter in another two centuries. But, as the Jews stood at the edge of disaster in the middle of the second century A.D., the light that guided them was beamed from the small town of Jabneh, in devastated Judea.

It had been the preservation of the Jewish idea in the face of total Diaspora that had obsessed Rabbi Jochanan ben Zakkai when, with the flames of burning Jerusalem on the horizon, he had established his Jewish academy in Jabneh. Here were Rabbi ben Zakkai and his rabbis. In the world around them the Jews were scattered. How does one go about preventing the disappearance of a people which has lost its country, which has been fragmentized into thousands of segments, and which has been strewn over vast land masses amidst alien tongues and alien religions? What measures does one take to preserve the identity of such a people, and how does one enforce such measures when there is no political power, no police, no army to make these measures enforceable?

What were the dangers which Rabbi ben Zakkai and his successors foresaw? There was the danger of the Jews disappearing through the slave markets of the world; the danger of the Jews forgetting their language; the danger of the Jews forsaking their heritage; the danger of the Jews being overwhelmed by dominant majorities. There were the dangers of being lured away to other religions, of no longer caring whether they continued to exist as Jews, of no longer believing in being the Chosen People. One by one

Rabbi ben Zakkai and his successors examined each of these problems, formulating the ideas which, they hoped, would permit the Jews to survive. The laws which they formulated over a thousand-year span, many of them becoming part of the Talmudic code, were disseminated to the Jews through a unique "courier service" known as *Responsa*, which did not need any political power for enforcement. The Jewish people had developed such a strong inner discipline that as long as their leaders transmitted vital and practical ideas which their "Mosaic antennae" could pick up, they obeyed voluntarily. Jewish charismatic power had passed from God to the Law of Moses, to the Old Testament, to the priesthood, and now to their men of learning—the rabbis. The age of the Jewish intellectuals was at hand.

Disappearance of the Jews through slavery was an immediate and practical problem. To avert this danger, Jewish leaders formulated the principle that every Jew was his brother's keeper, and that all Jews were brothers. In those days when someone was sold into slavery, he was a doomed man, unless he came of a prominent family, in which case he might be ransomed. The Jews devised an entirely new concept. Henceforth, any Jew sold into slavery had to be ransomed within seven years by Jews in the nearest community. To prevent the Hebrew language from becoming fragmentized into hundreds of dialects, Jewish scholars set about writing the first Hebrew dictionary and grammars. Though modern Hebrew has grown in the number of words, anyone able to speak Hebrew today can read the Hebrew of the ancient Israelites, the Hebrew of the Jews in the Islamic civilization, or the Hebrew of the Jews in the Middle Ages, without special guide books.

To prevent the Jewish religion from developing such divergences that Jews from different parts of the world would not recognize each other's holy services, the liturgy in the synagogues was standardized. Just as great Christian composers were to set Christian prayers to immortal music, so the greatest Jewish poets wrote the immortal prayers of the Jewish liturgy, prayers which have never been surpassed in sheer verbal beauty. They are prayers which have defied adequate translation. The decree of Ezra and Nehemiah that part of the Torah must be read aloud to the people two weekdays and on Saturday was continued, but with this change: The reader of the Torah no longer had to be a specialist, but could be anyone from the congregation, provided he had dignity and bearing. From this dictum grew the tradition for dressing oneself in one's best clothing when going to the synagogue as a mark of respect for God and His Word.

But if Jews were required to enforce discipline upon themselves, they would need social organization. This the Jewish leaders also provided on several levels. Any time ten Jewish males over thirteen years of age lived within commuting distance, they had to establish a religious community (*Minyan* in Hebrew). As soon as 120 males over thirteen years of age lived within commuting distance, they had the authority to establish a social community, including a court of their own to adjudicate those disputes among themselves which did not conflict with the laws of the nation within which they resided. Each such community had to incorporate certain principles. Every community had to impose taxes upon itself in addition to those taxes demanded by the state. These taxes were to go toward making the Jew self-supportive so that at no time would there be any need to go to a pagan or Christian government for financial help. This money was used mainly for education and charity. Every community was responsible for a school system which had to provide universal education. This education was to be free to the fatherless, to orphans, and to all needy. It was compulsory for all boys, but it could not be denied to any girl who wanted to continue schooling beyond reading and writing. These laws specifically stated that teachers must make good salaries so as to make the profession attractive and honorable. No one could go hungry. Charity had to be provided with dignity to all needy and to anyone demanding it. No Jew must ever ask for charity from the state, only from his own Jewish community. From this date stems the Jewish custom of always taking care of its own needy. This is still a cardinal principle of Jews all over the world.

To make sure there would be no depopulation of the Jews, severe penalties were imposed upon infanticide and celibacy. The community had to supply a dowry to all brides too poor to supply one for themselves. A ban was also placed on intermarriage. Again it must be stressed that it was the Jews who first rejected the pagans and Christians, not they who first rejected the Jews. It must also be noted that there is a psychological difference between the Jewish discrimination against gentiles and the discrimination practiced by whites against Negroes, for instance. The Jews imposed the restrictions on themselves, not on others, not out of a feeling of superiority, but out of the necessity of preserving their small numbers against dilution. The whites in the South, or the Dutch in South Africa, impose their restrictions, political and otherwise, on others out of a feeling of superiority or fear. Rightly speaking, then, the Jews do not discriminate, they merely restrict themselves.

To insure the right of self-rule and their rights against the accusation of treason, the Jews formulated four laws, unique in the history of mankind. The first one was that no Jew should ever have to obey a Jewish law which was beyond the power of a religious Jew to observe. If such a law which had been workable in one generation proved unworkable in another, then that law would have to be either repealed or re-interpreted. The second law stipulated that Jews must recognize the validity of a non-Jewish document in both a Jewish and non-Jewish court, and that all oaths taken in any court, in any language, were valid. The third law enunciated the principle that all laws of a country in which Jews resided had to be obeyed, so long as they did not arbitrarily forbid a religious practice, force them to practice incest, worship idols, or commit murder. So, for instance, if the country's laws of damages differed from those of Jewish law, the Jew must abide by the non-Jewish law if the non-Jewish court so decreed. On the other hand, if a law should arbitrarily demand that the Jew had to eat foods specially forbidden to him by his religion, then he had a right to refuse to obey such a law, since such a refusal in no way would imperil the state. The fourth law is one which has been adopted by men all over the world, upon finding themselves in a situation similar to that in which the Jews found themselves after 135 A.D. This law declared that Jews must fight in the defense of the country wherein they lived, even if it meant fighting against fellow Jews in another country at a time of war.

One additional decision made at this time had far-reaching psychological effects on the Jews, changing their character for twenty centuries. That decision was to abandon the idea of reconquering Palestine and of establishing another Jewish state there. Henceforth Palestine would be a spiritual homeland only, where pious Jews could go to die. Just as the Jews in the tenth century B.C. had discarded their nomadic life to become men of war, so in the second century A.D. they became men of peace. Though they would fight in the defense of the country in which they resided as a sign of gratitude for sanctuary, they would not fight as a militaristic people and would not attack anyone. Not until the twentieth century, when political Zionism came of age, advocating that Palestine once again be the political homeland for the Jews, did they again take up arms, as Jews, fighting to restore their ancient homeland.

At this juncture of their history, the Jews also gave up active proselytization. As Jewish leaders had no political power to enforce their decrees, but had to rely solely on voluntary acceptance, they were afraid that too many new converts would weaken the will to survive as Jews in succeeding generations. Henceforth pagans and Christians had to come to the Jews to ask permission to join their religion. Only if after much dissuasion the applicant still insisted was he permitted to become a convert. Even with these obstacles placed in the way, Judaism was still so attractive to many that in the sixth century the Church, in order to stop the wave of conversions, imposed the death penalty on any Christian who converted to Judaism.

More than anybody else the Jews realized that "no man is an island, entire of itself." They formulated laws not only for the survival of Judaism, but for the conduct of Jews among their gentile neighbors. If a Christian died in the midst of a Jewish community, he had to be buried by the Jews according to Christian ritual. Jewish physicians had to heal the ill, whether Jews or non-Jews, and do so without a fee if poverty prevented payment. Jews had to support not only their own communities, but also had to contribute toward the welfare of the general gentile community. Non-Jewish invalids had to be visited by Jews, if no one else came to see them. Charity had to be provided for anyone who demanded it—Jew or non-Jew. No matter how poor a Jew is, he always feels there is someone poorer than he, and a Jew living on charity sees nothing incongruous in giving some of his charity money as charity to someone else. Unlike the Christians, Jews did not feel that non-Jews were excluded from heaven. On the contrary, they held that the "righteous among the nations of the world have a share in the world to come."

All these laws formulated during the fateful centuries before the collapse of the Roman Empire had far-reaching effects on the Jews. These laws permitted them to identify themselves with the cultures of peoples in every land in which they resided without having to lose their identity. The Jews had learned the art of separation of church and state.

The span of five centuries between 100 and 600 A.D. was a transitional period for the Jews. There was no one dominant civilization during this vast stretch of time. Hellenism was on the decline and the Roman Empire was dying. But the Roman Empire did not come to an end in one great *Götterdämmerung.* It petered out, and two most unlikely events contributed to its final downfall. The first had its origin in a small town in Judea, the second in China. The first was the growth of Christianity; the second was the migration of the Huns. As subsequent Jewish history is inextricably woven into the fabric of early Christian origins, let us explore these origins before we examine the nature of Rome's psychosomatic trauma as the creed of the Christians assaulted her mind and the arms of the Huns reached for her body.

# III

# MOSES, CHRIST, AND CAESAR

*An unorthodox account of the establishment of the Christian "Son religion" in competition with the Jewish "Father religion," and how it challenged the might of Rome to become the creed of Europe.*

# WHEN CHRISTIANITY WAS BORN
## 100 B.C. TO 600 A.D.

| ROMAN HISTORY | | JUDEO-CHRISTIAN HISTORY |
|---|---|---|
| Age of revolutions and coming of Caesarism. Rome master of known world. | 100 B.C. to I A.D. | Judah becomes a Roman province. Herod the Great made King of the Jews. Jesus Christ is born. |
| Age of Emperors Nero, Vespasian, Titus. Britain conquered. | 1 to 100 | Jesus crucified by Romans. Paul takes Jewish Christian sect to pagans. Jerusalem destroyed. Pauline Epistles written. Gospels composed (70–120 A.D.). |
| Age of Emperors Trajan, Hadrian, Marcus Aurelius. Internal economic and moral collapse. | 100 to 200 | Second and third Jewish uprisings against Rome. Roman persecutions of Christians increase. Schisms plague new Church. |
| Pressure on Rome's frontiers by Germanic tribes in North and Parthians in East. Military dictatorships. Empire divided. | 200 to 300 | Jews become Roman citizens. Christian ranks raked by heresies. Christians branded subversives by Romans. |

| | | |
|---|---|---|
| Emperor Constantine temporarily reunites empire. Age of Theodosius. Empire split permanently in two. First Vandal invasion. | 300 to 400 | Emperor Constantine recognizes Christians. Church Council of Nicaea held. New Testament canonized (395). First laws limiting rights of non-Christians. |
| Vandals, Goths, Huns pour across frontiers. Rome sacked. Barbarian kings seize throne of Rome. Feudal Age settles over Europe. | 400 to 600 | Church solidifies its position in the empire. Papacy established. Jews only non-Christian body left in sea of Christianity. |

# MESSIAH AND APOSTLE

Throughout the centuries, Jews have accused Christians of calculated injustices of which they are innocent, and Christians have accused Jews of crimes of which they are not guilty. But what seems like planned prejudice or irreconcilable hostility could be only psychological astigmatism or a plain garden variety of human frailty afflicting both sides. Early Jewish-Christian relationships must be placed in a new frame of reference if we are to have a better understanding of them.

Who originated Christianity? Who spread it, and how was it able to become a dominant world religion? For centuries the opinion prevailed that the concepts of Christianity were totally the innovations of Jesus. Then, in 1947, an electrifying event occurred. Manuscripts dating back to 100 and 200 B.C. bearing a striking resemblance to the Christian creed were discovered. The so-called "Dead Sea Scrolls" had been found, and with them the mystery of the origin of early Christianity may have been solved.

The discovery of the Dead Sea Scrolls ranks as one of the greatest finds in archaeology, overshadowing in importance even Heinrich Schliemann's discovery of Troy and the Mycenaean civilization. No fiction writer would have dared invent the circumstances under which the Scrolls were found. No great scholars or planned expeditions were involved. The discovery was made in the early spring of 1947, by a young Bedouin black marketeer named Muhammed the Wolf, at a time when he was stealthily crossing the Arabian-Palestine lines on his way to Bethlehem with a flock of contraband goats.

Palestine was in a crisis. The defunct League of Nations' Mandate over Palestine was about to end. The British, who had administered that Mandate since World War I, were preparing to leave the following spring, and the Arabs were threatening to invade the moment the British left.

Practicing for invasion day, the Arabs were sniping at the Jews and the Jews were meeting fire with fire. As the British sided with the Arabs, the Jews sabotaged the British to hasten their departure. The British hanged the saboteurs and the Jews reciprocated by hanging British soldiers. Palestine was a proverbial powder keg.

These were the trying conditions under which Muhammed the Wolf had to earn a living. To reach the lucrative black market in Bethlehem where he could sell his flock of goats at a handsome profit to the Jews, Muhammed had to elude both Arab and British patrols. A native of the region, he took a little-known path along the desolate, hilly western shore of the Dead Sea. In pursuing a stray goat, Muhammed passed a strange cave and idly threw a stone into it. To his astonishment and fright he heard the sound of breaking pottery. He ran away but came back later with a friend engaged in the same profession, and together they explored the cave.

Inside the cave the two youths found tall clay jars, the kind Rachel might have used at the well when Jacob met her, or Zipporah might have used in tending her father's flock when Moses first saw her. Inside the jars Muhammed and his friend found scrolls of parchment with what turned out to be ancient Hebrew writing on them. They were biblical and Essene religious manuscripts dating back to 100 and 200 B.C. The two young Bedouins had stumbled upon an Essene *genizah*, a storage house for religious manuscripts.

Eventually these scrolls found their way into the hands of competent biblical scholars, who identified them as genuine Old Testament manuscripts and as hitherto unknown works of Essene writings. What astounded the scholars was the incredible resemblance of this Essene Judaism as revealed in these scrolls to early Christianity.

Subsequent expeditions to the scene led to the discovery of other caves and other scrolls. Even more incredible, the ruins of an early Jewish Essene monastery were found in the vicinity where John the Baptist and Jesus had preached. The resemblance of early Christianity to the Essene religion grew into a mirror image.

Among the many complete scrolls and fragments of Essene writings, the most important were those documents now entitled *Manual of Discipline, Habakkuk Commentary, The War of the Sons of Light with the Sons of Darkness,* and *Zadokite Fragments.* These manuscripts formed the heart of the Essene religious creed, and in these scrolls, many scholars now contend, are embedded the origins of early Christianity.

Briefly, the Essenes, whose political origins we have already explored, believed in a divinely sent messiah whom they called the "Teacher of Righteousness," and who had died a violent death at the hands of the Sons of Darkness. The followers of the Teacher of Righteousness called themselves the "Elect of God" and their religious community the "New Covenant." Members of the New Covenant were initiated through baptism. They had a protocol for seating which is almost identical to that of the Last Supper as described in the New Testament. The *Manual of Discipline* describes a ritual which could be mistaken for the Christian Communion. The many striking resemblances between the Essene and Christian creeds have best been summed up by A. Dupont-Sommer, a professor at the Sorbonne:

> Everything in the Jewish New Covenant heralds and prepares the way for the Christian New Covenant. The Galilean Master, as He is presented to us in the writings of the New Testament, appears in many respects as an astonishing reincarnation of the Teacher of Righteousness. Like the latter, He preached penitence, poverty, humility, love of one's neighbor, chastity. Like him, He prescribed the observance of the Law of Moses, the whole Law, but the Law finished and perfected, thanks to His own revelations. Like him, He was the Elect and the Messiah of God, the Messiah Redeemer of the World. Like him, He was the object of the hostility of the priests, the party of the Sadducees. Like him, He was condemned and put to death. Like him, He pronounced judgment on Jerusalem, which was taken and destroyed by the Romans for having put Him to death. Like him, at the end of time, He will be the supreme judge. Like him, He founded a church whose adherents fervently awaited His glorious return. In the Christian Church,

just as in the Essene Church, the essential rite is the sacred meal, whose ministers are the priests. Here and there, at the head of each community, there is the overseer, the "bishop." And the ideal of both Churches is essentially that of unity, communion in love—even going so far as the sharing of common property.

All these similarities—and here I only touch upon the subject—taken together constitute a very impressive whole. The question at once arises, to which of the two sects, the Jewish or the Christian, does the priority belong? Which of the two was able to influence the other? The reply leaves no room for doubt. The Teacher of Righteousness died about 65–53 B.C.; Jesus the Nazarene died about 30 A.D. In every case in which the resemblance compels or invites us to think of a borrowing, this was on the part of Christianity. But on the other hand, the appearance of the faith in Jesus—the foundation of the New Church—can scarcely be explained without the real historic activity of a new Prophet, a new Messiah, who has rekindled the flame and concentrated on himself the adoration of men.*

Up until the discovery of the Dead Sea Scrolls, only a handful of historians and scholars, among them Josephus, Philo, and the Roman scholar Pliny, had made any references to the Essenes and their religious observances; and few people had paid any heed to them. In 1864 a British scholar with the unlikely name of Christian D. Ginsburg published a monograph entitled *The Essenes: Their History and Doctrines*, in which he intuitively asserted what the Dead Sea Scrolls prove. But this too was dismissed as the meaningless work of a foolish scholar who speculated about something for which he had no concrete evidence.

But with the discovery of the Dead Sea Scrolls the scholars were vindicated. Josephus, Philo, Pliny, Ginsburg—all had been right. "Christianity" had existed at least two hundred years before Jesus, its greatest and noblest spokesman, but not its originator.

Instead of a loud reverberation through Christian and

---

*A. Dupont-Sommer, *The Dead Sea Scrolls: A Preliminary Survey.*

Jewish institutions at this momentous discovery, there was nothing but silence. The Christians were not anxious to impute to Jewish rabbis the total origin of their religion, feeling it enough that Jesus was Jewish. Neither were the Jews anxious to assume credit for the complete authorship of Christianity, feeling they had contributed enough by providing the central figure in the Christian religion. Thus the Essene Dead Sea Scrolls remained the property of little-known scholars who continued to write about this great discovery in esoteric magazines, or became the playthings of popularizers who diluted their essential meaning with so many soothing clichés that their importance was reduced to trivia.

In the troubled land of Judea, in the first century A.D., bleeding under Rome's tyrannical rule, many prophets, preachers, and holy men, representing most of the twenty-four religious sects in the country at the time, went about proclaiming the coming of a messiah who would deliver the Jews from the evil of the Roman yoke. Each sect preached its own brand of salvation, but the most numerous of these itinerant prophets and preachers were the Essenes. History has shown us that the most important of them all was Jesus.

*Jesus Christ* is Greek for "Joshua the messiah," and the word "messiah" comes from the Hebrew word *mashiah*, meaning "one who is anointed," that is, a messiah. As scholars disagree about the dates of Christ's life, we will give only approximate ones. Depending, then, upon what authority is used, Jesus was born between 7 and 4 B.C. either in Bethlehem or Nazareth* during the reign of Herod the Great in Judea, and was crucified either in 30 or in 33 A.D.** The Gospels according to Luke and Matthew trace

---

*Cecil John Cadoux, *The Life of Jesus Christ* (Pelican Books, page 27). Cadoux, professor of New Testament and professor of Church History, Oxford University, makes a strong case for his belief that the birth of Jesus took place at Nazareth, not at Bethlehem. This is the view generally held by scholars today.

**Astronomical evidence points to 33 A.D. rather than 30 A.D. All four Gospels agree the crucifixion of Jesus took place on a Friday, during the Feast of Passover, celebrated by the Jews on the fifteenth of Nisan, commencing on the evening when the full moon occurs. In 30 A.D., Passover was held on a Thursday, whereas in 33 A.D. it was held on a Friday, as the full moon occurred on those days.

his ancestry to the royal house of David, each through different and conflicting genealogies; the other two Gospels
make no such mention. When Jesus was about twelve years
old he was taken to Jerusalem, where he listened to
learned rabbis discuss the Torah, but, as in the case of
Moses, we know little else of his childhood and nothing
about his early manhood. In the light of the findings of the
Dead Sea Scrolls, it seems likely that he spent that period
in the Essene monastery so recently discovered in the very
neighborhood in which the New Testament says he spent
his youth.

After his visit to Jerusalem at the age of twelve, Jesus
disappears from the pages of the Gospels until he reap-
pears somewhere between 28 and 30 A.D., at the age of
thirty, at which time he is baptized by John the Baptist, so
called because John taught in accordance with the Essene
creed, that men could cleanse their souls symbolically
through "baptism," that is, through immersion in water.
This was not an unorthodox or heretical notion among the
Jews, who for centuries had practiced one or another form
of water purification ritual. John also proclaimed that he
was the messenger of God, and that his mission was that of
ushering in the kingdom of God. Neither Pharisees nor
Sadducees thought this a blasphemous notion, because
John was never brought to any trial by them. John was not
put to death for any political or religious reasons, nor was
he put to death by the Jews. John met his death at the
hands of the Idumean king, Herod Antipas, appointed
ruler of Galilee by the Romans, because John openly denounced the marriage of Antipas to his niece as illegal and
incestuous.

Jesus' public life as a savior begins with his baptism. His
ministry lasts but one year according to the Synoptic
Gospels,* and three years according to John, depending on
how one interprets the reference to the number of
Passovers mentioned in that Gospel.

Jesus took up the life of a teacher, preaching his own
gospel. There was nothing different or un-Jewish in his

---

*The first three Gospels are "Synoptic," because the narratives paral-
lel each other, which is not the case with the Gospel According to
Saint John.

teachings. He was a liberal; he was against all injustice, in the tradition of the Prophets. He taught the observance of the Mosaic law, compassion for the poor, mercy, and tolerance. He spoke in a soft voice and with a loving heart. He was an inspiring teacher who expressed himself in crystal-clear parables. His messages went straight to the hearts of his listeners. He was an oasis of comfort in a desert of Roman misery. The humble people flocked to him to take solace in his words, to find comfort in his vision, and to take heart in the hope he held out. Nothing he preached, taught, or said was in contradiction to what other Jewish prophets, rabbis, or sects said or taught. Jesus was not in danger from the Jews. He was in danger from the Romans, for it was no longer safe to teach justice in a land ruled by terror. Judea was sitting on the powder keg of an incipient rebellion, and the Roman cure was to seize all suspects and flay them alive or crucify them head down.

In the year 33 A.D. Jerusalem was crowded with pilgrims who had come from every part of the world to celebrate the Feast of Passover. Excitement ran high. A rebellion in the provinces had just been quelled. Rumors of another rebellion were rife. People were talking about a new messiah who had arrived in the city on the back of an ass, in the manner Jewish legend prophesied. To the Romans this talk about a messiah spelled trouble. These messiahs could inflame the people with words quicker than a torch could set fire to paper. Any small incident might incite the Jews to another rebellion. The procurator of Judea, Pontius Pilate, left his mistress in Caesarea, the administrative capital, to come to Jerusalem. He brought his legionnaires with him, ringing the city with steel.

The messiah the people were talking about was Jesus. This was the political atmosphere into which he stepped when he made his decision to come to Jerusalem. This was the time he had chosen to reveal publicly that he was the messiah. His destination was the Temple. His aim was the reform of some of its practices. From a political viewpoint, he had chosen the worst possible time to hasten Temple reforms.

The events which follow are shrouded in obscurity. They are viewed with hindsight by New Testament readers, who are baffled by what to them seems like blindness on the part of the Jews for not accepting immediately the Temple reforms which Jesus wanted to institute. That is how it may seem today, but not in Jerusalem in the year 33 A.D. What New Testament readers forget is that on the day Jesus entered Jerusalem no one, with the possible exception of a few of his closest disciples, knew that he was the messiah, because at this point Jesus had not as yet revealed it. This he did not do until later, after the incident at the Temple. Just exactly at what point Jesus revealed who he was is hard to say, as all four Gospels are contradictory at this point. But when Jesus entered Jerusalem his adherents had no knowledge that he was, or would soon declare himself, the messiah. How could it then be expected that the people in Jerusalem, who had never heard of him, would know what his followers themselves did not know?

Another point which New Testament readers forget, or are not aware of, is that it was the Prophets who began the reformation of the Temple cult, eight hundred years before Jesus. In the days of Jesus there existed, side by side, two Judaisms, one the Judaism of temple and sacrifice, the other the Judaism of synagogue and prayer, just as two Christianities exist side by side today, one Catholic, the other Protestant. Jesus, then, was not the first reformer of the Temple cult. When he appeared on the scene, the reforms instituted by the Prophets were already doing away with the entire Temple cult itself. In this dying Temple cult, Jesus aimed to do away with two practices, the selling of sacrificial animals and the handling of money on Temple grounds.

It was a long-established custom in those days to sell sacrificial doves and pigeons outside the Temple, just as it is the custom to sell candles and crosses inside churches and cathedrals today. As Jewish pilgrims came from many lands to offer their sacrifices in the Temple, it was also a custom for vendors to make change from one currency to another as a service to these pilgrims. Some Sunday-school textbooks hint that there was gambling involved, an understandable elaboration, but this theory is not supported by any of the four Gospels. Jesus objected, not to the making of change, but to the handling of money on Temple grounds, just as he might object to the custom of handling money inside churches and cathedrals today when collection plates or baskets are passed to worshipers.*

When Jesus arrived at the Temple, smashing the tables of the vendors and driving the money-changers down the Temple stairs, those Jews who wanted these services were as outraged as Christians would be today if someone were to storm into their churches during Easter services, smash the candles and crosses offered for sale, and drive the gentlemen passing the collection plates down the church steps. Does anyone doubt that such an intruder would be arrested at the orders of the priest or minister? Yet the Jews did not arrest Jesus at this time. They wanted no trouble with the Romans and hoped the incident would be forgotten.

But this hope was not to be realized. News of the commotion in the Temple tensed the Romans. Was this the event that would set off a riot? An uprising? A rebellion? Responsible Jewish citizens, fully aware of the danger of the slaughter, rapine, and torture which would take place if the Roman legions were unleashed, might have felt that Jesus should be restrained until after Passover, until the excitement had died, until the legionnaires had departed and the semisiege lifted. Cautiously they waited to see what would happen. The adherents of Jesus were now for the first time beginning to speak of him openly as "king of the Jews" and as "the messiah," further arousing the suspicions of the Romans. The Jews, according to the Gospels, arrested Jesus on the third day after his appearance at the Temple.

Twelve eventful hours in the history of mankind now took place. The only accounts we have of the twelve hours which followed the arrest of Jesus are contained in the Four Gospels, which were written forty to ninety years after the event itself. Their many contradictions aside, the Gospel accounts say essentially this: Jesus was arrested at night by orders of the Sanhedrin, the highest court in the land, and condemned to death by the Sanhedrin for the

---

*This custom, incidentally, does not exist among Jews, who do not allow the handling of money inside their temples or synagogues. They either pay annual dues or make pledges to pay certain sums toward the support of their religious institutions.

crime of blasphemy, or religious corruption, at the palace
of the High Priest with the aid of suborned witnesses. The
Gospel versions then go on to relate that Pontius Pilate,
who had to approve the sentence, did so most reluctantly
because he was afraid of the Jewish multitude.

Any person familiar with Jewish judicial procedure in
biblical times will find it difficult to take the Gospel accounts literally. According to Jewish law at that time, no
one could be arrested at night. It was illegal to hold court
proceedings after sundown on the eve or the day of the
Sabbath or a festival. The Great Sanhedrin could convene
only in the Chamber of Hewn Stones, never in the palace
of a High Priest or in any other dwelling. Nor could the
Sanhedrin initiate an arrest. No one could be tried before
the Sanhedrin unless two witnesses had first sworn out
charges against him. As there was no prosecuting attorney,
the accusing witnesses had to state the nature of the offense to the court in the presence of the accused, who had
the right to call witnesses in his own behalf. The court then
examined and cross-examined the accused, the accusers,
and the defense witnesses. The Talmud, in fact, decreed
that even as a condemned man was led to his place of execution, a herald had to precede him crying out to all: "So
and so, the son of so and so, is going forth to be executed
because he has committed such and such an offense, and so
and so are his [accusing] witnesses. Whoever knows anything in his favor, let him come and state it."* These facts
make it very unlikely that a Jewish High Court would defy
every law in its own code and act contrary to time-honored
custom. Such action by the august body of the Sanhedrin is
as inconceivable as the United States Supreme Court's
seizing a man at night, searching for "witnesses" during the
night to accuse him of a crime, condemning him to death
without a trial, and clamoring for immediate execution—
all within the space of twelve hours.**

A historian familiar with the cruelty and rapacity of
Pontius Pilate will find it equally difficult to accept the por-
trayal of Pilate as a tender and merciful judge, zealous for

---

*The Talmud, *Sanhedrin*, Mishna 43 a.
**As one wit expressed it: "Some Christian scholars do not believe
Jesus existed, but they are all convinced that the Jews killed him."

the welfare of one Jew. In fact, Pilate's cruelty and rapacity became so notorious that the Emperor Tiberius had to remove him because he brought dishonor to Rome. It demands too much credulity to think that this Pontius Pilate, a Roman general in command of many legions surrounding the city, was cowed by a Jewish "multitude" armed with nothing more fearful than phylacteries (small amulets wrapped around one arm during prayer).

Does it not seem more probable that Jesus was arrested by the Jews to *protect* him from the Romans (who never had any compunction about crucifying one Jew more or less), that this protective arrest was to no avail, and that the Romans demanded that the Jews turn Jesus over to them for punishment? There is evidence in the Gospels themselves for such a theory. According to the Gospels, it was the Roman soldiers who scourged and tortured the body of Jesus. It took Roman fiendishness, not Jewish compassion, to press a crown of thorns on his head, and to hang the mocking sign, "King of the Jews," on his body.

We cannot but be touched by the poignancy of Christ's agony, when he turned his eyes heavenward and uttered the now familiar cry, "*Eli, Eli, lama sabachtani*"—My God, my God, why hast Thou forsaken me?* The Gospels themselves relate that it was the Jewish multitude that wept at the scene of his crucifixion, not the Romans. The Romans were busy playing dice for his mantle. All the internal evidence points to a Roman atrocity, not a miscarriage of Jewish justice. Jews never in their history crucified anybody, nor ever demanded crucifixion for anyone. In fact the Jews came out in the defense of the Christians, as evidenced in the New Testament itself. Acts 5:34–39 states that the Pharisee Rabbi Rabban Gamaliel openly opposed the Roman persecution of the Christians. Josephus mentions that when James, the brother of Jesus, was executed by the Romans, it was none other than the Pharisees who risked their lives by protesting this wanton killing.

With Jesus dead, Christianity seemed doomed. It was

---

*It could be that Jesus was praying in the traditional Jewish manner, for the words come from the Old Testament, Psalm 22:2. The Psalm of course uses the Hebrew word "asavtani," whereas Jesus uses the Aramaic equivalent "sabachtani" (Matthew 27:46, Mark 15:34).

saved by the Jewish doctrine of resurrection. Jews throughout Judea were familiar with the idea of resurrection after
death, and freely speculated about the hereafter. We find
innumerable references to this in the apocryphal writings
of the Pharisees and in the Dead Sea Scrolls of the Essenes, written at least a century before the time of Jesus.
We should, therefore, not be surprised to read in the
Gospels that on the Sunday following the crucifixion of
Jesus some women went to his tomb to pray and found the
stone in front of it rolled away and the tomb itself empty.
One of the women had a vision of Jesus. Two disciples had
that same vision.* News of this miracle quickly spread
among the dispirited remnants of the followers of Jesus.
All were convinced that he had risen from the dead. Not
only Jesus, but Christianity had been resurrected.

In the first two decades after the death of Jesus, from 30
to 50 A.D., all Christians were Jews, and Christianity as a
Jewish sect differed little from the many other Jewish sects.
New converts came mostly from the ranks of other Jews,
and those pagans who joined the new religion had to become Jews first before they could be accepted into the
Christian faith. All Christians were regarded as Jews in the
same way that a Catholic turned Protestant, or a Protestant turned Catholic, is still regarded as a Christian. The
great schism between Christians and Jews did not occur
until after 50 A.D., when the Christian sect was taken to the
pagans and made a world religion. This was both the decision and the accomplishment of one man, another Jew, the
real builder of the Christian Church. His name is Saul of
Tarsus, generally known by Christians as Paul. He became
to Jesus what the Talmud became to the Torah—a commentary and a way of life.

To the German philosopher Friedrich Nietzsche, Paul
was a man "whose superstition was equaled by his cunning." To Martin Luther, he was a "rock of strength." Paul
was born about the same time as Jesus. He was a citizen of
Rome, intellectual and arrogant. He was educated in
Roman law and Greek philosophy, yet he was a devout and

---

*This is a composite of the four Gospel accounts, since each Gospel
tells part of the story only and the separate accounts contradict one
another in a number of details.

observing Jew, a Pharisee. He journeyed to Jerusalem at
about the same time that Jesus came to preach in that city,
but the two never knew each other. In Jerusalem, Paul also
came in contact with the works of Philo and was greatly influenced by them. He could have become a great scholar of
the Torah. History made him a Christian saint.

If Paul had lived today, he might have ended up on a
psychiatrist's couch. Throughout his life he was overwhelmed with an all-pervasive sense of guilt which pursued him with relentless fury. From early paintings and
from descriptions in New Testament accounts, both his and
others', we have a rather repellent physical portrait of him.
Ernest Renan characterized him as "the ugly little Jew."
Paul was of slight stature, bowlegged, blind in one eye, and
probably had some deformity of body. He was given to re-
current attacks of malaria, had repeated hallucinations,
and some scholars believe he was subject to epileptic
seizures. He was celibate, exhorted others to celibacy, and
advocated marriage only in extreme instances.

In his early years Paul was bitterly opposed to the new
Jewish sect, Christianity. He attacked its members sav-
agely, even appearing as a witness against (and probably in
the stoning of) that sect's first martyr, Stephen, who had
been the first to proclaim that Jesus was equal to God,
which in those days was as great a blasphemy as proclaiming today that Mary Baker Eddy, the founder of Christian
Science, is the daughter of Jesus and equal to God.

According to Acts 9:1–2, Paul ". . . went unto the high
priest . . . and desired of him letters to Damascus to the
synagogues, that if he found any of this way (as Christians
then were referred to), whether they were men or women,
he might bring them bound unto Jerusalem." It was on the
road to Damascus, on this mission, that Paul had his famous vision of Christ, so reminiscent of Abraham's encounter with God two thousand years earlier. But the
events that follow are entirely different. "Why dost thou
persecute me?" Jesus asks him. Paul is blinded by this vision of Christ and has to be led helpless to Damascus. Here
another Jew, a member of the Christian sect, named Ananias, cures Paul's blindness by laying his hands upon him
and converts him to Christianity.

We shall ask the same question at this point as we asked

at the time Abraham encountered God: "Did this really happen?" We shall answer it in the same way. From a historical viewpoint it makes no difference whether Christ actually appeared to Paul, or whether Paul had a hallucinative experience. The fact remains that for two thousand years this account of Paul's conversion has played a dominant role in the Christian religion. This is the reality we must deal with, for this is the reality which creates history.

In spite of this encounter with Jesus, the cure from blindness, and conversion to Christianity, little is heard of Paul for fourteen years, until a disciple named Barnabas, in the year 45 A.D., asks Paul to accompany him on a journey for the new Church. It is now that Paul's remarkable missionary work begins, and he soon surpasses his mentor, Barnabas.

After his return from this first mission Paul made his fateful decision to break with the Jews. Twice he had appealed to the Apostolic Church in Jerusalem to make him an apostle, and twice it had refused him this honor. Then he had a quarrel with James, the brother of Jesus, about the procedure in converting pagans. The custom had been for non-Jewish converts to become Jews first, then be admitted into the Christian sect. Paul felt that pagans should become Christians directly, without first being converted to Judaism. Rebuffed by the apostles of the Church, and defeated in his views on new converts by the brother of Jesus, Paul made three decisions which eliminated the Jewish element from the Christian sect and made it a separate religion.

Since the Jews would not have Christianity, Paul took it to the pagans. To make it easier for them to join his new religion, he made a second decision, that of abandoning Jewish dietary laws and the rite of circumcision. His third decision was to substitute Christ for the Torah, and this was the most crucial one, for it caused the final and unalterable break between the Father and the Son religions. The Jews believed then, as they do now, that man can know God only through the word of God as revealed in the Torah. The Pauline doctrine stated that man could know God only through Christ. The schism between Jew and Christian was total.

After his break with the Apostolic Church in Jerusalem

and his fight with James, Paul set out on his now famous missionary journeys, and it was at this time that he changed his Jewish name of Saul to the Roman name of Paul. On most of his journeys he was accompanied by one or both of two companions, Silas and Timothy, the latter of whom he had personally circumcised. It was also during these journeys, between 50 and 62 A.D., that he wrote the Pauline Epistles. These are the earliest Christian writings; the Gospels did not appear until later, the first some time between 70 and 74 A.D., the fourth around 120 A.D., or perhaps as late as 140 A.D.

The accounts of the history of Christianity in the Pauline Epistles and the Gospels, especially as the latter relate to the trial of Christ, become understandable now that we realize they were written not for the Jews but for the pagans. They were written for the Thessalonians, the Galatians, the Corinthians, the Romans, the Colossians, the Philippians, the Ephesians. It is understandable that neither Paul nor the Gospel writers would want to antagonize those whom they were seeking to convert, or anger the rulers whom they had to mollify, especially since they could be punished for such offenses by being thrown to the lions or being crucified head down.

As Paul journeyed from city to city, from country to country, he used the synagogue as a pulpit for his missionary sermons, for the synagogue was a most tolerant institution, permitting many divergent views. Paul, however, was not as tolerant. ". . . If any man preach any other gospel unto you than you have received [from me] let him be accursed" (Galatians 1:9). Paul did more than take Christianity away from the Jews. Slowly he changed early Christianity into a new Pauline Christology.

To the early Christians, Jesus had been human with divine attributes conferred upon him after resurrection. To Paul, Christ was divine even before birth. To the early Christians, Jesus had been the Son of God. To Paul, Christ was coequal and cosubstantial with God. Jesus had taught that one learned to love God by loving man. Paul taught that one learned to love Christ by incorporating him into oneself. Paul also shifted the early emphasis from Jesus the messiah to Christ the redeemer of sin. Paul's thinking was dominated by the concept of original sin. According to

Paul, man was contaminated by the guilt of Adam, the first sinner. Man could find redemption from sin only through Christ, the first "atoner," that is, the first one to atone for man's sins through his expiatory death.

So powerful was the Pauline appeal to the pagans, that within fifteen years they outnumbered the Jews in the Christian sect. The Jewish Christians, now a minority, became known as the Ebionites—"poor ones"—and soon fell into obscurity. Christianity was no longer a Jewish sect, for Paul had abandoned the Mosaic tradition. The Romans no longer looked upon the Christians as Jews, but as members of a distinct and separate religion of no specific nationality.

Where did Paul get his organizing ability? We don't know that any more than we know where Trotsky got his organizing ability. Just as Trotsky, the Russian-Jewish ghetto intellectual, took a bedraggled, beaten Russian Czarist Army and transformed it into a victorious Red Army, so Paul, the Roman-Jewish cosmopolitan intellectual, took a handful of dispirited disciples of Christ and transformed them into the Church militant. At the time of Paul's death in Rome in 62 A.D., when according to tradition he was beheaded by order of Emperor Nero, Christianity was a world movement to be reckoned with by the Roman Empire.

TWELVE

# THE CHURCH TRIUMPHANT

It was a miracle that the Christians survived their first three hundred years. One schism after another within their ranks threatened to obliterate them. In this early struggle for survival, the Christians had no time for the Jews. Wrangling over the many doctrinal viewpoints cropping up concerning the nature of the divinity of Christ and his relation to God, the Father, occupied all their energies.

Maintaining their number was also a full-time occupation. No sooner had Christianity become a separate religion than it was looked upon with suspicion by the Romans, who now branded the Christians as subversives and subjected them to relentless persecution. A good portion of their membership was eaten by the lions in the Roman amphitheaters, which was the Roman cure for Christianity, instituted by Nero and continued for three more centuries. Most of the losses in their ranks, however, came from recantations. Christianity was outlawed by the Romans in the same way Communism was later outlawed by some countries. When a Christian accused of being a subversive was brought before a Roman tribunal, he was given the choice of life, by denying he was a Christian, or death, by affirming it. Usually he chose life by recanting his Christianity. As the German jurist Rudolf Sohm so succinctly states in his *Outlines of Church History*, "The Church conquered, not because of the Christians, but in spite of them—through the power of the Gospels."

The Christian position in the Roman Empire resembled, in fact, that of the American Communist position in America during the 1950s. This is pointedly illustrated by two existing Roman documents, one a letter from Pliny the Younger, Governor of Bithynia, written to Emperor Trajan in 112, and the Emperor's reply. Pliny wrote:

It is my rule, Sire, to refer to you in matters where I am uncertain. For who can better direct my hesitation or instruct my ignorance? I was never present at any trial of Christians; therefore I do not know what are the customary penalties . . . I have hesitated a great deal on the question whether there should be any distinction of ages; whether the weak should have the same treatment as the more robust; whether those who recant should be pardoned, or whether a man who has ever been a Christian should gain nothing by ceasing to be such; whether the name itself, even if innocent of crime, should be punished, or only the crimes attaching to that name.

Meanwhile, this is the course I have adopted in the case of those brought before me as Christians. I ask them if they are Christians. If they admit it, I repeat the question a second and third time, threatening capital punishment; if they persist, I sentence them to death. For I do not doubt that whatever kind of crime it may be to which they have confessed, their pertinacity and inflexible obstinacy should certainly be punished . . . an anonymous pamphlet was issued, containing many names. All who denied that they were or had been Christian I considered should be discharged . . . Others named by the informer first said that they were Christians, and then denied it; declaring that they had been, but were so no longer, some having recanted three years or more before and one or two as long as twenty years ago. They all worshiped your image and the statues of the gods and cursed Christ. . . .

The matter seemed to me to justify my consulting you . . . for many persons of all ages and classes and of both sexes are being put in peril by accusations, and this will go on. . . .

And Emperor Trajan replied:

You have taken the right line, my dear Pliny, in examining the cases of those denounced to you as Christians, for no hard and fast rule can be laid down, of universal application. They are not to be sought out; if they are informed against and the charge is proved, they are to be punished, with this reservation—that if anyone denies that he is a Christian, and actually proves it, that is by worshiping our gods, he shall be pardoned as a result of his recantation, however suspect he may have been with respect to the past. Pamphlets published anonymously should carry no weight in any charge whatsoever. They constitute a very bad precedent, and are also out of keeping with this age.*

The age of Trajan was but a brief respite. The persecution of the Christians was stepped up by his successors, and their exclusion from the mainstreams of social life more rigorously enforced. This persecution and social exclusion gave the early Christians certain character traits reminis-

---

*Documents of the Christian Church* (Oxford University Press, 1947).

cent of the character traits ascribed by the Christians to the Jews during the Middle Ages. Edward Gibbon, in his *Decline and Fall of the Roman Empire*, expresses it this way:

> As the greater number [of the Christians] were of some trade or profession, it was incumbent on them . . . to remove suspicion which the profane are apt to conceive against the appearance of sanctity. The contempt of the world exercised upon them the habits of humility, meekness and patience. The more they were persecuted, the more closely they adhered to each other.

In the end, however, the power of the Gospels conquered. For every step back taken by the Christians, the power of the Gospels took them two steps forward. Though they had served as food for the lions in the first century, been regarded as subversives in the second century, and been despised in the third century, in the fourth century they became the masters of the Roman Empire.

The question to be asked is not only How did this come about? but also Why were the Christians so universally despised and so relentlessly persecuted by the Romans? We have already quoted Edward Gibbon on the religious toleration of the Romans, who regarded all religions as equally true, equally false, and equally useful. None, except the Christians, were ever singled out by them for religious persecution. The measures of repression by the Romans against the Jews had always been in retaliation against Jewish opposition to their rule, and the cruelty practiced against them differed in no way from the cruelty practiced, for instance, against the Carthaginians, who, like the Jews, had rebelled against Roman authority.

But few historians seem interested in the question of why the Romans persecuted the Christians. Most of them merely record the fact that it happened. Edward Gibbon, who is one exception to this general rule, is, unfortunately, more entertaining than impartial on this subject. Agnostics love his famous, sardonic chapters on the growth and history of the early Church. But devout Christians dismiss Gibbon's observations on Christianity as a product of his ignorance, though they do think his caustic remarks about the Jews are profound. The Jews agree with this verdict on Gibbon, but in reverse. They dismiss his annotations on the Jews as a product of ignorance but regard his ironic observations on the Christians as expressions of profundity.

Having made this reservation, a kernel of truth, nevertheless, does reside in Gibbon's explanation of why the Romans should have singled out the Christians for persecution. The Jews, said Gibbon, constituted a nation and as such, in the Roman view, were entitled to have their religious peculiarities. The Christians, on the other hand, were a sect, who, being without a country, subverted other nations. The Jews took an active part in government and, when not fighting Rome against injustice, fought side by side with Roman legionnaires to preserve the empire. The Christians, again, withdrew themselves from the mainstream of life, from the responsibility of government, and from the duty of bearing arms. It was for these reasons, says Gibbon, that the Romans felt that the crime of the Christian was not in anything he did but in being what he was.

There is no mystery attached to when and how the Christians assumed power in the Roman Empire. The year was 324, and it was Emperor Constantine the Great who gave them that power. At the beginning of the fourth century the Christians were the largest single religious body in the empire, though they still were a minority. This large, cohesive plurality could have a stabilizing influence in propping up his tottering empire. He followed the axiom, "If you can't lick 'em, join 'em." Accordingly, he not only recognized Christianity as a legal religion, but also made it the only legal religion in the land. The Christians at this time did not number over 20 percent of the total population.

Accession to power did not bring peace to the Church; one wave of trouble after another threatened to drown it. In giving the Church political power, Constantine also bequeathed it a dubious heritage—Oriental despotism. At the Church Council of Nicaea, which he convoked in 325, a creed, known as the Nicene Creed, was adopted; after that, all Christians had to believe in its principles; all other opinions were banned and declared heretical. The monopolistic character of the early Church was set. Whereas in the past the Christians had settled their sectarian differences by conciliation, they now resorted to the sword to enforce religious conformity. Gibbon estimates that the Christians killed more of their own number in the first hundred years after coming to power than did the Romans during the three previous centuries.

With the problem of one uniform Church also went the problem of one uniform Scripture. The history of the canonization of the New Testament parallels that of the Old Testament. The first attempt to bring order into the chaos of a multitude of Gospels, many more or less contradictory and all purporting to be true, was made about the year 170. It was at this time that the first exploratory list of books to be included in the New Testament was made, and known as the Muratorian Canon. The New Testament, as we know it, did not come into being until 362 years after the death of Jesus, that is, not until 395 A.D. Only those texts which most closely hewed to the official creed were accepted into the new canon. The others were banned. What other gospels contained, we have no way of knowing. To possess them was heresy, and heresy was punishable by death.

The final canonization of the New Testament coincided with the final split in the Roman Empire. Upon the death of Emperor Theodosius in 395, his son Arcadius took the eastern part of the empire and established his capital in Constantinople, and his son Honorius took the western half, with Rome as the capital. Though the shrunken frontiers were still intact, four sets of circumstances, set in motion by Jews. Romans, Christians, and barbarians, respectively, so corroded the empire internally that she fell apart in the next century.

The first set of circumstances, brought about by the Jews, has already been discussed, namely, the three Roman-Jewish wars. These three wars made Rome's subject people restive, and placed enemies in arms at her borders, waiting for an opportune moment to strike. This called for added taxation and additional reinforcements on the frontiers which further helped to drain the resources of the empire. Rome's frontiers never expanded after the first Jewish war, and they began to shrink after the third one.

The second set of events responsible for weakening the empire was caused by the Romans themselves. Slavery had displaced the middle classes, and work had become something to be disdained. Loose sexual morals had undermined the family institution. The corrupt and unjust taxation against which the Jews had rebelled now corroded the empire itself.

The third set of circumstances contributing to the fall of Rome is ascribed by many historians to the Christians. Because the early Christians believed that the end of the world was at hand, they did not take the burdens of governing seriously, and, as a result, centralized government collapsed. Monasticism and a stress on virginity, carried to the extent of unconsummated marriages, led to depopulation. An over-emphasis on the hereafter and a concentration on theology led to a neglect of civic duty, patriotism, and learning.

These three sets of circumstances, accelerating in their destructive effects in the first four centuries of this era, were combined in the fifth century with a fourth set of events, the barbarian invasions.

The origins of these barbarian invasions into Western Europe in the fifth century stretch five hundred years back into history, all the way to China. In the first century B.C. the emperors of China decided to rid themselves of all unstable elements within their borders, the millions of nomads who would not settle down on the farms or take jobs in the cities. A series of wars on these harmless itinerants—wars not to exterminate them, but to send them packing across the borders of China—set a law of physics in motion. This law operates on the principle of the corset—if you tighten it in one place, something has to bulge in another. When these nomadic peoples (known as Huns, from the Chinese Han dynasty which instituted these mass migrations) were squeezed out of China, they bulged into other countries.

These evicted nomads squatted in northern India, southern Russia, and the Balkans. But here dwelt other nomadic tribes—the West Goths (known as Visigoths), the Vandals, and the East Goths (known as Ostrogoths). Just as the Chinese emperors had driven the Huns out of China, so the Huns in their turn forced the Visigoths, Vandals, and Ostrogoths out of their lands, driving them into Western Europe—Germany, France, Italy, Spain. The Visigoths were the first to invade the Roman Empire in the fourth century. They were followed by the Vandals, and joined by the Gauls from the north, in the fifth century. All took turns sacking Rome.

But now a new threat, overshadowing all others, hovered over Europe. The Huns, who by sheer weight of numbers had been able to force the Vandals and Goths to leave their lands and migrate into Europe, now themselves crossed the frontiers of that continent. They had found a new leader, Attila, who changed these unorganized Asiatic nomads into a murderous military cavalry. With raw meat packed between saddle and horse for provisions, they rode into France on a carpet of blood and devastation. It is said that grass never grew again where the Hun cavalry passed. For the first and only time in recorded history Europe was in danger of becoming an Asiatic, tribute-paying colony. The Visigoths and Vandals, who a hundred years earlier had invaded France and had been looked upon as the scourges of mankind, came to the rescue of Europe. They defeated the Huns at the crucial Battle of Troyes, also known as the Battle of Châlons, in 451. Attila withdrew his forces to Italy and threatened Rome. His sudden death averted quick disaster. The Huns, now without a leader, dispersed and vanished from history.

But the incursion of the Huns had sapped the strength of the empire, broken down the frontiers, and disorganized the government. Other invading tribes from the east and north obligingly finished the work of the Huns. Sacking Rome became a habit, and Rome could stand only so much sacking. The western half of the former Roman Empire collapsed completely. The population had been intermingled thoroughly with the invaders. New nations were forged. Gothic and Vandal kings who took over the power knew little of the art of governing. What was left of the empire began falling apart into hundreds of little states and principalities. The glory that was Greece and the grandeur that was Rome had come to an end. The Feudal Age settled over Europe.

The Church had carried on a valiant battle against the barbarians. As she could not stop them by the force of her arms, she began to absorb them into her faith. By converting the invading pagans, the Church also endangered herself. The acquisition of so many unbelievers in so short a time threatened to dilute her dogma. The Eastern religion of Jesus Christ changed under the stress of its practical application in the West as much as Western Marxism changed under the stress of its practical application in the East.

The establishment of the Papacy in the sixth century gave the Church a strong central rallying point. The last of the old dissident sects were stamped out; the last of the pagans in the former western half of the empire were converted. The Church could now afford to breathe more easily and to survey its domain in tranquillity. The Jews, who had been virtually ignored by the Christians for six centuries, were now rediscovered.

Why was this so? The answer has already presented itself. Until their recognition by Constantine, the Christians were far too busy saving themselves from the Romans to bother much about the Jews. In the ensuing three hundred years after the death of Constantine, the Christians were far too occupied fighting the battle of heretical creeds and godless barbarians to pay much heed to the Jews, who minded their own business. This rediscovery of the Jews presented the Christians a king-size problem. The Jews were the only undigested remnant of non-Christians in a sea of Christianity which engulfed them. What should the Christians do? Baptize them, forcibly if need be, as they had done with nonbelieving pagans? Exterminate them as they had done with those barbarians who did not accept the true faith?* Or leave them alone, which might constitute a danger to Christian faith? This dilemma of the Christians and the precarious position of the Jews became the paramount Jewish problem in the Middle Ages.

Though the first six centuries of Christianity were rather tranquil for the Jews, many Jewish historians have made it appear as though they were studded with persecution. As evidence, they cite a law here and a law there, to show that the Jews were banned from this or that office or were denied one or another right. What these historians forget in their search for injustice is that the Jews lived on

---

*Forcible conversion was prohibited by the popes in the seventh century, after the Papacy had been firmly established. As will be discussed later, it was the popes who were the greatest protectors of the Jews during the Middle Ages.

a continent and in an age full of injustice and violence for everyone. Six hundred years is a long span of time, and occasional injustices do not constitute an official, universal, and consistent program of persecution.

Emperor Caracalla in 212 A.D. had granted the Jews in the empire not only equality but citizenship. Emperor Constantine, in recognizing the Christian Church, withdrew some of these rights from the Jews but did not revoke their citizenship. A fluke of history almost wiped out all the gains of the Christians and almost swept the Jews back to Jerusalem, Temple, and Sanhedrin. When Emperor Julian, known understandably by the Christians as "the Apostate," came to power in 361, he renounced Christianity, forbade the practice of that religion, turned what was left of the empire back to paganism, restored all the privileges of the Jews, and promised the Jews he would help them rebuild Jerusalem and the Temple. Julian was ripe for conversion to Judaism. Two years later he died. With him died the fears of the Christians and the hopes of the Jews.

It was the generation following the destruction of the Temple which brought about a final rupture between Jews and Christians. Though Paul had taken the Jewish-Christian sect to the pagans, the Christians flocked to Jewish synagogues in the Diaspora for protection against the Romans. In these synagogues they continued their proselytization efforts to convert Jews to Christianity. Feeling their hospitality abused, Jewish leaders inserted a prayer in their liturgy against heretics. As the Christians could not recite this prayer, the practice of using the synagogue as a sanctuary died out. In the third rebellion against Rome, when the Christians were unable to accept bar Kochba as their messiah, they declared that their kingdom was of the other world, and withdrew themselves completely from Judaism and everything Jewish. The alienation process was completed. Judaism and Christianity became strangers to each other.

Now that they had disassociated themselves from the Jews, the Christians were caught on the horns of a dilemma: They had to discredit the Old Testament, which was still held in great esteem by the Greeks and Romans, but they also needed the Old Testament to give sanctity to the New Testament as a way of combating the many attempts made to identify Jesus with pagan gods such as Attis, Osiris, and Adonis, who, like Jesus, were the center of a resurrection rite of one form or other. This dilemma the Church solved neatly by reading a prophecy of the coming of Christianity in the writings of the Old Testament. As one Jewish scholar summed it up:

> Thereupon they [the Christians] proclaimed themselves and the members of their churches to be the true "heirs of the promise," applying every favorable reference and blessing to themselves and every rebuke and curse to the Jews. This fantastic travesty was followed by an official version of Jewish history which portrayed the Jews as the followers, not of Moses, Aaron, David, Samuel, Jeremiah and Isaiah, but of Dathan and Abiram, Ahab and Manasseh. . . . The cherished words of the prophets were taken by the Christian zealots to be so much damning testimony against the Jewish people. A wall of misunderstanding and hate was erected by the narrow zealotries of the two faiths. And in the turbulence of passion, the light of either faith became invisible to those whose eyes were accustomed from childhood to the illumination of the other. In the darkness of the medieval period only the philosopher was aware of the unity of the Judeo-Christian tradition that underlies the diversity of creed and ritual.*

As Christian scholar James Parkes expressed it, "No people has ever paid so high a price for the greatness of its own religious leaders."

Generally speaking, in the three centuries from 300 to 600, four sets of laws were passed containing discriminatory provisions against the Jews in the Roman Empire—the Laws of Constantine the Great (315 A.D.), as noted above; the Laws of Constantius (399 A.D.), forbidding intermarriage between Jewish men and Christian women; the Laws of Theodosius II (439 A.D.), prohibiting Jews from holding high positions in government; and the Laws

---

*Jacob Bernard Agus, *The Evolution of Jewish Thought*, page 144.

of Justinian (531 A.D.), prohibiting Jews from appearing as witnesses against Christians.

On the face of it, these laws do appear discriminatory, disparaging, and derogatory. But if we are to get a true picture and understanding of Jewish life in the ensuing Middle Ages, we must first clearly understand the intent of these laws so as to perceive the difference between these and the laws passed a few centuries later. To properly evaluate these laws, they must be viewed with a sixth-century mind, not with the hindsight of the twentieth century. These laws did not apply to Jews alone, but, in the words of their framers, they applied equally to Jews, Samaritans, Manichaeans,* heretics, and pagans. These laws had two purposes: to protect the infant religion from the competition of other religions, and to protect key posts for coreligionists. When Jews are singled out by historians as the only victims of these laws, we are given a false picture of their intent.

In spirit these laws were no different from laws in America today, but no one questions these, because they wear the cloak of nationalism instead of religion. Just as citizenship is a prerequisite for holding public office in the United States today, so the ecclesiastical state made religious membership the prerequisite for holding office in medieval times. Just as early America protected its infant industries from European competition by erecting protective tariff barriers, so the early Church protected itself from the competition of the Eastern religions by erecting protective legislation against them. Even today, no Protestant can hold public office in Catholic Spain. No Catholic can become president in Lutheran Finland.

Though the Jews voluntarily had given up proselytizing in the second century, Judaism still proved a strong attraction to many pagans and Christians. To stop this trend the Church decreed the death penalty for any apostate Christian. Many slaves converted to Judaism because of the lenient treatment they received at the hands of the Jews, who, in accordance with Mosaic law, set them free after

---

*Members of a mystic Oriental religion which was carried by Roman soldiers from Asia Minor to Europe. It became so popular with the masses that it represented for a while a threat to the new Church.

seven years' servitude. The Church therefore decreed a ban against Jews possessing slaves. Jews as husbands held an especial attraction to Christian women, because they were reputed to be good providers who stressed education for their children. The Laws of Constantine therefore specifically forbade such marriages; but marriages between Christian men and Jewish women were not forbidden, as they usually brought converts into the fold of Christianity. The Jews were not too disturbed about these discriminatory marriage laws. In fact, many welcomed them, since the Jews had long ago imposed upon themselves similar laws against intermarriage.

The newly converted, formerly nomadic, illiterate Vandals, Visigoths, Gauls, Ostrogoths, and Huns were no match for the literate, sophisticated Jews, so recently educated in Greek science, literature, and philosophy. By natural law these educated Jews floated to the top posts which every country had to offer, and the barbarian emperors tried to stop this natural law with artificial legislation. But these laws were enforced more in the breach than in the observance. Just as Benjamin Disraeli was Prime Minister at a time when Jews in England were forbidden by law to hold seats in the House of Commons, so the Jews, by and large, continued to hold positions of judges and magistrates, scholars and merchants, workers and farmers in this Christian world.

Though occasional persecution did take place here and there during these three centuries, though an occasional edict against the Jews did deny them one or another liberty, though unjust taxation was now and then levied against them—all these were but sporadic actions, occasionally enforced, and generally ignored. One must not forget that these were three bloody centuries for Christians and pagans as they fought a life and death struggle for dominance. The wonder is that the Jews survived at all, as Visigoths and Vandals, Huns and Gauls, Christians and pagans slaughtered each other with careless abandon. If the Jews expected a newly converted Vandal to make a subtle distinction between an unconverted Jew and an unconverted Gaul, they expected too much.

But the Jews survived the turmoil. In the sixth century they were sitting astride the thresholds of three new emerging civilizations—the Byzantine, the Islamic, and the feudal. A sterile cultural death and physical expulsion awaited them in the Byzantine Empire. A brilliant intellectual career was in store for them in the Islamic world. Sorrow and greatness was their lot in the Feudal Age. The question is, How did they survive?

# THE INVISIBLE
# WORLD OF
# THE TALMUD

*The incredible tale of how a handful of Jews scattered among alien cultures in three continents grew into an influential "intellectual world" by virtue of the invisible power of Talmudic learning, and how that learning finally consumed itself in the ghettos of medieval Europe.*

# TALMUDIC PERIOD
## 500 B.C. TO 1700 A.D.

| WORLD HISTORY | | TALMUDIC HISTORY |
| --- | --- | --- |
| Persians defeat Babylonians; restore Jewish freedom. Greeks destroy Persian Empire. Jews come under Hellenic influence. | 500 B.C. to 200 | First seeds of Talmud sown with Midrash, sermonic interpretations of Torah. |
| Jews overthrow Greek rule; establish Hasmonean dynasty. Romans annex Judea. Christianity founded. Jews rebel against Romans; Jerusalem destroyed. | 200 B.C. to 200 A.D. | Tannaitic Period: Mishna, first amendments to Torah appear. Beginnings of Oral Law. |
| Christianity made Roman state religion. Sassanians establish empire over former Babylonian and Parthian regions. Rome declines. First Vandal invasions. | 200 to 400 | Amoraic Period: Mishna canonized. Further additions prohibited. Interpretations known as Gemara begin. First Jewish academies founded in Babylonia. |

| | | |
|---|---|---|
| Barbaric kings seize power in Europe. Byzantine Empire created of former eastern half of Roman Empire. Islamism born. Sassanid Empire disintegrates. | 400 to 700 | Palestinian Gemara closed. Babylonian Gemara continues to grow. Gains intellectual ascendancy. Saboraim entrusted with task of compiling Mishna and Gemara, now known as Talmud. |
| Muslims conquer Near East, Palestine, Egypt, North Africa, Spain. Christian Dark Age. Jewish Golden Age. Charlemagne rises to power. | 700 to 1000 | Gaonic Period: Further Gemara forbidden. Responsa literature. |
| Islamic Empire broken up into Sultanates, further weakened by new invasions and first wave of Crusades. | 1000 to 1200 | Age of Maimonides. Talmud becomes Jewish law in Diaspora. |
| Islamic Empire crumbling under impact of Crusades and Mongolian invasions. Turks seize Egypt; Christians reconquer Spain. Jewish life shifts from East to West. End of Islamic Empire. | 1200 to 1500 | Rashi founds yeshiva in France. Talmud codification by Alfasi. Yeshivas established all over Europe. |

| Byzantine Empire falls to Turks. Renaissance ends and Reformation begins. Century of religious wars. End of West European feudalism. | 1500 to 1700 | Shulchan Aruch, third codification of Talmud. End of Talmud as growing organism and liberal influence. |
| --- | --- | --- |

# GROWTH OF THE TALMUD

*Torah—Five Books of Moses*
*Genesis, Exodus, Leviticus, Numbers,*
*Deuteronomy*

| WHEN? | WHAT? | COMMENTARY |
|---|---|---|
| 445 B.C. | Torah Canonized | Written in Hebrew. Canonized by Ezra and Nehemiah in Jerusalem. |
| 400 to 200 | Midrash | First beginnings of Talmudic learning. Unofficial interpretations of Mosaic law and biblical exegesis, in Hebrew. |
| 200 B.C. to 200 A.D. | Mishna | Written in Hebrew. Composed of two disciplines: Halacha — Aggada; Law — Narration |

**MISHNA ENDS AND GEMARA BEGINS**

| | | |
|---|---|---|
| 200 to 400 | Palestinian Gemara | Written in Aramaic; some Hebrew. Had three main sections: Halacha Aggada Midrash; Law Narration Sermons |
| 200 to 500 | Babylonian Gemara | Written in Aramaic; some Hebrew. Took essentially same forms as Palestinian Gemara, but intellectually more brilliant. |

| | | |
|---|---|---|
| 500 to 700 | Saboraim | Name given to scholars entrusted with editing and writing down the Mishna and Gemara, now known as Talmud. |
| 700 to 1100 | Gaonim | Titular name of heads of Babylonian universities disseminating Talmudic learning. |
| 1100 | Rashi Commentaries and Tosaphot | Rashi, born in France. Modern reinterpretation of the Talmud. Written in Hebrew. Commentaries by his children and grandchildren known as Tosaphot. |

## CODIFICATIONS BEGIN

| | | |
|---|---|---|
| 1100 | Alfasi | Rabbi Alfasi, born in Fez, North Africa; codifies the Talmud. Written in Hebrew. |
| 1200 | Mishna Torah | Maimonides, born in Córdoba, Spain. Second main codification of the Talmud. Written in Hebrew. |
| 1600 | Shulchan Aruch | Rabbi Joseph Caro, born in Toledo, Spain. Third main codification of the Talmud. Written in Hebrew, in Palestine. |

# The "Ivy League" Yeshivas

Deep in the heart of the Sassanid Empire, formerly
Parthia, formerly Seleucia, formerly Persia, formerly Babylonia, there flourished, between the fourth and twelfth centuries A.D., at Sura, Pumpaditha, and Nehardea, three
unique Jewish institutions of learning. These "Ivy League"
*yeshivas*, or academies, played the same intellectual role in
Jewish life then as Harvard, Oxford, and the Sorbonne play
in Western life today, and served as a prototype for the first
European universities in the twelfth century. Here Jewish
thought was crystallized into a body of knowledge known
as the *Talmud*, or "learning."

The Talmud was the instrument for Jewish survival and
exercised a decisive influence in directing the course of
Jewish history for fifteen hundred years, as it meandered
through the Sassanid, Islamic, and feudal civilizations. It
was the drawbridge which connected the Jewish past in the
East to the Jewish future in the West. One end of this
bridge was anchored in the Written Law, and the other end
lowered into the Oral Law. Over this bridge rode the mes-
sengers of the *Responsa*, bringing "the Law" to the Jews in
Egypt, Greece, Italy, Spain, France, Germany—wherever
Jews lived. This was the Talmudic Age of Judaism.

Talmudic learning, or Talmudism, accomplished three
things: It changed the nature of Jehovah: it changed the
nature of the Jew; and it changed the Jewish idea of government. The Prophets had transformed Jehovah into a
God of justice and morality, into a God of mercy and
righteousness; the Talmudist injected God into the everyday activities of life, demanding that the actions of the
Jews themselves be tinged with these attributes of God.
The Torah had created the religious Jew; the Talmud expanded his interests into scientific and theoretical speculations. The Bible had created the nationalist Jew; the
Talmud gave birth to the universally adaptable Jew, pro-

viding him with an invisible framework for the governance of man.

But the Talmud had not always been known by that name. Though its seeds had been sown in the fifth century B.C., the name "Talmud" was not applied to this growing body of knowledge until the sixth century A.D. The historic function of the Babylonian yeshivas was to fuse the traditions of the past into the Jewish culture of the future, to give Jewish law the flexibility it needed in order to protect the rapidly changing fortunes of the Jews in the centuries ahead. Let us, therefore, trace the origin of the Talmud in Palestine to the Babylonian yeshivas and from there follow its further development until its final stultification in the eighteenth-century ghettos of Europe.

The seeds for Talmudism were sown inadvertently. The idea took root back in the fifth century B.C. when the two Persian Jews, Ezra and Nehemiah, canonized the Five Books of Moses, closing the door to further revelation, implying that God and Moses had said all there was to say, and that no new "divine" laws could be added. But, heedless of the consequences, life remained indifferent to the implications of this canonization. Life did not stop at the command of Ezra and Nehemiah the way the sun had stopped at the command of Joshua; it went right on throwing new problems into the unappreciative laps of the descendants of Abraham. As Mosaic law did not seem to answer the new needs, the question became: Should the Jews discard a seemingly outmoded Torah, or should they constrict life within its limits?

The Christians were faced with this same dilemma after the death of Jesus. To prevent a future "teacher of righteousness" from proclaiming himself a messiah in accordance with prophecy, they followed the precedent set by the Jews; they canonized the New Testament and forbade all further revelation. This froze Christianity into a mold; no change was permitted, no new way of life tolerated. Western civilization became a "closed society" for almost a thousand years, until the internal pressures of heresy and revolution exploded the feudal world.

The Jews did not fall into the same trap. They neither closed their way of life, nor threw the Torah away. They amended, or reinterpreted, the Mosaic laws in the same way Americans are amending or reinterpreting the Constitution, in order to cope with new problems. Instead of squeezing new challenges into the pattern of the past, the Jews fashioned new patterns to fit new circumstances.

The amending of the Torah began haphazardly and unintentionally. Ezra and Nehemiah had decreed that when the Torah was read aloud in the synagogues, interpreters had to be on hand to explain difficult passages. But the questions asked were not of the nature this Persian-Jewish team of reformers had hoped for. Instead of inquiring what an obscure Hebrew word or phrase meant, the listeners were more interested in how an outdated injunction in the Five Books of Moses could be reconciled with the current, contrary facts of life.

Who can resist the temptation to be a sage? Flattered by the wisdom imputed to them, the interpreters of the Torah began seeking answers to the questions raised. The most sagacious became the most popular. Like their contemporaries the Greek philosophers in the fifth and fourth centuries B.C., the Torah interpreters began to compete for customers in the marketplace of ideas. Instead of contending that the Five Books of Moses did not meet the realities of everyday life, they maintained that the Torah not only contained all the answers but anticipated such questions. It was only a matter of searching into Scripture with superior knowledge, they held.

The first reinterpretations of Mosaic injunctions may have been based on nothing more than cleverness. But soon the interpreters were carried away by their own inventiveness. To outdo each other, they sought for profundity instead of mere ingenuity, and a new biblical science was born, that of *Midrash*, or "exposition." Though nobody knew it then, the seeds for the future Talmud had begun to grow.

The tranquil life under the Persians came to an end with Grecian domination in the late fourth century B.C. We have seen how Jewish life reeled under the impact of Hellenism. Jewish youth, imbued with Greek skepticism, no longer accepted the naïve biblical exegesis of the earlier Midrash. They asked point-blank: Could or could not the Torah solve their problems?

Though the Jews had inveighed against the Greeks publicly, they had studied Greek philosophy and science privately. Enriched with Platonic thought, Aristotelian logic, and Euclidian science, Jewish scholars approached the Torah with new tools. They developed more sophisticated and scientific methods of stretching the Mosaic cloth to fit Hellenistic existence. They proceeded to add Greek reason to Jewish revelation. This refined method was called *Mishna*, the Hebrew word for "repetition."

The Mishna, which originated independently in Babylonia and Palestine, began seeping into Jewish life about 200 B.C. It was not accepted with equanimity by all Jews. The Sadducees fought it vehemently, and the Pharisees defended it with equal vehemence. The Sadducee arguments against the Mishna resembled the arguments of the early Christian Church against heretical creeds. God's word, they argued, was plainly revealed in Scripture, and no man could set himself above it, or interpret away the plain meaning of the text.

The Pharisees held the contrary view. The Torah, they contended, had not been given to the priests exclusively; it had been given to everybody. The priests had been elected by man to perform Temple ritual, not appointed by God to be the exclusive distributors of His word. Surely, if God had given His Torah to man, He intended all solutions to be in it, and if man did not perceive the total truth at once, it did not prove that the Torah lacked depth, but that man lacked insight. The Mishna, said the Pharisees, was man's way of searching for God's intent.

The arguments of the Pharisees triumphed over those of the Sadducees. Judaism became the property of the layman, and anyone who studied the Torah could become its spokesman. The new sages of the Torah came from every walk of life—rich man, poor man, noble, and peasant. Only learning counted. The Jewish populace was dazzled by this intellectual tour de force. To the people, the Mishna was another manifestation of God's omnipotence, a God who had foreseen in the days of Abraham and Moses the problems they now encountered.

This popularity of the Mishna worried the rabbis. They were afraid that the Mishna would eventually rival the Torah in authority and that the people might in time forget the source and venerate the deduction. To prevent this from happening it was forbidden to write down any Mishna. It had to be memorized, and therefore became known as Oral Law.

Two schools of Mishna developed about 35 B.C. One was that of Hillel, the other that of Shamai. Both men exerted great influence, but a wide humanistic gulf separated them. Shamai held to a narrow, legalistic interpretation, with a stress on property rights, whereas Hillel held to broad, flexible principles, with a stress on human rights. The Shamai interpretations tended to become conservative and sectarian; Hillel's became liberal and universal. This dual struggle in Jewish life during the first century B.C. resembles the American Hamiltonian-Jeffersonian struggle in the nineteenth century, with Shamai representing the Hamiltonian and Hillel the Jeffersonian ideals.

It was the liberal tradition of Oral Law that Rabbi ben Zakkai wanted to safeguard. This is why the academy at Jabneh was so important to him after the destruction of Jerusalem in 70 A.D. Here at Jabneh, and later in Babylon, ben Zakkai and a succession of rabbis, patriarchs, and sages formulated the laws for Jewish survival in alien lands, discussed in Chapter 10, "A New Deal for Diaspora."

Though the Jews recovered quickly from the devastation of the Hadrianic reprisals in the aftermath of the third unsuccessful revolt in 135 A.D., Palestinian intellectual life itself was dealt a death blow. In the same way that Nobel prize winners under Hitler's domination of the European continent fled to America, where they enriched her academic life, so Jewish intellectuals under the fury of Hadrian's rage fled Palestine to Babylon, where they enriched that country's scholastic life.

Palestine nevertheless produced one more great man before she went into a two-thousand-year political slumber, from which she was finally awakened by Zionism, her nineteenth-century suitor. This man was Judah Hanasi, the scholar friend of a Roman emperor, presumably Marcus Aurelius Antoninus. Judah Hanasi viewed with great alarm the ever-growing popularity of the Mishna. He was the Søren Kierkegaard of his time, intuitively divining then the dilemma now haunting science-dominated twentieth-century man. Judah Hanasi feared that the teachers of the Mishna would develop a philosophy of ethics based on reason rather than the Torah and would create a morality based on science instead of God's commandments. If such a state were to come about, he felt, man eventually would reject both ethics and morality, because they would be man-made instead of God-inspired. Science could make no value judgments. To put an end to this implied threat, Judah Hanasi forbade all further development of Mishna. In effect he "canonized" it, closing what he hoped would be all further growth of Oral Law. He died deluded in this hope. He had locked the front entrance but had neglected to close the back door.

It was at this point that the Babylonian yeshivas came into being. Two of Rabbi Judah's most brilliant protégés and one disciple were swept into Babylon in the third century with the general exodus from Palestine to escape the Roman reprisals. Here each founded an academy of his own, the three yeshivas which were to achieve such renown in the coming centuries. Degrees from these schools opened the doors to the wealthiest families and led to the most lucrative marriages. Their graduates furnished most of the names in the Jewish *Who's Who* for seven centuries.

Faced with the injunction for a closed Mishna but pressed by the demands of millions of Diaspora Jews for more *Responsa*, Rabbis Arrika and Samuel, the two former students of Rabbi Judah, and Rabbi Ezekiel, the disciple, entered the "House of Mishna" through the unlocked back door. They developed a new branch of interpretation to the Torah, calling it *Gemara*, or "supplement." Actually, Gemara was nothing but warmed-over Mishna, served orally in Aramaic, instead of in Hebrew, and disguised as amendments to the Mishna. A series of brilliant expounders elevated the Gemara to a status on a par with the Torah itself.

In the same way that the "conservative" Jews in the second century B.C. had protested that the Mishna violated the sanctity of the Torah, so the "liberals," who had fought for the Mishna, now complained that the Gemara violated its sanctity. But to no avail. The riders of the *Responsa* carried the new Gemara to the four corners of the Jewish world. Again nothing was written down. Like Topsy, the Gemara kept growing and growing. All of it, along with Midrash and Mishna, was committed to memory.

The man of learning among Jews began to acquire ever greater social prestige. The scholar was held in higher esteem than the captains of industry and stars of stage and screen are held in our society today. The hero in Jewish legend became the man who, with intellect, slew the dragons of ignorance, instead of the knight who, with sword, slew the monsters of violence. Illiteracy was regarded as something shameful, and the ignorant, whether rich or poor, were held in contempt. A learned bastard, the Jewish rabbis held, took precedence over an unlearned scion of a noble family. Pregnant mothers clustered around the yeshivas in the hope that their unborn would be imbued with the spirit of scholarship. Potions reputed to contain magical powers were given, not to facilitate the seduction of a reluctant maiden, but to induce a reluctant youth to take up the study of the Torah. Thus even superstition was put into the service of education.

For three hundred years, from 300 to 600 A.D., these Babylonian academies, unhindered, dominated Jewish thought and learning. Then a swift turn of events brought about a drastic change in the political fortunes of the Jews, forcing the rabbis to reverse their edict against writing down the Oral Law. A new religious intolerance was on the march.

Zoroastrianism, the enlightened religion of the Persians and Sassanians, founded in the eighth century B.C., had been strongly influenced first by the Judaism of the Prophets, later by Christianity. In the sixth century A.D., a fierce Zoroastrian religious sect known as the Magii seized political power and ended the rule of tolerance by carrying on a holy war against Christians and Jews alike. Under the Magii the old freedoms vanished.

Unrest prevailed not only in the Sassanian but also in the Roman Empire, for this was the century of the great barbaric invasions. Masses of people were on the move, old norms were uprooted, new forces were seizing power, empires crumbled, and violence was the current exchange of social amenities.

The rabbis feared that in this upheaval Jewish learning was in danger of being wiped out, for each time a Saracen or Vandal sword clove a scholastic skull, 2,500,000 words of Mishna and Gemara fell dead in the gutter. Against their better judgment the rabbis permitted the Mishna and Gemara to be written down. This compiling was entrusted to a school of scholars known as *Saboraim*, versed in Hebrew and Aramaic. Their combined text is the Talmud.

The task took over two hundred years and would have taken even longer but for the fact that some of the students of Oral Law had been cribbing. Many had kept written notes as aids to memory. But so wondrous are the ways of God that even a transgression could serve a good cause. Like their predecessors, the Saboraim yielded to the temptation to be lawgivers. Whenever they came across an unresolved disputation, they used their own erudition to resolve it, thus adding a little unofficial Gemara to the official text. These interpolations still stand as a monument to their inventiveness.

Three mainstreams of Jewish thought flow through the Talmud, the first two through the head, the third through the heart. Intertwined through its thirty-five volumes and 15,000 pages* are the complicated brain twisters of jurisprudence known as *Halacha*, or "law"; the philosophical dissertations on ethics, morals, conduct, and piety known as *Aggada*, or "narration"; and the beautiful, tender passages on Bible stories, wise sayings, and tales known as *Midrash*, or "sermons."

Because law and jurisprudence, ethics and morality, deal with many phases of human life, it is not surprising to find that the Talmud also touches upon the sciences, such as medicine, hygiene, astronomy, economics, government. The varied contents of the Talmud opened new vistas for the Jews, expanding their intellectual horizons, permitting them to discard the old and acquire the new. The study of the Talmud not only made the Jews jurists, it also made them physicians, mathematicians, astronomers, grammarians, philosophers, poets, and businessmen. With a background of universal education and ten to fifteen years' study of the Talmud, is it any wonder that the Jews showed such an affinity for the scientific, the intellectual, and the theoretical?

Let us now trace a Mosaic injunction as it is enlarged by the Talmudist into a system of ethics.

---

*This is an estimate, as the 63 Tractates of the Babylonian Talmud usually come in large folio volumes.

Of all Jewish customs, that of dealing with things *kosher*, or ritually clean, is the most perplexing to non-Jews. To the average Christian, the complicated kosher question is condensed into one bit of knowledge—Jews don't eat pork. Generally speaking, *Kashruth*, as the Jews call the system, rests on three injunctions in the Five Books of Moses—namely, not to seethe a kid in its mother's milk; not to eat carrion; and not to eat (a) animals which do not chew their cud and have no cloven hoofs, (b) birds which do not fly or have no feathers, and (c) fish which have no fins and no scales. It is not, then, that Jews have a conspiracy against pigs, but rather that the pig refuses to comply with the Torah. The pig qualifies on one count—he has cloven hoofs—but loses out on the second count—he does not chew his cud. Many Jews have long since forgiven the pig for this noncompliance and enjoy a ham sandwich at the soda fountain next to Christians.

Though the injunction not to seethe a kid in its mother's milk had its origin in prehistoric ritual and is common among many primitive tribes, the Jews raised this tribal custom into a universal ban against cruelty to animals. The Talmud condemned the practice of forcing premature deliveries in order to obtain the fine skins and tender meats of preborn animals, a practice, incidentally, as yet not outlawed in the United States. The Talmud also held that no animal or its young could be used as a beast of burden until the young were weaned. In order that the Jews should not forget these principles, the Talmud commanded that the meat of a slaughtered animal should not be cooked in one of its own products, like milk or butter, or served together at one sitting. Today, many Jews feel that after three thousand years they have learned the lesson and can safely have a meat sandwich with a glass of milk.

The Torah forbids the eating of carrion. But what is carrion? asked the Mishna and the Gemara. Their answers led to the question of the proper methods of slaughtering animals, based not on what was most convenient or profitable, but on the ethical principle that it was wrong to inflict pain. The Talmud held that any animal dying in pain, for any cause whatsoever, including slaughter, was carrion. What then was a painless death? The rabbis who were schooled in medicine held that an animal had died without pain if death was caused instantaneously by means of one clean, untorn cut across the jugular vein and carotid artery from a sharp knife without blemishes. This method of slaughtering also enabled the drainage of blood to fulfill the biblical commandment against eating or drinking blood. Throughout the centuries Jews have been aghast at the brutal slaughtering methods of their non-Jewish neighbors, who have killed animals in any way they pleased, by clubbing, shooting, puncturing, or repeated incisions with any instrument at hand. Not until the 1920s were such methods abandoned in the United States, after Upton Sinclair's protest novel *The Jungle* so aroused popular indignation that legislators were forced to enact laws for more humane slaughter.

Let us illustrate how the *Responsa* worked with an example from life today. Let us suppose that the yeshivas of Babylon still exist and that a Jewish community in suburban St. Louis has asked one of them to solve the vexing problem of "the automobile, the suburb, and the synagogue." This is the dilemma. The Torah forbids work on the Sabbath. In 1900 A.D. a yeshiva court ruled that driving a car is work. Now, many years later, the suburbs have developed. The synagogue no longer is a few blocks away, but miles out in the country, and the distance is too formidable to walk. The congregation is faced with the prospect of an empty synagogue or committing the sin of driving to the place of worship. What should be done?

The question is turned over to the yeshiva and the problem placed on the docket. When the case comes up, the yeshiva court will begin a hearing much as the Supreme Court reviews a case. The argument might go something like this: "Certainly God did not intend to have empty synagogues, nor to have His commandments broken. But who said that driving to the synagogue was work? Certainly not God or Moses. To force the aged to walk for miles in the hot sun or in the cold of winter is a peril to health. Attending services should be contemplated with joy, not with fear and trembling. Did not the sages say that 'he who takes upon himself a duty that is not specifically required is an ignoramus'? And furthermore, did not Rabbi Judah ben Ezekiel, back in the third century, say that 'he who would order his entire life according to strict and literal interpretation of Scripture is a fool'?"

The yeshiva court would then begin a search for precedents, just as lawyers arguing a brief before the Supreme Court would search for precedents favorable to their case. After due deliberation, the court might decide that in their opinion the court back in 1900 had erred, and that driving a car to the synagogue is not work but pleasure, much in the same way that the United States Supreme Court in the 1890s held that equal but separate facilities for Negroes was constitutional, but in the 1950s reversed itself, holding that it was unconstitutional. Once a verdict is reached, it is sent to the other yeshivas, where similar hearings are held and a joint agreement disseminated through the *Responsa* to every Jewish community.

But as there is no longer such a central Jewish authority, each rabbi, or aggregation of rabbis, is more or less an authority unto himself. Today, the orthodox Jew stays out of the suburbs so he can walk to his synagogue;* the conservative Jew drives to his synagogue with mixed emotions; and the reform Jew is superbly confident that driving to the Temple on the Sabbath is not only a pleasure, but also a *mitzvah*—a religious duty.

Let us return now to the Saboraim, whom we left compiling the Mishna and the Gemara into the Talmud. If the sixth century was a bleak one for the Jews, the seventh century held out high hopes, and the eighth century took them to dizzying heights of new power and prestige.

FOURTEEN

# Bibliosclerosis of the Talmud

Talmudism, which began in fifth-century Persia and traveled through Grecian, Roman, Islamic, and feudal history until 1800 A.D., had the function of cementing the Jews into a unified religious body and a cohesive civic community. While it coursed through Jewish history, it had to provide

---

*A group of orthodox rabbis have recently ruled that it is better not to attend the synagogue than drive a car on the Sabbath.

new religious interpretations to fit changing conditions of life, and new, expanding frameworks for government as old empires crumbled and young states arose. As the Jewish world expanded, the framework of Talmudic thinking and activity had to expand to be on hand at the right time and with the right solutions, to insure the survival of Jewish ideals.

In the previous chapter, we saw that as everyday Jewish life changed with historic conditions, Jewish religious orientation also changed. In this chapter let us look at the other side of the Talmudic coin and see how its conceptualization of the state grew from the provincial to the universal. For this, we must go back to 500 B.C. to the Jews in Persia, because Talmudic expansion into the field of government was made possible only because of the existence of certain historical conditions which began under Persian domination and continued through the succeeding civilizations in which the Jews dwelt.

Historical events do not take place in a vacuum. The unfolding of history resembles the unfolding of a dream. The dreamer at first is aware only of the manifest content, that part which he remembers upon awakening, vivid, real, and absurd. But behind it lies the latent content, the hidden meaning of the dream, which he does not remember. We tend to view history by its manifest contents only, instead of interpreting the surface events by the latent forces shaping them. The latent force behind Talmudism was Jewish self-government. Whenever the Jews showed they could govern themselves at a greater benefit to their victors, the victors permitted them this self-government.

We have already touched upon the paradox running through Jewish history: Though the Jews lost their independence, they gained their freedom; though they lost their land, they did not lose their nationality; though their country was devastated, their government remained inviolate; though in one decade they were annihilated on the battlefield, in the next they sat at the tables of popes and emperors, kings and nobles, sultans and caliphs, as friends, as physicians, as scholars. As a cork bobs to the surface of the sea the moment the pressure holding it down is released, so Jews bobbed to the surface of each civilization the moment the repressive force was removed. The heads of the Jewish governments in exile did not approach their conquerors hat in hand; they held ambassadorial status and were accorded the honors due to heads of state. And yet, the Jews had no state.

In the days of the first exile from Palestine, Jews held high government posts in Babylonia. The Persian conquerors, the next to subjugate the Jews, were impressed with their learning and intellect, and we read in the Old Testament that Nehemiah was "cupbearer" to the Persian king before he became governor of Palestine. The Greeks, Ptolemies, and Seleucids, impressed with the Jewish ability for self-government, not only continued the lenient policies of the Persians, but gave the Jews even greater freedom of political expression. Under the Romans, the Jews had their own kings until the rule of the procurators.

When the rule of the procurators ended in 70 A.D., after the first Jewish rebellion, the Romans instituted a new form of Jewish self-rule, that of the Patriarchs. The Patriarchs were the rabbis claiming descent from the house of Hillel, who in turn claimed descent from the house of David through a genealogy as complicated as that of those Gospels tracing the descent of Jesus from David. The Patriarch was addressed as *Nasi*, or "Prince," and was given official status by the Romans as though he represented an actual state. The recognition of these "descendants of David" continued from Gamaliel II in 85 A.D. to Gamaliel VI, who died in 425 without heirs.

Jews owe the Romans a tribute for the lenient treatment they received, considering that they rebelled three times against the empire. The Romans were animated in their reprisals, not by anti-Jewishness, but by problems of state. No sooner had Emperor Hadrian banished the Jews as a precautionary measure against a fourth uprising than his successor, Antoninus Pius (138–161 A.D.), allowed them to return. His admiration of the Jews was great, and they sat in the councils of the high.

It was on the permissive soil of these different civilizations, from 500 B.C. to 500 A.D., that the tree of Talmudic learning took root. Without it, Jewish ideas of the universal state could not have grown and the growth of the Talmud would have been impossible.

The Sassanians, inheritors of the former Persian Empire

in the third century A.D., granted the Jews even greater freedom than had the Greeks and Romans. Here, in four tranquil centuries, the Jews acquired both an "emperor" and a "pope," a temporal and a spiritual ruler. The political head was known as *exilarch*, or "prince of Diaspora." His rank was that of head of state, and the office was hereditary. The exilarch lived in great splendor and had his own royal court and access to the ear of the Sassanian emperor at all times. He could collect taxes and appoint judges. The spiritual leaders were none other than the heads of the Babylonian academies. They were addressed as *Gaon* ("Your Eminence") and were held in great esteem by Jews and Sassanians alike. The exilarchs held the administrative and judicial power, but the Gaonim held the legislative power.

When, in the seventh and eighth centuries, the Muslims carved out their empire from parts of Sassanid, Byzantine, and Roman territories, they inherited a sizable problem in the nonassimilable elements of Christians and Jews. The Christians, who, in Europe, could not understand why the Jews did not convert to their faith, now refused, with the same obduracy as the Jews, to convert to Islam. What had been a Jewish fault became a Christian virtue. When the Muslim rancor against Christians and Jews for refusing to accept the religion of Islam died, the Muslims relegated the Christians to the status of second-class citizens and recognized the Jews as a political entity. Under Islam, the Gaon was made head of state and the presidents of the Jewish Babylonian academies became the Eminences of Judaism. Who but history would have had the ingenuity to invent such improbable events?

A Jewish traveler, Benjamin of Tudela, Navarre, who visited Baghdad in the twelfth century, has left a vivid, first-hand report of the homage accorded a Gaon by both Jews and Muslims:

And every Thursday when he goes to pay a visit to the great Calif, horsemen—non-Jews as well as Jews—escort him, and heralds proclaim in advance: "Make way before our Lord, the son of David, as is due unto him," the Arabic words being *Amilu tarik la Saidna ben Daoud*. He is mounted on a horse, and is attired in robes of silk and embroidery with a large

turban on his head, and from the turban is suspended
a long white cloth adorned with a chain upon which
the seal of Muhammad is engraved.

Then he appears before the Calif and kisses his hand,
and the Calif rises and places him on a throne which
Muhammad had ordered to be made in honor of
him, and all the Muslim princes who attend the court
of the Calif rise up before him.*

During all these centuries the Talmudic concept of government underwent a change parallel to that of the changing concept of Jehovah. The Prophets changed Jehovah
from a Jewish God to a Universal God. The Talmudists
changed the Jewish concept of government for Jews exclusively to ideas applicable to the universal governance of
man. The Prophets conceived of Judaism as containing specific commandments for the Jews and general principles
for people at large. The Talmudists designed laws which
permitted the Jew to continue to live not only as a Jew, but
as a universal man. To the Talmudist, the Jews in all lands
symbolized mankind split into nationalities. Laws had to
be formulated for the particular needs of each national entity, and laws had to be formulated to enable all nations to
live together in a united nation of man. The Talmud's universal concepts of government became the flesh put on
Isaiah's dreams of the brotherhood of man.

As long as strong unified empires existed, the Talmud
could work on a universal scale. As the empires of the
world fell apart, the universal influence of the Talmud also
waned. When in the twelfth century the Islamic Empire
began to disintegrate, the splendor of the Gaonim vanished like the palaces in the tales of *A Thousand and One
Nights*. Where once the spirit of enlightenment had
reigned, now the spirit of intolerance became the rule and
swiftly spread from Baghdad toward Spain. The Jews fled
westward just a step ahead of it. By the fifteenth century
this transition from East to West had been completed.

Jews had lived in Western Europe since Roman days. By
the ninth and tenth centuries they had established the first

---

*Jacob R. Marcus, *The Jew in the Medieval World*.

yeshivas in Italy, Germany, and Spain. As these European yeshivas were enriched with the scholars fleeing the East, they gained in repute over the declining Babylonian yeshivas. The yeshivas in Italy and Germany achieved wide renown, but their influence was short-lived; those in Spain were less well known, but destined to great future importance. In the fifteenth century, classic Talmudic learning split off in two directions. The Italian and German schools, continuing in the former Babylonian traditions, led to an affirmation of the past. The Spanish schools, resurrecting the Greek tradition, led to an inquiry into the future. The former produced a few more brilliant Talmudic scholars, whose influence died with them; the latter produced philosophers like Maimonides and Spinoza, whose influence lived after them. But before we take up the thread of the new rationalist school, we must pursue the classic Talmudist to his grave.

The exception was France. The mantle of the Gaonim fell on a French Jew, affectionately known as Rashi (from the initials of his name, Rabbi Shlomo Itzhaki), who became the most loved, if not the greatest of all Talmudists. A popular saying has it that "if not for Rashi, the Talmud would be forgotten in all Israel," and, as one of his biographers said, Rashi "attained a fame during his lifetime usually reserved for the dead."

Rashi was born in Troyes, northern France, in 1040. He worked his way through the yeshivas in Germany as a wandering student. After graduation he settled in his hometown where he founded a yeshiva of his own. Build a better yeshiva and Jews will beat a path to its door. Here in Troyes, with a total population of 10,000 Frenchmen and 100 Jewish families, Rashi's yeshiva attracted Jewish scholars from all over the world. These scholars found lodgings with the Christians. Contrary to the popular prevailing notion that a gulf of hostility separated Jews and Christians from each other during the Middle Ages, Rashi and the Jews of Troyes had active social dealings with their Christian neighbors. From his college days, Rashi retained a great love for the songs of the Christians. He was greatly interested in the hymns of the Church, taught the local priests Hebrew melodies, and translated French lullabies into Hebrew.

Throughout their history, Jews have always believed that at the right time, the right man would appear. Rashi was the right man for the times. Life in eleventh-century Europe no longer related to many precepts in the Talmud. The people did not understand Aramaic, did not understand the phraseology, and did not understand its application to modern life. The *Responsa* was dying. There was a need for a universal Talmud which could be understood without interpreters. It was this need that Rashi served. His great contribution to Jewish life was his reinterpretation of all relevant passages into the vernacular of the day, in such clear, lucid language, with such warmth and humanity, with such rare skill and scholarship, that his commentaries became revered as scripture and loved as literature. Rashi wrote Hebrew as though it were French, with wit and elegance. Whenever he lacked the precise Hebrew word, he used a French word instead, spelling it with Hebrew letters. As over three thousand of the French words he used have disappeared from the language, Rashi's writings have become important source books on medieval French.

Rashi's commentaries and biblical exegesis had a great influence on Christian theologians, especially Nicholas de Lyra, who made extensive use of Rashi's writings. Lyra's theology in turn had a profound effect on the religious development of young Martin Luther.

Rarely do great men's children follow in their fathers' footsteps, but in the case of Rashi not only his children but his grandchildren, after his death in 1105, continued where he had left off. Because of him, interest in the Talmud was reawakened, and the demand for a new *Responsa* grew so great that his progeny instituted a new school of Talmudic commentaries, disguised as footnotes to the Gemara. They were known as *Tosaphot*, or "additions." The Talmud was finally and definitely closed at this point. What the rabbis had feared back in the second century B.C. happened in the twelfth century A.D. The Talmud was appealed to more often than the Torah as a source of knowledge—the deduction was venerated more than the source. This time the rabbis locked all the doors, and the windows too. No more amendments; no more footnotes; no more "closings." The age of the codifiers of the Talmud was at hand.

The twelfth to fifteenth centuries were portentous ones

for the Jews. During these centuries the Islamic Empire died, eight Crusades were launched, the Renaissance was born and began to die, and the forces of Reformation gained strength. European feudalism was crumbling and a new nationalism was being formed. Jews were banished from the West European states and spilled into Eastern Europe, where they were increasingly confined in cramped quarters. As times changed, so did the function of the Talmud. Whereas in previous centuries it had served an expanding Jewish universe, now it had to serve a shrinking one. More than anything, in this age of peril, when their communications were cut off, when their yeshivas were closing, they needed a workable "do-it-yourself kit" of Jewish jurisprudence which would provide handy answers to swiftly descending new problems.

This need was anticipated as early as the eleventh century and was answered in three main successive stages. The first was a codification of the Talmud, in the eleventh century, by a seventy-five-year-old Moroccan Jew named Alfasi. Alfasi went through the Talmud like a wastrel through an inheritance. He threw out everything except pertinent law, keeping only basic Gemara decisions. Brilliant though Alfasi's effort was, it was a hit-and-miss proposition, touching upon a law here and a law there. There was a need for a more complete but simplified, modernized, abridged, and indexed Talmud which any literate man could use as a reference book. Again Jewish history provided the right man at the right time. He was Rabbi Moses ben Maimon (1135–1204), known to the Jews as Rambam and to the Christians as Maimonides, the first of a series of great Jewish rationalist philosophers to illuminate the Western world.

Maimonides stood astride two civilizations, the Islamic and the Christian. He was born in Córdoba, Spain, into a distinguished family, which included judges, scholars, and financiers. But he was born in an age when the empire of the Moors in Spain was dying. Liberal Christians, Moors, and Jews, caught in a nutcracker squeeze between zealous Catholics invading from the north and fierce Almohade barbarians invading from the south, fled, not so much because of anticipated persecution as because they regarded the invaders as culturally inferior. The Maimonides family settled in Fez, North Africa, then a great center of learning, where Maimonides studied both the Talmud and medicine. As the Almohades extended their power into Africa, the Maimonides family fled farther eastward, settling finally in Cairo, Egypt, which was still under the enlightened rule of the Fatimid dynasty. Here Maimonides became the physician to Saladin, Caliph of Egypt. So great was the fame of Maimonides that Richard the Lionhearted, King of England, offered him a post as his personal physician, but Maimonides refused, feeling more at home in the culture of Arabic civilization than in the barbaric atmosphere of feudal Europe.

The historic function of Maimonides was to restore Prophetic Judaism as a spiritual lifeline to the Jews. Significantly, he chose the title *Mishneh Torah*, the "Second Torah," for his codification of the Talmud, to remind his readers that its authority still rested on the Five Books of Moses. He digested the Talmud with such precision that within fourteen volumes he packed all the important Gemara precepts and laws. He also attacked superstitions, and interpreted miracles rationally. Rambam (Maimonides) and the Talmud became synonymous.

To the Jews, Maimonides is famous for his *Mishneh Torah*; to the rest of the world his fame rests on his philosophical works, of which his *Guide to the Perplexed* is best known. Here he maintained that both the Jewish and the Greek systems were equally true. Maimonides was so imbued with the Greek philosophers that Aristotelian views crept into even his religious writings. One cannot but be amazed at the enlightenment, the tolerance, the rationalism of this twelfth-century man, this forerunner of renaissance humanism whose nonreligious works were studied more avidly by Muslims and Christians than by Jews. He was also a prophet before his time, and in keeping with the times, some Jews consigned his philosophical works to the flames in 1232, prophetically heralding the first burning of the Talmud by the Christians twelve years later.

Maimonides was an intellectual snob, however, who deliberately wrote only for the learned, feeling that nobody else would understand him; but he wrote with the beauty and clarity of a great novelist, and made even the most complex reasoning seem simple. His religious writings were as revered by the masses as his philosophical writings were ignored by them.

As Christian horizons expanded in the fifteenth and sixteenth centuries from state, to continent, to world size, and the Jewish world shrank from universal proportions, to a continent, to a country, to a province, to a city, to a ghetto, the Talmud, which had roamed the humanities, became preoccupied with daily existence. As the roots of learning were cut off from the Talmud, the tree itself began to show signs of withering. New ideas could no longer flow freely through its hardening arteries. The age of the yeshivas was over. The most the Jews could hope for was to fight illiteracy with local schools. An everyman's edition of the Talmud was needed, a pocket Talmud which would have the final word on everything.

The man who lovingly accomplished this was one of Judaism's gentlest scholars, a cosmopolitan Jew by dint of circumstance, not through love of adventure. But this third codification of the Talmud proved to be a curse as well as a blessing. Joseph Caro (1488–1575), born in Toledo, Spain, was among those caught in the Spanish expulsion of Jews in 1492. His parents settled in Constantinople, then under Turkish rule, but as the Turks at this point of their history favored Jews resettling in Palestine, Caro moved to Safed, north of Jerusalem, in 1525, where he founded a yeshiva.

Caro's "everyman's Talmud" (published in 1565) was appropriately named *Shulchan Aruch*, that is, "The Prepared Table." It was the busy man's Blackstone, a judicial smörgåsbord, where every Jew could help himself to the appropriate law. The mysteries of the Talmud were there codified, clarified, digested, and indexed for him. With the formulas in this book on his tongue, any Jew could equal the greatest of scholars. With the *Shulchan Aruch*, every Jewish ghetto could have self-government, every Jewish community could be autonomous.

But, in philosophical parlance, the *Shulchan Aruch* contained the seeds for its own destruction. Now the Jews began to force life into the limits of the *Shulchan Aruch*, and this froze Judaism into the image of sixteenth-century ghetto life. Anything in the Talmud came to be regarded as Judaism itself, any deviation was viewed with a horror usually reserved for apostates. It became a straitjacket constricting the universal ideas of the Jews. But, paradoxically, it also saved the Jews for a place in the sun when Napoleonic imperialism shattered the walls of the ghetto. Here, in cheerless, bleak classrooms, the pale ghetto students of the Talmud were taught subtle rules of law and logic. At an early age they came into contact with the humanism of Rashi and rationalism of Maimonides. They learned to think in abstract terms, to apply obsolete laws to nonexistent situations, to deal with imagination in concrete terms.

When the ghetto crumbled, these scholars blinked at the bright sunshine of the outside world, where ahead of them lay new careers in many instances shaped by what they had taken out of the Talmud. Some took from the Talmud a passionate love for justice, liberty, equality, and became the idealists who fought for a better world; others took from it its compassion and humility, its reverence for life and beauty, and became the humanistic philosophers and authors of belles-lettres; still others took from it the abstractions of the Greek philosophers, and became the theoretical scientists and mathematicians. Those who saw in the Talmud nothing but dry-as-dust facts of bygone eras rebelled against Judaism and found in conversion their "passport to European civilization."

# V

# MUHAMMAD, ALLAH, AND JEHOVAH

*The improbable but true tale of a camel driver's establishment of a world empire in the name of Allah, wherein the Jews rose to their Golden Age of creativity, only to be plunged into a Dark Age with the eclipse of the Crescent and the ascent of the Cross.*

# ISLAMIC PERIOD
## 500 A.D. TO 1500 A.D.

| ISLAMIC HISTORY | | JEWISH HISTORY |
|---|---|---|
| No history. Nomadic tribes wander across face of Arabia, worshiping moon, stars, and Kaaba Stone. | 5000 B.C. to 1 A.D. | 5000 B.C. to 2000 B.C.—None. 2000 B.C. to 1 A.D.—From Abraham to Jesus. |
| Beginnings of Arabic civilization. First organized commerce. Growth of towns. | 1 A.D. to 500 | Jews trickle into Arabian peninsula. Extend commerce, introduce handicraft. Jewish monotheism admired by Arabs; Jews known as "People of the Book." |
| Growth of cities. Commerce and industry extended. Muhammad creates new creed of Islam. Abu Bekr extends Islam by the sword. | 500 to 700 | Jews emigrate in large numbers to Arabia as Byzantine and Sassanid empires are locked in death struggle. Help to found new cities; refuse to join Muhammadan faith. Brief period of persecution. |

| | | |
|---|---|---|
| Muhammadan faith spreads from Caspian Sea across North Africa to Spain; stopped in France by Martel. Muhammadan Golden Age. Empire breaking up into Sultanates and Caliphates. | 700 to 1000 | Golden Age of Judaism. Period of great religious toleration; Jews rise to posts of great eminence. Karaite revolt begins. Jews become cosmopolitans; translations of Greek works begun. |
| Crusaders attack from Europe; Mongols invade from East. Turks annex Egypt; Almohades seize North Africa; Christians reconquer Spain. End of Islamic Empire. | 1000 to 1500 | Age of Judah Halevi. Christians and Jews flee invading barbarians of Islamic Empire. Center of Jewish life shifts from East to West. Age of Rashi and Maimonides. End of Karaite revolt. End of Golden Age of Judaism. |

# FIFTEEN

# HISTORY TRAVELS TO MECCA

Marxist and other materialist historians would be hard put to explain the phenomenon of the eruption of a Muhammadan empire in the Arabian desert in the seventh century A.D. The mode of production of the Bedouins in that century had not changed from that of previous centuries. The climate was the same then as it had been before. Unless we ascribe this phenomenon to God's inscrutable will, we will have to turn to the theory of the "hero in history" for an explanation. This is the idea of the individual who creates history by seizing opportunity at the right moment and bending it to his will. Muhammadanism (Islam) was the creation of such a man—Muhammad.

Muhammad's messiahship was in the new tradition of "humility" introduced by the Jews. Prior to the Jews, all religious leaders had been nobles or princes, as, for example, Buddha, Confucius, and Zoroaster. Abraham may have been a Babylonian merchant prince before he set out for his journey to Haran, but the Old Testament made him a sheepherder. Moses may have been brought up as a prince in the Egyptian court, but when he receives the divine call, he is a hired hand tending his father-in-law's flocks. Jesus was a carpenter. And Muhammad was a camel driver.

Muhammad is one of history's more improbable figures, an Arab imbued with the fervor of Judaism, proclaiming all Arabs descendants of Abraham, and calling for Jews and Christians alike to join him in a true brotherhood of man in the name of Allah. He was the successful Don Quixote, the prophet armed, who, convinced of his delusion, made it a reality by defeating the narrow-minded, armed only with reason. The rise of this camel driver was breathtaking in its swiftness. Within less than a hundred years his empire embraced half of the then known world. Islam had succeeded where Christianity had failed. In one century this new faith swept the lands encircling the southern half of the Mediterranean.

Arabia is the world's largest peninsula, attached through Israel to Egypt, and through Syria to Turkey. The rest of her body floats in the Red Sea, Arabian Sea, and Persian Gulf. Like a cleric's tonsure, a fringe of green land, beaded by a few cities, surrounds the 500,000 square miles of desert forming her heartland. This country has been the homeland of Bedouin and Quraish Arabs since unrecorded history. It has bred no civilization, but its fecund women for five thousand years bred an abundance of Semitic Arabs for export to the Sumerian, Akkadian, and Babylonian city-states, infusing strength into these effete civilizations with their barbaric vigor.

The religion of the Arabs was a diffused nature worship, democratically including heaven, stars, trees, stones—anything capable of being elevated to divinity by man's ingenuity. This diversification found unity in the centralized worship of a black meteorite, the Black Stone, enshrined in the Kaaba (cube), in Mecca.

The Bedouin Arabs were the sand dwellers, living in the desert; the Quraish Arabs dwelt along the coastal areas, where they had established trading villages at the end points of caravan routes. Here the Bedouins came to exchange the luxuries, robbed from caravans, for the necessities of life. But it was not until the end of the first century A.D., when the Jews began to arrive, that commerce and industry began to hum, cities to flourish, and art to proliferate. The trickle of Jews into Arabia beginning after 70 A.D. reached the proportions of a flood in the fifth and sixth centuries, when a power struggle between the Sassanid and Byzantine empires squeezed Jews out of Syria and Palestine into Arabia.

Like the Ptolemies and Seleucids before them, the Sassanians and Byzantians constantly warred over Syria and Palestine. Fickle fate gave neither a decisive victory, and finally, out of sheer exhaustion, a treaty of mutual toleration was signed. Jews, Syrians, Lebanese, and others who had the misfortune to live in the disputed areas suffered the classic fate of all civilians caught in the path of clashing armies—inglorious, impersonal deaths. Many Jews, once they were convinced it was going to be a protracted war, headed toward the western half of the Roman Empire, having been warned by fellow Jews that Byzantium was not a haven of liberty. Others, who had studied the situation for long-term yields, decided to head eastward, into territory where warring armies seldom ventured. They chose Arabia.

Here in their new homeland in Arabia the Jews introduced handicrafts, the goldsmith's art, and the date palm, which became to the Muslims what the potato became to the Irish. Here they founded Medina. Here they helped the Quraish convert their villages into cities. With their great numbers and twenty-five hundred years of experience, the Jews gave Mecca a cosmopolitan air.

In gratitude for the sanctuary given them, the Jews joined the Arabs in defeating invading Christian armies which came to proselytize and to plunder. Though Christianity was kept out, Judaism crept in, not by the sword, but by the exemplary conduct of the Jews. As with the Greeks and Romans, many pagan Arabs liked the nonsexualized symbols of Judaism, its ascetic monotheism, and the devotion of the Jews to family life and education. The Arabs called the Jews "the People of the Book," and Jew and Arab lived side by side in peace.

In the same way as the Septuagint prepared the way for the teachings of Paul among the pagans in the Roman Empire, so a general knowledge of the Old Testament among the Arabs helped prepare the way for the coming of Islam. The stage was set for the hero in history to fuse the nature worship of the Arabs, the salvation doctrine of the Christians, and the monotheism of the Jews into a new God image. The hero was Muhammad; the creed was Islam; the motivating ideology was Judaism.

Prophets should perhaps never be viewed with less than two millenniums of hindsight, to allow a lapse of time to blur human attributes into divine features. Muhammad is still young, as prophets go, and the impatient historian may be excused if he has not as yet fully perceived the divinity already discernible to the devout.

Muhammad (569–632 A.D.) lost both parents before he was six. He was brought up first by his grandfather, and later by an uncle. Both forgot to have him tutored in reading and writing, an oversight quickly remedied in later life when Muhammad learned the art of instant reading by revelation. As with Abraham, Moses, and Jesus, we know nothing of his early youth, except that at the age of twelve he was taken by caravan to Syria, where he for the first time came into contact with the Jewish and Christian religions. From this encounter he carried away a lifelong respect for "the Book" of the Jews. The Jewish Patriarchs became his heroes, heroes whom he later enshrined in the Koran, the Bible of the Muslims. At the age of twenty-five he married a wealthy, forty-year-old widow, with whom he lived in monogamy for a quarter of a century. After her death, in Muhammad's fifty-first year, his penchant for younger women between the ages of seven and twenty-one found its full expression. His later harem of ten wives and two concubines contained houris of various ages and stages of experience.

Muhammad was of medium height. His long black hair met his beard, and his beard fell down to his waist. Though he seldom laughed, he had a keen sense of humor, always, however, kept within the confines of dignity. Muhammad was proud of his Arab heritage, but deeply sensitive to the immature paganism of his brethren and their lack of a spirit of nationhood. Like Moses, he dreamed of uniting the dissident, warring tribes into one people, giving them a unifying religion, and raising them to an honored position in the world. The wish became father to the deed. The conviction that he was the prophet destined to bring this about for his people grew into revelation.

The "I and Thou" encounter between Muhammad and God took place in a cave, where Muhammad, then forty, brooded on the problem of bringing salvation to his people. Here he had an experience which to the faithful was conclusive proof that Muhammad was the true successor to Moses and Jesus, but to the infidels merely confirmation that Muhammad was familiar with the Bible. As unto Abraham, Moses, and Jesus, so God manifested Himself unto Muhammad, in the form of the angel Gabriel. The Koran, written by Muhammad, says that Gabriel showed Muhammad a tablet, which, though he was illiterate, he suddenly could read at Gabriel's command. The message stated that Allah, the true God, had appointed Muhammad to be His messenger on earth.

Muhammad first sold his new religion to his wife, then to his relatives, and then to his more distant cousins, and finally to strangers. Here he met with the first sales resistance. Like the Christians before him, Muhammad made his first converts among the slaves. This earned him the suspicion of the Quraish, to whom Muhammad was a radical threatening the economy of the country. After ten years of effort, the bitterness was such that in 622 Muhammad had to flee from Mecca to Medina, where he hoped the large Jewish population would support him.

Muhammad was convinced that the Jews, upon whose religion so much of his own was based, would recognize his claim as successor to Moses and Jesus and would join him in battle against the pagans. But when the Jews firmly rejected his offer, Muhammad turned against them. Though illiterate, he had native intelligence. Since the Jews would not help him, he decided to confiscate their wealth to serve his cause. He felt certain that a war against the Jews would not arouse the suspicions of the Quraish, who were envious of Jewish riches, even though tolerant of their religion. But instead of sharing the loot with the Quraish, Muhammad used his newfound wealth to equip an army of ten thousand men which he marched against Mecca. It was too late for the Quraish to regret their mistake in not aligning themselves with the Jews; seeing Muhammad's strength, they capitulated. Within two years all Arabia fell under Muhammad's rule. Islam, the name of Muhammad's new creed, was the religion of the land. In 632 Muhammad died.

"If we judge greatness by influence, he was one of the giants of history," said Will Durant of Muhammad. Just as Muhammad was the "conquering word" of Allah, so Abu Bekr, friend and successor to Muhammad, was the "conquering sword" of Allah. It was Abu Bekr who carried the Koran to a world which was not waiting for it, but which heeded the swish of the scimitar that spread it.

In the sixth century the Arabs were desert nomads, in the seventh century they were conquerors on the march, in the eighth century they were masters of an empire that made the Mediterranean an Islamic lake, and in the ninth century they were the standard-bearers of a dazzling civilization, leaders in art, architecture, and science, while

Western Europe was sinking deeper and deeper into a dark morass of its own making. One by one, countries in the path of the Arabs fell before their onslaughts—Damascus in 635, Palestine in 638, Syria in 640, Egypt in 641. The defeat of the Sassanid Empire in 636 deserves a sympathetic footnote. The day the numerically inferior Arabs attacked, a sandstorm blinded the superior Sassanid armies. Their defeat was as uncalled for as the defeat of Peter the Great of Russia at the hand of King Karl XII of Sweden at the battle of Narva in 1700, when 8,000 Swedes won over 80,000 Muscovites because a snowstorm blinded the latter. At the battle of Poltava, nine years later, however, Peter, who prudently chose a day in July, had his revenge over the Swedes. The Sassanids too had a second chance, but it ended in disaster, when their army of 150,000 was annihilated by 30,000 Arabs. It was the end of the Sassanid Empire.

By 700 A.D. the eastern half of the Byzantine Empire and all of North Africa had fallen into the hands of the Muslims. In 711 a mixed force of Arabs and Berbers led by a freed slave named Tariq invaded Spain, and by 715 they had crossed the Pyrenees. There was nothing to stop them except bad luck. As in the case of the Huns, who were stopped by the French at the Battle of Châlons, so the French, under the leadership of Charles Martel, stopped the invading Muslims at Tours, in 732. This battle resulted in a power stalemate for both Muslims and Christians. Although the spread of Islam was checked in the East by the Byzantine Empire and in the West by France, the spread of Christianity into Africa and Asia was checked by the counterforce of Islam.

The Muslims intellectually divided the people in their empire into two groups, those interested and those not interested in science. In the first they included Jews, Greeks, and Persians; in the second they lumped Chinese, Turks, and Christians. They looked with respect upon the former and with contempt upon the latter. The Christians, though they far outnumbered the Jews, produced neither great men nor a distinct culture of their own in the Muhammadan Empire. The Jews, on the other hand, produced a Golden Age during this period, generating great names in philosophy, medicine, science, mathematics, linguistics—in every area of human endeavor except art, which the Jews did not enter until the Modern Age.

Soon after the death of Muhammad, the hostility against the Jews, manufactured out of political expediency, vanished. Whatever legislation against non-Muslims existed was usually ignored in practice. The Muslims were even more tolerant of other people's religions than the Romans.

Of interest in this connection is the Pact of Omar (637 A.D.), enacted after the conquest of Christian Syria and Palestine, one of the few discriminatory pieces of Muhammadan legislation we know of. The remarkable thing about this pact is that it mentions Christians only, though it is presumed, but by no means certain, that it also applied to Jews. In accordance with this pact, Christians could not display crosses on churches or in the street, carry religious images in public, chant loudly at funeral processions, strike any Muslim, shave the front of their heads, wear distinctive dress, imitate the True Believers, prevent a Christian from converting to Islam, convert Muhammadans to Christianity, harbor spies in their churches, or build houses taller than those of their Muslim neighbors. They were to rise up in deference to any Muslim who entered their assemblies, and so on.

Technically, all non-Muslims had to pay a head tax for protection, which exempted them from military service and denied them the right to hold public office. But as far as the Jews were concerned, these were neglected laws, for the Jews seldom had to pay such a head tax, often served with great distinction and high rank in Muslim armies, and rose to the highest posts in government service, including grand vizier and princely rank.

The span of the Jewish Golden Age in the Muhammadan civilization corresponded to the life span of the Islamic Empire itself. When the latter broke up, the Jewish Golden Age broke up. The empire of the Muslims took as long in dying as did the empire of the Romans, beginning to break up about 1000 A.D. and coming to an end by 1500. We can only note its passing with a brevity that does great injustice to its quixotic complexity.

A curious schizophrenia ran through the ruling dynasties, alternating between unbounded profligacy and extreme penury. One caliph would ruin the treasury by spending vast sums on luxuries, and his successor would swell the coffers by total miserliness. Because the spenders were able rulers and the misers bad administrators, the spenders enhanced the country's culture while ruining its finances, and the misers ruined its prestige while leaving favorable balance sheets. As long as gold kept flowing in from an expanding empire, the country could afford its luxuries. Soon the Muslims had the world's most beautiful cities, most sybaritic rulers, and most unstable governments. Governors of provinces stepped into this power vacuum, seized their respective provinces, and proclaimed themselves rulers of their own domains. By the year 1000, the solid Muhammadan Empire was no more. It consisted of a series of independent caliphates.

With the old unity gone, the Islamic Empire became prey to barbaric tribes. In the thirteenth century, the Mongols under Genghis Khan invaded the empire from the northeast. It was not a mystic destiny which led them west; they followed their cattle. Genghis Khan's Mongols wore ox-hides, ate anything that lived—cats, dogs, rats, lice—and drank human blood for want of anything better. In their first encounter with the Mongols, an army of 400,000 Muslims was defeated. Genghis gutted the city of Bokhara, slew 30,000, and continued his march into the circle of civilization, burning libraries, sacking cities, and beheading people, stacking their heads into grisly pyramids as neatly as the Nazis stacked concentration camp corpses. Barbarians, yes! But not untidy. When Baghdad capitulated, 800,000 civilians were put to death, the city laid waste, its wealth plundered, and its women violated and sold into slavery. Urged on by their victories, fate dealt the Mongols an unexpected blow from a most unexpected source. The Egyptians stopped them at the Battle of Damascus in 1303. But the Mongolian defeat came too late. The devastation they had wrought was so great that this part of the world has not fully recovered to this day.

What was left of the Muhammadan Empire became vulnerable to other forces. Timurids and Moguls seized the Arabian Peninsula; Ottoman Turks annexed Egypt, Palestine, Syria, and Iraq; savage tribes known as Almohades became the rulers of North Africa; and the Spaniards, under Ferdinand and Isabella, eventually managed the final reconquest of Spain from the Moors. By 1500 the world's most incredible empire—tolerant and enlightened, luxuriant and sybaritic, full of mathematicians and poets, warriors and sycophants—had come to an end.

SIXTEEN

# THE JEWISH RENAISSANCE IN MUFTI

The image modern man holds of the Jew in the Islamic Age in no way corresponds to reality. He differed from the biblical Jew as much as the New York "Cafe Society" Jew differs from the ghetto Jew. A renaissance—a reawakening— had transformed the biblical Jew into a totally new individual, bearing little resemblance to the past. In this age he was a hedonist and philanderer, a *bon vivant* and sophisticate, a worldly philosopher and scientist, a secular writer and poet.

Yet there was something strange about this renaissance of the Jews—it was not Jewish. Hidden underneath the new Muhammadan mufti was not Judaism, but Hellenism. The "Jewish Renaissance" was not a reawakening of Judaism, but a resurgence of Hellenism. The Jews, who during their Greco-Roman period had fought the Hellenizers, had inveighed against the Epicureans, and had thrown their hands up in horror at the Greek philosophers, now welcomed the Jewish emancipators, succumbed to luxury, and praised rationalism. New, unheard-of occupations became respectable Jewish professions. The Jews became astronomers, mathematicians, alchemists, architects, translators, finance ministers, and international businessmen with branch offices in Baghdad, Cairo, and Córdoba. Wine was not only a drink for benediction, but a toast to a woman's lips; love meant not only the study of the Torah, but also the pursuit of a promising smile; song was not only a lamentation, but also a paean to the joy of life. And yet, though the door to assimilation into Islam was wide open, the Jews staved in the house of Judaism.

How had Hellenism found its way back into Jewish life in an Arabic world? The simple fact was that in rescuing Greek works for the Arabs the Jews became imbued for the first time with the true essence of Hellenism, not its outer trappings. As the early Christians had no use for the writings of the heathen Greeks, and the invading barbarians had no use for the Greek language, most of the former were lost and the latter forgotten. Greek literary and scientific works, however, survived in Syriac translations and in the libraries of wealthy and cultured Jews and unconverted Roman pagans. When the Arabs heard of this wealth of knowledge, they encouraged its translation into Arabic, and the task fell mainly to the Jews, the cosmopolitans of that age, who spoke Hebrew and Arabic, Greek and Latin, Syriac and Persian, with equal facility.

"The channels to Europe," as Moses Hadas, a contemporary scholar, calls the transmission of Greek science and humanism to Europe, were reopened by the Jews in the eighth century, and the work continued through 1400. Their first translations were from Greek and Syriac into Arabic, but soon they began to translate Greek and Arabic works into Hebrew, and finally Hebrew literature and philosophy into Arabic. A two-way cultural communication had been established. It soon included a third partner.

The enlightened crowned heads of Europe heard of these Jewish achievements and invited Jewish scholars, linguists, and translators to come to their capitals to translate the works of the Greeks and the Arabs, as well as their own Hebrew literature, into Latin, at that time the international language of European scholarship. So, for instance, Frederick II, crowned King of the Romans in 1212, King of the Germans in 1215, King of Jerusalem in 1229, and twice excommunicated—a pitiless, arrogant, yet brilliant ruler—appointed Jewish scholars to teach Hebrew at the university of Naples.

One of the earliest and most prominent of these Jewish intellectuals imported by the rulers of Western Europe, was Ibn Daud, who not only translated Hebrew, Greek, and Arabic literature into Latin, but also introduced Arabic numerals and the concept of the "zero" into European

mathematics. Euclid's *Elements* and the works of the Babylonian Talmudist Saadyah Gaon found their way into Latin
through Jewish scholars who sat side by side with Muslims
and Christians in synagogue, mosque, and church, translating Plato and Sophocles, Arab mathematicians and astronomers, Jewish philosophers and poets, into the
language of the Holy Roman Church.

How did all this affect the Jews themselves? It almost
turned them into Greeks. In their first encounter with Hellenism, after their conquest by the armies of Alexander the
Great, the Jews had not been prepared to meet this challenge. The biblical Jews were firmly convinced that theirs
was the only true religion, and they had divine Scripture to
prove it. They needed no further proof. Because they did
not doubt, they had no need to fortify their beliefs with
philosophy, logic, or science, for these three disciplines are
born out of skepticism. When Alexander and his Greeks
ran into the Jews, neither was prepared for the other. It was
the first time that Greek reason had run into faith, and the
first time that Jewish faith had run into reason. Jewish
leaders were astute enough to realize that their primitive
arsenal of ideas would never stand up in an idea-to-idea
combat with the Greeks. They therefore borrowed
weapons of logic and philosophy from the Greeks. It was
Jewish faith enriched with Greek thought that proved
stronger than Greek thought without faith. The Greeks
vanished and the Jews survived, the accidental inheritors
of the Greek *paideia*—cultural tradition.

The Jews could resist everything except their own intellectual curiosity. Now that there was no danger of being
absorbed into Hellenism, they began to examine more
closely the "idea of Hellenism." They had opened a Pandora's box of reason. They discarded the old lenses of blind
faith and tried on the new glasses of rational scrutiny. The
result was inevitable. A split between faith and reason developed. Into the breach rushed the conservatives to explain that reason and faith were but opposite sides of the
same coin, and the liberals to prove that they were incom-
patible. A new tension in Jewish life developed. Out of this
tension grew Jewish philosophy and science.

From this tension also evolved new attitudes. Until then
everything the Jews had written was in relation to Holy

Scripture. Now Jewish writing broadened to include relations to the outside world and to the individual. This expansion of interests led to a need for new words, and
writers coined them. Grammarians framed new rules
within which to fit a language of secular literature. Dictionaries came into existence. The Hebrew language was revi-
talized and expanded.

The Jews now became aware of their own history as the
unfolding of destiny. Poets explained the phenomenon of
Jewish survival in symbol and imagery. They coined a poetic metaphor, "Exiled Jew," which through the ages became the stereotype "Wandering Jew," striking the
Christians with awe and the Jews with fright. It was the
poets, too, who conceived of the Diaspora not as a result of
natural causes but as a punishment by God for the sins of
the Jews which doomed them to homelessness until God
Himself chose to return them to their homeland. This idea
took hold of the Jews like an obsessive neurosis, and they
lost their political initiative until Zionism, in the nineteenth century, shifted the burden from God back to the
shoulders of the Jews.

This Jewish Age of Reason took the same course that,
centuries later, was taken by its Christian counterpart. The
Age of Reason in Europe, born in the eighteenth century
with the French Encyclopedists, collapsed in the twentieth
century revolutionary age of totalitarianism. The Jewish
Age of Reason, born in the eighth century with the great
Talmudists, collapsed in the sixteenth-century revolutionary age of the Reformation. Like Europe's Age of Reason,
the Jewish Age of Reason produced not an eternal citadel
but an illusory castle. Was not the warmth of faith needed
to keep the idea of Jewishness alive? Could it be that "cold
reason" was freezing Jehovah out of Judaism? Slowly the
pendulum swung back to faith as the people rejected the
mechanistic Jehovah of the rationalist philosophers and responded to the humanistic Jehovah of the Romantics. By
the time the Muhammadan Empire collapsed, the Jew had
made the transition back to faith, which was to sustain him
in Europe's ghettos where reason might have led him to
hang himself or to give up his magnificent obsession that
he was destined to lead mankind into a brotherhood of
man as prophesied by Isaiah.

The life of the poet Judah Halevi symbolizes this shift from rationalism to romanticism at the same time that it illuminates the life of the Jews in the Islamic Empire. Judah was born in Toledo, Spain, in 1075. His well-to-do parents sent him to the best and most proper schools, where he studied algebra, grammar, Arabic, astronomy, and poetry. For postgraduate studies in the Talmud, he went to the famous yeshiva in Lucena, in southern Spain, a city not only reputed to have been founded by Jews but also called "Jews' Town" because of the many Jewish students attending the academy. By the age of twenty-four he had become a successful physician and had married into one of the most prominent Jewish families of Toledo. Respectability, probity, and wealth were his.

But inside Judah Halevi gnawed anxiety disguised as indefinable passions, yearning to express himself, to find himself. As Paul Gauguin gave up a banking career and abandoned his wife and children to go to Tahiti to paint and live out his destiny, so Halevi gave up his career as a physician and abandoned his wife and children to take up the life of a wandering poet. He walked through Spain, composing and singing songs to those who cared to listen to him. His wandering took him to Córdoba, the Paris of that age. Here, in this immoral, amoral, luxurious, cosmopolitan city, the home of every vice and virtue, superstition and wisdom, Halevi took root. He abandoned himself to its pleasures, found solace in its wit, and composed his love poems so reminiscent of Omar Khayyám's *Rubáiyát* and Shakespeare's sonnets. It was here he penned such lines as:

> *Awake, O my love, from your sleep,*
> *Your face as it wakes let me view;*
> *If you dream someone kisses your lips,*
> *I'll interpret your dream for you.*

But soon the pleasures of the senses palled; currents deeper than verse and love eddied into his consciousness. He was consumed by the question of Judaism, its meaning, and the mission of the Jews. From a versifier of love, he became a "Troubadour of God." It was not the love of a woman he now craved, but God's love:

> *When I remove from Thee, O God,*
> *I die, whilst I live; but when*
> *Clinging to Thee, I live in death.*

In a torrent of romantic poetry he cautioned his people not to be led into stagnation by reason:

> *And let not the wisdom of the Greeks beguile thee,*
> *Which hath not fruit, but only flowers.*

Nineteenth-century Jewish nationalism was foreshadowed in Halevi's great philosophic poem, *Ha-Kuzari*, modeled after the Book of Job. The theme revolves around a fantastic episode in Jewish history, which, were it not so well authenticated, would be dismissed as a fabrication.

In the year 740 a Tataric people living in the kingdom of Khazar on the western shore of the Caspian Sea between the Volga and the Don rivers, speaking Greek, and practicing a religious blend of Christianity and paganism in equal parts, were converted to Judaism under the vigorous promptings of their King Bulan. The fact that the Tatars now professed Judaism in no way changed their Tataric habits or nature. They remained the dreaded warriors of the steppes, feared equally by Persians, Byzantines, and the dukes of Kiev, who annually had to reaffirm their friendship with huge tributes.

The power and influence of the Khazars lasted for 250 years, until, finally, the permutation of events brought forth a weak king in Khazar and a strong duke in Kiev. In 969 Duke Sviatoslav defeated the Khazars and incorporated their territory into the new Russian state he was founding. His mother, Princess Olga, had twice been converted to Christianity—some scholars say this was to be sure it would take; others say it was to give her an excuse to make the journey twice to gay Constantinople—but as both she and her son considered Christianity the prerogative of nobles, the Russian *muzhiks* (peasants) remained pagan. Sviatoslav's successor, Vladimir, did not share this attitude, and he gave Christianity to all the Russian people, for which a grateful Church bestowed sainthood upon him. And so it came about that the former Jewish kingdom of Khazar became part of Mother Russia, and its people made the sign of the cross to the Russian Orthodox formula *Gospodi pomilooy* instead of bowing reverently to the Hebrew *Shema Yisroel*.

The conversion of the pagan Khazars to Judaism forms the theme in Halevi's poem. King Bulan, in search of a new religion, listens to a Muslim and a Christian arguing for their respective faiths. His interest is aroused when both refer to Judaism as the Father religion. He sends for a Jewish scholar, who presents Judaism not as a creed revealed to one man, but as a historic occurrence in which God manifested Himself to 600,000 Jews gathered at Mount Sinai to receive the Torah. It was, argues the Jewish scholar, a religion given to the people at once, complete and final. The growth of Judaism is maintained, he says, not by successive mystic revelations to individuals, but by a person-to-God and God-to-person experience. The visible presence of God, he says, is everywhere, but His invisible presence is found only in Jerusalem, the City of God. It is to Jerusalem that the author, Halevi, sends the Jewish scholar after converting Bulan.

As if seduced by his own arguments, Halevi, too, set out for Jerusalem to be reunited with the spirit of God and the destiny of his people. History traces him as far as Damascus; after that he disappears.

Does the life of Halevi also symbolize the life of the Jews in the Islamic civilization? Like Halevi, the Jews were brought up on the Talmud. Like him, the Jews became rich and famous in their new professions, abandoned themselves to the pleasures of life, and became imbued with the spirit of rationalism. Like Halevi, the Jews rejected their rationalism for faith and returned to the Torah. But did Halevi reach Jerusalem, the citadel of the Jewish spirit, the sanctuary for the invisible presence of Jehovah? Would the Jews reach Jerusalem, or would they, like Halevi, disappear?

The spirit of Halevi's new "social contract" with God caught the imagination of the Jewish people, and it grew into an irresistible force for survival. A new idea had seized them, that of a Jewish destiny which must find its fulfillment in Jerusalem. Their new "idea of Jewish history" created a new Jewish history.

# SEVENTEEN

# THE RISE AND FALL OF THE JEWISH PROTESTANT REVOLT

A religious schism, most closely resembling the rift between Catholicism and Protestantism, almost tore Judaism asunder in the Islamic Age. Talmudic wisdom, Hellenic rationalism, and Muhammadan tolerance had combined to produce Jewish literature and prosperity but had failed to achieve spiritual harmony. A Jewish heresy known as the Karaite Revolt against the rabbis developed in the eighth century and was not fully put down until the fifteenth century. So closely did this Karaite Revolt parallel the sixteenth-century Protestant revolt that Catholics hurled the epithet "Karaites" at the Protestants during the Reformation.

The burning of Huss (1415) and Savonarola (1498) heralded the entrance of Luther, leader of Protestantism. The violent deaths of two false Jewish messiahs (710 and 740) preceded the entrance of Anan ben David, leader of Karaism. Though the mainsprings of the Protestant and Karaite revolts were the same, each took an entirely different course. The Catholic Counter Reformation came too late to prevent the final schism in Christianity, but the Jewish rabbis acted quickly and prevented a final schism in Judaism. They stole all the valid ideas of Karaism, reformed abuses, and vitiated the arguments of the Karaites, then held up an image of reformed Judaism to the public, asking innocently, "What's all the commotion about?" But it was a touch-and-go struggle for close to seven hundred years, before the Karaite revolt gradually dissipated and finally ceased to be a threat to conventional Judaism.

Like so many other Jewish ideas, Karaism originated in Babylonia. It began as a revolt of the village Jews against the city Jews. Jewish life in the remote hamlets and villages of the Islamic Empire differed little from what it had been centuries before. The country people did not need the complex Talmudic laws so necessary for sophisticated city life. Talmudism to them was nothing but layers of trickery compiled by city rabbis to separate them from the Torah. There was a longing to return to the simplicity of the Five Books of Moses, to the explicit meaning of the "Word," not its derived interpretation. The word "Karaism," in fact, comes from the Hebrew word *karah*, "to read" Scripture, hence literally meaning "Scripturism" as opposed to "rabbinism."

The early beginnings of Karaism are shrouded by acrimony and a lack of facts. Before the appearance of the apostle of Karaism, there had been several "messianic pretenders"—that is, aspirants for the crown of messiahship who did not succeed. The first (about 700 A.D.), whose name is unknown, acted on bad advice, divine or otherwise. He set himself up not only as a prophet of the Jews, but also as a prophet of the Muslims, proclaiming he had the "word" that would free the Jews of the Talmud and the Muslims of the Koran. Arabs and Jews worked as a team; the Arabs caught him, both declared him guilty of heresy, and he was sentenced to death by a bipartisan court. So died the Huss of the Jews.

Thirty years later, about 740, a second messiah arose, like his predecessor, in Persia. He was a humble tailor by the name of Abu Isa, who had a gift of tongue and a genius for military leadership. Abu Isa denied the Talmud, denounced the rabbinate, called the Jews to his standard, and before anyone quite realized what had happened, an army of 10,000 Jews had sprung up, hailing him as prophet and messiah. This success went to his head and beclouded his judgment. Convinced that God would help him, he declared war upon the Persians and Arabians. This was the end of the Jewish Savonarola; he died proclaiming to the last his faith in Judaism.

Where these two had failed, Anan ben David (740–800), the Jewish Luther, succeeded. Anan ben David ran counter to the humble-origin tradition of religion givers. He was a wealthy prince, a descendant of the house of David, the legitimate heir to the "throne" of the Gaonim. Two utterly contradictory versions of subsequent events exist, and since there is no common ground between the two except Anan ben David's name, the historian has a chance to present both sides, leaving the reader to ponder upon which is true and which is false, a task as complex as for a Muslim to decide which is the true version of Luther, that of the Protestants or that of the Catholics.

This is the rabbinic version: Fearing that Anan's brilliance was tainted with heresy, the rabbis appointed his stupid younger brother as Gaon. In revenge, Anan set out deliberately to bring about a schism in the solid ranks of Judaism by preaching heresy, just as the rabbis had feared. Arrested and tried by the Muslim caliph, Anan ben David was sentenced to death. In prison he met a Muhammadan heretic awaiting death for a similar crime against the Islamic faith. The Muhammadan gave Anan some sage advice. "Surely," said he, "there are points of differences in Judaism. Bribe the vizier, prostrate yourself before the caliph, and ask him whether your brother has been made ruler over one religion or two. When the caliph answers, 'Over one religion,' then say to him, 'But I and my brother rule over two different religions,' and be sure to expound on some differences between your new faith and the faith of your brother."

Whereupon Anan had a vision in which the Prophet Elijah appeared to him and commanded him to denounce the Talmud and lead his people back to the Torah. The stratagem worked. The caliph set him free, and Karaism was born.

Not so, cry the Karaist apologists! Anan was the most prominent of all scholars, a pious, humble man who loved God and eschewed evil. He had been elected Gaon by the righteous of Israel, and as Gaon he wanted to restore the Torah to its former glory. The rabbis feared this man of righteousness who cited the Torah rather than the rabbinical elaborations of the Talmud. They therefore slandered and defamed him to the caliph, asking that he be put to death for heresy. But the caliph, struck by the gentleness of Anan, intuitively divined that Anan was a messiah and set him free. Anan, realizing that the rabbinate would not listen to him, that they had set their hearts against him, scorned the throne of the Gaon and received permission from the caliph to go to the Holy Land to preach his new gospel of the supremacy of the Torah.

The reader will have noted how these two interpretations cast their shadows into the past and into the future. With but a few changes it is the drama of Christ reenacted. With but a few changes it is the accusation and counteraccusation hurled by the Catholics against Luther, and by the Lutherans against the Catholics. Was Anan's new sect born out of desperation, or was it born of revelation in prison? We do not know. But within two hundred years, whatever its origin, Karaism had invaded every stratum of Jewish society in Diaspora.

Like the message of Jesus, the message of Anan was a simple one before it was seized by his disciples and enlarged into dogma in his name. According to these disciples, Anan preached the gospel of the messianic hope that the kingdom of God, as revealed in the Torah, was at hand. In the main, anything the Talmud imposed the Karaites rejected, much as the early Christians at the time of Paul rejected the teachings of the Pharisees. Many Talmudic dietary laws were abolished; the wearing of phylacteries was abandoned. Karaites also foreswore all medicine and did not consult physicians, for did not Scripture say, "I am the Lord that healeth"? This Karaite tenet might be the basis for Christian Science.

To reject all Talmudic law in the eighth century A.D. was one thing, but to live literally by a Torah given in 1200 B.C. was another. Soon the Karaites were caught in the pincers of their own making—modern life and outdated laws. Like the first teachers of the Mishna, the more enlightened and realistic Karaite scholars began to develop an "Oral Law" disguised as textual amplifications of Scripture. But as the Karaites had no central dogma, every man could be his own interpreter of Oral Law. Anarchy developed. Anan's successor, Benjamin Nahavendi, modified his master's viewpoint and organized the dissident sects into a unified Karaite movement.

At first the rabbis thought they could kill Karaism by ignoring it, but its rapid spread alarmed them. To contain the movement, they launched a war of words against it, but to little avail. The Karaite heresy spread. Unlike the Catholics and Protestants, the rabbinic and Karaite forces were in no position to declare open hostilities. Would war and bloodshed have occurred if the Jews had lived as a nation in Palestine? Judging by such previous schisms in Jewish history as those which resulted in the conflicts between the Hellenizers and anti-Hellenizers in Grecian times, between the Pharisees and Sadducees in Hasmonean times, between the Zealots and Peace Party members in Roman times, the answer is probably yes. But as the Jews had no armies, the paper war against the Karaites intensified.

The rabbinic-Karaite war of invective turned in favor of the Talmudists with the entry of a scholar who had the appearance of a saint and the cunning of a Machiavelli. Saadyah Gaon was the first of the "Jewish-Hellenic-Arabic-Renaissance" intellectuals, the first of the rationalist philosophers to introduce Aristotelianism into the Talmud itself. Born in Egypt in 882 A.D., he was made head of the most prominent of the Babylonian academies at an early age. He was a born campaigner who loved a good fight. It was he who drew the main battle lines, first for containing Karaism, then for weakening the movement.

Saadyah Gaon saw much that was fine in the Karaite religion, and recognized the legitimate aspirations of the people who joined the sect. His first move was to translate the Old Testament into Arabic, so the people, who no longer knew Hebrew, would not have to depend upon Karaite preachers to learn what was in the Torah but would be able to read it themselves, just as Luther, in the sixteenth century, translated the Bible from Latin into the vernacular German so the German people could read for themselves what was written in the two Testaments. Next Saadyah Gaon set out to incorporate into the Talmud the best precepts of Karaism. And finally, he penned a series of brilliant and devastating attacks against Karaism itself.

The Karaites, seeing their movement stolen from under their noses, fought back in kind. They reformed themselves. They had the good luck to develop a series of brilliant scholars whose prestige attracted new members. These scholars took up the scientific study of Hebrew, developing Hebrew philology to an advanced stage and liberalizing the entrance requirements into Karaism in much the same way that Paul liberalized entry into Christianity. The rabbis countered by trumping the Karaite ace. They studied Hebrew even more assiduously, developed even better Hebrew grammars, made the Bible even more accessible to the people, interpreted laws even less stringently. By the fourteenth century the tide was turning against Karaism. By the eighteenth century the movement that had threatened to engulf Judaism had almost vanished. Today there are only about 10,000 Karaites in Lithuania and the Crimea, and about 2,000 in Israel, lingering like undigested meals of history.

The Karaite revolt had not been in vain. It prevented Talmudism from becoming static at this point of its history, making it come to grips with life again instead of remaining preoccupied with its own cleverness. It was a salutary lesson. Judaism learned to defend itself, not by closing ranks but by opening them to new ideas. It taught the Jews two lessons: first, that in complete liberty lies anarchy; and second, that in total conformity lies death.

Thus the Jewish saga in the Islamic Empire ends. It was conceived by fate, supported in splendor, nourished by intellect, and buried by fate. By the fifteenth century, Jewish life in the East emptied into Western Europe at a juncture of Jewish history when the roads for the Jews led to the ghetto. But before we leave the Muhammadan stage of Jewish history and retrace our steps to sixth-century Europe, where we left the Jews after the fall of the Roman Empire, it is only fitting that tribute be paid the magnificent Arabic people who wrought a dazzling and enlightened civilization out of the desert.

Though the Muhammadan Empire is dead, the human element which shaped its grandeur is still living. The Arabic culture was not built on the plunder of other countries and the brains of other men. It sprang from deep wells of creativity within the people themselves. For seven hundred years Arab and Jew lived side by side in peace and with mutual respect. If Jews today in the Arabic world live under the most squalid conditions, it is not because Arabs pushed them there. These conditions were created for Jew and Arab alike by subsequent conquerors.

Today, the Arab world is arising from its slumber. If the Arabs can use the Jews to hoist themselves out of the abyss into which history hurled them, they can be blamed no more than other nations which are playing similar power politics. It is up to Jewish leaders, in their own national self-interest, to convince Arab leaders that the Arab world can achieve its legitimate aims with the friendship of the Jews, as in days past. Astute statesmanship can relax the present Israeli-Arab tensions, because they are not caused by deep-rooted racial and religious antagonisms but by temporary political expediencies. History has shown that Jew and Arab can live together without strife and with mutual profit.

# VI

# THE PRINCE AND THE YELLOW STAR

*How the Jews with only a gesture—conversion—could have saved themselves from banishment to the ghetto, but instead chose the yellow star of ignominy, yet became indispensable to the medieval prince because they were the only ones who carried the torch of learning and the spirit of enterprise in an age of darkness.*

## MEDIEVAL PERIOD
### CHRISTIAN: 500 A.D. TO 1500 A.D.
### JEWISH: 500 A.D. TO 1800 A.D.

| EUROPEAN HISTORY | | JEWISH HISTORY |
|---|---|---|
| Rome falls. Ostrogoths found Italy, Visigoths Spain, Franks and Burgundians France. Western barbarians Christianized. Dark Age and feudalism settle over Europe. Era of salvation. | 500 A.D. to 800 | Masses of Jews forcibly converted in Spain. Jews invited to settle in Italy, France, Germany; asked to help found cities and encourage trade. Become Europe's middle class. |
| Charlemagne unites heartland of Europe into Frankish Empire. Popes gain secular power. Viking invasions. Centralized government collapses. Dark Age intensifies. More salvation. | 800 to 900 | Charlemagne invites Jews to his realm. Jews organize large mercantile establishments in Europe. First Kabalistic work appears. |
| Eastern and Northern Europe Christianized. William the Conqueror invades Britain. Dark Age begins to lift. Holy Roman Empire founded. Still more salvation. | 900 to 1100 | Jews come to England with William the Conqueror. Expand money-lending activities; become Europe's bankers. Continue translating Greek works. Have highest educational standards in Europe. |

| | | |
|---|---|---|
| Two centuries of Crusades. Greek Orthodox Constantinople sacked by Roman Catholic Crusaders. Albigensian heresy. Fourth Lateran Council. First European universities founded. And still more salvation. | 1100 to 1300 | Jews flee Rhineland in wake of Crusades. Settle in liberal Poland, develop its economy. First ritual-murder and Host-desecration libels crop up; first burning of Talmud. Jews banished from England. Kabalistic work, Zohar, appears. |
| Age of Renaissance. Foundations of new humanism. New heresies plaguing Church. Mercantilism growing; middle classes gaining more power. Feudalism beginning to crumble. End of salvation era. | 1300 to 1500 | Jews banished from France (1400); banished from Spain and Portugal (1500). Persecutions become economically motivated. Jewish commercial interests decline in West, grow in East. Kabalistic writings assume metaphysical character. |
| End of Renaissance. Era of Reformation. Century of religious wars. Counter Reformation. Treaty of Westphalia. Emergence of nationalist states. Growing power of burghers. Scientific discoveries reshape Europe's thinking. | 1500 to 1700 | Jews relegated to ghettos in Italy, Germany, Central Europe. Jews settle in Russia. Pale of Settlements established. Still more Kabala. The Sabbatean heresy. Jews readmitted to England, Holland, France. Appearance of Court Jews. |

| | | |
|---|---|---|
| Russia, Prussia emerging as strong states. Poland carved up. Rousseau's *Social Contract* sets foundation for new concept of state. Louis XVI overthrown; French Revolution shakes Europe's institutions. Napoleon seizes power. Age of Industrialism. | 1700 to 1800 | The Frankist heresy. Rise of Hasidism. Deterioration of Jewish learning. Beginnings of psychological anti-Semitism. |

# EIGHTEEN

# CRUSADES, RENAISSANCE, AND REFORMATION

## THE AGE OF SALVATION

To most Christian scholars, Jewish history during the Middle Ages is a barely discernible thread in the feudal tapestry. Many Jewish historians see this thread as a rope suffocating the Jews. To our eyes, medieval Jewish history seems more like a multicolored strand of threads woven into an overall design, corollary to the main motif. If we lose sight of this design, Jewish history becomes a succession of meaningless events, unmotivated persecutions—a boring dirge. If, on the other hand, the design is brought into sharp focus, a fascinating constellation composed of religious, economic, and psychological forces emerges in the fabric. There is a progression to medieval Jewish history, inverse to the unfolding of medieval Christian history. As the fortunes of the Christians recede, those of the Jews advance; as the fortunes of the Christians go up, those of the Jews go down.

The medieval world developed essentially three overlapping attitudes toward the Jews. The first one began to crystallize itself in the sixth century and faded out in the eleventh. The second embraced four hundred years—the two centuries of the Crusades and the two centuries of the Renaissance. The third began with the Reformation and spanned the three centuries between 1500 and 1800. Let us examine each of these attitudes against the historical background of the Judeo-Christian drama.

After the conquest of Judah by Pompey, Jews and Romans became "inseparable." Behind the Roman armies carrying the Imperial Eagles marched the Jews carrying the banners of free enterprise. The Jews were in Italy in the second century B.C., in France in the first century B.C., in

Spain a hundred years later. At the end of the third century A.D. they had penetrated as far north as Cologne, Germany. When the barbarians from the East invaded Western Europe the Jews had been there for centuries.

By the sixth century, the invading barbarians, the Ostrogoths, Visigoths, Vandals, Huns, Franks, and Burgundians, had accomplished most of their damage. Ignorance was universal, rights of man had disappeared, and poverty united all in a common misery. Toward the end of the eighth century, roughly, four European kingdoms, now known as Italy, France, Spain, and Germany, were emerging. Though reshaped into different power patterns, these four states, with England a fifth member in the eleventh century, formed the heart of European history until 1500.

Ostrogoths settled in Italy, producing against all odds a great king, Theodoric the Great, who pulled the country out of chaos. Visigoths plundered their way into Spain, where they established a kingdom and in 587 under King Reccared were converted to Christianity. The Vandals sacked their way into France, ate all that was eatable, raped all that was rapable, sold all that was salable, and destroyed the rest. They founded a wretched kingdom in North Africa, which mercifully came to an end in 600. Vandals, mixed with Franks and Burgundians, formed the first Frankish kingdom and were converted to Catholicism in the late fifth century under Clovis. Germany was a hodgepodge of Huns, Slavs, Alamanni, Frisians, Saxons, Bavarians—all barbarians. Southern Germany was more or less Christianized by 600, backslid in 700, and was rebaptized in 800. It was at this time that Charles the Great, known as Charlemagne—six feet tall, fluent in Latin, conversant in Greek, unable to write, but an enlightened ruler who encouraged arts, sciences, and Jews—united the heartland of Europe into one kingdom. On Christmas Day in the year 800, florid-faced, long-mustached Charlemagne was crowned emperor, and the Pope knelt before him in homage. Had a new Caesar brought civilization back to Europe, like a suitor bringing a gift to his mistress? Alas, Charlemagne's glued-together empire crumbled under the inept fingers of his pious, pompous, and vain son and grandsons who succeeded him.

That same century another calamity befell Europe—a

new barbarian invasion. From the north, from the mists of Scandinavia, came strange-armored men in boats built like birds of prey. They were oared by Vikings—men of the sea—bent on plunder. Armed with *skeggøx*\* and *scramasax*,\*\* they marauded their way through Europe, killing with skill gentile and Jew, burning with ardor temple and church. Then, as suddenly as they had appeared, they vanished, and cassocked monks carried the cross of Christ to Scandia's scraggy shores.

Christianity, which first took hold in Southern and Western Europe, now was carried to the East and North. By the early tenth century the Gospels had taken root in what is now Poland, Bohemia, Bulgaria, and Russia; by the late tenth century they had spread to northern Germany, Denmark, Sweden, Norway, and Iceland. Finland and Lithuania were the last two countries in Europe to be Christianized. Vainly, for a century, Swedish crusaders tried to convert their pagan Finnish neighbors; but the magic of Ukko, Finnish god of the air, mired the Swedish armies in Finland's marshes. In the end, miracle prevailed over magic. The event took place in 1155, on the shores of Pyhäjärvi, the Holy Lake, where the Finns were forcibly baptized by being thrown into the water. During this ceremony, even as the Finns drowned, their souls were saved. Confronted by this miracle, Ukko fled. The surviving Finns converted to Christianity, whereupon they promptly were made loyal serfs to Swedish lords. Lithuania converted to Christianity about 1250 as a political expediency to protect herself from the crusading zeal of Teutonic knights, but after a decade she lapsed back into paganism. The second conversion took place a century later, when the pagan Grand Duke of Lithuania, Jagiello, married the Roman Catholic Queen of Poland, Jadwiga, and Christianity trickled down to the Lithuanian masses as the nobility of the two countries gradually assimilated.

But the tenth century, so rich in the acquisition of Christian converts, was also the nadir of Europe's Dark Ages. Not a single Christian university dotted the entire continent until the twelfth century. The ignorance of the sixth

---

\*A razor-sharp, hooked ax, shaped to hug a hull or cleave a skull.
\*\*A one-edged sword, scriptured with runes for god-blessed results.

century had ripened into a dull stupor, rights of man had become crimes against Church and state, and poverty had progressed to squalor. It was an age where only salvation of the soul mattered. The year 1000 was a turning point for both gentile and Jew, but in opposite directions.

The Jews escaped the general devastation of this first phase of their medieval experience with remarkably good fortune. Lest the admittedly large number of Jews killed during these four centuries seem oppressive to those who make it a business to gather Jewish statistics only, let us comfort them with Montaigne's epigram, "There is something altogether not too displeasing in the misfortunes of our friends," and cite the fact that Rome, a city with a population of 1,000,000 before the barbarian invasions, was reduced to 50,000 after the barbarians had taken turns sacking the city. Until they were Christianized, Goths and Vandals, Franks and Vikings never inquired into the religious affiliations of those they killed.

In Italy, Theodoric the Great (c.454–526) invited the Jews to settle in every city in his domain—Rome, Naples, Venice, Milan, and his new capital, Ravenna. They were merchants, bankers, judges, farmers, jewelers, artisans. Perhaps as many as a third of the Jews in Italy were not descendants of Abraham and Moses but the descendants of Romulus and Remus, inasmuch as their ancestors were former pagans who had converted to Judaism as far back as 100 A.D.

The story was much the same in France and Germany. Charlemagne encouraged Jews from other parts of the world to come to his empire. Specifically, he wanted the Jews to settle in cities, to foster industries, to extend the frontiers of commerce, and therefore he granted them liberal charters of self-government. Many found high posts in his court, especially in the diplomatic service. The reason for these special grants was simple enough. The feudal system provided for only three social classes, which, in the words of an eleventh-century wit, were "the nobles—who did the fighting; the priests—who did the praying; and the serfs—who did the work." There was no burgher or merchant class. This field was left open to the Jews.

In Spain the picture at first was slightly different. King Reccared, with the fearful zeal of a new convert, spread his newly found Christianity with a sword so fierce that not only were the Visigoths baptized, but a large number of Jews as well. When the Muslims conquered Spain and granted everyone religious freedom, many of these forcibly converted Jews did not return fully to the Mosaic religion. Many "crypto-Jews" became the cosmopolitan world citizens who moved with elegance and aplomb in the courts of viziers and grandees, marrying into the families of both. They were destined to form the nucleus of a most vexing and controversial problem in Spain, which exploded with calamitous results in the late fifteenth century.

We can now see how the forces shaping Jewish history in the early Feudal Age began with two paradoxes. Not only were the Jews the only non-Christians left in the entire Christian world, but, ironically, they lived in freedom outside the feudal system, while the gentiles were imprisoned within it.

Why had the Jews not been converted or killed as had the other pagans and nonbelievers? Why had they received special exemption? Why did the Church protect them?

The Church had maneuvered itself into this paradoxical impasse by the force of its own logic. Because the civilization of the Middle Ages was religiously oriented, it was important that the Jews be converted to Christianity. For how could the Church claim that Jesus was universally divine if his own people disclaimed him?

At first every conciliation was held out to the Jews as an inducement to accept Christianity. The Jews would not convert. The Church was in a dilemma. If the Jews were ignored, it might be equal to an admission that Jesus was not universally divine. On the other hand, if the Church exterminated his people, as it had the heathens, then the Church could never claim that the Jews had acknowledged Christ divine. The Jew was an ambivalent figure in the Western world. He could be neither converted nor killed. To prevent his religion from infecting the Christian believer with doubt, the Jew, therefore, was excluded from the feudal system. The Church did not realize that with this act it had jailed its own people and set the Jew free.

Some of the laws enacted against the Jews in these centuries were not new. They were, in fact, patterned after Old Testament and Talmudic laws against non-Jews. Old Jewish laws forbade a non-Jew being appointed king of Israel, or holding a post from which he could govern Jews. To prevent too great an intermixing between Jews and Greeks, Palestinian law forbade a Jew to sell land to a non-Jew. The Christians enacted like laws against the Jews. These cannot be judged as good or bad in terms of today's society. They were an expression of society in those days.

There is little historical material for those who might want to cast early medieval Jewish history in the mold of martyrdom. As with the laws of Constantine, Constantius, Theodosius, and Justinian, the occasional edicts against Jews were observed mostly in the breach. Impatient eager beavers, rushing history, did, here and there, now and then, issue laws expelling Jews from this or that city, in this or that year. But the Jews were soon recalled with apologies, since feudal society had not yet developed a merchant class of its own. These exceptions did not constitute official Church policy any more than the lynching of a Negro constituted official United States policy seventy years ago. From the pronouncement of Pope Gregory the Great (591), forbidding the forcible conversion of Jews, to the decree of Pope Innocent III at the Fourth Lateran Council (1215), instituting the yellow badge for Jews, the Jews lived in comparative freedom and moderate prosperity.

Until the eleventh century, the Church could take a lenient attitude toward the obstinate Jew, hoping time would convince him of his error. The Church was supreme, the princes obedient, the people docile. Then, dramatically, after the eleventh century, developments with unforeseen consequences took place, changing the fabric of medieval Jewish life. Such serious restrictive legislation as the humiliating garb, ritual-murder charges, Host-desecration libels, and confinement to the ghetto were not the heritage of the early Dark Ages but the heritage of the Crusades, the Renaissance, and the Reformation.

## THE AGE OF MORE SALVATION

If "salvation" was the key to the first phase of medieval history, then "more salvation" was the key to the Crusades, for, as with gold, one can never have enough. Although the origins of the Crusades were deeply rooted in the religious, political, and social texture of the age, these origins had no bearing upon Jewish history, but the Crusades themselves did.

We must be careful how we focus the lens of history on this period. If we keep it focused on Jews exclusively, then this interlude becomes a gory story of pillaging Jewish settlements, killing Jewish people, looting Jewish wealth, and, of course, committing the inevitable rape that so alliteratively goes with rapine. But if we enlarge our sector of vision to include Jews and Christians, an entirely different picture emerges.

A great many of the Crusaders were pious Christians fired with the idea of freeing the Holy Land from the infidel and turning Jerusalem into a Christian shrine. Many others were in quest of loot and the opportunity to kill with impunity. The days of chivalry, when only knights and their pages were permitted to lay down their lives on the field of battle, had vanished. The common man was now also extended the privilege of dying for honor, but this knightly prerogative did not fire him with joy. Therefore, to stir up zeal for a Crusade in an age where no universal conscription existed, serfs were promised freedom, criminals were offered pardon, sinners were granted absolution.

As a result of this propaganda barrage, unruly mobs, full of ardor and energy but low on discipline and supplies, sprang up all over. Long before the Crusaders reached the Holy Land they ran out of provisions. Armed detachments began attacking defenseless villages in the path of their march. At first it was Jewish communities. The Western world protested to the Pope against these outrages, and in many instances other Christian citizens came to the aid of the Jews. The looting now became general, Christians too became victims, and the fighting spread. More Crusaders died en route to the Holy Land than lived to fight for it.

As Crusade after Crusade met with either total defeat or only partial victory, it became more and more difficult to enlist the support of the populace for succeeding Crusades. As the nature of the Crusades shifted from that of freeing the Holy Land from the infidel to that of pillaging the rich Byzantine Empire, the enemy became the Greek Orthodox Catholics instead of the Muslims. What had started out as desultory looting of Jews ended up as a bloodbath for Christians.

Relations between Constantinople and Rome, never cordial since the founding of the Byzantine Empire in the fifth century, hardened through the years into hatred, and in 1094 the pontiffs of both cities pronounced anathema upon each other. "Political mistrust made the Latins hate and suspect the Greek schismatics, while the Greeks despised and loathed the rough Latin heretics."* The history of the Byzantine Empire was, to quote Gibbon, a "tedious and uniform tale of weakness and misery." Its military strength was offset by its intellectual weakness. During its eleven hundred years, the Byzantine civilization produced only three art forms—Byzantine churches, Byzantine painting, and castrated Byzantine choirboys; it did not produce a single new idea, philosopher, writer, or scientist of note.

It was a triple blessing for the Jews that they were expelled from the Byzantine Empire before the start of the Crusades.** They escaped the massacre, they escaped the blame, and they escaped those chroniclers who would have chalked up the fracas as another manifestation of Jewish persecution. In 1183, Byzantine Greeks killed all Italians in the realm, and in 1204 Italians in the fourth Crusade took their revenge with a carnage almost unparalleled in history. The bestiality of the Crusaders shocked Pope, prince, and people, but their horror in no way stopped the slaughter. Byzantium was carved up by the Crusaders like a cadaver, and its towns were tossed as loot to the Italian city-states which had financed this Crusade. Though the Greeks recaptured Constantinople fifty years later, the empire had been weakened. In 1453 she fell before the onslaught of the Turks, and the Christian stronghold in the East was lost.

---

*Steven Runciman, *Byzantine Civilization*, page 100.
**According to Runciman, the Jews were expelled from the Byzantine Empire during the reign of Romanus 1 (919–944), but were later readmitted. To use the words of Gibbon, the history of the Jews in the Byzantine Empire was also a "tedious and universal tale" of misery and persecution, even though, Runciman adds, "It is noticeable that the persecutors were the lay powers, not the Church." (*Ibid.*, page 105.)

The fifth Crusade met with indifferent success. With the sixth and seventh the zeal was gone. After the eighth Crusade, the fire was extinguished. Christian and Jew alike rejoiced that it was all over. But the Crusades, ironically, had the opposite effect from the one intended. It had been hoped that the capture of Jerusalem would rally the faithful into a more closely knit Christian community. Instead, the faith of the Christians in their own superiority was badly shaken. Thousands had been exposed to the superior culture of the Muslims. Serfs, freed during the Crusades, did not want to go back to the farm after they had seen Constantinople and the splendor of the Saracen (the Roman name for the Arab). They settled in the towns, swelling them into cities. A spirit of restlessness pervaded Europe. This spirit found its expression in two ways: through the creative outlet of the Renaissance, and in the religious protest of the Reformation. In the former the Jews participated fully, and succeeded brilliantly. In the latter they tried hard to stay out of the family quarrel and failed miserably.

Though Europe was ready for the Renaissance, it was the Italians who first saw her, grabbed her, and had the men of genius on tap to shape the inchoate yearnings of the age into an intellectual force which illuminated the European scene for over two hundred years, from about 1320 to 1520. Not all of Italy was involved in this humanistic resurgence. It was boxed in a rectangle bounded by Naples in the south, Milan in the north, Venice in the east, and Genoa in the west. It was ushered in by humanists (Dante, Petrarch, Boccaccio) and died with artists (Cellini, Titian, Michelangelo). To make the grade in between, one had to have such names as Leonardo da Vinci, Fra Filippo Lippi, Bellini. The melancholy task of the Jewish historian is to record the fact that no Jew qualified.

In Italy, the Renaissance took essentially a nonreligious course, with the accent on the individual. In Northern Europe, the Renaissance, running a hundred years behind, took essentially a religiously oriented course, as exemplified by Johann Reuchlin in Germany. Reuchlin (1455–1522) had a profound influence on the history of Europe, because, more than any other, he helped to lay the foundations for Protestantism through the influence of his

writings on the development of Luther's theological thinking. Reuchlin's humanistic philosophy was undisguisedly
Hebraic. Though a Christian, brought up on Latin, he
spoke Hebrew fluently, was familiar with Hebrew literature, and was a student of the Kabala, a Jewish mystic and
metaphysical philosophy which seeped into the writings of
Jewish and Christian scholars and scientists during the Renaissance. At the risk of his own life, when a deviation from
dogma meant death, Reuchlin protected the Jews against
slander, defended the Talmud against calumny, and popu-
larized Jewish thought among Christian intellectuals.

Because of Reuchlin's work, the part which Hebraism
played in the spread of humanistic learning in Germany is
readily obvious. Not quite so obvious in the creation of the
Renaissance is the supporting role played by the Jews.
Scholars are in agreement that it was the reintroduction of
Greek learning into the stream of European culture which
gave birth to the Renaissance, and they generally credit
Petrarch with this work. But it is more than a curious coincidence that the Renaissance sprang to life in just those
areas where Jewish life had been and again became most
active. The Renaissance did not originate in England, in
France, or in Germany; it originated in that geographic
area where Jews had been engaged most heavily for three
centuries in the translation of Greek, Arabic, and Hebrew
classics into Latin. We must remember it was to Naples, a
Renaissance center, that Frederick II had invited the Jews
to translate the works of the Greeks and to teach Hebrew
to Christian scholars. Petrarch followed in the footsteps of
the Jews. These coincidences do not, of course, constitute
proof, but perhaps here is a field for scholars to investigate,
to document, to assess.

## END OF SALVATION

Too late, popes and emperors discovered that the Renaissance was not only beautiful but dangerous. It set men's
minds free. It made them think. It made them question the
established order of things. The emergence of science, especially, shook Christian man in all his cherished prejudices. Too late did the men who permitted the opening of

this Pandora's box try to close the lid. Only Spain succeeded, mainly because she did it before the Renaissance could gain a foothold in that country and ruin the purity of the Spanish mind. In 1305 Spain banned the study of all science, and among the first victims of the Inquisition were not Jews but Christian scientists. Galileo did not make the trek to the stake, because he was sensible enough not to die for his beliefs but to live for them. When brought before the Inquisition in Italy, he recanted in public and went on with his studies in private. So effectively, however, did Spain close its doors to science, that to this day no major scientific discovery has been made by any Spaniard.

The dangerous current of the Renaissance merged with heretical currents of protest against the established Church. Of the heresies, the Albigensian one in the twelfth and thirteenth centuries is of particular interest because it led directly to the establishment of the Inquisition and indirectly to the banishment of the Jews from Spain.

Zealous princes undertook to punish the Albigensian Christians in southern France who dared question the dogma of the Church. As loss of property generally went with loss of life, the nobles soon discovered that there was a direct ratio between the number of heretics purified by death and the amount of gold which accumulated in noble coffers. Heresy hunting was profitable, no doubt about it. In one French town, 20,000 Albigensians were piously slain and their property solemnly confiscated.* The Papacy became alarmed at all this bloodshed, forbade the private hunting of heretics (as it was later to forbid the local hunting of Jews), and instituted the Inquisition (from the Latin *inquisitio*, meaning an "inquiry") in order to determine whether an accused actually was a heretic. During the first centuries of its existence, the Inquisition had no power to deal with Jews, Muslims, or any other nonbelievers, only with Christians.

As the Church abhorred the shedding of blood, it was decided that those convicted should be burned. Ironically,

---

*Historians estimate that over 1,000,000 Frenchmen suspected of being Albigensians were slain in thirty years by the Crusaders. The highest estimated number of Jews killed during the two hundred years of the Crusades is 100,000.

modern man looks with horror upon burning someone for his religious beliefs, yet sees nothing incongruous in shooting or hanging a man for his political convictions. Also, ironically, the authority for killing a heretic stems from the Old Testament itself, from Deuteronomy 17:2–5, "If there be found in the midst of thee . . . man or woman, that does that which is evil in the sight of the Lord thy God in transgressing His covenant, and has gone and served other gods, and worshipped them . . . and it be told thee . . . then shalt thou bring forth that man or woman . . . thou shalt stone them with stones that they die." Because only Christians could commit heresy in the eyes of the Church, this Mosaic law, with an updated punishment, was applied only to them. And thus came about the twist of fate which brought Jews comparative safety from the Inquisition while Christians burned one another at the stake.

As the Albigensian heresy spread from France to Germany and thence into Eastern Europe, Spain became apprehensive lest she too be contaminated. She had special cause for concern, because in her midst dwelt a large body of converted Jews, who later became known to the Spaniards as *Conversos*, "converted ones," and to the Jews as *Marranos*, the Spanish word for "swine" or "pigs." It would be of interest to know who coined the name "Marrano," the Jews or Spaniards, why the name stuck, and why the Jews to this day persist in calling the Spanish crypto-Jews "Marranos" (that is, "swine"), even as they loudly mourn their tragic fate.

The problem of the converted Jews in Spain dates back to the sixth century, when the zealous King Reccared converted as many as 90,000 Jews to Christianity. How many remained Christian, how many returned to Judaism, and how many chose to profess both religions when the Moors conquered Spain in the eighth century is not known. It was not until the fourteenth century that the names Conversos and Marranos were applied to these Spanish crypto-Jews.

During the Christian reconquest of Spain from the Moors, the soldiers of the Cross at first had difficulty recognizing the difference between Jew and Muslim, as both dressed alike and spoke the same tongue. *Reconquistadores* understandably killed Jew and Arab with impartial prejudice. But as the Spanish dukes and grandees became reacquainted with Jewish learning and industry, they offered the Jews every inducement to remain in Christian Spain in order to enrich her trade and to enhance her culture. Once Spain was safely back in the Christian column, however, a national conversion drive was launched. It was so successful that by the end of the fifteenth century the Marranos, not the Jews, constituted a problem to the Spanish government.

By virtue of their learning and sophistication, the Marranos had risen to positions of power. They had married into the noblest families of Spain and had become not only grandees and kissing cousins of royalty, but also bishops and archbishops. This was galling to many natural-born Christians who could not aspire to such lofty positions and were incensed at seeing orthodox Christianity flouted. This was equally galling to many orthodox Jews, who were incensed at seeing orthodox Judaism flouted. We can divine this resentment from the fact that both Maimonides and Rashi found it necessary to issue special edicts for Jews to treat the Marranos more kindly, to show them greater consideration in case they should want to return to the Jewish faith.

The Marrano problem was a festering sore in the Spanish clerical body. With uneasiness the Church viewed the growing influence of the Marranos, who put enjoyment of life above mortification of the flesh. Many felt that it was time to apply the Inquisition and stamp out the problem, as had been done with the Albigensians. Finally, in 1482, the decision was made and Inquisitorial powers were assigned by the Spanish Church to Thomas de Torquemada to stamp out any heretical tendencies, first among the Marranos, and then wherever else found.

The Jews have held up Torquemada as an archvillain, and the Spanish Inquisition as an instrument designed especially for their torture. There is no intent here to whitewash Torquemada or to play down the horror of the Inquisition. But to understand Jewish history as something more than a succession of persecutions, Torquemada and his function must be understood in the perspective of the social structure of his times, and the Inquisition must be understood in its larger, more frightening dimensions. Though Torquemada's fanaticism horrifies twentieth-century rational man, he was no barbarian butcher. He was more concerned with saving Catholic Christianity than with exterminating Jews. The Jews who had resisted conversion and remained Jews did not come under the jurisdiction of the Inquisition. Those who were consigned to the flames of the autos-da-fé, or acts of faith, were Christians as well as Marranos convicted of heresy. Death came to them as an act of mercy after excruciating days and weeks of torture. Some Jews, of course, died violent deaths during these decades, but they were mainly the victims of mob rule. They were not tried and they were not condemned by the official Church Inquisition.

When the "Marrano heresy" was checked, Torquemada appealed to the Pope for authority to expel the Jews from Spain on the ground that as long as the Jews resided in Spain, Judaism was a clear and present danger to the Catholic faith. The Pope refused. Convinced that he was right and the Pope wrong, Torquemada, who was Queen Isabella's father confessor, applied pressure on her to banish the Jews. Queen Isabella and King Ferdinand, whose marriage had been arranged by a Spanish Jew named Abraham Senior, were reluctant to do so, but the clamor from the Spanish Church became too great, and they finally consented.

If we are to believe a story persistently cropping up in the annals of Jewish history, this plan almost came to naught through the intercession of Don Isaac Abravanel, a rabbi and scholar with a penchant for making vast fortunes. Hearing of the contemplated expulsion of the Jews, Abravanel, then finance minister to the Spanish court, offered the royal couple such a fantastic sum of gold to rescind the order that they wavered. At this moment a suspicious Torquemada, who had been listening behind the door, burst into the room. Throwing caution to the wind, he held a crucifix high over his head and shouted, "Behold the Saviour whom the wicked Judas sold for thirty pieces of silver. If you approve this deed, then sell Him for a great sum." Frightened, the royal couple signed the order for the expulsion of the Jews in the same year and month that Columbus received his orders to undertake the voyage that led to his discovery of America.

Like Moses leading the Children of Israel out of Egypt,

Don Abravanel led the Jewish exodus from Spain. Of the 150,000 Jews in Spain at that time, an estimated 50,000, whose ancestry dated back for fifteen hundred years in Spain, did not want to leave their homeland and paid the price for staying—conversion to Christianity. Of the remaining 100,000, some 10,000 perished, about 45,000 eventually settled in Turkey, approximately 15,000 in North Africa and Egypt, 10,000 in southern France and Holland, 10,000 in northern Italy, 5,000 scattered in various other parts of Europe, Africa, and Asia, and 5,000 of these wanderers were among the first settlers in South America. Abravanel settled in Italy, where he became employed in the service of the king of Naples, and later as a counselor to the doge of Venice.

Throughout North Africa, Egypt, and the Ottoman Empire, the Jews enjoyed almost complete religious and economic freedom for several centuries. Though the Turks were looked upon by the Christians as the scourge of Christendom, Turkish policy toward the Jews for many years approximated that of the former Islamic Empire.

Portugal also instituted an Inquisition among her Marranos and in 1496 threatened to expel the Jews. Fleeing Portuguese Jews resettled in North Africa, the northern Italian states, and the Ottoman Empire. In the latter half of the sixteenth century many Marranos who had remained in Spain and Portugal fled to Holland and South America.

After the main body of Jews had been banished from Spain and had fled from Portugal, the Inquisition was turned against converted Moors, who were expelled from all of Spain in 1502. It was now the Christians who were examined by the Inquisition, and in the sixteenth, seventeenth, and eighteenth centuries the fires of the autos-da-fé spread like a rash all over Europe. The Church lost control of both Inquisition and autos-da-fé, and Christians and Jews then shared the same fate. But for every Jew executed there were a thousand and one Christians.

## THE ECONOMICS OF HERESY

The curious inverse progression of Jewish political history in its relation to Christian political history in the Middle

Ages is paralleled in the economic sphere. As the material welfare of the Christians during this period took a turn for the better, that of the Jews took a turn for the worse. No abstruse Marxist economics or advanced social theories are needed to explain this phenomenon. It was governed by an ancient, universal, and exceedingly simple law. When feudal man realized the superiority of the Jewish way of doing things, he absorbed Jewish know-how, kicked the Jews out to eliminate competition, and went into business for himself. The Christians, streaming out of their "feudal ghettos" in the thirteenth, fourteenth, and fifteenth centuries, seeing all posts already occupied by Jews, legislated them out of their jobs and into Jewish ghettos, and took over the economic functions previously performed by them.

As this happily coincided with a rethinking of the Jewish question by the Church, the Church did not object to this new turn of events. As long as heretic sects had been small and isolated, the Church felt it could easily eradicate them with a severity born out of love. But as heresies multiplied instead of diminishing, the Church became less indulgent. It could no longer afford to be tolerant of a Jewish minority religion in its midst, because by their refusal to convert, the Jews kept the idea of religious freedom alive. As more and more Christian intellectuals turned to the Jews for instruction in Hebrew and Scripture, the obstinacy of the Jews in not converting, which at first had merely confounded the Church, now, understandably, exhausted its patience. The Jews had to be taken out of the mainstream of Christian life. Confinement in ghettos seemed like a good solution.

The fears of the Church first found expression in the Fourth Lateran Council called by Pope Innocent III in 1215. Three general items were on the agenda: a redefinition of dogma; the threat of the Albigensian heresy; and the danger of unconverted Jews. It was at the Fourth Lateran Council that laws against Jews were shaped with the purpose of isolating them further from the Christian community. It was decided that Jews must wear a badge on their clothing to identify them as Jews.

Thus began a new era for the Jews. Hostilities against them intensified. The first burning of the Talmud took place, and ritual-murder charges cropped up. The Church had not intended matters to go this far. It issued bull after bull against these false accusations, with little effect. The tide could not be turned. The new Christian middle class wanted the Jews dispossessed.

The case in England is illustrative of this trend, because it was here that the first ritual-murder accusations were made, and it was here that the first expulsion of the Jews took place. Jews arrived in England in 1066 at the invitation of William the Conqueror, who depended on Jewish capital to forge a strong English state. As in France, Italy, and Germany, Jews in England rose to positions of wealth and influence. King William Rufus, successor to William, even forbade Jews to convert to Christianity because that would "rid him of a valuable property and give him only a subject." By 1200, English and Italian moneylenders began to supplant the Jewish moneylenders. By 1290, the kingdom felt it could get along without the Jews and expelled them.

The juggernaut of economics and history had been set in motion. The expulsion from England not only foreshadowed the expulsions of the Jews from other countries, but also foreshadowed the momentous clash between social and religious forces in Christendom. By the fourteenth century the Jews had been expelled from France. During the fifteenth century they were banished from various German states. At the end of that century came their expulsion from Spain and their flight from Portugal. By banishing the Jews, these states hoped to avert the brewing revolt on the comforting theory that the Jews, not the economic and social ills, were the troublemakers. But this remedy was like taking aspirin for a headache caused by a tumor. When Martin Luther nailed his ninety-five theses to the door of the church in Wittenberg (1517), the long-heralded challenge to the supremacy of the Catholic Church had been nailed to the body of the Church as unalterably as the body of Jesus had been nailed to the Cross by the Romans.

There was no room now for Renaissance and Jews. Both were luxuries and both had to go. In 1516 Venice introduced the first ghetto for the complete isolation of the Jews. In 1550 the Jews were expelled from Genoa. By 1569 they had been expelled from most of the Papal States. By the middle of the sixteenth century, Western Europe, which for one thousand years had been the center of European Jewry, had practically no Jewish population left. The Jews had not been murdered or exterminated. They had been banished. Where did they go?

They went east, to Germany, Poland, Austria, Lithuania, where dukes and kings invited them to settle for precisely the same reason they had been invited to come west in the sixth and seventh centuries. For instance, Casimir the Great, the Charlemagne of Poland (1333–1370), invited Jews to settle in Poland, giving them permission to rent land and villages—provided they brought commerce and industry to the country, helped settle her cities, and strengthened the economy. By 1500 the Jewish center of gravity had completely shifted to Eastern Europe.

The Reformation was to have a profound effect on Jewish history, as it changed not only the social but the economic fabric of Jewish society. We must therefore examine the nature of the Reformation to understand its impact on Jewish events.

The Reformation did not spring full-blown out of German soil like Pallas Athene from the forehead of Zeus. Its coming had been heralded for close to a century. The burning of Huss in 1415 and Savonarola in 1498 subdued for a while the spirit of revolt but did not extinguish it. The Christians had no Talmudic alchemists who could synthesize faith and reason into a politically harmless but socially useful mixture. In the sixteenth century the continent exploded into a series of religious revolts, led by Luther in Germany, Zwingli in Switzerland, Calvin in France, Knox in Scotland.

On every front the Catholic Church tried to stem the sweep of Protestantism, but to little avail. All of Scandinavia, England, Scotland, northern Germany, Holland were lost. The revolt spread to France. There is no massacre of Jews in all the medieval centuries to equal the bloodbath of St. Bartholomew's Day (August 24, 1572), when the Catholics within twelve hours slew 30,000 Huguenots in their beds. Nor did many, if any, Jewish communities ever experience the utter cruelty which took place when cities like Magdeburg were infested during the Thirty Years' War by the dragoons of Pappenheim, Tilly, and Wallenstein. Now it was the turn of Catholics and Protestants to experience some of the misfortunes of the Jews as countries professing one faith expelled or murdered fellow Christians of the other faith. This is not mentioned to make light of Jewish deaths during the century of religious wars which convulsed Europe, but to set the stage for a later distinction to be made between what constitutes impersonal history and what constitutes specifically anti-Jewish acts.

As the battle between Catholics and Protestants seesawed back and forth, the Jews assumed a great importance to both sides. Their learning, idealism, and ethical conduct were esteemed by millions of Christians who did not believe all the slurs against the Jews. Both Catholics and Protestants felt it would be a persuasive argument for millions of waverers between Catholicism and Protestantism if the Jews would join their side.

It was with superb confidence that Luther asked the Jews to join him and the Lutherans. In an article entitled, "That Jesus Was Born a Jew," dated 1523, Luther wrote:

> For they [the Catholics] have dealt with the Jews as if they were dogs and not human beings. They have done nothing for them but curse them and seize their wealth. I would advise and beg everybody to deal kindly with the Jews and to instruct them in Scriptures: in such a case we could expect them to come over to us. . . . We must receive them kindly and allow them to compete with us in earning a livelihood . . . and if some remain obstinate, what of it? Not everyone is a good Christian.

The refusal of the Jews to accept his sincere offer came to him as an unexpected and cruel blow, and he turned bitterly against them. In fairness to Luther, it must be said that by this time he was a sick man, disillusioned by many setbacks and betrayed by many friends. He turned not only against the Jews, but also against the German peasants who were using Protestantism to free themselves from serfdom. Nobody was listening to him any longer, except the devoutly religious. The others were using his Protestantism for their own economic and political ends.

The Thirty Years' War (1618–1648), as the great show-down between Catholicism and Protestantism is called, changed not only the religious complexion of Europe but its political and economic contours as well. The northern half of Europe became in the main Protestant and indus-trial. The southern half remained in the main Catholic and agricultural. The western states in the northern section be-came capitalistic. The eastern states in that sector became a mixture of feudalism, mercantilism, and capitalism. Wherever Protestantism won decisively, feudalism began to perish. In the wake of the Reformation, a new social class arose, which in turn shaped the modern industrial so-ciety.

## DYNAMICS OF REVOLUTION

We must understand the social forces that seized the Re-formation in order to understand the phenomena that re-shaped Jewish history. The answer lies in the peculiar relationship which existed between Church and feudal state. The Church and the feudal state had grown up to-gether, the Church protecting the feudal institutions and the feudal institutions protecting the Church. The tensions between Pope and emperor were not over the institutions of Church and feudal state, but merely a question of who should have how much power over whom. Neither institu-tion ever thought of doing away with the other. Popes and emperors removed each other with happy abandon, but the institutions themselves continued.

The solid edifice of Catholic Church and feudal state re-ceived its first jolts from the Crusades and the Renais-sance. The Crusades, as we have seen, freed the body of the serf from the manor and lord; the Renaissance freed the mind of man from dogma and scholasticism. The freed serfs settled in towns and changed their occupations from tillers of the soil to producers and sellers of goods. They sold these goods for money in free markets at a profit. This had been the function of the Jews previously. This shift in Christian occupation marked the end of feudalism and the beginning of capitalism. All qualities which helped in this exchange of goods for money at a profit became good qualities, everything that impeded this exchange became bad qualities. The marketplace, not the Church, now determined morality.

These new men of trade needed a supply of labor to help them create more goods, they needed more free markets, and they needed greater freedom from the restrictions of feudal laws. But these new needs conflicted with the wishes of the feudal nobles, who wanted to preserve the old order in which they were lord and master. They were not wicked men, merely prudent men who wished to preserve the feudal system which benefited them, in the same way that we wish to protect the economic system from new experiments which might take the benefits we enjoy away from us.

As trade continued to expand, as greater wealth was concentrated in the hands of the new middle class, that class became more powerful. Soon it dared to challenge the feudal princes openly, and as the Church supported the feudal state, the Church also became involved in the struggle for power. Therefore, alongside the social struggle, a religious struggle was also taking place.

No doubt the Church needed reform, as evidenced by the Counter Reformation instituted by the Catholic Church to clean out its own former abuses. But it came too late. Though Protestantism had begun as a strictly religious reform movement, the people behind the new economic forces seized the Reformation and bent it to their own economic needs. The new religion, Protestantism, slowly began to permit what the old religion, Catholicism, had forbidden. Imperceptibly, from 1521 and the Diet at Worms, where Luther had laid down his challenge to the Pope, to 1648 and the Treaty of Westphalia, where Catholicism and Protestantism had drawn a west-east truce line through the center of Europe, a religious protest had turned into a social revolution. As the modes of production in Europe changed, the people responsible for these changes searched for a state that would legalize what they were doing and for a religion that would sanctify it. They adopted the Protestant religion and made it embrace the capitalist state. The two went hand in hand like bride and groom.

If we now examine the chronological sequence of

events from the beginning of the Crusades to the end of the Reformation, an interesting timetable emerges in which the destiny of the Jews is correlated to the social upheavals of the gentile world. The Jews were expelled in 1290 by a Catholic feudal England and readmitted in 1655 by a Protestant and mercantile England. They were expelled from a Catholic and feudal France between 1400 and 1500, and readmitted in the seventeenth century by a reformed Catholic and mercantile France. They were expelled from various Catholic and feudal German states in the fourteenth, fifteenth, and sixteenth centuries, and readmitted in the sixteenth and seventeenth centuries by various other German states, mostly Protestant and mercantile. The Jews who were expelled from Spain and from several Italian states in the fifteenth and sixteenth centuries were not readmitted until modern times. In other words, the Western, Catholic, feudal countries did not want the Jews for religious reasons, and, having no economic need of them, did not readmit them, whereas the Protestant countries, having an economic need of the merchant Jews, did readmit them.

The East European states, though still Catholic, readmitted the Jews wherever they had banished them, because their economies had not, at that time, developed a middle class which could take over the functions of the Jews. Many East European feudal princes, however, having seen from events in Western Europe that such a class was a threat to their own existence, did not want a Christian burgher class. They "imported Jews" to act as a middle class. The Christian serfs were locked up in the prison of feudal institutions, the Jews were locked up in their ghettos, and the lords could go hunting without having their states taken away from them during their absence. However, as the Jews served the nobles, they became identified as an exploiting class by the serfs, and when the wave of revolutions hit Eastern Europe, Christian nobles and Jewish merchants were slaughtered with equal hatred.

The crazy quilt of anti-Jewish laws passed between the sixteenth and eighteenth centuries begins to make sense. It was not until the sixteenth century that the laws one generally associates with the entire medieval period came into being—laws which not only were aimed at isolating the Jews more and more from the Christians, but were also designed to make them objects of scorn and derision, to deprive them of any symbol of dignity, and to make people forget their former learning. These new laws tended to make Jewish persecutions more and more abstract until the very reason for their origin became obscured, then forgotten, until only a dehumanized symbol of a denigrated Jew remained. First he was given the yellow badge. Then he was isolated in the ghetto. He could not own land. He was forced to wear special clothing. He had to step aside when a Christian passed. He could not build synagogues. He could not strike up friendships with Christians. He could engage only in a restricted number of professions and trades.

New generations of Christians who did not know of the proud, learned Jew of other days, saw only a queerly dressed ghetto Jew, wearing a black caftan, a yellow patch of ignominy, a ridiculous peaked hat—an object of derision and scorn.

There is a faint, familiar echo to these laws. There is nothing original here. These are the very same laws we encountered in the Pact of Omar, which restricted the rights of Christians in Muslim lands. The Christians had turned around and applied the same laws against the Jews, but with one important difference. The laws in the Pact of Omar only restricted the legal rights of the Christians—they did not strip them of their human dignity.

This was the end of the line for the Jews. The Jewish medieval period began with the Jew as the "ambivalent man" in Western society. When his medieval period ended, he was the symbol of the "abhorrent man" in Western eyes.

But "the dark was light enough." If the Christians looked with derision upon the ridiculous ghetto Jews, the Jews looked with contempt upon those who jeered at them. As a group, they were still the most learned men in Europe, the only ethnic group having universal education. Into the ghetto they took with them their 3,500-year-old cultural heritage, their Talmud, the Old Testament which illuminated their bleak physical existence with intellectual and religious comfort.

But even as Western man called the Jews by the vilest of

names, he begged them to solve his economic problems. Even as he heaped calumny upon their heads, he invited them to sit at the tables of state. Even as he spat on the Jew, he was rejected by the Jew. With but one word, with but one gesture—conversion—the Jew could have become the most honored of citizens in Europe. The moment he was baptized, his "evil" became no evil, his "malevolence" became no malevolence, the "dirty dog" became no dirty dog. He became a good Christian. Though some Jews did take this "passport to European civilization," as Heinrich Heine termed baptism, most Jews did not. They transcended whatever ignominy was heaped upon them with the firm conviction that their values were superior to the values of their detractors.

Shakespeare, in his uncanny way, correctly sums up this whole Jewish-Christian complex in his play *The Merchant of Venice*. Though both Antonio and Bassanio call Shylock all sorts of evil names, Bassanio, nevertheless, invites Shylock to his house for dinner, and it is Shylock who refuses this friendly offer, saying:

*I will buy with you, sell with you, talk with you, walk with you, and so following; but I will not eat with you.*

After Shylock has been outwitted by Portia, what is the penalty imposed on him for having, in essence, wanted to take Antonio's life? One would think it would be the death penalty at least. Not at all. The Duke, acting as judge, decrees, at the suggestion of Antonio, that Shylock must become a Christian. Thus, by becoming a Christian, all Shylock's "bad" qualities would be transubstantiated into virtues, much as moneylending became virtuous after it was taken away from the Jews by the Christians. It will be recalled, however, that Shylock does not promise to convert, but proudly walks off the stage, still a Jew, unbowed, uncowed.

One more thing remains to be said about this era. If the Christians in their derision for the Jews blinded themselves to the magnificence of the Jewish achievement, the Jews in their contempt for their persecutors blinded themselves to the magnificence of the medieval achievement. Out of that age came van Eyck and Dürer, Ghiberti and Verrocchio,

Dante and Chaucer, Ockham and Copernicus, Leonardo da Vinci and Michelangelo. Under their genius, stone came to life, paint spoke with eloquence, and words etched ideas in men's minds. The Gothic cathedrals stretching their lofty spires to the sky were not testaments to any one faith, but tributes to the spirit of man and to God.

## N I N E T E E N

# CONCERTO FOR VIOLENCE

In no other phase of their history were the Jews subjected to such unremitting efforts to convert them to Christianity as in the Christian Middle Ages. In no other age had they been subjected to such unremitting persecution for rejecting conversion. The Babylonians, Assyrians, and Persians had only asked them to be nice tax-paying Jews. The Greeks and Romans had only asked them to throw a little incense at the feet of their gods as a mark of respect. No one cared whether the Jews converted to paganism or not. Jews had been slain, hanged, crucified, decimated, beheaded, tortured for all the reasons people have always been slain, hanged, crucified, decimated, beheaded, tortured—in anger, in justified indignation, in battle, for sheer pleasure, as an object lesson, as a punishment for rebellion, for not paying taxes—but never for not converting.

The Muslims may have looked down upon both Christians and Jews for their inability to perceive the superiority of Allah over Christ and Jehovah. But the Muslims never made it their mission in life to convert Christians and Jews to Islam. The Romans would have regarded the Christian effort as sheer lunacy. The Greeks would have been faintly amused. Other pagans would have been utterly bewildered. The Jews were all for leaving the Christians alone. The trouble was that the Christians would not leave the Jews alone.

The score for persecution in this medieval concerto for violence followed an almost predictable progression. There were three distinct movements: the first, a solemn religious adagio; the second, a frenzied economic allegro; and the third, a chilling psychological andante.

Of all three movements, the first, the religious adagio, is the most interesting, because it shows the variety of righteous excuses man can invent for taking another man's life. The medieval Church did not view the taking of a man's life as lightly as does the modern state. Even the ignorant laity hesitated to kill a Jew unless it had a good excuse for doing so. The murder of millions, according to formula, without moral scruples, is an innovation of the twentieth century.

The persecution of the Jews was rather desultory and of little historic consequence until the eleventh century, when the religious phase of Jewish persecutions began, with four main motifs standing out in the overall design. These were ritual-murder accusations, Host-desecration libels, burnings of the Talmud, and religious disputations.

The ritual-murder charge stemmed from the superstitious belief that upon each Passover the Jews slew a Christian male child and used his blood to spray over their Passover *matzos* (the unleavened bread Jews eat during this holiday). It was easy for such a notion to take hold in the medieval mind, because the Old Testament was not translated into the languages of the people until the sixteenth century. Until then, the people received all their Bible stories secondhand, as digested legends. It was in such secondhand fashion they heard the story of Exodus and learned how the Lord had smitten the male children of Egypt in order to force Pharaoh to let the Israelites go. Was it not logical that now the Jews were similarly smiting Christian children? The fact that human sacrifice was something the Jews had fought against since the days of Abraham, while the Druids in England and Germany still practiced it in the first century A.D., or the fact that Jews never eat the blood of animals, which is prohibited in the Old Testament, while Christians did, and still do, even to this day, never crossed the medieval Christian mind.

In 1144, a boy disappeared in the township of Norwich, England, and an apostate Jew swore that the Jews had killed him in observance of a "Passover blood ritual." Hysteria swept England, but before any overt acts against the Jews broke out, the dead body of the boy was found, without any evidence of murder. For some reason, unfathomable to the modern mind, the boy was sainted and enshrined in his hometown church.

A hundred years later, the Norwich incident was revived when a rumor cropped up that the Jews had kidnapped another boy, crucified him, and used his blood to color their Passover cakes. The king, fearing bloodshed, declared all Jews under arrest, and to calm the population, charged twenty Jews with the crime. Their guilt was established to everyone's satisfaction, except the Jews', when under proper torture all twenty signed prepared confessions, and all were executed. Later, when the boy's body was found, with all the blood still in it, and no sign of a crucifixion, it could plainly be seen that a miracle had taken place. He too was sainted and enshrined.

The pattern had been set, and in the ensuing two centuries ritual-murder accusations against the Jews reached epidemic proportions throughout the continent. The popes became alarmed at the spread of these false ritual-murder charges and in numerous papal bulls forbade them, stating such accusations were a mockery of Christ. Emperor Frederick II, whose enlightened rule illuminated his century, joined the popes and punished with death those who spread such rumors. By the fifteenth century, ritual-murder accusations had died out, although they were briefly revived in seventeenth-century Poland and late czarist Russia.

Closely resembling these ritual-murder charges were the Host-desecration libels, which were given birth to in the twelfth century with the enunciation of the Doctrine of Transubstantiation. This doctrine holds that in the drinking of the wine and in the eating of the wafer, or Host, the wine becomes the blood and the wafer the body of Christ. The rumor now became widespread that the Jews reenacted the crucifixion of Jesus by stealing the wafer and piercing it with a sharp instrument to make it bleed. Two remedies against such desecrations developed, in addition to general pillaging. The first was to burn a synagogue and erect a church upon the site. A church so situated often became a miracle-producing center. The second was to remit all debts to Jews. This remedy was a popular one.

The stealing-of-the-Host hysteria reached its height in

fourteenth-century Germany. Here a fanatic named Rindfleisch whipped the populace into a frenzy with an account
of how he had seen Jews crush the wafer in a mortar, after
which he led the howling mobs through Jewish quarters on
a murder spree. German authorities, alarmed at the growing power of Rindfleisch, figuring that a hanging in time
would save nine, hanged him unceremoniously. By the end
of the century, Host-stealing accusations also died out. The
Jews had begun to flee Germany, and the rulers, seeing the
economies of their duchies stagnate, quickly stopped the
Host-desecration canard by hanging those who spread
such false accusations. The Jews were invited to return,
with assurances that such charges would never again be
brought against them.

The first burnings of the Talmud took place in 1244 in
Paris and Rome. It was burned four more times in
fourteenth-century France, and then there were no more
burnings for two hundred years. The two best years for Talmud burning were 1553 and 1554, when it went to the stake
twelve times in various Italian cities. It was burned twice
more, in Rome in 1558 and 1559, and then the fashion
ended. In Eastern Europe, the Talmud was burned but
once, in 1757.

The interesting aspect about Talmud burning is not that
the Talmud was sent to the stake, for in the Middle Ages
translations of the New Testament in languages other than
Latin were consigned to the flames more frequently than
the Talmud. The interesting aspect is that the Old Testament in Hebrew was never sent to the stake. Though Torah
scrolls often were trampled underfoot by screaming mobs
looting synagogues, or burned with the synagogue itself,
such acts were never sanctioned by the Church, and the
Torah was never officially condemned. Though Judaism
was reviled as a blasphemy, though Jews were killed for
being unbelievers, the Torah itself was looked upon with
respect, for it was the Law of God. As one Pope expressed
it, "We praise and honor the Law, for it was given to your
fathers by Almighty God through Moses. But we condemn
your religion and your false interpretation of the Law."

It is of interest to note here that these anti-Jewish ritual-
murder accusations, Host-desecration libels, and Talmud
burnings all were first conceived by converted Jews. A dis-

section of their motivations for turning so bitterly against their former brothers would make an interesting psychological study. Perhaps such a study would give us a clue why the New Testament writers, some of them converted Jews, inveighed so bitterly against those Jews who were not baptized with them.

The "religious disputation" was also the innovation of apostate Jews. Many of these converted Jews were well versed in the Talmud and, to show off their learning to their new Christian brothers or, perhaps, to curry favor with the Church, they whispered in the ears of the powerful that if, in a public disputation, it were shown how wrong the Jews were, then the entire Jewish community might convert.

These religious disputations, called "tournaments of God and faith," were a combination of intellectual chess and Russian roulette. If the Jewish scholars could not disprove the charges of the Christian scholars arrayed against them, then an entire Jewish community stood the threat of a forced march to the baptismal font. If, on the other hand, they mocked the Christian scholars with superior Jewish scholarship, they ran the danger of being put to death. It took gamesmanship of the finest order to walk the thin line of a ploy which ceded victory to the other side without yielding on the main points. Only those with strong nerves survived, and the judges, which might include a pope or an emperor, were often left agape at the Jewish display of scholarship, audacity, and deftness. The Jews usually won by not checkmating their opponents but by stalemating them. The trick was to drive the opponent into a corner where, if he claimed victory, he would have to deny the authority of the Old Testament, which would have been heresy. Luther, who was familiar with such disputations, borrowed this technique in his disputation with the Catholic, Johann Maier von Eck. When Eck, after having cited a fourth-century saint as his authority, asked Luther whom he claimed as his, Luther triumphantly shouted, "Saint Paul." Who dares to trump Saint Paul?

It was one of these disputations which led to the first burning of the Talmud. Arraigned against four rabbis was a converted Jew named Nicholas Donin and his panel of experts. Present were the queen mother and the archbishops of France. Though the judges declared the rabbis had lost and ordered the Talmud burned as a work of Satan, the queen mother and the archbishops realized the cards had been stacked and tried to set the verdict aside. But Donin appealed to the king of France. It took four years of wrangling before the original decision was upheld in 1244, out of political considerations, and the Talmud was finally burned.

The most famed of these gamesmanship disputations took place in 1263, before King James I of Aragon, when the scholar Moses ben Nachman was challenged to a verbal duel by an apostate named Fra Paulo Christiani on the subject of the arrival of the messiah. Nachman introduced a little wit into this disputation with such grace that the king, though adjudging him loser for his own safety, gave him a handsome gift of money and the compliment that "never before had he heard such an unjust cause so nobly defended."

The Jews of the Middle Ages probably had the distinction of being the first captive audience in the world. A fifteenth-century pope conceived the idea of mass conversionist sermons. The Jews were herded into cathedrals, where bishops and archbishops, and sometimes even the Pope himself, would sermonize them on the evils of Judaism and the beauties of Christianity. Vigilance was the word for survival, as falling asleep would be a discourtesy for which death alone could atone. The Jews attended these sermons with trepidation, applauded with enthusiasm, and forgot with modesty. These compulsory conversion sermons lasted until late in the eighteenth century, not because of any practical results, but, may it be suggested, because no speaker could resist being flattered by such attentive audiences.

Even the Black Death, or bubonic plague (1348–1349), which carried off a third of Europe's population, was put into the service of killing Jews. Before the Black Death swept Europe, it had hit Mongolia and the Islamic Empire. Mongols, Muslims, and Jews had all died together without anyone having thought of blaming the Jews. But to medieval man it did occur. In an age when the concept of the germ was sheer lunacy, he could think of no other explanation for the plague except that it was an artificially induced malady and that the Jews had poisoned his wells, a scientific explanation which appealed especially to the German mind. Even as the good Germans were dying of the plague, they dragged Jews, also dying of the plague, to the stake. In September 1348, Pope Clement VI denounced the allegations against the Jews, saying that "... the Jews have provided the cause ... for such crimes is without plausibility."

Though the centuries between 1200 and 1600 were four agonizing centuries for the Jews, they were equally agonizing centuries for the Christians. Because the charges against the Jews bore such labels as "ritual murder" and "Host desecration," instead of "witchcraft" and "heresy," this should in no way mislead us. The same psychology, the same thinking, the same type of trial, the same type of evidence, the same type of torture went into both. Even as Jews accused of ritual murder were hauled to the stake, Christians accused of witchcraft were burned in adjacent marketplaces. The screams of Jews and Christians as they were burned alive went up together to our Father in Heaven, who must have wondered what on earth was going on.

There was, however, one rank discrimination against which Jews thus far have registered no formal protest. Whereas the executed Christians received grand send-offs, accompanied by magnificently sung cantatas, Kyries, Alleluias, Introits, and Jubilates, the Jews received fourth-class funerals, accompanied by lamentations sung off-key.

The second movement in this medieval concerto for violence, the economic allegro, began before the first movement was over. As the Reformation slowly changed from a religious revolt to an economic revolution, the nature of anti-Jewish violence shed more and more of its religious coloration and took on more and more of an economic overtone. By the sixteenth century, coincidentally with the Reformation, and as a result of the successive Jewish banishments from the West, Jewish life had shifted preponderantly to the East. Because the history of Jewish persecution in Eastern Europe between 1000 and 1800 is more or less a recapitulation of the history of Jewish persecution in Western Europe between 600 and 1600, we need only briefly review Jewish events in three East European countries, Poland, Russia, and Prussia, to show the remarkable parallelism.

German Jews, fleeing to escape the marauding Crusaders in the Rhineland, settled in Poland as early as 1100. Here they prospered. More and more, the Jews fled Germany and Austria for Poland, and the Polish nobility welcomed them with open arms. King Boleslav V, the Chaste, granted the Jews liberal charters of self-government (1264). And why not? The Jews were helping him to build cities and to found industry and commerce, enabling him to compete economically with the West. Like the nobles, the Jews owned land and large estates. They lived in city and village. Casimir III, the Great, the Charlemagne of Poland, founded universities, encouraged trade, and imported even more Jews to accelerate the hum of commerce and industry. Vitovt, Grand Duke of Lithuania, opened that country for Jewish settlement.

By 1400 the evils which had befallen the Jews in the West hit the East. A ritual-murder charge against the Jews was whipped by the clergy into hysteria that swept all Poland. Casimir IV tried to reassure the uneasy Jews, but the Roman Catholic clergy, alarmed at the heretical trends sweeping the West, linked the Jews to the new heresies. Host-desecration charges were leveled against both Jews and Protestants. The first pogroms, that is, organized attacks against Jews, broke out in Poland around 1500.

Stronger kings, not intimidated by the clergy, restored temporarily the former order. Sigismund I and II were both outraged at the Host-desecration infamies. Sigismund II denounced them as a fraud, saying, "I am shocked at this hideous villainy, nor am I sufficiently devoid of common sense as to believe there could be any blood in the Host."

Poland held the scepter of greatness in her hands in the fifteenth century, but a succession of weak kings and strong nobles lost it for her in the sixteenth century. The situation was complex, confused, and explosive. Weak governments were dominated by powerful nobles and a fanatic clergy. German tradesmen trying to corner the Polish market fostered anti-Jewish sentiment in order to drive the Jews out. The peasants, oppressed by the nobles, cheated by the Germans, squeezed for taxes by the Jews who served the Polish nobility as tax collectors, and kept in a feudal prison by

the priests, lavished their hate on all four and waited for
*der Tag* ("the day"), when revenge would be theirs. It came
in 1648.

Greek Orthodox Cossacks, living on the border lands
between medieval Poland and Turkey, rebelled against the
hated Roman Catholic Poles. They were led by a shrewd,
cruel chieftain named Bogdan Chmielnicki, whose small
son had been flayed alive by a Polish noble. Against Bogdan's ill-clad, smelly, sharp-sabered roughriders of the
steppes, the colorful, perfume-scented cavalry of the Polish
nobility had no more chance than did the Polish cavalry
against Hitler's tanks in 1939. They were mowed down like
the infantrymen in the fields of Flanders during World
War I. The Polish serfs, seeing their chance for revenge,
joined the Cossacks.

The Cossack savagery knew no bounds. The enemies
were the Polish nobility, the Roman Catholic priests, the
German traders, and the Jews. Why the Jews? Why not?
They lived in Poland and they were not Greek Orthodox.
The Cossacks sawed their prisoners into pieces, or flayed
them alive, or roasted them into brown crisps over slow
fires. They slit infants in two with their swords, ripped open
the bellies of nuns, noblewomen, and Jewesses; into them
they sewed live cats. They had two favorite formulas for
hanging. The first was a quartet consisting of one Polish nobleman, one German merchant, one Roman Catholic
priest, and one Jew. The second was a trio consisting of a
Jew, a priest, and a dog. If a dog was not available, a hog
was used, which could later be hauled down and eaten
after a good day's work of sawing people into pieces.

The Jews fled the fiends from the steppes to seek sanctuary in the cities, but there too massacre overtook them.
The wily Cossacks promised the Poles in the cities that
their lives would be spared provided they turned the Jews
over to them. This the Poles did. Then, weakened by the
loss of the Jewish defenders, the Poles were easy prey for
the Cossacks, who slaughtered them with glee. Perhaps as
many as 100,000 Jews perished in the decade of this revolution. It is difficult to estimate how many hundreds of
thousands, if not over a million, Poles were killed, equally
cruelly. The fields of Poland resembled a carnage house,
with the limbs of the massacred and tortured strewn over

the countryside. After ten years, when the Cossacks were exhausted, a measure of peace crept into the land.

But poor Poland was to know no surcease from her afflictions. The second half of the seventeenth century saw another Cossack uprising, bloodier than the first, two invasions by Sweden, and a disastrous war with Turkey. The eighteenth century brought no relief. Poland was invaded by Russia, then had a civil war. An unholy alliance—Russia, Prussia, and Austria—partitioned Poland three times until no Poland was left. The Jews in Poland had come into the orbit of Russian, German, and Austrian history.

The early history of the Jews in Russia is a unique tragicomedy. The harder Russia tried to get rid of her Jews, the faster she acquired them. Finally she gave up, drew a *cordon sanitaire* along her western border, saying "up to here but no further," and sat back to wait for the consequences. They were long in coming.

Russia, as we know it today, did not come into being until 1700, with Peter the Great. In its earlier centuries, Russia was a mammoth crazy quilt of dukedoms, with Tatars and Cossacks all over the place. Jews settled in the various dukedoms and cities along the western periphery and lived there in peace until 1500, when a fantastic episode set the church bells in Moscow ringing with alarm.

Two Lithuanian Jews had converted two Greek Orthodox priests to Judaism. These two converted priests took their new religion seriously and, in the fashion of St. Paul, went out and proselytized among the Russians in the hinterland. The totally unexpected happened. The Russians liked Judaism and converted in droves. This new Russian Judaism became so popular in Moscow's court circles that even the daughter-in-law of the Duke of Moscow became a Jewess. The frightened Russian Orthodox Church decided to stamp out this Jewish heresy as ruthlessly as the Roman Catholic Church had stamped out the Albigensian heresy in France. First, all Russian apostates were dealt with, for dead converts cannot proselytize. Then came the turn of the Jews. The Russians, familiar with the mass conversion technique of King Eric IX of Sweden, first tried that. But after three hundred Jews had been drowned in the Polotsk and Vitebsk rivers without a miracle taking place, the impatient Russians gave up and banished all Jews from Russian territory, with orders not to come back.

The Jews did not come back. They were hauled back. It was Russia's luck to acquire new Jews faster than she could banish her old ones. In 1655, just when the Russian Church believed that she finally had rid herself of all Jews, Russia acquired more Jews with the annexation of parts of Lithuanian territory wrested from Poland. The work began all over again. Then, when most of the Jewish newcomers had been banished, Peter the Great inherited (by the Treaty of Nystadt, 1721) a new multitude of Jews residing in the former Swedish territory along the Baltic coast which now became part of Russia. Though Peter was as fearful of the Jews as his ancestors had been, he protected their rights and liberties. In 1762, Catherine the Great, by a stroke of the pen, as the saying goes, made all Russia off-limits to the Jews. Ten years later she had more Jews in Russia than there were in all of Europe. The three successive partitions of Poland (1772, 1793, 1795) placed 900,000 Jews in her lap.

Catherine and her successors gave up the struggle. They also realized that the Jews were essential to the economies of the newly conquered territories. But the mind of the *muzhik*, the Russian peasant, had to be kept docile and ignorant. Though the Jews could roam throughout Poland, Lithuania, and the Ukraine, in Holy Mother Russia itself, where dwelt the *muzhiks*—95 percent of the population—they could not. Catherine and her successors succeeded in keeping the minds of their *muzhiks* untrammeled. When, in 1917, after the Russian Revolution, *muzhiks*, arriving in Moscow, beheld their first streetcar, they fell to their knees and crossed themselves with a loud *Gospodi pomilooy*, for they had beheld either the devil or a Jew.

The territory along Russia's western border, where the Jews were permitted to settle, was known as the *Pale of Settlement*, or simply the *Pale*. Here the Jews established their own self-government. In the century between 1700 and 1800, Russian intellectual life was dormant, and so was Russian Jewish life. With but few exceptions, such as the great Talmudist known as the Vilna Gaon and a few lesser Talmudic scholars, the Jews in this century vegetated. The era of Russian pogroms, the age of the intellectual flowering of both the Russians and the Russian Jews, was an eruption of the nineteenth century.

Quite different was the Jewish experience in Germany. Many historians feel there is enough evidence to show that by the second century A.D. Jewish-Roman soldiers were stationed along the northern frontier of the Roman Empire as border guards against the German barbarians. Roman emperors generally regarded the Germans as subhuman, therefore not worthy of being conquered.

It could well be that the Jews were the first civilized settlers of Germany. We know Jews were in Mainz, Cologne, and other German cities in the Rhineland in Roman days. It is generally assumed that in the eighth century Jews resided in such cities as Magdeburg, Worms, and Augsburg, but documentary evidence of flourishing Jewish communities in most large German cities dates from about the tenth century. As in the rest of Europe, we hear very little of any persecution of Jews until the Crusades. The peculiar composition of the Holy Roman Empire saved the Jews from total expulsion when that fashion started in Germany with the thirteenth century. The Holy Roman Empire (the name coined by its Emperor Frederick I, 1152–1190, known as Barbarossa, or "Red Beard") was a colorful tartan of federated states with autonomous powers. If one duchy banished the Jews, another welcomed them.

The Germans, perhaps because they were still closest to the barbaric strain which had nursed them, were the most barbaric in their persecutions. Most of the anti-Jewish measures one popularly attributes to the entire Middle Ages were of German-Austrian origin, and grew only on German soil. Here the ritual-murder charges, the Host-desecration libels, the Black Death accusations were used to whip the population into a frenzy by sadists and fetishists. One such group of fetishists was known as *Armleder* (arm-leather), because of the strips of leather its members wore around their arms. The manner in which they committed their murders betrayed their own psychopathic state rather than hatred for Jews.

It was here in Germany that the cheating of Jews reached its noblest and purest forms. Local German princes enticed Jews to their realms with sacred promises to protect them and solemnly gave them liberal charters, swearing on the cross they meant it all, only to rob them later of their wealth, confiscate their land, and then sell them protection, gangster style. One can but marvel that in spite of it all, the Jewish spirit survived, and Jewish cultural life continued. Talmudic learning still exerted its power, something realized by Jean Jacques Rousseau, who in 1762 wrote in his *The Social Contract:*

> Through it alone [the Talmud and its ritualistic legislation] that extraordinary nation so often subjugated, so often dispersed and outwardly destroyed, but always idolatrous of its Law, has preserved itself unto our days. . . . Its mores and rituals persist and will persist to the end of the world. . . .

An unusual disputation, which had repercussions in the Reformation, took place in sixteenth-century Germany when Johann Reuchlin defended the Talmud against an apostate Jew with the name of Johann Joseph Pfefferkorn. Herr Pfefferkorn had been a butcher who, when caught stealing, decided to be baptized to escape punishment by the Jewish court. To the Jews he was an ignoramus, but to the ignorant German populace he was a scholar. When Herr Pfefferkorn said the Talmud blasphemed against Christianity, he was given the job of purifying Jewish literature of anti-Christian elements. The Jews appealed to the emperor, who appointed Johann Reuchlin to examine the case.

The battle lines were drawn between the intellectuals and the anti-intellectuals, without regard to religion. Siding with Pfefferkorn were such secular institutions as the universities of Paris and Mainz. Siding with Reuchlin were theological seminaries like that of the University of Vienna, a number of cardinals and archbishops, and even the Elector of Saxony. Martin Luther too was drawn into the disputation on the side of Reuchlin, and the controversy broadened to become a plank in the Reformation platform. Though the entire matter was finally decided against Reuchlin, for practical considerations, it resulted in a disastrous defeat for Pfefferkorn. The ban against the study of the Talmud was lifted, and Jewish literature was allowed to flourish without Pfefferkornian help.

With the defeat of the Pfefferkorn forces, the current of

the German temper also ran against the sadists. The last of them was a baker named Vincent Fettmilch (Fatmilk), who organized a mob which he led against the Jewish quarter in Frankfurt. As Fettmilch's cohorts outnumbered the Jews, they bravely killed women and children. Two years later, Fettmilch and the leaders of his gang were arrested, by order of the emperor, and their heads were chopped off in the marketplace of Frankfurt. The era of setting oneself above the law in Germany was temporarily over.

The last movement in the concerto, the psychological andante, began with the seventeenth century. By this time history had taken the Jews back to Western Europe. This "return to the West" began with Jews settling in the Netherlands (1593), after the Dutch had overthrown the tyrannical rule of the Spaniards, in England (1655) at the invitation of Oliver Cromwell, and in France (1648) by default, when she acquired the province of Alsace by the Treaty of Westphalia which ended the Thirty Years' War.

Even though the origins of psychological anti-Semitic sentiments are embedded in the Jewish Middle Ages, its full effects were not felt until the modern period. As a new class emerged in Europe with the Industrial Revolution, personal anti-Jewish hostility, motivated by economic considerations, slowly changed into anti-Semitic race prejudice, motivated by deep-seated, psychological anxieties. Of all three movements, the psychological andante—anti-Semitism—was the most deadly, not for the Jews but for civilization itself.

TWENTY

# The Yellow Badge of Courage

The Middle Ages produced two Judaisms, each having a distinct way of life, literature, and philosophy, but the same Jehovah. One way of life was dominant from 600 to 1500 A.D. The other gained ascendancy in the sixteenth century. The first was *Sephardic*, or Spanish Judaism; the second was *Ashkenazic*, or German Judaism.

Of the two, Sephardic Judaism was the older and more sophisticated. It was a blend of Torah and Talmud, Aristotle and Averroës,* metaphysics and science, ecclesiastical and secular literature. It was a way of life distilled through Babylonian, Persian, Grecian, Roman, and Islamic civilizations. From 900 to 1500 A.D. it was the Sephardic Jews who set the pattern for Jewish culture in dress, manners, morals, and scholarship.

The Ashkenazic framework of Jewish life emerged in discernible outline with the dawn of the sixteenth century. History had pressured the Jews from Western to Eastern Europe, and the changing conditions of life hammered out a new Jewish cultural design. The Sephardic world had been an unhurried one. The Jews had had the time to write elegiac poetry and to explore the secrets of mind and matter. In the new Ashkenazic world, there was no time for poetry, no need for science. Religion had to be put into the service of preserving life. True, Talmudism regressed to its archaic forms and became preoccupied with the minutiae of everyday life, but it preserved the Jews. The Sephardics had expanded their horizons in the Spanish, French, and Italian languages. The Ashkenazis manned their shrinking frontiers with Hebrew, Torah, and Talmud to fortify themselves against the blandishments of the baptizers.

By the sixteenth century the Sephardic way of life was engulfed by the dominant Ashkenazic culture. Thus the history of Sephardic Judaism is essentially the history of the Jews in Western Europe until the expulsion from Spain, and the history of Ashkenazic Judaism is essentially the history of the Jews east of the Rhine from the fifteenth century onward. Let us examine more closely these two medieval Jewish cultural patterns.

We have already compared Christian feudal life to a vast prison. The bars were the all-encompassing restrictions placed upon the daily life of the people. Inside the bars were the peasants, the so-called Third Estate, who comprised about 95 percent of the total population. Outside the bars but tied to them by invisible chains were the

---

*Averroës was the outstanding scholar of the Islamic world, never studied by the medieval Christians because the Church placed his works under the ban.

other two estates, the priests and the nobles. Neither inside the prison nor tied to the bars outside it were the Jews, the unofficial "Fourth Estate."

The restrictions placed on the feudal serfs, as the peasants were called, pursued them from "womb to tomb." There could be no movement from one estate to another except through the ranks of the clergy, and then only for the exceptionally gifted child. Restrictions on travel kept the serf tied to the soil. He usually saw nothing of the world except that within walking distance. Though he technically was a free man, he could own no property. He could be sold with the land by his lord. Even freedmen, as late as 1500, could not sell their property without their lord's permission. The peasant had to grind his flour in the lord's granary, bake his bread in the lord's bakery—all for a fee, paid either in goods or in labor. He could own only wooden dishes, and one spoon was all he was allowed for his entire family, no matter what its size. The kind of cloth he could buy, sell, or wear was regulated. The lord was allowed to sample everything his serfs had, including their brides. In three aspects, however, the serf and noble were almost equals—they were usually equally ignorant, equally illiterate, and equally superstitious.

The nobles, too, were fettered with regulations. Society prescribed their roles with rigidity, and they had to act out these roles to the letter. They had to wear the right clothes, fight for the right causes, participate in the right games, render the right homage, marry the right girl. Life was one continuous ritual dance. Deviation from social restrictions meant loss of caste or ostracism. Deviation from religious regulations meant anathema or the stake.

None of these restrictions applied to the Jews. They were free to come and go, marry and divorce, sell and buy as they pleased. Whoever "designed" the feudal system had forgotten to provide for tradesmen, artisans, merchants, doctors, bankers. The priests were excluded from work, the nobles did not want to work, and the serfs were not allowed to enter the bourgeoisie or middle-class professions. There was no one left to do this work except the Jews, who therefore became indispensable. The Jews were the oil that lubricated the creaky machinery of the feudal state. This is why the Jews were granted charters of free-

dom by Pope, emperor, and prince. This is why they were
invited to settle in towns, villages, and provinces.

During these "tranquil centuries," Jewish life flowed in
an even tempo. There exists a popular misconception
about this entire era, that the Jews were stuck away in the
dark, dank, ghetto prisons for twelve hundred medieval
years. Actually the medieval Jewish ghetto experience was
a localized incident between 1500 and 1800, and prevalent
only in northern Italy, the German-speaking countries, and
a few Polish cities. The confusion stems from the indis-
criminate use of the word "ghetto," as opposed to "Jewish
quarter." There is a great difference between these two
ways of life. The Jewish quarter was voluntary and self-
imposed. The ghetto was involuntary and imposed from
without. One spelled freedom; the other brought imprisonment.

At first, the Jews lived dispersed among their Christian
neighbors, in towns and villages. As life became more urbanized, the Jews began to congregate in the larger cities
of Europe. Here they voluntarily settled in their own Jewish neighborhoods. They were proud of their districts and
before they would settle in a new city they demanded that
the king grant them such rights by special charter. Nor
were these Jewish quarters exclusively Jewish. On the contrary. Many nobles and rich burghers preferred to live in
the Jewish quarters in the same way that many Christians
today prefer to live in Jewish sections because they like the
air of intellectual ferment which they think Jews generate.
The Jewish homes squatted between cathedrals and
palaces. When the first Roman ghetto was instituted in
1555, on the left bank of the Tiber, the Pope did not create
anything new. The Jewish quarter already existed. His
problem was not getting the Jews into the Jewish quarter,
but getting the Christians out. They liked it there, and only
successive turns of the Inquisitional screw forced them out.
It took over a century before Rome's Jewish quarter became a hundred-percent Jewish ghetto.

Until 1500 most so-called *Judenstädte*—Jew Cities—in
Germany, Austria, and Bohemia had the same freedom as
the Jewish quarters in the West. Prague's *Judenstadt* was
especially famous. The average American thinks of the Puritan fathers as having invented the idea of the town hall,

with its bell summoning the free to exercise their inalienable right to vote. The Jews in Prague were a little ahead of them, for already in the fifteenth century they had their own town hall in their *Judenstadt*, including a large bell which summoned them to special town hall meetings to vote upon laws not covered by the *Responsa*.

What was everyday Jewish life like during the first half of its medieval history? Jewish Renaissance life can be brought into sharp enough focus to permit a closer look. Admittedly, all of it does not fit every country and century, but, granting variations, the motivating spirit and mode of life was the same.

The Italians recognized the Jews as a learned people and intuitively, without formal invitation, absorbed the Jews into the Renaissance. They learned philosophy and science from them, medicine and mathematics, but far surpassed the Jews in art and architecture.

The Jews participated in practically every profession, trade, and occupation existing in those centuries except farming. They were doctors, surgeons, scholars, poets, astronomers, druggists, finance ministers, royal ministers, silversmiths, goldsmiths, scientific-instrument designers. They were lion tamers, jugglers, mule sellers, soldiers, shoemakers, tailors, sailors, peddlers. They were fur-cloth-and-silk merchants, pawnbrokers, spice dealers, weavers, importers, and exporters, and they engaged in such manual occupations as blacksmiths, metal workers, day laborers. But the Jews also were in occupations which would have made the hair of a nice eighteenth-century Polish-ghetto Jew stand up in horror. These Renaissance Jews were playwrights and stage directors, actors, dancers, painters, and sculptors. Though the Jews did not produce any Corelli or Vivaldi, they nevertheless experimented in polyphonic music and composed sonatas and madrigals, canzonets and *balletti*. They wrote melodramas which for sheer corn rivaled the best America has ever produced.

Women, too, rose to new positions of prominence. They became doctors and bankers, went on the stage, and looked for careers in singing, dancing, and acting. Because of the great wealth concentrated in the hands of the Jews, they, like the contemporary nobles, became patrons of art and vied with prince and doge in buying the art of the

Cellinis and Verrocchios. They engaged famed architects to design their homes and synagogues, and those which survive show the unmistakable grandeur and beauty of the Renaissance touch of genius.

The problem of Jewish manners and morals during the Renaissance invites comparison with the Hellenistic period. Jewish youth in the Renaissance was subjected to the same pull between the lure of hedonism and the call of Talmudism as in the Hellenic period. Though orthodox Jews raised the same hue and cry against the "immoral Italians" as they had against the "immoral Hellenizers," their disapproval lacked the fervor and spontaneity of former days. A Jewish maiden's life no longer was one virginal romp from adolescence to the marriage bed. Cecil Roth, in *The Jews in the Renaissance*, quotes a rabbi, who, upon passing through Sicily in 1487, had wryly noted "most brides came under the marriage canopy when they were already pregnant." Jewish and Christian *maisons particulières* abounded, not only outside Jewish quarters but inside. Here Christian and Jewish youth could experience interfaith relations. As no Christian or Jewish Cellini, Casanova, or Don Juan has set down in his memoirs any qualitative differences in the professional attainments of these Renaissance *poules de trottoir*, it is to be presumed that at least on this level no serious schisms existed.

A well-bandied secret was the fact that many a prominent Jewish man had an adoring wife in the Jewish quarter and an appreciative mistress in town. Occasional homosexual scandals among well-known Jewish intellectuals and scholars helped pull an otherwise boring dinner party out of the doldrums. However, in one sphere the Jews did not contribute anywhere near their proportionate share, and that was in crimes of violence. Though occasionally a hotheaded Jewish youth stabbed a rival with a dagger in Renaissance fashion, sadistic acts, premeditated murders, forcible rapes, child molestation, were practically nonexistent among the Jews. The expulsion order of the Jews from Spain, for instance, contained no charge against them other than they were not Christians.

In spite of the satires and derogatory allusions to Jews in the literature of the times, the Jews in the main were not held in contempt by their contemporaries. When the Talmud was burned in Italy, a Christian wit quipped that now that the code of the Talmud had been declared blasphemous, the Jews were free to live by the code of the *Decameron*.

This way of life, culminating in Renaissance Italy, died with the expulsion of the Jews in thirteenth-century England, in fourteenth-century France, in fifteenth-century Spain, and in sixteenth-century Italy. When in the sixteenth century the Reformation rammed into the Renaissance, the Church had to prepare itself for the coming struggle with Lutheranism. The stakes were big, and the Jews were but incidental pawns in the game. The Jews, since they would not embrace Catholicism, had to be banished or locked up in ghettos. The age of good-fellowship was over. A century of religious wars was at hand.

A new way of Ashkenazic ghetto life was now being hammered out in Central Europe, with Germany as the vortex. It was here that most of the ignominies were heaped upon the helpless Jews. It was here, in three brief centuries, in this small land mass, that the new denigrated ghetto Jew was created.

The word "ghetto" originated in Italy, but its derivation is still not clear. Explanations are many—that it is a Latinization of the Hebrew word *get* ("divorce"), which is spelled *gueto* in Italian; that it comes from the Italian *borghetto*, meaning "little quarter"; and, the most commonly accepted, that it comes from the Italian word *gheta*, meaning "cannon foundry," because the first Jewish ghetto in Venice was adjacent to such a foundry.

The Jews had originally moved into their Jewish quarters, not to segregate themselves from the Christians, but out of necessity. As cities grew in size, they had to move closer and closer to their public institutions, the synagogue, the cemetery, the town hall, since Jewish life and death were bound up with them. When Pope and prince made the ghetto compulsory, the Jews were, for the first time, forcibly separated from the Christians.

The typical ghetto in Germany, Austria, and Bohemia consisted, as a rule, of one main street, with a synagogue at one end and a cemetery at the other. The size of the Jewish community generally averaged between one hundred and five hundred souls. A thousand inhabitants was the exception. The entire ghetto was walled, with but one gate which served as exit and entrance. Modern man tends to view this as another example of Jewish imprisonment, but in medieval days all cities were walled and the gates locked at night. Jews did not protest against this feature until 1700, when it disappeared from Christian life but was retained for the ghetto.

Ghetto life could easily have degenerated into slum life, but Talmudic laws and farsighted rabbis prevented it. Just as much slum property in African-American neighborhoods today is owned by wealthy white men, so most ghetto property in medieval days was owned by wealthy Christians. Had the Jews not stood up to them, rents in the crowded ghettos would have become millstones around their necks. The rabbis passed ordinances prohibiting Jews from outbidding each other for living quarters. No Jew was permitted to oust another Jew from his home, nor could a Christian landlord raise the rent by getting rid of one tenant for another one by selling his property to another Christian. Landlords soon learned that if they tried these tricks, the ousted Jews would simply move in with relatives, no other Jew would rent the property, and it would stay vacant to doomsday unless the landlord met the terms of the community. The Popes realized the reason for these Jewish laws and showed their understanding by sanctioning them. The Jews kept the ghettos clean and in constant repair.

Except in a few large cities in Poland, the ghetto did not exist in the non-German-speaking countries in Eastern Europe. Here most of the Jews lived in villages or small towns known as *shtetls*. Here there were no dead-end main streets, no walls, no gates to be locked. Jews could come and go as they pleased in pursuit of their trades, as long as they stayed out of Mother Russia itself.

The ghetto isolated the Jews; the *shtetl* drew gentile and Jew together. The *shtetl* could be either the main town in a province, or it could be the main street in a town, like the American main street. The Jews kept chickens, goats, sheep, cows, horses, as did their gentile neighbors, who also kept pigs. These pigs loved the kosher Jewish garbage, and it was a common sight to see a sow, educated in the ways of Jewish life, leading her piglets to the nearest kosher garbage can for the leftover of the Sabbath meal, *gefüllte fish, tzollnt, tzimes.* As the Christian peasants never had to worry that a little piglet would disappear in a Jewish cooking pot, it was an all-around agreeable arrangement. The Jews got rid of their garbage, the gentiles got a free meal for their pigs, and the pigs got a welcome change from the diet of their masters, cabbage soup, potatoes, and herring.

Israel Abrahams, in *Jewish Life in the Middle Ages,* lists sixty occupations of Jews in the Prague ghetto around 1600, but though the list still includes doctors, goldsmiths, printers, booksellers, writers, architects, musicians, and singers, the stress is more on tailors, shoemakers, tanners, furriers, butchers, wagonmakers, barbers, and the like. By 1700 the list had shrunk considerably, as legislation drove more and more Jews out of even the most humble of trades, until in 1800 peddling and petty shopkeeping became the two chief occupations.

A common feature of ghetto and *shtetl* life was the quest for *yichus,* an untranslatable word most closely akin to "prestige" and "status." Possessing *yichus* was much like charm in a woman—if she has it, it makes no difference what else she lacks, and if she does not have it, it makes no difference what else she has. *Yichus* was an amalgam of family background, tradition, learning, and occupation, which usually was inherited, but which could be possessed through the acquisition of knowledge. Good conduct was essential to keep *yichus* in the family. Whoever possessed it had to set for himself high standards in deportment, learning, charity. He could not be a drunkard or a cheat. The word of a man of *yichus* was law, and he would rather go to the torture rack than break it. He early learned to look a gentile defamer straight in the eye with such dignity that it made the detractor ill at ease. Whereas it was forgiven the *prost,* the common man, to cringe in deference to a gentile, the *yichus* man would lose status if he ever did so.

The *prost* could aspire to *yichus* through learning. The most important item in the budget of a Jewish household, no matter how poor, was education. Even more than the father, it was the mother who yearned for an education for all her sons. She would cheat on her meager household money and put away a few *pfennige* or *kopecks* each week so "maybe the younger brother could get an education, too." The Christians admired this quality in the Jews. As a pupil of Peter Abelard expressed it:

> If the Christians educate their sons, they do so not for God, but for gain in order that the one brother, if he be a clerk, may help his father and mother and his other brothers. . . . A Jew, however poor, if he had ten sons he would put them all to letters, not for gain, as the Christians do, but to the understanding of God's Law, and not only his sons, but his daughters.*

Jewish education was at its height in twelfth-century Western Europe. For example, the ordinary Jewish curriculum included Bible, Hebrew, poetry, Talmud, the relation of philosophy and revelation, the logic of Aristotle, the elements of Euclid, arithmetic, the mathematical works of Archimedes and others, optics, astronomy, music, mechanics, medicine, natural science, and metaphysics. This is how the Irish historian and moralist, W. E. H. Lecky, described the Jewish intellectual position in the Middle Ages:

> While those around them were grovelling in the darkness of besotted ignorance; . . . while the intellect of Christendom, enthralled by countless superstitions, had sunk into a deadly torpor, in which all love of enquiry and all search for truth were abandoned, the Jews were still pursuing the path of knowledge, amassing learning, and stimulating progress with the same unflinching constancy that they manifested in their faith. They were the most skilful physicians, the ablest financiers, and among the most profound philosophers.**

But Mama's *pfennige* and *kopecks* no longer brought the quality education they used to buy. By the fourteenth century, Jewish education began to deteriorate, and by the fifteenth century Christian education surpassed it in quality. By the seventeenth century, the curriculum had dwin-

---

*Great Jewish Personalities in Ancient and Medieval Times*, edited by Simon Noveck, page 240.
**Rationalism in Europe*, volume II, page 271.

dled to reading, writing, Bible, and Talmud. To obtain a higher education, the Jews had to send their children to gentile universities.

Ghetto and *shtetl* life accentuated the psychological gulf between Jews and gentiles. What set them apart was the accent each gave to spiritual and cultural values. Jewish children soon sensed the difference between their values and the values of the barefooted, gentile urchins playing on the Sabbath day in gutter and barnyard. To Jewish children, everything intellectual, scholarly, and spiritual was a Jewish value, and everything sensual, gross, and menial became a gentile attribute. In spite of the limited range of ghetto education, the Jews as a group remained the most educated in Europe. No matter with how much disdain the gentiles may have looked upon them, the Jews looked with greater contempt upon the gentiles, for in their minds there was no doubt that their culture, their values, their ethics were superior to those of their detractors.

Next to the stultifying effect of ghetto life, the most hated feature was the special badge the Jews had to wear for identification, which the Jews living in the *shtetl* did not have to wear. Though decent Christian folk left them alone, this badge invited abuse by hoodlums. Yet the Jews wore this badge, often yellow and star-shaped—it took on many different shapes and colors from country to country, century to century—with a courage that often elicited the admiration of Christians who knew that all the Jews had to do to become equals was to be baptized.

It must not be supposed that the majority of the Christians hated the Jews. Quite the contrary. Only a small segment were Jew-baiters. When left to themselves, Jew and Christian lived peacefully side by side. Most Christians, though they viewed the Jews as a rather strange people, admired their veneration for learning and respected them for their closely knit family relations. It must also be remembered that the ritual-murder charges, the Host-desecration libels, and pogroms took place over a period of seven hundred years and over an entire continent. By and large, most of the ghettos and *shtetls* were not affected by pogroms or general maraudings.

In spite of the outward semblance of sameness in life, a vast psychological gulf separated ghetto and *shtetl* Jews.

The ghetto represented urban, cosmopolitan life, and the *shtetl* represented rural village life. In spite of their shrinking frontiers, the Jews in the ghetto did come into contact with the outside world, with its men of learning, its science and business, whereas their brothers in the *shtetls* dealt only with ignorant peasants and vain, arrogant, uneducated feudal landlords. The Jews in the West were aware of the new scientific achievements; they were embroiled in the new political movements. The Jews in the East were sinking deeper into mysticism and superstition. When the Jews in Germany, Austria, France, Holland, and England were riding high on the crest of science, industry, and finance, the Jews in Poland, Russia, Hungary, and Lithuania still were part of the world of villages and peasants.

TWENTY-ONE

# THE GHETTO CAPITALIST

In each age the Jewish genius has manifested itself in a different sphere. In the Pagan Age it was in religion, in the Greco-Roman Age it was in humanism, in the Muhammadan Age it was in philosophy, in the Modern Age it is in theoretical science. In the Middle Ages it was in economics, and some Christian scholars even credit the Jews with having originated capitalism at that time.

Jews accept with reluctance the credit for being the originators of Christianity and communism, but they throw off the crown of capitalism whenever anyone tries to press it on their heads, vehemently denying they are its authors. Ever since the German economist Werner Sombart published his highly controversial book *The Jews and Modern Capitalism* (1911), pointing out that perhaps the road to capitalism began in the ghetto, most Jewish scholars, instead of substantiating his interesting speculations, have spent their energies refuting him. Only now are the more valid aspects of Sombart's thesis being reexamined. No clear verdict either way has yet been given.

The reasons for the Jewish reluctance to accept this

credit are not hard to find. Today's anti-Semites and communists depict Jews as "predatory capitalists." Sombart himself turned Nazi in 1933. But it must be remembered that these same anti-Semites work both sides of the fence and also depict the Jews as "predatory communists," if it suits their purposes. The Nazis also denounced the Jews for having given birth to "such a sickness as Christianity." These are rantings of psychopaths and murderers, and they should be so dismissed. To be the originators of something and to embrace that something are two entirely different actions. Whatever "stigmas" may attach to Christianity, capitalism, and communism are more "Christian stigmas" than Jewish ones, since Christians embrace these three philosophies in greater numbers and percentages than do the Jews.

We should, therefore, not dismiss too lightly the idea that the Jews did indeed originate capitalism. It originated in the western half of Europe, precisely at the time when Jews did live there, trade there, perform banking functions there. As this is a history of "the idea of Jewish history," it is perfectly permissible to examine this thesis more closely without asserting that it is true. That will be for future scholars to determine.

Business, industry, and trade have been carried on by all peoples and nations since earliest pagan days. Why had not capitalism originated in India, China, Egypt, Greece, Rome—nations and empires which at one time or another possessed more silver and gold than any medieval European nation? Another question which comes to mind is: If, as is suggested, the Jews invented capitalism, why did they not invent it earlier—in Greece or Rome, for instance, where they lived in equally great numbers and for many centuries? Other puzzles are: In what way did trade in the Middle Ages differ from trade in all other ages? In what way was the Jewish contribution unique in the medieval civilization?

We have already discussed how the Jews were able to create distinct Jewish cultures within each of the civilizations wherein they dwelt, each such culture taking on the coloration of the host civilization. Until the Middle Ages, the Jews had always been considered members of the civilizations in which they lived. Medieval civilization was the first exception. In the Middle Ages the Jews were outside the framework of the feudal system. We must again stress that the feudal system had only three estates—clergy, nobles, and serfs—and the task of providing a merchant class fell to the Jews. But because the Jews were not part of the feudal state machinery, because they did not own land, because they were not backed by the power of the state (but only individually as chattels of the king), the Jews had to create an "abstract economy," which functioned outside the feudal state machinery, in contrast to their former "concrete economies" in other civilizations, which functioned within the state organism.

Historically, the Jews were prepared for the task of surviving in an "abstract world." External conditions were favorable for such a transition. The Diaspora had already produced a situation where Jewish economic strongholds existed on three continents and in three civilizations. Here Jews could carry on commerce in an international atmosphere. But this was not enough. Free-enterprise capitalism, to take root, demands several other conditions. What are they?

Some economists use the word "capitalism" rather loosely to denote almost any form of economic activity, thus proving that capitalism has existed since time immemorial. Such "capitalism" as amassing wealth, lending money at a profit, speculation, gaining riches through the spoils of war, have, it is true, always been with us. But this does not represent capitalism in the true economic sense of the word. In an economic sense, capitalism is generally regarded as a specific application of wealth to create "surplus wealth," which is used in the creation of further wealth along certain established principles. Such capitalism depends upon the existence of a free wage-earning class, mobility of labor and capital, free markets, international law, sanctity of contracts, availability of credit, negotiable securities, and liquid wealth.

In former ages, trade was *concrete*—that is, "cash on the barrelhead." The trader bought goods in one country and disposed of them at a higher price in another country. The Jews in the early medieval centuries began introducing new methods, based on credit and negotiable securities. This seems simple and elementary today, but in Roman

and medieval days these were strange and wicked ideas.
The Roman law of *obligatio* and much medieval law which
was based on it held that all indebtedness was personal,
and therefore the creditor could not sell a note of indebtedness to someone else if he himself became pressed for
money before the note was due. German law, for instance,
was specific on this point. The debtor did not have to pay
anyone else except the original creditor, and if the creditor
died, he didn't have to pay the debt. In England, until
about 1850, for example, a claim could not be transferred
from one individual to another. Talmudic law, on the other
hand, recognized impersonal credit arrangements, and a
debt had to be paid to whoever presented the demand, just
as such demands are honored by all reputable banking institutions today. Instead of going into tedious details as to
why such a system of negotiable securities permits greater
flexibility and a greater accumulation of wealth, just imagine what would happen today in the Western world if all financial transactions were based on Roman and medieval
laws—no checks, no drafts, no notes, no installments, no financing.

With the new easy credit arrangements and the honor-
ing of all debts, business between nations was facilitated,
leading to international capitalism. There is nothing sinister in that concept. It merely means free-enterprise trade
between nations. But in order for such international capitalism to flourish, several conditions must first be met:
Governments must enforce all international agreements,
must protect the flow of free trade, must allow the exchange of one another's currencies, must enforce contracts,
must protect foreign investments, and must guarantee
against the expropriation of property. The Diaspora created just such conditions for the Jews, and the Talmud provided the legal framework for them.

The Diaspora Jews, though dispersed over three continents and in three civilizations, represented but one law.
They were organized as "states within states" with the permission of the various gentile governments of the countries
in which they lived. These "Jewish states" were governed
by the laws and ethics of the Talmud, and they were knit by
the Talmud into a commonwealth of Jewish nations. In the
Talmud, then, the Jews had an international law, which reg-

ulated their moral, ethical, and business conduct, as well as their religious life. Section IV, dealing with torts, trade regulations, damages, real estate, commerce, the sanctity of oaths, and the enforcement of contracts, made the Talmud an ideal system of international law to regulate the far-flung enterprises of the Jews. Rabbis had to know not only ritual observances but commercial regulations as well. Scholars and philosophers became embroiled in economic questions. Maimonides, incidentally, held the view that the lending of money for equitable interest was a prerequisite for modern (1300 A.D.) business.

Through the Talmud, then, the Jews had an international law that regulated business conduct between Jew and Jew, between Jew and state, between Jew and non-Jew. The Talmud held that a Jew was under an even greater obligation to honor all commitments to non-Jews. The feudal system itself contributed greatly to the development of capitalism among the Jews. Because the Jews did not belong to any of the three estates, most of the Jewish working force was put at the disposal of commerce, industry, and the professions.

A far-flung Jewish commercial network was already in existence by the tenth century. Not only were the Jews in Europe, North Africa, and the Near East, but they had trading posts in India and in faraway China, where their positions of eminence in commerce made Marco Polo take note of them and their achievements in his travels to the latter country in the thirteenth century.

To facilitate their business transactions, the Jews had informal clearinghouses where loans could be obtained and notes negotiated. Such a clearinghouse, for instance, was Montpellier, a seaport in southern France. Benjamin of Tudela, the twelfth-century Jewish Marco Polo, said, "You meet here with Christian and Muhammadan merchants from all parts; from Portugal, from Lombardy, from the Roman Empire, from Egypt, Palestine, Greece, France, England." Montpellier not only had a large, flourishing Jewish community, but also was the seat of a renowned yeshiva to which came students from every part of the world.

In fact, in the eleventh, twelfth, and thirteenth centuries, most Mediterranean seaports were beehives of Jewish commercial activity. In his account, Benjamin of Tudela carefully noted the Jewish glass-manufacturing industries and the many Jewish shipyards, where new ships for expanding trade were built. By 1500, before the Jews were banished from Spain, they were predominant in the wool and silk trades, and they were chief importers of sugar, pepper, and other spices. Before the Jews of Italy were banished or placed in ghettos, they dominated that country's silk and dyeing industries and carried on vast commercial dealings with India. When the Jews migrated to Eastern Europe they took their business ability with them. Poland, which until the Jews arrived had little domestic or foreign trade, hummed with industrial activity after the Jews settled there. Soon the Jews had developed inland trade routes, competing with even the mighty Hanseatic League; and cities in East Europe such as Warsaw, Prague, and Vienna became important trading centers.

W. E. H. Lecky* makes the point that for many centuries the Jews were, if not the only, then the most important segment in keeping international trade moving, because of their organized systems of monetary exchange, their knowledge of the needs and products of countries, and their willingness to risk their capital in long-term investments. If this be so, we see nothing in it to be ashamed of. The world has simply emulated their example.

But in the early Middle Ages these were not respectable activities. The Jews earned the contumely of the Christians for engaging in them, until these professions became "too good for the Jews" and were taken away from them by the Christians. Of these functions, moneylending was the most reviled. Yet moneylending was perhaps the most important contribution by the Jews to medieval society. Without it the entire feudal system might have collapsed.

It was to the Jews that feudal man went when his harvest failed and he needed money to buy grain for next year's sowing. It was to the Jews he turned when disease carried off his cattle and he had to buy new ones, when he was ill and there was no food, or when he needed money with which to pay his taxes and avoid forfeiting his meager belongings to predatory lords. The nobles, too, needed the money of the Jews to buy new castles, to pay for costly

---

*Rationalism in Europe, Volume II, page 272.

tournaments, and to defray the expense of maintaining the feudal way of courtly life. The Church used the money of the Jews to build new cathedrals, to commission new murals, to finance new monasteries. This function of money-lending by the Jews was so important that when the city of Ravenna, for instance, asked to be permitted to join the Republic of Venice, one of the conditions was that Jews should be called in to open loan banks to assist the poor who stood on the edge of disaster. Florence, even as she basked in the sunshine of her Renaissance, begged Jews to come to the city to keep up its flow of capital.

Why were the Jews the only ones engaged in this moneylending? Why did not the Christians themselves go into banking? Why were the Jews so reviled for performing this essential service? The answers hinge on a definition. The Church called the lending of money not "banking" but "usury." To modern man the word "usury" means the lending of money at exorbitant rates; in medieval times it simply meant the lending of money for interest, no matter how low. Any Christian today who accepts 3 percent interest on his bank savings or government bonds would have been regarded as a blackhearted usurer by the medieval Church, for the simple reason that the Church viewed the lending of money at interest as a mortal sin. How then could it permit Christians to lend money if that meant that their souls would go to hell? With the Jews it was another story. As the Jews were not Christians and in the eyes of the Church were headed for hell anyhow, one more sin—that is, moneylending—could not add much to the punishment they would receive in the hereafter. One could suggest that the Church kept the Jews as "bankers" in the same way Jews kept Christians as "Sabbath-goys" (Sabbath gentiles)—to perform functions for them which they were not allowed to perform for themselves. (Jews could perform no work on the Sabbath.)

The Jewish attitude toward lending money in medieval days was what it is in the Western world today. The Talmud forbids usury in today's sense of the word—that is, the taking of excessive interest—and it compares usurers to murderers. The Talmud was as sensible two thousand years ago as ethical Christian bankers are today. It encouraged the lending of money as an aid to business and commerce, and left it to the rabbis to set permissible rates of interest, which constantly fluctuated with the available supply of money, just as banks today set the permissible rate of interest as the money market fluctuates. In actuality, in medieval days, it was not the rabbis who set the rates of lending money to Christians, but the Pope himself, or else the emperor or prince.

When the Jews were dispossessed from their occupations by the rising Christian middle class, the Jewish professions, which had been so scorned in previous generations, became respectable. One of the first professions the Christians went into was moneylending, even though the Church still forbade it. Christian cynics shrugged their shoulders and quoted the epigram of the day—"He who takes usury goes to hell, and he who does not goes to the poorhouse." When the Jews still proved too much competition for them, the good burghers went into silent partnership with the nearest noble or prince, who then banned the "bad" Jews so the "good" Christians would have a chance.

But no sooner had the Jews been banished than up went the money rates, so much so that Popes themselves openly accused the Christian moneylenders of being heartless. They were usurers in the modern sense of charging exorbitant rates of interest. So notorious was their rapacity that Dante, in his *Divina Commedia*, consigned these Christian usurers to the lowest rung in Purgatory. Communities in England, France, Italy petitioned their kings and princes to allow the Jewish moneylenders to return. But it was too late. Moneylending was too profitable for these Christian usurers, who were protected by princes receiving a cut of the take. Besides, the Jews had already moved to the East, to Poland, where their services during these centuries were appreciated by the state.

The Reformation brought vast social and economic changes for gentile and Jew. Because it established itself first in the western half of Europe, it was precisely here that the most drastic changes occurred. Out of the debris of the Thirty Years' War rose a new economic class which built a new social order. Economists generally date the foundations of capitalism from this period.

How had a religious reform movement been changed

into a social revolution? Did Protestantism give birth to capitalism, as Max Weber holds, or did capitalism give birth to Protestantism, as the dialectical materialist insists? Did the Jews create capitalism, as Werner Sombart contends, or did capitalism just create itself, as some college textbooks in economics maintain? Or did all have a hand in shaping capitalism? Perhaps here the materialist philosopher can shed a little light.

The materialist philosopher believes that the way we produce things, the way we go about making and selling things to one another, shapes our politics and our religion. He argues that when people are engaged in productive activity, they automatically enter into specific relations with one another. These specific relations arise independently of the will of the people themselves. The total sum of these new relations, which arise out of these new methods of production, go into making up the economic structure of that society. The way we do business, says the materialist philosopher, determines how we behave in an economic sense, and how we behave is simply an expression of how we do business.

It is at this point that the materialist philosopher comes to the crux of his argument. He claims that the economic structure is the real foundation upon which we build our social, legal, political, and religious institutions. We build these institutions to protect not only what we are doing but also the way we are doing it. For instance, the American way of doing business is built on a system called "free enterprise." Our laws say this is the legal way, our politicians run on tickets endorsing free enterprise, and our religion says this is the only moral way. But, if our methods of production were to change, then the social, legal, political, and spiritual laws—that is, our ideologies—would also change, and we would have a new society.

This can be illustrated with a simple example. When much capital was needed to build this country's productive arsenal, the great moral stress was on thrift and saving, exemplified by Benjamin Franklin's motto "A penny saved is a penny earned." Today, when it is of paramount importance that we consume the vast amounts of goods turned out by our productive machinery, spending becomes a virtue, not saving. The moral aspect of spending has changed from "profligacy" to "faith in the economy." It is not the consciousness of men that determines their existence, says the materialist philosopher, but, on the contrary, it is the social existence that determines the consciousness of men.

No one, then, is a hero or a villain in the materialist theory of economic evolution. But the new capitalism, formed in the wake of the Protestant revolution, was not a readily accepted way of life. The invective which the United States Chamber of Commerce so recently hurled at communism is but 3 percent abuse compared to the 100 percent vitriol the Catholic and Lutheran churches heaped upon the early capitalists. Capitalism had to struggle for over two hundred years before it became a respectable word at church suppers.

The Thirty Years' War, being not only a religious war but also a social revolution, gave rise to a new concept of state, which happened ideally to suit the rising middle classes. The social ideal changed from loyalty to one's religion to loyalty to one's state. To be a Frenchman, an Englishman, a Dutchman, counted for more than being a Christian, Protestant, or Catholic. Also, before the Reformation, the king derived his power from the nobles. After the Reformation, he began to derive his powers from the new, constantly growing middle class. It was a slow, imperceptible, but inexorable process. In the past, the nobles had supported the king with men, arms, and money, and they had paid the cost of administering their respective provinces. Now these activities became the function of the state itself, and the state was faced with the necessity of raising the money needed to supply the national army, the money for an administrative staff, the money to pay for a bureaucracy without which a modern state cannot function. Invariably, in this dilemma the rulers of Europe turned to the Jews. In Werner Sombart's words,

A cursory glance would make it appear that in no direction could the Jews . . . have had less influence than in the establishment of modern States. Not one of the statesmen of whom we think in this connection was a Jew—neither Charles the Fifth, nor Louis the Eleventh, neither Richelieu, Mazarin, Colbert,

Cromwell, Fredrick William of Prussia, nor Fredrick the Great. However, when speaking of these modern statesmen and rulers, we can hardly do so without perforce thinking of the Jews.... Arm in arm the Jew and ruler stride through the age which historians call modern.... Their interests and their sympathies coincided. The Jew embodied modern capitalism, and the ruler allied himself with this force in order to establish, or maintain, his own position. When, therefore, I speak of the part played by the Jews in the foundation of the modern State, it is not so much their direct influence as organizers that I have in mind, as rather their indirect cooperation in the process. I am thinking of the fact that the Jews furnished the rising states with the material means necessary to maintain themselves and develop; that the Jews supported the army in each country ... and the armies were the bulwarks on which the new States rested.*

The rulers of seventeenth- and eighteenth-century Europe were quick to sense the Jewish genius in financial affairs. Jews were recalled to the West, and there they created international banking institutions that made history. But this phase of Jewish history in the West properly falls in the Modern Age.

More properly part of medieval Jewish history and an amazing new phenomenon is the *Court Jew*, who arose in Central Europe, especially in German-speaking countries. It is only recently that historians have taken his role seriously. Modern historians who are examining the Court Jew and his functions are coming up with new verdicts.

The Court Jew was the prototype not so much for the international banker of the 1900s as he was for the Secretary of the Treasury or for the Chancellor of the Exchequer today. His function was not only to serve as quartermaster general for the army, financial agent for the prince, master of the mint, but also to create new sources for revenue, negotiate loans, float debentures, devise new taxes. In short, the Court Jew set the pattern for emancipating the ruler

---

*Werner Sombart, *The Jews and Modern Capitalism*, pages 49–50.

from the nobles by modern financing methods. Of the two hundred main grand duchies, principalities, and palatinates* in the Holy Roman Empire after the Thirty Years' War, almost all had Court Jews. Even Charles V, the most Catholic of all emperors, beholden to the Jesuits, had a *Hofjude*, Court Jew, Jossl of Rosheim, who was his mintmaster and financier, and so powerful that the Emperor dared not dispense with his services.

The Court Jews were absolutely loyal to the prince who protected them. They could come and go as they pleased. They wined and dined with the heads of state. Often they were the possessors of titles. But they never forgot their brothers in the ghettos. The Court Jew was their intermediary and contributed heavily to their weal. Though most Court Jews could have risen to the highest positions of state had they only converted, the remarkable aspect is that they refused to do so. But this refusal to convert is not what merited them the hate they sowed in the hearts of the nobles. The Court Jew was a revolutionary figure who heralded the coming of the radical capitalist state, which would do away with the power and privileges of the nobles. In the Court Jew the nobles correctly foresaw their doom.

The three centuries of Court Jews produced many colorful individuals and adventurous careers. Perhaps the most colorful and adventurous was that of Joseph Süss Oppenheimer (1698–1738), finance minister to Duke Charles I (Karl Alexander) of Württemberg. Oppenheimer is looked upon today as the prototype of the modern financier-statesmen, who by their skillful financial innovations set the pattern for emancipating the kings from the nobles. For this, Oppenheimer was bitterly hated by the nobles of Württemberg, who, not realizing that their system had already been relegated to the backwash of history, attributed all their troubles to him.

Oppenheimer's dramatic career became the theme for Lion Feuchtwanger's historical novel, *Power*. According to Feuchtwanger, Joseph Süss Oppenheimer was the son of the beautiful Jewish actress Michaele Süss, and the handsome Christian, Marshal Heydersdorff, Duke of Wolfen-

---

*After the Treaty of Westphalia the Holy Roman Empire consisted of 2,000 independent units, some only a few square miles in area.

büttel. Her husband, Oppenheimer, was the director of a Jewish theatrical road company. According to Mosaic law, Joseph was Jewish, since any offspring, legitimate or illegitimate, of a Jewish mother is counted as Jewish, no matter who the father is. According to Christian law, he was a Christian, of the royal house of Württemberg.

Young Joseph, unaware of his paternity, studied languages, mathematics, and law at the University of Tübingen. He loved the company of aristocrats and royalty, and as he was rich, handsome, witty, and brilliant, his company was not only tolerated, but sought after. Much of his time was devoted to married and unmarried ladies of the aristocracy, both in and out of their bedrooms. A series of financial arrangements involving a stamp tax for a palatinate and a minting contract for a free city brought his name to the attention of royalty, who now vied for his services. Dint of circumstance attached him to the court of Württemberg.

At court, Oppenheimer became popular with the ladies in the bedroom and with society in the drawing room. But in spite of the constant companionship of Christian nobility, he frequently visited the ghettos, did all he could to help the Jews in their plight, and had contempt for his Jewish half brother who had converted to Christianity in order to hold high government office.

As the nobles felt their power slipping, as they saw more and more of their privileges vanish, they concentrated their hate on "Jew Süss," as he was called. The death of Karl Alexander gave them their opportunity to strike at him. A conspiracy was formed and Süss was arrested for treason. In prison, while awaiting sentence, Süss learned of his identity. All he had to do to be set free and live the life of European royalty was to announce who he was, the son of the revered Marshal Heydersdorff. Instead, he accepted the death sentence in silence. He had lived as a Jew, and he was going to die as one. He went to the gallows on a snowy day in 1738, with a Christian mob pelting him with dung and the Jews chanting *"Shema Yisroel, Adonoi Elohenu, Adonoi Echod"* (Hear O Israel, the Lord is our God, the Lord is One).

That night, risking death, the Jews cut down the body of the son of Marshal Heydersdorff and substituted an unknown cadaver. The body was spirited away to a different duchy, dressed in fine silks, and lowered into a Jewish grave with the blessing of the God of Abraham, the God of Isaac, and the God of Jacob intoned over him.

With him was interred not the spirit of the new capitalism but the spirit of the Middle Ages.

T W E N T Y - T W O

# Kabala and Kinnanhorra

We have traced the physical survival of the Jews through the medieval phase of their history, as they hopscotched the feudal checkerboard from danger zone to safety zone until they ran out of space and time. But how did Judaism spiritually survive these twelve centuries? Was there a common element in this phase of Jewish history which gave Judaism a psychic unity? If "salvation" and "more salvation" sum up the spirit of the Christian Middle Ages, then perhaps "Kabala"* and "more Kabala" sum up the spirit of the Jewish Middle Ages.

Mysticism was not something new in Jewish life. It began with Judaism itself and existed before the giving of the Torah at Mount Sinai in the twelfth century B.C. With the giving of the law, however, Jewish mysticism was relegated to a minor position. According to the Kabalists, the Kabala was given simultaneously with the Torah; but, whereas the Torah was given to all, the Kabala was revealed only to a few select saints, who, according to tradition, handed it down to a very small group of mystics.

Throughout the centuries, this current of mysticism ran alongside Torah and Talmud, but always underneath their majestic achievements. It was regarded by its devotees as a second Oral Law, claiming authority from Scripture. It grew up with the Torah, but in its shadow, in the back alleys

---

*The word "Kabala" comes from the Hebrew word *kabeil*, meaning "to receive"—hence "tradition," or "revelation." It was the name given to Jewish mystic philosophy.

of Jewish occult philosophy. It fed on noncanonized prophecy, Zoroastrian resurrection mythology, Greek science, numerology, gnostic heresies. This was the material Jewish saints and scholars worked on for centuries, distilling it, shaping it, blowing life into it.

Not until the eighth century A.D. did the first of these undercurrents of mysticism break through to the surface with the publication of the *Book of Formation*, compiled in southern Italy. In the thirteenth century, the second undercurrent emerged into medieval Jewish civilization with the appearance of the *Zohar*, written and compiled in Spain. The *Book of Formation* is concerned mainly with the ecstatic experience of God. The *Zohar* can best be described as an encyclopedia of occultism and metaphysical speculations on God, universe, and science. These two books combined constitute the Kabala, a body of mystic and occult thought, a distinctly Jewish metaphysical philosophy.

With the appearance of the *Zohar*, Kabalism did not continue for long to course through Jewish life as a unified current, but branched out into two streams. One stream sought out the rational and the scientific and became metaphysical in its orientation. This current led to Spinoza and the rationalist school of Western philosophers and scientists, finding adherents among both Jewish and Christian scholars. The other stream had its source in Germany and coursed for centuries through Eastern Europe. It began with mysticism and degenerated into superstition with *Kinnanhorra** as its central theme.

Both the *Zohar* and the *Book of Formation* were translated into Latin and other Western tongues, and the writings of Jewish and Christian scholars, humanists, and scientists, based on or inspired by the Kabala, were widely disseminated throughout universities. This body of Kabalistic work may even have had a large share in the sudden efflorescence of science in the seventeenth century. This was the century when Kabalism reached the height of its

---

*The word "Kinnanhorra" is a Yiddish contraction of one Yiddish (the first) and two Hebrew words, *kein ayyin ha'ra'ah*, that is, "no evil eye," which symbolized Jewish superstition in the Middle Ages. From this comes the Bronx contraction "canary," as in "Don't give me a canary," meaning "Don't give me an evil eye."

influence and also saw the beginnings of its demise, per- haps because it was no longer needed after science was re- born.

Because logic alone could not explain their doctrine of the "exalted experience of God," the Kabalists introduced symbolic thinking and symbolic language into their specu- lations. They abandoned the ordinary meanings of words, gave numerical values to letters, and attributed mystical properties to both letters and numbers. This symbolic lan- guage consisted of the first ten numbers and all the letters in the Hebrew alphabet, and together they formed the Ka- balistic thirty-two avenues to wisdom. With this abstract shorthand the Kabalists developed a fantastic metaphysi- cal world where one element was transformed into an- other, where numbers stood for properties possessed by objects, and the world revolved around its own axis. These Kabalists also had an ear for language and a flair for style. They wrote great poetry, which survives in Hebrew liturgy and literature.

It may throw some light on the sudden eruption of sci- entific genius in Western Europe in the seventeenth cen- tury if we examine the role of the medieval Kabalists as scientists. Because their works have been overshadowed by later non-Jewish scientists such as Galileo and Newton is no reason why the contributions of these early Jewish scientists should not be assessed. New ideas do not spring up in a vacuum. They bloom only in well-prepared intel- lectual soil.

In the twelfth century Abraham bar Hiyya, one of these early Jewish scientists, not only translated Greek and Ara- bic scientific works into Latin, but also wrote several orig- inal works on geography, astronomy, mathematics, and scientific methodology, all of which were translated into Latin. It was he who developed the first Hebrew scientific methodology.

A scholar who coupled Kabalism and science was the Spanish Jew Abraham ibn Latif (1220–1290). He wove Ka- balism, Aristotelianism, mathematics, and natural science into a unified system. His works were translated into Latin and caught the attention of Raymond Lully, a Christian scholar, and the outstanding scientist of thirteenth-century Spain. Lully, searching for a way to break through the stranglehold which Scholasticism* had upon science, used the Kabala and the works of ibn Latif as the basis for his book on logic, *Ars Magna*, which was widely used in medieval European universities. The Muhammadans stoned him to death for preaching the gospel in North Africa.

A French-Jewish mathematician and astronomer, Immanuel Bonfils, is credited with having invented the decimal system in the fourteenth century, 150 years before it was accepted by European scientists. His works introduced new mathematical concepts, and his astronomical tables were in wide use by mariners. In that same century, Levi ben Gerson criticized the faulty methodology of contemporary scientific theories and introduced a new trigonometric system which became the basis for modern trigonometry. He also invented the quadrant known as "Jacob's staff," which was used by such navigators as Magellan, Columbus, and Vasco da Gama.

It was in the fifteenth and sixteenth centuries, however, that Kabalism received its greatest dispersal in the Christian world. In the later fifteenth century, for instance, Pico della Mirandola, a Renaissance humanist and philosopher, translated the *Zohar* into Latin. But the Christian scholar who did the most to popularize Kabalism was, of course, Johann Reuchlin, who, early in the sixteenth century, freely asserted that his theological philosophy was based on the Kabala.

A new metaphysical philosophy was injected into Kabalism in the sixteenth century by one of the great Kabalistic scholars, Isaac Luria (1534–1572), known as *Ari*, "the lion." Luria held that all matter and thought evolved through a three-stage cycle—*tzimtzum*, literally "contraction" or thesis; *shevirat hakeilim*, literally "breaking of the vessels" or antithesis; and *tikkun*, literally "restoration" or synthesis.

Western philosophy and science, which had died with the Greeks and Romans in the second century A.D., was reborn in the sixteenth and seventeenth centuries. A fifteen-hundred-year philosophical and scientific dark age lies

---

*A medieval system of philosophy that tried to unify Christian orthodoxy with the newly discovered science of Aristotle. Instead of liberalizing Christianity, Scholasticism strangled science.

between Epictetus and Marcus Aurelius on the one hand and Bacon, Descartes, Locke, Leibnitz, Copernicus, Kepler, Galileo, and Newton on the other. Something must have sparked this rebirth, but what? Did, perhaps, the Kabalistic metaphysical speculations of such Jewish and Christian scholars as Latif, Lully, Pico della Mirandola, and Reuchlin (1300–1600) and the contributions of such Jewish scientists as Hiyya, Bonfils, and Gerson (1200–1500) have something to do with laying the intellectual foundations for the seventeenth-century rebirth of philosophy and the establishment of scientific methodology in Western Europe?*

We are again confronted with one of those curious coincidences of history. This burst of Christian scientific and philosophical activity did not take place in the centuries between 1100 and 1500, nor did it take place in Eastern Europe. It took place in the seventeenth century, in Western Europe, in the area where Jewish Kabalists and scientists had flourished for four hundred years. There is no reason to doubt that Copernicus, Kepler, Galileo, Newton, Bacon, Descartes, Locke, Leibnitz, and others were familiar with both Kabalistic thought and the scientific writings of the Jews. In the seventeenth century all these writings were available in Latin and widely distributed in the libraries and universities of Europe.

Of course, such coincidence does not constitute proof. But why did Western science and philosophy take this bold leap in the seventeenth century? Though scholars call this sort of reasoning *post hoc ergo propter hoc* (meaning "after this, therefore in consequence of this," or a logical fallacy from a supposedly false cause), we nevertheless maintain

---

*"One outstanding fact about the Scientific Revolution is that its initial and in a sense most important stages were carried through before the invention of the new measuring instruments, the telescope, and microscope, thermometer and accurate clock, which were later to become indispensable for getting accurate and scientific answers to the questions that were to come to the forefront of science. In its initial stages, in fact, the Scientific Revolution came about rather by a systematic change in intellectual outlook, in the type of questions asked, than by an increase in technical equipment. Why such a revolution in methods of thought should have taken place is obscure." (A. C. Crombie, *Medieval and Early Modern Science*, Volume II, page 122.)

that here we have an area where scholars could use their searchlights to reveal more meaningful answers than those they have hitherto given.

In Eastern Europe, as has been mentioned, the Kabala took an entirely different direction and coloration. We must recall that Jewish life shifted between the thirteenth and sixteenth centuries from Western to Eastern Europe, and that Jewish history was now being shaped in the East, not the West. Here the Kabala was put in the service of alleviating the misery of the Jewish people. With its doctrine of the imminence of the messiah, the Kabala held out hope for the Jewish people.

Ever since the appearance of the *Book of Formation* in the eighth century, mystics had attempted to use its secret formulas as a means of hastening the coming of a Jewish messiah. If man could get close to God, argued the mystic Kabalists, they would be able to influence Him to send the messiah sooner, end the afflictions of the Jews sooner, and thus thwart the designs of their oppressors. These Kabalistic doctrines fired the imagination of the people and prepared them for the coming of the messiah. They were not disappointed. A "messiah" arrived in practically every medieval century, but not in the way the prophetic Kabalists had hoped for or anticipated.

The Kabala was increasingly removed from the people by its most devoted adherents. In the West, as we saw, it became the possession of metaphysicians, philosophers, and scientists who used the Kabala in their speculations on the essence of matter and universe. In the East, again, it became the possession of scholars and mystics who used the Kabala in their speculations on the nature of God and heaven. As Kabala scientists, philosophers, and mystics did not give the people what they wanted, charlatans and crackpots stepped in where scholars feared to tread. They brought the Kabala to the people, in their own version, but one the people could understand. The soil of superstition had been prepared for the degradation of the Kabala.

Jewish history has been so replete with revered prophets, rabbis, and scholars, that it is a pleasure to interrupt the tedium of so much saintliness with a select gallery of the most magnificent psychos and crackpots, adventurers and charlatans the world has ever beheld. Because they were by-products of the Kabala, they are as such part of Jewish history.

Abraham Abulafia (1240–1291) is one of the more important false Kabalistic prophets. Abulafia, the descendant of a most distinguished, noble Spanish-Jewish family, immersed himself at an early age in the Kabala. On a pilgrimage to Jerusalem he heard a voice urging him to go back to Spain and there declare himself a prophet. Nobody took him seriously; everyone knew him as a rich man's son. In 1280 he heard another voice and a more startling message. This voice urged him to convert Pope Nicholas III to Judaism. A voice is a voice, and one does best to heed it. So Abulafia went to see the Pope, who gave him an audience. But when Nicholas III heard Abulafia's mission he hit the holy ceiling and condemned Abulafia to the stake. The exertion was too much for the Pope, who died three days later. Abulafia "Kabalized" his judges out of burning him—no mean feat for a Jew in the Middle Ages—and then went to Sicily, where the voice spoke to him again, upgrading him to the status of messiah. But Abulafia was too thin-skinned for a messiah. He could not take the harassment of the rabbis, who accused him of being an impostor, and he went off on another journey. Another and last voice took him out of history.

One spring morning in 1502, Asher Lemmlin, a young Kabala student in Venice, woke up with the realization that he was the Prophet Elijah who had been returned to announce the coming of the messiah that very year, provided the people would fast and purify themselves for the event. The Jews flocked to his cause, kissed the hem of his garment, adored him as a prophet, and suspected that Lemmlin himself was the messiah, that only modesty prevented him from announcing it. Even his own grandfather, in spite of the apothegm that a prophet has no honor in his own hometown, destroyed his oven for baking Passover *matzos*, because he was that certain that the following year he would be baking them in Palestine in partnership with the new messiah.

The year 1502 also proved a bonanza year for the Christians in the number of new Jewish converts to Christianity. Disillusioned at the failure of their promised messiah to arrive, the pious fathers, who had purified themselves for the event, had themselves baptized in order to prevent a total loss of their investment in fasting.

That same century another colorful adventurer teamed up with a deluded saint to make the messianic headlines, and they involved a Pope, a king, and an emperor in their grandiose schemes. One sunny day in Venice, in 1524, an incongruous figure appeared on a glittering, prancing, white Arabian steed. Atop the horse was a dark, gnomelike dwarf, David Reuveni, who announced he was the brother of the king of the Tribe of Reuben, the commander of thousands of fierce Jewish warriors in Arabia in the rear of the Turkish lines. He had come on a diplomatic mission for his brother to win the support of the Pope for a Jewish Crusade against the infidels.

So magnetic was this gnome's personality that Pope Clement VII gave Reuveni an audience. The Pope wanted to be convinced. Catholic Christendom was beset with troubles. The Protestant heresy had broken out into the open. The Christian world was in a crisis. The Turks were marching into Europe. An army in the rear of the Turks, led by Jews, Christ's own people! Even the Pope's astrologers saw favorable signs. The Pope consulted the king of Portugal, an authority on Far Eastern affairs, who certified Reuveni as a bona fide emissary from a bona fide kingdom, and offered to help. With the blessings of the Pope, Reuveni set sail for Portugal with a Jewish flag flying from the mast. The Jews were jubilant. The Pope himself had given audience to an ambassador of the king of one of the lost Ten Tribes! The king of Portugal had certified his authenticity. In the eyes of the people, Reuveni was, perhaps, even the messiah!

Meanwhile, in Lisbon, King John III and Reuveni were in deep discussions as to what lend-lease weapons should be sent to the fierce soldiers of the Tribe of Reuben behind the Turkish lines in darkest Arabia. So thoughtful was the king that he even stopped the persecution of the Marranos during these serious summit negotiations. But pandemonium broke out in Portugal. Marranos came out from their hiding places to hail Reuveni as the messiah, while Inquisition priests busily scribbled down names for future reference. Christians began converting to Judaism. King and priests became alarmed, and Reuveni, feeling suspicions being fastened upon him, quickly set sail for Italy. King John III went back to persecuting Marranos, and the newly converted Christians went to the stake.

Back in Italy, Reuveni was joined by one Diogo Pires, a "crypto-Christian" Portuguese Marrano. Diogo, who knew nothing of Judaism, converted, was circumcised, changed his name to Solomon Molko, and now miraculously all of Judaism was instantly and divinely revealed to him. But the Inquisition did not take kindly to Jewish revelation, so Molko fled to Palestine, where he added scholastic Kabalism to his divinely acquired Talmudism. A few years later he was back in Italy, preaching an imminent Judgment Day with such confidence that he convinced himself and declared himself the messiah. In the "old tradition," he preached to the poor, the sick, the lame, the blind, the scabrous, and the leprous, and such became his esteem that the Pope granted him immunity from the Inquisition.

Reuveni and Molko joined forces in Venice and traveled together with banners flying, to Regensburg (then known as Ratisbon), to offer Emperor Charles V of the Holy Roman Empire an alliance against the Turks and to enlist his support in the cause of the Jewish king in Arabia. It is doubtful whether even a little knowledge of Charles V would have deterred them. Charles V, whose mother was an imbecile, had secured his election as Emperor by a vast amount of bribery, and been crowned by the Pope after he had pillaged Rome, the last German emperor to be crowned by a Roman Pontiff. The Emperor, who had never acquired the habits of reading and writing, acquired intolerance early. With the rapid increase of Protestants, Charles V put the Inquisition on a crash program, proclaiming that all Protestants "who remained obstinate in their errors should be burned alive, and those who were admitted to penitence were to be beheaded." Every Friday and during Lent, in the company of monks, the Emperor scourged himself until blood was drawn.

It was this Charles V who listened to the story of Reuveni and Molko, clapped them both in irons and turned them over to the Inquisition. Molko was given a chance to recant his Jewishness and save himself from the auto-da-fé, but, still convinced he was the messiah, he offered himself as a scapegoat in order to redeem man and was burned in 1532. For many centuries his adherents believed he had been resurrected, but having no leadership, the Molko sect eventually died out.

The fate of Reuveni is undetermined. Some say he perished at the stake, others that he rotted in prison, others that he talked himself out of his predicament. None really know who he was or what happened to him. From his diary it would seem he was a Polish Jew. Be that as it may, he was an adventurer in the spirit of the Renaissance.

Of all the messiahs produced by the Kabala, however, Sabbatai Zevi (1626–1676) was the most interesting, the most complex, and the most important to Jewish history. He appeared at a time when Europe was lying prostrate after the Thirty Years' War, when Christian and Jew alike were sick unto their souls of all the carnage. When Sabbatai Zevi proclaimed his messiahship it seemed like an answer to everyone's prayers. Over a million Jews, from every stratum of society, rich man, poor man, scholar, and worker, from Turkey to England, all hailed him as the long-awaited deliverer.

Sabbatai was born in Smyrna, Turkey, where his father was a broker to an English merchant. Sabbatai was sent to the finest schools, was fluent in Hebrew and Arabic. In early life he came under the influence of the Kabala, and early began to exhibit those signs which today would be diagnosed as paranoia but then were signs of holiness. He heard voices from heaven ordering him to redeem Israel. Acting in response to these voices, he blasphemed by uttering the ineffable name of the Lord, abolished all Jewish fasts, and inveighed against the Talmud, much in the manner of the Karaites back in the eighth century. He proclaimed himself the messiah, and people flocked to his tent to hear the new gospel.

Sabbatai's evangelistic itinerary took him to Egypt, and here the century's most talked-about marriage took place. He was betrothed to Sarah, an international, peripatetic prostitute. Sarah is so implausible she could not have been invented. At the age of six she had been taken to a convent after her Jewish parents had been killed in a Polish pogrom. Early in her teens she made her escape, deciding to see Europe before settling down. Her quick wit, bucolic beauty, and ready body preserved her life as she trekked from Poland to Amsterdam. Here she had a double hallucination, one voice informing her about Sabbatai Zevi and another voice telling her to become his bride. This team of saint and whore is not a unique one in Scripture. Hosea was married to the prostitute Gomer, and legend proclaimed that the messiah would marry an unchaste bride.

After his marriage, Sabbatai went to Palestine, where the masses hysterically adored him as the messiah. The rabbis felt it was time to take action and excommunicated him. Sabbatai returned to Turkey, where he was joyfully welcomed by the Jews as the savior. There was also a rumor of a Jewish army hanging around in Arabia waiting for the messiah to give the order to unleash it against the Turks. Sabbatai fell for this rumor. He announced he would march against Constantinople to depose the sultan. The sultan, not knowing what to do with this madman, and fearful of making him a martyr by executing him, threw him into prison. Here, thousands upon thousands came to visit Sabbatai, who from his prison held court and spread his influence. Alarmed, the sultan gave him a choice between death or conversion to Muhammadanism and freedom. Sabbatai chose conversion and freedom.

The conversion shook the Sabbatean movement to its foundation but did not kill it. Confirmed Kabalists merely said this was precisely what the Kabala had prophesied, that the messiah would be "good within and bad without." But the converted Sabbatai could not stop playing his role as Jewish messiah, and as the movement showed every sign of gaining new strength the sultan threw him back into prison, where he was kept until he died. To the end, the devout came to Sabbatai's cell to venerate him. As the Sabbatean movement had no Paul nor Abu Bekr to organize it after the master's death, it slowly died out.

Though there are still arguments as to whether Sabbatai was a deluded saint or a charlatan, there can be no doubt that Jacob Frank, the man who claimed his mantle, was an out-and-out fake. An etching of Frank shows a handsome face, powerful piercing black eyes, a long aquiline nose, a black mustache perched over sensuous lips, and a Turkish fez at a rakish angle over one ear. He was a traveling salesman, born in 1726 in the Ukraine, whose business took him to Turkey, where he studied the Kabala and where he became a member in the *Donmeh*, a Sabbatean sect. Here Frank founded a new concept of Sabbateanism. Anybody, according to him, could find redemption through purity. The unique way of finding redemption was through impurity. Accordingly, Frank's mystical séances were enlivened with sexual orgies.

The rabbis, learning of Frank's sexual practices in the name of religion, excommunicated him. The Turks cooperated by sending him across the borders as an undesirable alien. Frank then went to Poland, where he announced he was the reincarnation of Sabbatai Zevi and preached his creed, which resembled the Christian Trinity, consisting of the Father, the Holy Ghost, and Sabbatai.

As adherents poured gold and silver into his coffers, Frank's living standards went up. He lived in a ducal castle, dressed like a prince, drove in a magnificent equipage, and styled himself "Baron de Frank." The Jewish community in Poland excommunicated him for heresy and licentiousness. But the Frankists appealed to the local Christian bishop, arguing that they were not Jews but "Zoharists" engaged in a deadly struggle with the Talmudists. A disputation was called by the bishop, after which the Talmud was burned for the first and only time in Poland. A second disputation ended in the conversion of the Frankists, who marched in great numbers to the baptismal font, with the nobles of Poland as their godfathers and the king of Poland himself as the godfather of Frank.

Many of these baptized Frankists, coming from scholarly Jewish backgrounds, did not lose their learning at the baptismal font. They rose to the highest government posts in Poland and Russia, married nobility and royalty, and may even have fathered liberal elements in the subsequent history of these two nations.

Frank continued to live in ever greater splendor, but his glory soon came to an end. When the Church found out about his "Trinity doctrine," it threw him into prison, not daring to burn so recent a convert whose godfather was the king of Poland. Here he languished for thirteen years, until set free by the Russians when they invaded the country. Frank then went to Austria, where he became the darling of Viennese society. Even the Empress Maria Theresa looked upon him as the "man with the gospel." His livery-men dressed like Uhlans, riding with long pointed lances, flying pennants inscribed with Kabalistic signs.

Frank died in 1791 of apoplexy, but Frankism was a few more years in dying. It was carried on by his charming daughter Eve, in the tradition of her father. A contemporary portrait shows her wearing a low-cut dress, coyly shielding a minimum of her ample bosom. She preserved the dues-paying membership of Frankism by combining the scholasticism of the *Zohar* with the mysteries of her bedroom into a lucrative religion which enabled her to live in the grand style of her father. The Kabala had not taught her how to retain her youth, however, and her membership dwindled as her middle-age spread increased. Our Jewish Theodosia died in 1817, in Dickensian debt and poverty. Fondly she was remembered by those who knew her in the earlier days as "the Holy Lady."

What was there in the Kabala and the Sabbatean movements to exert such an obsessive, powerful hold on the Jews? Even though charlatans exploited them, underneath the manifest comedy was compressed a latent drama, seeking ways to express itself, which undeniably influenced Jewish life. The mystic elements in the Kabala represented perhaps a return to the primitivism of feeling, a way out from the rigorous logic of the Talmud. The Kabalistic philosophy differed from the Talmudic philosophy in that the Talmud searched for truth with the aid of reason, whereas the Kabala tried to experience truth by intuition. It was a return to "mythology," in which truth and insights could be symbolized. In myth, the sorely beset Jewish people could find an escape from the indignities medieval life heaped upon them. The Kabala gave them the feeling they could again hold their destiny in their own hands. With the Kabala they could influence the coming of the messiah instead of being reduced to a helpless waiting for him.

Sabbateanism held another appeal to the people. On an unconscious level, it was a return to a former stage of Jewishness, where Jewishness was not one of definition but one of feeling. Karaism was a fight for a free inquiry into the Torah, without being bound by the Talmud. Sabbateanism went a step further and reached out for Jewishness beyond the Talmud and the Torah. In the Sabbatean view, it was not Torah nor Talmud which made Judaism, but Judaism which made Torah and Talmud. It was only logical that Sabbatai should have dissolved all 613 *Mitzvoth*, or commandments of the Torah, for in his mind the "idea of Judaism" by itself could hold the Jews together. We dimly perceive that perhaps all this happened once before, way back in Jewish history, when the Jews wandered in the desert after the exodus from Egypt. Here, too, they rebelled against the rigors imposed on them by their new God, Jehovah, and went back to their earlier, primitive rites, back to mythology. Frankism carried this type of unconscious rebellion too far, back to the primordial days of fertility rites. This excess shocked the Jews to their senses.

But the spirit implied in Sabbateanism was not easily forgotten. Subconsciously the East European Jews were waiting for someone to give these unexpressed feelings expression, someone who would not trample this spirit in the mud of obscenity, someone who would exalt the soul with the mysticism of God. It was on this psychological soil that a new Jewish religious movement arose in eighteenth-century Europe, in the twilight of the Jewish Middle Ages. The savior whom this segment of the Jewish people had been waiting for burst on the Jewish scene unannounced, unheralded. He was Bal Shem Tov. With him the gospel of *Hasidism*\* was born.

In a sense, the conditions in Eastern Europe in 1700 were similar to those in ancient Palestine in the first century A.D. of the time of Jesus. Life then had degenerated to a daily struggle for existence under the oppressive rule of the Romans. The country was inundated with cross-currents of Judaisms in strife with one another. Intermingled with the stern morality of Judaism were foreign currents—the Zoroastrian resurrection beliefs, pagan fertility rites, Adonis and Osiris dying-son cults, Oriental mysticism, a hodgepodge of beliefs. In Christianity, all these inchoate yearnings, all these dissident opinions, found a unification. Christianity took the best of these resurrection

---

\*Hasidism is not to be confused with the Hasidean party at the time of the Maccabean rebellion. There is no connection between the two.

cults, dying-son beliefs, mysticism, myths, and rites, and it forged them into a new, lofty religion of redemption for man and promise of heaven.

In the same way, the new religion of Hasidism grew out of a similar soil—political oppression, social unrest, Sabbatean messiah worship, Frankist sex rites, mystic cults, revelation, penance. Hasidism transcended all this in the way Christianity had transcended the Oriental religious cults. Hasidism forged all the yearnings of the people into a new stream of Judaism, sloughing off the obscene, the gross, the sexual in Sabbateanism and Frankism, leaving only the essence of a new religious movement which tried to exalt the spirit. But just as Christianity in its early forms was unrealistic in its attitude toward the state, so early Hasidism was unrealistic in its attitude toward the dual role man has to play on earth—his role in relation to state, and his role in relation to God.

Hasidism was not a simple thing; it was a complex syndrome. It was the triumph of ignorance over knowledge. The Talmud said that no ignorant man could be pious. Hasidism preached the reverse. It affirmed the Jewish spirit without the Jewish tradition. It created its own tradition by proclaiming itself more Jewish than Jewishness itself. Hasidism was strength through joy, an affirmation of the ecstatic, not the ecstasy of the senses as with the Frankists but the ecstasy of knowing God. In one fell swoop, Bal Shem Tov turned weakness into strength, defeat into triumph. Just as Jesus had opposed the Pharisee intellectuals, so Bal Shem Tov opposed the Talmudic intellectuals. Hasidism and early Christianity were kindred spirits.

Israel ben Eliezer, known by his disciples as Bal Shem Tov (Master of the Good Name), the founder of Hasidism, was a contemporary of Jacob Frank, born about 1700 in the same region in the Ukraine. His life, as outlined by his disciples, remarkably paralleled that of Jesus. An angel appeared to Bal Shem Tov's parents, when they were at an advanced age. God, said the angel, was going to bless them with a son in their old age, even as He had blessed Abraham and Sarah, and this son would carry the message of the Lord to man on earth.

Bal Shem Tov's parents, who conceived him late in their lives, died early in his. When he was six years old, the elders of the community, as required by the Talmud, gave him a free education. His early manhood was spent in the wilderness, in utter poverty, performing miracles which his disciples speak of with wonder even today, such as healing the sick with a touching, walking across deep water, causing a tree to burn by looking at it, banishing a ghost by uttering the secret "Name." Once he intervened with the populace of a town which had turned against a prostitute. Bal Shem Tov touched her, whereupon she became whole and saintly. He had direct intercession with God in heaven. One word from him could release a tortured soul from hell. Wherever he went, a radiance hovered over him.

This is the account of his disciples. Others are less kind. One dissenting school holds that Bal Shem Tov was lazy and stupid, an irresponsible failure who succeeded in nothing he undertook, who was fired from every job he ever held. His disciples, again, aver that actually Bal Shem Tov slept days because he secretly studied nights, that he deliberately created an impression as a ne'er-do-well until God revealed the time for him to announce who he really was. This Bal Shem Tov did at the age of forty-two.

Bal Shem Tov wrote nothing, and we are dependent upon his disciples for what he did say. Most of it is preserved, as in the case of Jesus, in allegories and parables. When Bal Shem Tov died, in 1760, he had about 100,000 adherents. At its high point, Hasidism may have embraced half the Jews in Eastern Europe.

His disciple Dov Ber spread the Hasidic gospel throughout Europe. However, fierce opposition to Hasidism developed early, and within a century after the death of its founder, Hasidism had lost its force, not so much by the attacks upon it as by its own internal weakness. New religions, like revolutions, must be quickly institutionalized, because they contain the seeds for their own destruction. Hasidism was no exception. As there was no organization to establish tradition or give the movement direction, it took off without tradition in all directions. Each Hasidic rabbi seized a piece of territory, and soon the Hasidic map resembled that of the Holy Roman Empire, with hundreds of Hasidic "principalities," "duchies," and "palatinates," each maintaining its rabbi like a prince.

These offices became hereditary, and soon wisdom and ability yielded to nepotism and politics.

Whereas Christianity found in Paul an organizer and survived as an established religion, the Hasidic movement never found such a practical man and, as a consequence, within a century and a half practically died out. But its influence is not dead, for out of its still warm ashes sprang the Jewish renaissance, the so-called *Haskala*, or "Enlightenment," and the contemporary school of Jewish theological existentialism, as exemplified by its foremost exponent, Martin Buber.

Viewing the twelve hundred years of Jewish medieval history with hindsight, we can see it as a dark age for both Jew and Christian, although it was not so dark or so bloody as it so often is depicted. Yet, the question still remains: How did the Jews survive it? The answer has been summed up by one historian in a sentence: "The secret of a nation's endurance is its ability to accept defeat." The Jews survived because they never thought of giving up. Judaism is not a religion of defeatism. It has no doctrines of Judgment Day. It teaches, on the contrary, that to despair of the future is a sin. There is but one place to live, and that is here on earth, in joy, and in the name of God.

Throughout Jewish history the dialogue between Jew and God has continued unabated. Only the tune changed, reflecting the changing moods of Jewish philosophy, which always have had a tendency to branch off from the mainstream of Talmudism. But after a century or so of straying, these digressive philosophies usually emptied themselves back into the Talmud. There were three exceptions, and to the Talmudist these three exceptions had the sound of heresy.

Thrice in Jewish history a digressive Jewish philosophy dared challenge the Talmud. The first threat to Talmudism was Christianity in the Greco-Roman Age; but, cutting itself off early from this Jewish sect, Talmudism was able to keep its independence. The second threat, in the Islamic Age, was Karaism; by incorporating the main tenets of Karaism into itself, Talmudism nullified that threat too. In the Middle Ages came the third threat to Talmudism, in

Kabalism, a chunk of dissent so huge that the Talmudist could neither cut it off nor swallow it. For several centuries Kabalism ran alongside Talmudism, and often it was anyone's guess which of the two constituted the main current in Jewish life. So great was the challenge of Kabalism that, though it has lost its force as an influence on Jewish life today, it is a moot question whether Talmudism itself will survive. Today Talmudism is a minor force, though its undercurrents are still strong and its sources far from dried up.

The medieval period was not a useless experience in the history of the Jews. It educated them for the Modern Age. Because the Jew was not part of the feudal system, it did not tie him to any of its institutions, but allowed him to become a cosmopolitan in his life and a universalist in his thought. He spoke the languages of the world, and appreciated its cultures. Because he had no prejudices he could carry ideas and commodities from one nation to another. Because he was an outsider with an education, he could view societies objectively and assess their weaknesses and strengths. He became the social critic and the prophet for new social justice.

Popes and princes of the Middle Ages could have wiped out the Jews completely had they wanted to, but they did not want to. They realized the Jews were indispensable to them. The Jews were their physicians, their ambassadors, their businessmen, their financiers, their men of learning in an age of darkness. But it would be an injustice to the spirit of the Middle Ages to leave the implication that if the Jews had not been useful they would have been exterminated. When, because of social, economic, or even religious pressures, the presence of the Jews became unwanted, they were banished, not killed. The Church endowed all human beings with a soul, and it took a man's life only to save his soul. It was only when religion lost its deterrent hold on man that Western society could entertain the idea of coolly murdering millions because it felt there was no room for them.

Someday, perhaps, the real role of the Jew in the Middle Ages will be given its rightful recognition by history. Then the Jews will no longer be looked upon as an expendable people who wore yellow patches, or whose twelve-hundred-year sojourn in the Middle Ages was no more than an insignificant, meaningless thread in the rich medieval tapestry. Then the Jews will be looked upon as a people which helped usher in the Enlightenment to Europe, a colorful and integral part of the grand design of medieval history.

# VII

# ON THE HORNS
# OF MODERN "ISMS"

---

*The second Jewish Exodus—from the ghetto into a rapidly shrinking world of freedom, where the Jews become prime ministers, generals, merchant princes, and the charter members in an intellectual avant-garde that was to change the destiny of the world and hurl new challenges to Jewish survival reminiscent of Babylonian times.*

---

# THE MODERN PERIOD

| WORLD HISTORY | | JEWISH HISTORY |
| --- | --- | --- |
| American continents discovered; southern sector explored and settled by Spain and Portugal, northern areas by British and French. The Netherlands becomes Protestant; wins independence from Spain. Britain defeats Spanish Armada. Dutch rise in commerce begins. | 1500 A.D. to 1600 | Jews fleeing Spain and Portugal; are among first settlers in South America. The Netherlands first country to readmit Jews into Western Europe. |
| Holland revives Europe; age of Rembrandt and commerce. Cromwell gains power in England, establishes precapitalism. Dutch lose sea supremacy and her North American colonies to England. British colonial expansion in North America; the Thirteen Colonies formed. | 1600 to 1700 | Jews rise to high financial and commercial posts in the Netherlands; achieve renown in scholarship. World greets Spinoza's writings with silence. Jews readmitted to England; permitted to stay in France. First Jews arrive in the Thirteen Colonies. |

| | | |
|---|---|---|
| Austria, Russia, Prussia become European powers; usher in eras of enlightenment. French Revolution shakes Europe. Napoleon reshapes map of Europe. Strife between Colonies and England leads to American Revolution and establishment of the United States. | 1700 to 1800 | Jews begin to leave ghettos of Austria and Germany. March to baptismal fonts begins. Moses Mendelssohn founds Reform Judaism. Hasidism spreads in Russia and Poland. French Revolution bestows French citizenship on Jews, Napoleon incorporates them in French life. Age of Zunz and Vilna Gaon. Trickle of German Jews to America. |
| Russia snatched from brink of enlightenment by her Romanov czars. Napoleon defeated. Holy Alliance restores former monarchies and revolutions bring back suppressed liberties. Nationalism sweeps Europe. Greeks win independence from Turks. Italy is unified. German states united. Industrial Revolution reshuffles Europe's economic frontiers. Stock exchange becomes a power. Africa carved up by European imperialists. Franco-Prussian War. | 1800 to 1900 | Jewish fortunes in Russia fluctuate with whims of rulers, finally degenerate from poverty to pogroms. Spread of Hasidism checked. Haskala born. Secular Hebrew and Yiddish literature flourish. Enlightenment in Western Europe sweeps Jews to high posts in literature, finance, and politics. Become members of Europe's elite and intellectual avant-garde. Anti-Semitism becomes political movement. Karl Marx founds Communism. Dreyfus Affair. |

America expands to Pacific Ocean; inundated with millions of immigrants.

Herzl founds political Zionism. Immigration tides wash waves of German and Russian Jews to the United States.

**1900 to Present**

Nobel prizes founded. Eight million men perish in World War I. Russia goes communist. League of Nations dedicated. Hitler rises to power in Germany. World War II, greatest holocaust in human history, is won by the Allies. United Nations established. China goes communist. America becomes world power and wages Cold War with Soviet Union, and fights Korean War and Vietnam War. Germany and Japan become major economic powers. European communism collapses. Breakup of Soviet Union.

Rosenzweig and Buber shape Jewish existentialism. Freud and Einstein revolutionize the modern mind. Balfour declaration. Palestine mandated to Britain. Zionism motivates hundreds of thousands of Jews to Palestine to wrest land from desert. Nazis murder 12 million, 5 million of them Jews. United States offers haven for 300,000 German-Jewish refugees. State of Israel is born. Jews defeat five invading Arab armies, secure their own frontiers. American Jews inherit intellectual scepter from European Jews. Rise of terrorism threatens Israel. Three more Arab-Israeli wars won by Israel. Peace signed with Egypt. Lebanese War. Large infusion of Russian refugees. End of Gulf War leads to beginning of peace talks.

# TWENTY-THREE

# ANATOMY OF EMANCIPATION

Medieval European history began with the Church supreme, the princes obedient, and the people docile. Modern European history began with the king in power, the Church obsequious, and the people in revolt. The medieval state, built around the concept of a man-God relationship, strove toward a universal brotherhood of man united by one Catholic faith. The modern state is centered around the concept of a "social contract" between man and state. The pattern of political power shifted from the ecclesiastic to the secular, from faith to reason, from noble to banker.

Medieval Jewish history ended in England in 1300, in France in 1400, in Spain in 1500, with the successive expulsions of the Jews from these countries. Modern Jewish history began with the readmittance of the Jews to the West in the seventeenth century. In Germany it began with the eighteenth century, as the first wave of the Enlightenment breached the walls of the ghetto. In Eastern Europe the modern period of the Jews began with the nineteenth century.

But, whereas Jewish history in the medieval period progressed inversely to the unfolding of Christian history, in the Modern Age it runs parallel to it. The ideas which engulfed the Christians also engulfed the Jews. The devaluation of religion found its adherents among both. Christians and Jews fought side by side for democracy. They became the victims of the same tyrannies, and both knelt at the altar of the same new god—science. It is within these changed man-God relationships in Western civilization that the modern act of the Jewish drama unfolds in all its grandeur and tragedy.

Modern Jewish history can be viewed as an existentialist syndrome in five symptoms—a West European illusion, an East European regression, an American amnesia, a Nazi nightmare, and an Israeli awakening. To unravel this tangled skein, we must first retrace our steps to the seventeenth century and follow the historical events which led the Jews back to the West, then work our way to the East to examine the anatomy of their emancipation, which came as a result not of direct Jewish action but of a change in Christian attitudes. We must break Jewish history into arbitrary, component parts, and examine each in turn before we unify it in Israel, a state created mainly by direct Jewish action.

## The Westward Trail

After the decline of Charlemagne's empire, the map of Europe was reshaped more in the bedrooms of royalty than on the battlefield, for who married whom also determined who ruled what. Spain especially had her royal offspring in practically every court on the Continent, including that of the Netherlands. Through a genealogy more complicated than any in Genesis, much-married Philip II of Spain, a bureaucratic Hapsburg autocrat and revengeful religious fanatic, inherited the Protestant and capitalist Netherlands in 1556. To stamp out this dual heresy, Catholic and feudal Philip II introduced both the Inquisition and the Duke of Alba, who, like the Roman procurators in Judea, thought that ideas could be stamped out by massacre. The Dutch rose in revolt, and the Puritan Virgin Queen of England, Elizabeth I, fearful of Romanism and Spain's growing power, joined the cause of the Netherlands. To break this alliance, Philip II organized his invincible Armada of 132 ships and 3,165 cannon. But history was unimpressed, as was Sir Francis Drake, who put the Armada to flight (1588). A storm sank the remnants of the fleet off the coast of the Hebrides. Hundreds of seamen were washed ashore on Ireland's coast, where many a Spanish sailor was hospitably received to the bosom of many an Irish lass in holy matrimony, which may account for the numerous black-haired Irishmen with Spanish names.

Here in the Netherlands we are again confronted with one of those inexplicable coincidences that receive such scant attention from historians. Within twenty years of her liberation, this little country challenged the commercial supremacy of all European powers. By 1602 she had formed the Dutch East India Company, the chief arm of her imperialism. By 1650, she was the commercial center of Europe, and her capital, Amsterdam, was the financial center of the world. Uncannily, this rise of Dutch supremacy coincides with the arrival of the Jews and their proliferation in trade and finance during this period. The first Jews to arrive in the Netherlands in 1593 from Spain were the descendants of those Jews who, rather than leave Spain in the expulsion of 1492, had converted to Christianity and then, in turn, had become Marranos.

Tradition has it that the first Jews, settling unobtrusively and unofficially in the Netherlands, aroused the suspicions of the Dutch Protestants by their secret practice of Judaism. Suspecting a Papist plot, the authorities swooped down on the Amsterdam Jewish congregation while at prayer on the Day of Atonement, thinking they had corralled a nest of Catholics. As the Jews could speak no Dutch, disaster faced them. Fortunately their spokesman, a Latin scholar, found a Dutch Latin scholar to whom he explained the situation in the language of the Holy Roman Church, promising that if allowed to stay the Jews would persuade other Marranos in Spain and Portugal—all men of means and learning—to come to Amsterdam to help the Dutch in their struggle against Spain. The Dutch, confused, consulted their legal notables, who ruled that the Jews were neither Catholics nor Papists, but members of the Hebrew nation. Permission to reside in the land was granted, provided they would not marry Christians or attack the state religion. As these two conditions coincided with the Jewish view of things, an accord was reached. Jews streamed into the Netherlands from Portugal, Spain, and the nearby German ghettos.

Soon Amsterdam was known as "New Jerusalem," to which Spanish and Portuguese Marranos brought their vast learning, their skills, and their connections. They established business branches in every seaport—in the Mediterranean, in India, in the Ottoman Empire, in South and North America, including New York, then known as New Amsterdam. They founded new industries and new trade routes, built new factories, and established famed banking houses. They sat on the board of directors of the

Dutch East India Company, and were instrumental in making Amsterdam the center of the world jewelry trade. They became subjects for Rembrandt's paintings. Toward the end of the seventeenth century there were about 10,000 Jews in Amsterdam.

Dutch supremacy in world commerce came to an end, however, in the middle of the seventeenth century, with the ascent to power in England of Oliver Cromwell, a plain man in ill-fitting clothes, who combined revolt, reformation, and capitalism into a single victory. Cromwell served the capitalist cause in England in the same way Luther had served it in Germany. Under the mantle of his Ironsides—as his soldiers were called—free enterprise entrenched itself in British life. Cromwell became Lord Protector—another name for dictator—of England. Just as the Jews in the Middle Ages had been dispossessed from their posts by the rising Christian middle class, so the Catholics in Britain and Ireland were dispossessed from all better-paying jobs to make room for deserving Protestants. Capitalism was firmly entrenched in the new order, and all ill-gotten gains were deeded to the new owners. England turned to trade, and soon her ships were carrying the cargoes of the world.

The Jews in Holland quickly sensed this new spirit of capitalism in Cromwell's England, and the Amsterdam Jews sent an emissary to explore the possibility of a return to that island from which the Jews had been banned in 1290. Cromwell viewed the Jews with the appraising eye of an employer looking for good men to staff his growing business. He could see the activity of the Jews in Amsterdam, could see them in many dominant posts, busily spreading the gospel of commerce. He looked forward to meeting their deputy, Rabbi Manasseh ben Israel.

Rembrandt's etching of Manasseh shows a countenance and a mode of dress more associated with the musketeer Porthos in Dumas's novel than with the popular concept of a Jew of the 1650s. The Vandyke beard, with the matching mustache, neatly displayed on a starched white collar, and a wide-brimmed hat perched on the head in a casual fashion give more the image of the man on a horse than the man with the Talmud. At the age of eighteen, child prodigy Manasseh had become rabbi of the Jewish congregation in Amsterdam, where he founded the first Jewish printing press. Through the translation of his writings into Latin and Spanish, he came to represent contemporary Jewish scholarship to the Christians.

Correctly appraising the Puritan mind, Manasseh appealed to the spirit of Protestantism. Expecting a presentation on how much the Jews could contribute to England's commerce, Cromwell and the assembled notables instead heard Manasseh tell how the British themselves could hasten the Last Judgment by admitting Jews to England. His reasoning was simplicity itself. Had not the Book of Daniel prophesied that there could be no redemption until after the Jews had been scattered from one end of the earth to the other? How then, he asked, could this be fulfilled if there were no Jews in England?

The approach worked. Not knowing how the people would take to Jews who would compete with them, but convinced the Jews were essential both to their redemption and to their economy, the notables decided not to make any official decision. Instead, the word was passed to the Jews that they could settle in England without a formal invitation.

Again we are confronted with uncanny coincidence. As the Jews were forced to stay out of retailing by law, they went into banking, finance, and international trade; and, as in the Netherlands, the Jews in England quickly rose to high posts. Soon they had far-flung commercial enterprises, sat on the Royal Exchange, acquired great wealth. Soon Britain began challenging the Dutch. After her navy had defeated rival fleets, she surpassed all other European powers in trade.

British rulers in the seventeenth century specifically asked the Jews to break the stranglehold of the ring of usurious Christian moneylenders who had dominated England's money market since the expulsion of the Jews in the thirteenth century. It was for his successful effort in this struggle that William III (William of Orange) knighted the Jewish banker Solomon Medina. William Pitt asked the Jews to help him finance England's struggle against France, in the Seven Years' War. He also turned to them for help in the government's fight against a group of Christian bankers who were monopolizing all treasury issues at extortionate rates, services for which several Jews were again knighted. Though Jews in the banking field could have benefited personally from higher interest rates, they fought for social legislation prohibiting ruinously high interest charges. In time, the competition of Jewish bankers forced interest rates down.

A hundred years after the first Marranos settled in England, Jews began arriving from the ghettos of Germany and Russia. But the two strains of Jews never merged. Each went its separate way, the Spanish or Sephardic Jews regarding themselves as superior to the German or Ashkenazic Jews in the way a Boston Brahmin regards himself as superior to an Italian immigrant. In fact, not only did they not merge, they diverged. As the Sephardics rose in scholarship and wealth, they absorbed more and more English culture. What the Spanish had not been able to accomplish with force, the English accomplished with indifference. Sephardic Jews applied for baptism in the Anglican Church. The Church welcomed these Jewish "truants" with open arms, and the Jews welcomed the patents of nobility that so often accompanied the certificate of baptism. The German and Russian Jews, again, secluded themselves in their own quarters, waiting for the nineteenth century before making their debut in British high society.

The Jews reentered France during the reign of Louis XIV strictly as a by-product of history. With the signing of the Treaty of Westphalia (1648), France not only gained Alsace from Austria but also inherited a sizable Jewish ghetto population, destined to make no impact on French culture, science, or finance for 150 years. Petty moneylending and old-clothes peddling were their lot for another century and a half, though famed Court Jews served all four Louises (XIII through XVI). Why did not the Jews prosper and advance in French society the way they had in the Netherlands and England? The answer is simple. There was no need in France at this time for the Jews and their specialized skills, because France at this time was neither Protestant nor capitalist.

## FROM GHETTO TO BAPTISMAL FONT

In the West, the problem for the Jews had been to get in. In the East the problem was to get out, that is, out of the ghettos where they had been since 1600. In Austria this exodus began when the Spanish-born Empress Maria Theresa was handed that war-torn Catholic country by her father, Emperor Charles VI. Lusty and matriarchal, shrewd and ambitious, enlightened and superstitious, she mothered sixteen children, corresponded with Voltaire, had the finest artillery in Europe, and was frightened by Protestants and Jews. Like the Greeks and their Hellenization program, Maria Theresa tried to fit an Austrian *Kultur* skirt on her subject peoples—Bohemians, Silesians, Magyars, Moravians, Poles, Romanians, Jews—and failed. She then adopted a policy of force and conciliation. Many former feudal restrictions were abolished and the lot of the peasants was improved. But she banished the Jews from both Prague and Vienna, only to recall them a few years later under the pressure of mixed emotions—a pinched treasury, the censure of world opinion, and her own sense of fairness. Yet at all times she retained the services of the best Court Jews in Europe to keep her army well provisioned and her finances in the black.

Much as Maria Theresa feared unbaptized Jews, she loved baptized ones. A converted Jew could reach practically any position he aspired to, including a career in the clergy or nobility. The career of ghetto-born Joseph von Sonnenfels illustrates the great cultural and humanistic impact baptized Jews had on eighteenth-century Austria. Von Sonnenfels, converted at an early age, served as a private in the Austrian army, studied law, wrote the legislation abolishing torture in Austria, founded the Austrian National Theater, and became president of the Royal Academy of Arts, director of literature, and a personal friend of both Maria Theresa and her successor, Joseph II.

"I love humanity without limitations," declared Joseph II when he inherited the throne of Austria; and European royalty shivered. To preach enlightenment was elegant, but to practice it was downright vulgar. A year after his accession to the throne, Joseph II issued his Patent of Tolerance, which included both Jews and Protestants. It was not his intent to place them on equal footing with the Catholics, but for many Jews the Patent did mean that they were free to leave the ghetto, free to discard dress distinctions, free to learn any trade they pleased, free to engage in commerce, open factories, send their children to public schools, and attend universities.

Under the tolerant reign of Joseph II, a new type of Jew made his appearance in Austrian society, the *Salon Jude*, or "Salon Jew." As in their Greco-Roman and Islamic Ages, the Jews used education as a lever to success, and because they became rich, because they were talented, brilliant, witty, interested in the theater, music, literature, the Christian intelligentsia found itself drawn to the Jewish salons. After an inspiring Mass on Sunday morning, it was wonderful to relax in the elegant, sophisticated atmosphere of a Jewish drawing room where one could meet royalty, aristocracy, and the latest celebrities of stage, arts, and letters.

But such was not the way of life for all Jews, only for a favored few. By 1800, Jewish life in Austria had hardened into three strata: a great mass of ghetto Jews who, though free to leave, were tied to the ghetto by poverty; a small brilliant coterie of Salon Jews; and an even smaller number of converted Jews who had gained entry into the clergy, nobility, and government.

Jewish fortunes in Protestant Prussia paralleled those in Catholic Austria. The founders of modern Prussia were four Fredericks of the house of Hohenzollern. They built the Prussian state with a calculated mixture of cruelty and enlightenment, and their work was preserved with Europe's most formidable standing army, numbering 83,000 men out of a population of 2,500,000. Torture as an aid to justice was abolished, a measure of freedom was given the serfs, compulsory primary education was introduced, and religious toleration was granted to Catholics and Jews.

It was during the reign of the Great Elector, Frederick William (1640–1688), that the first Jews settled in Berlin, and in 1712 the Jews in Berlin formally dedicated their first synagogue. The cause for the Great Elector's interest in the Jews is still debated. The Freudian school holds to the theory that it sprang from a romantic, though illicit, attachment to the beautiful but not too virtuous wife of his Jewish court jeweler. The Marxist school hews to the line that it stemmed from the substantial revenue the Jews brought into his realm by stimulating industry. Whatever the cause, it was not sufficient to open the doors to freedom for all Jews, only to a select few who, by luck or by knowing the right people, moved out of the ghetto into the expanding German cities. Business and scholarship were the bent of these emancipated German Jews, and here, as in all other countries where restrictions were removed, they soon soared to the top.

In Prussia and the other German states, the Salon Jew too appeared, and the voluntary procession to the baptismal font also began. There were no emancipation leaders to give meaning to a Judaism outside ghetto walls, and Jews seemed to assimilate the moment they were emancipated. Again, the right man appeared at the right time, the hero in history who singlehandedly shaped the first Jewish reform movement.

No stage director would have dared select an ugly, ghetto hunchback as the central character in this Jewish *Kultur* drama. But history dared. It selected Moses Mendelssohn (1729–1786), a hunchback from the ghetto of Dessau, to reintroduce a knowledge of Judaism to the Christians, and, even more incredibly, to sell Christian cultural values to the ghetto dwellers. It was he who overcame the conviction that ghetto life was Jewish life. It was he who brought secular learning back to the Jewish schools. It was he, more than anyone else, who prepared the Jews of Germany for the freedom hiding around the corner of history.

At the age of fourteen, Moses Mendelssohn hitchhiked to Berlin for a secular education. Here he was swept into the German Enlightenment (*Aufklärung*), which, influenced by Rousseau and Voltaire, revolted against all traditional beliefs. He became a friend of Immanuel Kant and of Gotthold Lessing, then Germany's foremost dramatist. Lessing's play inspired by him, *Nathan the Wise*, swept the European stage and changed the popular image of the Jew from that of a ghetto dweller to that of the proud Jew of former days, the inheritor of a rich culture. Mendelssohn's philosophical works earned him the sobriquet "German Socrates"; his reviews on literature made him the leading German stylist; and his critical essays on art made him the founder of modern aesthetic criticism.

Mendelssohn became a Salon Jew, and his *Aufklärung* trail was leading him to the arms of the Christian church. His recall to Judaism did not come about through an encounter with the Deity; it came about through a fluke of history. He was challenged publicly to quit straddling the religious issue and either refute Christianity or be baptized. In wrestling with his conscience, Mendelssohn became reinfected with the spirit of Judaism.

Mendelssohn clearly saw the dilemma of and the danger to the Jews. If they remained in the ghetto, they would stagnate into a meaningless existence. If, on the other hand, they were catapulted out of the ghetto by the new social forces shattering feudalism, without being prepared for the Enlightenment, they would be swallowed up by the dominant Christian majority. Mendelssohn saw his task as twofold: first, to give the Jews a tool for their own emancipation; second, to prepare a new basis for Judaic values once the old religious norms were rejected. The way Hercules diverted the flow of two rivers into the Augean stables to clean out decades of accumulated refuse, so Mendelssohn channeled the currents of the *Aufklärung* into the ghetto to sweep out centuries of accumulated orthodoxy.

The German language was to be the tool whereby the Jews would lift themselves out of the ghetto. It was with this in mind that Mendelssohn translated the Pentateuch into a beautiful, lucid German, written in Hebrew letters. His surmise, that once the Jews learned German they would also start reading German secular literature and science, proved correct. Ghetto education began to lose its hold upon Jewish youth as it came in contact with Western science, mathematics, literature, and philosophy. Jewish youth left the ghetto. But they did not walk out into an unfenced field. Mendelssohn had shaped the first outlines of the coming Reform Judaism to hold the newly enlightened Jews in the fold. In a series of books and pamphlets, he formulated the principles upon which modern Judaism was to be built. He reformulated Rousseau's social contract to apply to the Jews, but that contract did not exclude God.

Secular laws formulated for survival in one age, argued Mendelssohn, should not become divine laws in another age which no longer needed them. There was no reason why the Jews should cling to a "Jewish state" within a feudal state that was dying. Every Jew should be free to dissolve his bonds with the "ghetto government" and "sign a contract" with the gentile state in the same way Christians were abandoning their feudal ties and becoming citizens of the state. Emancipation of the Jews, argued Mendelssohn, could only be achieved by throwing off those laws which bound them to the ghetto past. Jewish religion should be concerned with eternal truths, not with the minutiae of everyday life.

To survive as Jews, he held, it was not necessary to cling eternally to temporary national injunctions, but it was necessary for survival as Jews to keep those commandments which bound them to the divine past.

Up to this point, Mendelssohn's arguments were modern restatements of those of the Pharisees, who, back in Greco-Roman days, had argued for a liberal Mishna and Gemara. Mendelssohn added two new ideas: First, the breaking of a religious law, he said, was an individual offense, not a state offense; second, the power of excommunication must not be used to enforce religious conformity.

Mendelssohn proved a prophet before his time. The questions he raised on the relationship of the modern Jew to the modern state were precisely those which Napoleon was to raise thirty years later, and the answers the Jews were to give then were in essence the solutions Mendelssohn had prescribed.

The Jewish "eighteenth-century story" in Russia never even received a chapter heading. The Russian Enlightenment did not touch the life of the Jews, and it barely touched the Russian people. While the Jews in the Netherlands and England rose to great prosperity, while the Austrian and Prussian Salon Jews entertained Christian nobility in their drawing rooms, while Mendelssohn spread his gospel of the Enlightenment in Germany, the Jews in Russia and her buffer countries from Lithuania to Romania vegetated until they were shaken out of their mental and political torpor by an event whose import they could not fathom at the time, and by a man about whom more books have been written than have been written about Jesus. The event was the French Revolution, and the man was Napoleon Bonaparte.

## NAPOLEONIC IMPERIALISM AND
## JEWISH EMANCIPATION

The destiny not only of nineteenth-century Europe but also of her Jews was forged in eighteenth-century France. Whatever affected France affected all Europe, for as one historian succinctly phrased it, "When France sneezed, Europe caught a cold." The history of France was no longer shaped by her kings but by her intellectuals. Not hunger stirred the masses, but ideas. Four eighteenth-century French intellectuals, none Jewish, were changing the thinking of Europe. Voltaire's slashing wit undermined the foundations of the Church, Diderot's *Encyclopedia* of reason, science, and art undermined the value of faith, Rousseau's *Social Contract* undermined the old concepts of state, and Condorcet's philosophy of the "infinite perfectibility of man" gave hope for a new rational human being.

Of all these works, Rousseau's *Social Contract* played the greatest role, not only in fueling the French Revolution but also in kindling the intense nationalism of the nineteenth century. It holds that the first government began with a mutual contract between people and ruler for the general good of both, but that through the ages, through the intervention of science, art, and politics, this contract became corrupted, and then lost. The state, Rousseau held, should be a popular expression of the will of the people, not that of the ruler. The governed must surrender certain rights to the state for the welfare of all. But the governed also have the right to terminate this contract if the ruler should usurp the powers delegated to him by the people.

The question again presents itself, Which comes first, the new ideas which overthrow old institutions, or the crumbling of old institutions which give rise to new ideas? Do new modes of production make the established order obsolete, or does a dying old order give rise to these new ideas? Whichever came first, there is no doubt that the leaders of the French Revolution seized these concepts of the rationalists and used their words as slogans to sweep the people along with them. The muskets of Louis XVI's Swiss mercenaries were unable to prevent the germs of Equality, Fraternity, and Liberty from infecting the political body of France.

The French Revolution began as a revolt against a king whom the people could not understand, and developed into a hysteria which their leaders could not contain. Reason clouded humanity, and terror became the instrument of reason. Events followed in quick succession. The Bastille was stormed. France was declared a republic, the king and queen were executed, the Terror was instituted, and the nobles were marched three hundred fifty a month to the guillotine. In November 1793 God was formally dethroned, and in June 1794 Robespierre was venerated as high priest.

But one by one, those who had made the Revolution died by its dynamics. Marat was assassinated in his bathtub by Charlotte Corday for having betrayed the Revolution. Danton was guillotined by Robespierre for having stood in the way of the Revolution. Robespierre was beheaded by his own party because he had not been corrupted by the Revolution.

When the Revolution began, the Jews were high on the priority list of enemies of the Republic. Pure reason proved it. The Church was an enemy of the Revolution, and since Church and Jews recognized the same Old Testament it stood to reason that the Jews also were enemies of the state. But for the ghost of Mendelssohn and a famous French aristocrat, Count Mirabeau, the Jews of France might have vanished in the backwash of the French Revolution. Mirabeau, famed orator and one of the few Revolutionary leaders who died in bed, had met Moses Mendelssohn in Berlin and through him had become acquainted with the 3,500-year-old Jewish cultural tradition.

When, after the storming of the Bastille, Jewish leaders appeared before the Tribunal to state their rights as equal citizens, it was Mirabeau who took up their cause. A great debate ensued, and finally the issue was put to a vote by the people. The anti-Jewish factions, confident of the outcome, received a stinging setback. Of the sixty districts in Paris, fifty-three voted overwhelmingly for Jewish equality. In 1791, the 70,000 Jews of France became citizens with equal rights.

But the new French Republic and the new freedoms of the Jews were in peril. With trepidation the crowned heads of Europe had seen the common people in America rebel against their king in England, take law in their own hands and establish a revolutionary, radical republic based on an inflammatory doctrine known as the Declaration of Independence, obviously modeled on that left-wing book *The Social Contract*, written by that lascivious megalomaniac, Rousseau. Now with even greater trepidation, the kings of Europe saw the same thing happening in France, in their own backyard. It had to be stopped, by force. The armies of Austria, Prussia, Spain, and England converged on France to stamp out this heresy of liberty.

To aid the invading armies, the French nobles organized a fifth column inside France and staged a white counterterror of their own, getting set to take Paris by a *coup d'état*. But they had not counted on a twenty-four-year-old general of artillery named Napoleon Bonaparte. With one "whiff of grapeshot," as he termed it, Bonaparte broke the back of the uprising by a point-blank fusillade into the ranks of the nobles. From then on until 1815 the history of Europe was the biography of this little Corsican, "a scion of the poor gentry of Ajaccio."* One by one he devoured the states of Europe, handing their crowns like wedding gifts to his numerous family members. "I am not the successor to Louis XVI but to Charlemagne," he proclaimed, upon placing the famed iron crown of Milan upon his own head.

Napoleon enthroned himself and took over the functions of both dethroned king and God. The allegiance of man was now unofficially transferred from God to goods. He domesticated the clergy, confirmed with his Code Napoleon the social and material gains of the Revolution, established educational institutions controlled by the state, and created the Legion of Honor, a badge to reward bourgeois virtues.

How did all this affect the Jews? The Jews in the Middle Ages, it must be remembered, were a separate corporate entity, almost completely self-governing. As no one had equality in the Middle Ages, it is meaningless to assert that the Jews did not have equality. But they did have their own courts, their own police, judges, and taxation system. As such they acted as a state within a state, enjoying liberties

---

*Lucien Romier, *A History of France*, page 347.

and rights not enjoyed by most Christians in feudal society. Though their general status had been below that of the nobility and the higher-ranking clergy, it was far above serf, villein, yeoman, and burgher in the period before the Jewish banishment to the ghetto. Now that the feudal state no longer existed in France, Napoleon was faced with the problem of what to do with the "Jewish state" within his empire's boundaries, and with the "Jewish states" existing in the countries he was conquering and annexing to that empire.

With his flair for showmanship, Napoleon convoked a National Assembly of Jewish Notables, where he stunned them by asking twelve seemingly pointless questions. Some of the questions asked were: Do Jews sanction polygamy? Do they permit divorce? Would a Jew be permitted to marry a Christian? Do French-born Jews consider themselves Frenchmen? Are Jews willing to obey French laws? What police powers do the rabbis exercise? And so on. The Notables, seething with rage because they did not understand the full import of the situation, nevertheless had the sense to treat the questions with a gravity they did not seem to merit. Within a few weeks they gave the answers Napoleon had anticipated, namely that Jews did not believe in polygamy and did permit divorce, that France was the country of French Jews and they would insist on defending her against all enemies, that the rabbis exercised no police functions, that Jewish marriage prohibitions extended to heathens only and Jews did not view Christians as heathens, and so on.

Napoleon then played his trump. He convoked the first Great Sanhedrin in eighteen hundred years, a Sanhedrin which had not held a meeting since the destruction of the Temple by the Romans. Napoleon wanted the Jews to reaffirm their answers before this special Great Sanhedrin and thus make their answers binding on all Jewry. The Jewish leaders, though now divining his intent, were nevertheless unable to hold back tears of pride that that august body would once again preside in Jewish life. The news swept through the Jewish world. The name of Napoleon became known to every Jew. Special services were held for him in synagogues throughout Europe and America.

The Great Sanhedrin, which collapsed as soon as it had

accomplished Napoleon's ends, confirmed the answers of the Assembly of Notables. By doing so, it also proclaimed to world Jewry that the Mosaic laws were religious, not secular, in nature, that Jews owed allegiance to the state, that the jurisdiction of rabbis did not extend into civil and judicial affairs, and that the Jews no longer had a special corporate state but were part of the nation. From that moment on, whatever Jewish feudal entities still existed were anachronistic remnants waiting for history to end them.

Napoleon's military defeat came with Waterloo, his political end with the Congress of Vienna (1815), where Emperor Francis of Austria played host to the reactionary rulers of Europe who arrived with wardrobes of brilliant uniforms, retinues of glittering mistresses, and a firm resolve to set the clock back. They signed a pact known as the Holy Alliance. The old order was to be restored. They slammed the lid on all further social and economic progress, and swore they would come to the aid of each other in case any democratic revolutionaries tried to overthrow any monarchies.

The result was a series of revolutions the like of which Europe had never seen. A breeze of freedom spread the flames of revolt across the continent, fanning the outbreaks of 1820, 1830, and 1848. Democracy was defeated again and again, but it persevered and in the end was triumphant. The French rebelled against the restoration of the Bourbons, the Greeks overthrew their Turkish masters, Italy was unified, Bismarck forged the German state. Jews fought side by side with the Christians, on the side of reaction at times, but mostly on the side of democracy. They fought as Frenchmen, Italians, Germans, Austrians, Englishmen, all infected with the same slogans of nationalism. While men waved their respective flags, talked of the brotherhood of man, and shot each other, steam and electricity forged new patterns of life, the Industrial Revolution elevated a seat on the stock exchange above a seat on the throne, and a new German state rose to challenge the supremacy of England's place in the sun. The world, without knowing it, was rushing headlong into World War I.

The nineteenth-century emancipation of the Jews in Italy paralleled the seesawing fortunes of nineteenth-century European history, and typified the pattern of Jewish emancipation in the rest of Western Europe. The liberation of Rome by Napoleon's armies was dramatic. In a torchlight ceremony the commanding French general read to a cheering multitude Napoleon's proclamation granting Italians and Jews freedom, equal rights, and religious toleration. All over Italy ghetto gates were torn down. Italians greeted rabbis as "citizen rabbi," linked their arms with the arms of bewildered Jews, and marched jubilantly with them into freedom. Liberty Trees were dedicated everywhere.

Napoleon's Waterloo also spelled a Waterloo for Jews and democratic Italians. The moment Napoleon fell, the exiled rulers dusted off their uniforms and, with the help of the signatory powers of the Holy Alliance, were restored to their thrones in a carved-up Italy. Down came the Liberty Trees. The Pope, who had been led into captivity, was restored, the Inquisition was reintroduced, the Jews were driven back into the ghetto, and the civil rights of the Italians were revoked.

But it was too late. The Italian people liked the idea of individual freedom. Revolutionary sentiment grew, and secret societies to combat the reactionaries multiplied. The most influential of these was the *Carbonari*, a movement inspired by Christian ideals, supported by Jewish money, and composed of fighting members of both religions. In 1820 the first revolt broke out in the open. It was doomed to failure by the intervention of the Holy Alliance. Bayonets and bullets were the answers to demands for liberty and groceries. But though that battle was lost, the war for freedom went on. Giuseppe Mazzini launched a new revolutionary society with the aim of freeing Italy from both papal rule and foreign domination. Rabbis preached recruitment sermons and the Jews flocked to the banners of Mazzini's Young Italy. This was the second revolution (1830–1831), and it too met with bitter defeat.

A new national hero then appeared on the scene, Giuseppe Garibaldi. In the revolution of 1849, Garibaldi, together with Mazzini, succeeded in the first unification of Italy. Jews streamed into Rome from all over the country to hail the liberators, to hear the new Italian Republic proclaimed. Their devotion and sacrifice earned them high posts in the government of this new republic, which was short-lived. It was again crushed by the Holy Alliance, and again Italy was carved up. The underground fight for unification continued. Jews joined Count Cavour's Risorgimento, marched with Garibaldi's Thousand Redshirts to take Sicily and Naples, fought in Mazzini's new legions, and shouted themselves hoarse with the Italians when success at last followed and the new constitutional Kingdom of Italy was proclaimed in 1861.

In the new Italy, Jews were elected and named by Italians to high and glittering posts, a ringing affirmation of faith in the Jewish people. Luigi Luzzatti, the Jewish founder of the People's Bank in Italy, was finance minister five times, as well as prime minister. General Giuseppe Ottolenghi, the first Jew to serve on the Italian General Staff, fought in the Risorgimento, and became minister of war. Another Jew, Sidney Sonnino, was prime minister twice, and as foreign minister during World War I was instrumental in breaking the Triple Alliance between Germany, Austria, and Italy to bring Italy into the war on the side of the Allies. Catholic Rome elected Ernesto Nathan as its mayor. Ludovico Mortara, who systematized Italian civil law procedure, was president of the Italian Supreme Court and served as minister of justice.

The story of the Jews in nineteenth-century Germany was much the same as in Italy. The first German ghetto to fall, in 1798, was in Bonn, the birthplace of Beethoven, where singing Germans marched to the gates and tore them down. One by one the German ghettos disappeared, and the Jews became citizens. As in Italy, they took part in the revolutions and counterrevolutions taking place in Germany, joining the Germans in their fight for a modern state with liberty for all. The Jews served the Prussian state as officers and privates, as statesmen and bureaucrats. They worked with the Kaiser and Bismarck to unify Prussia with the Confederation of German States, which had replaced the Holy Roman Empire after the Congress of Vienna. When Napoleon III declared war on Prussia in 1870, over 7,000 Jews marched with Bismarck's armies into France. The spirit of *Deutschland über Alles* was as endemic with the German Jews as with the German Christians. German Jews jubilantly hailed the victory with their German Christian comrades in arms, and French Jews swore with French Christians to take revenge.

In Austria, Jewish emancipation first hit a snag, then took much the same form as it had taken in Germany. When Joseph II died, his Patent of Tolerance was buried with him. It was replaced with a free reign of reaction. Jewish and Christian gains were thrown into a coffer of repression, and the lid was slammed shut and sat on by the hosts of the Vienna Congress and the signers of the Holy Alliance. Inside, Christian and Jewish liberals fomented the Revolution of 1848, which blew the royal sit-downers off the lid and out of power, restoring to the Austrians their former gains. An ironic footnote is the fate of Prince Metternich, whose hand had guided the Congress of Vienna. Threatened with a rope by the revolutionaries, Metternich beseeched the help of Baron Salomon Rothschild, one of the century's last Court Jews, who helped him escape and subsidized him in exile.

## SERFS, SLAVOPHILES, AND JEWS

While the emancipation of the Jews progressed rapidly west of the Vistula, Jewish political life in Russia and her buffer states regressed equally rapidly. Jews roamed the Pale of Settlement at will, after the partition of Poland, but remained isolated among illiterate Russian peasants and ignorant landholders. Their life continued to stagnate, their heritage buried in the daily, meaningless activities of village life, their children cut off from secular learning. It was a physically safe dead-end street which spelled intellectual death. Then, suddenly, in the nineteenth century, Russian Jewish history reversed itself. Life became physically dangerous but intellectually challenging.

Five Romanov czars ruled Russia in the nineteenth century. Between them they managed to snatch Russia from the brink of enlightenment and plunge her back into feudal despotism. They had no consistent policy, but ruled by whim, with a blend of ruthlessness and paternalism. They gave freedom to the serfs, but no land. They abolished torture, but instituted a police state. They preached enlightenment, but kept the masses illiterate. Their policy toward the

Jews was equally paradoxical. They abolished the Jewish corporate state, but refused the Jews citizenship. They urged the Jews into agriculture, but would not let them own land. They tried to integrate the Jews with the Russians, but restricted them to an ever-shrinking Pale. In the end, their good and bad intentions alike earned them the hate of Russians, Poles, and Jews.

Russia's one million Jews hailed Alexander I as a liberator, when he ascended the throne in 1801. He granted amnesty to political prisoners, abolished torture, permitted anyone who wished to set his serfs free. Jews were allowed to pursue any occupations they desired. They could attend Russian schools and universities, even settle in Moscow and in Great Russia. Most of these liberties were on paper only. Nevertheless, many Jews whose parents were peddlers and goatherds managed to become merchants and manufacturers, professionals and scholars. Though most still lived in the Pale, the average Jew was better off than the average Russian, who at the dawn of the nineteenth century still lived in a thatched mud hut with his animals, slave to his master's knout, illiterate and superstitious.

At the Congress of Vienna, however, Alexander I drank too much of the wine of reaction and began to view with fright his own liberalism. He clamped a police-state straitjacket over all Russia, and embarked upon a policy of herding all Jews back into a smaller Pale. He died before he could put these ideas into effect, but his successor, Nicholas I, shared his older brother's fears, and Russians, Poles, and Jews all felt his tyrannical hand.

Jews were banned from their professions and banished from the cities into the Pale. Overnight, 100,000 Jews were made penniless and homeless. A special military conscription policy made Jewish children between twelve and eighteen years of age eligible for twenty-five years of military service. Once a Jewish youth was thus drafted his parents never saw him again. He either died before his term expired, or converted under the pressure of taunts and torture. Civil disobedience developed, giving rise to a new Russian occupation, kidnaping. These military kidnapers— or *"choppers"* (literally snatchers), as they were known by the Jews—prowled Jewish communities, kidnaping Jewish boys to fill military quotas, much as the British impressed

Americans into their merchant marine, prior to the War of 1812.

One other edict would have practically wiped out Jewish communal life but for the ingenuity of the Jews. Jewish self-government was to be dissolved and the Jews were to be placed directly under Russian administration, in much the same manner as in France under Napoleon. When the Jews in the West gave up their corporate state, however, they received citizenship in exchange. But Russia had not given up its feudal state and did not grant the Jews citizenship. The Jews had a justifiable disrespect for Russian justice and administration. To have depended upon the mercies of Russian justice would have led to destruction. Corruption and venality ran through the Russian state like venereal disease through Napoleon's troops in Spain.

How, then, did the Jews of Russia survive, without either a state of their own or a host state to protect them? They devised a pocket-size, instant government known as *hevras*, or "societies." The Jews broke down the functions of government into component parts and formed a society for each function. There were societies for orphans, funerals, education, marriageable poor maidens, soup kitchens, arts and crafts—anything one could name—each with its rules and bylaws which the members had to abide by. Whenever a dispute arose, the Jews went to the proper "society" for justice. There always happened to be a rabbi or two as a member in each *hevra* to render a verdict. Seldom did a Jew resort to a Russian court.

By 1850 the Pale had shrunk to half its original size, and most Jews lived on the edge of poverty, starvation, and despair. When Czar Nicholas I was lowered into his grave with the unified hatred of Russians, Poles, and Jews, in 1855, the first act of the Romanov drama ended.

With amazement Russia watched the second act of this unpredictable royal play. Alexander II boldly freed 40 million serfs, curbed the powers of the Greek Orthodox Church, cracked down on the nobles, and cleaned out the Augean stables of his corrupt judiciary. He ended the forcible conscription of Jewish juveniles, made education available to all, and opened the doors of Russia to the three million Jews living in the Pale.

Once more the history of the Jews took on the now familiar forms. Because of their connections with European banking houses, because of their ready credit, Czar Alexander turned to them to help him develop Russia industrially. It was to the Jews that he entrusted the building of Russia's banking system. Samuel Poliakov, known as Russia's "railroad king," linked Russia's East and West with arteries of iron, for which he was knighted. Banking, law, architecture, medicine, industry became the occupations of Jews in Russia. This new mode of life applied only to 5 percent of the Jewish population, however. The vast majority still lived in the Pale. But with no twenty-five-year military-service terms threatening their children, with the avenues of education open, hope again swept through the Russian Jewish communities.

Then, as if overnight, the second act of liberalism was over. The stage was struck, down came the scenery of enlightenment and back went the props of Act One. A wave of reaction swept Russia. The Jews were hurled back into the Pale, and anyone who looked like a liberal ended up in front of a firing squad or behind the Urals. Everything went wrong for Alexander II. The Poles rebelled. Russia's land mass was rubbed raw by the sores of pauperized peasants, landless serfs, underpaid factory workers, oppressive working conditions, disaffected minorities. Russia was sick unto her Slavic soul.

Alexander II, never noted for his originality, resorted to an "aspirin cure"; to heal the sick Slavic soul of his country, he applied a new Russian brand of nationalism known as "Slavophilism." The Slavophiles held that Russia should stop imitating the West and return to the source of her greatness, the "Slavic soul." It was a movement to gain unity by a denial of fact. The Slavophiles created an image of Russia that hid its ignorance, illiteracy, poverty. Those who saw these things were held to be myopic and subversive. "One Russia, one creed, one Czar" was the Slavophile slogan. Obedience to the Czar (the Little Father of Russia) and to the Church (the Holy Mother of Russia) was the mystic cement which held the pan-Slavic state together—with a little help from the secret police and terrorist gangs.

The Russian people countered terror with terror. One nice day in 1881 the Nihilists blew Alexander II to bits with a homemade bomb, but instead of gaining amelioration for their desperate plight they reaped weak-minded Alexander III. The new Czar was completely in the hands of the aristocrats, who could see no further than their privileges. Their leader was Pobedonostsev, head of the Holy Synod, a Slavophile who looked upon democracy as a leprous disease and upon voting as dangerous. It was he who instituted the pogroms, officially sponsored uprisings against the Jews as tactics to divert the Russians from their miseries. His formula for solving the "Jewish question" was "one third conversion, one third emigration, and one third starvation." The pogroms he encouraged were a diversion for the masses, like the circuses of the Romans, but instead of tossing Christians to the lions he tossed Jews to the peasants. A series of such calculated pogroms erupted all over Russia, and the entire world protested. Twenty thousand Jews were expelled from Moscow. Jews emigrated by the hundreds of thousands to the United States, which still had unrestricted immigration. But the millions for whom there was no avenue of escape lived in fear and poverty, kept alive by the help that poured in from voluntary Jewish relief organizations in Europe and America.

The Romanovs, like the Bourbons, never learned. Nicholas II, the last of the Russian autocrats, also met with bullets the demands of his people for bread. In despair, Russians joined the revolutionary movements, from parliamentary reformism to communism. The day of reckoning was not far off.

When World War I broke out, the promise to "make the world safe for democracy" was meant only for the western front, for on the eastern front as the Russian armies retreated Russian reactionaries advanced. The liberal parties had rallied patriotically to give their support to the government, but Nicholas II arrogantly failed to recognize them or support their aspirations. As one military defeat after another crippled Russian prestige and power, the Czar announced he would take personal command of the armies, a declaration which threw Russia into consternation, for even his most sycophantic nobles did not credit him with even a modicum of military genius.

With Nicholas II on the front, Empress Alexandra, who could not even spell the word "democracy," took over domestic affairs. She was completely in the power of an illiterate, lustful monk named Grigori Rasputin, who through hypnosis, it was alleged, was able to prevent her hemophilic son from bleeding to death. Rasputin was a member of the Khlysti sect, whose main tenet was the necessity for carnal sinning in order to obtain salvation. Into his hands, with black bands of dirt under the long fingernails, fell the rule of Russia.

Russia was dying. Disease, starvation, and death stalked her people. War casualty figures mounted. Disorganization, shortages, strikes plagued her. Many Russians who had hoped that parliamentary reforms could save her were now convinced that nothing short of overthrowing the present regime could help. Rasputin was assassinated and eased into a hole in the ice of the River Neva. Parliament seized power and forced the abdication of the Czar. The Communists overthrew the interim government and established the Soviet state. Czar Nicholas and his entire family were shot in Ekaterinburg. The rule of the Romanovs was over.

During the reign of the last two czars, a new attitude had transformed the Jew of Russia. New ideologies had penetrated into the Pale. For a hundred years the Jews had passively put up with czars who had blown hot and cold. They had petitioned the Little Father of Russia to let them live and make a living. They had stayed away from politics. But Jewish youth grew tired of going to Jewish funerals. They tired of caution. A century of appeasement had brought nothing but ignominy, starvation, pogroms. The Jews had had enough and were ready to fight. They began to demand liberties, instead of begging for them. They went into politics, they joined underground movements, and they ran for office in spite of all warnings when the Czar was forced to grant elections for a representative parliament, or Duma. Jewish liberals were hanged with other liberal Russians, after the Czar dissolved the Duma. And some joined the Red Army organized by Leon Trotsky to fight the five invading armies led by White Russian generals attempting to restore the rule of the Romanovs.

Eastern Jewish history now mingled with Western Jewish history, in the fields of battle where Jews in Russian uniform fought against Jews in German uniform, in the field of ideas where the politics of the left clashed with the politics of the right, in the field of theology where orthodoxy clashed with reform, and in the field of Judaism where Jews embraced each other as brothers.

Modern Jewish history, then, begins with the Jews impatiently knocking on the portals of the eighteenth century, seeking admittance to full citizenship. The French Revolution left Jewish emancipation as a residue on the bottom of the revolutionary crucible. As Napoleon's armies advanced, the walls of the ghetto crumbled.

But, mercifully, the emancipated Jews were unaware of the assault to be made upon them by a new degeneracy of man—racism. In subsequent chapters we shall first dissect the anti-Semitic symptom of racism, then trace the development of two new currents in Jewish life: a Western one, seeking identification with the surrounding gentile culture, and an Eastern one, leading to a new affirmation of Jewish values. We shall then see these two currents merging into an ironic trilogy of thesis, antithesis, and synthesis—first, a fusion in America through successive waves of immigration; then, an appointment with death in the concentration camps of Hitler; and, finally, a reunion in the re-created state of Israel.

TWENTY-FOUR

# REHEARSAL FOR RACISM

Toward the end of the nineteenth century we come face to face for the first time with a unique phenomenon which, more than any other single factor, has influenced the course of Jewish history since 1850. This is the phenomenon of anti-Semitism. We must understand not only its nature but also its origins, because the mixture of anti-Semitism, nationalism, and racism created the barbarism of our age and was responsible for the mass murder of five million Jews. When and why did it originate? What is its nature? How did it spread?

Most people think of anti-Semitism as having existed for four thousand years, ever since Jewish history began, mainly because the term has been conferred retroactively by so many historians on past events which outwardly resembled anti-Semitism. Any act of violence involving Jews, regardless of cause, was classified as an anti-Semitic act, when it should have been classified in some other manner, as "anti-Jewish" perhaps. Contrary to the popularly held opinion, anti-Semitism did not come into being until 1800. The word "anti-Semitism," in fact, did not exist until 1879,* when it was coined by a German to fit the emergence of an entirely new historic pattern of Jewish-Christian relationships.

We are obviously dealing with a semantic problem, where various acts of violence, all having different motivations, have fallen under the same descriptive mantle. Consequently, in order to understand the specific course Jewish history took in the Modern Age, as well as to understand how this modern history differed from that of other ages, we must make a distinction between an "anti-Semitic" and an "anti-Jewish" act, because each connotes a different value judgment.

How essential semantic distinctions are, in making value judgments, can be illustrated with a simple example. Suppose there were only the word "murder" to cover all situations where one man has killed another. Then any killing would have to be classified as murder. This would do away with such recognized degrees of killing as "self-defense," "accidental homicide," "murder in the second degree," and the like. But the law does recognize different degrees of killing, and the motivation behind each killing determines its degree. There are different psychological motivations behind anti-Semitic and anti-Jewish acts, just as there are different motivations behind premeditated murder and manslaughter. What are some of these differences?

Four qualities distinguish anti-Semitism from anti-Jewish violence. Anti-Semitism is illogical and irrational,

---

*The word "anti-Semitism" was first used in a pamphlet published that year, entitled *The Victory of Judaism over Germanism*, a violent, intemperate attack on the Jews by an apostate half-Jew named Wilhelm Marr. Again, the apostate, running like a curse through Jewish history.

and stems from unconscious forces. First comes the prejudice; then follows the rationalized justification for that feeling. Anti-Jewish violence, on the other hand, stems from logical, rational, and conscious motivations. First comes the motivation, then comes the act of retaliation. Second, anti-Semitism is directed toward the "Jewish race" and has nothing whatever to do with the individual Jew, his faults, or his virtues. Anti-Jewish violence is directed toward the Jew as an individual, in the same way and for the same reasons that violence is directed toward individuals of other religions and nationalities. Third, anti-Semitism deliberately seeks out Jews, and Jews only, for its targets, excluding all others who might be equally "guilty" of whatever the Jew is accused of. Anti-Jewish violence often is only an incidental factor in the general violence committed by the attacker. Fourth, anti-Semitism does not seek a solution, does not hold out "redemption" to the Jew, and does not offer an alternative for being Jewish. In anti-Jewish violence, which is directed specifically at Jews, the object is to convert them to the religion of the attacker.

People who do not like Jews must not be confused with anti-Semites. There is no more reason for Jews to be universally liked than for Americans, Englishmen, or Frenchmen to be universally liked. Voltaire did not like Jews, but that did not make him anti-Semitic. He thought of all Jews as ignorant and superstitious, but held that this was no reason why they should be burned. Herein lies the difference. If one does not like someone, one simply does not associate with that person. One does not advocate that he should be debased or annihilated. To the true anti-Semite, the crux of anti-Semitism is the "crime" of being Jewish. This "crime" of Jewishness cannot be obliterated or atoned for, even if the Jew gives up his religion, whereas in the Middle Ages, the moment the Jew was baptized he became an honored citizen. Anti-Semitism is a psychological problem, residing in the mind of the anti-Semite. A few examples from history will illustrate this point.

When Cato exhorted the Romans to exterminate the Carthaginians, it was fear which motivated him, because three times the Carthaginians had challenged the Romans. Carthage was leveled to the ground and the inhabitants were either slain or sold into slavery, as a protective measure against a Fourth Punic War. If we look with equal objectivity upon a similar historic event involving the Jews, we can see that it was not anti-Semitic prejudice which led the Romans to lay Jerusalem waste in the second century A.D. and banish the Jews from Palestinian soil. Like the Carthaginians, the Jews had rebelled three times against the Romans, and like the Carthaginians, then received the same punishment. That this political act was undertaken without prejudice is supported by the fact that subsequently the Romans conferred their coveted citizenship upon all Jews.

The Jewish experience in Spain affords us another example. As stressed in Chapter 18, "Crusades, Renaissance, and Reformation," the Spanish Inquisition was applied only to Christians suspected of heresy, not to the Jews. The Marranos, the converted Jews, were regarded by the Church as Christians, and the Inquisition was applied to them for the same reason it was applied to other Christians, to stem the spread of heresy. The Jews, who could not be touched by the Inquisition, were banished. The fires of the autos-da-fé continued to burn for three hundred years after the Jews were expelled. Its victims were mostly Christians. Jews were the incidental victims of the age, not selected scapegoats because of their race or the innate "crime" of Jewishness.

Is the present feeling against Jews in the Arabic world motivated by illogical, nonobjective factors, or is it engendered by objective, partisan, and political considerations? Rightly or wrongly, the Arabs think they have good cause to fear the Jews, because in their eyes the Jews have dispossessed them from what they consider their land. The Arabs are playing the political game the way it has always been played, mobilizing fears to unify dissident factions. It is anti-Jewish, yes, but certainly not anti-Semitic.

Contrast these acts of violence, motivated by various fears, to the persecution of the Jews in Germany during the days of Hitler, motivated by prejudice. The Jews had never rebelled against Germany, spread no heresy, annexed no German territory. They had, in fact, contributed greatly to her culture and fought valorously side by side with non-Jewish Germans in World War I. The "crime" of the Jews existed only in the mind of the Nazis. The "guilt" of the

Jews was in *being Jewish*. Any human being suspected of having as little as one-tenth Jewish blood was guilty of that "crime." The Nazi philosophy envisioned not only a Germany, but an entire European continent, which would be *Judenrein*—"free of Jews." This was to be accomplished not by conversion or by banishment, as in medieval days, but by murder. Viewed in this light, anti-Semitism no longer appears as an opinion one entertains among other opinions. It becomes an aberration of the mind.

Irrational race anti-Semitism, as we have seen, was unknown in the pagan, Grecian, Roman, Islamic, and medieval cultures in which the Jews lived from 2000 B.C. to 1800 A.D. We have seen how during these 3,800 years Jews were slain, massacred, tortured, sold as slaves—but who was not treated much the same way in those days? Anti-Jewish violence differed in no way from the violence directed at other minority nations and groups. One has but to scan a list of the nations which have disappeared from history during these thirty-eight centuries to realize the magnitude of the carnage practiced. The history of anti-Jewish violence in the Middle Ages was more complex than in the previous ages, but it was not irrational anti-Semitism, embodying the four points in our definition. Medieval Christian anti-Jewish violence stemmed from the refusal of the Jew to become Christian. Anti-Semitism is based upon the complete reverse of this concept. The anti-Semite hates the idea of Jewishness, not the individual Jew. Since it is a concept he hates, the conversion of the Jew alters nothing in his mind.

How did anti-Jewish animosity become anti-Semitic prejudice? How did this change in thinking take place? The transformation was accomplished in three stages, successive but overlapping. First, the soil for modern anti-Semitism was mulched in a new insecure social class created by changing economic conditions. Second, nationalism was manipulated into racism to give this new social class a philosophy of superiority. Third, to quell the inner anxieties of this new class, anti-Jewish feeling was distilled into anti-Semitism and used as a political tranquilizer.

We have seen how the Reformation dealt a deathblow to feudalism, and how a new mercantilism developed in the wake of Protestantism—the spirit of free trade and enterprise. This new spirit also affected the ethical thinking of man. Previous religious precepts were weakened. No longer did the masses believe in church-oriented society. Religion became divorced from government. And, as religion lost its full significance, it became less and less important to the Western world whether or not Jews converted to Christianity. In fact, many are puzzled today that this should ever have been a serious issue.

By 1800 capitalism and colonialism were in full flowering. Another development had also taken place, the Industrial Revolution. It is a little difficult to realize today that the Industrial Revolution is barely two hundred years old. It is also a little difficult to realize that in 1850 the average industrial enterprise employed fewer than fifty people. With the growth of industrialism, intimate personal relationships between worker and owner disappeared. Foremen and department managers now stood between them. Absentee management appeared. The multiple plant developed. Employees became estranged from each other; five thousand workers in a plant became a "lonely crowd."

Hand in hand with these new developments in industry, yet another estrangement took place. Handiwork disappeared. In the past, man had taken pride in his product—the horseshoes he forged, the footwear he created, the suit he tailored. He was in those days a creator of total and complete things. That pride and that relationship to society disappeared with the assembly-line method of production. The worker became estranged from the finished product. Now he created only a small part of the finished product—a fragment.

These economic changes in man's life had far-reaching social implications and deep psychological effects. As machinery reduced the ranks of the workers, an entirely new social class came into being, a class which created no goods but rendered services instead. In the past hundred years this service-rendering class has grown progressively larger, as the parent body of workers upon whose productivity it feeds has grown smaller. We are in the process of creating a society in which fewer and fewer people produce concrete objects and an ever-increasing number of people are engaged in paper activity, all more or less connected with the disposal of these goods.

This new and ever-growing social class is composed of bureaucrats, bookkeepers, hack writers, petty academicians, marginal advertising, publicity, and professional men, small functionaries, lower-echelon office workers, and others, whose feet are in the parlor of the worker and whose heads are in the living room of the manager. This is the group which forms the heart of that amorphous mass of modern society which Hannah Arendt in *The Origins of Totalitarianism* calls *déclassé*, the "declassed" segment of society, so called because it has lost its former class status and former security. We shall also refer to this group as the "frayed-white-collar class," in contrast to the "white-collar class" of professional and managerial people. It is among the insecure in this declassed, frayed-white-collar group that we find most of the potential adherents of modern anti-Semitism. It is from this group that Hitler recruited his most ardent followers.

As the religious forces holding society together weakened, the psychological forces holding man's unconscious hostilities in check also weakened. The social breakdown brought insecurity; the psychological breakdown brought anxiety. The social group which was most affected by the economic changes taking place, the group which became most estranged from its former values and status symbols, was and is this new frayed-white-collar class. Because it is the most insecure group in modern society, it is also the most anxiety-ridden. In order to quell, to pacify, to alleviate these frightening feelings of insecurity and anxiety, the frayed-white-collar class looked around for leaders who would restore to them their lost prestige and former security, and for a philosophy which would quell their anxieties. Religion had once served that function. Something else was now needed to fill the void.

Charles's law applies to politics as well as to gases. Politicians began to pander to this group in direct proportion to its political usefulness. Because the modern state had given the franchise to the declassed, they became important to politicians seeking power. A new power struggle developed in western Europe. On the one hand were the forces standing for strong centralized states, fighting against the emerging working class in the same way the feudal state had fought against the emerging middle class.

On the other hand were the liberal and democratic forces, advocating the assimilation of the working class into the new society by allowing them a greater participation in the affairs of state and a greater share of its goods. Depressions and dislocations of industry were pushing the frayed-white-collar class into a marginal existence, threatening its members with absorption into a working class they despised. The declassed also feared the new philosophies of socialism and communism which would transfer power from them to the working class.

The mid-nineteenth century, the period of contagious revolutions in Europe, the period that saw the birth of socialism and communism, was also the period in which politicians suddenly found a new use for the frayed-white-collar class and the Jews. The declassed could be used as a buffer. They were wooed by the politicians of the right to offset the encroachments of the politicians of the left. The insecurity of the declassed was explained not in terms of social and economic conditions but in terms of Jewish evil-doing. The Jew was held up to them as the exploiting capitalist when it was capitalism the declassed feared, or as the plotting communist when it was communism they feared. If not for the Jew, these arguments ran, every member of the declassed would be an important pillar in society.

This was the beginning of anti-Semitism. It was not a political movement, as someone once remarked, but a political weapon. Existing anti-Jewish feeling, left over from the Middle Ages, was slowly transformed into anti-Semitism by its constant application to this new use. The religious politician in the Middle Ages had asked for the banishment of the Jews so that they would not infect the Christian believer with doubt. The secular politician of the Modern Age did not ask for the banishment of the Jews, because it would not have served his purpose. If the Jews were banished, the declassed would immediately see that their condition had in no way improved. The way the first manipulators of anti-Semitism saw it, the Jews had to be kept around as perpetual scapegoats. What they had not foreseen, or wished for, was the emergence of a new breed of totalitarian politician who would advocate the actual extermination of Jews. They had not foreseen that their own irresponsible propa-

ganda would be seized by neurotics and sadists and shaped
into a philosophy of murder.

The process began imperceptibly, like any cancerous
growth. Even as the declassed listened to the anti-Jewish
diatribes of the politicians, their own anti-Jewish feelings
took on more and more disturbing aspects. Those who felt
the need for anti-Semitism also felt uneasy about it. Behind the violence of their anti-Semitic slogans there lurked
another anxiety from the realization that their reasons for
hating the Jews had nothing to do with the Jews but was
something within themselves. If only they had leaders who
could assuage their doubts, leaders who could make respectable these disturbing feelings of hate! Their prayers
were answered.

The declassed were given a comforting ideational "race
religion" by three late-nineteenth-century race theorists
who extolled the meager virtues of the frayed-white-collar
class into superior products. In addition, anti-Semitism was
given a scientific veneer by three books which had the
quality of transforming disturbing anxiety into respectable
hate. The three race theorists were Count Arthur de Gobineau, a Frenchman; Friedrich Nietzsche, a German; and
Houston Stewart Chamberlain, an Englishman. The authors of the three pseudoscientific books were Édouard
Drumont, a Frenchman; Sergei Nilus, a Russian; and Alfred Rosenberg, a German.

"Race thinking" was not born in Germany; it began in
the early 1800s, festering on the exposed body of European
nationalism. The race theorists were at first held in contempt, but toward the end of that same century they had
gained esteem, an ominous indication of the drift of the
times. Nationalism was conceived by honorable parents
with good intent—Rousseau, Burke, Jefferson, Fichte,
Locke, Mazzini—none of whom were Jewish. From
Rousseau, who was born in 1712, to Mazzini, who died in
1872, the lives of these six social philosophers overlapped,
as did their social philosophies. These philosophies essentially centered around the idea of man as a citizen of the
state instead of a subject of God. Pseudointellectual para-
sites fastened themselves onto these philosophies of nationalism, sucked out their humanism, and spawned
virulent ideas of a nationalism based on race instead of on

equal rights of man. These race philosophers made "blood" the fount of grace, and the "superman" supplanted the Gospels as a source of power.

The first of these race philosophers, Count Gobineau, was a minor official in the French diplomatic service, embittered at never having advanced to a post of importance. In his book *The Inequality of Human Races*, published in 1853, he advanced what may have been the first systematic theory of white racial supremacy. As Hannah Arendt expressed it, "He was only a curious mixture of frustrated nobleman and romantic intellectual who invented racism almost by accident." Gobineau introduced the concept of one single cause behind the fall of all civilizations, the dilution of the superior blood in aristocracy by the inferior blood of the common people. In essence, Gobineau held that the blood of the Aryan elite was being diluted with the blood of a non-Aryan mass through the process of democracy. He does not mention the Jews. It is the middle- and lower-class French he views with fear, for it is they who carry the taint of inferior blood, infecting the French aristocracy, which he claims was descended from Nordic Aryans. The French at first ignored Gobineau, but the Germans immediately embraced his theories. His book gained him the friendship of Friedrich Nietzsche, creator of the concept of the superman.

A whole school of apologists has recently arisen, making Nietzsche the ethical successor to the humanists. Nietzsche, however, with all due regard for his nervous, brilliant prose, is the "father" of Nazism, and his ethic is not the ethic of Torah and Testament, but the limited code of the Nazi. "Write with blood," advises Nietzsche, "and you learn that spirit is blood." In *Beyond Good and Evil*, Nietzsche also laid down the foundation for the morality of his superman with such maxims as "You I advise not to work but to fight," and "You I advise not to peace but to victory," and "A man shall be raised as a warrior, a woman for a warrior's recreation," and "Are you going to women? Do not forget your whip." His superman is beyond good and evil, for, says Nietzsche, "the falseness of an opinion is for us no objection to it . . . and we are fundamentally inclined to maintain that the falsest of opinions . . . are the most indispensable to us." His philosophy led, indeed, to a complete defiance of Christianity, to a complete reversal of the teachings of Gospel and Decalogue. His works, the cornerstone for the Nazi state, were written during the decade before his insanity, and he died insane. It may be that Nietzsche did not advocate what he wrote, but that he foresaw with the clarity of a prophet the morality of the new age ahead. But we are not passing value judgments on the man; we are concerned with the effects of his philosophy. Nietzsche the man did not create history. His books did.

Houston Stewart Chamberlain, an Englishman living in Germany, combined the social theories of Gobineau, the philosophy of Nietzsche, and anti-Semitism in his book *Foundations of the Nineteenth Century*, published in 1899 in German and in 1911 in English. In this work, Gobineau's supremacy of the aristocracy became Nordic supremacy; race and blood were welded into a pseudoscientific sociology upon which the final Aryan-race and superman theories were fashioned. Like so many other racists, Chamberlain became a traitor to his country, defecting to the Germans during World War I.

As the race theorists enlarged upon their philosophies, anti-Semites gave them practical application. Jewish history was vulgarized, distorted, and changed to fit the new needs. The first of these books to synthesize racism and anti-Semitism was Drumont's *La France juive*, published in 1886. It helped give people who entertained anti-Semitic feelings a reason for feeling the way they did.

For the first time in 3,900 years of Jewish history an entirely new picture of the Jews arose—that of the Jews as conspirators. In the Middle Ages the Jew had been depicted as a stupid, uncouth, flea-bitten lout, in order to create such an abhorrent image of him that no self-respecting Christian would want to convert to the Jewish faith. In the new catechism of the anti-Semites, the Jew was conceded to have superior intellect, learning, skill, and capacity to excel. But these virtues were now evil, for these were the qualities which the frayed-white-collar class realized it did not possess. By making these qualities vices, Drumont made mediocrity a virtue. His book attempted to show how the Jews, with their intellect, learning, and skill, would soon dominate France and turn it into a Jewish state. Drumont had correctly appraised the psychological needs of the declassed. The denigrated Jew of the Middle Ages—the hunchbacked peddler with the yellow patch—was an out-dated medieval symbol. This type of Jew could not be a threat. But the diabolical Jew with superior cunning—this was the enemy! Overnight the symbol created by Drumont took. *La France juive* became the bible of the declassed.

Unfortunately for the anti-Semites of the world, Dru-mont's book gave this alleged Jewish plot only national proportions. Only Frenchmen could have cause for con-cern. What about the Germans, the Austrians, the Romani-ans, the Hungarians? Sergei Nilus remedied this flaw. He expanded the Drumont "conspiracy" to international scope.

The origin of Nilus's notorious *Protocols of the Elders of Zion*, published in 1903, is so fantastic that the truth it-self is hardly believable. As it became increasingly difficult to convince the ignorant Russian peasants of the necessity to kill innocent Jews in order to alleviate their own miser-able condition, Czar Nicholas II commissioned Nilus, a monk, to come up with something to damn the Jews. Nilus forged a set of documents, based on a French novel which had no Jews in it. This Nilus forgery purported to show how a group of conspiratorial Jews, known as the Elders of Zion, planned to conquer the world. It did not convince the Russian peasants, but it convinced the world's anti-Semites. The forgery served their preexisting needs.

The Drumont and Nilus fantasies of a Jewish conspiracy to seize power gave the anti-Semites a peg on which to hang their perplexing and disturbing anxieties. Now they could say, "We don't hate the Jews. Some of our best friends are Jews.* It's the Jews themselves who are forcing us to protect ourselves and our country from their conspir-acies."

This reasoning is similar to the reasoning of a paranoid psychotic. The paranoid has "feelings" that he is perse-cuted, and this causes him anxiety, because he is at a loss to explain his disturbing feelings. He therefore invents "logi-cal" reasons for them—a particular person or group is out to "get" him. His logic is clear and consistent. But, because

---

*Adolf Otto Eichmann, even as he murdered millions of Jews, felt the need to boast about "Jewish friends."

the premise is based on a delusion, these answers never quite satisfy him. To convince himself that his reasoning is correct, he has to "defend" himself against his "accusers" by punishing them. These tensions finally build up to such proportions that the paranoid becomes capable of murdering an innocent person unless given medical treatment in time. Because Western man did not incarcerate the paranoid anti-Semite in its midst, social paranoia eventually erupted in mass murder.

In Drumont's and Nilus's books, the anti-Semites were supplied with defense mechanisms for feeling the way they did. But they lacked a philosophy which would ennoble their anti-Semitism and elevate their violence to a civic duty. Such a comforting philosophy was supplied by Alfred Rosenberg, a dedicated Nazi party member, with the publication in 1930 of his book *The Myth of the Twentieth Century*. Here the way to total anti-Semitism was found, the road to the gas chambers of Belsen and Auschwitz paved. Even Catholics and Protestants did not realize the nature of the peril, as only the refrain "kill the Jews" was heard. When they did understand the siren song, the sirens were upon them too.

In brief, the thesis of Rosenberg's book was that Germany should be rebuilt not on Christian principles but on the philosophy of Nietzsche. It was to be the state of the superman, the state without principles. Christianity, Rosenberg argued, was to be extirpated as a Jewish disease. The Germans and those "spiritually" akin to them should dispense with such "Christian nonsense" as guilt, sin, and morality. Instead they devised a "new Christianity" from which St. Paul was purged. Jesus was Nordicized and given a Syrian mother and a Roman father, pure pagans both. A new myth was formulated, the myth of the mystique of Aryan blood.

This was the ranting of a Nazi madman, and it was given a gruesome reality by 15 million German bayonets. Yet the world was so anesthetized by the pseudoscientific writings of racists and anti-Semites that it rarely raised a voice in protest when it saw murder perpetrated in the name of nonsense.

Thus, imperceptibly, nationalism, the hope of the eighteenth-century humanists, was transformed into the philosophy of racism in the nineteenth century. Thus the religious anti-Jewish feeling of the Middle Ages was turned into racist anti-Semitism. By 1870 the first openly anti-Semitic political parties had been formed in Germany, and politicians vied for the votes of anti-Semites by whipping their anxieties into fears. The balance of power held by the declassed became so enormous in Germany that even Bismarck, who at first had scorned them, catered to their votes to hold on to his power, thereby giving anti-Semitism its first coat of respectability. Anti-Semitism spread to the declassed of Eastern Europe and France, where, with the celebrated Dreyfus Affair, it exploded into a dress rehearsal for the total anti-Semitism of the twentieth century.

Though the Jewish Captain Alfred Dreyfus made his entrance as the central figure, he soon relegated himself to a minor role as he fought the case on the narrow lines of personal injustice only. The real heroes were two Christians, an army colonel and a novelist, who realized that the Dreyfus Affair represented a case of the state conspiring against the individual. They challenged not only the injustice to Dreyfus, but the right of the state to put itself above justice. In 1894, injustice to one man could still inspire the indignation of the world. *L'Affaire Dreyfus* was fought in court and ballot box, in sidewalk cafés and world headlines. It tore France apart politically, but she emerged the spiritual victor.

The Dreyfus drama began in 1893 with the philanderings of a dashing, handsome, fierce-mustached, impecunious, Paris-born French aristocrat of Hungarian descent. Major Ferdinand Walsin Esterhazy, an engaging scoundrel who meant no harm as he ruined others. He had served in the papal army against the Italian Risorgimento, fought with the French against the Prussians in 1870, and had been decorated for valor. He married a lady of dubious charm but of impeccable aristocratic lineage and high financial standing, whose fortune he soon squandered. Esterhazy then became part owner of a fashionable house of prostitution, but when even this could not support him in the style he thought was his due, he augmented his income by selling military secrets to the German embassy.

The French counterespionage, working to uncover the

spy in their midst, came into possession of a document to be known as the *bordereau*, written by Esterhazy, which listed five items of military information he had delivered to the Germans. Suspecting that the leak came from someone on their own General Staff, French intelligence officers ran through their files, comparing the handwriting of its personnel to the handwriting in the *bordereau*. When the card with the name "Alfred Dreyfus" came up, the search automatically ended. Alfred Dreyfus was the only Jewish officer on the French General Staff, and the General Staff, still intensely royalist and antirepublican, was prepared to do anything to get rid of the only Jewish member foisted upon it by a republican regime.

There is nothing much to say of Captain Alfred Dreyfus himself, except that history proved him innocent. He was an undistinguished Jew. Blue-eyed, pale, taut, reserved, uncommunicative, he appeared haughty, overbearing, and snobbish. Besides his wife and two children, he had no friends. He had joined the army out of a deep love for it, and by virtue of being better than average, by possessing an immense capacity for work, he was subsequently commissioned a lieutenant in the artillery and promoted to captain. He was a man of great personal wealth, a man always correct, a man without vice—in short, a bore. He would have made an ideal officer for a minor staff job, had he not been Jewish.

Dreyfus was arrested on the charge of espionage. Soon after the arrest, the General Staff discovered that Esterhazy, not Dreyfus, was the guilty party. But to accuse a French aristocrat and career officer of espionage was something the General Staff could not countenance. It would mean loss of prestige for the army. The decision to sacrifice Dreyfus was made. He was court-martialed and sentenced to life imprisonment on Devil's Island, after a public dishonorable discharge from his command. The court-martial was a victory for Édouard Drumont, who had been in the vanguard of the rioters demanding the conviction of Dreyfus. This publicly confirmed Drumont's thesis that Jews were conspiring to take over France. The army was pleased; it had vindicated its honor. The public was pleased; the army had protected it from traitors. The Jews were confused; they did not know what to think.

Nobody, least of all the army itself, had figured that if a nemesis came it would come in the shape of a slender, ascetic-looking, devoutly Catholic career officer, Colonel Georges Picquart, Chief of Intelligence. Picquart, promoted to this post after the Dreyfus conviction, accidentally stumbled across the fact that the notorious *bordereau* had been written not by Dreyfus but by Esterhazy. He excitedly took his findings to his superiors, who coolly informed him to keep quiet. As one general expressed it, "Why should you care about this Jew?"

To defy the army meant loss of his career; to come out for a Jew meant loss of status. But Picquart saw the situation for what it was, not a question of the innocence of one Jew, but a question of the state having the power to conspire against an individual. Like the Prophets of old, Picquart placed justice above his personal safety. He spoke out in public, demanding a reexamination of the facts and a new trial for Dreyfus. The army responded by demoting him and sending him to the Tunisian front lines in the hope he would be killed fighting against Arab tribesmen.

But Picquart's public statements had aroused that segment of the people which also places justice above state expediency. Overnight, it seemed, France was divided into two camps, a small minority, the "Dreyfusards," clamoring for justice, and the "anti-Dreyfusards" branding the Dreyfusards as traitors for demanding that the army incriminate itself. The anti-Dreyfusards had Church, state, army, and press behind them. Newspapers screamed anti-Dreyfusard slogans, street fights developed, and the Jews, in the main, not realizing that a mob can never be appeased, tried to appease it by quietly staying out of the fight.

But the hysteria did not abate. As the people's doubt grew with the clamor of the Dreyfusards, the army decided to put on a show to exonerate itself. In an elaborately faked trial in which Major Esterhazy was tried on charges of espionage brought by Colonel Picquart, tons of irrelevant materials, purporting to show his innocence, were introduced with great gravity by Esterhazy's defense. Opposing counsel was prevented from asking pertinent questions under the pretense that answers would give military information to the enemy. Major Esterhazy was unanimously acquitted, and Colonel Picquart, who had not been killed on the Tunisian front, was arrested for having dared to accuse Esterhazy.

Many who had believed Dreyfus guilty now began to have doubts. Men in and out of public office saw the affair for what it truly was—a plot of reactionaries, hiding behind the façade of anti-Semitism, to undermine the republican state. Among those who saw through the fraud were Émile Zola, world-famous novelist, and Georges Clemenceau, publisher of *L'Aurore* and former correspondent with General Ulysses S. Grant's army during the Civil War. It was the concerted action of these two men which broke the Dreyfus case wide open.

In January 1898 Zola's famous letter entitled *"J'Accuse"* (I Accuse) appeared as a headlined front-page editorial in Clemenceau's paper. Over 500,000 copies had to be printed, as Parisians fought for them. In the letter Zola openly accused the government and the army of deliberately conspiring against Dreyfus to cover up its own infamy. He accused them of fraud and degradation of justice, calling the Dreyfus affair a "crime of high treason against humanity."

The government tried to intimidate the opposition by arresting Zola, who fled to England. But Zola's letter had broken the back of the anti-Dreyfusards. People who, out of ignorance of the facts, had joined the mob now became Dreyfusards. Colonel Joseph Henry, an intelligence officer on the General Staff who had helped fabricate the incriminating evidence against Dreyfus, committed suicide. Major Esterhazy finally confessed that he had written the *bordereau*. In 1898 a new trial was ordered for Dreyfus at Rennes, but he was again convicted, five to two, of high treason. Because of "extenuating circumstances," however, he was sentenced to only ten years' imprisonment.

An even greater shock to the Dreyfusards than the unexpected verdict of guilty was the behavior of Dreyfus himself, who was deferential to the generals trying to convict him and haughty toward Colonel Picquart trying to clear him. When an attaché in dismay asked Clemenceau how much Dreyfus understood of his own case, Clemenceau replied, "Nothing. He is the only one who has not understood it at all. He stands abysmally below the Dreyfus Affair." The opinion of Léon Blum, later Jewish

Premier of France, was that if "Dreyfus had not been Dreyfus but someone else, he would not even have been a Dreyfusard." Those who watched Dreyfus were convinced that had he sat on the court-martial board he too would have convicted the accused in order to save the honor of the army.

But Dreyfus had become a symbol and his mediocrity did not matter. The world protested the travesty of the court-martial at Rennes, and a new President of France ordered a review of the Dreyfus case. In 1906 the French Supreme Court set him free, exonerating him of all charges. He was promoted to major and given the Legion of Honor. He died in 1935, an undistinguished man who had allowed his symbol to overshadow him. Colonel Picquart's subsequent career was a brilliant one. He was made a general and became minister of war. Zola was honored by his country for his fearless fight for justice. Clemenceau became Premier of the Republic and the head of the French delegation to the Peace Conference at Versailles.

The fate of one vociferous anti-Dreyfusard makes an interesting sidelight to this celebrated affair. He was Henri Philippe Pétain, who became Commander in Chief of the French Army in World War I, was made Marshal of France in 1918, and in 1940, after the defeat of France by Germany, headed the collaborationist Vichy government. He was tried for high treason in 1945 by the French and was sentenced to death, the sentence later being commuted to life imprisonment.

And so the first state-sanctioned political manipulation of anti-Semitism failed. The world had not as yet become fully indifferent to injustice. But what failed in France was to succeed in Germany. The mechanism had been tested. With a little more experimentation it would become a formula. By 1900, anti-Semitism had become the mode of political life in Eastern Europe, with Germany as the manufacturing center of anti-Semitic doctrines.

But this nineteenth-century unpremeditated rehearsal for twentieth-century racism was also the stage for the resurgence of Jewish intellectualism. The nineteenth century for the Jews most closely resembled a century of the Italian Renaissance. Within the framework of Western civilizations the Jews produced two cultures, one a unique contribution to the dominant Christian values, the other designed for ethnic survival of the Jews in an age of chaos. Let us examine the nature and source of this creativity before raising the curtain on the twentieth-century racist drama being perfected in Germany for its debut.

TWENTY-FIVE

# WESTERN EUROPE:
# THE NEW ENLIGHTENMENT

The nineteenth century came to an end not with a whimper but with a bang. It did not end neatly in 1900 but stretched through World War I to 1918. It died in the rubble of Verdun and was buried with its accumulation of nineteenth-century values in the fields of Flanders. Never did the Jewish "Diaspora law of talion"—a culture for a culture— apply more fully than during this period. As Western Europe became extrovert, developing a culture of utilitarianism and science, the Western Jews also became extroverts and developed a utilitarian and scientific culture. As Eastern Europe became introvert, examining its own soul and drawing new strength from the past, the Eastern Jews too became introverts, and turned their intellectual searchlights into their Jewish past to find affirmation for the future. The Jews in the West produced a Westernized culture, the Jews in the East a Jewish culture. Both became part of the tapestry of contemporary civilization.

We have traced the ebb and flow of the fortunes of the West European Jews in the Modern Age, without touching upon their intellectual life. What did they contribute to Western Europe as their admission price to the circle of culture-producing people?

An unhistoric people is acted upon by events. A historic people acts upon events. The Jews have remained a historic people through the centuries because they have always been active agents instead of passive bystanders. The Modern Age was no exception. The Jews were not only acted upon by historical forces but they themselves also acted upon history. They created ideas that indelibly imprinted themselves upon the face of the world and affected the future of mankind.

This era in Western Europe was a magnificent period in the history of man, perhaps the most significant in his career on earth. In this period man innovated more than he had in any one millennium in all his previous existence, including his accomplishments in the Greco-Roman Age. In this period tower the figures of Hegel, Schopenhauer, Mill, Darwin, Spencer. This century viewed for the first time the paintings of Goya, Turner, Delacroix, Renoir, Cézanne, Gauguin, Van Gogh. It heard the music of Beethoven, Schubert, Chopin, Wagner, Verdi, Brahms. It read the works of Goethe, Keats, Balzac, Shaw, Yeats. In this century the combustion engine was developed, the X ray was discovered, and pasteurization became a household word.

But the image is blurred if we leave out the names of the Jewish contributors. In this period tower also the Jewish figures of Marx, Freud, Bergson, Einstein. This age also viewed the paintings of Pissarro, Soutine, Chagall, Modigliani. It heard the music of Mendelssohn, Offenbach, Saint-Saëns, Bizet, Mahler. It read Heine, Proust, Maurois, Romains. It witnessed the development of theoretical physics, known as *Judenphysik* by the Germans, and followed with interest the advance in medicine through the works of Wassermann, Ehrlich, and Schick. During this time the Jews helped extend the frontiers of mathematics, biology, and chemistry, and were awarded more Nobel prizes in science than any other national group. They became viceroys, prime ministers, generals, and avant-garde intellectuals who helped shape the map of Europe and chart the course of world history. All this in spite of the fact that the Jews in Western and Central Europe at this time constituted less than one half of one percent of the total population.* All this in spite of the fact that the Jews were

---

*In 1870 the Jews in Germany, Austria-Hungary, France, England, Holland, Spain, Portugal, Italy, Switzerland, and the Scandinavian countries numbered a little under one million, out of a total population in these countries of slightly over 200 million.

still emerging from the ghetto into a climate of growing anti-Semitism.

If someone objects that some of these contributions were not "Jewish" in character, that some of these contributors are only half Jews, converted Jews, or Jews who rejected Judaism, our answer is that we are not concerned with whether a contribution is "Jewish" or "non-Jewish" in character, merely with whether the contributor is Jewish. Whether half Jew, converted Jew, or apostate, the contributor still comes from a Jewish heritage, not a Chinese, Hindu, or deeply rooted Christian tradition.

The nineteenth-century Jewish Enlightenment was like a beam of light refracted through a prism into a spectral band of brilliant intellectual colors spread across Western Europe. The prism through which Jewish thought was refracted was a Jew born in Amsterdam in 1632, a Jew so modern in his thinking that the second half of the twentieth century has not yet caught up with him. Excommunicated by the Jews in the seventeenth century, abhorred by the Christians in the eighteenth century, acknowledged "great" in the nineteenth century, Baruch Spinoza will perhaps not be fully understood even in the twenty-first century. But perhaps by then Spinoza's philosophy will become the basis of a world religion for neomodern man.

Spinoza's father had a successful business, but Spinoza had no talent for business. Instead, he took up the study of Torah, Talmud, and Kabala. Soon outstripping his rabbinic teachers, he turned first to Maimonides, then to the Greek philosophers, to Descartes, and to the rationalists. His teacher now was Francis van den Ende, a Dutchman who combined scholarship and conspiracy in an unsafe proportion, a miscalculation which cost him his head in an abortive plot against the king of France. Spinoza courted van den Ende's beautiful daughter, until a richer, less shy suitor came along and married her. That was the end of romance for Spinoza, who never married.

Meanwhile Spinoza's excursions into the philosophies of the godless philosophers worried the Jewish burghers, who were afraid that their Dutch hosts might think all Jews were atheists. When Spinoza rejected an offer of an annuity by the Amsterdam Jewish community in which he lived, provided he would maintain cordial external relations with the synagogue, he was excommunicated. Spinoza spent the rest of his life in solitude, earning a living grinding lenses and writing the four books which were to bring him world fame. Though he spoke Hebrew and Spanish fluently, he wrote in Dutch and Latin with the preciseness and conciseness of a Talmudist. But his works are still difficult to comprehend because of the terseness with which he expressed his thoughts.

Though we cannot here expound the philosophy of Spinoza, we can pause to note briefly some of its aspects. It attempted to lay foundations for a new, free society, ruled by law, yet also in accord with divine nature. On the one hand, Spinoza presented religion as a product of the imagination, leading, in the main, to piety. On the other hand, Spinoza held that reason and intuition led man to a union with the source of all things, which he calls the intellectual love of God. God, he says, is nature; God is whatever truly *is*. In knowing Him we love Him, and it is this knowledge of Him which makes man's mind immortal. In those days this was a dangerous doctrine of immortality, and laid Spinoza open to misunderstanding and invective. Yet God Himself was ever-present in all of Spinoza's writings, so much so that one commentator has aptly called him the "God-intoxicated man."

Spinoza also laid down a great number of theorems about human passions and right conduct, demonstrating them in Euclidian fashion, "in exactly the same manner, as though I were concerned with lines, planes, and solids." It was a bold attempt to state the principles of a unified master science. Had Spinoza lived beyond the age of forty-four, he would doubtless have applied these principles not only to ethics, politics, and religion, as he did, but also to physics and mathematics, as he planned to do.

Spinoza's philosophy shows the direct influence of the Talmud and Kabala, of Maimonides, the Christian Scholastics, and Descartes. When he died in 1677, his philosophy was almost buried with him. But in 1882, when a statue of him was unveiled in The Hague, Ernest Renan said, "The truest vision ever had of God came perhaps here." It is ironic to speculate that had Spinoza been born a Christian he might have been burned as a heretic, as was the Italian philosopher Giordano Bruno, in 1600, or, had he been born five centuries earlier, in the Islamic Age, he would have been hailed as the great philosopher he was.

Some of the currents in Spinoza's philosophy—the need for piety, the passion for freedom and justice, the rational ordering of all thought, and the conception of an all-embracing science of the universe—were in turn personified by four great, modern Jewish thinkers: Leopold Zunz, Karl Marx, Sigmund Freud, and Albert Einstein.

The first of these Spinozian currents to be felt in Jewish life was that of a "rational piety," or "science of faith." As the fever of emancipation spread through Western Europe, more and more Jews used Mendelssohn's formula to hoist themselves out of the ghetto into the rich cultural life around them. But Mendelssohn's vague and idealistic reform Judaism was not sufficiently practical or elastic to contain all the emancipated Jews within the gates of Judaism. The line to the baptismal font grew. The spirit of the age demanded a scientific foundation for Judaism, a Spinozian presentation of Judaism as an evolving system of the mind, as a form of universal reason.

The task of fashioning such a Judaism fell on Leopold Zunz (1794–1886), a German ghetto Jew who, with his white sideburns and high wing collar, resembles the school-room pictures of Ralph Waldo Emerson. Born to poverty and educated on scholarships, Zunz ate the bread of humiliation long after his fame had been established. But before his death at the age of ninety-two, he had shaped "the science of Judaism." His vast body of work began with a slim monograph on rabbinic literature, which attacked the nonsense written about Jews by Christians who posed as Judaic scholars. Zunz argued for recognition of the great contributions made by Jews to so many civilizations. He founded the first Jewish "Organization for Culture and Science," and published a biography of Rashi, the first systematic study of a Jewish scholar. It was his monumental *History of the Jewish Sermon*, however, which won him his greatest renown. This is perhaps the single most important "Jewish work" produced in the nineteenth century. It traced the growth of the synagogue and its functions through the centuries, and showed how prayer had been practiced by Jews long before Christianity existed. It gave specific dates and illuminated the origins of Jewish beliefs and practices. Zunz showed that Judaism did not become a fossilized remnant of history after the birth of Jesus, but continued as a living creed, a growing ethic, and a valid science.

Zunz's subsequent works dealt with interpretations of Jewish literature and biblical exegesis. One book traced the origin of names to Jewish sources including many names usually thought of as Christian. More than anyone else, Zunz disabused the Christian mind of its stagnant, stereotyped, medieval notions about the Jews. His scientific Judaism gave Reform Judaism not only an intellectual fortress from which the Jews could defend their faith, but also advance outposts from which they could venture on intellectual forays into "enemy territory."

The flow to the baptismal font slowed to a trickle. Reform Judaism did not become the religion of the poor and the ignorant, like Hasidism, but the religion of the rich, the cultured, and the learned. The synagogues were again artistically adorned. Services were modernized and music was made part of the devotional hour. Prayers in the vernacular were instituted. Men and women were allowed to sit together, and the wearing of a hat during services was no longer required. Reform Jews could worship this way because Zunz had shown that Orthodox ghetto practices were not the eternal forms of Judaism, but merely the accretion of ghetto customs. He had shown that music, prayer in the vernacular, a different order of prayers, and the like, were not sacrilegious, but at one time or another had all been part of Jewish temple and synagogue practice.

As Leopold Zunz had sought a scientific formula for modern Judaism, so Karl Marx sought a scientific formula for social justice. It is necessary in any discussion of Marx to touch upon the influence of his doctrines on world history. But we shall avoid becoming entangled in value judgments of these doctrines just as we avoided becoming entangled in value judgments on the doctrines of Paul and Muhammad.

Karl Marx, the son of well-to-do Jewish parents, was born in 1818 in Trier, Germany, the hometown of Saint Ambrose, and was baptized at the age of six. Growing up between two cultures, Marx early rejected the values of Judaism and Christianity, because he felt both sets of values were the residues of iniquitous social systems. Expelled from Prussia for attacking the state, he moved first to Paris, then to London. For a while he held a job as correspondent for the New York *Tribune*, but most of his life he spent in the British Museum, where he wrote *Das Kapital,* the "secular bible" of world communism.

History, said Marx, is motivated by economic forces, not psychological or religious ones, which, he believed, were by-products of man's economic struggle. Change the social order, and the religious and psychological complexions of man would also change, according to his view. Social inequalities, he held, stemmed not from any inherent evil in man, or from any preordained "crime-punishment" doctrines, but from the very nature of an acquisitive society. By changing the capitalist order to a socialist state, a new society would emerge. As with Christianity, communism was seized early by the gentiles and given to people Marx had never dreamed would become communist. Marx was convinced communism could succeed only in states with advanced forms of capitalism, because it would need an advanced technology to establish itself. Instead the advanced nations have remained capitalist,* whereas backward nations with undeveloped economies, like Russia and China, became communist. The industrial economy communism needed had to be built by an enslaved population. The social justice envisioned by Marx was abandoned.

When Karl Marx died in 1883, communism was as weak a movement in world affairs as Christianity was after the death of Paul. But whereas it took one thousand years for Christianity to convert the pagans of Europe, one billion Christians and Asiatics were converted to communism within one hundred years after the death of Marx, and as with the spread of early Christianity, most of the spread of communism was accomplished by force, conquest, and

---

*The reason is a simple one. When Karl Marx wrote *Das Kapital*, large corporations with social-benefit plans and large unions did not exist. The idea that workers would be paid salaries large enough for them to buy back the things they produced would have seemed utopian to Marx. The capitalism Marx inveighed against has disappeared, and the communism he recommended has long since been scrapped. Yet these concepts of 1850 vintage were bandied about as realities in a world where they no longer existed.

proselytization. Almost a third of the world was communist, united by a belief that communism eventually would bring salvation on this earth instead of in the hereafter. As of 1993, communism had fallen in most nations, having been corrupted to the point of being more akin to totalitarianism than communism.

Everyone seems prone to ascribe everything to Marxism, but few want to ascribe anything to psychoanalysis, which has affected man's view of himself as profoundly as Marxism has affected man's view of society. Sigmund Freud (1856–1939), an Austrian Jew educated in Paris and Vienna, revolutionized the entire field of psychiatry with his theory of psychoanalysis. "Because I was a Jew," Freud once wrote, "I found myself free from many prejudices which limited others in the use of their intellect, and being a Jew, I was prepared to enter opposition and to renounce agreement with the 'compact majority.' "

At the time Freud attended medical school, society generally left the question of mental illness to philosophers, priests, and a brand of psychiatrists known as "nosologists"—men who defined mental illnesses they could not understand by symptoms, without regard to cause. In this way, patients having hallucinations from such diverse causes as syphilis of the brain, senile dementia, or paranoia could end up neighbors in the same dungeon. Freud was the first to make the distinction between organic mental illness caused by physical factors and functional mental disorders caused by psychic factors. With him modern psychiatry was born, the odium of degeneracy or sin was lifted from mental illness, and the psychotic were treated as sick people instead of people possessed.

The desolate silence which had greeted Freud's *Interpretation of Dreams*, the first breakthrough in the understanding of mental illness, was shattered by the loud invective given the publication of his books dealing with child sexuality and the role of sexuality in the causation of mental illness. From obscurity to notoriety to fame, Freud's name became known around the world. Though Freud himself often stated that a medical basis for treating mental illness must be found, because psychoanalysis as a therapy is too involved, modern psychiatrists, even while standing on the shoulders of Freud, ignore the contribution he made in enlarging their field of vision. Today, psycho-analysis plays a major role in our understanding of criminology and cultural anthropology, and it throws further light on our understanding of art, religion, and the humanistic sciences.

When Nazi stormtroopers invaded Freud's study in Vienna after the *Anschluss* in 1938, they were stopped by his serene, steadfast gaze. A cultural distance of a million years separated the civilized man and the Nazi beast. Such was Freud's fame, however, that the Nazis did not dare to harm him. Freud and his family were allowed to leave for London, where he died a year later.

The fourth in the Spinozian quartet, Albert Einstein (1879–1955), was another product of the German-Jewish Enlightenment. It was he who completed the work of Spinoza by destroying the mechanistic concept of the universe which Spinoza had undermined. Einstein clearly saw the ideological ties binding him to Spinoza. When a Boston cardinal warned American youth to beware of Einstein because he was an atheist, a New York rabbi called Einstein asking, "Do you believe in God?" Einstein replied, "I believe in Spinoza's God, who reveals himself in the harmony of all being." Today Einstein's thinking, even more than that of Marx or Freud, dominates world thinking.

Einstein entered the world scene in 1905, when he published his now famed theory of relativity. His views on Brownian motion and his interpretation of the meaning of the photoelectric effect brought him further fame and a Nobel prize. In all his theorizing, Einstein was "Kabalistic." He relied not on external experimentation but on intellect, logic, and intuition. "The logic of a theory," said Einstein, "must stem from an inner coherence, not because external evidence makes it the most logical over other theories."

In 1933, the superior Nordic Aryans drove Einstein out of Germany. He came to the United States, where he was appointed professor of mathematics at the Institute for Advanced Study at Princeton. He died in 1955.

It was in the field of science, where Freud and Einstein had broken new ground, that the Jews made their greatest contribution to Western civilization, not as "practical men" but as theoreticians. They were innovators of methods, creators of new ideas, pioneers in new fields, founders of scientific publications. They were the motivating spirit behind new institutions.

In medicine, as early as 1850, Jewish scientists argued for the existence of microorganisms which cause contagious disease, and laid the foundations for modern heart therapy, bacteriology, and clinical pathology. They first advanced theories that chemical processes within the cell were responsible for glandular activity, proposed serum immunity for contagious diseases, discovered phagocytes, pioneered in the chemistry of muscles, and made blood transfusions possible through the discovery of the different blood types. It was Jewish scientists who advanced the first hope man had of ever finding a cure for the ravages of venereal disease, through Neisser's discovery of the gonococcus, Wassermann's test for the early detection of syphilis, and Ehrlich's first cure for it, with his drug salvarsan.

Why the Jews, who had just come out of the ghetto, Talmud in hand, should suddenly become leading mathematicians, is a mystery, unless Freud's explanation for his own genius is valid. Here we can only adumbrate a few of their contributions to indicate the extent of their activities. Karl Jacobi founded modern mathematical physics with his theories of dynamics and partial differential equations, and developed the theory of elliptic functions, the theory of Abelian functions, and the functional determinants known as "Jacobians." Georg Cantor introduced the concept of transfinite numbers, outlined an approach to set theory, and paved the way for the logical positivists and Wittgenstein's school of mathematical philosophy. Hermann Minkowski fathered the geometry of numbers and first formulated the concept of relativity of time and space. Leopold Kronecker won fame for his work in the theory of numbers and in the theory of equations. Luigi Cremona furthered the study of synthetic geometry and developed the Cremona birational transformation theory. Tullio Levi-Civita, in association with Gregorio Ricci, formulated the absolute differential calculus, which, according to Einstein, made possible the mathematics of general relativity.

Jews won fame gazing at the stars. Sir William Herschel, the first to measure the distances of stars from the sun, formulated a theory for the behavior of double stars, in addition to discovering the planet Uranus. Karl Schwarzschild made contributions to the study of the internal composition of stars. To confound that school of anti-Semitism which holds the Jews responsible for communism because of Karl Marx, and to comfort that school of anti-Semitism which holds the Jews responsible for capitalism without knowing why, let us point out that David Ricardo is regarded as the father of capitalism with his development of a theory of rent, property, and wages, and of a quantity theory of money. We urge caution, however, for the anticapitalist anti-Semites; Ricardo's father held a symbolic Jewish funeral service for his son when he was converted and married into English gentry.

The modern chemical and dye industries rest on German-Jewish achievements. Jewish chemists were the first to synthesize indigo, the first to discover phthalein dyes, and the first to produce ammonia synthetically (the Haber process, named after Fritz Haber). A Jew founded the German potash industry. Jewish chemists devised methods for estimating vapor density, studied coefficients of expansion for gases, worked out theories of valencies, developed molecular theories, and classified organic compounds. Nobel prize winner Richard Willstätter determined the composition of chlorophyll and the role of enzymes in the chemical process of life.

In physics, the Jewish contributions are so numerous that this list must be even more cursory. Jewish physicists discovered the Hertzian wave, investigated photoelectric phenomena, were codiscoverers of the gamma rays. They isolated isotopes, worked in electron kinetics, and pried into the secret of the atom. They were the founders of the entire school of relativity, which led to the splitting of the atom. This trail began, of course, with Albert Einstein, then led to Lise Meitner, codiscoverer of protactinium, element 91, and her nuclear fission theory. The next stop led to Enrico Fermi (a non-Jew) and Leo Szilard, who developed the chain reaction system, and then to Niels Bohr, who investigated the structure of atoms and the radiations emanating from them. Thus the intellectual and theoretical formulations for the atomic bomb were laid. All—Einstein, Meitner, Fermi, Szilard, Bohr—were driven out of Europe by Hitler. All came to the United States. To make the circle complete Albert Einstein, as an American citizen, threw his scientific prestige behind the "insane idea" of nuclear energy by fission, and convinced President Franklin Delano Roosevelt that such a superbomb could be made. From here on it was merely a matter of technology, which any country with money enough could follow through on, as subsequent events proved.

In the arts and the humanities, the Jews were equally numerous. One could not walk into a salon of West European nineteenth-century intellectuals without meeting a Jew. They performed on Europe's concert stages, conducted orchestras, staged the great dramas of the world, introduced new art forms. Before the advent of the Nazi, Max Reinhardt reigned in the theater, Sarah Bernhardt was the queen of the stage, and Lotte Lehman, Joseph Szigeti, Artur Schnabel, were in the music world headlines.

In politics, finance, and industry, the rise of the Jews was equally phenomenal. Time after time, overwhelming majorities of Christians from Rome to London, from Paris to Vienna, voted Jews to high office, appointed them Cabinet members, made them Supreme Court justices, promoted them to high military rank.

Most well known of all the Jews in England was probably Benjamin Disraeli, who began his career as a novelist and became founder and leader of England's Conservative party and Prime Minister. Disraeli was the one man most instrumental in building the British Empire, for which he earned the gratitude of Queen Victoria, whom he made Empress of India. Sir Moses Montefiore, Queen Victoria's financial adviser, established the Provisional Bank of Ireland. A champion of human rights, his name became a byword among the oppressed, both Jews and Christians, who everywhere benefited from his philanthropies. Sir Rufus Isaacs, first Jewish Chief Justice of England, later knighted, served as Viceroy of India.

In France, Adolphe Crémieux, Minister of Justice, abolished Negro slavery in the French colonies and instituted legislation abolishing the death penalty for political prisoners. Isaac and Émile Pereire developed the credit feature in modern banking and built the first railroad in France. Achille Fould was Minister of State and Minister of Finance during the Second Empire. Léon Blum was Premier of France several times.

In Germany, more than anywhere else in Europe, Jewish preeminence in every field helped to create the German Zeitgeist—the German "spirit of the times." It was in Germany that Ferdinand Lassalle organized the world's first trade-union movement. Lassalle, though a political realist, was privately a romanticist. More skilled in polemics than with the rapier, he was killed in a duel over the honor of a baroness, whose favors were worth living for, but not dying for. Gabriel Riesser championed general constitutional reforms and equal opportunities for all Jews. He was elected to the parliament held at Frankfort, and was the first Jewish judge in Germany. Jews served with distinction as Cabinet ministers, Reichstag members, chief justices, bankers, and industrialists.

The Court Jew disappeared. The banker took his place. With his expanding credit and international loan facilities, the modern banker was able to finance great governmental undertakings, underwrite vast industrial expansion plans, and risk huge sums of capital in the service of the state. The history of the house of Rothschild, the prototype of now famed Jewish banking houses which sprang up all over Europe, needs no retelling here.

This is not to suggest that Jews dominated the financial structure of the countries in which they generally dwelt. Far from it. Jewish banking institutions and Jewish money constituted but a fraction of the economy of Germany, England, or France. The reason the Jews were so prominent in Europe's economic life was not their numbers or the dominance of their institutions, but the new ideas of banking they infused into European commercial thinking.

Jewish bankers were innovators, idea men. Werner Sombart, in *The Jews and Modern Capitalism*, suggests that the Jews were the originators of the system of securities and the practice of discounting bills. He asserts that the Jews played a large part in founding the stock exchange, and that they played an important part in the development of bank notes in their modern use as negotiable securities. As early as 1812, the Jews were predominant on the Berlin Stock Exchange, and two of its first four presidents were Jewish. The Rothschilds made the stock market international. Modern man is a little incredulous that at one time this was cause for anger at the Jews. But in the beginning of the nineteenth century, the stock exchange was a wonder of Europe, and the public could, for the first time, invest in foreign capital. Jewish innovations were described at the time as unfair competition, though they have since become the standard form for all banking, financing, and international trade, Christian or otherwise.

Though Western European governments may have yielded to the pressure of anti-Semitic groups for political reasons, they leaned heavily on Jewish loyalty when they were in financial trouble. They relied on the discretion of their Jewish bankers, on their ideas, on their loyalty. Most important of all they had implicit faith in their honesty, for, though millions in currency passed through their hands during a century, financial scandals involving Jews were few. This Jewish influence in European banking and finance lasted until the end of the century, after which governments slowly began to take over many of the functions formerly carried on by private banking.

This then is the true image of the Western Jew in the Modern Age. Nevertheless, it strains credulity that such a ridiculously small minority, so recently deprived of all rights of citizenship, often looked upon as narrow, bigoted, and ignorant, could have attained such preeminence in politics, in industry, in science, in the arts, and in the humanities. How was this possible?

The answer is a complex one, yet it can be narrowed to three main themes. The Jews used the same tool they had used in Babylonian, Persian, Grecian, Roman, Islamic, and early medieval times—namely, the survival tool of education. Now, after finishing their three-hundred-year term in the ghetto, the Jews, to overcome their handicap of being both outsiders and latecomers, had to be twice as good as their Christian competitors. They did not hesitate to study for any profession, no matter how hopeless it seemed to gain a foothold in it. They studied day and night for years, until they became renowned in their fields. Universities could not ignore their scholastic records or their world-acclaimed achievements. Governments could not ignore their contributions to science, industry, and commerce. As they became renowned in their fields, more and more Christians sought them out for advice in law, to heal their sick, to design their buildings, to build their businesses.

How did the Jews develop this flair for scholarship, this ability for theoretical thought, this passion for justice, this ability to peer into society and view it with such precision? The answer is that such scholarship was not an overnight growth but the very heart of the Judaic design for survival. Even in the ghetto, even when denied the educational facilities of the outside world, the Jews created their own educational institutions. The Talmud, though it did not answer the needs of modern living, was still the same Talmud of Grecian, Roman, and Islamic times, the Talmud of abstractions and legal logic that sharpened the mind. The Jewish passion for justice was part of an inherited tradition. Given a heritage that respected learning, that imparted justice, that taught its doctrines in abstractions, was it any wonder that the Jews should excel in the field of learning?

One more question may be asked. Though the Jews produced a Spinoza in philosophy, a Marx in economics, a Freud in medicine, an Einstein in physics, why did they not produce men of equal stature in literature, music, and painting? Perhaps the answer lies in the very fact that the Jews were outsiders, excluded and excluding themselves from sharing in the spiritual life of the nations in which they existed. Such giants as Goethe and Keats, Beethoven and Brahms, Renoir and Van Gogh were expressions of their Christian culture. This tie to their past gave their work its individual aspect; their genius gave it universal appeal. Because the Jews were spiritually tied to another faith, they could not identify themselves with the Christian heritage. The abstractions of Spinoza, Marx, Freud, and Einstein are universal, not identifiable expressions of a creed.

It is interesting to note that those Jews who have approached greatness in painting are the modern ones, who no longer express themselves in faithful reproductions but in abstractions. Here the prohibition against making graven images no longer obtrudes. Since abstract painting is also a universal mode of painting, the Jew can express himself on the abstract universal canvas without soul-tying identification with other religions.

The Jews will create their Goethe and Keats, their Beethoven and Brahms, their Renoir and Van Gogh when their own men of genius take up themes which capture the four-thousand-year drama of their survival and then distill that drama, that survival, into a universal mythology of man.

TWENTY-SIX

# EASTERN EUROPE:
# THE NEW HUMANISM

Like tides, European Jewish history has ebbed and flowed between Western and Eastern Europe, leaving differently hued cultures in its wake. Jewish history in the Middle Ages began in the West and rolled slowly and inexorably toward the East. Jewish history in the Modern Age began in the East and rolled slowly and inexorably back to the West. In Western Europe, emancipated Jews—a panoply of scientists, musicians, painters, writers—created a culture identified with Western values. They expressed themselves in the languages of their host nations—in German, in English, in French, in Italian. In Eastern Europe, unemancipated Jews created a culture, known as the Haskala, identified with Jewish values. But the Haskala produced no scientists, no musicians, no painters.* It did produce a humanistic literature, written not in Russian or Polish but in Hebrew and Yiddish, one the classical, the other the folk language of the Jews.

Of the two cultures, the Eastern Jewish humanism was far more important for Jewish survival than the Western Jewish Enlightenment. The contributions of the Jews in the West were merely ornamental columns added to the stately cultural edifice of the Western Christian achieve-

---

*East European Jews with a talent for painting, like Marc Chagall and Chaim Soutine, moved to Paris, and scientists, like Hermann Minkowski, moved to Germany.

ment. The innovations of the Jewish humanists in the East were the pillars which supported the Jewish Diaspora. As the Western Enlightenment edged itself toward the drab *shtetls* of the East, these Jewish humanists turned it into the *Haskala* (from the Hebrew word meaning "awakening" or "rebirth"). But whereas the Enlightenment was the philosophy of the rich, and Hasidism the religion of the poor, the Haskala expressed the cultural nationalism of the middle classes. It was the Jewish Renaissance arriving three hundred years late.

Like a Freudian libido flowing through the unconscious, attaching itself to previous psychic experiences, the Haskala flowed through the body of Judaism, attaching itself to former Jewish values and creating new ones. It attached itself to Hebrew and Yiddish, creating a new literature. It attached itself to Jewish religion and created Jewish existentialism. It attached itself to politics and created Zionism. Zionism fused the Jews in Eastern and Western Europe with the Jews in the United States and created the new State of Israel. This vast transformation and fusion began with a few Talmudic students fighting the Hasidists, who were preaching a return to primitivism of feeling as a way of relating themselves with God.

Hasidism had not died with the death of its founder, Bal Shem Tov, in 1760. His disciple Dov Ber spread the Hasidic gospel and soon half of Eastern Europe's Jews belonged to the Hasidic sect. The rabbis, fearful of this new gospel because it undermined their authority, tried to stifle it, but in vain. In only one part of Europe, Lithuania, did they succeed, due largely to the efforts of one man, Elijah ben Solomon (1720–1797), an ambivalent figure in Jewish history. Elijah's unwitting historic function was to serve as a bridge over which the Talmudic students could troop into the camp of Enlightenment and slay Hasidism with modern weapons.

Had Elijah ben Solomon (known as the Vilna Gaon— "His Eminence from Vilna") been born in the twelfth century he would have been a great philosopher. In the eighteenth century he was an anachronistic man, torn between orthodox scholarship and science. As his sobriquet implies, he was born in Vilna, Lithuania, and as one would expect of an eighteenth-century Jew referred to as "Gaon," he had mastered the Torah at eight and the Talmud at nine.

But what one would not have expected was that at the age of ten he would want to become a scientist. His horrified father turned him from science to Talmud, but though he became the most famed Jewish Orthodox scholar of his time, he never forgot his early interest in science.

The Vilna Gaon was drawn early into the Hasidic dispute, and, though not a rabbi, he excommunicated the sect. So great was his reputation as a scholar among the orthodox that the excommunication was effective. He failed, however, to understand the psychological motivations underlying Hasidism, viewing the Hasidists merely as Jewish ignoramuses. The Vilna Gaon was the last of the great Jewish scholars of Talmudism, revered by the orthodox but ignored by the moderns. He died in 1797, never having had a prophetic vision of the future. But through his interest in science, he had shown his Talmudic students the way to Western Enlightenment. The seeds for the coming Haskala were sown when the Vilna Gaon had encouraged not only his but other Talmud students to translate scientific works into the language of the Prophets.

History repeated itself. As in Greco-Roman and Islamic days, when these eighteenth-century Jewish youths came in contact with new ideas, they also became imbued with them. From science their interests wandered to Western philosophy, to the social sciences, and to literature. They were impressed with these ideas of the Western world, but they also were in love with their Jewish heritage. They wanted to Westernize themselves without becoming Christianized. They wanted to compromise between the orthodox who conceded nothing, and the assimilationists who yielded everything. They wanted to create a Jewish culture which could also be used by the West, instead of a Western culture which could also be used by the Jews.

As they looked about them, these harbingers of the early Haskala saw half of Eastern Europe's Jews infected with the Hasidic doctrines of salvation. The Hasidists, they realized, were their enemy, and they aligned themselves with the reluctant rabbis to weaken that enemy. Unlike the Vilna Gaon and the rabbis, these first Haskala intellectuals did not view the Hasidists as ignoramuses, but viewed Hasidism as the "opiate of the people"—as an escape from the miseries of physical existence.

To bring their ideas to the people, the Haskala writers first had to have an audience. To capture the attention of the people they resorted to writing escape novels of the type so popular in the nineteenth century. To make sure, however, that whatever they wrote would not become Russian or Polish in its orientation, the way the Jewish Enlightenment in the West had become German in its orientation, they wrote in Hebrew. Their aim was to undermine the influence of Hasidism.

These Hebrew escape novels were set mostly in Palestine. Jews were the heroines, the lovers, the villains. Since the decline of the Jewish Golden Age in the Islamic Empire, Jews in Jewish literature had been depicted as paragons of virtue to whom sex hardly existed except in medical tomes. Now Jewish history was divided into a romantic past, where love was joyously indulged in, and a miserable present, where sex was hidden under long, drab, unaesthetic skirts. These escape novels accomplished a useful purpose. They helped to destroy the image the Jews had of themselves as eternal ghetto dwellers. Not always had the Jews been such derided creatures, these novels implied. Once they had been romantic lovers, brave warriors, people of destiny. These novels also implied that perhaps the Jews could change their present situation by taking political action, instead of passively sitting around waiting for a messiah.

By 1850, Hasidism was beginning to lose its force. It had stopped growing and had begun to wither away into quibbling sects, mainly because of its inability to institutionalize itself. But the romantic novels had also had their effect. Many Jews no longer looked upon Hasidism as a return to Judaism, but as a regression from it. The image of the romantic, brave Jew in the novels was more to their liking than the hymn-singing, dancing Hasid of the revival meetings.

As their audience became more discriminating, the Haskala writers turned to more serious themes, to the meaning of Judaism and to an examination of the Jewish condition. They began to write in two languages, in Hebrew for the intellectuals and in Yiddish for the masses. Within one century, Eastern Europe gave birth to a series of great Hebrew and Yiddish writers who, like the humanists of the Renaissance, influenced both literature and life.

Five thousand years of recorded history has produced only four great literary periods—the prophetic writings of the Jews in biblical days, the Greek tragedies in the Periclean Age, the poetic dramas of the reign of Elizabeth, and the soul-searching novels of the nineteenth-century Russians. In fifty brief years, Pushkin, Gogol, Turgenev, Dostoevski, and Tolstoy gave the world an immortal literature. True to the Jewish Diaspora formula of a culture for a culture, the Russian Jews also produced a literature, not to be compared with the achievements of these Russian literary giants, but a unique achievement nevertheless.

Just as the heroes in the Russian novels have Russian names but are actors in a universal human drama, so the heroes in the Jewish novels have Jewish names and are also actors in a universal human drama. Just as the great Russian writers probed deeply into the Russian soul for inner values, so the Hebrew and Yiddish writers probed into the Jewish soul for inner values. In the main, the Yiddish writers wrote fiction, the Hebrew writers essays and poetry. The Yiddish writers turned from the romanticism of the early Hebrew novels to realism, and the Hebrew writers turned to Zionism, a new Jewish aspiration for a political homeland in Palestine.

One of the first and most important of these early Hebrew essayists who influenced the course of Jewish history while enriching Hebrew literature was Ahad Ha-Am (1856–1927), born to riches and orthodoxy in the Ukraine. Ahad Ha-Am supplemented his Torah and Talmud education with courses at the universities of Vienna, Berlin, and Breslau, though he never graduated from any of these institutions. He lived in Odessa, then in London, and in 1922 settled in Tel Aviv, Palestine. Through his writings he infused the emerging political Zionism with a sense of cultural responsibility. The function of Zionism, as he saw it, was to solve not only the political but also the spiritual problem of Judaism—the problem of a continuing and unifying Jewish culture. It was not the state that bound the individual to his nation, but his culture. The Jews in the Diaspora, he held, had to have a unifying culture to weld them into a national organism, and only a spiritual center in Palestine could serve such a function. As Israel Friedlaender summed it up, "According to Ahad Ha-Am, Zion-

ism must begin with culture and end with culture, its con-
summation being a center for Judaism."* He was a critic,
not a leader. He provided the butter on the Zionist bread
Herzl had baked.

Whereas Ahad Ha-Am was primarily an essayist,
Russian-born Hayim Bialik (1873–1934) was a poet comparable in stature to Judah Halevi, and poet laureate of the
Hebrew language. He was self-educated, a truant from the
Talmud, a rebel against traditionalism, and his whole life
was an agonized revolt against the remnants of *shtetl* orthodoxy. He drifted to Odessa, became a timber trader,
taught school, fled to Berlin, and finally settled in Tel Aviv.
His poem "In the City of the Slaughter" prophetically de-
picts the 1903 Russian pogrom in Kishinev as a prelude to
world tragedy, just as Picasso in 1937 foreshadowed the
horrors of totalitarian war with his painting "Guernica,"
which depicted the German slaughter in that town during
the Spanish Civil War of 1936–1939. Bialik's poem caused
thousands of Jewish youths to cast off their pacifism and
join the Russian underground to fight Czar and tyranny.
Among his many translations into Hebrew are works of
Shakespeare, Schiller's *Wilhelm Tell*, and *Don Quixote*.
More than anyone else, Bialik gave life and verve to modern Hebrew.

Quite different from the lives of Ahad Ha-Am and Bialik was the life of Crimean-born Saul Tchernichovsky
(1875–1943), who never saw the inside of a Talmud-Torah.
Though his parents were observant Jews, they let their
child grow up with Russian urchins, and with them he
roamed the steppes. At the age of seven his education
began, not in Yiddish, which he never learned, but in Hebrew, and through that language he grew to love his people. In 1899 he enrolled at the University of Heidelberg,
where he studied medicine and where he was continually
embroiled in love affairs. His good looks and education
gained him entree into both Jewish and gentile high society. Many of his most beautiful poems in Hebrew were
penned to his Christian amours, and he finally married a
Greek girl. He served as a physician in the Russian Medical Corps during World War I, took part in the Russian

---

*Past and Present: A Collection of Jewish Essays*, page 421.

Revolution, moved to Germany, and in 1931 settled in Palestine.

It was this sophisticated cosmopolitan Jew who in impassioned poetry exhorted the Jewish people to stand up and fight their oppressor, to free Jehovah whom the Talmudists "had bound in phylacteries." Like all modern Hebrew scholars, he too was a linguist. He translated Molière and Goethe as well as the *Iliad* and the *Odyssey* into Hebrew, so masterfully that they read like Hebrew classics. Strangely enough, he also mastered the Finnish language, with its fifteen cases, and translated into Hebrew the strange, unrhymed, trochaic, alliterative Finnish epic poem the *Kalevala*, as well as Longfellow's *Song of Hiawatha*, a poem inspired by and written in the meter of the *Kalevala*. But, above all, Tchernichovsky was a Jewish nationalist, and his poetry repeatedly touched upon the theme of a political reawakening of the Jews and a return to their historic destiny.

Side by side with this secular Hebrew literature grew Yiddish literature, the first such literature in Jewish history. Hebrew was the language of the Torah and prophetic writings, the classic language of the Jews, four thousand years old. Yiddish, on the other hand, was the folk language, barely seven hundred years old. It was born in the Rhine Valley, in the twelfth century, the illegitimate child of a union between the German language and the Hebrew alphabet. The Jews spoke German among themselves. But when they wrote German, they wrote it with Hebrew letters. Through the centuries, German words were modified, Hebrew words were added, and this spoken and written idiom developed its own syntax. As the Jews moved eastward, they carried with them this new language, now called Yiddish, adding Polish, Russian, Lithuanian words as they settled in those countries. By the eighteenth century, the great majority of European Jews spoke Yiddish only; Hebrew was reserved for scholars and for praying.

To reach the masses of the Jews, many Haskala writers turned to Yiddish. Because Yiddish was a folk language, fluid and without discipline, it had certain literary limitations and also certain advantages. It did not lend itself to heroic epics or subtle psychological moods, but it was perfect for lyric expression and satire. It could not be made to express ambiguity, but it could be made to exude empathy. As Dante shaped the Italian language, as Chaucer shaped the English language, as Luther shaped the German language, so the Haskala writers shaped the Yiddish language.

The genius of the Haskala writers forged a literature that did not die with the Yiddish-speaking Jews in the German concentration camps. Though born in that strip of land known as the Pale, located in an outpost of history, and written for three million Jews who were thought of as anachronisms of history by the gentile world, this Yiddish literature created characters that still live, long after the already vanished *shtetl* Jews. In these heroes of the "insulted and injured," the Jewish Haskala writers created universal figures. By pure chance, the first three of these Haskala Yiddish writers were also its three greatest—Mendele Mocher Sforim (Mendele the bookseller), Sholem Aleichem, and I. L. Peretz.

Mendele Mocher Sforim was a typical Talmud student "led astray" by the Haskala. He was born in Lithuania (1836–1917) into a family whose rabbinic ancestors were as numerous as shields in a British castle. Educated on Talmud and more Talmud in one-room *shtetl* schools and various yeshivas, he rebelled against this traducement of Jewish culture and educated himself on the literature of the West. At first he wrote in Hebrew, but discarded that language for Yiddish, then regarded as mere jargon by the intellectuals. Mendele inveighed against the narrow-mindedness and dogmatism of the Jews in the Pale, but behind his vitriol the Jews could sense his love for his people. In all his writings he tried to recreate a subconscious Jewish community of feeling. There is such a universality about his Jews in the Pale that someday, when his works are more adequately translated, he may be accorded some of the praise now lavished on the great Russian writers.

In the nineteenth century, careers in literature were frowned upon by most Jewish parents in the Pale, for "what was there to write about that had not already been written?" Sholem Aleichem's father was one of the exceptions; he encouraged his son to write. At the age of seventeen, Sholem Aleichem (1859–1916), brought up on traditional *shtetl* educational fare, rebelled and began writing in Hebrew and teaching Russian to earn a living. His first literary effort was a dictionary listing his stepmother's extensive vocabulary of colorful Yiddish curses. He married a wealthy landowner's daughter, administered a large estate, lost his fortune on the stock market, and went back to writing, in Yiddish this time. He left Russia to live in Switzerland, moved to Denmark, and finally to the United States at the outbreak of World War I.

Sholem Aleichem was both an artist and an entertainer, the Jewish Mark Twain, who, because he loved the Jews, was allowed to spoof them, the ghetto, and their rituals. He held before them a comic image of the "Chosen People" and made them laugh at themselves. In one sentence spoken by his favorite character, Tevye, the dairyman, Sholem Aleichem summed up the plight of the Jew in the Pale. "I was, with God's help, born poor," says Tevye. Sholem Aleichem wrote about the helpless masses and defended the "sanctity of the insulted and the injured." With Tevye, the Jewish people could agree on the plight of being a Jew in the Pale, "If He wants it that way, that's the way it ought to be—and yet, what would have been wrong to have it different?" But even as they laughed, the Jewish people paused and reflected.

Polish-born I. L. Peretz (1852–1915) grew up with one foot in his Hasidic inheritance and the other in the Haskala. He was university educated, practiced law for ten years, then became a writer and editor. His first published work was a volume of Hebrew poetry, but Yiddish fiction soon dominated his writings. Peretz brought the nineteenth century to the *shtetl* Jews of Eastern Europe. In many of his stories he turned away from the *shtetl* to write of Jewish life in the big town, of the urbanized, proletarianized Jews. He wrote like a modern novelist, with rapid, subtle strokes.

A century of Haskala Hebrew and Yiddish writers began to have its effect. The Jews in the Pale got the points of the stories—that their afflictions were not part of an eternal design or a punishment for their sins; that orthodoxy was not synonymous with God's commandments; that Hasidism was not a paradise on earth. As more and more Jews rebelled against orthodoxy, the rabbinate lost more and more of its power. Jews began to think of their liberation not in terms of better prayers but in terms of better organization.

Because the Haskala succeeded in creating Jewish values with which the young emancipated Eastern Jews could identify themselves, there were no lines of Jews standing in front of the baptismal fonts in Russian and Polish churches. Instead, they searched for new answers to the perplexing question of faith in an age of reason. They did not search for scientific answers, like Zunz and his school, but for philosophic answers. In this search they were joined by Western Jewish intellectuals who became convinced, through the growing anti-Semitism of the West, that baptism was not the answer. Imperceptibly the Haskala of the East and the Enlightenment of the West began moving closer toward each other in viewpoint, and by 1900 a symbolic merger had been made. Out of this merger grew Jewish existentialism, and appropriately, the two foremost proponents of this new philosophy, Franz Rosenzweig and Martin Buber, were born on the borderland between Eastern and Western Europe. Both were products of the Western Enlightenment, and both seized upon the underlying psychological base of Hasidism for their new, modern approach to Judaism.

Franz Rosenzweig (1886–1929) was born into an assimilationst German-Jewish family and educated at the universities of Freiburg and Berlin, with degrees in both philosophy and medicine. About this time, he decided to convert to Protestantism, because he could discern no rational philosophy in Judaism. He had never had a Jewish upbringing, and he felt it would be intellectually more honest if he entered Christianity as a former Jew instead of a mere agnostic. As the day before his appointment with Christianity happened to be the Jewish Day of Atonement, Franz casually sauntered into the nearest synagogue for a perfunctory "I and Thou" introduction. While listening to the prayers, he experienced a Jewish reawakening. Instead of entering Christianity, he reentered Judaism.

It was at the eastern front in World War I that Franz Rosenzweig composed his main work, *The Star of Redemption*, written between battles, advances, and retreats, on postcards and bits of wrapping paper which he sent to his mother, who transcribed his notes. In this and other works Rosenzweig tried to rescue Judaism from what he considered its three enemies—orthodox Jewry, who confused their Talmudic legalisms with the Torah; the Hasidists, who confused their ecstasy for God with God; and the political Zionists, who thought of Judaism only as a form of nationalism. Whereas Rosenzweig formerly had seen faith as a contest between the mind of man and the commandments of God, he now realized that faith could be apprehended only as an encounter between man and God. Faith, he said, was an involvement with one's self and not an involvement with one's mind.

The last days of Rosenzweig were tragic. He was struck by an illness which paralyzed his entire body except for one thumb. He "wrote" his subsequent works strapped in a special chair; with his thumb he indicated to his wife each individual letter, painstakingly forming first words, then sentences, paragraphs, and books.

Rosenzweig was strongly influenced in his views by Martin Buber, a scholar who, in his own lifetime, has come to be looked upon as a prophet and acknowledged by Jews and Christians as one of the most influential modern-day philosophical theologians. Buber developed the Jewish existentialist philosophy which has influenced the Protestant theologian Paul Tillich and the Catholic humanist philosopher Nikolai Berdyaev. Today, Buber's thinking, like that of Freud, permeates Western culture and has influenced the writings of educators, sociologists, psychiatrists, psychologists, philosophers, theologians, and poets.

Buber, born in 1878, of wealthy Viennese parents, was brought up by his grandfather in Galicia (Poland), where he early came in contact with Hasidism. After a traditional Jewish upbringing, he attended the universities of Vienna and Berlin, studying philosophy and art, graduating from the latter with a doctorate in philosophy. He joined the Zionist movement and, together with a Catholic theologian and a Protestant psychiatrist, edited a journal on social problems relating to religion. It is his philosophical works on Hasidism and theology, however, which have brought him world fame.

Men, said Buber, are capable of a twofold relationship. The first aspect of this relationship, which he calls "objective," permits man to order his environment. The second, which he calls "realization," permits him to perceive the inner meaning of his own existence (or, as the German philosophers call it, *Existenz*); hence, "existentialism." Buber also holds that one cannot explain religion in terms of science any more than one can explain science in terms of religion. He leans heavily on Freudian psychoanalytic insights for an understanding of the mind of man. Unlike Freud, though, Buber does not reject religion as an "illusion" but accepts it as a reality.

Man has a soul, says Buber, his unconscious national soul. This unconscious soul in the individual Jew is a mirror image of the collective soul of the Jewish people, a soul which compresses four thousand years of Jewish history within it. Therefore, in order to know himself, the Jew must at all times be aware of the history of his people. The Old Testament, in Buber's view, is the affirmation of the collective experience of the people of Israel with God. Each Jew can reexperience this collective encounter with God on an individual basis, because of the Jewish heritage preserved in his unconscious. This is the meaning of Buber's now famous phrase, "I-and-Thou encounter." The key to salvation, then, according to Buber, is both a collective and an individual encounter with the Deity through faith—a faith which needs no dogma. Such a belief neither contradicts reason nor opposes science, and it answers the need of man for faith.

Buber's philosophy is also a protest against the depersonalization of man in modern society because of the dominance of the "I-It" relation between man and things. The strength of a true community can arise only out of an "I-Thou" relationship with God, says Buber.

> Existence will remain meaningless for you if you yourself do not penetrate into it with active love and if you do not in this way discover its meaning for yourself. . . . And for this very reason the answer to the silent question asked by the modern world is found herein. Will the world perceive it? But will Jewry itself perceive that its very existence depends upon the revival of its religious existence? The Jewish State may assure the future of a nation of Jews, even one with a culture of its own; Judaism will live

only if it brings to life again the primeval Jewish relationship to God, the world, and mankind.*

In 1938, at the age of sixty, Buber was forced to flee Nazi Germany. He settled in Palestine, where he became professor of social philosophy at the Hebrew University in Jerusalem.

The Haskala died with the nineteenth century in the rubble of World War I. Born in the West, child of the German Enlightenment, and reared in the East, ward of the Jewish intellectuals, the Haskala was Jewish humanism painted over Western Enlightenment. By having held up the mirror of grandeur to the Jewish past, the Haskala writers were able to make the people of the Pale realize the sordidness of their present. By reviving Hebrew as a secular language and elevating Yiddish to a literary status, they enriched Jewish culture. The Enlightenment of the West and the Haskala of the East revived the Jewish will to survive.

This new expression of the will for survival as Jews was born with Zionism. And it was Zionism which fused Jewry in Eastern and Western Europe with Jewry in the United States. For two and a half centuries the Jews in America had played a minor role in Jewish world affairs, but in the twentieth century they became a force in Jewish destiny. As the history of the American Jews now commingles with that of the European, we must cross the Atlantic Ocean for a closer view of this American segment of the Jewish people, as it vies for the leadership of Diaspora Judaism.

---

*From "The Silent Question," in *The Writings of Martin Buber*, edited by Will Herberg, page 314.

# TWENTY-SEVEN

# UNITED STATES:
# THE NEW BABYLON

Jewish history in America is a strange mixture of the familiar and the prophetic. It arrived in South America in the sixteenth century with the Hispanic explorations, and flowed to North America in the seventeenth century with the tides of Anglo-Dutch colonial expansion. For its first 250 years, Jewish history in America was a curious reversal of Jewish history in Europe. From 1650 to 1900, American Jewry was spiritually and intellectually dependent upon European Jewry, producing no new ideas of its own. Just as America before 1900 was regarded by nineteenth-century European intellectuals as an inferior nation and people, so European Jews looked upon American Jews as intellectual inferiors. And just as America after World Wars I and II began to assume leadership of the Western world, so the Jews in America in the twentieth century began to grope for leadership of world Jewry.

What is the explanation for the opposite intellectual directions taken by Jewish history in America and in Europe? One explanation can be found in the parallel drawn by some historians between the relationship of Rome and Greece on the one hand, and of America and Europe, on the other. If Americans, as such historians contend, are anti-intellectual in outlook, followers in literature, copyists in art, and technicians in science, in contrast to Europeans, who are pace setters in literature, innovators in art, and theoreticians in science, then this parallel clarifies the relationship between American and European Jews, for whatever American Jews created prior to about 1900 was but a pale imitation of the original European pattern. This also fits in with our "Diaspora law of talion"—a culture for a culture—because Jewish American culture was as anti-intellectual and pragmatic

369

as Christian American culture. This antithesis is exemplified in the fates of the four waves of Jewish immigration to the United States. The first two waves, spanning two and a half centuries between 1650 and 1880, were culturally sterile; the second two waves, between 1880 and 1950, were culturally fertile.

The Spanish Jews, who arrived as early as 1621, were not prominent in Colonial affairs, nor did they help shape events in the American Revolution. They did not become philosophers, scholars, and statesmen in America as they had in Europe. They became tradesmen and merchants. A similar fate befell the German Jews who arrived between 1825 and 1880. They became well integrated, well adjusted, and prosperous, but, until 1900, played only a minor role in United States history, developing none of America's heavy industries, leading no vanguard of progressive social legislation, and gracing no list of contributors to the literary "flowering of New England."

Then, paradoxically, between 1880 and 1920, when history washed ashore 2,000,000 despised, poverty-stricken Russian Jews, Jewish intellectual life suddenly took root in America. With the fourth immigration wave, which carried on its crest 300,000 German Jews made homeless and stateless by the Nazi terror, American Jewish intellectual life began to flourish. The center of Jewish intellectual life shifted from the Old World to the New, just as the center of Jewish intellectual life in biblical days had shifted from Palestine to Babylonia after the fall of Judah in the sixth century B.C.

Jewish history in the New World begins with the very discovery of the Western Hemisphere, and Jews played a far greater part in its discovery, exploration, and settlement than present-day historians accord them. Who dares place Jews on the ships that made these historic voyages, or ascribe to them a share in the planning? Jewish mathematicians and scientists worked for a century in laying the groundwork for these expeditions. Abraham Cresques, a Majorcan cartographer, known in Europe as "Master of Maps and Compasses," charted the maps European navigators used to find their way across the seas. His son Judah, known as the "Map Jew," served under the name of Jacomo de Majorca as the director of the Nautical Observatory at Sagres. When Portugal's Prince Henry the Navigator needed a director for his famed Academy of Navigation, he gave the post to Master Jacob, a leading cartographer who came from Majorca's renowned school of Jewish scientists.

After the Jews were expelled from Spain, the Jewish astronomer Abraham Zacuto, whose books on astronomy had been translated from Hebrew into Spanish and Latin, became astronomer at the court of King John II of Portugal. Vasco da Gama consulted Zacuto before setting out on his expedition to India. These medieval Jewish scientists, cartographers, and astronomers were, as the French scholar Charles de La Roncière expresses it, "the bedrock of the great discoveries, from the voyage around Africa to the discovery of the New World."

Jewish history in America begins with the expulsion of the Jews from Spain in the same year and month that Columbus set sail on his first voyage in search of a trade route to India. Jews served on board his small flotilla as able-bodied seamen, map readers, interpreters, and surgeons. As a footnote to history, we must record the fact that the Indians on the Caribbean island where the flotilla first landed were greeted in Hebrew and Arabic by one Luis de Torres, a Jewish interpreter aboard the flagship, for Columbus was certain the natives spoke either Hebrew or Arabic. It was de Torres, incidentally, who discovered maize and brought it to Europe, where, with the potato, it enriched the diet of Western man. Leaving ourselves open to the charge that we credit the Jews with "everything," we must also note that it was not Sir Walter Raleigh who introduced tobacco to Europe, but de Torres and his Christian companion Roderigo de Jerez.

The first settling of Jews in the New World came about through the signing of a compact between King Manuel the Great of Portugal and a Marrano, Fernando de Loronha. In exchange for the privilege of settling in Brazil, de Loronha agreed to explore three hundred leagues of Brazil's coast every year and build a fort wherever he and his passengers settled. In 1502 de Loronha's five ships, filled with Marranos fleeing the Inquisition, set sail for Brazil. Among his few Christian passengers was Amerigo Vespucci, whose name was given to the American continents.* In 1503, de Loronha's Marranos built their first fort on Brazilian soil.

Jewish settlements in South America grew rapidly as the Jews expelled from Western Europe searched for sanctuary. By the end of the sixteenth century, they had cultivated extensive tobacco and sugar plantations, and had developed a sizable merchant and financier class engaged in exporting raw materials and importing finished goods. Right on their heels, however, followed the Inquisition, to establish branch offices on the new continent. Instead of allowing the new economy to develop freely, the Inquisition, in close cooperation with the Spanish and Portuguese governments, established feudalism. Christian settlers, instead of arriving to trade and cultivate, as had the Jews, arrived to despoil and plunder. But for the Inquisition, the dominant civilization might well have been in South America instead of North America.

Spain and Portugal did not hold colonial monopoly in the New World for long. Learning of the gold and silver filling Spanish and Portuguese coffers, England, France, and the Netherlands sent their own fleets to search for their own Eldorados. The Dutch, seeing allies in the Brazilian Jews fleeing the Inquisition, asked them for help in seizing Brazilian trading posts from the Portuguese. The Dutch soon gained a toehold in Brazil, but, unfortunately, they were expelled by the Portuguese in 1654, and the Jews fled in all directions. Jewish history in the United States is generally dated from September of that same year, when twenty-three of these fleeing Jews arrived in New York City, then known as New Amsterdam, and asked its choleric governor, Peter Stuyvesant, for permission to stay.

Though small, New Amsterdam was cosmopolitan, its 750 inhabitants speaking eighteen languages, but not Hebrew. A good organization man who saw no need for Jews in his organization, Stuyvesant, a "vice-president" of the

---

*This was Amerigo Vespucci's second voyage to South America, the first having been made in 1500 in the service of Spain. After his second voyage, Amerigo published an account of it, stating his conviction that not India, but a new continent had been discovered. This led a geographer, Martin Waldseemüller, to suggest the new continent be called "America." Amerigo himself never set foot on North American soil.

Dutch West India Company, sent a note to the home office asking for permission to expel them. The Jews petitioned to stay, on the grounds that they had helped the Dutch in Brazil, and their petition was granted. In 1657 they became Dutch citizens, but hardly had they become acclimated to their new political status than they became British subjects by an act of war. In 1664, when the British ousted the Dutch from North America, the former refugees of the Brazilian autos-da-fé became British colonials.

Jewish history in the Colonies is the history of individuals rather than communities, for during this period entire Jewish communities did not emigrate from Europe, only individuals and families. As soon as new groups arrived, they dispersed throughout the vast American landmass and were absorbed into the American social system.

This absorption was facilitated by two conditions, one the nature of America's social structure, the other the nature of Puritanism. Because the Colonies never developed a feudal corporate state, there was no need for a specially exempt "Jewish middle class." The colonists themselves made up the middle class. Furthermore, because no one threatened their existence, the Jews had no need for self-government. Because they could get justice in American courts, they did not need their own judgment. In fact, the entire idea of Jewish self-government never took root in America.

Another reason for the quick integration of the Jews into the American scene was the Judaic nature of the Puritan spirit in New England. The Puritans regarded themselves as the spiritual heirs of the Old Testament, looking upon the New Testament only as the story of Christ. It was to the Old Testament they looked for God, which was one reason that in England the Puritans were viewed as "Jewish fellow travelers." The Puritans compared their flight to America to the flight of the Jews out of Egypt, and they thought of the Massachusetts Bay Colony as the New Jerusalem. When Harvard was founded, Hebrew was taught along with Latin and Greek. In fact, there was even a proposal that Hebrew be made the official language of the Colonies, and John Cotton wanted to adopt the Mosiac Code as the basis for the laws of Massachusetts. Out of this Puritan spirit came many embodiments of the Mosiac Code in the American Constitution.

The founding fathers and the American people had a steadfast belief in the Old Testament. The development of constitutional law through the body of decisions by the Supreme Court has acted, in a sense, like a Talmud in interpreting and clarifying the Constitution, and those decisions have come to function in American political life much as the Talmud has in Jewish life. "Proclaim liberty throughout the land, unto all its inhabitants," from Leviticus (25:10), is inscribed on the Liberty Bell, which rang out its message at the first reading of the Declaration of Independence.

American Jewish communities were slow to form in the colonial period, developing haphazardly, without plan or organization. There were Jewish settlements as early as 1621 in Virginia, 1649 in Massachusetts, and 1658 in Maryland. By 1733, with the settlement of Jews in Georgia, they were represented in all thirteen colonies.

The colonial period came to an end with the American Revolution. Jews participated on both sides, as did the other colonists, but, as in Europe, most joined the side of freedom. General Washington relied on Jewish as well as Christian financiers and brokers to supply his armies and to back the valueless bills of exchange with whatever fortunes they had at their command. No proof exists, however, for the legend that Haym Salomon backed the Revolution with a personal fortune of $300,000 (a fabulous sum in those days). In his many advertisements, Haym Salomon represented himself as "Broker to the Office of Finance," and his job was that of a banker today, selling "war bonds" to the public.

The Jews of the colonial wave of settlers were at first preponderantly of Spanish descent, but after 1700 their ranks were diluted by an admixture of German Jews trickling into the colonies. By 1750 they already outnumbered the Spanish Jews, though the latter still remained dominant socially for another half a century. Some of these Jewish immigrants and their descendants became prosperous shipowners. Others joined Christian colleagues in the brisk slave trade. Some pressed with the pioneers into the American hinterland. A few became cultured gentlemen, who had their portraits painted by Gilbert Stuart and sent their sons abroad to study. Most, however, were petty tradesmen who never rose out of historic obscurity. They did not help frame the Constitution, were not elected to Congress, and were not appointed to any important judicial or governmental posts.*

By the close of the first phase of Jewish immigration, which spanned roughly 175 years, from 1650 to 1825, the Jewish population in America numbered about 10,000 individuals. Except for their religion they were indistinguishable from the general population. They wore no yellow badges, no ridiculous peaked caps, no earlocks, no black caftans. They Americanized their names. They shed their Spanish, German, Hebrew, and Yiddish, and spoke English. As there were no synagogues in the Colonies until 1730, religion slowly lost its hold upon these Jews, and an American form of creeping assimilationism set in. Whereas the Jews in Europe were baptized, in America they just faded out of Judaism via intermarriage, with no formal renunciation of faith. But against these losses must be set increased fecundity and a trickle of immigration, which kept the Jewish population rather stable until 1825.

During the second immigration wave, from 1820 to 1880, the Jewish population swelled from 10,000 to 250,000, as Jews fled to America in the company of seven million Christian refugees to escape the sanguinary revolutions and counterrevolutions which convulsed Europe during those years. Providentially, these events in Europe coincided with the requirements of the United States. Expanding nineteenth-century America needed these European refugees as farmers, laborers, and merchants. The West was opening up and becoming agricultural. The East was investing its agricultural profits in industry. The country needed farmers to settle the West and a merchant class to service both East and West. The Christian refugees, mostly peasants, headed westward and became farmers. The Jewish refugees, mostly middle class, became free enterprisers.

Many of these Jews, most of them German, did not stay long on the eastern seaboard. Musket on shoulder, pack on back, they headed southward and westward, for Louisville

*The first Jewish representative was not elected until 1841, and the first Jewish senator not until 1845, both from Florida.

and New Orleans, for Cincinnati and Cleveland, for Chicago and St. Louis. Those who arrived with the Gold Rush headed farther westward and were among the first to settle in San Francisco, where their descendants now constitute some of the oldest and most elite families. The newcomers worked night and day, lived frugally, and saved their pennies to accumulate capital to invest in business. The peddler's tray became the drygoods store, and the drygoods store expanded into the department store.* But in the scramble for riches, learning and scholarship were forgotten.

The slavery issue divided the Jews the way it divided the rest of the country. Though a few dealt in slaves, most were strongly abolitionist. Southern Jews fought for the South, not because they believed in slavery, but because they loved the South. And the Southern Jewish elite sympathized with the Southern aristocracy, which, in the main, was more liberal and better educated than the Northern bluebloods. When the Civil War broke out, Southern rabbis exhorted Jews to volunteer for the Confederate gray, and Northern rabbis exhorted Jews to volunteer for the Union blue. When the war was over, there were nine Jewish generals and hundreds of Jewish field officers in the Union Army. The count was proportionately the same in the Confederate Army. The Confederacy also gave the Jews their first American statesman in Judah Benjamin, who served as Secretary of State under Jefferson Davis.

After the war, American industrial expansion created vast empires in steel, oil, railroads, shipping lines, chemicals, coal, and banking, but, with the few exceptions in banking, the Jews were almost totally excluded. There was a vacuum—which nature is said to abhor—in the retail field, however, and the immigrant Jews were sucked into that vacuum. As a consequence, most American Jewish fortunes were made not in industry but in retailing. Later generations funneled large shares of this wealth into art and philanthropy. Families like the Guggenheims, the Warburgs, the Strauses, the Schiffs, the Rosenwalds, have become bywords in American philanthropic and cultural enterprises.

---

*Most of modern America's giant department stores are outgrowths of these early Jewish peddlers' work and ingenuity.

They have donated fabulous collections of paintings and other art works to museums. They have made up the deficits of symphony orchestras and opera companies, and have given millions for the building of concert halls and museums. They have established trust funds for scholarships and professional chairs in the arts and sciences.

Though nineteenth-century Jews produced businessmen of note and philanthropists of distinction who contributed to the social and cultural consciousness of America, they still did not produce great statesmen, jurists, scholars, or scientists. And the Romantic Revolution, as Vernon Louis Parrington calls the literary period between 1800 and 1860, included not a single Jewish name. The picture was equally dismal in Jewish scholarship. No enlightenment appeared to stimulate a Jewish contribution to American culture. No Haskala was born to enrich American Jewish life. But when, in the 1880s, America was given an infusion of Russian Jews, the picture changed dramatically. Again a benign providence timed an immigration wave with the country's economic needs.

In the 1880s, the alchemy of history combined two events into a most unlikely result. The crack-up of the feudal system in Eastern Europe sent millions of immigrants to the United States, two million of them Jews; and the anti-Jewish measures of Alexander III and Nicholas II squeezed the Jews out of Russia by an enveloping pincers of pogrom and starvation. These Russian Jews arrived just as the great westward expansion was coming to an end, at a time when America was settling down to digest the continent she had swallowed, at a time when America was strengthening her economic foundation and renovating her social structure. Cities were gaining political ascendancy over rural areas, industry was subordinating agriculture, and the organization man's voice was beginning to be heard in the nation's capital.

Great gaps in the economy remained to be plugged, however. America needed millions of unskilled laborers to tend the vast industrial complex she had created. She needed additional millions in the "service industries" to feed, to clothe, and to entertain the people in her swelling metropolitan centers. The immigrations of 1880 to 1920 fitted these needs as if they had been filled by an employment agency. The Poles, the Russians, the Romanians—brawny peasants and unskilled workers—were siphoned into the steel mills of Pittsburgh and Youngstown, into the factories of Detroit and Cleveland, into the mushrooming industries of the Midwest. The immigrant Russian Jews were tradesmen and artisans, scholars and professionals, who settled in the cities. They quickly discovered that advancement in industry was dominated by gentiles, and that the important commercial positions had already been filled by the "established" Jews. The opportunities, they quickly sensed, were in the professional fields, in the arts, in the sciences, and in government.

These were long-range goals, however. There was the immediate question of making a living. These Russian Jews were *Luftmenschen** whose skills had been essential for survival in Russia, where the czars had disenfranchised them from land and job and then had taxed them on what they had been robbed of. In their desperate struggle for survival, they had perfected skills as needleworkers, cigar makers, petty tradesmen. If a new skill was needed for survival, they acquired it. All were united in a common poverty and a common dislike of unskilled labor.

Those having skills demanded by the American economy, especially in the needle trades, found immediate employment. Those having obsolete skills took to the peddler's tray. Those who could scrape together a little capital opened "hole-in-the-wall" enterprises—candy stalls, tailor shops, grocery stores. Few looked upon their lowly positions as permanent. Most saw hope for betterment, if not for themselves, then for their children. Life was meager and hard, but self-sustaining.

The majority of these immigrants had arrived penniless, all their worldly belongings wrapped in a bundle. Yet not until every other means had been exhausted, including the love of relatives, did they seek aid. Asking for help was something they abhorred. They looked upon charity as something to give, not something to get. Only illness, catastrophe, or a dire emergency sent them to a relief agency, and even as they themselves were receiving aid they saw

---

*Literally, "people made of air." They were the Jews of the Pale, who, without visible means of support, had to coax a living out of thin air.

nothing incongruous in putting aside a few pennies for the poor in Russia or Palestine. As soon as they found a job, however humble, they scurried off the relief rolls. Jews who had to seek aid did not go to public relief agencies, but to Jewish social bureaus organized by the German Jews. At first the prosperous, established, Americanized German Jews had recoiled in horror at the arrival of the pauperized, bearded, orthodox, Russian "slum Jews." They had withdrawn to their fashionable flats, hoping the immigrants would disappear if ignored. But American newspapers, hammering away at the miserable plight of these people, shamed the German Jews into action. After their initial shock, they rushed to aid the penniless immigrants with a generosity unequaled anywhere, any time. They established relief organizations, vocational schools, recreational centers, hospitals, and old-folks' homes. The social agencies and services they created at this time served as models for many New Deal agencies during the Great Depression.

Most of these immigrants arrived in New York. Some made their way into other cities, Philadelphia, Boston, Detroit, Cleveland, Chicago, but the majority remained in New York, settling in the Lower East Side of Manhattan, which had been a fashionable district during Civil War days but had since been reduced by genteel poverty to a neighborhood of the poor. Sociologists, with their impressive charts showing the number of toilets (or lack of them), the number of people per room, the low per capita income, paint a dismal picture of the Lower East Side Jewish slum. But their charts do not capture its uniqueness. Though it bred tuberculosis and rheumatism, it did not breed crime and venereal disease. It did not spawn illiteracy, illegitimate children, or deserted wives. Library cards were in constant use. There were books in many flats, not in fine bindings in mahogany cases as part of the interior *décor*, but secondhand books with dog-eared pages lined up on shelves made of unpainted planks.

Academic honors were snatched away from bluestocking neighborhood public schools as the Jewish immigrant children attending slum public schools brought home scholastic prizes. Families saved their pennies and sent their children to colleges and universities, to law and medical schools. Within one generation Jewish occupations changed radically, Today the Jews have practically no representation in unskilled labor, and less than a third of them are clerks and salesmen. The rest are either entrepreneurs or professionals—manufacturers, factory representatives, retailers, government career men, doctors and lawyers, writers and artists, teachers and professors, scientists and scholars.

With the 1920s began the exodus from the slums. As Jews improved their economic condition they moved to better neighborhoods, and the gentile population fled to the suburbs. The Jews caught up with them in the 1940s, but this time the gentiles no longer fled. The Jews were now men of learning or prosperous businessmen. In today's suburbia, it is difficult to tell which of two Bermuda-shorts-clad gentlemen guiding their power mowers is the Jewish businessman and which is the gentile vice-president.

How was this transformation from a peddler in the slums to a businessman in a split-level ranch home achieved in one generation? The answer lies in a qualitative difference between the Christian and Jewish immigration waves. The Christians who fled Russia, Poland, Romania, Hungary, were peasants and workers. The rich, the intellectuals, and the aristocrats did not leave their countries. With the Jews it was a different story. The entire community was oppressed; therefore entire communities fled—rich man, poor man, worker and scholar, orthodox and radical—taking their entire culture with them. They were not uprooted. They were transplanted.

World War I put a stop to the boatloads of arriving European immigrants. Instead, boatloads of American soldiers were shipped to Europe to "make the world safe for democracy." After the war, immigration was resumed, but it soon ended as the American mind reacted to events abroad. Communism was sweeping Eastern Europe and in each steerageload of immigrants who disembarked at Ellis Island, many Americans saw bearded Bolsheviks, with the *Communist Manifesto* in one hand and a bomb in the other, bent on destroying the United States. An anti-Red hysteria swept the country, and grass-roots pressure was put on Congress to stop the influx of foreigners. Coincidentally, by this time America had all the labor she needed.

Consequently, Congress responded to the will of the people, and between 1921 and 1924 a series of bills was passed to block the flow of immigration.

The anti-Red hysteria of the post–World War I period contained no anti-Semitism, only a fear of Russian Bolsheviks, East Europeans, college intellectuals, and labor leaders. When Leon Trotsky's plan for world revolution failed and Joseph Stalin decided to build "socialism in one country" only, the hysteria subsided. America returned to normalcy and developed that exhilarating age of nonsense and literature known as the "Roaring Twenties." But with the Depression of 1929 anti-Semitism crept into American history.

Until 1880 anti-Semitism in America had been practically nonexistent. Occasional injustices to Jews must not be confused with anti-Semitism, for injustice is not exclusively reserved for Jews. Anti-Semitism flared up briefly during the agrarian depression of 1880–1890, but quickly died out when the slump in farming ended. This Bible-belt anti-Semitism was not national in scope but was confined to the farming areas affected by the depression. It was, in a sense, a homegrown hate, the expression of a fear trying to find a reasonable explanation.

The anti-Semitism of the Great Depression of 1929 was entirely different. It was manufactured in Germany and imported by American Nazis of German descent as part of a plot to undermine the American will to fight Hitler's brand of fascism. Many Americans, unable to comprehend the nature of a depression in the world's richest country, fell prey to Hitler's paid propagandists. In the end it was not the United States that declared war on Germany, but Germany that declared war on the United States.* Significantly, anti-Semitism in America, as in Germany, took hold, not among the rich and not among the working class, but among the declassed. They were among the most ardent followers of the "prophets of deceit" who spread their

---

*It is astounding how many Americans are unaware of this fact. The Japanese attacked Pearl Harbor on December 7, 1941, and on December 8 the United States declared war on Japan. On December 10, Germany declared war on the United States, her chargé d'affaires handing the formal declaration to the Secretary of State on the morning of December 11. In the afternoon of that same day, the United States responded with a declaration of war on Germany.

hate doctrines throughout the nation via pulpit, press, and radio. Anti-Semitism as a movement in America died, not because the people who had embraced it considered it false, but because the Depression ended.

German anti-Semitism did serve, however unintentionally, to enrich America's cultural life. After 1935, Congress relaxed its immigration laws to permit the entry of 300,000 Jews and thousands of Christians who were fleeing Europe to escape Nazi totalitarianism. Many of the refugees in this wave were scientists, scholars, or writers. The vacuum created by their departure from Europe made itself indelibly felt on the intellectual balance sheet. In the thirty-eight years between 1901 and 1939, for instance, only fourteen Americans were awarded Nobel prizes in physics, chemistry, and medicine.* In the thirteen-year period between 1943 and 1955, after the flight of Germany's intellectuals to America, twenty-nine Americans received prizes in these categories. In Germany, it was the reverse. In the first thirty-eight-year period, Germany received thirty-five Nobel prizes, whereas in the second thirteen-year period the country received only five. For the next thirty-five years, these figures are even more revealing. From 1955 to 1990 one hundred and thirty-two Nobel prizes were awarded to Americans with only thirteen going to Germans.

The cultural contributions of this newly arrived Jewish intellectual elite enriched the contributions already being made by American-born Jews. But just as the Jewish Enlightenment in nineteenth-century Western Europe had been Western in its orientation, so this twentieth-century cultural contribution was American in its orientation. Though impressive, these Jewish contributions in America did not have the brilliance of Jewish contributions in Europe. The European contribution was almost exclusively intellectual, whereas the American tended more toward the popular arts.

The modern American stage was nourished by the Frohman and Shubert brothers, Abraham Erlanger, and David Belasco. Jews founded early experimental theaters such as the Group Theatre and the Theatre Guild. The

---

*No Nobel prizes were awarded for the years 1940 through 1942.

plays of George S. Kaufman, Lillian Hellman, Arthur Miller, Elmer Rice, Clifford Odets, Sidney Kingsley, and Irwin Shaw have received international recognition. The American movie industry was founded by Jews, and many of its finest directors, actors, and script writers have been Jewish. The modern musical comedy became a world art form through the genius of Richard Rodgers and Oscar Hammerstein II. The tunes of Sigmund Romberg, Jerome Kern, Irving Berlin, and George Gershwin have achieved semiclassical status. Benny Goodman made jazz respectable by bringing it to Carnegie Hall.

But with the twentieth century, American Jews also became scientists, statesmen, jurists, and publishers. Among others, Albert Abraham Michelson, famed for his studies in measuring the velocity of light and his experiments on the relative motion of matter and ether, was America's second Nobel prize winner (1907) in the sciences.* Isidor Isaac Rabi won acclaim and a Nobel prize for his research in quantum mechanics and his studies in the magnetic properties of molecules and atoms. Jacob Lipman, chemist and biologist, advanced scientific farming in America through his research in soil chemistry. Hermann Joseph Muller won a Nobel prize for his pioneering work in the artificial transmutation of genes through X rays. Selman Waksman isolated streptomycin, biochemist Casimar Frank discovered vitamins, and Jonas Salk introduced the first vaccine against polio. Since its inception in 1969, seven American Jews have been awarded the Nobel prize in Economics, and Henry Kissinger was awarded the Nobel prize for Peace.

Benjamin N. Cardozo, Felix Frankfurter, and Louis D. Brandeis were appointed to the Supreme Court. Bernard M. Baruch served American presidents from Woodrow Wilson to Dwight D. Eisenhower. Oscar S. Straus was the first American Jew to serve as Cabinet member. Herbert H. Lehman was four times governor of New York and later a United States senator. Adolph S. Ochs established the *New York Times* as one of the world's leading newspapers. Joseph Pulitzer founded the *St. Louis Post-Dispatch*, the school of journalism at Columbia University, and the

*Theodore Roosevelt won the Nobel prize for peace in 1906.

Pulitzer prizes for outstanding achievements in journalism, literature, and music. The social thinking of such men as Samuel Gompers, David Dubinsky, and Sidney Hillman has become so much a part of the American sense of social justice that no political party would think of turning back the clock. Writers Isaac Bashevis Singer and Elie Wiesel received Nobel prizes for literature.

America won renown on the concert stages of the world through the performances of such naturalized Americans as pianists Vladimir Horowitz and Artur Rubinstein; violinists Mischa Elman, Efrem Zimbalist, Jascha Heifetz, Nathan Milstein, Isaac Stern, and Itzhak Perlman; cellist Gregor Piatigorsky; and Beverly Sills for her contributions to the world of opera. The world will long remember Serge Koussevitzky, the late conductor of the Boston Symphony Orchestra and the founder of the Berkshire Festival. The names of conductors Bruno Walter and Fritz Reiner are familiar to lovers of classical music, as are those of American-born conductor Leonard Bernstein and violinist Yehudi Menuhin.

Just as the third and fourth immigration waves wrought vast transformations in American cultural and intellectual life, the second wave wrought a great transformation in Jewish religious life. Because there was no ghetto tradition in America to overthrow, the German Reform Movement of Mendelssohn, Zunz, and Geiger,* brought over by these immigrants, established itself quickly in the United States. It succeeded largely through the efforts of one man, Bohemian-born Rabbi Isaac Mayer Wise (1819–1900). When the congregation of the orthodox Beth El Synagogue in Albany, New York, engaged Wise in 1846, it little realized it had acquired a stormy petrel in the twenty-seven-year-old rabbi who had arrived in New York only the week before with a wife, a child, and no passport. Rabbi Wise began to "reform" his congregation and begat a rebellion. Undaunted, he accepted another orthodox rabbinic post in Cincinnati and, having learned caution from his previous experience, brought Reform Judaism in

---

*It was Abraham Geiger (1810–1874), born in Wiesbaden, Germany, who formalized Reform Judaism at the first conference of Reformed Rabbis, which he convened in 1837.

through the back door of diplomacy instead of the front door of ultimatum. In 1875 he founded the Hebrew Union College, the first American rabbinical seminary, and in 1900 he died revered as the father of American Reform Judaism.

It was this Reform Judaism which greeted the orthodox Russian Jews when they arrived. The Russian Jews looked upon the hatless, clean-shaven, English-speaking, Americanized German Jews as apostates. The German-American Jews looked upon the bearded, caftaned, Yiddish-speaking, Russian Jews as apparitions from the Middle Ages. The impact these German Jews had upon the youth of the Russian Jews was as great as the impact of the Greeks upon Jewish youth in Hellenic days. Russian-Jewish youth soon began to imitate the German Jews in manners, mores, and dress. When parents would not yield some of their rigid orthodoxy for fear they might lose their Judaism, they lost their children instead, who in rebellion joined Reform temples, intermarried with Christians, or faded out of Judaism through the back alley of agnosticism. To hold on to their children, the orthodox Jews reformed their orthodoxy. But like so much else in American Jewish life, this "reform orthodoxy" too was a European innovation. As the development of reform orthodoxy, or "neo-orthodoxy," is important to an understanding of modern Judaism, we must digress to discuss briefly its origins.

Prior to the German Reform Movement developed by Mendelssohn, Zunz, and Geiger there had been only one Judaism, based on Torah and Talmud. In the centuries before the confinement of the Jews in the ghettos, Talmudism had been flexible, and great rabbis had constantly tailored it for survival in changing times. But three hundred years of ghetto life had hardened the Talmudic arteries, because ghetto rabbis permitted no change. When, therefore, ghetto rabbis refused to accommodate the Western Enlightenment, a large segment of Jews broke away to join the Jewish Reform Movement. By 1850 it had become the dominant Jewish religion in Germany, and old, ghetto Judaism was in danger of dying out.

The course Jewish religious history took in Western Europe after 1850 resembles the course Western Christian religious history took after 1550. The Catholic Church, alarmed at the inroads made by the Reformation, instituted a Counter Reformation at the Council of Trent (1545–1563), modernizing and liberalizing the outward forms of Catholicism without changing its central dogma. Ghetto Jews, alarmed at the inroads made by the Jewish "Reformation," also instituted a "Counter Reformation," modernizing the outward forms of their Judaism without changing its central dogma.

Thus there existed in the late nineteenth century two Judaisms—Reform and neo-orthodox, which we shall from now on refer to as "Orthodox." Both believed, however, in the same God, the same Torah, the same Prophets. But whereas the latter believed in the divine revelation of religion, the former believed in its scientific evolution. The great everyday difference between them is revealed in their attitudes toward dietary laws, rules for observing the Sabbath, and the composition of liturgy. Just as the Pharisees in Greco-Roman days held that the cult of priest and sacrifice was not essential for the preservation of Judaism, so the Reform rabbinate holds that Judaism is neither undermined by the eating of a ham sandwich nor strengthened by exhaustive praying in Hebrew.

The Orthodox "Counter Reformation" stopped the stampede to Reform Judaism with a program of internal renovation. It Westernized itself by raising the standards of learning and introducing secular subjects into its yeshivas, by permitting choirs in the synagogues, and by sermonizing in the vernacular. It was to this new orthodoxy that many Russian-Jewish immigrants turned in order to keep their children in the fold and at the same time save what they thought constituted the essence of Judaism. An eighteenth-century Russian Jew of the Pale would look upon an American Orthodox Jew of today as an apostate.

But Reform Judaism also reformed itself. In their zeal to modernize, the early reformers had thrown overboard so much tradition that the residue was barely distinguishable from some Protestant sects. The final step that almost took the Reform Movement out of Judaism was the founding by Felix Adler in 1876 of a "secular religion" known as the Society for Ethical Culture. Its creed, a synthesis of Jewish and Christian morality applied to everyday life, linked Jews and Christians by one common ethic. As a result, as Reform Judaism began to lose more and more of its membership to Protestant and Catholic churches, Reform rabbis quickly made the "Hebrew Word flesh" and began to serve a slightly more kosher liturgy to their members. Since then, the American Reform Movement has steadily gained strength and today has 850 congregations with a membership of more than 299,000 families.

Inadvertently, America also gave birth to Conservative Judaism, a modern movement, founded by Romanian-born Solomon Schechter (1850–1915). Son of Hasidic parents, Schechter attended the yeshivas of Lemberg (Lvov) and Vienna, where he stumbled on the Haskala. He switched from Talmud to Hegel and from yeshiva to university. His scholarship attracted wide attention, and in 1890 he was appointed Lecturer in Talmud at Cambridge University, England, where he became famed not only for introducing British wit into Talmudic discussions, but also for identifying the original manuscript of Ecclesiasticus from a fragment, which led to his discovery of other fragments in a synagogue in Cairo. In 1901 Schechter was brought to the United States by the Jewish Theological Seminary in New York as its president, with the mission of raising Jewish scholastic standards in America. His fame attracted many of Europe's renowned Jewish scholars to America.

Schechter, who while in Germany had come under the influence of the doctrines of sociologist Max Weber, held that Judaism was shaped as much by changing social and economic conditions as by its own inner dynamics. Therefore, he felt that Judaism, if it wished to survive, would have to absorb part of the civilization in which it lived as well as to establish its own cultural values. This unique blend of Torah and modern sociology was the basis for Schechter's new Conservative Judaism, which drew to itself the conservative elements in Reform and the liberal elements in Orthodox Judaism. It relaxed some of the dietary restrictions, lifted some of the Sabbath blue laws, permitted an organ in the synagogue, and sanctioned the use of some prayers in the vernacular. It also allowed its members to adopt many of the modes, manners, and mores prevalent in gentile society. Today all three main branches of Judaism—Orthodox, Conservative, and Reform—are one interlocked faith without any serious, weakening schisms.

This is not to say that the American Jewish future is set in stone. Today the American Jew, standing in the lobby of history, is again being warned about their decreasing numbers. He is still searching for ways to educate their youth; how to overcome the results of creeping assimilation and intermarriage with resultant losses to Judaism of the children of these marriages; how to fight anti-Semitism; how to interest the unaffiliated Jews and the affiliated Jews who do not attend religious services.

In nineteenth-century France, a French Jew said: "The grandfather believes, the father doubts, the son denies. The grandfather prays in Hebrew, the father prays in French, the son does not pray at all. The grandfather observes the holidays, the father Yom Kippur, the son becomes a deist ... if not an atheist." Is this very different from what we are being told today? If he, as well as many other "doomsayers," had been correct, Jews would not be here today. But they are—still viable, still strong. Perhaps this French Jew was not farsighted enough. He stopped counting too soon. He did not tell us what the great-grandson did.

Are the dire predictions by American Jews more accurate today than were those we heard in the past? Only the future will tell. But we do know that past predictions were not. There were always leaders who refused to give up. These "Diaspora Designers" wrote the scripts that enabled Jews to continue as culture-producing creative people, through two thousand years in the Diaspora. Today the creative impulse is alive and well. Who would have foreseen in the early 1900s that by the end of the century Judaism would have Jews forming their own Havurahs,* with their own leaders and services, some even leading breakaway congregations? Or women rabbis who would play major roles in the rabbinate? Or the shift to Orthodoxy by some while others are leaving Orthodoxy, all searching for closer ties to Judaism? Or the role of the Jewish Commu-

---

*Small groups that join together in the spirit of friendship to explore their Judaism.

nity Center Associations in competing for membership and leadership with congregations?

How shall we assess Jewish history in America? But for a few minor exceptions it was, until the twentieth century, little more than a banal succession of events, an accretion of Jews through a series of migrations. The American "Judaism of plenty" before 1900 was culturally as sterile as was the Russian "Judaism of poverty" before the Haskala. Then two historical events—the mass migrations of Russian Jews to America and Hitler's destruction of European Jewry—swelled the number of Jews in the United States to over five million and made this country the center of Diaspora Judaism.

Do we have here a superficial resemblance to past events or a genuine repetition of history? In the sixth century B.C. the Babylonians destroyed the Palestinian center of Judaism just as in the twentieth century A.D. Hitler destroyed the European center of Judaism. But the idea of Judaism did not die with either destruction. When history presented the Jews of Babylon with a passport to return to a reconstituted Palestine, they declined the invitation, just as American Jews declined a similar invitation to return to a reconstituted Israel. By their refusal the Babylonian Jews created the Diaspora; by their refusal the American Jews perpetuated the Diaspora. In Babylonia, Diaspora Judaism slowly gained intellectual ascendancy over Palestinian Judaism. In the twentieth century, history placed the scepter of Diaspora Judaism in the willing hands of the American Jews.

American Judaism was not shaped by a blueprint; it evolved out of what was done. It lived itself into existence and thus created its own brand of Judaism. The first Jews who arrived in Colonial America devised ways to remain Jews by willingly amending the nonessentials in Judaism while holding on to the nonnegotiable items. American Judaism is the first and only noncoercive Judaism in Jewish history, and only those aspects that the Jews wished to retain have survived. Radically changing attitudes toward religion in America have also influenced the Jews. There is more diversity and more freedom of choice than ever before.

Judaism in America has been re-forming itself since

the first Jews set foot in New Amsterdam in 1654. Although today we are facing some of the same problems as in the past, the environment is different. In Europe the need was to keep the Jews as Jews so they would not be absorbed into the civilization in which they lived. In the United States the task is to find ways to keep the Jews as Jews while they are participating and contributing partners of that society, teaching youth *why* to be Jewish, not just how.

Can American Jewry produce a series of intellectual giants capable of hammering out the ideas needed for Diaspora survival? Before 1900, the answer would have been "no." After 1900, after the influx of Europe's intellectual elite into the mainstream of American Judaism, the answer could be "yes." If this influx results only in a physical mixture of European intellect and American pragmatism, then any present American Jewish intellectual preeminence is transitory, an illusion that will vanish soon after the immigrant intellectuals have died out. But if, on the other hand, this infusion results in a chemical reaction wherein the American Jews will have absorbed the intellectual vitality of the European Jews and will have expanded on it, then the United States may well play the role of Babylonia for the Judaism of the twenty-first century.

Are we perhaps already beginning to see the emergence of a new Judaism on American soil, just as a new Judaism emerged on Babylonian soil, where the cults of sacrifice and priesthood died and where the institutions of rabbi, prayer, and synagogue were born? In American Reform Judaism these three institutions are beginning to assume different functions. The rabbi is no longer only an interpreter of Talmudic Judaism but a counselor and an interfaith mediator; prayer is no longer an exclusively personal intercession with God but praise of the Creator; the synagogue or temple is no longer exclusively a place of worship but also a social community for expressing one's ties to Judaism. Just as the Pharisees discarded the third of the Torah and Talmud dealing with sacrifice and priesthood, so Reform Judaism discarded another third of the Torah and Talmud dealing with dietary and ritual laws, leaving the last third, which it considers the core of Judaism—its code of ethics, morality, and justice. And a whole new institution has been developed in America and adopted by Jews all over the world—organizational Judaism, which includes organizations such as Jewish Federations, National Council of Jewish Women, Jewish Community Center Associations, American Jewish Committee, Hadassah, B'nai B'rith and its Anti-Defamation League, among many others. Will it be the historic role of American Jewry to usher in the Spinozian Age of Judaism—the universalist phase?

Before proffering an answer we must pick up the thread of Jewish history in Europe from World War I in 1914 to the establishment of the State of Israel in 1948. Between these two events occurred a world tragedy which left a blot on the escutcheon of man and the mark of Cain on the German people.

TWENTY-EIGHT

# THE BROWN-SHIRTED
# CHRIST KILLERS

On January 30, 1933, history played a trick on the world and made Adolf Hitler Chancellor of Germany. Jubilant Germans spilled into the streets "heiling" the brown-shirted stormtroopers marching in triumph down Unter den Linden, little knowing that in a few short years they would drench the world in blood and go down in history as the barbarian's barbarians; little suspecting that within one decade they would choke in the sands of the Sahara, drown in the waters of the Atlantic, die on the steppes of Russia, and be crushed in the ruins of their own cities.

From that first day in power to that April day in 1945 when, with Berlin ablaze, Hitler shot himself through the mouth, the Germans exterminated with systematized murder 12 million men, women, and children, in concentration camps, by firing squads, and in gas chambers. Of these 12 million victims, 7 million were Christians and 5 million were Jews*—1.4 Christians for every Jew. But because the Nazis shouted "Kill the Jews," the world blinded itself to the murder of Christians.

The irony is that, in spite of all the murder and the bloodshed, it did not impede the march of Jewish history. The Third Reich, which Hitler boasted would endure for a thousand years, perished after twelve. The Jews, whom Hitler boasted he would eradicate, survived to create a new, independent Jewish state.

The perplexing question is, how could the Nazi infamy happen in Germany, a culture creator in Western civilization? The answer is that Germany is a fusion of two contradictory strains of thought and feeling. One is the Germany of Beethoven and Brahms, of Goethe and Schiller, the Germany of lofty idealism, of the open universe, of unlimited possibilities of human achievement. It is this Germany which evolved and nurtured her humanism, art, music, and literature.

But there is also another Germany of the authoritarian philosophers and militarists, of Fichte and Hegel, of Bismarck and Kaiser—the instigators of the closed universe and the *masse-mensch* (mass man). It is this authoritarian Germany which subverted the liberal and idealistic strains of the other Germany, calling them "Judaizing influences." This judgment may well be true, for the sublimation of the evil in man—a sublimation essential for the survival of society—is precisely the universal function of religion, the function of Judaism.

World War I marked the visible turning point in Germany's history, when these authoritarian influences gained

---

*The figure usually quoted for the number of Jews murdered by the Nazis is 6,000,000, but facts tend to support a figure of 5,000,000. Justice Jackson at the Nuremberg trials cited 4,500,000 Jews killed by the Germans. Today, the highest estimate is 5,600,000, the lowest 4,200,000. This difference is accounted for by guessing Jewish losses in territories held by the Soviet Union. Gerald Reitlinger gives the figure of 5,000,000. "I believe it does not make the guilt of the living Germans any less if the figure of six million turns out to be an overestimate," he says. (*The Final Solution*, p. 469.) Howard M. Sachar puts the figure at 4,200,000 to 4,600,000, stating that "the figure of 6,000,000 released at the end of the war has since been discounted." (*The Course of Modern Jewish History*, p. 452.)

total ascendancy and total power. "The Hun," said Winston Churchill, "is either at your throat or at your feet." After four years of fighting in World War I, the Germans capitulated. As long as they fought in someone else's territory, they could stand the devastation they wrought. But when the war was carried to their own soil, they did not have the stamina the French had. German sailors, their submarines no longer supreme, mutinied. German soldiers threw down their rifles. And the Kaiser, instead of standing by his nation in her hour of defeat, fled to Holland. After the Peace Treaty of Versailles, Germany whined about her hardships, begged for money, and blamed the Jews for her defeat in order to save her "honor." "We Germans did not lose the war," was the German song of the twenties. "It was the Jews who betrayed us." Self-pity gnawed away at her former greatness, leaving only a hollow shell as prey for men who would force her into barbarism.

World War I brought devastation not only to Germany but to Eastern Europe as well. The Jews especially fared badly. They had tactlessly chosen to live in a sector of land where German and Russian armies locked for four years in a gigantic struggle for power. When the Russians retreated in bitter defeat, they killed Jews for being German sympathizers. When the Germans were forced to make "tactical withdrawals," they killed Jews for being Russian informers.

The end of World War I brought a brief period of hope for a better life to Europe's millions, Christians and Jews alike; but this hope was soon laid to rest with other dead hopes. At the urgent promptings of President Woodrow Wilson, certificates of democracy were handed out to people who had no conception of what democracy was, and to rulers who had no intention of enforcing its principles. Overnight, Wilson created the new "democracies" of Estonia, Latvia, Lithuania, Poland, Hungary, Yugoslavia, Albania—all formerly parts of the Russian, Austrian, and German empires. It was in this borderland of twenty-four-hour democracies that German anti-Semitism found immediate acceptance and became the highest form of statesmanship. The only two exceptions were Finland and Czechoslovakia, also created at this time.

Why should there have been such a ready acceptance of anti-Semitism in Eastern Europe? A review of economic reality offers an explanation. World War I had shattered the feudal economies of these newly created states. Artificial boundaries cut across their economic lifelines. After the surgery on Austria-Hungary, for instance, Austria got the scenery and Hungary got the coal and iron deposits. The landed gentry and aristocrats who, before the war, had regarded work as demeaning and the professions as fit only for Jews, now had to find jobs or starve. The middle class was destitute. Workers, pressed to the point of starvation by falling wages in "democracies" that had little social legislation, cast flirtatious eyes on communism as a solution to their problems.

Instead of countering these threats with injections of democracy as Finland and Czechoslovakia did under similar circumstances, the rulers of these East European countries resorted to the tranquilizer of fascism. The specter of a communist danger was dangled before the declassed, who were told over and over again that if the "Jewish problem" were solved, then the problems of the declassed would be solved. The worried and impoverished white-collar class welcomed this soothing political philosophy. The Jews were legislated out of the professions and out of industry so that the aristocrats could take over jobs they had formerly despised. As economic conditions worsened, anti-Semitic legislation was increased. It is ironic that the states that tried to save themselves from communism by cooperating with the Nazis now came under the domination of communism. And it is in some of these states that former hatreds burst into flames with the fall of communism in the early 1990s.

The German Weimar Republic that rose out of the chaos which the fleeing Kaiser had left was weakened by the cynical men who were appointed to administer it. They paid lip service to the new democratic institutions, but they allowed assassination to undermine the Republic. Between the years 1918 and 1925, right-wing terrorist organizations murdered more than three hundred prominent liberal men in office—Catholics, Protestants, and Jews. The ruling clique gave tacit approval to these acts of violence by imposing wrist-slapping sentences on the criminals when they were brought to "justice."

It was in this general atmosphere of terrorism that a defunct general named Erich von Ludendorff and a jobless house painter named Adolf Hitler staged the now notorious 1923 Munich beer hall *putsch*, with the avowed intention of overthrowing the Bavarian government. The *putsch* failed. Ludendorff was set free by the minions of Munich law enforcement, and Hitler was given a five-year sentence, of which he served less than one.

The career of Hitler the Führer had begun. Without the help of Junkers, industrialists, and militarists who made the error of thinking he was their tool, it would have been impossible. Adolf Hitler's road to power was a straight one. He preached a simple political gospel. The communists, the Jews, and the Versailles Treaty had brought on the evils which had befallen Germany. By outlawing communism, by exterminating the Jews, and by repudiating the Versailles Treaty he would make Germany great again. In increasing numbers the declassed voted for Hitler's party, which, with each election, increased its representation in the Reichstag. In 1929, the aged General Paul von Hindenburg—a symbol of Kaiser, Junker, and *Herrentum*—was taken out of mothballs and trotted out as a candidate for president to run against Hitler. Hindenburg won the election, but four years later he yielded to the threats of Hitler and made the former Austrian house painter Chancellor of Germany. Within ten years of his release from prison, Hitler was the sole ruler of the Third Reich, as Germany was now called, and his party, the NAtional SoZIalistische Deutsche Arbeiterpartei, known as NAZI, became the only legal party in the land.

Who was this Adolf Hitler, this contemporary Hun, who, by pandering to the bestial in man, triggered the most heinous blood orgy in history? Biographers have sought in vain for deep, hidden motives in his make-up which would account for his actions. Sinister though he was, it is difficult to take him seriously. Insignificant in appearance, undistinguished in face, his countenance would be easily forgotten if not for the Charlie Chaplin mustache and the ersatz Napoleon hair lock. Perhaps there was no depth to seek.

Adolf Hitler's father, Alois Schicklgruber, the illegitimate son of a vagrant and a servant girl, was thrice married. Out of the third union with a peasant girl twenty-three years younger than he, Adolf Hitler was born in 1889. His whole life was a cliché. He was a poor student, an undistinguished soldier, an unsuccessful house painter, and pathetic in his ambition to become an artist because he had no talent. Statesmen who came into contact with him were appalled by his ignorance and vulgarity.

What then was the nature of the hold Hitler had on his followers? Wherein did he differ from other racists? To say that he had hypnotic, spellbinding powers is to say nothing. Perhaps the answer is that whereas other racists merely toyed with the idea of making murder a civic virtue, Hitler made it a reality by opening the Pandora's box of man's unconscious mind. Hitler freed those evil impulses which man has tried to chain and tame in the name of civilization ever since his emergence from the primeval forest. It was not by accident that those who rose to the highest posts in Hitler's inner circle were drug addicts like Goering, sadists like Heydrich, and murderers like Himmler.

Once Hitler had political power there was no holding him back. The entire state was organized for brutality. In 1935 the Reichstag passed the so-called "Nuremberg Laws," disenfranchising all those deemed to have "Jewish blood"—which included anyone with one Jewish grand-parent. It is interesting to note that Hitler considered the Jewish strain four times stronger than the Aryan. One by one the Nuremberg Laws stripped the Jews of their pro-fessions and their businesses; blackmail stripped them of their liquid assets. The businesses of the Jews fell into the appreciative hands of the Germans. The liquid assets found their way into the pockets of Nazi party officials. Hundreds were hauled off to concentration camps, where they were greeted by the Christian prisoners who had preceded them.

"The fact that German anti-Semitism had evolved into anti-Christianity must be considered a highly significant symptom," said the Russian Orthodox Catholic theologian Nikolai Berdyaev.* This basic anti-Christianity of German Nazism is something that is almost totally overlooked by popular historians and journalists. Though Nazi ideologies had proclaimed anti-Christian doctrines ever since the party was formed in 1919, only anti-Semitic slogans were

---

*Christianity and Anti-Semitism*, page 2.

stressed in world headlines. Yet the Nazis wanted to obliterate Christianity as much as they wanted to expunge Judaism. In the Nazi view, Christianity represented a danger because it weakened the Aryan strain of blood through proselytization. They held that "Aryan Christianity" had been betrayed by St. Paul; they contended that Christian churches were a sham and a fraud; and they preached that the Catholic Church was the most dangerous of all because it was both Jewish and international. The Nazis taught that National Socialism was the only true gospel, the sole faith and salvation of the German people, and that Hitler was the sole savior.

This gibberish is incorporated in official Nazi works from which stemmed both anti-Semitic and anti-Christian doctrines. If one believes the anti-Semitic, one should also believe the anti-Christian, for both had a single purpose. Hitler's aim was to eradicate all religious organizations within the state and to foster a return to paganism.

In 1933 Germany signed a concordat with the Vatican, guaranteeing the freedom of the Catholic Church. A year later Dr. Erich Klausner, head of the Catholic Action organization, was murdered by Hitler's stormtroopers. In an attempt to discredit the Church, monks were brought to trial on immorality charges. In 1935 the Protestant churches were placed under state control. Protesting ministers and priests were sent to concentration camps. They had become "subversives" on a par with the Jews and communists. Pope Pius XI, realizing the anti-Christian nature of Nazism, charged Hitler with "the threatening storm clouds of destructive religious wars ... which have no other aim than ... that of extermination." But the Nazi shouts of "Kill the Jews" drowned out the warning voice of the Pope and the agonized cries of the tortured in the concentration camps.

The first concentration camps were collection points where the Gestapo—the German secret police—could send people they wanted to terrorize into submission. Most early inmates were the so-called "politicals"—communists, socialists, liberals, republicans, ordinary Germans who opposed Hitler's policies of violence, including, of course, the personal enemies of high Nazi functionaries. During the first five years of the Nazi regime, therefore, most concentration camp inmates were Christians. Jews were relatively late arrivals, the result of German anti-Semitism, which progressed in five stages, picking up at each stage a momentum of violence from its own inner dynamics. The first stage began in 1933, with the Nazi accession to power, and consisted mostly of the looting of Jewish shops, occasional beatings, and a boycott of Jewish businesses. The second stage set in with the enactment of the Nuremberg laws in 1935. The third stage began in 1939 with the mass arrest of 20,000 Jews, bringing with it the first systematic physical violence and the first mass detentions in concentration camps.

Until 1939, Jews had been allowed to leave Germany upon the payment of a ransom to the German state, and by that year 300,000 of Germany's 600,000 Jews had left the country. In 1939 the ante for emigration was raised to the total wealth possessed by each individual Jew. At this time Nazi statesmen also conceived the idea of holding Germany's remaining 200,000 Jews as hostages for the payment by world Jewry of a ransom of one and a half billion Reichsmarks. Negotiations were begun in Geneva, but with the invasions of Czechoslovakia and Poland, Germany broke off all talks. The fourth stage began in 1940 with the deportation of all German and Austrian Jews to specially created ghettos in Poland, where they were allowed to die of disease and starvation.

The fifth and last stage, the so-called "final solution," was instituted by Hitler himself. It was after the invasion of Russia in 1941 that the purpose of the concentration camps changed from that of detention to that of extermination, and murder became a full-time occupation for Germans. The "final solution," as envisaged by Hitler, included not only the murder of all Jews in Europe, but also the enslavement of "Christian subhumans" like Russians, Poles, Romanians, Hungarians, and Yugoslavs, and their reduction in number through a ruthless program of planned extermination. The enslavement was to be accomplished by exporting these nationals to Germany as slave laborers; their murder was assigned to special task forces known as *Einsatzgruppen*.

As millions of able-bodied Germans were drafted from fields and factories to fight on the Russian front, millions of Christian civilians were sent from the occupied countries to Germany to work as slave laborers. When they became too ill or too feeble to work, they were shipped to the new model concentration camps to be disposed of. An unending stream of such slave labor poured into Germany—7,500,000 in five years. Here, in the one thousand camps which had mushroomed in Germany and adjacent territories, several million Russians, Frenchmen, Poles, Belgians, Yugoslavs, Dutchmen, and other European nationals died horrible deaths from starvation, disease, and torture.

Though a few hundred thousand East European Jews were sent as slave laborers to Germany, and then disposed of in the same manner as Christian slave laborers, most were "liquidated" (to use the language of dehumanization) by the four *Einsatzgruppen* assigned to the four German fronts in Russia. Each *Einsatzgruppe* consisted of 500 to 900 men commanded by a general. Their mission was to march behind the *Wehrmacht*—the regular German Army—to round up civilians, Christians as well as Jews, and shoot them. Most *Einsatz* troops were Nazi party members who had volunteered for this dangerous job.

Their procedure for mass murder was as follows: Jews, or Czechs, or Poles, or Russians were rounded up, marched to a deserted area and forced to dig pits or trenches, after which they were forced to undress, lined up in front of the trenches, and machine-gunned. Those that fell along the edges, dead and wounded, were shoveled by soldiers or bulldozers into the pits, and dirt was thrown over all, the dead and the living, the adults, the children, and the infants. Altogether, the *Einsatzgruppen* were responsible for the murder of several million Christians and a million Jews.

Though the Nazi hierarchy did not question the bravery or hard work of the *Einsatzgruppen*, they were dissatisfied with its methods, not on the grounds that these methods were inhuman, but because they were too slow and too costly. Nazi science was asked to step in and offer a solution. Freed of the restraints of any "Judaizing tendencies," Nazi scientists could exercise their ingenuity to the fullest. They experimented—on human beings, of course—by injecting air into the veins, severing arteries, testing various poisons, and so on, but these methods were rejected because of the time and labor involved. Serendipity succeeded where ingenuity failed. A jubilant Nazi reported he had stumbled upon the perfect method. Having some 600 Russian prisoners of war to dispose of, he had experimented with an inexpensive, easy-to-manufacture gas known as Zyklon B, a hydrogen cyanide. Within a few minutes all 600 Russians were dead. An effective way of quickly disposing of millions had been found.

The entire Jewish phase of the "final solution" was placed in the hands of one Adolf Eichmann, a slender, owlish, failure-prone salesman of oil products, who, through a rapid rise within the Nazi hierarchy, had become a cynical, boastful, sycophantic S.S. lieutenant colonel, with a frumpy wife and a glamorous mistress. When apprehended fifteen years after the war by Israeli agents, Eichmann modestly disclaimed any credit for his achievement, but we must not underestimate the enormity of the task that faced him back in the exhilarating days when German armies were victoriously slashing their way into Russia.

The old concentration camps had to be modernized for mass murder. Additional camps, large enough to handle hundreds of thousands of Jews at a time, had to be built. Means for transporting millions of Jews from all over Eastern Europe to these camps had to be provided. New railroad spurs had to be built, as these camps were off the main arteries. Corps of special camp attendants had to be recruited and trained, records kept. Soon a sizable segment of the German population was diverted from the war effort for the planning, building, and staffing of these murder camps. Generals on the Russian front complained that winter uniforms for the troops were arriving late because trains had been diverted; industrialists complained they were being pirated of skilled labor. But nothing was allowed to interfere with the "final solution."

Though there was a shortage of steel for tanks and airplanes, there was no shortage of steel to build furnaces for the disposal of the cadavers. This excerpt from a business letter from the director of the Didier Works in Berlin gives proof of the knowledge German industrialists had of the use of their products:

For placing the bodies into the furnaces, we suggest simply a metal tray moving on cylinders. Each furnace will have an oven measuring only 24 by 18 inches, as coffins will not be used. For transporting corpses from the storage points to the furnaces we suggest using light carts on wheels, and we enclose diagrams of these drawn to scale.

With German efficiency, chambers for the administration of Zyklon B gas were built to resemble large shower rooms. Arrivals were informed they would have to take a shower, were ordered to undress, and then were herded into the "shower rooms." Small children were often thrown in after the adults. The steel doors to the gas chambers were shut. Then the amethyst-blue Zyklon B crystals were funneled through the large-holed shower nozzles into the hermetically sealed room. The hydrogen cyanide gas released from the crystals slowly rose to the ceiling, slowly gassing the people in the room, slowly turning the gasping, retching bodies into bright pink, green-spotted, convulsed corpses. Peepholes in walls and ceiling, protected by safety glass, were provided for Nazi officials who had a compulsion to view the agonized writhings of naked men and women choking to death. Through these peepholes they could watch, entranced, several performances a day.

New industries develop special skills, and the concentration camp industry was no exception. Adept *Sonderkommandos* learned to apply grappling hooks with skill to separate the bodies. Trained technicians learned to pry dead lips apart and deftly knock out gold-filled teeth. Talented barbers dexterously shaved the heads of dead women. Six days a week, the new elite worked in the concentration camps. On Sunday they rested, went to church with their wives and children, and after church talked with horror about the eastern front where Russians were killing German soldiers, and commented on the barbarity of the Americans who were dropping bombs on civilians.

At the Auschwitz concentration camp seven thousand Germans were thus employed. Here, seventeen tons of gold were collected from the dead. The hair from the shaven heads was used in the manufacture of cloth and mattresses. The ashes of the bodies were used as fertilizer for German victory gardens. *Mens sana in corpore sano*— a sound mind in a sound body. Fatty acids were salvaged for making inexpensive soap. This is a good formula, according to a Danzig firm: "Take 12 pounds of human fat, 10 quarts of water, and 8 ounces to a pound of caustic soda and boil for two or three hours, then cool."

Why did the Jews not fight back? The answer is not as complicated as some psychologists and sociologists have made it out to be. This "pacifism" of the Jews has been attributed to such diverse causes as a Jewish death instinct, collective guilt complexes, self-hatred obsessions, and self-punishment wishes. Such answers betray the inner anxieties of the writers more than they illuminate the dilemma of the Jews.

The fact is that the Jews, as well as the rest of the world, were at first totally unaware of the existence of the "final solution," which was kept in strictest secrecy by the Nazis. When the horrible truth did begin to seep out, the Jews, along with the rest of the world, refused to believe that anyone could be so inhuman. Not until 1943 did the Jews begin to realize that the rumors of death camps were all too true. But by this time it was too late for effective resistance. Jewish communities had been broken up, Jewish communications had been shattered, and Jewish leadership had been killed. The Jews at this point could offer no more resistance than could the American soldiers on Bataan once they had surrendered. When the American soldiers found out about their death march, there was nothing they could do except march, fall by the wayside, and die. The Jews, too, marched, fell by the wayside, and died. But in the end the will to survive triumphed, and both Americans and Jews lived to see their enemies vanquished.

Why did not the Jews kill a Nazi or two before they were exterminated? They did, but not for long. The Nazis were too cunning for them. They knew the love the Jews had for their children. As brought out at the Nuremberg and Eichmann trials, the moment a Jew showed the slightest sign of rebellion, the Nazis tortured not him, but his or some other Jew's children. An infant would be torn in two by its legs in front of its parents; a child's head would be smashed against a tree and the bloody remains handed to the mother; a teenage girl would be raped and then impaled on a bayonet while her brothers and sisters were forced to watch. It was not Jewish morale which was low, but German. The fact which shames German psychologists and sociologists is that the suicide rate of the Jews inside the concentration camps was lower than that of the Germans outside. In the few instances where Jews retained some community organization, communications, and leadership, they did rebel and take up arms against the Germans.

The most spectacular of several such rebellions was that of the Warsaw ghetto in 1943. Warsaw was one of the collection points for Jews from Eastern Europe. Just as the Romans during the siege of Jerusalem built a wall around that city, so the Germans built a wall around the Warsaw ghetto, sealing it off tightly. Here, in an area meant for 50,000 people, were enclosed as many as 450,000 Jews; here they were herded and "stored" until shipped to the gas chambers of Treblinka, Belsen, Maidanek, Auschwitz.

There were 40,000 Jews left in the ghetto on that fateful day in January 1943, when the first armed resistance took place. Only 7,000 could bear arms. Through ingenuity, bribery, and raids the Jews had built a small stockpile of arms—World War I rifles, machine guns, and a collection of Molotov cocktails (bottles of gasoline with flammable wicks for use against tanks). The uprising took place when four companies of stormtroopers—eight hundred men— under the pretense of looking for factory workers, arrived in the ghetto to escort their next haul of Jews to the concentration camps. But this time they were met with lead instead of supplication. Shocked, the black-booted SS men scurried for cover. For three days the battle raged. In the end it was not the Jews but the Nazis who were forced to retreat.

The Nazis were outraged at this rout of their SS troops, but not beyond prudence. The campaign to crush these rebellious ghetto Jews was put under the command of General Jürgen Stroop, who was rushed to Warsaw at the head of a special combat group with attached artillery units.

The Jews feverishly prepared for the German counterattack, converting cellars into bunkers, mining the streets, and establishing a maze of connecting passages through the sewers. They expected to hold out a week at the most; so did Germany's propaganda minister, Herr Joseph Goebbels, who noted in his diary, "The Jews have actually succeeded in making a defensive position of the Ghetto. Heavy engagements are being fought there which led even to the Jewish Supreme Command issuing daily communiqués. Of course this fun won't last long."* But both Jews and Goebbels were wrong. The Jews resisted for six weeks.

General Stroop, after careful planning, launched his counteroffensive in March. From a safe distance his artillery batteries laid down a barrage over the ghetto. Block by block the artillery fire raked the buildings, forcing the defenders to take refuge in cellars and sewers. Then the black-uniformed SS men attacked with automatic rifles and machine guns, mortars and tanks. Armed with rifles, a few machine guns, hand grenades, and Molotov cocktails, the Jews first fought the Nazis to a standstill, then slowly forced their retreat. Jewish youths gave their lives to smash burning bottles of gasoline against German tanks, and Jewish partisans fired point-blank into the frightened faces of the SS men as they tried to escape their burning tanks.

The shelling of the ghetto was resumed. It became a hell of exploding shells, crumbling buildings, and moving walls of flame. In desperation the Jews appealed to the Polish underground for help, but in vain. The Poles hoped the Germans would solve their "Jewish problem" for them. Little did they realize the surprise that history had in store for them. When, in July 1944, the Polish underground staged its own uprising against the Germans, the Poles begged the Russians to come to their aid. But just as the Poles had refused to come to the aid of the Jews, so the Russians refused to come to the aid of the Poles. The well-armed Polish underground army of 150,000 men was annihilated. The Germans had solved Russia's "Polish problem" for her.

As the outcome of Jerusalem's fight against Rome was inevitable, so the end of the ghetto fight against Germany was also inevitable. Disease, starvation, and mounting casualty figures from the murderous artillery fire took their toll. There was no one left to fight, and the defense collapsed. It is estimated that the Germans expended more artillery shells in subduing the Warsaw ghetto, defended by a handful of bedraggled Jewish partisans, than they did in

*Louis P. Lochner, ed., *The Goebbels Diaries*, 1948, page 351.

the initial capture of Warsaw in 1939, when it was defended by the Polish Army. General Jürgen Stroop wrote a seventy-five-page battle report to the Führer in Berlin, and a proud Hitler awarded the general an Iron Cross to ease his *Halsschmerzen*.* When General Alfred Jodl, Chief of Operations of the German Armed Forces High Command, heard this report read at the Nuremberg Trials, he could not contain himself. "That dirty, arrogant SS swine," he shouted. "Imagine writing a seventy-five-page boastful report on a little murder expedition, when a major campaign fought by soldiers against a well-armed enemy takes only a few pages."**

The world, however, took little note of the Warsaw uprising. It was too busy following the daily communiqués of the two-front World War. But Adolf Eichmann noted it, and in his diary set down that a chill of fear swept through Germany upon the news. Even Goebbels was apprehensive. "It shows what is to be expected of the Jews when they are in possession of arms," he jotted in his diary.† And the Jews too noted it, Jews in concentration camps, Jews in America, Jews in Russia, Jews in Palestine.

In Germany orders were issued that henceforth there were to be no large concentrations of Jews anywhere. Their extermination was to continue to the bitter end, at an accelerated pace. Even as German armies retreated in Russia and France, the death trains with their human cargoes kept rolling to Germany's gas chambers, and the chimneys continued to belch fine layers of warm human ashes over the countryside and to fill the air with the sickening-sweet odor of the "bakeries," as the Germans jestingly called the crematoriums. Only when Allied soldiers crossed Germany's borders did a frantic scramble begin to eradicate all traces of concentration camp activities. But the Allied advance was too swift, and what the world had refused to believe remained intact for all the world to see.

---

*Literally "neck pains," a derisive term used by German soldiers to describe the pains generals felt around their necks until they could promote an Iron Cross for themselves. They sacrificed men in desperate military gambles and exaggerated battle accounts in the quest of balm for such *Halsschmerzen*.
**G. M. Gilbert, *Nuremberg Diary* (Signet, 1961), page 68.
†Louis P. Lochner, ed., *The Goebbels Diaries*, 1948, page 351.

Three million Jews perished in these death camps. Most were Jews from Eastern Europe, with a small minority from the West. To the glory of France, Belgium, Holland, and Italy, let it be said that they refused to cooperate with Germany in the deportation of their Jewish nationals. In Italy the Pope denounced German atrocities and called upon the Italians to resist German demands to hand over the Jews.

The Fenno-Scandian countries (Finland and Scandinavia) deserve a standing ovation from the world. Under the nose of their Quisling government, the Norwegians helped most of the country's Jews to escape into Sweden. The King of Denmark publicly wore the yellow Star of David, which the Nazis had prescribed for the Jews, and took part in the planning of an "underground" organization of students and Boy Scouts which led Denmark's Jews to a flotilla of fishing boats waiting to take them to Sweden, which, in true Christian spirit, welcomed all Jewish refugees. Though allied with Germany in a war against Russia, Finland's Field Marshal Karl Gustav Mannerheim informed the Germans that if but one of Finland's 1,700 Jews were seized, Finland would turn around and declare war on Germany. The Finns, said the Field Marshal, would not stand for the murder of any of their citizens. Mannerheim also ordered all Jewish soldiers attached to units fighting under the Nazi and Finnish flags to be transferred to units fighting under Finnish flags only.

Quite different was the story in Eastern Europe. Poland's action was the most shameful. Without a protest she handed over 2,800,000 of her 3,300,000 Jews to the Germans. Poor Poland was to discover that the Germans had even more contempt for her than for the Jews. The Germans slaughtered like cattle over 1,500,000 Poles. In Romania and Hungary, the picture was almost equally dismal. Half the Jews perished in these two countries; only the arrival of Soviet troops saved the remainder.

As for the fate of the Jews in Soviet Russia, the picture is a confused one. How should one classify the hundreds of thousands of Jewish refugees who fled to Russia from the East European border states? When Germany invaded Russia, she rounded up refugee Jews and Russian Jews, as well as Russian partisans, to be slain by the *Einsatzgruppen* or sent to the death camps. At no point, however, did the Russian people or government abandon Jews to the Germans.

History must note the heroic actions of Yugoslavia, Greece, and Bulgaria, whose peoples put the principle of human dignity above safety and expediency. Nazi reprisals in Yugoslavia were especially vindictive. They slaughtered 1,380,000 people—10 percent of Yugoslavia's population. The Greeks, never anti-Semites, put up a fierce resistance, and the Germans declared the death penalty for anyone harboring Jews. King Boris II, archreactionary, willingly signed away the citizenship of the Bulgarian Jews, but when the Bulgarian people found out the hideous fate awaiting the Jews they staged a huge mass demonstration. The Church also protested. No more death trains left Bulgaria, and in September 1944 the Germans were driven out.

World War II was coming to an end. In the spring of 1945, the Russians were driving 12 million German soldiers across Germany's frontiers. On the western front the Allies crossed the Rhine into Germany. German cities were ablaze, the Führer shot himself, and the Germans begged for peace. The Nazis, who had boasted to the world that they would fight to the last man in their mountain redoubts, did not even put up a token resistance. It was "*Kamerad*, don't shoot." The intrepid *Einsatzgruppen*, who had resolutely followed the German armies, now led the retreat. Whereas the *Wehrmacht* soldier wore his uniform with pride, the SS Nazi troops dishonored their uniforms, shedding them in cellars, fields, and ditches, garbing themselves in the protective coloration of peaceful peasants. The *Nazi* soldier did not surrender—he deserted.

Most of the Nazis branded as war criminals by the Allies were eventually ferreted out and brought to trial. All pleaded innocent; all betrayed the Führer to whom they had sworn undying fealty; all accused him of being an archmurderer and fiend; all pictured themselves as sheep merely following orders, as if to execute an order for murder exonerates the murderer instead of making him an accessory. Some begged for their lives, others committed suicide, few walked with dignity to the gallows. Hitler little realized how apt was the punishment he himself decreed for his would-be assassins after the attempt on his life on

July 20, 1944. The Aryan conspirators were stripped naked, hanged with piano wire from meathooks on the walls, and left dangling like carcasses in a butchershop.

World War II represents the biggest killing spree in the history of man. Never before had so many been killed in so short a time at so high a cost. With the war over, the world could assess the price it had had to pay for Hitler and anti-Semitism. In six years of war, 17,000,000 able-bodied men of military age were killed in battle; 18,000,000 civilians were killed as a direct result of war; and an additional 12,000,000 people were murdered by the Nazis. The Germans, who in 1933 had jubilantly "heiled" their Führer, could now mournfully count their dead: 3,250,000 battle deaths, 3,350,000 civilian dead, and some 5,000,000 wounded. Of 20,000,000 buildings, 7,000,000 were completely destroyed or severely damaged. The Germans, who time after time had complained to the world that they were destitute and had begged America and England for money, somehow found $272,000,000,000 to spend for their six-year war. Hitlers do not come cheap.

This chapter in ignominy is now completed. How do the Jews feel about this episode in their history? In the main, their feelings can be summed up succinctly. For the Nazis: contempt for abasing man below the level of the beast. For the Germans: pity for not having had the courage to fight the cancer that debased them. For the world: shame at its failure to fight for the dignity of man until forced to fight for its own life. But there is also a grim moral in this wholesale betrayal of the Jews. Those who curried favor with the Nazis betrayed not only the Jews but also their own people. Those who collaborated most with the Nazis in the end became their victims.

Since the war, holocaust museums have been set up all over the world to commemorate the dead—in Europe, in the United States, in Israel. But this history of the Jews in Nazi Germany would be little more than the story of a meaningless interlude of murder if we failed to place it in a larger context. If we do not bury these dead millions with honor, safeguard their dignity, and give meaning to their sacrifice, then future generations will regard them merely as so many sheep led to the "slaughter-bench of history," like the forgotten millions murdered by Attila. We *must* recognize the fact that Nazism was not just anti-Semitic but anti-human. Because Nazi beliefs of racial superiority had no basis in fact, Nazism was like a nightmare, unfolding without a past or future in an ever-moving present. Because none but German Aryans were qualified to live in the Nazi view, it stood to reason that everyone else would be exterminated. The chilling reality is that when the Russians overran the concentration camps in Poland they found enough Zyklon B crystals to kill 20 million people. Yet there were no more than 3 million Jews left in Europe. The ratio of contemplated mass killing was no longer 1.4 Christians for every Jew, but 5.3 Christians for every Jew. Nazi future plans called for the killing of 10 million non-Germanic people every year.

The world will perhaps disbelieve this as it once disbelieved the existence of gas chambers and death camps. The imagination of the rest of the Western world could not encompass such antihuman concepts, because the Western mind was still imbued with Jewish and Christian humanism and concerned with spiritual values, whereas in Germany these had been expunged by Nazism. If the Christian reader dismisses what happened in Germany as something which affected a few million Jews only, he has not merely shown his contempt for the 7 million Christians murdered by the Nazis but has betrayed his Christian heritage as well. And, if the Jewish reader forgets the 7 million Christians murdered by the Nazis, then he has not merely let 5 million Jews die in vain but has betrayed his Jewish heritage of compassion and justice. It is no longer a question of the survival of the Jews only. It is the question of the survival of man.

Once out of the Nazi cul-de-sac, Jewish history regrouped its forces and continued toward its previously announced goal of creating a new Jewish state. The motivating force behind this course was Zionism, which had its origins in the Haskala and Western Enlightenment. We therefore must return to nineteenth-century Europe to retrieve the ideological strands of Zionism which Jewish leaders wove into a design for Jewish survival.

# TWENTY-NINE

# THE WILL TO WIN:
# FROM ZIONISM TO THE
# STATE OF ISRAEL

May 15, 1948, was a bad day for the United Nations. On that day the armies of five Arab countries—Egypt,* Transjordan, Iraq, Syria, and Lebanon—invaded Israel with the avowed intention of annihilating that new state, which only the day before had so proudly proclaimed its independence. It was clear, of course, that there was nothing the United Nations could do. Helplessly it closed its eyes and braced itself for the inevitable. Poor Jews! They had again met tragedy. But such, alas, seemed to be their fate!

After a few weeks, however, the sound of shooting took on the ominous quality of a Jewish victory. Alarmed, the United Nations opened its eyes and saw the Arabs losing the war. Means for quick action were found. The General Assembly met in special session and Count Folke Bernadotte was dispatched on a peace mission to Israel before a Jewish victory could take the Jews to Cairo.

From the attic of their history the Jews had taken down the symbolic shield of David and the armor of bar Kochba. Once again, after 2,000 years, they were marching under Jewish generals giving commands in Hebrew. Shattered was the stereotype held by the West of the Jew as a man of meekness. What had happened?

What, indeed, had happened? The Jews had had no armies of their own since 135 A.D., when bar Kochba had

---

*Strictly speaking, Egypt, of course, is not an Arab nation, though 90 percent of its people profess the Muslim faith. The vast majority of today's Egyptians are of Hamitic descent, with the Arab Bedouins composing the largest minority group. Only a small minority, the Copts, are true descendants of the ancient Egyptians.

led them in their third uprising against Rome. Where had these Jewish armies advancing on Cairo come from? Since the sixth century A.D. the Jews had been a minority in Palestine. Now they were fast becoming the dominant majority. As late as 1900, Palestine had been a barren, stony, cactus-infested patch of desert. Now it was a modern agricultural and industrial state, its desert serrated by fertile fields and planted with beautiful cities. Where had the scientific farmers, the industrial workers, the managerial and professional hierarchy who had wrought this transformation come from? Here was a modern democratic state, with a parliament, a Supreme Court, and an independent judiciary. How had all this come about as if overnight? The world had seen revolutions before, but never one like this.

Contrary to popular opinion, revolutions are not started by the oppressed masses, nor are they overnight phenomena. They are generated by intellectuals who come from the bourgeoisie or the aristocracy. Revolutions also have long incubation periods, which often take half a century before the infecting idea breaks out into the rash of revolt.

Before a successful revolution can deliver its promised state, it must undergo three stages of gestation, each in charge of a set of specialists whom we shall call "intellectuals," "politicals," and "bureaucrats." First come the intellectuals, who question existing institutions, point out their inefficiencies, and draw blueprints for a new society. The intellectuals behind the French Revolution were such men as Voltaire, Rousseau, Montesquieu, Condorcet. The ideas which inseminated the American Revolution belonged to a quartet of English philosophers—Locke, Hobbes, Bacon, Burke. The intellectual parents of the Russian Revolution were Marx and Engels. These intellectuals were not the offspring of workers and peasants, but the progeny of the bourgeoisie and the aristocracy.

The ideas of the intellectuals slowly germinate in the minds of other men, giving birth to the politicals, whose function it is to carry the new gospels to the people, organize them into armed opposition, and establish the new state. The politicals are, as a rule, "hotheads" who keep events in constant turmoil, hindering the establishment of a stable government. In due course, the politicals in France, America, and Russia seized the revolutionary ideas of their respective mentors and fomented their revolutions—Robespierre, Danton, and Marat in France; Adams, Jefferson, Hamilton, Madison, and Franklin in America; Lenin, Trotsky, and Stalin* in Russia—none, incidentally, workers or peasants.

The task of the bureaucrats, who sooner or later must supplant the politicals to insure the success of the revolution, is to restore tranquillity and to institutionalize the radical new ideas into a normal way of life. French history after the entry of Napoleon is too complicated to be summarized in one sentence, but the revolutionary ideas which he codified were so firmly established that they survived more than a century of turmoil. Fifty years after the American Revolution, the revolutionary principles of 1776 were so firmly embedded in the national consciousness that an era of good feeling welded together the diverse elements of the nation's heterogeneous population. In Russia, bureaucracy was so firmly entrenched thirty years after the revolution that the Russian premier could leave the country without fearing it would be stolen from him during his absence.

The war in Israel was also the symptom of a revolution—the Zionist Revolution—which, except for one unique difference, followed the classic pattern. The difference was the addition of a fourth set of specialists, the "motivators," who were essential to the Zionist Revolution. To Robespierre's axiom that "omelets are not made without breaking eggs," we must add the maxim that revolutions cannot be made without people. The Zionists were fully aware that there were not enough Jews in Palestine to establish a nation. The historic task of the Zionist motivators was to *motivate* enough Diaspora Jews to migrate to Palestine to assemble the parts for a new Jewish state.

---

*Stalin could with equal right be classified either as a "political" or as a "bureaucrat," because he stood midway in the revolutionary process. Though he was one of the triumvirate who made the Russian Revolution, it was also he who began its bureaucratization, although he never succeeded in giving it stability because he kept it in revolutionary turmoil through purges. Stalin's background, too, shows this split. He stood midway between the white-collar and worker class. His father was a petty artisan, a cobbler, and Stalin himself studied for the priesthood until dismissed from the seminary for his revolutionary leanings.

The Zionist Revolution, just like the French, American, and Russian Revolutions, began with the work of intellectuals. The Haskala Zionists were the revolutionary intellectuals who criticized the existing state of Jewish affairs and outlined the idealistic blueprint for a new state. Next, the motivators went to work, diverting waves of European emigrants to Palestine. They, in turn, were followed by the politicals, who spread the new gospel of Zionism among the Jews. After they had established the new state of Israel, the bureaucrats, following historic precedent, took over.

Actually, "Zionism" was a new name for an old ideology; it simply signifies "a return to Zion"*—that is, a return to Jerusalem. The idea of such a return has permeated Jewish thinking ever since the earliest days of the Diaspora. Though the Jews had lost physical possession of Palestine, they had never given up their hope of someday again establishing their capital in Zion. Modern Zionism differed in one important respect from this old aspiration. Until modern Zionism, most Jews had always thought that a messiah would lead them back to the Promised Land. The Zionists shifted this responsibility from the shoulders of a messiah to the shoulders of the Jews. Having saddled themselves with this responsibility, the Zionists reappraised this "Zion," this future homeland of the Jews. What had happened to Palestine, since the days of the abortive rebellion of bar Kochba in 135 A.D.?

Palestinian history from Emperor Hadrian in the second century to Ben-Gurion in the twentieth century is a fascinating study in the rape and conquest of a country that refused to acquiesce gracefully or die expediently. After Hadrian's death the Jews returned to Jerusalem, acquired Roman citizenship, and shared in the spirit of amity which suffused the third-century Roman Empire. This era of domestic tranquillity, exemplified by the progressivism of Emperor Alexander Severus, who kept statues of Moses and Christ in his private chapel, came to an end in 325 with the accession to power of the Christians.

Forty years later the two royal brothers, Valens and

---

*Zion was the original name for the Jebusite stronghold in Jerusalem. When the city was captured by King David, he made "Zion" a symbol for Jerusalem itself.

Valentinian, split the Roman world in two. Palestine, after six hundred years of Western influence under the Greeks and the Romans, was taken back to Orientalism by the Byzantine Empire, as the eastern half of the Roman Empire was then called. During two and a half centuries of Byzantine rule, the Jewish population in Palestine for the first time dwindled to a minority through death and migrations. Palestine became a battleground for clashing Byzantine and Persian armies, a stage for warring Christian sects, and the scene of an intense relic hunt. The first two were physically dangerous; the last was psychologically enervating.

Especially ferocious was the Athanasian-Arian controversy regarding the homoousian or homoiousian nature of Christ—that is, whether Christ was "consubstantial" or "of like nature" with God. "The furious contests which the difference of a single diphthong excited," to use the words of Edward Gibbon, led to the slaughter of tens of thousands of Christians and of any stray Jews who got in the way of the argument.

With the hardening of Christian dogma, the belief grew that if part of a saint or martyr were placed in a church or a cathedral, that edifice would become sanctified. As most early saints and martyrs had died in the Holy Land, Palestine became the scene for the most intensive hunt for relics in the history of man. Throughout the land the search went on for an arm, a finger, a toe, even a single bone with which to consecrate an altar or a sacristy.

The Jews and Christians who remained in Palestine welcomed the Persian victors in 614, but they barely had time to become acquainted when, in 638, they had a new set of masters, the Muslims. The subsequent five-hundred-year Arab rule was broken by the Crusaders when they captured the Holy Land in 1100. For almost two hundred years the Crusaders held on to their precarious toehold, until they were ousted by an incredible species of men known as Mamelukes—the Arab name given to the Turkish slaves in Egypt.

The Mamelukes rebelled against their Egyptian masters in 1250, seized power in Egypt, defeated the Crusaders, made Palestine an Egyptian province, stopped the Mongol invasion of Genghis Khan, and held the frontiers of Egypt

intact for 267 years. They were fine horsemen, but inca-
pable of political organization. Forty-seven Mameluke sultans, either illiterate or insane, held the throne of Egypt for
an average tenure of less than six years each, and as a rule
vacated the throne the way they had acquired it—by assassination. Yet they built magnificent universities and
mosques, made Cairo the showplace of the world, and
without effort reduced the populations of Egypt and Palestine by one third. Their end came in 1517 when the Ottoman Turks annexed Egypt and Palestine to their
ascending empire.

A century of magnificent Turkish rule brought tranquillity and Jews back to Palestine. Marranos, Kabalists, Talmudists flocked to that country to build businesses,
establish schools, write books. Then the Ottoman Empire,
aided by corruption and privilege, settled on a course of
steady decline. Jewish hopes for an amelioration of conditions revived briefly in 1798 when, having bypassed Lord
Nelson's fleet in a Mediterranean fog, Napoleon landed in
Alexandria with 32,000 men, the number Alexander the
Great had used in conquering the ancient Eastern world.
Napoleon captured Jerusalem and drove north to Acre but
was forced to retreat when he could not take that stronghold. Palestine was recaptured by the Turks, and by 1860
the "land of milk and honey" was a barren desert which
could barely support 12,000 Jews. It was at this juncture of
Jewish Diaspora history that the idea of transforming the
Palestinian desert back into a land of milk and honey took
hold. Under the stimulus of Zionism, the Jews again became active agents in Palestinian history. But it was not
until the 1920s, when the Ottoman Empire was disbanded
by the Allies after World War I, that the Arabs, too, became
active agents in Palestinian history.

World events and the needs of the Zionists embraced
each other at the most propitious moments as if on a divinely prearranged "planned parenthood" schedule, foster-
ing five Palestinian immigration waves at the right times
and in the right succession. In the first wave of 1880–1900
came the tillers of the soil to break the ground. In the second wave of 1900–1914 came the scientific farmers and laborers to build the country's agriculture. In the third wave
of 1918–1924 came the young people, the entrepreneurs,

and the speculators, to build cities, found industries, organize an army, and establish educational institutions. In the fourth wave of 1924–1939 came the intellectuals, the professionals, and the bureaucrats, to draw blueprints for democracy and statehood. In the fifth wave, after World War II, came Jews from every walk of life to fill the gaps in all ranks. By 1948 the Zionist intellectuals, motivators, and politicals had accomplished their tasks. The Jews had an army and a blueprint for their state. An idea for survival had been forged into a tool for survival.

The chain reaction from the idea of Zionism to the reality of Israel was touched off about 1860, at which time the messianic concept of a "return to Zion" began to change into the political concept of a "return to Palestine." This change in Jewish outlook coincided with the beginnings of the transformation of the anti-Jewishness of the·Middle Ages into the anti-Semitism of the Modern Age. Jewish intellectuals divined the difference between anti-Jewishness and anti-Semitism. They maintained that the Jew could no longer find peaceful existence by fleeing from one country to seek asylum in another, but could save himself only by establishing a country of his own. In the way the rhapsodic Prophets had taught that God wanted morality, not sacrifice, so the political Zionists taught that God wanted self-reliant Jews, not submissive ones.

The road from the Diaspora back to Jerusalem was paved with a succession of ideas contained in a series of books published between 1860 and 1900, the first of which was prophetically entitled *Rome and Jerusalem*, an intensely Jewish book written in 1862 by Moses Hess (1812–1875). Handsome, fiery Hess married a French prostitute to show his defiance of orthodox Jewish traditions. Contrary to dire predictions, Hess lived happily with his grisette, who dearly loved her strange Jew and his strange life in a world of ideas she had never known existed. Hess, strongly influenced by Spinoza, had argued as early as 1841 for a humanistic United States of Europe, had joined the Socialist movement, and was for a while associated with Marx and Engels. He had participated in the German Revolution of 1848 and had been sentenced to death, but had escaped to Paris.

Because Hess viewed socialism as a humanitarian ideal,

he could not accept the communist materialistic interpretation of history or the idea of class war. He broke with the left-wing movement, returned to Judaism, and brooded upon the problem of the Jews. The result of his cogitation was *Rome and Jerusalem*. Its ideas foreshadowed Zionism and influenced the future leaders of the movement. In this book Hess advocated the return of the Jews to Palestine, there to create a spiritual center for Diaspora Judaism.

These ideas were polished and refined by Russian-born Peretz Smolenskin (1842–1885), another refugee from orthodoxy. At the age of eleven, Smolenskin had seen his slightly older brother impressed into the Russian army by *"choppers"*;* at the age of twelve he had absorbed the Talmud by rote and rod; by the time of his *bar mitzvah* (confirmation) he had had enough of *shtetl* life and ran away from home. For twelve years he wandered across the face of Russia. At the age of twenty-five, Smolenskin appeared in Vienna, where he became an intellectual. There he founded the Hebrew literary monthly in which he published his now famed essay *The Eternal People*, asserting that the Jews were a nation of intellect, kept together by the Hebrew language. Smolenskin also prophesied that Jewish intellectual values would someday become the cherished possessions of mankind, and that Palestine would once again become a world center where Jewish genius would flourish.

In the 1880s Zionist intellectuals began to run into Zionist motivators, such as Rabbi Samuel Mohilever (1824–1898), who launched the first Zionist immigration wave to Palestine. Mohilever founded a political action organization, Lovers of Zion. A plank in its platform called for the purchase of land in Palestine for its members, and its slogan "On to Palestine" echoed through the *shtetls* of Russia and Poland.

The Lovers of Zion found one of its most able leaders in a Haskala intellectual, Judah Pinsker (1821–1891), a former officer in the Russian Medical Corps. Seeing his fellow Jews massacred in the Odessa pogrom, even as he preached the integration of Jews and Russians, Pinsker ex-

---

*Army officials who "grabbed" Jewish children and carted them away for military service.

ecuted an about-face and denounced assimilationism as a futile sop to the anti-Semites. In a pamphlet, *Auto-Emancipation*, he urged the Jews to seek territorial independence and to return to a Jewish national consciousness. Anti-Semitism, said Pinsker, was a peril which no Jew could escape by migrating from a minority status in one country to a minority status in another. He also raised a new, or rather old, battle cry, that of Rabbi Hillel of Roman days—*"Im ayn anee lee, mee lee?"* (If I am not for myself, who is?) It was a call to stand up on one's feet and fight instead of sinking down on one's knees to pray. The way had been paved for Theodor Herzl (1860–1904), the founder of what is now termed Zionism.

Herzl, the pampered son of a wealthy, half-assimilated Jewish family in Budapest, was raised in an atmosphere of luxury and German culture. He was greatly attached to his mother; his only playmate as a child was his sister; and his adolescent heroes were Goethe, Napoleon, and Bismarck. He studied law in Vienna, but became a journalist.

As one views the portraits of this strikingly handsome, unsmiling, prophetic figure, dressed in elegantly tailored suits, it is hard to imagine that during his early manhood he was a successful playwright, author of cream-puff bedroom comedies in which wives were constantly being seduced by handsome young rakes and husbands made amiable cuckolds. As a journalist, Herzl affected a supercilious, cynical literary style which made him the darling of Viennese society. One simply had to read Herzl every morning with one's croissants and coffee.

The turning point in Herzl's life was the Dreyfus Affair. Herzl had been sent to France by his Vienna employers to cover this celebrated case. At first, he felt certain that Dreyfus was guilty, but, after becoming convinced of the captain's innocence, he joined the Dreyfusards. A prevailing cliché about Herzl is that the Dreyfus Affair made him aware for the first time of the existence of anti-Semitism. Actually, anti-Semitism had been one of Herzl's constant problems and he had even toyed with the idea of baptism as a way out. *L'Affaire Dreyfus* made him come to grips with his problem.

For the first time Herzl realized that anti-Semitism stemmed from the social structure, and that personal salvation could not be gained through baptism. Once Herzl chose to identify himself with the Jews and Judaism, he became great almost overnight. Once he turned to the problem of Jewish survival, all superciliousness, all mocking pretense left him. With a cry of the French mob, "Death to the Jews," still echoing in the depths of his soul, Herzl sat down to write his *Der Judenstaat* (The Jewish State), published in 1896. In this slim book he outlined the Zionist ideal, turning the messianic currents of longing for a return to Zion into a political force. The book created a sensation.

Herzl threw himself into the task of organizing an international Zionist movement and in 1897 convened the historic First Zionist Congress held in Basel, Switzerland. To a wildly cheering delegation, Herzl proclaimed the aims of the Zionist movement—"to create for the Jewish people a homeland in Palestine secured by public law." Zionism was not to be a trickle of individually subsidized Jews returning to Palestine, but a mass movement of farmers and workers, managers and entrepreneurs, scholars and intellectuals.

The world at large took little note of this Zionist Congress in Basel. To the world press it was only a crackpot Jewish organization holding another meeting. Nor did the world note the replica of the Jewish coin used in the days of the bar Kochba rebellion against Rome, which each member in the Zionist organization received. But the Basel Congress touched off a conflagration among the mass of Jews. The rich Jews, the assimilationist Jews, rejected Herzl and his Zionist ideas. Many Reform rabbis attacked him. But the poor, the ignorant, and the orthodox flocked to his banner. It was no accident that Zionism originated in the West, not in the East; out of the European Enlightenment, not the Jewish Haskala. It was not the Jew in Herzl but the universal man in Herzl that brought forth secular Zionism. But it was the Jews from the East who gave it dimension. They did not look upon Zionism as mere nationalism; they looked upon it as a continuation of the Jewish tradition, thus making it something that it was not but what it was to become.

What was the hold this man Herzl, this rich, handsome ex-assimilationist, had on the imagination of the poor, the oppressed, the orthodox Jews of Eastern Europe? It was threefold. First, there was a grandeur and a dignity in Herzl's concept of a voluntary exodus, not to a wilderness, but to a Jewish state from which the voice of the Jews would again be heard in the councils of the world. Second, there was an impelling majesty in his entire approach—an impatience with caution, a lofty disregard for detail. The strength of Herzl was his total ignorance of Judaism. His mind was not confused by irrelevant facts. He had a vision that made all old facts irrelevant as it created new ideas. Herzl's Zionism was not a piecemeal program, but a total concept. By merely identifying themselves with this as yet nonexistent state, the impoverished Jews in Eastern Europe gained status in their own eyes. And finally there was Herzl himself, his stately image, his commanding appearance, and his imperious knock that opened the doors of royalty. To the Jews, Herzl was already the ruler of this state-to-be, their *Herzl hamelech*—"Herzl the King."

Herzl committed one great blunder before he died, but such was his popularity that, although this blunder would have proved fatal to anyone else, it was overlooked in him. A split had developed in the ranks of the Zionists between the Herzl motivators, who felt that persistent diplomacy would win the fight for a Jewish state, and the Zionist politicals, who felt that not "hat-in-hand" but "gun-on-shoulder" would decide the issue of Palestinian independence. At the Zionist Congress in 1903, when Herzl proposed that the Zionists abandon Palestine for Uganda* (where the British government had promised him land), a magnificent furor broke out. The great Herzl was accused of being a traitor. Realizing his blunder, he joined the opposition in order to preserve a unified Zionist organization. He died the following year, at the age of forty-four.

The Zionists decided to redeem Palestine by buying land on a grand scale for all Jewish settlers. Suddenly, the scraggy soil of Palestine, neglected for fifteen centuries by

---

*It is said that in 1903, when Weizmann heard that Britain had offered Uganda for Palestine, he asked, "Suppose I were to offer you Paris instead of London, would you take it?" The answer came: "But, Mr. Weizmann, we have London." "That is true," said Weizmann, "but we had Jerusalem when London was a marsh."

its alien custodians, acquired value. Though prices asked by Arab and Turkish landholders were outrageous, the Zionist Jewish National Fund paid them. By 1948, when the State of Israel was founded, the Jews had paid millions of dollars for 250,000 acres of desert land, had settled 83,000 Jews on the land, had founded 233 villages, and had planted 5,000,000 trees on soil which but fifty years previous had been barren. Before 1880 there had been about 12,000 Jews in Palestine, mostly the pious and orthodox who had come to live out their days and be buried in the Holy Land. From 1880 until World War I, Hess's *Rome and Jerusalem*, Smolenskin's *The Eternal People*, Pinsker's *Auto-Emancipation*, and Herzl's *The Jewish State* motivated 115,000 Jews to settle in Palestine. The "intellectuals" and the "motivators" had done their work. After World War I the "politicals" took over.

World War I almost killed the Zionist movement. Britain had counted on Turkey to come into the war on the side of the Allies. Instead the Ottoman Empire sided with the Germans, portending calamity for both the British and the Jews. To Britain it meant that her Suez Canal lifeline was in danger. To the Palestinian Jews it spelled physical disaster. Every Jew suspected of sympathy with the Allies—the knowledge of a little English was considered proof of sympathy—was hanged; 12,000 Jews were deported because they were not Turkish citizens; and Zionism itself was declared illegal.

During World War I the now famed Balfour Declaration was born. It was an expression of gratitude from the British government to the Jewish people for the part they played in the Great War. England's brilliant chemist, Chaim Weizmann, had been called into the British War Office to find a way of producing synthetic cordite, an explosive essential to the British war effort, previously manufactured from acetone, a chemical imported from Germany before the war. Weizmann discovered such a process and turned it over to the British government.

Weizmann was both a chemist and a Zionist, and he knew little beyond these two disciplines. He was a man of dignity and strength. The Jewish masses viewed him, like Herzl, with awe—a Jewish scientist who could mingle with the elite. He spoke flawless English, but he also spoke the

Yiddish of the Jewish masses. He was a Jew, yet he walked with gentiles. His wit was that of a Jewish ghetto man, parochial and universal. American Zionists viewed with suspicion his love for Britain; indeed, he saw British democracy through the eyes of the upper classes—he did not see their soldiers with bayonets on the frontier of empire. Regarded with misgivings by many Jews, he was tolerated by them because he was the only one who had easy access to British ministers. And, in fact, though outwardly democratic, he thought his own judgment infallible. He could mimic the masses, but underneath it all he had a contempt for them. His love was for the aristocracy. Yet he remained a Jew—unashamedly so—and a staunch Zionist.

When, therefore, in 1917, Weizmann approached the British government with a request that it assume a protectorate for a national Jewish home in Palestine, Jewish contributions to the British War effort (his among them) helped assure a favorable reply. Through Lord Balfour, the Foreign Secretary, the British government let it be known on November 2, 1917, that "His Majesty's Government view with favor the establishment in Palestine of a national home for the Jewish people. . . ." As a deeply religious man, Balfour felt that Christianity owed the Jews an immeasurable debt. He was a Christian Zionist who, like Lloyd George, J. C. Smuts, Sir Mark Sykes, and many other Englishmen, saw the Bible as a living thing and believed fully in its divinity. To them, instead of sounding like preposterous nonsense about the Jews returning to Zion after a 2,000-year absence, it sounded like fulfillment of prophecy.*

Jubilation among the Jews was great. "We hear the steps of the Messiah," Weizmann exclaimed after the signing of the Balfour Declaration.

During World War I, in exchange for the promise of an Arab revolt against the Ottoman Empire, Britain secretly also gave her qualified support for Arab independence. The artificial boundaries in the Arab world that we now

---

*There was hardly a British statesman who was not convinced that the universal, the international Jew represented a force that was good for Britain to have as a friend in these perilous times. The image of the Jew in the 1910s was totally different from that propagated by anti-Semites in the 1930s.

regard as engraved in stone did not exist until after World War I, when the Ottoman Empire was neatly dismembered by England and France in a series of clinical lessons known as "peace conferences." The divisions were not made for sound ethnic or geographical reasons but as repayment for favors granted and promises made during the war. Thus the Middle East was subdivided like pastureland for suburban development into lots called Syria, Lebanon, Transjordan, Iraq, and Saudi Arabia by a series of treaties anchored in oil wells and tied to Britain and France. This carving up of the Middle East complicated the Palestinian question, but not nearly as much as did the Arabs themselves when they exploded a diplomatic bombshell by making public the secret correspondence between the King of Hejaz and the former British High Commissioner in Egypt, Sir Arthur Henry McMahon. In this correspondence the British guaranteed the Arabs certain Middle Eastern territories if they would revolt against the Turks, which they subsequently did under the leadership of the famed Lawrence of Arabia. The Arabs insisted that Palestine was part of the promise, though the McMahon correspondence did not mention Palestine by name.

There is no reason to doubt the good faith of either the Arab or the British claims. The confusion stemmed from the wording in the correspondence, which can be interpreted either way. Neither is there any merit in arguing which took precedence, the Balfour Declaration or the McMahon correspondence; they were documents of equal validity. The subsequent course of Palestinian history would have been essentially the same even if neither had existed. The fundamental issues boil down to this: The Arabs claimed the right to be the sole rulers of Palestine by virtue of Muhammad's conquest of that country in the seventh century and by virtue of constituting a majority of the population at the end of World War I. The Jews claimed the right to Palestine by virtue of their conquest of that country in the twelfth century B.C., and by virtue of having been a majority in that country far longer than the Arabs. All else is rationalization.

Between 1918 and 1936 about 150,000 Jewish immigrants settled in Palestine, speeding its transformation from desolation to fertility. Towns sprang up in the desert and boomed into cities. Villages, factories, schools and orange groves dotted the formerly barren fields from Haifa to Ascalon. As with America during frontier days, Palestine too was being built on faith, hope, and speculation. Robber barons and speculators in quest of the quick buck followed behind the Jewish settlers, buying land, speculating in real estate, and selling "futures" in blue-sky enterprises. Instead of scorning them, we shall praise them. They were in many instances responsible for the success of otherwise impossible ventures. These scalawags and snollygosters who descended on Palestine between 1918 and 1936 anchored down corners for hotels, and for office and apartment buildings, where prudent virtue saw only sand and cactus. They helped build Palestine as surely as their Christian counterparts had helped build America a century earlier.

Arabs also benefited by the Jewish introduction of Western science and industry into Palestine. Before the arrival of the Jews, Arab *fellahin* (peasants) stood next to the Chinese coolies on the lower rungs of the world's income ladder, working for a pittance from morning till night for the *effendis* (landholders) who owned most of the land. Of the 650,000 Arabs in Palestine in 1922, over 100,000 were desert nomads, and the rest, with the exception of the small class of *effendis*, were landless peasants who lived no better than European serfs at the time of the Crusades. The *fellahin* burned camel dung for fuel, slept in the same huts with their animals, faced a life-expectancy of thirty-five years, and, until death came, had no hope for a better future.

This mode of existence began to change drastically with the arrival of the Jews, who paid equal wages to Jew and Arab. *Effendis* no longer could get cheap labor to till their soil. *Fellahin* went to work for the Jews in factories and in the white-collar occupations opening up in the cities. The modern sanitation methods and free clinics introduced by the Jews benefited the Arabs especially, infected as they were with trachoma, venereal disease, and rickets.

By 1930 the trend toward higher living and health standards for the Palestinian Arabs was well established and constituted a clear and present danger for the feudal system throughout the Middle East. Feudal Arab leaders, afraid of losing their privileges, embarked on a program to destroy the seat of democratic infection, cleverly using the forces of emerging Arab nationalism. The British sat by and did nothing, not because they were anti-Semitic—which they were not—but because they had an empire to preserve. The course of British policy would have been no different had the Jews not been Jews, but Frenchmen or Italians.

The historic fact was that the Jews in 1918 had been confronted with a monumental challenge and had committed a monumental blunder. They underestimated the force of nascent Arab nationalism and followed the British lead in opposing it. Even before the end of World War I, some Zionist leaders had foreseen the impending struggle for power and realized that even if the Jews were to conquer Palestine with the hoe, they would have to hold it with the gun. The establishment of a Jewish army, they argued, was absolutely essential.

The father of such an army was colorful, Russian-born Vladimir Jabotinsky (1880–1940), who, in his British officer's uniform, pince-nez, and riding crop, was the image of a Kipling *pukkah sahib*. Jabotinsky began his career as the Rome correspondent for an Odessa newspaper, but switched to being a mule skinner during the opening phase of World War I. He organized the Zion Mule Corps, placing it at the disposal of General Allenby, in command of British forces fighting the Turks in Palestine. In 1915 he also organized Jewish battalions to fight with the British against the Turks. It was the remnants of these combat-tested companies which Jabotinsky used to form the Haganah, the Jewish army in Palestine, and in 1920 it repelled the first Arab attack on the Palestinian Jews. For the effrontery of this Jewish victory, Jabotinsky was sentenced to fifteen years' imprisonment by the British, but was freed within a year. Jabotinsky retired temporarily, again taking up the pen, translating Bialik's poetry into Russian, and Dante and Edgar Allan Poe into Hebrew. He was to exchange the pen for the sword once again in 1934.

With the ascent of Hitler to power, a new type of Jew began immigrating to Palestine, propitiously timed with the country's economic development. By 1936 there were 60,000 German Jews in Palestine, providing her with much-needed scientists, engineers, managers, chemists, and research men to increase her productive capacity and to improve the quality of her goods. But even more importantly, eminent scholars now staffed Palestine's educational institutions, and financial experts and government career men provided her with the framework of self-government even while she remained ostensibly a mandated territory under Britain.

The Grand Mufti of Jerusalem and the *effendis* were not fools. They saw what was happening. If the Jews in Palestine were to be destroyed, it would have to be soon. Accordingly, Arab leaders in Palestine made a secret alliance with the Nazis. In exchange for German money and arms, Arab leaders promised to support Hitler in case of open conflict between Germany and England. Britain sat back and waited, having every expectation that Jews and Arabs would exhaust themselves, leaving the British in control. But such was not to be the case.

The expected violence flared up in 1936. Well supplied with arms by the Nazis, the Mufti and his forces struck with fusillades of rifle fire in city and countryside, on street and highway, from buses and cars. All Palestine was an armed camp, but the official Zionist policy was to use the Haganah for defense only, not for counterattacks. Jabotinsky violently disagreed with this policy, urging the Jews to strike back at both Arabs and British. He organized an underground paramilitary force known as the Irgun, whose threefold aim was to fight the Arabs to a standstill by taking the war to them, to force the British to leave Palestine, and boldly to declare Palestinian independence. As Arab terror increased, the ranks of Jabotinsky's Irgun swelled. The Arabs were adamant in their stand—Jewish immigration to Palestine must stop; Jews in Palestine must remain a minority group; and the leadership of the country must be vested in Arab hands. The Jews were equally adamant in their stand that Jewish immigration to Palestine must continue. Jews in Europe were fleeing the Nazi terror in increasing numbers, and as the doors to other countries were closing to them, Palestine was their only hope.

Alarmed at the increasing violence, the British appointed a six-member inquiry group, the Peel Commission, to look into the Palestinian mess and make recommendations, never suspecting that it would come up with the solution it did. The Peel Commission took a long look, found the British Mandate unworkable, and recommended that Palestine be partitioned into separate Jewish and Arab states. The Jews accepted the recommendation with misgivings and the Arabs rejected it with gunfire. To prevent a partition of Palestine, the British quickly came up with a compromise solution, the White Paper of 1939, which was accepted with reluctance by the Arabs and rejected with gunfire by the Jews. This White Paper proposed that Jewish immigration be limited to 15,000 a year for five years and then stopped altogether.

The White Paper led to the first open Jewish defiance of the British. Young Jews volunteered to serve in Jabotinsky's underground army. The attitude of the Irgun was that the British, in preventing Jewish immigration, had allied themselves with the Arabs and were therefore as much a target for attack as were the Arabs themselves. Arrogantly, Irgun youths tweaked the tail of the British imperial lion. The British lion roared in pain and went out in an Irgun hunt. But the Irgun was as agile as the lion was relentless. Jews and British were caught in an enmity neither had desired but which events had forced upon them.

When Britain became embroiled in World War II, 130,000 Jews clamored for enlistment in the British Africa Corps. The wary British feared to arm so many Jews. Nevertheless, out of sheer necessity, Britain did accept 30,000, who fought as independent companies. Grudgingly the British admired the courage of these Jewish soldiers; ruefully, Rommel's Afrika Korps found out that against Jews armed with guns they were not supermen.

As the British had suspected, the Jews fought not only for the pleasure of meeting the Nazis in combat, but also to train themselves for the inevitable future showdown in Palestine. Once the war was over, everybody jockeyed for position. When the curtain rose again in 1945 on the Palestinian drama, the actors sprang to life, taking the same parts they had in 1941; British policy was still the White Paper; Arab policy was still to oppose all Jewish immigration; and Jewish policy remained that of unrestricted immigration.

Terror again erupted in 1946 when the British refused to admit 100,000 Jews from Germany, as proposed by

United States President Harry S. Truman. Enraged by the British policy of barring Jewish refugees from Palestine and by the detention of refugee Jews on the island of Cyprus, Irgun leaders determined to force a showdown on the issue. Irgunists dynamited the King David Hotel, the Jerusalem headquarters of the British, killing eighty British officers and men, and wounding seventy others. Goaded into reprisals, the British ordered a boycott of all Jewish shops. Far from shattering Jewish unity, however, this solidified Jewish sentiment against British rule.

The British repeated history by embarking on the same futile policy that they had in American colonial times when the Americans had defied British rule. Instead of reexamining their policies in Palestine, instead of listening to the voices of conciliation in their own Parliament, the British imposed fines on anyone suspected of having helped or harbored a Jewish immigrant. In spite of this, in five years the Jews smuggled 113,000 immigrants into the country under the guns of the British. When Britain protested this mass violation of law to the Jewish Agency, it replied with some acerbity that the British were violating human law by denying the homeless European Jews their rightful sanctuary.

Britain retaliated by disarming the Jews, by mass arrests, by hanging Jewish leaders. But new weapons seemed to grow in the desert (where the Jews had hidden them), mass arrests bred mass defiance, and the hanging of Jewish leaders gave birth to an Irgun "law of talion"—the hanging of a British officer for a Jewish noncom, a higher British officer for a Jewish officer. The entire country was a seething camp of rebellion. In 1947, harassed Britain, beset with even more serious troubles in other parts of her empire, declared she had had enough of the Palestinian problem and dropped it in the lap of the United Nations.

The United Nations, meanwhile, had sent a special committee to Palestine to investigate the situation. It came back with basically the same recommendations made by the Peel Commission in 1937—that the British Mandate be terminated and that Palestine be partitioned into an Arab and a Jewish state. On November 29, 1947, the General Assembly voted 33 to 13 for partition. The Jews accepted the decision; the Arabs defied it. After twenty-six turbulent years, the British Mandate had come to an end.

In spite of what happened, in spite of the White Paper and the reprisals, the British must elicit our admiration. Under the most trying circumstances, they had behaved like civilized soldiers representing a civilized nation. They fought hard and lost courageously. They were not animated by evil intent or inhuman policies, but by affairs of state and the will to preserve their empire. The fact that friendly relations exist today between Israel and Britain testifies to the realization of the Israelis themselves that Britain had been a formidable foe, not an anti-Semitic enemy, and that Israel had won not because she was mightier, but because Britain was beset with other, more pressing problems.

As evacuation day, May 14, 1948, drew closer, Arabs began to flee. Between February and May before the British had left, thousands of Arabs had already fled. The first to flee were their leaders and the upper and educated classes. Why? Arabs say the Jews had frightened them with their threats of massacres. The Jews said the Arabs simply heeded the commands of their leaders to leave so the Arabs could "drive the Jews into the sea," after which the Arabs would return to reclaim their land, implying that those who remained would be regarded as renegades. Thus was laid the groundwork for the Arab refugee problem.

The State of Israel was officially born at 4:00 P.M., Friday, May 14, 1948, at the Tel Aviv Museum, where the Jews listened to Ben-Gurion proclaim the independence of the State of Israel. "By virtue of the natural and historic right of the Jewish people and of the resolution of the General Assembly of the United Nations, we hereby proclaim the establishment of the Jewish state in Palestine to be called Israel." After the declaration, Ben-Gurion issued a plea to the Arab states to cooperate with the Jewish nation, which was "prepared to make its contribution to the progress of the Middle East as a whole." Instead, Egypt sent a cable advising it would invade the new state to put an end to it. Three other Arab states—Jordan, Lebanon, and Syria— did not bother with formalities but followed Egypt's lead.

President Harry Truman, two hours after Israel was founded, was the first to recognize the new state. Four communist countries followed: Russia, Poland, Czechoslovakia, and Yugoslavia.

That evening the Israelis toasted their new homeland. The next morning they manned the front lines to defend it. Years later, I asked Ben-Gurion what he had thought on the eve of independence. Did he believe Israel could win? His answer indicated the seriousness of the situation but also the courage and will to win that prevailed at the time. He said he had believed firmly that the Israelis could win but that they would suffer 60,000 casualties. (They lost 4,000 soldiers and 2,000 civilians.) There was, he said, great apprehension. He had been informed that General Marshall had given President Truman an appraisal of Israel's chances of winning a war against the Arabs, the gist of which was that Israel would best be advised to forget about the state and come to an understanding with the Arabs who, numbering 30 million and with vastly superior arms and manpower, would annihilate the Jews in a horrible bloodbath. Most people at the time seemed to agree with General Marshall. But Ben-Gurion added that even after listening to this statement, Israel's governing body decided to stay the course.

The Israeli War of Independence (1948–1949) contained all the elements of drama, intrigue, and luck that one associates with a historical novel. This clash of destinies began when the British Empire folded its Palestinian tents, hauled down the Union Jack, and departed. Five Arab armies, led by the spiritual successor to T. E. Lawrence—General John Bagot Glubb, honorary Pasha—immediately swooped down upon Israel from all directions, announcing in their first communiqué that within a week the fighting would be over and the Jews driven into the sea.

And, indeed, it looked as if the Arabs were right. Of Israel's total population of 758,700, on the second day of her independence she had only 19,000 men to stem the invaders on five fronts. Many of the defenders who had never held anything in their arms except wives, children, and Torah, now held Bren and Sten guns. The Jews were outgunned by the modern weapons of the Arabs, acquired from British sources. In that first onslaught, Jewish lines first wavered, then fell back. On May 20, Old Jerusalem fell to the Arabs.

The mistake the British and the Jews had made in 1918 in underestimating Arab nationalism, the Arabs now made in 1948 in underestimating Jewish nationalism. A will to win swept Jewish ranks and the tide of battle turned. The Jews became imbued with the historic spirit of their struggle. Here, in this land, their ancestors had fought Assyrians, Babylonians, Egyptians, Sassanids, and Seleucids. Here they had challenged Rome in three uprisings. The tempo of fighting changed from desperate defense to confidence in victory. Lines solidified. Not an inch of soil was to be yielded; there would be no retreat, only advance. The Arabs ran into this wall of psychological resistance and were hurled back; they could not understand what had happened. As the French stopped the Germans at Verdun in World War I, so the Jews stopped the Arab onslaught on all five fronts. The war the Arabs had thought would be over in a week exhausted them after a month. On June 11 they gratefully accepted the truce terms offered by Count Folke Bernadotte of the United Nations.

Both sides used the truce to consolidate their forces, for neither had any intention of quitting. Under pretense of neutrality, the West placed an embargo on the sale of all arms, but Israel, anticipating this move, had made advance arrangements to purchase arms from Czechoslovakia.* In an airlift known as "Operation Black" because it was carried on at night, Israeli pilots shuttled rifles, machine guns, 75-mm artillery, and tanks to the Israeli front in a buildup for the next showdown. Jews who had served in the British and American air forces shuttled Flying Boxcars, Hurricanes, and Messerschmitts from the four corners of the world to Israel, refueling at bases clandestinely arranged for them in England, France, Corsica, and Yugoslavia by former comrades in the service. Impatiently the Jews waited for the Arabs to break the truce.

The Arabs were even more impatient for the truce to end. They had greatly improved their positions with British-made artillery and tanks. A recruitment drive increased their forces from 24,000 to 60,000, whereas Jewish strength increased only to 20,000. There was no doubt that this time victory was within Arab grasp.

---

*In a meeting with Ben-Gurion in Tel Aviv, I asked him how he felt about buying arms from a Communist country. He explained that with Israel "up against the wall" he would accept arms from the devil himself, and when the devil became the problem he would find a solution.

The moment the month-long truce ended, the Arabs launched an attack that carried them irresistibly forward, right into the muzzles of Israeli guns. Arab lines sagged; the Israeli counterattack swept everything in front of it, carrying the war into enemy territory. The second round of the war lasted but ten days. The Arabs cried for a truce, and the obliging Count Folke Bernadotte came running with white flags and a cease-fire order—without a time limit.

As with the first truce, the second one too was shamelessly violated by both sides. The Jews wanted just one more bout with the Arabs to consolidate their position. The Arabs, convinced their rout had been a fluke, wanted one more go at the Jews to finish them off. More arms poured in on both sides.

Only on the Egyptian front had the Arabs been successful. Here the Egyptians were in possession of the Negev Desert. Confident the next thrust would take them to Jerusalem, they broke the truce. The Jews were waiting for them. The momentum of the counterattack carried the Israeli armies across Egypt's borders to the outskirts of the main Egyptian army base of el-Arish on the Mediterranean. Its fall and capture would have left Egypt defenseless. England let it be known that if Israel did not retreat, it would mean war with England. Israel retreated. Egypt sued for peace, and one by one the other Arab nations followed suit. The war was over. Israel had been redeemed, not by money this time, but by the blood of her sons. God had been on the side of the better, not the bigger, battalions.

Even as the War of Independence was being fought, Israel's statesmen concentrated on building the new Jewish state on old Jewish democratic principles. The first national elections were held in 1949, and a new Constituent Assembly was proclaimed, with David Ben-Gurion as Prime Minister and Chaim Weizmann as President.* Weizmann was not in Israel when the state was declared, nor does his

---

*Boris Guriel, Secretary to Dr. Weizmann, told me this rather sad story: "A few days after Weizmann was appointed President, I found him staring out of a window in his study. As he turned around, I saw him crying, and I started to leave the room. 'No, Boris, stay.' [Weizmann said] 'I was just meditating about my role in history and why I did not become Prime Minister. Ben-Gurion was right. It was I who missed the boat.' "

name appear on the Israel Declaration of Independence. Just as Herzl had reached the summit with the first Congress at Basel, and Weizmann with the Balfour Declaration, so Ben-Gurion reached his zenith with the Declaration of Independence and the victory of 1948.

Ben-Gurion was a casting director's dream for the part of Israel's Prime Minister. White-haired and sun-tanned, shrewd and sentimental, tough and benign, Ben-Gurion played with historic conviction each of the four roles demanded by the Zionist revolutionary cycle. Born in Plonsk, Poland, in 1886, Ben-Gurion rebelled early in life against *shtetl* Judaism, exchanging it for the Haskala and Western Enlightenment. He fell easy and willing prey to the Zionist intellectuals, joining the movement and "motivating" himself to Palestine in 1906, where he became a tiller of the soil and where, in 1910, he founded a political party and a newspaper. In 1912, he was ready to change his role from a motivator to a political. He matriculated at the University of Constantinople Law School, but when he returned to Palestine he was promptly expelled by the Turks as a potential troublemaker. During World War I, he helped recruit Jewish fighters for Jabotinsky's battalions, and then enlisted himself. After World War I, Ben-Gurion became one of Palestine's most influential politicians, guiding, prodding, influencing members of the League of Nations and United Nations, his magnetic personality playing a great part both in the establishment of a Mandated Palestine in 1922, and in the vote for an independent Israel in the General Assembly in 1947.

The moment the Israeli state was proclaimed, Ben-Gurion shed his role as a Zionist political, realizing this phase of the revolution had become an anachronism the moment victory had been achieved. He became the statesman bureaucrat. Boldly he declared the Zionist party defunct, its mission over, having "committed suicide" by success. It was time for the bureaucrats to take over to solidify gains, institutionalize new mores, and domesticate revolutionary tempers into normal activity. A new democracy, based on "liberty and groceries," had to be secured.

There was to be no second-class citizenship for anyone in Israel. No Jew needed to pass tests to become an Israeli. All he had to do was to land on Israeli soil and proclaim himself a citizen. Citizenship was also extended to every Arab living in Israel. The franchise, universal education, and the right to hold jobs according to ability were granted to all, regardless of religion, sex, or previous condition of servitude. For the first time in history, Arab women could vote.

As Ahad Ha-Am, Bialik, and Tchernichovsky had preached, Israel was to be not the land of "milk and honey" alone, but also the land of education and culture. Schools sprang up all over the country. Education was compulsory. As villages, towns, and cities grew, so also museums and symphony halls, theaters and opera houses, art galleries and colleges appeared. Today a performance of *Peer Gynt* is attended by Israeli Arabs and Jews. The children of the "insulted and injured" sit with the children of the former Arab *fellahin* watching ballet or listening to a children's concert. In 1960, just twelve years after its birth as a state, Israel had more newspapers, magazines, and bookstores, more art galleries, museums, schools, and symphony orchestras per capita than any other nation.

Two factors make this achievement in so short a time even more remarkable. In 1922, Palestine embraced 45,000 square miles, which supported 750,000 people. By 1948, Palestine, through successive partitions by the British and by the United Nations, had been trimmed down to 8,000 square miles. Yet in 1960, Israel supported 2,000,000 people, of whom about 200,000 were Arabs; in 1990 there were 4,700,000 people of whom 3,800,000 were Jews and the balance Muslims, Christians, and Druze. Although only a small portion of its Jewish population is native-born, so strong is the Jewish idea that within a few years of their arrival, Jews from Yemen and Germany, Morocco and Russia, Turkey and Poland, Ethiopia and Iraq, Egypt and Syria have all been welded into a new Israeli ethos. The people which had been dispersed for 2,000 years have been reunited into one peoplehood, one nation.

But Israel was not yet to know the tranquillity of peace. In the autumn of 1956, the Egyptians, still smarting from their defeat, sent specially trained commandos, known as *fedayeen*, across Israeli borders to harass the Jews. They infiltrated the country at night, and, like Indians in American frontier days, put the farmhouses along the border to the torch, killed the inhabitants, and then vanished in the night to the safety of their own country.

As the Soviet bloc poured more arms and munitions into Egypt, the Egyptians became bolder in their attacks. The three Arab states of Egypt, Jordan, and Syria formed a military alliance under a unified command, Gamal Abdel Nasser announcing again, over worldwide radio, that he would destroy the Israeli state. Instead, in eight days, world headlines told a different story. What began as a hope for a quick victory for Egypt almost erupted into a third world war.

Quickly Israel mobilized her army, and on October 29, 1956, rushed it to the front in the Sinai in trucks, taxicabs, and private vehicles, greeting the surprised Egyptians with a clash of tanks, roar of airplanes, and an infantry advancing at will, taking vital positions near the Negev-Sinai border. Within three days the Israeli Army outmaneuvered and outflanked the Egyptian Army, slashed its way into the Sinai Peninsula, seized Egypt's stockpiles of military supplies, and stood poised at the Suez, ready to invade Cairo. The actual fighting was concluded in 100 hours. The Egyptian High Command ordered their troops to retreat on November 1, which turned into a rout.*

However, events suddenly took a turn that could have destroyed Israel. The war entered an international phase. In July, Egypt had nationalized the formerly international Suez Canal**; England and France attacked to regain the

---

*Israeli troops were shocked at what they saw on their way to El Arish. The Egyptian soldiers, abandoned by their officers, threw away their weapons and uniforms and trekked back west as the Israeli soldiers bypassed them on their way to Kanatra. El Arish was abandoned. The Egyptians, officers and soldiers alike, lost all sense of duty as they rushed for transport trucks. Even medical men left wounded soldiers on operating tables to die in order to get to the trucks on time. As Israeli soldiers entered El Arish, not a single medic was to be seen, only the wounded and the dead.

**A hundred and one miles long, 43 feet deep, and 796 feet at its narrowest waist, the Suez Canal stretches from Port Said in the north to Suez City in the south.

The bright idea for the canal was that of Ferdinand de Lesseps. Given France's blessing in 1854, the project did not get started until 1858 in the face of opposition by the British, who saw in it a challenge by France to her empire. An issue of 400,000 shares for 500 francs a

canal in October. This action brought the United States into an unanticipated international fray.

On the afternoon of October 30, the Anglo-French forces sent an ultimatum to Egypt and Israel to withdraw to ten miles from the immediate vicinity of the Suez Canal so their soldiers could station themselves along the banks of the Suez. Israel accepted. She did not want the canal; she only wanted the Sinai for a buffer zone. Since Egypt rejected the demand, the Israeli advance continued with infantry and armor supported by the air force toward the canal.

Luck saved the Egyptians. The United States and Soviet Russia forced England and France to withdraw from their military venture, and Britain in turn commanded Israel to withdraw her troops from Egyptian soil, which she did. By her action, however, Israel had served notice on the Arab world that any violation of her borders would bring military reprisals just as surely as would a violation of American, Russian, or English borders.

The result was that the Suez, Sinai, and Gaza were returned to the Egyptians, who were handed a magnificent victory out of a brutal defeat.* Never before had a defeated nation been so generously allocated the fruits of victory. For the West the consequences proved disastrous. Britain lost her power in the Middle East. For France, who had lost her status as a great power in 1940, this aborted invasion meant the end of empire. As for the United States, this debacle weakened her relationship with England and France for decades.

---

share was floated. Half the shares were bought by France, the other half by Egypt. The canal was finished in 1869.

Now began the intrigue. Egypt held 44 percent of the shares. The Khedive of Egypt, heavily in debt, sold his shares at a profit to the British in 1875 for £4 million. However, if they had waited another seven years they would have had it free, for in 1882, Britain occupied Egypt, ousting the French. She now owned the Suez Canal outright.

In 1888, all the maritime powers signed a convention that Suez should be an open shipping port to all in war and peace, which it remained until 1956.

*Richard Nixon, who was vice president at the time, wrote several years later in a letter to Julian Amory that "restraining Britain, France, and Israel was a major foreign policy mistake" and that Eisenhower shared this view.

Israel, pressured into giving up the Sinai and Gaza, was left holding a bagful of empty promises. Before the next war, Israel was to face the establishment of the Palestine Liberation Organization in 1964; the first PLO raid into Israel in 1965; and continuing Arab rhetoric threatening to annihilate it.

For the Arabs, an armistice was viewed as a continuation of war by other means. Thus it came about that instead of discussing peace, Egypt and her Arab allies prepared for a third war. Despite a United Nations Emergency Force in place, in 1966, Arab terrorist attacks against Israel were intensified. Finally, on May 17, 1967, ready to unleash her "fighting tigers" on Israel, an emboldened Egypt demanded the United Nations peacekeeping force be withdrawn. U Thant, Secretary General of the UN, obliged, thereby laying the groundwork for the Six Day War.

Meanwhile, sabotage, *fedayeen* raids, and shelling from the Golan Heights—all encouraged by Syria—increased. Israel finally responded on April 7, 1967, after an exchange of fire on the ground, striking at the artillery positions that were raking Israel. An air battle ensued. Syria ran to Egypt for help to punish the Israeli bandits who had dared to challenge her. Egypt responded by massing troops and tanks in the Sinai near the Israeli border. With the UN Emergency Force gone, Nasser was ready to strike in the south. He imposed a blockade, first in the Gulf of Akaba, then in the Suez Canal. He knew full well that Israel had repeatedly warned that blocking these straits would be tantamount to a declaration of war.

The United States stepped into the picture rather gingerly with a declaration that the straits comprised international waters and could not be blockaded. Nasser, in defiance, replied boldly that any act, by anyone, to break the blockade would be considered an act of war. The United States backed down, not wanting to go to war with Egypt over a body of water she did not need.

Encouraged by the U.S. retrenchment, Nasser taunted Israel with blood-curdling announcements, publicly baiting her to act on her threat that any closing of the straits would mean war. Nasser said he was "ready to destroy Israel." Cairo radio blared, "No Jew will remain alive." Syria, Jordan, and Lebanon chimed in on Nasser's side. The Soviet Union provided the weapons. The stage was set.

Israel knew she could not allow a war to be fought on her soil. She would have to move with ground forces head-on into the waiting Egyptian divisions. Using air power, she would have to prevent her cities from being bombed.

Surprise was of the essence. On June 5, Israel decided to strike when radar detected planes and tanks approaching the border. The Israeli air force swooped low in a semicircle over the Mediterranean into Egypt, almost totally destroying Egyptian air forces on the ground—300 of 340 planes were left in flames, with 20 planes shot down in the air. Israel issued no announcement.

King Hussein of Jordan, misled by Egypt's false military communiqués into believing Egypt was winning the war, and disregarding a message from the Israeli government that Israel had no designs on Jordan, decided to take his piece of the pie, confident his divisions could cut the narrow belt of Israel's waist in two and capture Jewish Jerusalem. Crossing into Israeli territory, he forced Israel to respond with a similarly devastating attack against Jordan. Syria's entry into the fray was met in like fashion.

In the first day of fighting, Israel lost 19 planes. Egypt, Jordan, and Syria lost 391. Israel first turned her military might against Egypt in the Sinai. On June 6, Israel recaptured Sharm El Sheikh, first by sea, then with paratroopers. After three days, the West Bank of Jordan, the Gaza Strip, and the Sinai fell. On June 7, the Old City of Jerusalem was taken.

On June 8, Egypt, aware of the havoc she had brought on herself, beseeched the United Nations, through Russia, to send in a truce team. Syria, still fortified and thinking herself safe, would not accept a cease fire. Israel, again forced to protect herself, took the Golan Heights on June 10. And thus it came about that Israel, with a military might of 275,000 Jews, had been given no choice but to beat the hell out of the Arab force of 440,000 Egyptians, Jordanians, and Syrians.

With the conclusion of the Six Day War, Israel was forced to administer the West Bank, Gaza, and the Golan Heights and prevent uprisings there. She also had to set up plans to keep the nation and the territories economically viable, as well as to train, educate, and absorb both the 372,000* immigrants who had arrived in the '60s and an equal number expected in the '70s, a total of 5.5 percent of her population.** In those same years the United States absorbed almost six million immigrants—only 1.5 to 1.7 percent of her population. Israel, left with territories many times larger than herself and a million more Arab inhabitants, would go on paying heavily for her victory in the years that followed.

At the time, the world was stunned by the brilliant victory and full of admiration for Israel, the new David in Jewish history. But the Arab League, meeting in Khartoum, Sudan, refused to negotiate with Israel, and the UN decided that Arab pride had to be saved—all for the ultimate good of Israel. A defeated Arab nation was a menace. The only hope for peace and harmony would be an Arab world assuaged.

The USSR and the UN agreed with this most peculiar logic. The United States did, at least, argue that Israel should not be required to withdraw from occupied territories without Arab acceptance of Israel's independence and security. But the Arabs, confident of further arms shipments from the Russians and support from the UN, haughtily refused and vowed revenge. Never before in history had the vanquished threatened a new war and the victors begged for peace! Can one imagine Hitler demanding to dictate the peace treaty and the Allies agreeing?

Israel, now trebled in size, held the Sinai, the Gaza Strip, the Golan Heights, and the West Bank (Judea and Samaria). But the most significant result of the Six Day War was that on June 27, 1967, for the first time since the War of Independence, Jerusalem was united. In 1948 Jordan had wrested the Eastern Sector of Jerusalem from the Israelis, destroyed the Jewish section including all religious buildings, and used the bricks to pave the streets. Israel

---

*This number in only a twenty-year period is larger than the number of Palestinians displaced in the Arab-Israeli wars (Palestinians no Arab country would accept, preferring to keep them in refugee camps). By 1951 Israel had already absorbed over 262,000 Jews from Arab lands.

**Since 1989 alone, Israel has resettled almost half a million newcomers—a ratio of one new immigrant to every nine Israelis.

now made Jerusalem its capital, much to the discomfort of the UN, the Arabs, and even the United States.

Meanwhile, the Palestine Liberation Organization remained active against Israel and eventually became a threat to Jordan. Egypt openly supported the PLO guerrillas in violation of United Nations Security Council cease-fire resolutions. In the second half of 1967 alone, there were 1,288 acts of sabotage and border incidents, with 281 Israeli soldiers and civilians killed and 1,095 soldiers and civilians wounded. By comparison, during the Six Day War there were 759 total Israeli fatalities. After the Six Day War, Arab guerrilla forces had also become a serious internal threat in Arab countries. Revolutions and attempts at revolutions occurred in Iraq, South Yemen, Somalia, Sudan, Libya, and Saudi Arabia.

At the same time, some political and administrative cooperation existed between Jordan and Israel. Israeli farmers were allowed to cross into Jordan to sell their crops. Eventually a two-way movement of all goods was permitted and then travel to and from each side was allowed. This was known as the "open-bridge" policy. Though Jordan indicated she was ready to accept Israel's right to exist, no other Arab country would consider this, which put Jordan in a difficult position.

In the West Bank, Israel's attempt to work with Arab officials came to naught. Fearful of reprisals from their Arab brethren should the West Bank be returned to Arab rule, they remembered how the Egyptians had punished the Gazans who had cooperated with Israel after the Sinai War.

Israel continued to administer the territories, trying to improve conditions for the Arabs, which they succeeded in doing to a great extent. The Arabs planned more terrorism and more wars, leaving Israel with no choice but to insist on a final peace settlement before she withdrew from any territory.

Even while cooperating with Israel on the "open-bridge" policy, Jordan openly said she supported the guerrillas, until they turned on her and demanded that they be allowed to use Jordan as the main base of operations against Israel. When King Hussein refused, Yassar Arafat, who had become leader of the PLO in 1969, launched an offensive in "all parts of Jordan," and King Hussein was faced with what Israel had been aware of all along: the reality of what the PLO stood for, their aims, and how they planned to achieve them. Arafat's plans called for a "scorched earth" policy to force Hussein to accede to his demand. Although most of the Arab world was against him, Hussein refused to sacrifice his country to PLO domination, and in 1970 the PLO lost all their bases in Jordan.

This conflict, called the Black September War, only one of many in which Arabs fought with Arabs, led to the PLO "invasion" of Lebanon and the eventual establishment of a "state within a state." It helped lay the groundwork for the Lebanese Civil War in 1975 and the eventual Syrian control of that country.

Israelis, meanwhile, went back to running their own country, content to set up programs to administer the new territories, hoping the Six Day War would lead to peace. What came instead was yet another war.

In 1969, a change in government brought Golda Meir, an implausible character on the Israeli scene, to power. As a young woman she came to Israel from her native United States and became involved in politics, often at the expense of her personal life and the neglect of her family. Because of her connections in the States, she had been instrumental in raising large sums of money for the War of Independence. She was also responsible for the extension of Israeli aid to emergent African nations and the establishment of friendly relations with them. By the time she became Prime Minister she was a grandmother, with a benign face, a golden heart, and two iron fists unsheathed by velvet gloves. She had smiled and slugged her way to power, rode in as a dark horse, and ended up an aged Jewish Joan of Arc who saved Israel in its hour of peril.

It was Saturday morning, October 6, 1973, Yom Kippur, the holiest day in the Jewish year and the Arabs knew it. At 4:00 A.M., word of an imminent attack was brought to Israel's political leaders. Instead of attacking, Prime Minister Meir called a meeting, and the decision was made to contact Western leaders to seek their last-minute intervention. The reply to her request was, "Don't preempt."

For months, Anwar Sadat, the Egyptian President, had practiced the game of political camouflage, and Israel had been getting signals of possible attack from Egypt and Syria. Each time Israel decided against mobilization. Each time it was a major gamble to avoid both the international criticism and the staggering costs that mobilization would have brought. This time the gamble almost failed.

Numerically superior in men and matériel, the Arabs achieved a strategic and tactical advantage. At 2:00 P.M. on October 6 Egypt and Syria launched coordinated attacks into the Sinai and the Golan Heights with an advantage in infantry forces immediately engaged of 20 to 1 and a tank advantage of 5 to 1. Partial mobilization in Israel had begun only four hours earlier. In the past, Israel had relied on the preemptive strike and fast-moving offensive armor. Now, while mobilizing, she had both to contain the Egyptian thrust in the Sinai and to stop the Syrian attack on the northern front. Not until October 9 was a decisive counterblow against Syria successfully executed.

The Israelis had been overconfident. Though they knew the Arabs had excellent weapons, they believed the Egyptians would not know how to handle them. They were wrong. The Arabs had succumbed to their own myths as well. They believed that a man with an IQ of 160 would be defenseless against an uneducated soldier with more sophisticated weapons. They also believed they would have won the Six Day War if they had struck first, and so they did just that this time. They, too, were wrong.

As Israel's very existence was threatened, the flow of history floated through Jewish minds in two contradictory strains. One was the thought of their ancestors' sacrifices to create and maintain a nation: Joshua, a former slave and head of a nomadic people, conquering the mighty tribes and kingdoms of Canaan; the first King Saul crushing the Ammonites and the mighty Philistines at Michmash, and King David uniting Israel and Judah to establish the first Jewish mini-empire. The other strain was the knowledge of what happened after the defeat by the Romans: exile, dispersion, second-class citizenship, anti-Semitism. Never again. The spirit of their past swept through the Jewish forces and carried them on a tide of historic fervor to victory. The Egyptians ran out of steam; the Israelis rallied.

Admiral Thomas H. Moorer, then Chairman of the U.S. Joint Chiefs of Staff, said after the war, "This war, like most, was decided primarily by the impact of leadership, ability, and training." It was a war of armies; neither side dared bomb each other's cities for each had the capacity to devastate the other. By October 24, when the cease fire was established, Israel had crossed the Suez Canal, seized 500 square miles of Egyptian territory, trapped 25,000 men in the Egyptian III Corps, and was free to move at will on the west bank of the Suez Canal. In Syria, Israel had moved closer to Damascus and held more ground than before the war started. Once again, it was only political pressure that halted Israel's advance.

The costs of the victory, however, were enormous. Within the first week, Israel was in dire need of military equipment. No one could have anticipated that the United States would resupply Israel, but, in answer to desperate pleas, Nixon and Kissinger responded with an emergency airlift. They sent 300,000 tons of critical weaponry between October 14 and November 14 and continued to send supplies as needed, in addition to a $1.1 billion congressional appropriation.

The U.S. Defense Department estimates that the Soviet Union's cost of the 1973 war was more than $2.6 billion, while American outlays during the war totaled nearly $1 billion, with emergency aid authorized for $2.2 billion. The cost to Israel was more than $250 million a day—two and a half times the cost of the 1967 Six Day War. Israel, in 1973, had to spend 40 percent of its gross national product on defense, all because the Arabs, the losing side, refused to sit down to talk about peace.

After the Yom Kippur War, how could the Arabs sustain the myth that they could conquer Israel if only conditions were right? They had struck first, and on a Jewish holiday, while almost everyone was at prayer. They had Russian support and sophisticated Soviet weapons. Conditions could not have been more favorable. Yet in only sixteen days, Egypt was begging Moscow and the United Nations to impose a cease fire to save the Arabs from another catastrophic defeat. And, as in the three previous wars, Israel was forced by the major world powers to stop before consolidating its victory. Golda Meir complained, "For God's sake, Sadat started the war . . . and he has been defeated. Then by political arrangements, he is handed a victory." Another Israeli official added: "The realization that Egypt could start a war and the rest of the world would stop it to save her from defeat is shattering."

Then the impossible happened; Israeli politics took a conservative tilt. Likud, Israel's conservative party, after losing all eight elections since 1948, survived to win the ninth in 1977. Menahem Begin, its leader, became Prime Minister, riding into power on a wave of unpopularity.

Begin found himself sitting at the poker table of state with the Arabs who had piles of chips stacked in front of them, while he had none. He knew the odds were against him. To even them, he decided to take a lesson out of American history involving the annexation of Texas: First send people to settle new territories; then the settlers ask for statehood. Begin decided to start settling the occupied territories with Jewish settlers and announced his policy boldly on his first visit to Washington. When a reporter asked him about the occupied territories, Begin answered, "What occupied territories? I only see Israel, Judea, and Samaria."

A cry of pain went through the Arab nations. All at once Begin had the occupied territories as bargaining chips. The Arabs would now have to bargain for land rather than Israel having to bargain for recognition and peace. Sadat eventually would do what no prior Labor government could do—trade land for peace.

If Begin was a realist, so, fortunately, was Anwar Sadat. He knew his country's economic condition was desperate. He, like many of his countrymen, had come to realize that Egypt had fought for her Arab "friends" to the last Egyptian. The Arabs had saved face and gained pride; Egypt had lost men, money, and matériel. The army had been saved only through Western intervention. The country had been devastated by defeat and loss of morale in spite of all that had been done for it. It was the last hurrah for the Egyptians. Once many settlers were comfortably ensconced in the Sinai there would be no way they could be evicted. Begin was the first to make peace overtures: Sinai for recognition of Israel.

The world watched on television as Sadat came to Israel to meet with Begin and receive a royal welcome from the

Israeli public. After prolonged negotiating, and with much "encouragement" from President Jimmy Carter, the agreement was made and signed at Camp David. Israel returned the Sinai to Egypt, including oil fields, air bases, and settlements, in exchange for Egypt's recognition of Israel's right to exist, as well as cast-iron guarantees for Israel's southern borders with Egypt.

The Egyptian-Israeli treaty demanded heavy sacrifices. It cost Begin some of his closest political friends. But it cost Sadat his life. In return for peace, the Israelis also agreed to make concessions over the West Bank and even Jerusalem. But once again, without even attempting to negotiate, the Palestinians and the other Arab countries threw away the opportunity. They rejected the Camp David Accords, thus forcing Israel to continue to retain control over Judea, Samaria, Gaza, and the Golan Heights.

The growth of Arab influences was great in those years. The Arabs tripled the price of oil, making huge sums of money—not to improve the life of their people, but to purchase arms, to finance terrorism, and to finance their leaders' luxurious lifestyles while keeping the Palestinians in refugee camps.* The UN passed a resolution equating Zionism with racism; Yassar Arafat was recognized by the UN as a head of state and appeared on its platform, gun in holster, as he gave his anti-Israel talk, making it clear that all of Israel was included as part of his plan for a Palestinian state. Meanwhile, Iraq had built a nuclear reactor, a "clear and present danger" to Israel. In June 1981, Israel bombed that reactor before it could be activated. The world was dismayed at this preemptive strike, viewing it as against international law. That dismay, of course, turned to pleasure when Iraq invaded Kuwait in 1990.

After failing to take over Jordan, and after Syria would not have them, the PLO moved into Lebanon in 1970. They demanded the end of government restrictions against them, freedom of commando movement and supply in Lebanon, and that they be allowed to use the country as a

---

*A Palestinian in the West Bank, when discussing the Black Panthers, Arab Death Squads, and the murder of Palestinians by Palestinians, said, "We do not need Arafat anymore. What we need is a Ben-Gurion." ("Meltdown," *New Republic*, Nov. 1992)

base for attacks against Israel. In essence, they wanted what they could not get in Jordan, a "state within a state," and they eventually achieved that end. The Lebanese ambassador warned the UN that if the PLO was granted this request, there would be a strong response from Israel. Lebanese President Charles Helou said the guerrillas must leave Lebanon and warned that if they used Lebanon's southern border, Israel would seize part of the country. Both warnings were ignored.

Thus the PLO had the freedom to infiltrate Israel and to launch their attacks into the northern part of Israel from Lebanon. And then there was the Syrian problem. At first Syria provided support for opponents of the PLO. Then, fearful that the Palestinian militias, allied to the more radical Lebanese militias, might push Syria into a new war with Israel, for which Syria was unprepared, Syria sent in an expeditionary force to restrain them, only to protect itself, not Israel. But neither Lebanon nor Syria stopped the PLO raids or the shelling of Israel. The situation became intolerable, and the Israelis decided to act.

Their objectives were to stop the raids and shelling with Katuysha rockets and to destroy the infrastructure of the PLO so that the raids and shelling could not soon be resumed. The Israelis were welcomed with open arms and cheers by the Lebanese in the south, who had been abused and intimidated and had their property stolen and their country devastated by the PLO. The Israelis had come to rescue them, and they did temporarily. When, along with the cache of arms and ammunition controlled by the PLO, the Israelis also found the PLO plans for the destruction of Israel, they were sure their mission was none too soon.

But once again the world could not stand by and watch an Israeli victory. Israel had almost succeeded in ousting the PLO from Lebanon when outsiders—the United States and the UN—interfered.* The United States pres-

---

*In Israel, through the years, suspicion had grown that the United Nations only responded when the Arab aggressors were about to pay the price for their aggression. This suspicion became a visible reality with the Yom Kippur War, although the signs were there after the Suez and the Six Day War. The Lebanese War confirmed whatever doubts had remained after the previous wars.

sured Israel to withdraw, conditioned on the Syrian withdrawal from the Bekaa Valley and a treaty was signed between Israel and Lebanon even while Israel warned the United States that without Syria's approval the treaty would fail. And it did. Syria did not withdraw. Under pressure from Syria, Lebanon canceled the accord in March 1984. The result was more shelling, bombing, and the near total political destruction of what was left of Lebanon. When the United States sent in a contingent of Marines to separate the warring factions in Beirut, an Arab car bomb leveled the American compound and killed two hundred forty-one marines. As a result, the United States withdrew its troops. The final irony was that the United States was left with a brutal hostage crisis in Lebanon that lasted from July 1982 to December 1991. Syria said it could do nothing. However, when it served Syria's purpose, after the Gulf War in 1991, the country assisted in the release of the American hostages and was thanked by the United States for doing so. But the crisis in Lebanon has remained central to the problems in the Middle East.

The Lebanese war did break the PLO and turned Arafat from a dominant factor in the Arab world into a beggar living in Tunisia. He eventually regained some of his power but not the political or military power he had before the war. The war in Lebanon, called Operation Peace for Galilee by Israel, did cut down the shelling of northern Israel and weakened the PLO militarily. Conversely, terrorism increased, and Islamic fundamentalism became stronger, growing into a danger to the Arab countries themselves and threatening to overthrow their regimes.

Why, after thirty-five years and four wars with the Arabs, did Operation Peace for Galilee create so much anger and accusation both inside Israel and out? For the Israelis, Lebanon both attracted and repelled. On the one hand there was clearly a need to defend the country and to protect the Jews in the northern section of Israel as well as the Christian Arabs in southern Lebanon. On the other hand, Israelis have always found the killing role of the state hard to accept, and the casualties and costs were particularly onerous when international action prevented a clear-cut result. As to the rest of the world, it is hard to understand why Lebanon's destruction by the PLO and its takeover by Syria were allowed to go on with so little effort to prevent them, with nowhere near the level of anger expressed against Israel. And it is hard to understand why the world could watch Arabs threaten and murder and terrorize each other as well as Israelis and Westerners but often only object when Israel fought back.

Was this a just war? If you ask the PLO, the answer is no. If you ask a citizen of the Galilee or a Christian Lebanese in southern Lebanon, the answer is yes. Henry Kissinger told the *Washington Post*, "Whatever our opinion . . . of the official reason given by Israel . . . there is no argument over its strategic justification. No sovereign state can tolerate endlessly the strengthening along its border of a military force wishing to destroy it."

Mr. Kissinger's statement could as well stand as a description of Kuwait's situation just before the Iraqi invasion in January 1991. The world, of course, had little difficulty deciding to act in that situation, but Saddam Hussein made the decision even easier by invading and destroying Kuwait, another Arab state, and one of the main oil producers in the region, and by threatening to invade Saudi Arabia and control the world's largest source of oil.

In an unprecedented move, an alarmed United Nations, led by the United States, voted against Iraq and approved the use of military force to eject Iraq from Kuwait. Behind this move lay not only the fear of Iraqi control of oil supplies, but the fear that Hussein might have an atomic bomb.

The world had loudly decried Israel's swift surprise air strike in 1981 against Iraq's nuclear reactor. It now viewed that act in a much better light. But the fear remained that Iraq had replaced that loss and also increased its supply of poison gas, a gas it had already used on its own people.

After unsuccessful negotiations with Saddam Hussein, U.S. President George H. W. Bush mobilized a coalition of Arab and world leaders to face Iraq with armed force. Hussein was forced to withdraw from Kuwait, and much of Iraq's infrastructure and industrial capacity were devastated, but not before Iraq had set fire to the oil fields of Kuwait, inundated the Persian Gulf with a huge oil slick, and fired Scud missiles into Israel and Saudi Arabia.

Though Israel was not directly a part of this Arab-against-Arab conflict, Hussein counted on decades of knee-jerk anti-Israel sentiment as part of his strategy to dominate the Middle East. By attacking Israel with missiles, he expected to gain the automatic support of nations like Jordan, Syria, and perhaps even Egypt, thus breaking up the coalition and stirring up further anti-American and anti-Saudi feeling among the Muslim masses.

Would this plan succeed? Jordan felt the pressure from her large Palestinian population and refused to join the coalition. Israel, ready to defend herself like the Jews in biblical times, now faced a dilemma. The coalition, especially the United States, implored her to ignore the danger, suffer the casualties, and do nothing. But Israel had always been saved by her insistence on defending herself; in the Middle East, any sign of weakness could be fatal. Should she strike back at Iraq to protect her cities, or was destabilization of the coalition the greater danger? Would the Arab world's anti-Israel reflexes once again lead them to disaster? Would they actually consider Israel a greater danger to the Arab world than Saddam Hussein?

In the end, threats by Israel to retaliate against Iraq were not carried out as a result of military and diplomatic initiatives by the United States. President Bush, after two phone calls to Prime Minister Yitzhak Shamir, dispatched Deputy Secretary of State Lawrence S. Eagleburger to Israel. At a meeting with Shamir and Defense Secretary Moshe Arens, he was assured that Israel would not retaliate at that time and pledged to consult with the United States before taking any action. While reserving the right to see to their own defense, the Israelis decided to trust their enduring friendship with the United States and wait out the Iraqi attacks. They accepted the American argument that this war had the potential to change attitudes in the Arab world, and they decided the possibility was worth the risk.

Though Saddam Hussein remained in power, the Gulf War was brought to a more or less satisfactory conclusion, with the U.S.-led UN coalition intact. And it did lead to actual peace talks—Arabs and Israelis sitting face to face, trying to solve the region's problems, just what Israel had been asking for since the War of Independence in 1948. The first tentative agreement between Israel and the PLO was signed on September 14, 1993. The next day, an agenda was agreed upon for Israeli-Jordanian peace talks. It is, of course, not yet possible to know if old attitudes will be rekindled or if the talks will finally lead to enduring stability and cooperation.*

The State of Israel has been established and has now endured for more than half a century. Will the peace talks lead to the fulfillment of Jewish destiny, or are they just another chapter in the inexorable march of Jewish history?

---

*Though the peace talks are still ongoing as of this writing, the situation changes from day to day. See Appendix for background to the peace talks.

# VIII

# CONCLUSION: A CULTURAL MOSAIC

*Concluding the odyssey of the Jewish people through four thousand years of history, venturing a historical explanation of the remarkable survival of this people, which is as modern and intellectually alive today as it was four millenniums ago.*

# EXILED TO FREEDOM

During the four-thousand-year odyssey of the Jewish people, from the twentieth century B.C. to the twentieth century A.D., they struggled, fought, fell, revived, regressed, and advanced over four continents and through six civilizations, surviving against all odds. After wanderings in Canaan, enslavement in Egypt, destruction in Judah, captivity in Babylon; after contact with the Greeks, strife under the Maccabeans, oppression by the Romans; after surviving as a capitalist class under feudal lords, as a "People of the Book" under Muslim rule, as children of the ghetto in the late Middle Ages, as statesmen, scholars, and concentration camp victims in the Modern Age, they returned at the end of a two-thousand-year absence to their ancient homeland as its rulers. *Jews, God, and History* has been a study of this survival, not in terms of kings, wars, and persecutions, but in terms of ideas generated by the Jews in response to the challenges hurled at them by the ever-accelerating force of history.

How should we evaluate this varied and vexing saga? Is the survival of the Jews a mere accident, their history a meaningless succession of events—all "bunk," as the Henry Ford school of history would contend? Or were there deterministic forces behind their destiny? Should we look to the Marxists for an answer? Was the survival of the Jews shaped, perhaps, by the material conditions of their lives? Did the way they tilled their soil and exchanged their goods give rise to their concept of Jehovah? Did the social systems of Omri and Josiah inspire their Prophetic writings? Or are the psychoanalysts right? Is Jewish history the product of what the Jews repressed in their unconscious? Does this explain Torah and Talmud, Karaism and Kabala, Hasidism and Zionism? Or should we turn to the philosophical historians for an answer? Can Jewish history be explained as a Spenglerian cyclical evolution? If so, why did the Jews not disappear after the usual life span of a civilization? Can Toynbee's "challenge and response" theory explain their survival? Must we accept his version that Judaism as a culture was nothing but a fossil left over from a Syriac civilization? Or have the Jews perhaps been aided by a divine force, according to an as yet undisclosed plan? Can theology give a satisfactory answer?

As it is the task of a historian not only to record the foibles of man but also to venture an explanation of them, we shall offer for those who cannot accept the theory of a guiding divinity, an explanation for Jewish survival consistent with natural law, never forgetting, however, that throughout this colorful panoply of events and ideas there runs a constant thread—the illusion or dream or revelation of Abraham that the Jews are God's Chosen People.

Because we have been taught to view history as Ancient, Medieval, and Modern, we often fail to perceive history in other molds, as, for instance, the ebb and flow of civilization motivated not by fortunes of war but by cycles of ideas. In all history, mankind has failed to produce more than twenty or thirty civilizations. Most of them are now dead, a few still struggle for survival, some are in their formative stages, none are at the height of creativity. How did these civilizations arise? What gave them force? Why did they die? Historians can only speculate. Perhaps the most valid of such speculations are those of two twentieth-century "metahistorians"—the "fatalistic" or "nonfree-will" theory of Spengler and the "free-will" theory of Toynbee. Man is powerless to change the course of his destiny, according to Spengler. Man has something to say about his fate, according to Toynbee. An explanation for the paradox of Jewish survival is implicit in the theories of these two men who have relegated Jewish history to a minor footnote. Yet how can Jewish history be explained by and incorporated into these two contradictory theories? Let us examine more closely the theories of each.

Once a people has been impregnated with the sperm of civilization, its future, in the Spenglerian system, is as predictable as the course and results of a pregnancy. We can predict a gestation period, the birth and infancy of a child, its adolescence and maturity, and finally old age and death. Each of these is comparable to a cycle in the Spenglerian evolution of a civilization—a spring phase, giving birth to a new religion and world outlook; a summer phase, culminating in philosophical and mathematical conceptualizations; an autumn phase, maturing into "enlightenment" and rationalism; and a winter phase, declining into materialism, a cult of science, and degradation of abstract thinking, leading to senility and death.

Quite different is the philosophy of Toynbee, who, in essence, contends that nature constantly presents new and unanticipated challenges to man. If people do not respond to the initial challenges, they remain unhistoric, like the Eskimos or the Hottentots, unable to harness their destiny to the chariot of history. If people respond to the initial challenges, but fail to continue with adequate responses, their civilizations become either fossils of history or cliffhangers left to rot with time. The sphinx of Toynbee's history never volunteers an answer to her riddles. If a civilization responds with the right answers to such challenges, it has the implied possibility of everlasting life.

Though the Jews have successfully answered the sphinx of history for four thousand years, both Spengler and Toynbee regard Judaism as an "arrested civilization" and exclude it from their lists of civilizations. Why? Because the Jews did not fit into their definitions of a civilization. But it is precisely in this paradox of Judaism as an "arrested civilization" responding successfully to the challenges of history that we can find the secret of Jewish survival. This paradox will be clarified if we define Judaism as a "culture" instead of a "civilization." The difference between these two concepts is clearly stated by Amaury de Riencourt in the introduction to his book *The Coming Caesars*.

Culture predominates in young societies awakening to life . . . and represents a new world outlook. It implies original creation of new values, or new religious symbols and artistic styles, of new intellectual and spiritual structures, new sciences, new legislation, new moral codes. It emphasizes the individual rather than society, original creation rather than preservation and duplication, prototypes rather than mass production, an aesthetic outlook on life rather than an ethical one. Culture is essentially trailblazing.

Civilization, on the other hand, represents the crystallization on a gigantic scale of the preceding Culture's deepest and greatest thoughts and styles, living on the petrified stock forms created by the parent Culture, basically uncreative, culturally sterile, but efficient in its mass organization, practical and ethical, spreading over large surfaces on the globe, finally ending in a universal state. . . .

Civilization aims at the gradual standardization of increasingly large masses of men within a rigidly mechanical framework—masses of "common men" who think alike, feel alike, thrive on conformism, are willing to bow to vast bureaucratic structures, and in whom the social instinct predominates over that of the creative individual.

In other words, culture, according to de Riencourt's definition, corresponds to Spengler's spring, summer, and autumn phases. The winter phase represents, in de Riencourt's terms, the civilization which feeds off its parent culture.

The Jews began their historic existence in the full Spenglerian sense—with a spring ushered in by a new religion and a new way of abstract thinking, which formed the nucleus for an emerging Judaic culture. In Toynbeean terms, they then responded to the challenges of nomadic existence, to the conquest of Canaan, to the establishment of a state. They responded to the challenge of survival in Babylonian captivity, and returned to Palestine, there to evolve into the autumn phase of their emerging civilization. But they never "progressed" to the decline of their winter phase—that is, they never made the transition from "culture" to "civilization." They remained suspended, so to speak, at the height of their culture, between their autumn and winter phases. What had freed them? As Spengler himself so perceptively observed, "Vespasian's war, directed against Judea, was a liberation of Jewry." The wars with Rome freed the Jews from the fate awaiting them as a civilization, by dispersing them into the Diaspora. The Jews were exiled to freedom. Into the Diaspora they carried with them a highly developed culture, packaged for export by Prophets, saints, and scholars. The Diaspora took them to many lands, to many civilizations. If a civilization went under, as the Islamic one did, the Jews went under with it. But even as one civilization was swallowed by history, another one always emerged, and the Diaspora Jews within the emerging civilization rose with it. The Jews could set up shop in any land and unfold their culture in any civilization. Their firm belief that they were God's Chosen People gave them the will to survive, the Torah nourished that will to survive, and their men of learning designed the tools for their survival—but it was the Diaspora itself that freed the Jews from time, from history, and from death as a civilization. They had stumbled on the secret of eternal cultural youth. With the Diaspora, the Jews became the civilization hoppers of history.

The existence of a Diaspora, then, has been the one essential condition for the cultural survival of the Jews beyond the normal life span of a civilization. Had they not been exiled, had they remained in Palestine, they probably would be no more of a cultural force in world history today than the remnants of the Karaites. Today, as once before, we have both an independent State of Israel and the Diaspora. But, as in the past, the State of Israel today is a citadel of Judaism, a haven of refuge, the center of Jewish nationalism where dwell only 3,750,000 of the world's 17,500,000 Jews. The Diaspora, although it has shifted its center through the ages with the rise and fall of civilizations, still remains the universal soul of Judaism.

Will the Jews continue to survive? If they maintain their will to survive as Jews, if they continue to fashion new tools for survival in response to new challenges, and if the Diaspora continues to be a constant factor in their history, then the Jews will continue to survive as a culture-producing people. But the will to survive and the ability to respond to challenges will not be enough without a permanent Diaspora. The Diaspora *must* be an ingredient in their history.

Where will be the next center of Diaspora Judaism? That will depend upon the historic forces that continually rearrange the patterns of Jewish dispersion. The United States could continue to be that center for the next two or three centuries, but the American citadel too may prove to be transitory. If Spengler is right, Western civilization—in which the American civilization is contained—may be in its winter phase, whereas the Slavic and Sinic civilizations may be in their spring. Should Western civilization decline, a Jewish Diaspora culture could spring up in Russia or in China.

Though the position of the Jews in Russia today is as anomalous as it was in Catholic Spain in the fifteenth century, it is not beyond belief for history to establish a Diaspora center there. In fact, the Jewish position in Russia today closely resembles that of the Marrano position in Spain. Though constituting but 1.5 percent of Russia's population, in 1970 Jews were an estimated 12 percent of Russia's top scientists, intellectuals, and scholars. With the demise of communism, Russia seems, for the moment, an unlikely site for the next dominant civilization. But we cannot know what fifty or five hundred years will bring. Since 1967 almost a million of Russia's Jews have gone to Israel and to America, but some will remain, and only time will tell how strongly the spark of Judaism burns among the ostensibly agnostic Russian-Jewish youth.

Nor is it beyond possibility that a Diaspora center could establish itself in China. In the tenth century, China played host to a flourishing Jewish community in Kaifeng, important enough for Marco Polo to mention. This community fell into decay by the nineteenth century, when history severed its ties with the Western Diaspora. Should a world civilization once again arise in China, it is no more farfetched for a Jewish Diaspora center to emerge in that vast nation than it was for Diaspora centers to be established in pagan Babylonia, Muslim Spain, or Catholic Poland.

A fourth possible center of world Jewish Diaspora could be South America, where the present history of the Jews resembles their early history in the United States. South America's Jews are today as dependent on the ideas and culture of the Jews of the United States as the latter were dependent upon the ideas of European Jewry before 1900. Although Judaism in South America today is diffused and decentralized, it would take only a sudden flare-up of intellectual life to make that continent a Diaspora center.

There still remains the question, Have the Jews been *divinely chosen* to fulfill a *mission*, or have they *chosen themselves* to fulfill a *divine mission*? Do we have a hint of the nature of this mission in Isaiah, who prophesies the brotherhood of man in the days to come? Will it be the function of the Jews to establish such a brotherhood of man and, having fulfilled such a predestined role, to disappear? Has Spinoza prepared us for this with his pantheistic theology for universal man? We cannot know. We can only speculate.

Let us view Jewish history as the unfolding of a vast Kabalistic drama in three acts, each act two thousand years long. In the first act—the *tzimtzum*, or "thesis"—a succession of Jews, like heroes in a Greek tragedy, are cast by a Divine Director in predestined roles. Without a firm conviction in his preordained role as the progenitor of the Chosen People, Abraham would have been a tragic figure. His faith makes him heroic. In this first act, God continues to assign roles—to Moses, to lead the Jews out of Egyptian bondage and to give them the Law; to Joshua, to take them to the Promised Land; to the Prophets, to enlarge the Jewish concept of God into a universal Deity; to Ezra and Nehemiah, to make sure that the Jews are not swallowed up in this new universality. Within the external strife of Jewish history develops the thesis of a Jewish destiny, binding the Jews together into a people. This internal unity is then shattered with the appearance of a Christian sect that claims Jesus as the messiah. Just before the curtain descends, the Christians boldly declare that the role of the Jews as God's Chosen People is over.

When the curtain rises on the second act of our Kabalistic drama—the *shevirath ha-keilim*, or "breaking of the vessels"—Jerusalem has been destroyed and the Jews scattered in the Diaspora. Having acted for two thousand years as God's Chosen People, however, they are not prepared to relinquish their former roles. We now observe a succession of rabbis, philosophers, and scholars fashioning new tools of Jewish survival—the Talmudism of the ivy-league yeshivas, the philosophy of Maimonides, the interpretations of Rashi, the poetry of Halevi, the codification of Caro, the mysticism of the Kabala, the humanism of the Haskala, and finally, near the end of the act, the nationalism of Zionism, which reunites a segment of the Diaspora Jews in Israel. The "vessel," broken for two thousand years, has been mended. The curtain has fallen on the twentieth century. The second act is over.

Has our drama ended, or is this only an intermission before the third act—the *tikkun*, or "restoration"—in the Kabalistic cycle? Are the Jews destined to survive another two thousand years to fulfill an as yet unrevealed role?

Throughout the centuries, the trinity of Jehovah, Torah, and Prophets, by accident or design, evolved two sets of laws, one to preserve the Jews as Jews, the other to preserve mankind. In their first two thousand years, the Jews used that third of the Torah and Talmud which deals with priesthood and sacrifice to maintain themselves as a Jewish entity in a world of pagan civilizations. In their second two thousand years, they used that third of Torah and Talmud which deals with ritual and dietary restrictions to maintain their ethnic unity even as they spread the universal aspects of Judaic humanism. Left now of Torah and Talmud are the universal contents only—the third that deals with morality, justice, and ethics. Does this progression suggest that Judaism is now prepared to proselytize its faith in a world ready to accept its prophetic message? Is this to be the destiny of the Jews in the third act?

If man views the Jewish achievement through materialistic eyes, seeing only an insignificant minority in possession of a little land and a few battalions, this will seem improbable. It will not seem improbable if man discards the blinkers of prejudice and views the world not as a "thing" but as an "idea." Then he may see that two thirds of the civilized world is already governed by the ideas of Jews—the ideas of Moses, Jesus, Paul, Spinoza, Marx, Freud, Einstein. Will the world in the next two thousand years embrace the morality of the Torah, the social justice of the Prophets, the ethics of the Jewish patriarchs? If so, then in the words of Isaiah, there will be "Peace, peace, to him that is far off and to him that is near."

# APPENDIX
## THE RECENT HISTORY OF
## PALESTINE/ISRAEL

Peace in the Middle East is essential, as both Arab countries and Israel realize. Their numerous wars, Arab-Israeli and Arab-Arab, have not solved the problems. Circumstances arising out of an incredibly tangled and complicated past have increased the dangers in the area.

Now, in the last decade of the twentieth century, Israelis and Arabs—with misgivings on both sides—are searching, face to face, for a way to live together in peace. No comprehensive discussion of these peace talks has been included in the text of the book, since neither their historical implications nor their possible results can even be guessed at.

Who is sitting at the table? On the one hand, a new nation with an old history—democratic, determined—a nation that would not have been born, much less survived, if it had had to rely on foreign guarantees or international support. Asked about U.S. guarantees, Golda Meir responded, "By the time you get here, we won't be here."

On the other hand, there is a people that has never been a nation, supported (and often enough mistreated) by an array of Islamic nations, each with its own agenda—none democratic nor united with the others, and with vast economic, geographic, and social differences among them.

The following Chronology is by no means comprehensive. It is not intended as a basis for a final conclusion about the subject, nor is it intended to apportion praise or blame among the parties. Rather it is hoped that by pointing out some past efforts, disappointments, and frustrations, by describing some of the baggage that each side brings to the negotiating table, it will suggest to the reader the complexity of the problems with which the parties have had to deal and emphasize the magnitude and the fragility of the recent agreements, which, it is to be hoped, will be the opening of a new bright chapter in the thousands of years of history recounted in this book.

# CHRONOLOGY

| JEWISH HISTORY | | ARAB HISTORY |
| --- | --- | --- |
| Jerusalem "mournful, dreary, and lifeless. Palestine sits in sack cloth and ashes." (Mark Twain, 1867) | Before 1914 | Palestine* not a separate political or administrative entity; part of the Ottoman Empire (1517–1917). |
| Religious Jews come to die and be buried in the Holy Land. First and second large waves of Jewish immigration. City of Tel Aviv established 1909. | | Arab population in 1882 is 260,000; most live in mud huts without sanitation; farms average 25 acres. |
| World War I begins; Balfour Declaration (1917) supports Jewish homeland. | 1914 to 1945 | Sykes-Picot Agreement (1916), secret French-British pact for postwar division of Holy Land. Britain encourages Arabs to revolt against Ottoman Empire with promises of political independence. |

---

*"Palestine" includes the present states of Israel and Jordan until noted otherwise.

Britain captures Jerusalem (December 9, 1917); 400 years of Ottoman rule ends. Mutual recognition of Jewish and Arab rights in Palestine in Weizmann-Feisal agreement (1919).

Arabs divided on acceptance of Weizmann-Feisal agreement. Hardliners win. Grand Mufti of Jerusalem, who had cooperated with Ottoman Empire on Germany's side during World War I, rejects cooperation with Jews. Grand Mufti instigates riots in 1920 and 1929 against Jews and in 1936 and 1939 against British and Jews.

1919–1923: Third wave of Jewish immigration (35,000).

After World War I, Middle East fractured into Arab "states"—Syria, Lebanon, Iraq, and Palestine (Transjordan); Arab demands for independent nations lead to numerous uprisings.

Jews believe Balfour Declaration means a homeland to include all of Palestine.

Britain partitions Palestine at Jordan River and recognizes Transjordan (March 27, 1921), giving Arabs approximately 80 percent of Palestine. Arabs believe entire Middle East was promised to them. Armed rebellion in effort to gain remaining 20 percent of Palestine.*

1920: Britain arrests Jews retaliating in self-defense. Jews organize self-defense units to defend settlements. The beginning of Haganah, the defense forces.

Riots instigated by Grand Mufti of Jerusalem against Jews. Britain does not arrest Arabs who rioted and attacked Jews.

---

*Hereafter, "Palestine" will refer only to this remaining 20 percent—not because this is historically accurate but because it has become common usage.

1922: League of Nations approves British Mandate for Iraq, Transjordan (present-day Jordan), and Palestine.

1922: League of Nations grants French Mandate for Syria and Lebanon.

1922–1946: Jewish development and increased opportunities draw 100,000 Arab immigrants to British mandated Palestine and Transjordan. Jewish and Arab economies interact.

1924–1928: More Jews immigrate to Palestine; purchase land from Arab *effendi* (landowners); develop land. Two underground military groups, Irgun and Stern, begin campaigns against British and later against Arab marauders.

Inter-Arab fighting for Arab Palestinian leadership. Arab leaders either murdered or terrorized to leave country. By 1939 victims exceed 3,000.

Arab attacks against Jews. Jews defend Jewish communities but do not retaliate against Arab villages.

Arabs from neighboring countries infiltrate to attack Jews: Arab uprisings against British (1936–39). 800 Arab victims.

Peel Commission Report (1937) recommends that Palestine be partitioned into Jewish, Arab, and British zones.

Palestinian Arabs and most Arab states (except Transjordan) reject Peel Commission Report; renew violence against Jews. Demand end to Jewish immigration and land purchases.

Churchill's 1939 White Paper sets immigration limits; forbids sale of most Arab lands to Jews.

White Paper promises Arabs most of what they want; Higher Arab Committee rejects White Paper. Arabs unite against Jewish claims to Palestine; violence reaches level of open war.

Secret talks between Ben-Gurion and Arab leaders. Jews reject White Paper because of need to offer asylum to Jews fleeing Nazi persecution.

When Arab National Defense Party tentatively accepts White Paper for negotiation, a member of the party is slain by Mufti terrorists. Arab leaders in Lebanon, Syria, and Palestine talk with Jewish leaders.

| | | |
|---|---|---|
| Palestinian Jews help supply British during North African campaign in World War II. Jews are restricted from fighting for British, who want an equal number of Arabs; 30,000-man Jewish Brigade fights in Italy and Germany. | | Britain has little support from Arab world during World War II. Defense of Egypt in British hands. |
| | | Arab politics and infighting continue to follow tribal structures. |
| UN votes for partition plan that will create a Jewish state: 5,500 sq. mi. to include 538,000 Jews and 397,000 Arabs. | 1945 to 1948 | UN votes for partition plan that will create a Palestinian state: 4,500 sq. mi. to include 804,000 Arabs and 10,000 Jews. |
| Jews accept plan; prepare to set up new government and to defend country against Arab attacks. | | Arab world rejects plan; prepares for war against new Jewish state. No plans begun for Palestinian government. |
| Britain expects Jews to lose war. | | Britain refuses to cooperate with partition plan. |
| British financial moves nearly bankrupt the new state (while aiding the Supreme Muslim Council). | | |

Strict embargo on
Jews entering
Palestine and
weapons acquisition.

Britain continues to
sell arms to Arabs.
Leaves office
buildings and
military posts to
Arabs as British
Mandate ends.

Arab leaders leave
Palestine, causing
collapse of political
institutions and mass
exodus of Arabs.
175,000 flee during
last week of British
Mandate.

Jews give up passive
defense; go on
offensive with
inadequate
manpower and
weapons.

Arabs destroy Jewish
military positions in
area allotted to Jews
in partition plan.

U.S. asks Jews to
delay announcing
new state. Jews reject
request.

Arabs control half of
Jerusalem, high
ground, road
networks, vital
stretches of highway
from coast.
Outnumber Jews in
manpower, quantity
and quality of
weapons.

Jewish underground force attacks village of Deir Yassin; kills Arab inhabitants. Jewish government arrests men responsible.

Arabs attack doctors and nurses on road to Hadassah Hospital; 77 out of 105 people killed.

*The War of Independence (1948):*

Britain pulls out. Ben-Gurion announces establishment of State of Israel. Calls for development of Mideast and cooperation from Arab states.

Arabs reject new state: Six Arab nations—Syria, Jordan, Egypt, Iran, Lebanon, and Saudi Arabia—invade Israel. Outnumber Jews 40 to 1.

Arab states invade Israel. Israel loses Old Jerusalem. Full-scale fighting erupts immediately. 250,000 Arabs flee. Jews fight on all fronts. UN does not oppose invasion. Encourages Arabs to leave. 100,000 more do so.

First truce: violated by Arabs and Jews. Arabs gain 30 percent of land allotted to Israel in Partition Plan.

Second truce: violated by Jews and Arabs. Israel regains lost territory plus additional land. Controls 73 percent of Palestine.

Jews say Arab leaders encouraged Arabs to leave, thus creating refugee problem. 156,000 Arabs remain in Israel after end of war.

Arabs say Jewish leaders encouraged Arabs to leave, thus creating refugee problem.

Israel defeats Arab armies; series of armistice agreements signed. 6,000 dead, 30,000 wounded, $500 million cost. Willing to discuss peace negotiations.

Arabs disregard armistice agreements; reject peace overtures. Demand Israel return to prewar borders. UN Security Council supports Arab demands. Gaza taken over by Egyptian administration; Transjordan renamed Jordan, annexes West Bank despite protests of most of Arab League. Refugee camps set up in both areas.

## *After War of Independence:*

Arabs entitled to full citizenship; 3 Arab members in first Knesset (1949).

1949 to 1953

Arab movements restricted in border areas. Arabs are not required to serve in Israeli military to avoid fighting fellow Arabs; their national and cultural loyalties remain tied to Arab world.

Israel rejects UN vote to internationalize Jerusalem. Israel guarantees religious freedom for all; Arab mosques under Arab control; Christian buildings under Christian control.

Jordan ignores armistice provisions. Refuses to allow Jews into West Bank, East Jerusalem, and to the Wailing Wall, considered the holiest place in Judaism. In East Jerusalem, Jordan expels all Jews, desecrates and destroys most Jewish cemeteries, uses headstones to pave streets, and destroys sacred places and all houses of worship.

1949 Armistice Agreement guarantees free access to international waterways.

Egypt restricts Israel's right to passage through Suez Canal and Strait of Tiran.*

*In 1888, the maritime powers had signed a resolution that the Suez Canal should be an open shipping route to all in war and peace, which it remained until 1956.

Israel protests to UN about restriction. UN resolution confirms right to use of waterways.

Egypt ignores UN resolution. Security Council takes no action.

Arab economic boycott of Israel. Penalties applied to companies in Europe, United States, and elsewhere for trading with Israel.

West Bank and Israeli borders not clearly delineated.

Jews take over property of Arabs who fled; Israel absorbs 400,000 Jews who flee or were expelled from Arab lands. Israel agrees to allow return of Arabs with wives and children left in Israel.

Arab countries force Jews to leave; confiscate property and wealth of 467,000 Jews, 400,000 of whom go to Israel.

Israel willing to discuss return of refugees who fled if Arabs will discuss meaningful peace. Will contemplate taking back as many as 100,000 Arabs.

Arabs insist refugee problem be solved before they discuss peace. UN sets up UNRWA (United Nations Relief and Works Agency for Palestine refugees in the Near East) to assist and train refugees and develop relocation projects, but Arab countries will not allow them to leave the camps.

## *Suez-Sinai Crisis:*

| | | |
|---|---|---|
| Over 1300 Israelis killed or wounded in guerrilla activities organized and assisted by Jordan and Syria. Ignored by the world, Israel retaliates vigorously. Security Council condemns Israel for retaliating. | 1953 to 1957 | *Fedayeen* raids into Israel from Egypt under Egyptian army control. U.S. Mixed Armistice Commission report states Syria violated armistice 108 times in 1955. |
| Britain refuses to sell arms to Israel; France eventually agrees to do so. | | Britain, Soviet Union, and Czechoslovakia sell arms to Egypt. |
| | | Continued violations of 1949 armistice. Egypt blockades Strait of Tiran against Israeli shipping. |
| Israeli forces join British and French and capture Egyptian bases in Gaza and Sinai. UN demands Israel withdraw unconditionally. | | Egypt nationalizes Suez Canal. British and French attack Egypt in effort to regain Suez Canal. |
| Israel gets international assurance of guaranteed shipping rights through Strait of Tiran. Returns Sinai to Egypt under pressure. | | Egypt promises to cease attacks and maritime blockades. Promises not kept. |

| | | |
|---|---|---|
| Retaliating raids against Palestinian terrorist attacks. | 1958 to 1962 | Terrorist attacks by Palestinian forces against Israel from Lebanese territory draw Lebanon into conflict with Israel. |
| | 1964 | PLO established. Fatah's first raid into Israel in 1965. PLO becomes central feature of Middle East. |
| | | Jordan and Egypt sign a mutual defense pact before Six Day War. |

### Six Day War:

| | | |
|---|---|---|
| | June 5, 1967 | Egypt orders UN to remove peacekeeping force; closes Strait of Tiran to Israeli shipping. |
| Israel takes preemptive strike against Egyptian air force on ground. Israel condemned by UN. | | Egyptian air force effectively destroyed. |
| | | Egypt moves massive forces through Sinai toward Israel. Jordan, Syrian, and Iraqi aircraft attack Israel. |

UN declares cease-fire; Israel does not observe it. Israel defeats Arab armies on three fronts; extends administration to West Bank, Gaza, Sinai, and the Golan Heights. Jerusalem united as Israel's capital.

Arabs do not observe cease-fire.

UN condemns Israeli annexation of Jerusalem; passes Resolution 242.* Not accepted by Israel until three years later.

Egypt and Jordan accept Resolution 242.

UN Security Council resolution calls for permanent peace settlement in Middle East. Arabs still refuse to talk to Israelis and continue to finance terrorists. Heads of Arab states in Khartoum adopt resolution of "Three No's": no recognition, no negotiation, no peace with Israel.

---

*Resolution 242 insists on "the inadmissibility of the acquisition of territory by war . . . need to work for peace . . . withdrawal of Israeli armed forces from territories occupied . . . sovereignty, territorial integrity and political independence of every State . . . freedom of navigation through international waterways . . . just settlement of refugee problem . . . and a UN Special Representative to visit Middle East to promote . . . a peaceful and accepted settlement."

### *After Six Day War:*

UN Jarring Mission (1967): suggests talks between Arabs and Jews.

Arabs turn down Jarring suggestions. Hussein of Jordan prepared to negotiate, but fear of overthrow or assassination prevents cooperation with Israel.

Israel develops relations with Arabs in territories; establishes departments for agriculture, education, mail, telegraph, commerce, and industry with local residents. Encourages investment in local industry and subcontracts work to West Bank Arabs.

First Palestinian administration in area.

No local industry or government offices in the West Bank under Jordan.

Government begins settlement activity in Bethlehem-Hebron area and plans for kibbutzim on the Golan Heights.

Open Door Policy
allows trade and
travel between Israel
and Jordan. Egypt
denies citizenship or
employment to
Arabs in Gaza;
approximately 50
percent unemployed
under Egyptian rule.

*War of Attrition:*

| | | |
|---|---|---|
| 4,000 casualties since Six Day War from guerrilla attacks and artillery shelling. | 1968 to 1970 | Egypt launches War of Attrition; almost daily artillery barrages across Suez Canal. Soviet SAM missiles placed along canal facing Israel. Soviet advisers in Egypt. |
| Israel objects to SAM missiles in Egypt aimed at Israel. U.S. supplies Israel with Phantom jets to counteract Russian strength in Middle East. | | |
| | 1969 to 1971 | Jordan convulsed by Palestinian guerrilla movements. Syria aids PLO in effort to overthrow King Hussein. Jordan's army eliminates guerrilla movement from Jordan. |

U.S. emissary Henry Kissinger asks Israel to act as buffer between Jordan and Syria. Israel saves Jordan from Syrian invasion.

Bazooka attack by PLO on Israeli school bus. Israeli armored units retaliate by "mopping up" terrorist bases in Tyre and Sidon in Lebanon.

450,000 Arabs living in Israel. Social and medical care keep death rate and infant mortality low. Social benefits equal for Arab and Jewish workers. Per capita income for Arabs rises 80 percent from 1967 to 1973; no Arab violence in territories at this time.

PLO moves its operations to Lebanon. Syria breaks relations with Jordan. Jordan expels 150,000 Palestinians and their families.

Arab states continue to subsidize PLO. Arafat invited to attend meetings of Arab leaders.

Lebanon too weak to prevent PLO terrorism against Lebanese and Israel.

PLO fires Katyusha rockets into Israel.

## Yom Kippur War:

| | | |
|---|---|---|
| U.S. advises Israel not to preempt Arab attack. Despite heavy losses from Egyptian SAM missiles, Israeli troops eventually cross Suez Canal, trapping Egyptian Army. | October 6, 1973 | Surprise attack on two fronts by Egypt and Syria. |
| | | Security Council meets but does nothing. Arabs satisfied with inaction, believing time to be against Israel. |
| | | Sadat's generals assure him situation is "not serious." This major error helps Israel. Egyptian Third Army trapped. |
| Israeli poll (November 1974) indicates 75 percent of Israelis would return all or nearly all land acquired in Six Day War for peace with Arabs.* | 1974 to 1976 | Arabs still will not discuss peace. |
| Israelis want bilateral and direct negotiations in any talks. | | Arabs demand indirect and collective negotiations in any talks. |

*Israel Institute of Social Research, November 22–23, 1974.

UN General
Assembly adopts
Syrian-initiated
resolution declaring
PLO sole
representative of the
Palestinian people.

PLO breaks into
Israeli homes, kills 41
including women and
children; seizes
school, kills 20
children, and wounds
70. Bombs planted in
hotel and Jerusalem
marketplace, killing
39 and injuring 114.
Israel retaliates
against PLO bases
hidden in refugee
camps in Lebanon.

Palestinian guerrillas
kill scores of civilians
in northern Israel.

Israel aids Christian
forces in Lebanon's
civil war; sets up
buffer zone (security
zone) in southern
Lebanon to protect
northern Israel.
Medical tent set up
at northern Israeli
border for Lebanese
citizens.

Civil War in
Lebanon. Syria sends
30,000 troops. 60,000
Lebanese killed.
Syria first supports
the PLO, then, to
maintain balance of
power, fights them.

Israel rescues
hostages from
Entebbe.

Air-France airliner
hijacked, forced to
land in Uganda. 103
Israeli passengers
held as hostages in
Entebbe, Uganda.

Likud Party defeats       1977
Labor Party (1977).        to
Prime Minister            1981
Menachem Begin
claims West Bank for
Israel as Judea and
Samaria; believes
concessions by Israel
lead only to more
demands from Arabs.

President Carter
helps negotiate peace
treaty between Israel
and Egypt at Camp
David in the U.S.

Sadat offers to come
to Israel to negotiate
land for peace with
Begin: Egypt gets all
of the Sinai
(captured in 1967)
back in peace treaty.
Jewish settlements in
Sinai dismantled.

Israel offers to
discuss autonomy for
Palestinians.

Arab states expel
Egypt from Arab
League; reject any
peace overtures.

115,000 Jews live in
occupied territories
in 142 settlements
among 1.6 million
Palestinians.

Israel continues to
respond to terrorist
acts by bombing
bases and hideouts of
terrorists and
searching out
terrorist leaders.

Arab world continues
to subsidize terrorism
against Israel.
International
terrorism against the
U.S. develops; planes
are hijacked,
diplomats killed, and
civilians held hostage.

Israel crosses border
to assist Christian
Lebanese to control
a swath of land in
Southern Lebanon
against attacks by
PLO and Muslims.
Withdraws in favor
of U.N. force.

Terrorist attacks
from Lebanon
continue.

Israel continues to
protect its northern
border with military
force.

Syria installs Soviet
surface-to-air missiles
facing Israel; refuses
to dismantle them.

Israel threatens to
destroy Syrian
missiles.

Israel destroys            1981      Sadat assassinated by
atomic reactor in                    Muslim
Iraq.                                fundamentalists.

Israel rejects Saudi                 Saudi Arabia suggests
suggestion; no talk of               peace plan same as
peace.                               original UN Partition
                                     Plan of 1940s: Israel
                                     to withdraw to pre-
                                     1967 borders;
                                     Palestinian state in
                                     West Bank and Gaza;
                                     East Jerusalem Arab
                                     capital.

Israel adds new settlements in West Bank. Leads to increased violence against Jews.

1982

To avoid war with Israel, Syria collaborates with Israel to contain extremists in Christian and Muslim camps in Lebanon. Tense relations continue. Israeli and Syrian forces fight in Bekaa Valley.

Israel retaliates; invades Lebanon, crushing PLO strongholds in Tyre and Sidon. Encircles West Beirut; traps 5,000 to 6,000 PLO guerillas. PLO forced to retreat to Tunisia.

PLO terrorizes Israel from Lebanon, which it effectively occupied from 1970 to 1982.

Israeli army condemned for not preventing Christian Arab slaughter of Palestinian refugees.

Christian militia massacres Palestinians in Sabra and Shatilla camps in Beirut.

Suicide attack by terrorists kills 241 U.S. servicemen. Leads to withdrawal of U.S. forces from Lebanon. 50 French soldiers killed.

| | 1983 | |
|---|---|---|
| Israel withdraws from Lebanon. Suffers casualties from Muslim opponents during pullout. | | Syria agrees to withdraw from Lebanon if Israel does, but refuses to do so as agreed in Israeli-Lebanese withdrawal agreement. |
| Israeli forces remain in southern Lebanon; maintain buffer zone between Lebanon and Israel. | 1984 | Syrian forces remain in Bekaa Valley. Terrorism against Israel continues. Syria receives 1 billion dollars a year from oil-producing states to finance terrorism. |
| Intifada (rebellion against Israel in territories) begins; viewed by Israel as "low-level violence and civil disobedience." | 1987 | Terrorism of intifada leads to fundamentalist Arab intergroup fighting; Arab death squads use beheading, mutilation, acid against "collaborators" with Israel and against political, religious, and personal enemies. By 1992, 800 Arabs are killed by other Arabs. |
| | | Fundamentalist and terrorist factions against Israel gain strength in Egypt and Jordan. Terrorists also active in other Arab countries. |

1989    Arafat makes public statement recognizing Israel's "right to exist"; renounces terrorism. U.S. dialogue with PLO ends in 1990 after PLO terrorist attack on Israeli beaches.

*Gulf War:*

1990    Iraq invades Kuwait; threatens Saudi Arabia. Causes major realignment in Arab world. Several Arab nations join U.S.-led UN coalition to defeat Iraq.

Jordan and PLO back Saddam Hussein. PLO sees him as anti-Israel and pro-Palestinian. Thousands of Egyptians and Palestinians flee Iraq.

Israel refrains from retaliation to help preserve UN coalition at request of U.S.

Iraq fires Scud missiles at Israeli cities and Saudi Arabia.

Kuwait and Saudi Arabia expel more than 1 million Arabs suspected of cooperating with Iraq.

Between 1985 and 1991 secret Israeli airlifts bring 26,000 Ethiopian Jews to Israel; 200,000 Soviet immigrants arrive; additional large migrations expected. Integration and absorption create new set of economic problems.

U.S.-Israeli alliance under Bush and Shamir weakened after Gulf War.

1991 to 1993

After Gulf War, alliances in Arab world alter drastically. Jordan and the PLO back Iraq. Saudi Arabia cuts off aid to PLO and Syria. With the Soviet Union's demise, Syria loses financial backing. U.S. strength in the region increases. Attitudes of masses and religious fundamentalists become more aggressive.

U.S. takes initiative to resolve Arab-Israeli dispute, stressing diplomacy and compromise. Talks start in Madrid October 20, 1991.

Arab countries agree to face-to-face talks with Israelis.*

Defeat of Shamir and Likud Party; Rabin elected head of Labor Party; Rabin's attitude seen as more conducive to peace talks and progress.**

Israel expels (temporarily) over 400 leaders and sympathizers from Hamas, an anti-PLO and anti-Israel group that terrorizes Israelis. Expellees evoke worldwide sympathy; UN condemns Israel.

Iran supports Hamas; Saudi Arabia transfers financial support from PLO to Hamas to direct energies against PLO and Israel. Iran continues to support fundamentalist groups and terrorists.

---

*David McDowell in *Palestine and Israel*, University of California Press, Berkeley, CA (1989), wrote: "Arabs and Jews may not agree on much, but even acceptance of the need for an impartial analysis of beliefs, myths, events and policies by both sides is a vital precondition to any progress toward peace."
**Rabin accepts Faisal Husseini, PLO member from East Jerusalem, as head of delegation at peace talks. After recognition, Husseini says, "Palestinians are 'committed to peace talks' " but that the intifada must continue "as long as Israel occupies Arab lands."

| | September to November 1993 | |
|---|---|---|
| Prime Minister Rabin recognizes PLO as representative of Palestinian people. | | PLO Chairman Arafat recognizes Israel's right to exist. |
| | | Jordan and Israel sign agenda for peace. |
| Egypt, Russia, and U.S. press for revisions of anti-Israel resolutions at U.N. | | |
| West Bank Jewish settlers burn Arab homes in retaliation. | | Jews murdered by terrorists. |
| | | Fatah officials— active supporters of peace plan— assassinated; Fatah sets up "secret police" in Gaza to protect Palestinians. |
| Plans for interim period of self-rule discussed with PLO. | | Plans for interim period of self-rule discussed with Israel. |

## EVENTS LEADING TO ISRAELI-PLO ACCORD

The end of the Cold War meant the end of Soviet support for the Arab positions, and the Gulf War prompted Arab-Arab and Arab-Western cooperation which created hope that solutions might be worked out in the Middle East. In 1991, at the urging of the United States, the Arabs and Israelis met for several rounds of talks in Madrid, Washington, and Moscow. The talks created considerable sound but were totally devoid of results.

Prior to the peace talks both sides agreed that the Palestinian delegation would include only Palestinians living in the West Bank and none with ties to the PLO. Nor would there be any discussion of the establishment of a Palestinian state until after an interim period of self-rule on the West Bank and Gaza.

The Arabs, nevertheless, created an advisory panel to serve as a liaison between the Palestinian delegation and the PLO, and insisted on discussing a Palestinian state before they would discuss an interim agreement. They refused to renounce the state of war that has been maintained by the Arab states against Israel since 1948.

Israel, for her part, would not give up territories captured in 1967 or consider a Palestinian state until the country could be assured, after an interim period of limited self-rule by the Palestinians, that there would be peace in the region.

The Syrian delegation insisted that Israel return the Golan Heights in exchange for peace but would not clarify what they meant by peace.

The bickering continued until September 1993 when Israel and the PLO announced they had been holding secret talks and had agreed to formally recognize each other. Then suddenly, in front of the White House in Washington, two ancient enemies met, spoke, shook hands. The image was stunning.

The agreement itself was limited, but the principle was not. The PLO promised to give up terrorism and remove from their Covenant the ultimate aim of destroying Israel. Israel agreed to the establishment of a governing body (a Palestinian Council with some legislative powers) and a police force to be set up under limited Palestinian self-rule in Gaza and Jericho. Both sides agreed this would be a first step toward future negotiations regarding Palestinian self-rule in the West Bank. If details were few, the mere fact of an agreement placed the Israelis and the Palestinians on a new path, away from the dead end of the bickering of the past toward the productive problem solving for the future.

Reactions from both Arabs and Israelis ranged from complete rejection to positive acceptance but most were in favor of the agreement. Additional breakthroughs did not follow speedily—the Arab boycott against Israel was not even eased—but the atmosphere seemed hopeful on several fronts, most notably in Jordan.

Syria, Jordan, and Lebanon are expected to play major roles in this drama. And the balance of the Arab world will have its share in influencing the future course of events in the Middle East.

Myriad obstacles have to be overcome in implementing and extending the Israeli-PLO accord. Opponents will try to prevent progress toward peace. The PLO will have to create political organizations, develop a stable economy and government structure, and obtain financial assistance for the West Bank and Gaza; Israel and the PLO will have to agree on territorial concessions, water distribution rights, and the status of Jerusalem, while ensuring physical security for all participants.

Perhaps the most difficult task will be learning to trust each other after so many years of hatred, killings, and mistrust.

This first difficult step is a ray of light leading out of a dark past. Whether it will lead to a durable peace and a solution to the age-old complex problems in the Middle East cannot now be foreseen.

# BIBLIOGRAPHY

Into the writing of *Jews, God and History* went twenty
years of reading in various fields—history, economics, psychoanalysis, philosophy, biblical exegesis, literature. To acknowledge properly every source consulted would result
in a long and wearisome catalogue of books and encyclopedias as well as hundreds of articles and periodicals of interest only to the specialist. Rather, we have listed only
those books which either were basic to the writing of this
history or may be of interest to the general reader who
would like to pursue a particular topic.

We do wish to make one exception, to pay tribute to
three one-volume encyclopedias—*The Standard Jewish
Encyclopedia* (Doubleday and Company, 1959), edited by
Dr. Cecil Roth, for its clarity of style, comprehensiveness,
and erudition; William L. Langer's *An Encyclopedia of
World History* (Houghton Mifflin Company, 1948), for its
wit, scholarship, and high literary standards; and *The
Reader's Encyclopedia* (Thomas Y. Crowell Company,
1948), edited by William Rose Benét, for its remarkably
concise summaries of complex ideas, written with verve
and taste.

## GENERAL JEWISH HISTORY

ABRAHAMS, ISRAEL: *Jewish Life in the Middle Ages*. New
York, Meridian Books, 1958. Reprinted by arrangement
with the Jewish Publication Society of America. An absorbing account, vivid and detailed.

AUSUBEL, NATHAN: *Pictorial History of the Jewish People*.
New York, Crown Publishers, 1953.

BARON, SALO W.: *A Social and Religious History of the
Jews*. New York, Columbia University Press, 1937; second edition, revised and enlarged, 1952. Eight volumes.
A great achievement in scholarship—a vivid, sweeping,
panoramic account of the Jew as a dynamic factor in the

civilizations in which he created his history, an account unfortunately ending with the 13th century A.D.

BAUER, YEHUDA: *From Diplomacy to Resistance: A History of Jewish Palestine*. Philadelphia, Jewish Publication Society of America, 1970.

BEN-GURION, DAVID: *Israel: A Personal History*. New York, Funk and Wagnalls, Inc., 1971.

BENTWICH, NORMAN: *Hellenism*. Philadelphia, Jewish Publication Society of America, 1920.

BENTWICH, NORMAN: *Israel Resurgent*. [New York,] Frederick A. Praeger, (no date).

———. *The Jews in Our Time*. Baltimore, Penguin Books, 1960. A study of the interaction of Jews in modern society and their contribution to Western civilization.

BRIGHT, JOHN: *A History of Israel*. Philadelphia, Westminster Press, no date. An ordained Presbyterian minister views the history of Israel with detached scholarship and a few Christian-oriented speculations.

COLLINS, LARRY, and DOMINIQUE LAPIERRE: *O Jerusalem*. New York, Simon and Schuster, 1972.

DIMONT, MAX I.: *The Indestructible Jews*. New York, An NAL Book/The World Publishing Co., 1971.

DUBNOW, S. M.: *An Outline of Jewish History*. New York, Max N. Maisel, 1925. Three volumes. Traditional Jewish history—a linear presentation with stress on suffering. A "Jewish classic."

DUNNER, JOSEPH: *The Republic of Israel*. New York, McGraw-Hill Book Co., 1950. Pedestrian but basic.

ELBOGEN, ISMAR: *A Century of Jewish Life*. Philadelphia, Jewish Publication Society of America, 1944. The "seventh volume" to Graetz's six-volume work, bringing Jewish history up to World War II in the stylized manner of the Graetz opus.

ELDAD, ISRAEL: *The Jewish Revolution: Jewish Statehood*. New York, Shengold Publishers, Inc., 1971.

EPSTEIN, ISIDORE: *Judaism: A Historical Presentation*. Baltimore, Penguin Books, 1959. The history of Judaism seen through its religious and philosophical effects.

FINKELSTEIN, LOUIS, ed.: *The Jews: Their History, Culture and Religion*. New York, Harper & Bros., 1949. Two volumes. Encyclopedic in its wealth of information. A monumental work, modern in its approach.

FRIEDMAN, LEE M.: *Pilgrims in a New Land*. New York, Farrar, Straus and Co., 1948. Random notes on Jews in American history.

GLAZER, NATHAN: *American Judaism*. Chicago, University of Chicago Press, 1953. First published in 1911. A 175-page record of Jewish life in America.

GOODMAN, PAUL: *A History of the Jews*. New York, E. P. Dutton & Co., 1930; New York, Everyman (paperback), 1951. A masterly, concise history of the Jews.

GRAETZ, HEINRICH: *History of the Jews*. Philadelphia, Jewish Publication Society of America, 1898. Six volumes. Teutonic scholarship—turgid, lachrymose, humorless, but a thorough work, which, in spite of its overemphasis on suffering and underemphasis on social and economic factors, remains a forceful classic.

GRAYZEL, SOLOMON: *A History of the Contemporary Jews*. New York, Meridian Books, 1960. A 192-page monograph on Jewish history from 1900 to the present day.

HANDLIN, OSCAR: *Adventure in Freedom*. New York, McGraw-Hill Book Co., 1954. The story of Jews in America.

HERBERG, WILL: *Judaism and Modern Man: An Interpretation of Jewish Religion*. New York, Farrar, Straus and Cudahy, 1951; New York, Meridian Books (paperback), 1959. A perceptive interpretation, recommended for Christians—and Jews.

HERTZBERG, ARTHUR, ed.: *The Zionist Idea*. New York, Meridian Books, 1960. Reprinted by arrangement with Doubleday & Co. and Herzl Press. A fine anthology of Zionist literature, with an analytic introduction and excellent prefatory essays to the selections.

JABBER, FUAD: *Israel and Nuclear Weapons*. London, Chatto & Windus, 1971.

JANOWSKY, OSCAR I.: *Foundations of Israel: Emergence of a Welfare State*, Princeton, N.J., D. Van Nostrand Co., 1959. A good outline with valuable statistical tables.

JOHNSON, PAUL: *A History of the Jews*. New York, Harper and Row, Perennial Library, 1988.

JOSEPHUS: *The Jewish War*. Baltimore, Penguin Books, 1959. A fascinating account of the fall of Jerusalem in the war against Rome, by the man who was there.

KAUFMANN, YEHEZKEL: *The Religion of Israel: From Its*

*Beginnings to the Babylonian Exile.* Chicago, University of Chicago Press, 1960. The one-volume English abridgment of Kaufmann's seven-volume work in Hebrew.

KIMCHE, JON AND DAVID: *A Clash of Destinies: The Arab-Jewish War and the Founding of the State of Israel.* New York, Frederick A. Praeger, 1960. A fascinating account of an incredible war.

KISCH, GUIDO: *The Jews in Medieval Germany: A Study of Their Legal and Social Status.* Chicago, University of Chicago Press, 1949.

LEARSI, RUFUS: *Israel: A History of the Jewish People.* Cleveland, World Publishing Co., 1949. Read the author's pseudonym backward and you have "Suffer Israel." Here Jewish history is viewed as a 4,000-year-long dirge.

MARCUS, JACOB RADER, ed.: *Essays in American-Jewish History.* Cincinnati, American Jewish Archives, 1958. Interesting essays on the most diverse subjects.

———. *The Jew in the Medieval World.* New York, Meridian Books, 1960. Copyright 1938 by Union of American Hebrew Congregations. Translations of original documents dealing with legislation against Jews as well as accounts by Jews and non-Jews of attitudes toward Jews.

MARGOLIS, MAX L. AND MARX, ALEXANDER: *A History of the Jewish People.* Philadelphia, Jewish Publication Society of America, 1927; New York, Meridian Books (paperback), 1959. A funerary march of Jewish history accompanied by scholarship and lamentations.

NEILSON, FRANCIS: *From Ur to Nazareth.* New York, Robert Schalkenbach Foundation, 1959. A fascinating account of early Jewish history by a British theologian who has subtitled his work "An Economic Inquiry into the Religious and Political History of Israel."

PARKES, JAMES: *A History of Palestine from 135 A.D. to Modern Times.* New York, Oxford University Press, 1949.

PRITTLE, TERENCE: *Israel: Miracle in the Desert.* New York, Frederick Praeger, 1967.

ROTH, CECIL: *A History of the Marranos.* Philadelphia, Jewish Publication Society of America, 1932; New York, Meridian Books (paperback), 1959. A vivid re-creation of an amazing chapter in Jewish history.

————. *A Short History of the Jewish People*, illustrated edition. London, East and West Library, 1953 (first published in 1936); New York, Schocken Books (paperback), 1961. The traditional "martyrdom" approach to Jewish history.

RUBIN, JACOB A. AND BARKAI, MEYER: *Pictorial History of Israel*. New York, Thomas Yoseloff, 1958.

SACHAR, ABRAM LEON: *A History of the Jews*. New York, Alfred A. Knopf, 1930; third edition, 1948. A sober, scholarly account of the fortunes of the Jewish people from Abraham to the establishment of Israel in 1948.

SACHAR, HOWARD M.: *The Course of Modern Jewish History*. Cleveland, World Publishing Co., 1958. A scholarly evaluation of Jewish history from Napoleon to the present day.

————: *A History of Israel: From the Rise of Zionism to Our Time*. New York, Alfred A. Knopf, 1976.

SCHAPPES, MORRIS U., ed.: *A Documentary History of the Jews in the United States: 1654–1875*. New York, Citadel Press (paperback), 1961.

SCHWARZ, LEO W., ed.: *Great Ages and Ideas of the Jewish People*. New York, Random House, 1956. A brilliant series of essays by outstanding present-day Jewish scholars on the idea of Jewish history.

SOUSTELLE, JACQUES: *The Long March of Israel: From Theodor Herzl to the Present Day*. New York, American Heritage Press, 1969.

TCHERIKOVER, VICTOR: *Hellenistic Civilization and the Jews*. Philadelphia, Jewish Publication Society of America, 1961. A modern account of the turbulent period when the faith of the Jews clashed with the culture of the Greeks.

#### TOPICAL JEWISH HISTORY

AGUS, JACOB BERNARD: *The Evolution of Jewish Thought*. London, Abelard-Schuman, 1959. An incisive study comprehensible, unfortunately, only to the person already familiar with Jewish religion.

BARON, SALO W.: *Modern Nationalism and Religion*. New York, Harper & Bros., 1947; New York, Meridian Books (paperback), 1960. A pioneer work of great implications for the future.

BEGIN, MENACHEM: *The Revolt: Story of the Irgun*. Stein-matzky's Agency Ltd., Jerusalem, (no date).

BELL, J. BOWYER: *The Long War: Israel and Arabs Since 1946*. Englewood Cliffs, N.J., Prentice-Hall Inc., 1969.

BUBER, MARTIN: *Hasidism*. New York, Philosophical Library, 1948. An existentialist approach to Hasidism.

——. *Israel and the World*. New York, Shocken Books, 1948. Beautiful, evocative essays on Jewish questions.

——. *Moses: The Revelation and the Covenant*. New York, Harper & Bros., 1946; Harper Torchbook (paper-back), 1958. A short philosophical study of the historic Moses and his meaning in Jewish eschatology.

CASPER, BERNARD M.: *An Introduction to Jewish Bible Commentary*. New York, Thomas Yoseloff, 1960.

COHEN, MORRIS RAPHAEL: *Reflections of a Wondering Jew*. Boston, Beacon Press, 1950. Philosophical inter-pretations of Jewish problems in a contemporary mood.

DAGAN, AVIGDOR: *Moscow and Jerusalem*. London, Abelard-Schuman, 1970.

DAVIS, MOSHE: *The Yom Kippur War: Israel and the Jewish People*. New York, Arno Press, 1974.

DIMONT, MAX I.: *The Jews in America*. New York, Simon and Schuster, 1978.

DUBNOW, SIMON: *Nationalism and History*. Koppel S. Pin-son, ed. New York, Meridian Books, 1961. Essays on the interpretation of Jewish history.

ELON, AMOS: *The Israelis: Founders and Sons*. New York, Holt, Rinehart and Winston, 1971.

GINZBERG, LOUIS: *Students, Scholars, and Saints*. Philadel-phia, Jewish Publication Society of America, 1928; New York, Meridian Books (paperback), 1958. Biographical, psychological, and philosophical insights into an odd as-sortment of Jewish scholars, illuminating Jewish atti-tudes from Babylonian to present days.

GOODENOUGH, ERWIN R.: *Jewish Symbols in the Greco-Roman Period*, Vol. IV, *Symbols from Jewish Cult*. New York, Pantheon Books, 1954. Though ostensibly a book on the prevalence of certain symbols during this age, it is also an absorbing account of Jewish life, customs, and beliefs during those centuries.

HADAS, MOSES: *Hellenistic Culture: Fusion and Diffusion*.

New York, Columbia University Press, 1959. Illuminates the interaction between Jewish and Greek thought.

———. *Humanism: The Greek Ideal and Its Survival*. New York, Harper & Bros., 1960. Traces the spread of Greek ideas into Western civilization.

HALASZ, NICHOLAS: *Captain Dreyfus: The Story of a Mass Hysteria*. New York, Simon & Schuster, 1955; New York, Grove Press (paperback), no date. A lively, readable, exciting account of a famous case.

HARKABI, Y.: *Arab Attitudes to Israel*. Jerusalem, Israel University Press, Israel, 1971.

HILBERG, RAUL: *The Destruction of the European Jews*. Chicago, Quadrangle Books, 1961. The most definitive book on concentration camps—788 pages of information, from blueprints to organization charts.

HIYSH, SEYMOUR M.: *The Samson Option: Israel's Nuclear Arsenal and American Foreign Policy*. New York, Random House, 1991.

HOWE, IRVING AND GREENBERG, ELIEZER, eds.: *A Treasury of Yiddish Stories*. New York, Viking Press, 1954; New York, Meridian Books (paperback), 1958. The finest anthology of its kind, with a long, illuminating introduction.

HUSIK, ISAAC: *A History of Medieval Jewish Philosophy*. New York, Macmillan Co., 1916; New York, Meridian Books (paperback), 1958. A basic introduction to the subject for the interested reader.

KAPLAN, MORDECAI M.: *Judaism as a Civilization*. New York, Thomas Yoseloff, 1934. Foundations for a new pragmatic American Judaism.

KATZ, SAMUEL: *Days of Fire: The Secret Story of the Making of Israel*. London, W. H. Allen, 1968.

KIMCHE, DAVID and BAWLEY, DAN: *The Arab-Israeli War of 1967: Prelude and Aftermath*. London, Secker & Warburg, (no date).

KRAELING, CARL H.: *The Excavations of Dura-Europos*, Final Report VIII, Part I, *The Synagogue*. New Haven, Yale University Press, 1956. Shatters the belief that the Jews had no pictorial representations in their early synagogues. Excellent color reproductions in the back of the book.

LACQUER, WALTER: *Guerrilla*. Boston, Little Brown & Co., (no date).

LIPSKY, LOUIS: *A Gallery of Zionist Profiles*. New York, Farrar, Straus & Cudahy, 1956. Reading for the ardent Zionist.

LITVINOFF, BARNET: *Road to Jerusalem: Zionism's Imprint on History*. London, Weidenfeld and Nicolson, 1965.

MCDOWALL, DAVID: *Palestine and Israel*. Berkeley, University of California Press, 1989.

MILLEY, C. ROSS: *The Prophets of Israel*, New York, Philosophical Library, 1959.

MINKIN, JACOB S.: *The World of Moses Maimonides*. New York, Thomas Yoseloff, 1957.

MODDER, MONTAGU FRANK: *The Jew in the Literature of England*. Philadelphia, Jewish Publication Society of America, 1939; New York, Meridian Books (paperback), 1960.

NOVECK, SIMON, ed.: *Great Jewish Personalities*. B'nai B'rith Great Books Series. New York, Farrar, Straus & Cudahy, 1959 and 1960. Two volumes. A public-relations-minded presentation: nevertheless, captivating "minute biographies."

RABINOVICH, ABRAHAM: *The Battle for Jerusalem*. Philadelphia, Jewish Publication Society of America, 1972.

RABINOVICH, IRAMAR: *The War for Lebanon, 1970–1985*. Ithaca, N.Y., Cornell University Press, 1985.

RABINOWICZ, H.: *A Guide to Hassidism*. New York, Thomas Yoseloff, 1960.

REITLINGER, GERALD: *The Final Solution*. New York, Beechhurst Press, 1953; New York, A. S. Barnes & Co. (paperback), 1961. A Christian writes a common-sense, balanced account of the murder of the Jews in Germany's concentration camps.

ROBACK, A. A.: *Jewish Influence in Modern Thought*. Cambridge, Mass., Sci-Art Publishers, 1929. The familiar restated.

ROTH, CECIL: *The Jewish Contribution to Civilization*. New York, Harper & Bros., 1940. Recommended reading for Christians who have wondered what the Jews did between the fall of Jerusalem and the present day.

———. *The Jews in the Renaissance*. Philadelphia, Jewish Publication Society of America, 1959. A wonderful study that reads like a novel.

RUNES, DAGOBERT D., ed.: *The Hebrew Impact on Western*

*Civilization*. New York, Philosophical Library, 1951. Especially recommended for its chapter "Hebraic Foundations of American Democracy."

SACHER, HOWARD M.: *A History of the Jews in America*. New York, Alfred A. Knopf, 1962.

SAFRAN, NADAR: *The United States and Israel*. Cambridge, Mass., Harvard University Press, 1963.

SCHECHTER, SOLOMON: *Studies in Judaism*. New York, Meridian Books, 1958. Essays reprinted by arrangement with the Jewish Publication Society of America. British wit in rabbinic essays by a Talmudic scholar who wrote with the flawless precision of Joseph Conrad.

SCHOLEM, GERSHOM G.: *Major Trends in Jewish Mysticism*. New York, Schocken Books, 1946. A scholarly book for scholars only.

SOMBART, WERNER: *The Jews and Modern Capitalism*. Glencoe, Ill., Free Press, 1951. A brilliant Part I has been buried under the abuse heaped on Parts II and III, wherein Sombart made assumptions not warranted by facts as presently known.

STERN, SELMA: *The Court Jew*. Philadelphia, Jewish Publication Society of America, 1950. A remarkable reevaluation of the function of the Court Jew, restoring him to his rightful place in history.

STRACK, HERMANN L.: *Introduction to the Talmud and Midrash*. Philadelphia, Jewish Publication Society of America, 1931; New York, Meridian Books (paperback), 1959.

SYKES, CHRISTOPHER: *Crossroads to Israel*. Cleveland, Ohio, The World Publishing Co., 1965.

TENENBAUM, JOSEPH: *Race and Reich*. New York, Twayne Publishers, 1956. A devastating account of the rise and fall of Nazi concentration camps.

TEVETH, SHABTAI. *The Tanks of Tammuz*. New York, The Viking Press, 1968.

TROEN, SELWYN ILAN, AND SHEMESH, MOSHE, Eds.: *The Suez-Sinai Crisis, 1956: Retrospective and Reappraisal*. New York, Columbia University Press, 1990.

UNTERMAN, ISAAC: *The Talmud*. New York, Record Press, 1952.

WEISGAL, MEYER W., and CARMICHAEL, JOEL, Eds.: *Chaim Weizmann*. New York, Atheneum, 1963.

WIRTH, LOUIS: *The Ghetto*. Chicago, University of Chicago Press, 1928; Chicago, Phoenix Books (paperback), 1956. Dispels a lot of nonsense about the ghetto.

YADIN, YIGAEL: *Masada*. New York, Random House, 1966. ———. *Bar-Kochba*. New York, Random House, 1971.

ZBOROWSKI, MARK AND HERZOG, ELIZABETH: *Life Is With People*. New York, International Universities Press, 1952. A nostalgic yet faithful re-creation of *shtetl* life.

## GENERAL WORLD HISTORY

ATIYAH, EDWARD: *The Arabs*. London, Penguin Books, 1955.

BEARD, CHARLES A. AND MARY R.: *The Rise of American Civilization*. New York, Macmillan Co., 1927; revised edition, 1934. If there is such a thing as instant understanding of American history, this book will give it.

BURCKHARDT, JACOB: *The Civilization of the Renaissance in Italy*. London, Phaidon Press, no date. A vivid picture of the Renaissance by the man who "invented" the period.

DURANT, WILL: *The Story of Civilization*. New York, Simon & Schuster. Six volumes—Vol. I, *Our Oriental Heritage*, 1935; Vol. II, *The Life of Greece*, 1939; Vol. III, *Caesar and Christ*, 1944; Vol. *IV, The Age of Faith*, 1950; Vol. V, *The Renaissance*, 1953; Vol. VI, *The Reformation*, 1957. Three cheers and three cheers more for these lucid volumes, re-creating history in a three-dimensional framework.

GIBBON, EDWARD: *The Decline and Fall of the Roman Empire*. New York, Viking Press, 1952. An excellent job of abridging Gibbon's masterpiece of 1788 into one short, comprehensive volume.

GILBERT, G. M.: *Nuremberg Diary*. New York, Farrar, Straus & Cudahy, 1947; New York, Signet (paperback), 1961. A deft composite of excerpts from the Nuremberg Trials and the reactions of the accused to the unfolding of the evidence.

HEIDEN, KONRAD: *Der Fuehrer: Hitler's Rise to Power*. Boston, Houghton Mifflin Co., 1944.

KIRK, GEORGE E.: *A Short History of the Middle East*. New York, Frederick A. Praeger, 1959.

LAFFONT, ROBERT, general ed.: *The Illustrated History of Europe*. New York, Doubleday & Co., 1960. A brilliant marriage of rich illustration with lucid text resulting in a remarkable insight into the men, ideas, and forces that shaped 2,500 years of European history.

LOCHNER, LOUIS P.: *The Goebbels Diaries*. Garden City, N.Y., Doubleday & Co., 1948. A master liar weaving history to his own conceit.

PARES, BERNARD: *A History of Russia*. New York, Alfred A. Knopf, 1946. A book that leads the reader safely through the labyrinth of Russian history.

PIRENNE, HENRI: *A History of Europe*. Garden City, N.Y., Doubleday Anchor Books, 1956. Two volumes. A book to be savored as a good *apéritif*. Brings to life European history from the end of the Roman world through the Reformation.

RIENCOURT, AMAURY DE: *The Coming Caesars*. New York, Coward-McCann, 1957. A stimulating interpretation of contemporary history in the light of past historical experience.

ROMIER, LUCIEN: *A History of France*. New York, St. Martin's Press, 1953. A versatile book written with grace, and giving as much insight into French history as a ten-volume work.

RUNCIMAN, STEVEN: *Byzantine Civilization*. New York, Meridian Books, 1956. First published in 1933. Runciman rescues Byzantine history from its dreary setting.

RUSSELL, LORD, of Liverpool: *The Scourge of the Swastika*. New York, Philosophical Library, 1954. A general outline of Nazi atrocities against Christians and Jews.

SHIMONI, YAACOV, LEVINE, EVYATAR, Eds.: *Political Dictionary of the Middle East in the 20th Century*. London, Weidenfeld & Nicolson, 1972.

SHIRER, WILLIAM L.: *The Rise and Fall of the Third Reich*. New York, Simon & Schuster, 1960. A rich source book for many little-known, interesting details behind the phenomenon of Nazi Germany. A massive journalistic achievement.

TOYNBEE, ARNOLD J.: *A Study of History*, Vols. I and II. New York, Oxford University Press, 1947 and 1960. The famed abridgments of Volumes I-X of Toynbee's famed work. Presupposes a knowledge of much history.

————. *Reconsiderations* (Vol. XII of *A Study of History*). New York, Oxford University Press, 1961. Remarkable for its Chapter 15, in which Toynbee reconsiders some of his earlier, harsher judgments on Jewish history.

WELLS, H. G.: *The Outline of History*. Garden City, N.Y., Garden City Publishing Co., 1920; revised edition, 1949. Best one-volume popular history we know of. The history of the world from protozoa to the United Nations in a 1,288-page nutshell.


RELIGIOUS SUBJECTS

ALBRIGHT, WILLIAM FOXWELL: *From the Stone Age to Christianity*. Baltimore, Johns Hopkins Press, 1940; Garden City, N.Y., Doubleday Anchor Books, 1957. A classic account by a gentleman and a scholar. First-rate.

BETTENSON, HENRY, ed.: *Documents of the Christian Church*. New York, Oxford University Press, 1947.

BURROWS, MILLAR: *The Dead Sea Scrolls*. New York, Viking Press, 1955. Sad saga of a scholar buried by his own facts.

CADOUX, C. J.: *The Life of Jesus*. West Drayton, Middlesex, Penguin Books, 1948.

DIMONT, MAX I.: *Appointment in Jerusalem: A Search for the Historical Jesus*. New York, St. Martin's Press, 1991.

DUPONT-SOMMER, A.: *The Dead Sea Scrolls: A Preliminary Survey*. Oxford, Blackwell, 1952.

————. *The Jewish Sect of Qumran and the Essenes: New Studies on the Dead Sea Scrolls*. New York, Macmillan Co., 1955. Bold, brilliant, and original speculations on the true meaning of the disputed scrolls.

GINSBURG, CHRISTIAN D.: *The Essenes and the Kabbalah*. New York, Macmillan Co., 1956. An interesting museum piece on the Essenes, written in 1864, a century before the discovery of the Dead Sea Scrolls.

GOLDIN, HYMAN E.: *The Case of the Nazarene Reopened*. New York, Exposition Press, 1948. Not recommended for fundamentalists whose most cherished prejudices might be shaken by this exciting trial in the modern manner of the four Gospel writers who are entrapped by their own contradictions and their accounts of what happened, challenged by voluble scholars and mute facts.

KAUTSKY, KARL: *Foundations of Christianity*. New York, S. A. Russell, 1953. A socio-economic interpretation of the rise of Christianity.

KELLER, WERNER: *The Bible as History*. New York, William Morrow & Co., 1956. A lively re-creation of biblical history in the light of archaeological discoveries.

KLAUSNER, JOSEPH: *From Jesus to Paul*. New York, Macmillan Co., 1943; Boston, Beacon Press (paperback), 1961. ". . . this reconstruction of the past is as much a contribution to Christian as to Jewish thinking," is the verdict of the *New York Times* reviewer. Fascinating reading.

———. *Jesus of Nazareth*. New York, Macmillan Co., 1946. A Jewish scholar loved by Christian fundamentalists because of his search for kernels of truth to support the Gospel accounts.

LEWY, IMMANUEL: *The Growth of the Pentateuch*. New York, Bookman Associates, 1955.

MARTY, MARTIN E.: *A Short History of Christianity*. New York, Meridian Books, 1959. The Protestant view of Christianity. Recommended for Catholics and Jews.

OESTERLEY, W. O. E., and ROBINSON, THEODORE H.: *An Introduction to the Books of the Old Testament*. New York, Meridian Books, 1958.

RENAN, ERNEST: *The Life of Jesus*. New York, Modern Library, 1927.

SANDMEL, SAMUEL: *The Genius of Paul*. New York, Farrar, Straus & Cudahy, 1958. A Jewish theologian examines the success of Paul.

———. *A Jewish Understanding of the New Testament*. Cincinnati, Hebrew Union College Press, 1956. Recommended reading for Christians of an outsider's view of their religion.

SMITH, W. ROBERTSON: *The Religion of the Semites*. New York, Meridian Books, 1956. Dull but didactic.

SOHM, RUDOLF: *Outlines of Church History*. Boston, Beacon Press, 1958. A miniature classic, crisp and epigrammatic, recommended for Protestants, Catholics, and Jews.

WELLHAUSEN, JULIUS: *Prolegomena to the History of Ancient Israel*. New York, Meridian Books, 1957. The "great" biblical scholar of the 1880s has been "modified" by subsequent findings into obscurity.

WILSON, EDMUND: *The Scrolls from the Dead Sea*. New York, Oxford University Press, 1955; New York, Meridian Books (paperback), 1959. The best brief popular account of the Dead Sea Scrolls that is likely to come our way for another generation.

## MISCELLANEOUS SUBJECTS

ABRAHAM, KARL: *Clinical Papers and Essays on Psychoanalysis*, Part III, Chapter 3, "Amenhotep IV: A Psycho-Analytical Contribution Towards the Understanding of His Personality and of the Monotheistic Cult of Aton." New York, Basic Books, 1955.

ACKERMAN, NATHAN W. AND JAHODA, MARIE: *Anti-Semitism and Emotional Disorder*. New York, Harper & Bros., 1950. Anti-Semitism on the psychoanalytic couch.

ARENDT, HANNAH: *The Origins of Totalitarianism*. New York, Harcourt, Brace & Co., 1951; New York, Meridian Books (paperback), 1958. The author should be sainted for having produced a most readable classic in her own times.

BAINTON, ROLAND H.: *The Travail of Religious Liberty*. Philadelphia, Westminister Press, 1951; New York, Harper Torchbook (paperback), 1958. A sobering book for Jews who think that only they died for their religious beliefs.

BERDYAEV, NIKOLAI: *Christianity and Anti-Semitism*. New York, Philosophical Library, 1954. Perceptive insights by an existentialist theologian.

BRINTON, CRANE: *The Anatomy of Revolution*. New York, Prentice-Hall, 1938; New York, Vintage Books (paperback), 1957. A dissertation on the dynamics impelling man into and out of revolution.

BURTT, EDWIN ARTHUR: *The Metaphysical Foundations of Modern Science*. London, Routledge & Kegan Paul, 1924; New York, Humanities Press, 1951. An examination of the assumptions underlying modern science, blasting the popular notion that science is based on "scientific" concepts.

BYRNES, ROBERT F.: *Anti-Semitism in Modern France*, Vol. I. New Brunswick, N.J., Rutgers University Press, 1950. An analysis of the social and economic factors behind anti-Semitism.

COLLINGWOOD, R. G.: *The Idea of History*. New York, Oxford University Press, 1946; New York, Galaxy Book (paperback), 1956. An urbane examination of history as a succession of ideas instead of as chronological events.

CROMBIE, A. C.: *Medieval and Early Modern Science*. Garden City, N.Y, Anchor Books (paperback), 1959. An illuminating history of science as a continuous evolution from Greek ideas.

DOBB, MAURICE: *Studies in the Development of Capitalism*. London, Routledge & Kegan Paul, 1946. A lucid account, steering clear of the Scylla of the Left and the Charybdis of the Right.

FRAZER, SIR JAMES GEORGE: *Folk-Lore in the Old Testament*. New York, Tudor Publishing Co., 1923. A "bricklayer" of facts, unable to perceive his own fascinating structure.

FREUD, SIGMUND: *The Future of an Illusion*. New York, Liveright Publishing Corp., 1949; Garden City, N.Y., Anchor Books (paperback), 1957. Dr. Freud's dour view of religion as an illusion—but not a delusion.

———. *Moses and Monotheism*. New York, Alfred A. Knopf, 1939; New York, Vintage Books (paperback), 1955. The book that caused as much controversy as his sexual theories.

———. *Totem and Taboo*. New York, W. W. Norton & Co., 1950; Modern Library (paperback), no date. A 161-page book, basic for an understanding of the psychoanalytic interpretation of the origin of religion.

FROMM, ERICH: *Escape from Freedom*. New York, Rinehart & Co., 1941. A chilling analysis of why men seek totalitarianism.

GERTH, H. H. AND MILLS, C. WRIGHT, Eds.: *From Max Weber: Essays in Sociology*. New York, Oxford University Press, 1946; New York, Galaxy Book (paperback), 1958. Penetrating views into contemporary society. Especially recommended are the chapters "Politics as a Vocation" and "Science as a Vocation."

GLUECK, NELSON: *Deities and Dolphins*. New York, Farrar, Straus & Giroux, 1965.

GRUN, BERNARD: *The Timetables of History: The New Third Revised Edition*. New York, Simon & Schuster, 1991.

HERBERG, WILL, ed.: *The Writings of Martin Buber.* New York, Meridian Books, 1956. A perceptive selection with a pellucid introduction.

HOURANI, ALBERT HABIB: *A History of the Arab Peoples.* Cambridge, Mass., Harvard University Press (Belknap), 1991.

JONES, ERNEST: *Essays in Applied Psychoanalysis*, Vol. II. London, Hogarth Press, 1951. Trenchant psychoanalytic exegesis of Christian dogma.

KRACAUER, SIEGFRIED: *From Caligari to Hitler: A Psychological Study of the German Film.* Princeton, N.J., Princeton University Press, 1947; New York, Noonday (paperback), 1959. A tour de force showing how Nazism was foreshadowed by German movies.

LECKY, W. E. H.: *Rationalism in Europe* (History of the Rise and Influence of the Spirit of —). New York, D. Appleton & Co., 1906. Two volumes. A nineteenth-century Irish moralist with more insight into the historical process than many twentieth-century rationalists.

LISSNER, IVAR: *The Living Past.* New York, G. P. Putnam's Sons, 1957. A popular account of the growth and death of ancient civilizations.

LOWENTHAL, LEO AND GUTERMAN, NORBERT: *Prophets of Deceit.* New York, Harper & Bros., 1949. A deadly analysis of the contents of anti-Semitic diatribes.

OSBORN, REUBEN: *Freud and Marx: A Dialectical Study.* New York, Equinox Co-operative Press, no date. Dialectical pyrotechnics to prove that Freudianism is not inimical to Marxism.

SARTRE, JEAN-PAUL: *Anti-Semite and Jew.* New York, Schocken Books, 1948. A brilliant and incisive monograph on the psychic factors behind anti-Semitism.

TAWNEY, R. H.: *Religion and the Rise of Capitalism.* London, J. Murray, 1926; New York, Mentor Books (paperback), 1941. A brief but illuminating study inspired by Max Weber's work.

WEBER, MAX: *The Protestant Ethic and the Spirit of Capitalism.* New York, Charles Scribner's Sons, 1930. An examination of the psychological conditions making capitalism the child of Protestantism. Not easy, but rewarding reading.

WELLISCH, E.: *Isaac and Oedipus.* London, Routledge &

Kegan Paul, 1954. Kierkegaard would have loved this short monograph on the inner meaning of the Abraham-Isaac story—the psychic road from Moriah to Golgotha.

WILSON, EDMUND: *To the Finland Station.* New York, Harcourt, Brace & Co., 1940; Garden City, N.Y., Anchor Books (paperback), 1953. A clear account of Marxism from Marx to Lenin by one of America's most readable literary critics.

# Index

Aaron, brother of Moses, 31

Abel, 85

Abelard, Peter, 261

abolitionists, 376

Abraham (patriarch): leaves city of Ur, xii; encounter with God, 17, 19, 139; son of Terah, 18; conceives idea of a covenant with God, 20, 27; conceives the idea of one God, 21; becomes father of Isaac, 22; grand illusion of, 23, 37; Jehovah as God of, 26; as instrument of God's will, 28; ancestor of Hebrews, 32; Hebrews as descendants of, 38; dream of unified Jewish people, 65; descendants of, 164, 218; perhaps Babylonian merchant prince, or sheepherder, 189; little known about youth of, 192; appearance to, of God, 192; struggle against human sacrifice since days of, 240; as progenitor of Chosen People, 459

Abraham bar Hiyya (12th century), 278

Abraham ibn Latif, see ibn Latif, Abraham

Abraham, Karl, 30n

Abravanel, Isaac, 228–29

absentee-landlordism, 43

abstinence, 22

Abu Bekr, 193

Abu Isa (c. 740), 205

Abulafia, Abraham (1240–91), 282

academicians, 329

academic life, acadamies, 64, 99–100, 163, 167–70, 176–78, 208

acculturation, 73

actors and actresses, 256, 274

Adam, 142

Adams, John, 412

Adler, Felix, 386

"Adonai" ("my Lord") as name of God, 19n

Adonijah, 85

Adonis, pagan god, 152, 289

Aegean Peninsula, Aegean Sea, 72

Aelia Capitolina, 103

Africa, 194, 229; *see also* South Africa
Age of Reason, 200
Age of Reason, Jewish, 200
Aggada ("narration"), 170
agnosticism, agnostics, 145, 385
agriculture, 18, 40–43, 61, 75, 234, 318, 375, 377, 411, 415
Agrippa I, grandson of Herod the Great, 96
Agus, Jacob Bernard, 152*n*
Ahab: son of Omri, 46; marries Jezebel, 46–47; wars of, 47
Ahad Ha-Am (Asher Ginzberg, 1856–1927), 360–61, 434
Ahaziah: son of Jehoram, 49; becomes king of Judah, 49
Ainu, 3
Akaba, Gulf of, 42
Akiba, Rabbi, 103–5, 113
Akkad, 18
Akkadians, 190
Alamanni, 216
Alba, Duke of, 300
Albania, 393
Albigenses, 225–27, 230, 248
Albinus, Roman procurator, 96
alchemists, 197
Alexander the Great, of Macedonia: quest for empire, 65; Alexandrian empire, 71, 75; dream of world conquest, 73; conquest of Persia, 73; founder of Greek cities in Middle East, 73; successors of, 74; Hellenic culture of, 75–77; invites Jews to settle in Greek cities, 79; former empire of, 87; number of soldiers in army of, 100; quest of Jews, 199–200; conquest of ancient Eastern world, 415
Alexander Janneus, 84–85
Alexander Severus, Roman emperor, 413
Alexander I, of Russia, 318
Alexander II, of Russia, 319–20
Alexander III, of Russia, 321, 377
Alexandra, wife of Alexander Janneus, 85, 90
Alexandra, of Russia, 321–22
Alexandria, Egypt: founding of, 73; uprising against Jews in, 110; Greek-speaking Jews in, 113; Philo a native of, 113–14; new Jewish cultural center in, 117; Napoleon's landing in, 415
Alexandrian Jews, 117
Alexandrians, 113
Alfasi (11th century), 180
Allah (Muhammadan name of God), 188, 192–93, 239
allegory, 114, 291
Allenby, Edmund Henry Hynman, 425
Allies (World War I), 316, 421

Allies (World War II), 407
Almohades, 180–81, 196
alphabet, 40
Alps, 100
Alsace, 252, 304
ambassadors, 293
Amenhotep IV: king of Egypt, 29; attempt to introduce monotheism, 29; death, 29
America, 8, 36, 39–40, 44, 82, 89, 116, 143, 167, 229, 271, 299, 313, 321, 323, 369–91, 411–13, 422, 434, 457; see also United States
American Constitution, see Constitution, U.S.
American Jews, 60, 75, 82, 112, 368, 369, 373–78, 382–91
American Judaism, 388–90
American legal system, 74–75
American Nazis, 381
American Reform Judaism, see Reform Judaism
American Revolution, 10, 370, 374, 411
Americanization, 379, 385
Americans, 89, 319, 381–82, 428
Amish, 82, 94
Amos, 57
amphitheaters, 109
Amsterdam, Holland, 301–2, 343
Anan ben David, leader of Karaism (740–800), 204–7
Ananias, early Jewish Christian, 139

anathema, 254
Anatolia, 72
Anglican Church, 304
Anglo-Dutch, 369
animals, 108, 171–72, 240
anthropology, 349
anti-Christianity, 396–97
anti-Communists, 380–81
anti-Dreyfusards, 338–40
Antigonus, son of Aristobulus II, 91
Antigonus, successor of Alexander the Great, 74
anti-Hellenists, anti-Hellenizers, 77, 78–79, 82–83, 93, 208
anti-intellectualism, xi, 89, 251, 369
anti-Jewish laws, 250; see also Discrimination
anti-Jewish persecution, see anti-Semitism; persecution of Jews
Antioch, 102, 111
Antiochus Epiphanes, of Syria: son of Antiochus III, 78; Hellenization program of, 78–79; place in Jewish history, 78–80; attack on Egypt, 79; rebuff by Romans, 79; slaughter of Jews by, 79; invites pagans to settle in Jerusalem, 79; forbids Jews to observe Sabbath and circumcision, 79; revolt against, by Maccabees, 80; defeat of, by Maccabees, 80; death of, 81; repressive measures of, 79, 93

Antiochus III, "the Great": Seleucid king, 77; seizes Palestine, 77–78; tolerance of, 77; plan to unify former Alexandrian empire, 77

Antipas, son of Herod, 92–93, 132

Antipater, 90

*Antiquities of the Jews* (Josephus), 98

anti-Semites, anti-Semitism, 7, 242–43, 245–46, 252, 262, 311, 323–27, 331, 333–36, 340, 343, 351, 354, 365, 377, 381–82, 394, 398–400, 408–9, 416, 418–19

Antoninus Pius (138–61), Roman emperor, 175

Antonio (character in *Merchant of Venice*), 238

"Apikorsim" (Epicurean Greeks), 67, 77

Apocrypha, 138

apostasy, apostates, 76, 182, 240, 244, 248, 324*n*, 343, 385

Apostles of early Christian Church, 140

Apostolic Church, of Jerusalem, 140

Arab religion, 189–90

Arabia, Arabians, 8, 48–49, 190–91, 193–94, 196, 205; *see also* Arabic people; Saudi Arabia

Arabian desert, 189

Arabian Sea, 190

Arabic culture, 9, 180–81, 198, 209

Arabic language, 5, 6, 198, 208, 224

Arabic numerals, 198

Arabic people, 209, 326; *see also* Arabia; Arabs

Arabs, 116, 127–28, 189–91, 194, 198–99, 205, 209–10, 226, 326, 410, 414, 421; *see also* Arabia; Arabic people

Arafat, Yassar, 440–41

Aramaic, 5, 64, 112, 168, 179

Arcadius, Roman emperor, 147

Arch of Titus, 102

archaeologists, archaeology, 23, 24, 40, 46, 76, 127

archbishops, 244, 251

Archelaus, son of Herod, 92

Archimedes, 261

architects, architecture, xi, 24, 37, 108, 193, 197, 257, 260, 320

Arendt, Hannah, 329, 332

Arians, 414

Aristobulus I, son of John Hyrcanus, 84

Aristobulus II, 85, 91

aristocracy, aristocrats, 77, 81, 321, 333, 376, 380, 394, 411

Aristotelianism, 278

Aristotle, Greek philosopher, 166, 181, 253, 261, 279*n*

arithmetic, 261

Ark, 41

Armada, Spanish, 300

Armleder, 250

army, armies, 17, 42, 44, 47–48, 51, 72–73, 80, 85, 104, 191, 194, 196, 217, 306, 312, 314–16, 404–5, 410–11, 414, 415, 425

Arrika, Rabbi, 168

*Ars Magna* (Raymond Lully), 279

art, arts, 5, 71, 89, 108–9, 116, 190, 193, 195, 216, 256, 306, 309, 319, 349, 352, 369, 376, 382–83, 392, 434; *see also* plastic arts

artisans, 218, 254, 378

artists, 223, 380

Aryans, 59, 72, 332, 335, 396–97, 408

asceticism, ascetics, 94, 191

Asherah, 38

Ashkenazic Jews, Ashkenazim, 252–53, 258, 304

Ashkenazic Judaism, 252–53

Asia, 3, 18, 194, 229

Asia Minor, 59, 72, 74, 75, 87

Asians, Asiatics, 149, 347

assembly, freedom of, 65

Assembly of Notables; *see* National Assembly of Jewish Notables

assimilation, assimilationists, 6, 21, 53, 57, 63, 113, 116, 197–98, 307, 358, 365, 375, 418

Assyria, Assyrians, Assyrian Empire: as nation of antiquity, 5; relations with Jews, 17, 93; as northern part of Mesopotamia, 18; power struggle with Egypt, 24; resistance of Israel and Judah to, 45, 431; Assyrian monument referring to Israel as "the land of Omri," 46; Ahab's battle against, 47; conquests, wars of Tiglath-Pileser III, 48; tribute paid by kings of Judah, 50; wars in Palestine, 50–51; defeat of Ten Tribes of Israel, 52–53, 72; policy, 57; attacks on Israel, 57; Parthia formed in part from remnant of, 92; payment of taxes by Jews, 239

Astarte, 55

astronomers, astronomy, 170, 199, 256, 261, 279, 350–51, 371

Athaliah, queen of Judah, 49

Athanasians, 414

atheists, 343, 349

Athens, Greece, 112

Atlantic Ocean, 115, 368

atomic age, atomic bomb, atoms, 3, 351–52

Aton: Egyptian sun-god, 29; religious sect, 29

atonement, 142

Attila the Hun, 149, 408

Attis, pagan god, 152

*Aufklärung, see* Enlightenment, German

Augsburg, Germany, 250
Augustus (Octavian),
    Roman emperor, 91
Auschwitz, 335, 401–3
Austria, Austrians, 232, 246,
    248, 250, 255, 258, 263,
    305–6, 312, 314, 316,
    393–94
Austria-Hungary, 342*n*, 394
Austrian Jews, 309, 348,
    366, 398
Austrian National Theater,
    305
authoritarians, 392–93
authority, civil, *see* civil au-
    thority
authority, rabbinical, 357
autocrats, 321
*Auto-Emancipation* (Judah
    Pinsker), 418, 421
autonomy, *see* self-
    government
autos-da-fé, 228, 229, 284,
    326, 373
Avaris, capital city of the
    Hyksos, 24–25
Averroës, Islamic scholar,
    253

Baal, Baal worship, 38, 47,
    55
Baala, female goddess
    (Asherah), 38
Babylon, 57–60, 116, 168,
    453
Babylonia, Babylonian
    Empire, Babylonians:
    disappearance as great
    power, 4; as great na-
    tion, 5; expulsion of
    Jews by, 6; relations
    with Jews, 17; Babylo-
nia as southern part of
    Mesopotamia, 18;
    power struggle with
    Egypt, 24; Abraham as
    Babylonian, 29*n;*
    Babylonian Code of
    Hammurabi, 33;
    armies of, 45; depar-
    ture of Abraham
    from, 47; rebellion of
    Judah against Neb-
    uchadrezzar, 51–52;
    deportation of Jews
    to, 51; conquest of
    Kingdom of Judah, 51,
    116; exile of Jews of
    Judah to, 53; defeat of
    other nations by, 53;
    Jews in Babylonian
    captivity, 59, 116; en-
    lightened kings of, 59;
    trade routes of, 59; de-
    feat by Cyrus the
    Great, 60; prosperity
    of Jews in, 59; mass
    exoduses of Jews
    from, 61, 65; destruc-
    tion of Temple in
    Jerusalem by, 61; Jew-
    ish scholarship in, 65;
    synagogue in, 65;
    Parthia formed in part
    from remnant of, 92;
    relations to Jews, 93;
    conquest by Persians,
    116; sojourn of Jews
    in, 116–17; creation of
    Jewish cultural Dias-
    pora capital in, 116;
    Parthia formerly
    Babylonia, 163;
    yeshivas of, 164, 168,

176, 178; origin of Mishna in, 166; government posts held by Jews, 175; city-states of, 190; origin of Karaism in, 204; Saadyah Gaon appointed head of Babylonian academy, 208; payment of taxes by Jews, 239; civilization, 253; shifting of Jewish life to, 370; emergence of new Judaism, 390; wars of Jews against Babylonians, 431; survival of Jews in Babylonian captivity, 456

Babylonian Jews, 58–62, 65, 189

Babylonian Talmud, 170*n*; *see also* Talmud

bachelorhood, 35–36

Bacon, Francis, 280, 411

bacteriology, 350

badge, Jewish, *see* yellow badge

Baghdad, 177, 196

Bal Shem Tov (Israel ben Eliezer) (1700–60), 289–91, 357

Balfour, Arthur James, 422

Balfour Declaration, 421

Balkans, 148

Baltic Sea, 249

Balzac, Honoré de, 342

banishment, *see* expulsions

bankers, banking, banks, 218, 254, 264, 268–70, 274, 301, 303, 320, 353, 376

baptism, 95, 129, 132, 217, 238, 243, 251, 262, 283, 287, 304, 345, 346, 365, 375, 418

barbarians, 73, 89, 108, 147, 148–49, 154, 169, 181, 196, 216, 218, 250

barbers, 260

Bar Kochba (Simon ben Cozeba), 103–4, 151, 410–11, 413, 419

Barnabas, Christian disciple, 140

Baruch, Bernard M., 383

Basel Congress, 419

Bassanio (character in *Merchant of Venice*), 238

bastards, 36

Bastille, 311

Bavaria, Bavarians, 216, 395

beauty, 109, 183

Bedouins, 410*n*

Beethoven, Ludwig von, 342, 355, 392

Begin, Menahem, 444

Belasco, David, 382

Belgium, 406

beliefs, Jewish, 345–46

belles-lettres, 183

Bellini, Giovanni, 223

Belsen, 335, 403

Ben-Gurion, David, 413, 429, 432–33

Benjamin, Judah P., 376

Benjamin Nahavendi, Karaite leader, 207

Benjamin of Tudela, 176–77, 267

ben Zakkai, Jochanan, *see* Jochanan ben Zakkai

Berbers, 194

Berdyaev, Nikolai, 10, 366, 396

Bergson, Henri, 342

Berlin, Germany, 306

Berlin, Irving, 383

Berlin Stock Exchange, 353

Bernadotte, Folke, 410, 431–32

Bernhardt, Sarah, 352

Bernstein, Leonard, 384

bestiality, 37, 101–2

Bethel, temple of, 28, 46

Beth El Synagogue, Albany, N.Y., 384

Beth Haknesseth, "House of Assembly" (designation for synagogue), 65

Beth Hamidrash, "House of Study" (designation for synagogue), 65

Bethlehem, 91, 131

Beth Tephila, "House of Prayer" (designation for synagogue), 65

*Beyond Good and Evil* (Friedrich Nietzsche), 332

Bialik, Hayim (1873–1934), 361, 425

Bible, 10, 18–19, 23, 25–26, 30, 44, 63–65, 85, 112, 128, 163, 170, 208, 240, 262, 370; *see also* Old Testament; Torah

Bible translations, 111–14, 208, 308

biblical exegesis, 31, 165–66, 179, 346

biblical Jews, 197, 199

biochemists, 383

biologists, biology, 342, 383

bishops, 244

Bismarck, Otto Eduard Leopold von, 314, 316, 336, 392

Bizet, Georges Alexandre César Léopold, 342

Black Death (1348–49), 244–45, 250

Black Stone, 190

blasphemy, 136

blood, 240

blood accusation, *see* ritual-murder accusations

Blum, Léon, 339–40, 352

Boccaccio, Giovanni, 223

Bohemia, Bohemians, 217, 258, 305

Bohemian Jews, 384

Bohr, Niels, 351

Bokhara, 196

Boleslav V, the Chaste, of Poland (1264), 246

Bolsheviks, 380–81

Bonaparte, Napoleon, *see* Napoleon Bonaparte

Bonfils, Immanuel (14th century), 280

Bonn, Germany, 316

"Book, the," *see* Bible

bookkeepers, 329

*Book of Formation* (8th century), 277, 281

books, 58, 59, 65

booksellers, 260

Books of Moses, *see* Five Books of Moses

Boris II, of Bulgaria, 407

Boston, Mass., 379

Bourbons, 314, 321

bourgeoisie, 254, 411

boys, 119

Brahms, Johannes, 342, 355, 392
Brandeis, Louis D., 383
Brazil, 371–72
Britain, British Empire, 100, 104, 303–4, 352, 421–29; *see also* England
British Mandate for Palestine, *see* Palestine Mandate
British people, 104, 127–28, 303–4, 318, 373, 421–29; *see also* English people
brokers, 374
brotherhood of man, 177, 189, 200, 299, 458–59
Bruno, Giordano, 344
brutality, 37
Buber, Martin, 10, 292, 366–68
bubonic plague, *see* Black Death
Buddha, 189
Bulan, Khazar king (A.D. 740), 202
Bulgaria, Bulgarians, 217, 407
Bulgarian Jews, 407
bulls, papal, *see* papal bulls
bureaucrats, 316, 329, 413, 416, 433
burgher class, burghers, 218, 236, 255, 313, 343
Burgundians, 216
burial, 121
Burke, Edmund, 331, 411
Bush, George, 448, 449
business, businessmen, 75–76, 170, 197, 263, 264, 267, 268–70, 271, 293, 301, 306–7, 377–78, 396; *see also* economic life, economics
butchers, 260
Byzantine civilization, Byzantine Empire, 117, 155, 176, 190, 194, 202, 221–22, 414
Byzantium, 191, 222

cabarets, 76
cabinet members, cabinet ministers, 383
Cadoux, Cecil John, 131*n*
Caesar, Julius, 88, 90, 100
Caesarism, 87
caftan, 237
Cain, 85
Cairo, Egypt, 181, 197, 415
calendar, 17, 24
Caligula, Roman emperor, 96, 113–14
caliphs, caliphate, 196
Calvin, John, 232
Cambridge University, England, 387
Cambyses, son of Cyrus the Great, of Persia, 60
Canaan, xiii, 19, 21, 22–23, 27–29, 32, 38–39, 453, 456
Canaanites, 38
"canonization" of Mishna, 168
canonization of New Testament, 147, 164
canonization of Old Testament, 147
canonization of Scripture, 54, 112, 164
Cantor, Georg, 350

capitalism, capitalists, 8, 42, 232, 234–36, 263–68, 269–72, 300–301, 303, 327–28, 330, 347, 351, 453

captivity, 53, 58; *see also* deportations; exile

Caracalla, Roman emperor (A.D. 212), 151

Carbonari, 315

Carchemish, Battle of (605 B.C.), 51

cardinals, 251

Cardozo, Benjamin N., 383

Caro, Joseph (1488–1575), 182, 459

Carter, Jimmy, 445

Carthaginians, 145, 325–26

cartographers, 370–71

Casimir III, the Great, of Poland (1333–70), 232, 246

Casimir IV, of Poland, 246

Caspian Sea, 60, 202

Cassius, 90

caste, 254

Catherine the Great, of Russia (1762), 249

Catholic Church, Catholicism, Catholics, 58, 134, 138, 153, 180, 204, 206, 207, 216, 228, 231–36, 258, 272, 283, 301, 302, 305–6, 316, 335, 386, 397, 458; *see also* Roman Catholicism; Spanish Church

Catholic Counter Reformation, *see* Counter Reformation, Catholic

Cato, 325

Caucasus, 60

Cavour, Camillo Bensodi, 316

celibacy, 95, 119, 139

Cellini, Benvenuto, 223

Celts, 104

cemeteries, 258

censuses, 92

Central Europe, 258, 273, 342

ceremonies, *see* customs; ritual

Cestus Gallus, Roman general, 97

Cézanne, Paul, 342

Chagall, Marc, 342, 356*n*

Châlons, Battle of (451), 149, 194

Chamberlain, Houston Stewart, 331, 333

charismatic power, 56, 118

charity, 4, 119, 378–79; *see also* philanthropy

Charlemagne (Charles the Great), 216, 218, 300, 312

Charles Martel (A.D. 732), 194

Charles I (Karl Alexander), Duke of Württemberg, 274–75

Charles V, 274, 284

Charles VI, emperor of Austria, 305

charters, 218, 246, 250, 254

chastity, 36, 77

Chaucer, Geoffrey, 239, 363

chemistry, chemical industry, chemists, 342, 351, 383, 421

Chicago, Ill., 376, 379

chief justices, *see* justices

children, 22, 36, 47, 73, 87, 95, 154, 241, 257, 260–62, 306, 317, 378, 379, 385, 402, 434

China, Chinese, 3, 4, 9, 75, 122, 148, 194, 264, 267, 347, 458

Chmielnicki, Bogdan, 247

choirs, 386

Chopin, Frédéric, 342

"choppers" (in Russia), 318, 417

Chosen People, 19, 28, 32, 56, 63, 117, 364, 454, 457, 459

Christ, see Jesus Christ

Christian Church, 3, 22, 143, 145, 146–47, 151, 153–54, 166, 178, 219–20, 225–27, 229, 230–31, 234–35, 243, 253n, 258, 269–70, 287, 293, 311, 326, 397; see also Christianity; Christians

Christian Science, 139, 207

Christian sects, see sects, Christian

Christiani, Fra Paulo, see Paulo Christiani, Fra

Christianity, Christian sects, 6, 25, 29, 41, 54, 72, 82, 113, 121–22, 127–31, 134, 138–42, 145–47, 150–51, 154, 164, 169, 191, 195, 203, 204, 208, 217, 219, 227, 244, 251, 258, 263, 275, 278–79, 290, 292, 299, 308, 328, 333, 335, 345–46, 347, 396–97, 459; see also Christian Church; Christians

Christians, Christendom, 3, 19, 25, 35, 37, 58, 76, 94–95, 100, 104, 110, 111, 113, 114n, 118, 120–22, 127, 131, 134, 137–54, 164, 169, 171, 176, 178–79, 180, 189, 191, 193, 194–95, 199, 200, 207, 215, 217, 219, 220–29, 229–39, 240, 245, 253n, 255, 257–58, 261–62, 264, 268–69, 275, 282–83, 292, 299–301, 303, 305–9, 313, 317, 326, 330, 343, 345–46, 347, 354, 372, 373–75, 382, 385, 386–87, 392, 398–99, 409, 414, 459; see also Christian Church; Christianity

Church, the, see Christian Church

churches, 4, 58, 121, 217, 241

church and state, separation of, 33–34, 120

Church Council of Nicaea, see Nicaea, Council of

Churchill, Winston S., 393

cigar makers, 378

Cincinnati, Oh., 376, 384

circumcision, 19, 21, 27, 33, 79, 107, 110, 140

cities, 17, 43, 71, 73, 75, 79, 190–91, 196, 218, 223, 232, 246, 249, 255, 258–59, 307, 377, 416, 434; see also towns; urbanization citizens, citizenship, 106, 151, 153, 311, 318, 323, 326, 331, 351–52, 354, 373, 413, 433–34

city-states, 17–18, 72, 222

civic life, 147–48

civil authority, civil government, 34

civil rights, 46, 315

civil war: in Kingdom of Israel, 43–46, 49–50, 51; between Pharisees and Sadducees, 83–84; between Hyrcanus II and Aristobulus II, 84; between Julius Caesar and Gnaeus Pompey, 88, 90

Civil War (American), 104, 376

civilization, 9, 17–18, 107–9, 116, 183, 193, 198–99, 209, 219, 252, 253, 264–65, 340, 341, 392, 454–58, 460

class war, 417

classes, social, 218, 328

Claudius, Roman emperor (A.D. 41), 114

Clemenceau, Georges, 339

Clement VII, Pope, 283

Cleopatra, queen of Egypt, 88

clergy, 227, 246, 254, 265, 306, 313

clerks, 380

Cleveland, Oh., 376, 379

climate, 8

clothing, 237

Clovis, Frankish king (5th century), 216

coal industry, 376

Code Napoleon, 312

Code of Hammurabi, see Hammurabi, Code of

codes (of law), see law codes

codifications and codifiers of the Talmud, 180–82

colleges, 379, 434

Cologne, Germany, 216, 250

colonialism, colonial period, 328, 369, 372–73, 428

colonies, American, 370, 373–75

colonists, American, 44, 373–75

Colossians, 141

Columbus, Christopher, 228, 279, 371

commandments, 19, 22, 56, 65, 168, 177, 309, 366

commandments (the 613), 289

Commandments, the Ten, see Ten Commandments

commentaries, 179

commerce, commercial life, 18, 43, 46, 59, 63, 75, 190, 218, 232, 246, 265–69, 300–303, 305, 353–54, 378; see also trade

common people, 332

communal life, 319

communion (in Christianity), 129

communism, communists, 3, 7, 8, 105, 143, 263–64, 272, 321, 330, 346–48, 394–95, 397, 417

communities, community, 367, 373
community, religious (Minyan), 119
community, social, 119
composers, 118
concentration camps, 335, 397–400, 401–2, 409, 453
Condorcet, Marie Jean Antoine, 310, 411
conduct, 170, 267, 344
conductors, 352, 384
Confederacy (American), 376
Confederate Army (Civil War), 376
Confederation of German States, 316
conformity, religious, 209, 309
Confucius, 189
Congress, U.S., 375, 380–81, 382, 383
Congress of Vienna (1815), 314, 317, 318
conscription, 318
conservatism, 168, 173, 199
Conservative Judaism, 387–88
Constantine the Great (A.D. 324), 146, 150, 220
Constantine the Great, Laws of (A.D. 315), 152, 220
Constantinople, 147, 222
Constantius, Laws of (A.D. 399), 152, 220
Constitution, U.S., 34, 39, 165, 373–74
constitutional law, American, 34
consuls (of Rome), 88

contract, social, see "social contract"
conversion, forcible, 150n, 217, 220
conversion to Christianity, 110, 139–40, 150, 154, 195, 202, 216–20, 226–29, 238, 244, 274, 282–83, 287, 301, 305, 306, 318, 328, 343, 365
conversion to Judaism, 91, 110, 112, 121, 138, 153–54, 202–3, 218, 248, 283–84
conversion to Muhammadanism, 193, 195, 239, 286
conversionist sermons, 244
Conversos, 226
Copernicus, Nicholas, 239, 280
Copts, 410n
Corday, Charlotte, 311
Córdoba, Spain, 180, 197, 201
Corinth, Greece, 72
Corinthians, 141
corporate Jewish state, 314, 318; see also "Jewish state"
corporate state, 373
Cossacks, 247–48
Cotton, John, 373
Council of Nicaea, see Nicaea, Council of
Council of Trent, see Trent, Council of
Counter Reformation, Catholic, 204, 235, 386
counterrevolutions, 316
Court Jews, 273–75, 304, 305, 317, 353

courts, 119, 120, 136, 319, 374
covenant, 19–20, 23, 27, 32
crafts, 319
Crassus, Marcus, 88
creation, 54, 114
credit, creditors, 265–66, 320, 353
Crémieux, Adolphe, 352
Cremona, Luigi, 350
Cresques, Abraham, 370
Cresques, Judah, 370–71
Cretans, 38
Crimea, 209
crimes, criminals, criminality, 36–37, 221, 257, 379
criminology, 349
Crombie, A. C., 280*n*
Cromwell, Oliver (1656), 252, 302
crucifixion, 107, 133, 137, 241
crucifixion (of Jesus), 131, 137–38, 241
Crusades, 180, 215, 217, 220–22, 225*n*, 234, 236, 246, 250, 414
crypto-Jews, 219, 226
cult, 57
cultural freedom, 74
cultural life, culture, 20–21, 59, 71, 75, 83, 89–90, 107–9, 113, 116–17, 122, 154–55, 164, 196, 199, 223–24, 227, 238, 251, 253, 262, 264, 304, 323, 341, 345, 354–55, 359–61, 366–68, 369–70, 377, 382–83, 384, 386–87, 392, 434, 453–56, 458
cuneiform writing, 18

currencies, 266
customs, Jewish, 110, 346; *see also* ritual
cynics, 76
Cyprus, 102, 110–11, 428
Cyrene, 102
Cyrus the Great, of Persia (560 B.C.), 60–61
czars, 317–22, 361, 378
Czechoslovakia, 393, 394, 398, 429, 431

"D" code (Deuteronomy), 31*n*, 55
da Gama, Vasco, 371
Damascus, Syria, 45, 47, 111, 112, 139, 194, 203
Damascus, Battle of (1303), 196
dancers, 256
Daniel (biblical book), 112, 303
Dante Alighieri, 223, 239, 270, 363, 425
Danton, Georges Jacques, 311, 412
Darius III, Persian king, 73
Dark Ages, 217–18, 220
Darwin, Charles, 54, 342
*Das Kapital* (Marx), 3, 347, 347*n*
David: as first king of Palestine, 41; warrior king, 41; makes Jerusalem political capital of Palestine, 41; death of, 44; as uniter of Israel, 44; place in Palestinian civilization, 52; attribution of Psalm 137 to, 59*n*; appoints Zadok first high

priest, 61*n;* plundering of tomb by John Hyrcanus, 84; extensive rule of, 84; Bar Kochba regarded as descendant of, 104; descent of Jesus traced from, 175

Davidic house, Davidic line, 49–51, 77, 131–32, 175, 205

da Vinci, Leonardo, *see* Leonardo da Vinci

Davis, Jefferson, 376

day laborers, 256

day of rest, *see* Sabbath

Dead Sea, 103, 128

Dead Sea Scrolls, 127–31, 138

death, 258

Deborah, judge, 40

debt, debtors, 87, 266

Decalogue, 21, 333; *see also* Ten Commandments

*Decameron* (Boccaccio), 258

decimal system, 279

Declaration of Independence, 312

declassed, the, 330, 334, 336, 381, 394

*Decline and Fall of the Roman Empire* (Gibbon), 145

*Decline of the West, The* (Spengler), 9

defeatism, 292

de Jerez, Roderigo, *see* Jerez, Roderigo de

Delacroix, Ferdinand Victor Eugène, 342

de Loronha, Fernando, 371

demagogues, 87

democracy, democrats, 34, 39, 53, 62, 87, 299, 314, 321, 330, 380, 393, 425

democracy, Jewish, 26, 33–34, 432

Denmark, 217, 406

department stores, 376

deportations, 49, 51; *see also* exile

depression (U.S.), 381

depressions, 330

de Riencourt, Amaury, 455–56

de Torres, Luis, *see* Torres, Luis de

*Der Judenstaat* (Herzl), 419

Descartes, René, 280, 343

despotism, 146, 317

Detroit, Mich., 378, 379

Deuteronomic Code ("D" document), 31*n*

Deuteronomy (biblical book), 32, 55, 63–64

Diaspora, 115–17, 151, 167, 200, 207, 265–66, 357, 360, 368, 413, 456–58; *see also* exile

dictators, dictatorship, 88

dictionaries, Hebrew, 118, 200

Diderot, Denis, 310

Diet of Worms (1521), 235

dietary laws, 110, 120, 140, 171, 207, 386, 387, 390, 460

dignity of man, 74

Dimont, Ethel, xi, xiv

Dimont, Gail, xiv

Dimont, Hyman, v

Diogo Pires, 284

diplomatic service, 218

Disciples (of Jesus), 142

discrimination, discriminatory laws, 120, 152–54, 195, 219–20, 230, 236–37, 305, 352–53; *see also* persecution of Jews

disenfranchisement, 378

dispersion, *see* captivity; exile

disputations, religious, 243–44, 251, 287

Disraeli, Benjamin, 154, 352

*Divina Commedia* (Dante), 270

divorce, 35, 254, 313

doctors, *see* physicians

dogma, 223–24, 230, 235, 367, 386, 414

Donin, Nicholas, 243–44

Donmeh (Sabbatean sect), 287

Dostoevski, Feodor Mikhailovich, 360

Dov Ber, Hasidist leader, 291, 357

dowry, 119

Drake, Francis, 300

drama, 352, 360; *see also* plays

dress, 253

Dreyfus Affair, 337–40, 418

Dreyfus, Alfred, 337–40, 418

Dreyfusards, 338–40, 418

druggists, 256

Druids, 240

Drumont, Edouard, 331, 333–35, 337

drygoods stores, 376

Dubinsky, David, 384

Duma, of Russia, 322

Dupont-Sommer, A., 129–30

Dura-Europos, 76n, 117

Durant, Will, 193

Dürer, Albrecht, 238

Dutch East India Company, 301

Dutch language, 301

Dutch people, 120, 252, 300–301, 303, 343, 372–73

Dutch West India Company, 373

dye (dyeing) industry, 268, 351

"E" document, 31, 46, 55

East (U.S.), 375

East European Jews, Eastern Jews, 289, 341, 356n, 356–57, 364–65, 368, 399, 406, 420

East Europeans, 380–81

East Goths, *see* Ostrogoths

Eastern Europe, 180, 226, 232, 236, 246, 253, 259, 268, 277, 281, 289, 291, 299–300, 336, 340, 341, 356, 359, 364, 377, 381, 393–94, 400, 403, 406–7

Eastern religions, 153

Eastern world, 3, 88, 92, 148, 163, 177–78, 194, 208–9, 216, 222, 263, 281, 323, 356–57, 365, 368

Ebionites, 142

ecclesiastical literature, 253

ecclesiastical state, 153, 299

Eck, Johann Maier von, *see* von Eck, Johann Maier

economic life, economics, 8, 40–41, 43, 53, 215, 229, 232, 234, 236, 242, 245, 252, 263, 265, 271, 293, 303–4, 314, 327–29, 347, 353–54, 355, 377–80, 394, 424–25

ecstasy, 290

Eddy, Mary Baker, 139

editors, 364

education, 4, 65, 85, 111, 119, 168–69, 191, 237, 260–62, 293, 306, 308, 312, 319, 354–55, 416, 426, 434

effendi, 424, 426

Egypt, Egyptians: Jews in, xii–xiii, 22–23, 453; Egyptian people today, 4; relations with Jews, 17; civilization, 17; slavery of Jews in, 22–23, 28–29; and Joseph, 22–23; early history, 24–25; exodus of Jews from, 25, 26–27, 38, 240; Hyksos invasion, 24–25; adoption of Moses, 26; revolution against Amenhotep IV, 29; judicial code, 33; return of Jeroboam from, 44; Assyrian attack, 47; invasion of Judah by, 49; pro-Egyptian party in Judah, 50; alliance of Judah with, 50; conquest by Cambyses of Persia, 60; liberation of Israelites from, 72; seizure by Ptolemy, 74; invasion by Antiochus III, 77; attacks by Antiochus Epiphanes, 79; conquest by Julius Caesar, 88; rebellion of Jews, 102; position of Jews in, 111; Jews of, 163; conquest by Muhammadans (A.D. 641), 194; defeat of Mongols (1303), 196; annexation by Ottoman Turks, 196; settlement of Spanish Jews in, 229; nonexistence of capitalism in, 264; invasion of Israel (state), 410; Mameluke rebellion (1250), 414–15; first war against Israel (state), 432; second war against Israel (state), 434–35; Moses chosen to lead Jews out of bondage, 459

Ehrlich, Paul, 342, 350

Eichmann, Adolf Otto, 334n, 400, 402, 405

Einstein, Albert, (1879–1955), 3, 342, 345, 349, 351–52, 355, 460

Eisenhower, Dwight D., 383

Elders, 39, 44

Elders of Zion, 334

*Elements* (Euclid), 199

Elijah ben Solomon (the Vilna Gaon) (1720–97), 357–58

Elisha, prophet, 47

Elizabeth I, English queen, 300, 360

Ellis Island, N.Y., 380

Elman, Mischa, 384

Elohim, as name for God, 19*n*, 28, 31

emancipation, 345

emancipation, Jewish, 300, 307, 314–15, 317, 323, 345, 356, 365

emigration, 321, 373, 398, 413; *see also* immigration; migrations

emperors, 87, 224, 234, 250, 255, 270, 274, 283, 413

*Encyclopedia* (Diderot), 310

Encyclopedists, 200

Engels, Friedrich, 411, 416

England: prestige of, 9; current divorce laws, 35; petition of American colonists to king, 44; as ruler of seas, 59; Benjamin Disraeli prime minister of, 154; becomes European power, 216; and Renaissance, 224; first ritual-murder accusation against Jews, 231; expulsion of Jews from, 231, 236, 258, 299, 303; Jews invited to come to, by William the Conqueror, 231; religious revolt of John Knox, 232; readmission of Jews to, 236, 252; Druids, 240; ritual-murder accusations, 240–41; high status of Jews in, 263; law of claims, 266; petitions for return of Jewish moneylenders, 270; end of medieval Jewish history in, 299; rise of Oliver Cromwell, 302; resettlement of Jews under Cromwell, 303; settlement of Marranos in, 304; Jews in English society, 304; prosperity of Jews in, 309; rebellion of American colonists, 311–12; opposition to French Revolution, 312; challenged by new German state, 314; notable Jews of, 352; colonization in New World, 372; Puritans, 373; and Ottoman Empire, 421; halts Israeli invasion of Egypt, 432; attack on Egypt, 435–36

English language, 112, 356, 363, 375

English people, 304, 314; *see also* British people

Enlightenment, 34, 294, 299, 365, 368, 385, 409

Enlightenment, German, 307–8, 349, 368

Enlightenment, Jewish, 343, 356–59

Enlightenment, Russian, 309

entrepreneurs, 380, 415, 419

Ephesians, 141

Epictetus, 280
Epicurean Greeks, Epicureans ("Apikorsim"), 67, 76–77, 197
Epistles (of Paul), 141
equality, equal rights, 151, 310–11, 312, 315, 353
"Equality, Fraternity, and Liberty," 310
Eric IX, of Sweden, 248
Erlanger, Abraham, 382
Esau, 85
Eskimos, 455
essays, essayists, 360–61
Essenes, 83, 94–97, 128–29, 132, 138
estates, the three, 265
Esterhazy, Ferdinand Walsin, 336–39
Estonia, 393
*Eternal People, The* (Peretz Smolenskin), 417, 421
Ethical Culture, Society for, *see* Society for Ethical Culture
ethical monotheism, 116
ethics, 8, 75, 167–68, 170, 233, 262, 266, 460
ethnarchs, 90
Etruscans, 86
Euclid, 199, 261
Euphrates River, 42
Europe, xi, 8, 65, 74, 89, 102, 148, 153, 164, 167, 176, 180, 183, 198, 200, 209, 216–17, 223, 229, 231–32, 238, 244, 252, 255, 262, 268, 273, 280–81, 283, 285, 289, 291, 294, 299–301, 303, 310, 311–12, 314–15, 331, 342, 347, 353,

369–75, 381–82, 393–94, 409, 426; *see also* Central Europe; Eastern Europe; individual countries; Northern Europe; Southern Europe; Western Europe
European Jews, 232, 356, 368, 375, 391, 399, 427, 458
Europeans, 75, 116
evil, 392
evolution, 54
excommunication, 309, 344, 358
exegesis, biblical, *see* biblical exegesis
exilarchs, 176
exile, 53, 57, 60, 98, 116; *see also* captivity; deportations
"Exiled Jew," 200
existential theologians, 10
existentialism, Jewish, 292, 357, 365–68
Exodus (from Egypt), 25, 33, 38
Exodus (biblical book), 26–27, 32–33, 63, 240
exporters, export trade, 256, 372
expulsions of Jews, 258, 299, 321, 371–72
Eyck, Jan van, 238
Ezekiel, rabbi, 168
Ezra: influence at Persian court, 62; scribe at Persian court, 62; reinstitution of Mosaic law by, 63; heads second mass exodus of

Ezra (*cont.*)
Jews from Babylonia to Jerusalem, 63; collaborator of Nehemiah, 63–64; forbids intermarriage, 63; introduction of Pentateuch by, 64; decrees reading of Pentateuch on Sabbath and during the week, 64; innovations of, 65; decree on reading of the Torah, 118–19; canonization of the Five Books of Moses, 164; decree on interpreters of the Torah, 165; role in Jewish history, 459
Ezra (biblical book), 62, 112

factories, 301, 306, 320, 378
faith, 199, 203, 233, 299, 310, 365–68, 457
false messiahs, *see* messiah
family life, 34, 43, 109–10, 148, 262, 379–80
farming, farmers, 43, 154, 218, 375, 381, 415, 419; *see also* agriculture
fascism, 7, 381, 394
fatalism, fate, 454
Fatimids, 181
Federal Constitution, *see* Constitution, U.S.
federal government (U.S.), 34; *see also* United States
fellahin, 424, 434
Fenno-Scandian countries, 406

Ferdinand, of Spain, 197, 228
Fermi, Enrico, 351
fertility rites, 22, 289
festivals, 136
Fettmilch, Vincent, 252
Feuchtwanger, Lion, 274
Feudal Age, feudalism, 8, 42, 149, 163, 173, 180, 215, 218–20, 230, 234, 236, 253–54, 265, 268–69, 276, 293, 305, 308, 313, 317, 327, 329, 372, 377, 394, 424–25, 453
Fêz, North Africa, 181
Fichte, Johann Gottlieb, 331, 392
fiction, 360, 364
finance, financiers, 3, 273–74, 293, 303–4, 353–54, 372
finance ministers, 197, 256, 316, 352
Finland, Finns, 48, 153, 393, 406
First Zionist Congress, Basel, Switzerland (1897), 419
Five Books of Moses, 25, 27–28, 40, 63, 112, 164–65, 181, 205; *see also* Pentateuch; Torah
Flavius Josephus, *see* Josephus
Florence, Italy, 269
Florus, Roman procurator, 96
Ford, Henry, 7, 453
foreign ministers, 316
foreigners, 380
Fould, Achille, 352

*Foundations of the Nineteenth Century* (H. S. Chamberlain), 333
founding fathers (U.S.), 40
Four Gospels, *see* Gospels
"Fourth Estate" (Jews), 254
Fourth Lateran Council (1215), 220, 230
Fra Filippo Lippi, *see* Lippi, Fra Filippo
France, 149, 163, 178, 215, 218, 225–26, 229, 231, 236, 242, 248, 252, 263, 270, 299, 304, 309, 310–13, 316–17, 319, 333–34, 336–40, 342*n*, 352, 372, 405–6, 411, 423; expulsion of the Jews from, 231, 236, 258, 299
franchise, 433, 434; *see also* vote
Francis, emperor of Austria, 314
Frank, Casimar, 383
Frank, Eve (died in 1817), 288
Frank, Jacob (1726–91), 286–88, 290
Frankfurt, Germany, 252
Frankfurter, Felix, 383
Frankism, Frankists, 286–90
Franklin, Benjamin, 271, 412
Franks, 216, 218
fraternity, 310
Frederick I, Barbarossa (1152–90), German emperor, 250
Frederick William, of Prussia (1640–88), 306
Fredericks, of Hohenzollern, founders of modern Prussia, 306
Frederick II, of Germany, 198, 224, 241
free enterprise, 271, 302, 327–28, 375
free men, freemen, 35, 44, 108, 254
free trade, 327
free will, 11
freedom, 26, 30, 45, 86, 108, 169, 174, 208, 254–55, 305, 306, 311, 314–17, 345, 374
freedom, cultural, *see* cultural freedom
freedom of assembly, *see* assembly, freedom of
freedom of religion, *see* religious freedom
freedom, political, *see* political freedom
French, the, 194, 225, 314, 317, 332, 393, 431
French Jews, 279, 312–13, 317
French language, 75, 178, 179, 253, 356
French Republic, 310–13
French Revolution, 10, 309, 310–12, 323, 411
Freud, Sigmund (1856–1939), 3–4, 8–9, 29–30, 31, 36, 342, 345, 348–49, 355, 366, 460
Friedlaender, Israel, 360–61
Frisians, 216
Frohman brothers, 382
Fromm, Erich, 11*n*
fundamentalism, 19–20
funerals, 319, 322
furriers, 260

Gabriel, angel, 192
Gaer, Joseph, xiv
Galatians, 141
Galileans, 84, 93, 97–98
Galilee, 83, 92, 93, 95, 97, 132
Galileo Galilei, 225, 278, 280
Gamaliel, Rabban, 137
Gamaliel II, 175
Gamaliel VI (died in 425), 175
Gaonim, 176–77, 206, 208
Garibaldi, Giuseppe, 315–16
Gauguin, Paul, 201
Gaul, Gauls, 86, 100, 149, 154
Gaza Strip, 436–37
Geiger, Abraham (1810–74), 385
Gemara, 168, 173, 179–80, 309; see also Talmud
generals, 342
Genesis (biblical book), 21–22, 27, 64
Genghis Khan, 196, 414
Genizah, 128
Genoa, Italy, 223; expulsion of Jews from, 231
gentiles, gentile world, 6, 30, 120, 217, 219, 236, 259, 262, 269, 308–9, 323, 347, 380, 387–88
geography, 278
geometry, 350
Georgia, 374
German Enlightenment, see Enlightenment, German
German Jews, 246, 304, 307–8, 316–17, 345, 346,

365, 370, 374–75, 379, 385, 398, 425, 427, 434
German Judaism, 252–53
German language, 208, 255, 273, 308, 356, 362, 375
German law, 266
German Reform movement, see Reform Judaism
German States, Confederation of, 316
Germans, 208, 233, 245, 246, 250–52, 314, 316–17, 332, 335, 391–93, 396–97, 402–5, 407–9, 421, 431
Germany, 86, 148, 163, 178, 216–17, 218, 223, 226, 231–32, 236, 240, 246, 250–51, 255, 258, 263, 299, 301, 304, 309, 314, 316–17, 326–27, 331, 335, 340–41, 342n, 353, 382, 385, 391–95, 396–99, 403–9, 426; expulsion of the Jews from states of, 231, 236
Gershwin, George, 383
Gerson, Levi ben, see Levi ben Gerson
Gerth, H. H., 42n
ghettos, 7, 164, 182, 220, 231, 236–37, 255, 258–60, 262–63, 268, 274, 299, 301, 304–8, 313, 315, 316, 323, 342–43, 345, 355, 359, 364, 385, 398, 403–4, 453
Ghiberti, Lorenzo, 238
Gibbon, Edward, 43, 145–47, 222n, 414

Ginsburg, Christian D., 130
girls, 119
Giving of the Law, see Law, Giving of the
glass-manufacturing, 268
Glubb, John, 430
gnostics, 277
Gobineau, Arthur de, 331–32
God, 11, 17, 19–22, 27–37, 40–41, 54–55, 58, 74, 81, 104, 109, 111, 114, 118–19, 139–40, 142, 163–64, 166, 177, 191–92, 200, 203, 239, 277, 281, 289–91, 299, 308, 311, 312, 331, 344, 349, 357, 366–68, 373, 386, 390, 414, 454, 459
God, Kingdom of, see Kingdom of God
God, Law of, see Law, the; Torah
God, Word of, see Law, the; Torah
gods and goddesses, 11, 21–22, 29, 36, 38, 47, 73, 76–77, 109, 152, 239
Goebbels, Joseph, 403–5
Goering, Hermann, 396
Goethe, Johann Wolfgang von, 342, 355, 392
Gogol, Nikolai, 360
Gold Rush, 376
Golden Rule, 35
goldsmiths, 191, 256, 260
Gomer, wife of Hosea, 286
Gompers, Samuel, 384
Goodman, Benny, 383
Gospels (New Testament), 25, 100, 131–38, 141, 143, 145, 147, 175, 217, 333; see also Synoptic Gospels
Goths, 148–49, 218
government, governments, 5, 21, 34, 40–41, 44, 62–63, 65, 149–50, 163, 170, 174, 177, 196, 246, 266, 306, 310, 319, 328, 354, 379, 380–81
governors, 383
Goya, Francisco José de, 342
grammarians, grammars, 170, 200, 208
grammars, Hebrew, 118
Grand Mufti of Jerusalem, 426
Granicus River, battle of, 73
Great Sanhedrin (of Napoleon), 313; see also Sanhedrin
Greco-Roman, 5, 39, 63, 68–70, 107, 109–12, 197, 263, 342, 386
Greece and the Greeks, xi–xii, 3, 4–5, 8, 17, 22, 38, 39–40, 45, 60, 66, 71–77, 79, 86, 87, 88–89, 93, 107–13, 114–15, 116–17, 163, 165–66, 173, 175–76, 191, 194, 198–99, 202, 220, 222, 239, 253, 264, 279, 314, 360, 385, 407, 414, 453; see also Hellenic world
Greek language, 5, 73, 75–76, 111, 198, 202, 224, 373
Greek Orthodox Catholics, Greek Orthodox Church, 221, 247, 248, 319

Greek philosophers and philosophy, 76, 108, 113–15, 165, 181, 183, 197, 343

Greek religion, 109–10

Gregory the Great, Pope (A.D. 591), 220

Group Theatre, 382

Guggenheim family, 376

*Guide to the Perplexed* (Moses Maimonides), 181

guilt, 335

Gulf of Akaba, *see* Akaba, Gulf of

gymnasiums, 75

*Habakkuk Commentary* (Dead Sea Scrolls), 128–29

Haber, Fritz, 351

Hadas, Moses, 198

Hadrian, Roman emperor (A.D. 117), 103–5, 167, 175, 413

Haganah, 426

Haggadah, 25

Haimo, Franklin, xiii

*Ha-Kuzari* (Judah Halevi), 202

Halacha ("law"), 170

Halevi, Judah, *see* Judah Halevi

half Jews, 343

Hamilton, Alexander, 167, 412

Hammerstein, Oscar, II, 383

Hammurabi: as king and lawgiver of Babylonia, 18; unites city-states into Babylonian Empire, 18; Code of, 33

Han dynasty, 148

handicrafts, 191

handiwork, 328

Hannibal, 100

Hanseatic League, 268

Hanukkah, 79–80

Haran, 19, 189

harems, 43, 192

Harvard University, 163, 373

Hasidean party, Hasideans, 77, 82, 93, 289*n*

Hasidism, 289–92, 346, 357–59, 364, 453

Hasidists, 77, 356–58, 366

Haskala (Jewish "Enlightenment"), 292, 356–59, 362–65, 377, 387, 409, 413, 417, 433, 459

Hasmoneans, 80, 81, 90–91, 94, 112, 208

hat, wearing of in synagogue, 346

Hazor, 38

head tax, 195

heart therapy, 350

heathenism, heathens, *see* paganism, pagans

heaven, 95, 122, 290

Hebraism, 224

Hebrew language, 5, 27, 31, 40, 64, 112, 118, 168, 178, 200, 208, 224, 230, 242, 253, 261, 357–64, 368, 373, 386, 417

Hebrew literature, *see* literature, Hebrew

Hebrew Union College, Cincinnati, 385

Hebrews, 19, 22–23, 27–29, 32–33, 38, 301

hedonism, hedonists, 71, 76–77, 109, 197, 257

Hegel, Georg Wilhelm
  Friedrich, 9, 342, 392
Heifetz, Jascha, 384
Heine, Heinrich, 238, 342
hell, 95, 269, 291
Hellas, *see* Greece
Hellenic-Roman world, 99
Hellenic world, Hellenists,
  Hellenizers, 5, 71–72,
  73, 75–79, 82–83, 93,
  108–9, 113, 122,
  165–66, 197–99, 204,
  208, 257; *see also*
  Greece
Hellman, Lillian, 383
Henry the Navigator, 371
Henry, Joseph, 339
hereafter, 148, 270, 348
heresy, heretics, 150–52,
  164, 166, 204–8,
  225–26, 230, 244–46,
  248, 282, 286–87, 300,
  326
Herod Antipas, 132
Herod the Great: an
  Idumean, 84; son of
  Antipater, 90; ap-
  pointed king of the
  Jews by Octavian, 91;
  murder of Hyrcanus II
  by, 91; defeats
  Antigonus, 91; cap-
  tures Jerusalem, 91;
  murder of the two
  sons of Mariamne by,
  92; Samaritan wife of,
  92; year rule of, 93;
  Agrippa I, grandson
  of, 96; birth of Jesus
  during reign of, 131
Herodotus, 50
Herschel, William, 350

Herzl, Theodor
  (1860–1904), 418–21
Hess, Moses (1812–75),
  416–17, 421
hevras ("societies"), 319
Heydersdorff, Marshal,
  Duke of Wolfenbüttel,
  274–75
Heydrich, Reinhard Tristan
  Eugen, 396
hieroglyphics, Egyptian, 18,
  24
High Priests, 55, 62, 74,
  78–79, 81, 90, 96, 136;
  *see also* priesthood,
  priests
Hillel, 35, 167, 418
Hillel, house of, 175
Hillel, school of, 167
Hillman, Sidney, 384
Himmler, Heinrich, 396
Hindenburg, Paul von, 395
Hindus, 4
historians, 98, 107, 189, 215,
  272
history, xi–xii, 4–5, 7–12, 39,
  42, 52–54, 59–60, 107,
  174, 189, 209, 216, 220,
  231, 252, 293, 299, 310,
  314–15, 341–42, 368,
  415, 453–57
history, Jewish, 10–11, 17,
  20, 22–23, 24–25, 45,
  52–53, 56, 58–59,
  95–96, 98, 105–6, 122,
  163, 173–74, 179–80,
  200, 204, 209, 215, 220,
  228–29, 229–32, 234,
  239, 248, 253, 255–56,
  265, 273, 276, 281, 289,
  292, 299–300, 317–18,
  319–20, 323, 333, 356,

history, Jewish (*cont.*) 359, 369–73, 385–86, 392, 408–9, 453–54, 457

*History of Jewish Sermons* (Zunz), 345–46

*History of the Jewish War* (Josephus), 98

Hitler, Adolf, 167, 247, 323, 326, 329, 351, 381, 389, 391–92, 395–98, 405, 407–8, 425

Hittites, 4, 53

Hobbes, Thomas, 411

*Hofjuden* (Court Jews), 274; *see also* Court Jews

holidays, 25

holiness, 109

Holland, 229, 232, 263, 302, 342*n*, 406; *see also* Netherlands, the

Holy Alliance, 315, 317

Holy Land, *see* Palestine

Holy Roman Empire, 250, 274, 291

Holy Scripture, *see* Bible; Old Testament; Scriptures

homosexuality, 36, 257

Honorius, Roman emperor, 147

Horeb, *see* Mount Horeb

Horowitz, Vladimir, 384

Hosea, prophet, 57, 286

hospitals, 379

Host-desecration libels, 220, 240, 241–42, 245, 250, 262

Hottentots, 455

House of Commons (England), 154

House of David, *see* Davidic house

House of Lords (England), 39

House of Representatives (U.S.), 39

Huguenots, 232

human rights, 167; *see also* rights of man

human sacrifice, *see* sacrifice, human

humanism, humanists, 35, 180–83, 223, 263, 277, 331, 335–36, 349, 356–57, 359, 368, 392, 409, 459

humanitarianism, 35

humanities, 352, 354

humanity, 57, 311

Hungarian Jews, 418

Hungary, Hungarians, 105–6, 263, 380, 394, 398, 406

Huns, 122, 148, 154, 194, 216

Hussein, Saddam, 448–49

Huss, John (1415), 204, 232

hygiene, 170

Hyksos, 24

hymns, 178

Hyrcanus I, *see* John Hyrcanus

Hyrcanus II, 85–86, 90

Iannaccone, Laurence, xiii

Ibn Daud, 198

ibn Latif, Abraham (1220–90), 278–79

Iceland, 217

idealism, idealists, 183, 233

idolatry, idols, 21, 43, 54, 80, 120; *see also* images

Idumea, 84, 90, 97

Idumeans, 84, 90, 132
ignorance, 216, 254, 290, 320, 358
illiteracy, 71, 85, 169, 182, 192, 254, 317, 320
images, 37; *see also* idolatry
Immanuel Bonfils, *see* Bonfils, Immanuel
immersion, 95
immigration, immigrants, 321, 323, 352, 370, 374–82, 384, 415–16, 421, 426–27; *see also* emigration; migrations
immorality, 10, 76–77, 148
immortality, 94, 344
imperialism, 183, 300
importers, import trade, 256, 267–68, 372
incest, 120, 132
indebtedness, *see* debt
India, 92, 115, 148, 264, 268, 352, 371
Indian Ocean, 60
Indians, 371, 434
individualism, 34, 43, 200, 360, 367
Indus River, 60
Industrial Revolution, 252, 314, 328
industry, industrialization, 7, 18, 43, 46, 63, 75, 153, 234, 263, 264, 267–68, 301, 318, 347, 351, 370, 375, 411
*Inequality of Human Races, The* (de Gobineau), 332
infanticide, 108, 119
injustice, 146, 150–51
Innocent III, Pope (A.D. 1215), 220, 230

Inquisition, 225–29, 255, 284, 300, 315, 326, 371–72
intellectualism, intellectuals, 36, 65, 89, 110, 116–17, 155, 163, 208, 230, 237, 251, 256, 261–62, 290, 310, 317, 341–42, 351, 359, 365, 368, 369–70, 379–80, 381, 383, 384, 411, 416, 458
intelligentsia, 306
interest, 266, 268–70, 303–4
interfaith relations, 390
intermarriage, 23, 43, 63, 73, 111, 119–20, 152, 313, 361, 375, 385
intermediary, intermediation, 58
international law, *see* law, international
international trade, *see* trade
*Interpretation of Dreams* (Freud), 348
interpretation of the Torah, 164–65, 168, 459–60
intolerance, 169
intuition, 344
Iranic culture, 9
Iraq, 17, 196, 410, 423
Ireland, 302
Irgun, 428
Irish people, 191
Isaac (patriarch), 22, 27, 32, 38, 85
Isaacs, Rufus Daniel (Marquis of Reading), 352
Isabella of Spain, 197, 228
Isaiah, prophet, 50, 57, 86, 200, 458–59

Ishmael, 3, 85
Islam, Islamic civilization, 6, 9–10, 41, 54, 63, 118, 155, 163, 173, 176–77, 189–91, 193, 195–96, 203, 204–5, 209, 229, 244, 253, 457; *see also* Muhammadanism
Israel (country), 37–38
Israel (Jacob), 27*n*
Israel (people), Israelites, 3, 18, 23, 27–28, 32–34, 38, 44, 46–49, 52, 58, 72, 118, 240, 367
Israel (modern state), Israelis, 8, 38, 60, 190, 210, 300, 323, 357, 389, 409, 410, 412–13, 420–21, 428–41, 442–43, 457
Israel ben Eliezer (Bal Shem Tov) (*c.* 1700–60), 289–91
Israel, Kingdom of, 26–27, 31, 42–50, 53, 57, 72, 93; *see also* Ten Tribes, Kingdom of the
Israeli War of Independence (1948–49), 426–33
Issus, battle of (334 B.C.), 73
Italian language, 253, 356, 363
Italian Renaissance, 340
Italian Republic, 315
Italian Supreme Court, *see* Supreme Court (of Italy)
Italy, Italians, 4, 45, 86, 149, 163, 178, 215–16, 218, 223, 225, 229, 231, 236, 255–58, 267–68, 270, 283, 314–16, 342*n*, 406
Italy, expulsion of Jews from several states of, 236
Italy, Kingdom of (1861), 316
Ivriim (Hebrews), 19

"J" document, 31, 46, 55
Jabneh, 100, 106, 117, 167
Jabotinsky, Vladimir (1880–1940), 425–26, 433
Jacob (patriarch), 22, 27, 32, 38, 85, 128
Jacob, Master, 371
Jacobi, Karl, 350
"Jacob's staff," 279
Jacomo de Majorca, *see* Cresques, Judah
Jadwiga, Polish queen, 217
Jagiello, Grand Duke of Lithuania, 217
"Jahveh" (Lord), 19*n*
James, brother of Jesus, 137, 140
James I of Aragon, 244
Janneus, Alexander, *see* Alexander Janneus
Japan, Japanese, 75, 381*n*
Jason, high priest and Hellenizer, 78
jazz music, 383
"JE" document, 31
Jebusites, 38, 42, 53
Jefferson, Thomas, 39, 167, 331, 412
Jehoash, king of Judah, 49
Jehoram, king of Judah, 49
Jehovah, 11, 17, 19–23, 26, 31, 56, 65, 80, 103, 116,

163, 177, 200, 203, 239, 252, 289, 362, 453, 459–60; *see also* Elohim; God; JHVH

Jehovah Elohim, 31

Jehu: king of Israel, 47; revolt of, 47; his murder of Ahaziah, 49

Jeremiah, prophet, 57

Jerez, Roderigo de, 371

Jeroboam, first king of Israel, 44

Jerusalem: expulsion of Jews from, 6; Temple in, 28, 41, 58; made political capital of Palestine by David, 41; and Jebusites and Philistines, 42; surrender to Babylonians, 51–52; destruction of, by Babylonians, 51; restoration to, 60; Jews permitted to return to, 60–61; renewed prosperity of, 61; second mass exodus to, from Babylonia, 61, 65; Jeshua anointed ruler of, 62; Nehemiah rebuilds walls of, 63; destruction of Temple by Romans, 65; destruction of, by Romans, 66, 168, 326, 459; visit of Alexander the Great, 73; represented at Greek games, 78; slaughter of Jews by Antiochus Epiphanes, 79; pagans invited to settle in, 79; recapture by Maccabees, 80; Simon the Maccabee high priest of, 81; destruction of, 82; preaching of Jesus in, 83; Jerusalem passes under the control of Rome, 88; capital of independent Palestine under Antigonus, 91; capture of, by Herod, 91; siege of, by Romans, 97–102; destruction of, by Titus, 100–101; forbidden to Jews by Romans, 105, 109; departure of Jochanan ben Zakkai from, 98–100, 106; art and culture, 116–17; as a cultural center, 117; sojourn of Jesus in, 132, 133–34; journey of Paul to, 139; promise of Julian the Apostate to restore, 151; view held by Judah Halevi, 203; fulfillment of Jewish destiny in, 203; capture of, by Crusaders, 223; return of Jews to, after death of Hadrian, 413; capture of, by Napoleon, 415; capture by Arabs (1948), 430

Jeshua, high priest, 61

Jesuits, 274

Jesus Christ, 3, 19, 25, 30, 35, 82, 83, 95, 104, 127–42, 147, 150, 152, 164, 175, 189, 192–93, 219, 231, 233, 239, 241, 290, 335, 373, 414, 460

Jethro, Midianite priest and father-in-law of Moses, 26

Jew-baiters, *see* anti-Semitism; persecution of Jews

Jew Cities, *see* Judenstädte

jewelers, jewelry trade, 218, 302, 306

Jewish Age of Reason, *see* Age of Reason, Jewish

Jewish Agency for Palestine, 428

Jewish-Christian relationships, 127

Jewish Christians, 96–97, 142, 151

Jewish existentialism, *see* existentialism, Jewish

Jewish history, *see* history, Jewish

Jewish law, 74–75, 136, 164

Jewish life, *see* life

*Jewish Life in the Middle Ages* (Abrahams), 260

Jewish literature, *see* literature, Jewish

Jewish mission, *see* mission, Jewish

Jewish National Fund, 421

Jewish Notables, National Assembly of, *see* National Assembly of Jewish Notables

Jewish people, *see* Israel (people); Jews

Jewish quarter, 255, 258–59

Jewish religion, *see* Judaism

Jewish Renaissance, *see* Renaissance, Jewish

Jewish schools, *see* schools

Jewish sects, *see* sects, Jewish

"Jewish state," "Jewish states," 308, 313, 318, 409

*Jewish State, The* (*Der Judenstaat*) (Herzl), 419–21

Jewish survival, *see* survival, Jewish

Jewish Theological Seminary of America, New York, 387

Jews, Jewish people, xi–xii, 3–7, 11, 21–23, 24–30, 34–41, 51, 53, 55–65, 71–82, 85, 88–96, 97–106, 107–15, 115–22, 128, 131, 132–33, 135–40, 146, 150–55, 163–70, 173–83, 189–95, 197–203, 204–7, 209, 215–33, 236–39, 239–51, 252–63, 263–76, 281, 287–94, 299–323, 325–27, 330–34, 338, 341–46, 349–55, 356–68, 369–90, 391–409, 410–33, 453–60

*Jews and Modern Capitalism, The* (Sombart), 273*n*, 353

Jezebel: a Sidonite princess, 46; marriage to Ahab, king of Israel, 46–47; mother of Athaliah, 49

*"JHVH,"* 19*n*

*"JHVH Elohim,"* 19*n*

Joan of Arc, 40

Job (biblical book), 202

Jochanan ben Zakkai, 98–100, 106, 117–18, 167

Jodl, Alfred, 405

John (New Testament gospel), 114*n*, 132
John the Baptist, 82, 95, 128, 132
John of Gisela, 100*n*
John Hyrcanus (Hyrcanus I): son of Simon the Maccabee, 83; crowned king and anointed high priest, 83; plunders tomb of David, 84; member of party of Pharisees, 84; and Sadducees, 84; introduces Hellenizing measures, 84; conquest of Idumean and Galilean territory by, 84; conversion of Idumeans and Galileans to Judaism, 84, 93; father of Aristobulus I, 84
John II, of Portugal, 371
John III, of Portugal, 283
Jordan (state), 435; *see also* Transjordan
Jordan River, 38
Joseph, son of Jacob, 22–23, 27–28, 32, 38
Joseph ben Mattathias, *see* Josephus
Joseph II, emperor of Austria, 305–6, 317
Josephus (Flavius Josephus), 95, 97–98, 130, 137
Joshua, 38, 44, 52, 164, 459
Josiah, king of Judah, 54–55, 65, 453
Jossl of Rosheim, 274
journalism, journalists, 383–84, 418

Judah (country), 38
Judah Halevi, 201, 361, 459
Judah Hanasi, 167–68
Judah, Kingdom of: Temple of, 28; place of origin of "J" documents, 31; government of king of Judah, 44; Rehoboam the ruler of, 44; history of, 45, 49; invasion of, by Egypt, 49; influence of Isaiah in, 50; invasion of, by Assyrians, 50; Zedekiah the last king of, 51; destruction of, by Babylonians, 52, 116–17, 370, 453; survival of the Jews of, 53; Prophets' preaching in, 57; and Persian nontolerance, 62; Nehemiah appointed governor of, 62–63; reestablishment of, by Maccabees, 81; conquest by Pompey, 85–86, 88, 90, 215; rulership of Rome over, 88; relations of Assyria and Babylonia to, 93; *see also* Two Tribes, Kingdom of the
Judaism, xii, 3, 6, 11, 20, 23, 25, 32, 35, 41, 53–54, 57, 62, 75, 82, 93, 99–100, 110, 111–15, 118, 121, 134, 140, 151, 153, 163, 166, 170, 176, 181–83, 191, 197, 200, 202, 204–5, 209, 218, 226–27, 242–44,

Judaism (*cont.*)
  252–53, 276, 283,
  288–89, 292, 301,
  307–9, 323, 346, 357,
  259–60, 365–66,
  384–91, 392, 418–19,
  453, 457–60
Judaism, Conservative, *see*
  Conservative Judaism
Judaism, Diaspora, *see* Diaspora
Judaism, Orthodox, *see* Orthodox Judaism
Judaism, Palestinian, *see*
  Palestinian Judaism
Judaism, Reform, *see* Reform Judaism
Judaism, Talmudic, *see* Talmudic Judaism
Judea, 38, 86, 90–93, 97, 98,
  102, 105, 122, 131, 138,
  300, 456
*Judenstaat, Der* (Herzl),
  419, 421
*Judenstädte* (Jew Cities),
  255–56
Judeo-Christian relation-
  ships, 215, 324
judges, 39, 40, 43, 62, 154,
  176, 218, 312, 353, 373;
  *see also* judiciary
Judgment Day, 292; *see also*
  Last Judgment
judiciary, 34, 319; *see also*
  judges
Julian "the Apostate,"
  Roman emperor (A.D.
  361), 151
Julius Caesar, *see* Caesar,
  Julius
Julius Severus, *see* Severus,
  Julius

Junkers, 395
Jupiter (Roman god), 88,
  103
jurisprudence, 170, 180
jurists, 170, 383
jury, 74
justice, 33, 39, 55, 57, 74, 87,
  133, 163, 183, 345,
  390–91, 409, 460
justices (and chief justices),
  353
Justinian, Laws of (A.D.
  531), 152–53, 220

Kabala, Kabalism, Kabal-
  ists, 224, 276–82,
  282–88, 293, 344, 415,
  453, 459
Kaifeng, China, 458
kaisers (of Germany), 316,
  392–93
Kant, Immanuel, 307
*Kapital, Das, see Das Kapi-
  tal* (Marx)
Karaism, Karaites, 204–9,
  285, 288, 292, 453, 457
Karkar, 47
Karl Alexander (Duke
  Charles I), of Würt-
  temberg, 274
Karl XII, of Sweden, 194
Kashruth, 171
Kaufman, George S., 383
Keats, John, 342, 355
Kepler, Johannes, 279–80
Kern, Jerome, 383
Khazar, Kingdom of, 202
Khazars, 202–3
Khlysti sect, of Russia, 322
kidnapers, military (in Rus-
  sia), 318
Kierkegaard, Søren, 167

Kiev, Russia, 202
Kingdom of God, 132, 207
Kingdom of Israel, *see* Israel, Kingdom of
Kingdom of Judah, *see* Judah, Kingdom of
Kingdom of the Ten Tribes, *see* Ten Tribes, Kingdom of the
Kingdom of the Two Tribes, *see* Two Tribes, Kingdom of the
kings, kingship, 32, 41–45, 49–50, 54–55, 58, 62, 246, 255, 265, 272, 273–74, 284, 299, 310, 311–12; *see also* monarchy; rulers
Kingsley, Sidney, 383
Kinnanhorra (medieval Jewish superstition), 277
Kish, a Mesopotamian city-state, 17
Kishinev, Russia, 361
Kissinger, Henry, 448
Klausner, Erich, 397
Knesseth (parliament of Israel), 65
Knox, John, 232
Koran, 192, 205
kosher foods, *see* Kashruth
Koussevitzky, Serge, 384
Kraeling, Carl H., 76*n*
Kronecker, Leopold, 350
*Kuzari* (Judah Halevi), *see* Ha-Kuzari

labor, laborers, 43, 87, 235, 265, 377–78, 380, 415, 424; *see also* workers
labor leaders, 381

*La France juive* (Drumont), 333–34
land, 220, 237, 246, 254, 265, 318, 320, 378, 420
land, law of the, *see* law of the land
landholders, 317, 424
landless class, 43
landlords, 259, 263
La Ronciere, Charles de, *see* Ronciere, Charles de La
Lassalle, Ferdinand, 353
Last Judgment, 303; *see also* Judgment Day
Last Supper, 129
Lateran Councils, 220, 230
Latin, 5, 198, 208, 224, 225, 242, 277–79, 301
Latvia, 393
law, laws, 5, 32–33, 46, 74–75, 170, 177, 180–81, 207, 309, 319
Law, American, *see* American legal system
law, civil, *see* civil law
law codes, 18, 33, 459
Law, Giving of the, 32, 37
law, international, 267
law, Jewish, *see* Jewish law
Law, Mosaic, *see* Mosaic Law
law, natural, *see* natural law
Law of God, *see* Law, the; Torah
law of the land, 119–20, 313–14
Law, Oral, *see* Oral Law
Law, Reading of the, *see* Reading of the Law
law, religious, 308–9
law, Roman, *see* Roman law

law schools, 379–80
Law, the, 32, 39, 94, 163, 242, 459; *see also* Mosaic Law; Torah
Law, Written, *see* Written Law
Lawrence, T. E. (Lawrence of Arabia), 423, 430
laws, 118, 119–20, 219–20, 266
laws, anti-Jewish, *see* anti-Jewish laws; discrimination
laws, discriminatory, *see* discrimination
lawyers, 380
laymen, laity, 166, 240
League of Nations, 127
learning, 65, 99–100, 106, 163–69, 177–78, 227, 233, 237, 251, 260–62, 293, 354–55, 379–80, 386; *see also* scholars; scholarship; study
Lebanon, 410, 423
Lebanese, 190
LeBert, Gordon, xiii
Lecky, W.E.H., 261, 268
legalism, 167, 366
legislation, restrictive, *see* discrimination
Lehman, Herbert H., 383
Lehmann, Lotte, 352
Leibnitz, Gottfried Wilhelm von, 279–80
Lemmlin, Asher (1502), 282
Lenin, Vladimir Ilyich, 10, 412
Leonardo da Vinci, 223, 239
Lessing, Gotthold, 307

letters, *see* literature
Levi, tribe, 26
Levi ben Gerson, 279
Levi-Civita, Tullio, 350
Levites, 28
Leviticus (biblical book), 32, 63
liberalism, liberals, 83, 167, 199, 309, 317, 320, 322–23, 330
liberty, *see* "Equality, Fraternity, and Liberty"; freedom
libraries, 280
life, 164–65, 170, 174, 179, 182, 204–5, 209, 220, 224, 227, 230, 245, 249, 252–56, 258, 281, 306, 314, 317, 323, 359
linguistics, linguists, 194, 200
Linnaeus, Swedish botanist (1707–78), 54
Lipman, Jacob, 383
Lippi, Fra Filippo, 223
literature, xii, 3, 5, 24, 71, 89, 108, 111, 154, 198–99, 204, 252, 257, 308, 355, 359, 362–63, 369, 392
literature, ecclesiastical, 253
literature, Hebrew, 224, 278, 359–61
literature, Jewish, 252, 345–46, 356–59
literature, rabbinic, 345
literature, secular, 253, 308, 362
literature, Yiddish, 362–63
Lithuania, 209, 217, 232, 246, 249, 263, 309, 357, 393

Lithuanian Jews, 248, 363
liturgy, 65, 118, 151, 278, 386
loans, 267, 273, 353
Locke, John, 279–80, 331, 411
logic, 114–15, 166, 199, 261, 278, 355
Logos, 114
lords, 254, 268
Loronha, Fernando de, 371
Lot, nephew of Abraham, 18
Louis XIII, of France, 304
Louis XIV, of France, 304
Louis XV, of France, 304
Louis XVI, of France, 304, 310
Louisville, Ky., 375
love, 6, 108, 197, 359
Lovers of Zion, 417
lower class, 332
Lower East Side (New York), 379
Lucena, Spain, 201
Ludendorff, Erich von, 394–95
Luke (New Testament gospel), 131–32
lullabies, 178
Lully, Raymond, 278–79
Luria, Isaac (1534–72), 279
Luther, Martin, 11, 58, 138, 179, 204, 207, 208, 232–33, 235, 243, 251, 302, 363
Lutherans, Lutheranism, 153, 207, 233, 258, 272
Luzzatti, Luigi, 316
Lyra, Nicholas de, see Nicholas de Lyra

Maccabees: revolt against Antiochus Epiphanes, 80, 93; conquest of the Maccabean Kingdom of Judah by Pompey, 86; Mariamne, Maccabean princess, 92; strife under, 453
Macedonian Wars, 86–87
McMahon, Arthur Henry, 423
Madison, James, 412
Magdeburg, Germany, 232–33, 250
Magellan, Ferdinand, 279
Magii (6th century), 169
magistrates, 154
Magna Carta, 41
Magyars, 305
Mahler, Gustav, 342
Maidanek, 403
Maimonides, Moses (Moses ben Maimon) (1135–1204), 178, 180–83, 227, 267, 343, 344, 459
Mainz, Germany, 250
Mainz, University of, 251
maize, 371
Majorca, 371
Malachi, prophet, 57
Mamelukes, 414–15
man, mankind, 3, 8–9, 10, 33–34, 41, 56–58, 76, 108, 140, 166, 200, 239, 290, 299, 331, 342, 344, 347, 366–67, 454–55, 460
man, dignity of, see dignity of man
man, rights of, see rights of man

Manasseh ben Israel, 302
Mandate, Palestinian, *see* Palestine Mandate
Manichaeans, 153
Manne, Henry G., xiii
Mannerheim, Karl Gustav, 406
manners, 253, 257
*Manual of Discipline* (Dead Sea Scrolls), 128–29
Manuel the Great (of Portugal), 371
manufacturers, 318, 380
Marat, Jean Paul, 311, 411–12
Marathon, battle at (490 B.C.), 72
Marco Polo, 267, 458
Marcus Aurelius Antoninus, Roman emperor, 167, 279–80
Marcus, Jacob R., xiii
Maria Theresa, Austrian empress, 287–88, 305
Mariamne, wife of Herod, 92
Maritain, Jacques, 10
Mark (New Testament gospel), 100*n*
Marr, Wilhelm, 324*n*
Marranos, 226–29, 283, 301, 304, 326, 371–72, 415, 458
marriage, marriage laws, 35–36, 95, 139, 148, 154, 168, 254, 313
Marx, Karl (1818–83), 3, 342, 345, 346–48, 355, 411, 416, 460
Marxism, Marxists, 8, 150, 189, 230, 347–48, 453

Maryland, 374
Massachusetts, 374
Massachusetts Bay Colony, 373
masses, the, 310, 317, 321, 328, 359, 364
materialism, 94, 110, 271, 455
mathematicians, mathematics, 3, 116, 170, 183, 194, 197, 256, 261, 278, 308, 342, 349, 455
Mattathias, the Hasmonean, 79–81, 86
Matthew (New Testament gospel), 91, 131–32
matzos, 240
Maurois, André, 342
mayors, 316
Mazzini, Giuseppe (died in 1872), 315–16, 331
Mecca, Arabia, 190–91, 193
mechanics, 261, 383
Medes, 59–60
Media, 60
medical schools, 379–80
Medici, 45
medicine, 3, 170, 194, 207, 256, 320, 342, 350
medieval period, medieval world, *see* Middle Ages
Medina, Arabia, 191, 193
Medina, Solomon, 303
Mediterranean Sea and seaports, 52, 60, 193, 267, 301
Meir, Golda, 441
Meitner, Lise, 351
Mendele Mocher Sforim (1836–1917), 363
Mendelssohn, Felix, 342

Mendelssohn, Moses (1729–86), 307, 311, 345

Menuhin, Yehudi, 384

mercantilism, 234–35, 327

*Merchant of Venice* (Shakespeare), 238

merchants, merchant class, 154, 218, 220, 236, 254, 256, 318, 372, 375

mercy, 133, 163

Mesopotamia, 17–18

Messiah, messianism, 40, 82, 94–95, 103–4, 129, 133, 141, 151, 164, 189, 204–7, 244, 281–86, 289–91, 359, 419, 459

messiahs, false, *see* Messiah

metal workers, 256

metaphysics, metaphysicians, 113–15, 253, 261, 277–81

methodology, 278–79

Metternich, Prince Klemens Wenzel Nepomuk Lothar von, 317

Michelangelo, 25, 223, 239

Michelson, Albert Abraham, 383

Middle Ages, 4, 6–7, 118, 145, 150, 153, 178, 215, 219–20, 229–30, 239, 242–45, 251–52, 258, 263–65, 268–70, 273–76, 289, 293, 299, 302, 312–13, 327, 330, 333–34, 336, 356, 416, 453

middle class, 147, 231, 236, 254, 270, 272, 302, 329, 332, 357, 373–75, 394

Middle East, 60, 64, 423

Midian, Midianites, 26–27, 30

Midrash (exposition of the Bible), 64, 165, 168, 170

Midwest (U.S.), 378

migrations, 148–49, 301, 303–4, 371, 374–75, 389, 413; *see also* emigration; immigration

Milan, Italy, 218, 223

militarists, 392, 395

military, military service, 7, 195, 318–19, 352, 376; *see also* soldiers

Mill, John Stuart, 342

Miller, Arthur, 383

Mills, C. Wright, 42n

Milstein, Nathan, 384

ministers of finance, *see* finance ministers

ministers of justice, 316, 352

ministers of state, 352

ministers of war, 316

Minkowski, Hermann, 350, 356n

Minyan, 119

Mirabeau, Comte de (Honoré Gabriel Victor Riqueti), 311

miracles, 181, 291

Mishna, 166–70, 173, 207, 309

Mishna, "canonization" of, 168

*Mishneh Torah* (Moses Maimonides), 181

mission, Jewish, 203, 458–59

missionaries, Christian, 140

Mithridatic Wars, 87–88

Mitzvoth, the 613, 289
Moab, Moabites, 46, 49
Moabite Stone, 46
Modern Age, modern life, modern period, 7, 195, 207, 252, 263, 273, 293, 299–300, 323, 324, 330, 341–42, 353–54, 416, 453
Modigliani, Amedeo, 342
Mohilever, Samuel (1824–98), 417
Molko, Solomon, 284
Moloch, Canaanite god, 38, 47
monarchy, monarchists, 41, 314; see also kings, kingship
monasteries, 95, 128, 132, 269
monasticism, 148
money, 265–71, 303–4, 353
moneylenders, moneylending, 87, 231, 238, 268–70, 303–4
Mongolia, 244
Mongols, 196, 244, 414
monotheism, 21, 29, 41, 45, 56, 111, 116, 191
Montaigne, Michel Eyquem de, 218
Montefiore, Moses, 352
Montesquieu, Charles de Secondat de, 411
Montpellier, France, 267
Moors, 180, 197, 229
morality, morals, 8, 45, 55, 57, 75, 76–77, 108–9, 163, 167–68, 170, 253, 257, 266–67, 289, 332, 335, 386–87, 416, 460
Mormons, 3

Moroccan Jews, 180, 434
Mortara, Ludovico, 316
Mosaic Law, Mosaic Code, Mosaic laws, 26, 32–35, 55, 77, 83, 118, 133, 153–54, 164–65, 226, 275, 314, 373
Mosaic religion, see Judaism
Mosaic tradition, 142
Moscow, Russia, 248, 318, 321
Moses (lawgiver and prophet), 132, 192; the code of laws of, 18, 32–35, 55; the Decalogue of, 21; the Exodus from Egypt under, 24, 38, 72, 459; the Five Books of (the Pentateuch), 31, 39; Moses as prophet, 24–37; his place in civilization of Palestine, 52; his enrichment of Jewish religious thought, 58; as author of the Pentateuch, 63–64; dream of a unified Jewish people, 65, 192; meeting with Zipporah, 128; the revelation of, 164; as shepherd, 189; appearance of God to, 192; descendants of, 218; importance of his ideas, 460
Moses and Monotheism (Freud), 29
Moses ben Maimon, see Maimonides, Moses

Moses ben Nachman, 244
Moses, Five Books of; *see* Five Books of Moses
mosques, 58, 415
motion picture industry, 383
Mount Horeb, 26
Mount Sinai, 18, 39, 52, 203, 276
Muhammad (569–632), 6, 189, 191–95, 346, 423
Muhammadan Empire, Muhammadanism, Muhammadans, 3, 4, 6, 189–96, 197, 200, 203, 204, 205, 209, 219, 223, 239, 244, 263, 279, 410*n*, 414; *see also* Islam; Muslims
Muhammed the Wolf, 127–28
Muller, Hermann Joseph, 383
Munich, Germany, 395
Muratorian Canon (of the New Testament), 147
murder, 37, 120, 257, 326–27, 330–31, 335, 392, 394, 399–400, 407–8
Muruba'at, 103
Muscovites, 194
music, musicians, 3, 118, 256, 260, 346, 352, 356, 384, 392
musical comedy, 383
Muslims, 58, 176–77, 181, 195–96, 226, 237, 453, 458; *see also* Islam; Muhammadanism
muzhiks (Russian peasants), 202, 249

Mycenaean civilization, 127
mysticism, mystics, 4, 114, 224, 263, 276, 281, 288–89, 459
*Myth of the Twentieth Century, The* (Alfred Rosenberg), 335
mythology, myths, 277, 288–89

Nabateans, 85, 90
names, 346
Naples, Italy, 218, 224, 316
Naples, University of, 198
Napoleon Bonaparte, 309, 312–15, 319, 323, 412, 415
Napoleon III, 316
Narva, battle of (1700), 194
Nasi ("Prince"), title of the Patriarch, 175
*Nathan the Wise* (Lessing), 307
National Assembly of Jewish Notables, 314
National Socialism, 397
nationalism, nationalities, nationalists, 7, 153, 163, 177, 180, 202, 310, 314, 320, 327, 331–32, 335–36, 357, 362, 366, 424–25, 430–31, 459
natural law, 454
natural science, 261, 278; *see also* science
naturalization, 384
nature, 344, 455
nature worship, 190
navigation, 24
Nazareth, 131

Nazi Germany, Nazis, Nazism, 47, 196, 264, 299, 326–27, 332–33, 349, 370, 382, 391–405, 406–7, 425–27; *see also* American Nazis

Near East, 65, 71, 102, 267

Nebuchadrezzar (Neb-uchadnezzar), Baby-lonian king, 51–52

needle trades, needlework-ers, 378

Negev, Negev Desert (of Palestine), 39*n*, 435

Negroes, 120, 173, 220, 259

Nehardea, 163

Nehemiah: descendant of Zadok, 62; appointed governor of Judah, 62, 175; social-reform laws of, 62; rebuilding of the walls of Jerusalem, 63; collaborator of Ezra, 63; forbids inter-marriage with non-Jews, 63; introduction of the Pentateuch, 63–64; decrees the reading of the Penta-teuch on the Sabbath and during the week, 64; the innovations of, 65; decree regarding reading of the Torah, 118–19; canonization of the Five Books of Moses, 164; decree re-garding interpreters of the Torah, 165; cup-bearer to the Persian king, 175; his role in Jewish history, 459

Neisser, Albert Ludwig Siegmund, 350

Nelson, Horatio, 415

neo-Orthodoxy, 385–86

Nero, Roman emperor, 97, 100, 142

Netherlands, the, 252, 300–302, 309, 372–73; *see also* Holland

New Amsterdam, 301, 372

New Deal, 379

New England, 373

New Orleans, La., 375–76

New Testament, 54, 64, 94, 129, 132, 133–34, 137–38, 147, 151–52, 208, 242, 332–33, 373

New Testament, canoniza-tion of, 147, 164

New Testament transla-tions, 242

New World, 370–72

New York (City), 301, 372, 379

New York (State), 383

*New York Times,* 383

newspapers, 383, 434

Newton, Isaac, 278, 270–80

Nicaea, Council of (A.D. 325), 146

Nicene Creed, 146

Nicholas I, of Russia, 318–19

Nicholas II, of Russia, 321, 334, 377

Nicholas III, Pope, 282

Nietzsche, Friedrich Wil-helm, 138, 331, 332–33, 335

Nihilists, 320–21

Nile River, Nile Delta, 22, 26

Nilus, Sergei, 331, 334–35
Nineveh: seizure of the throne by Tiglath-Pileser III, 48; Assyrian capital, 48, 51; sacked by Babylonians, 51
Noah: Shem, one of the three sons of, 18
Nobel prizes, Nobel prize winners, 3, 342, 349, 351, 382–84
nobles, nobility, 71, 218, 224, 234, 236, 247, 254–55, 265, 268–69, 272–74, 299, 304, 305–6, 310, 312, 320
Nodel, Julius J., xiii
nomads, 5, 21, 22, 33, 39, 45, 116, 121, 148, 154, 193, 456
non-Aryans, 332
nonbelievers, 219, 225, 242
non-Christians, 150, 219
non-Jews, 63, 121, 140, 171, 219–20, 267
non-Muhammadans, 195
Nordic Aryans, Nordics, 333, 349
North Africa, 8, 86, 194, 196, 216, 229, 267
North America, 301, 369, 372n, 373
Northern Europe, 223, 234
Northern Kingdom, 31; see also Israel, Kingdom of
Norway, Norwegians, 217, 406
Norwich, England, 241
Notables, National Assembly of, see National

Assembly of Jewish Notables
notes of indebtedness, 266, 267
novels, 359
nuclear energy, nuclear fission, 351–52
Numbers (biblical book), 21, 32, 63
numbers, numerology, 278
numerals, Arabic, 198
Nuremberg Laws (1935), 396, 398
Nuremberg Trials, 402, 405
Nystadt, Treaty of (1721), 249

oaths, 120
Occident, the, 71
occult philosophy, occultism, 277
occupations, 256, 260, 270, 318, 320, 380
Ochs, Adolph S., 383
Ockham, William of, 238–39
Octavian Augustus, 88; see also Augustus
Odessa, Russia, 417
Odets, Clifford, 383
Offenbach, Jacques, 342
office, public, see public office
old-folks' homes, 379
Old Testament, 19n, 28, 31, 40, 54, 57, 61–62, 111–12, 118, 128, 147, 151–52, 175, 191, 208, 219, 226, 237, 240, 242, 311, 367, 373; see also Bible
Old Testament, canonization of the, 147

Old World, 370
Olga, Princess, of Russia, 202
Omar Khayyám, 201
Omar, Pact of (A.D. 637), 195, 237
omnipotence (of God), 166
Omri: king of Israel, 46; wars of, 46; shifts of capital of the Kingdom of Israel to Samaria, 46; marriage of son Ahab to Jezebel, 46
Oppenheimer, father of Joseph Süss Oppenheimer, 275
Oppenheimer, Joseph Süss (1698–1738), 274
oppression, *see* persecution of Jews
optics, 261
Oral Law, 83, 94, 163, 167–68, 207, 276
ordeal, trial by, 74
organ, 387
"Organization for Culture and Science," 345
Orient, the, 71
Oriental religions, 289
Orientals, 109
original sin (in Christianity), 141–42
*Origins of Totalitarianism, The* (Arendt), 329
orphans, 119, 319
Orthodox Judaism, Orthodoxy, 19n, 76, 173, 227, 257, 308, 346, 358, 360, 366, 380, 386–88, 417, 419
orthodoxy, 323

Osiris, pagan god, 152
ostracism, 254
Ostrogoths, 148, 154, 216
Ottolenghi, Giuseppe, 316
Ottoman Empire, Ottoman Turks, 196, 229, 301, 415, 421
Oxford College, 163

"P" documents ("Priestly Code"), 31
Pact of Omar, *see* Omar, Pact of
paganism, pagans, 4, 5, 11, 17, 21–22, 36, 41, 45, 53, 71, 76–79, 84, 93, 110, 120, 140, 150–54, 191, 202–3, 217–18, 219, 239, 263, 289, 347, 397, 458
paideia, 199
painters, painting, 37, 116–17, 256–57, 355, 356; *see also* art
Pale of Settlement, 249, 318–20, 322, 363–64, 368, 378n, 386
Palestine, 6, 17, 25, 37–38, 41–45, 52, 61, 65, 74, 77–81, 84, 99, 111, 121, 127, 166, 167, 175, 182, 190, 194, 196, 207, 221, 326, 359, 360, 370, 379, 410–11, 412–17, 420–24, 425–27, 433, 456–57; *see also* Canaan
Palestine Liberation Organization, 437, 440–41, 446–48, 449–50
Palestine Mandate, 127, 426–27, 428, 433
Palestinian Jews, 74, 420–21

Palestinian Judaism, 389
pantheism, 459
Papacy, 11, 150, 216, 220, 221, 225, 228, 230, 235, 242, 244, 258, 259, 270, 282–83, 315, 397, 406
papal bulls, 230–31, 241
Papal States, expulsion of Jews from, 231–32
Pappenheim, Gottfried Heinrich zu, 233
papyrus, 24
parables, 133, 291
parents, parental authority, 43
Paris, France, 311
Paris, University of, 251
Parkes, James, 152
Parliament, Russian, 322
parliamentary reform, 321
Parrington, Vernon Louis, 377
Parthia, Parthians, 91, 92, 102–3, 105, 163
Passover, 25, 96, 108, 131n, 133, 240
Passover Haggadah, see Haggadah
Patent of Tolerance (of Joseph II, of Austria), 305, 317
paternalism, 317
pathology, 350
patriarch, 19, 22, 167, 175, 192, 460
patricians, 87, 111, 113
patriotism, 148
Paul (Christian apostle), 3, 19, 29–30, 95, 110, 113, 138–42, 151, 191, 207, 208, 243, 248, 292, 335, 346, 347, 397, 460

Pauline Christianity, Pauline Christology, 141–42
Pauline Epistles, see Epistles (of Paul)
Paulo Christiani, Fra, 244
pawnbrokers, 256
peace, Peace Party, 39, 41–42, 45, 47, 93, 99, 121
Pearl Harbor, 381n
peasants, 233, 246–47, 249, 253–54, 260, 263, 305, 317, 320, 334, 375, 378, 380, 424
peddlers, peddling, 256, 260, 318, 334, 376, 378, 380
pederasty, 108
Peel Commission, 426–27, 428
penance, 290
Pentateuch, 31, 63–64, 308; see also Five Books of Moses; Torah
Pentateuch, reading of the, 64
"People of the Book," 191
people, the, 310; see also common people
People's Bank, of Italy, 316
pepper trade, 268
Pereire, Émile, 352
Pereire, Isaac, 352
Peretz, Isaac Loeb (1852–1915), 363, 364
Periclean Age, Greece, 360
persecution of Jews, 150–51, 154, 227–28, 236–37, 239–42, 245, 250–51, 326–27, 417–18; see also discrimination; pogroms

Persia and the Persians: as a great power, 4, 59–60; relations of, to the Jews, 17, 112, 165, 175; as rulers of Asia Minor, 59; origins of, 59–60; founding of the Persian Empire by Cyrus the Great, 60; extension of, by Cyrus the Great, 60; nontolerance of royal house in Judah, 62; an Aryan people, 72; invaded by Greeks, 72; defeated by Greeks, 72–73, 117; conquered by Alexander the Great, 73; Parthia formed from the remnant of, 92; conquest of Babylonia, 116; Jews permitted to return to Palestine, 116; formerly Parthia, 163; Zoroastrianism (religion of the Persians), 169; beginnings of Talmudism, 173; Nehemiah appointed cupbearer to the king, 175; Sassanians inheritors of the former Persian Empire, 175–76; interest of, in science, 194; Persians' fear of Tatars of Khazar, 202; war declared on by Abu Isa, 205; payment of taxes by the Jews, 239; civilization, 253; wars between Persian and Byzantine armies, 414; victory in Palestine (A.D. 614), 414

Persian Gulf, 190

Persian Jews, 164–65

Persian language, 198

"personality cult," 10

Pétain, Henri Philippe, 340

Peter the Great, of Russia, 194, 248

Petrarch, 224

Pfefferkorn, Johann Joseph, 251

Pharaoh, ruler of Egypt, 22, 25–26, 30, 91, 240

Pharisees ("Separatists"), 82–84, 90, 93–94, 96, 98–99, 108–9, 132, 137, 166, 207, 290, 309, 386, 390

Pharsalus, battle of (48 B.C.), 88

Philadelphia, Pa., 379

Philadelphus (Ptolemaic king), see Ptolemy Philadelphus

philanthropists, philanthropy, 376–77

Philip II (of Spain), 300

Philippians, 141

Philistines, 4, 42, 49

Philo, Jewish philosopher (A.D. 35–40), 113–14, 130, 139

philology, 208

philosophers, philosophy, 3, 4, 6, 9, 33–35, 71–72, 76, 98–100, 108–9, 111, 113–14, 116, 154, 170, 178, 180–82, 194, 199–200, 208, 224, 252, 256, 261, 267, 271,

276–77, 276n, 279–81, 292, 307–9, 331–32, 343–44, 355, 358, 365, 367, 370, 411, 455, 459; see also Greek philosophers
Phoenicia, Phoenicians, 4, 5, 40, 45, 47, 49, 53
phylacteries, 137, 207, 362
physicians, 121, 170, 181, 201, 207, 254, 260, 293, 361, 380
physics, physicists, 3, 342, 350–51, 355, 383
Piatigorsky, Gregor, 384
Pico della Mirandola, Count Giovanni, 279
Picquart, Georges, 338–40
pietists, 77
piety, 170, 345
pigs, 171
Pilate, Pontius, see Pontius Pilate
pilgrims, 134
Pinsker, Judah (1821–91), 417–18, 421
Pissarro, Camille, 342
Pitt, William, 303
Pittsburgh, Pa., 378
Pius XI, Pope, 397
plastic arts, 37
Plato, 114, 166, 199
plays, playwrights, 256, 382–83; see also drama
pleasure, see hedonism
plebeians, 87
Pliny (Roman scholar), 130
Pliny the Younger, 143–44
Plochmann, George Kimball, xiv
Pobedonostsev, Konstantin Petrovich, head of the Holy Synod in Russia, 320–21
Poe, Edgar Allan, 88–89, 425
poetry, poets, 71, 116, 118, 170, 197, 199, 200–202, 253, 256, 261, 278, 360–62, 364
pogroms, 247–48, 249, 262, 321, 361, 377, 417
Poland, 71, 217, 232, 241, 245–48, 249, 255, 259, 263, 268, 270, 287, 317, 380, 393, 398, 406, 417, 429, 458
Poles, 246–47, 305, 318–19, 378, 398–99, 404–5
Poliakov, Samuel, 320
police, 312, 317, 320
Polish Jews, 47, 285, 433
political freedom, 73, 322
political Zionism, political Zionists, see Zionism, Zionists
politics, 42, 47, 50, 53, 82–84, 93–94, 210, 263, 299, 310, 318, 321–22, 330, 340, 352, 354, 357, 360
Poltava, battle of (1709), 194
polygamy, 43, 313
polytheism, 29
Pompey, Gnaeus, 85–86, 88, 90, 215
Pontius Pilate, Roman procurator, 133, 136–37
popes, see Papacy
"Popular Assembly" (of ancient Israel), 39, 62
pork, 171

Portia (character in *Merchant of Venice*), 238
Portugal, 229, 283, 301, 342*n,* 372
Portuguese, 372
Portuguese Inquisition, 229
Portuguese Jews, 229
potash industry, 351
poverty, 43, 87, 121, 216, 269, 306, 319–20, 345, 378–79, 419
*Power* (Feuchtwanger), 274
practices, Jewish, 345–46
Prague, Bohemia, 255, 260, 268, 305
prayer, prayers, 4, 20, 58, 65, 83, 118, 134, 151, 346, 388
prayer books, 65
prejudice, 127, 460
premiers, 340
priesthood, priests, 30, 34, 46, 56–57, 62, 78, 83–84, 85, 94, 118, 166, 218, 247, 248, 253–54, 386, 390, 460; *see also* High Priests
"Priestly Code," 31
prime ministers, 7, 316, 342, 352
primitivism, 357
princes, 250, 254–55, 258, 270, 293, 299
printers, printing presses, 260, 302–3
procurators, Roman, 92, 98–99, 133, 175, 300
professionals, professions, 237, 254, 256, 270, 318, 329–30, 354–55, 379–80, 394, 396, 416
"projection," 20

Promised Land, 26–27, 38, 459; *see also* Canaan; Palestine
property, property rights, 167, 259, 266, 351
prophecy, prophets, 23, 26–27, 32, 38, 47, 50, 56–58, 65, 75, 83, 114, 133–34, 152, 163, 169, 177, 181, 191, 277, 281, 360, 386, 417, 453, 456, 459
proselytization, 95, 110, 121, 151, 153, 191, 248, 397, 460
prostitution, 36, 38, 46–47, 108
Protestant Church, Protestantism, Protestants, 58, 134, 138, 153, 204, 207, 223, 233, 235, 246, 271, 283, 300–302, 305, 306, 327, 335, 365, 397
*Protocols of the Elders of Zion* (Sergei Nilus), 334
Proust, Marcel, 342
provinces, 255
Prussia, 248, 306–7, 312, 316
Prussian Jews, 309
Psalms, 59
psychiatrists, psychiatry, 3–4, 20, 348–49
psychoanalysis, psychoanalysts, 3–4, 8–9, 20, 348–49, 367
Ptolemaic Empire, Ptolemaic kings, Ptolemies, 74, 77, 81, 88, 190
Ptolemy, successor to Alexander the Great, 74

Ptolemy Philadelphus, 112
public office, 87, 111, 153, 195, 218, 287, 316, 322, 342, 352–53, 375, 383
public schools, 305–6, 379; *see also* schools
publishers, 383
Pulitzer, Joseph, 383–84
Pumpaditha, 163
Punic Wars, 86
punishment, 76, 95, 200; *see also* reward and punishment
Purgatory, 270
purification rites (ritual), 95, 132
Puritans, Puritanism, 35, 255, 303, 373
Pushkin, Aleksander, 360
Phyhäjärvi, Lake, 217
pyramids, 24
Pyrenees, 194

quadrant, 279
Quakers, 82, 94
quarter, Jewish, *see* Jewish quarter
Quisling, Vidkun, 406
Quraish Arabs, 190–93

rabbinic literature, *see* literature, rabbinic
"rabbinism," 205
rabbis, rabbinate, 36, 58, 74, 83, 85, 98, 103, 117–18, 131, 133, 137, 166–68, 172–73, 178–79, 205–7, 243, 259, 267, 270, 281, 282, 287, 291, 302–3, 313, 319, 357–58, 364, 376, 384–85, 386–87, 390, 419, 459

Rabi, Isidor Isaac, 383
race prejudice, racism, racists, 252, 323–25, 327, 330–33, 335–36, 340–41, 396, 409
Rachel (matriarch), 128
railroads, 352, 376
Raleigh, Walter, 371
Rambam, *see* Maimonides, Moses
Ramses, Egyptian name, 30
Ramses, new capital of Egypt, 25
Rameses II, Egyptian Pharaoh, 25
ransoming of slaves, 118
rape, 37, 216, 221, 257
Rashi (Rabbi Shlomo Itzhaki, 1040–1105), 178–79, 183, 227, 459
Rasputin, Grigori Efimovich, 321–22
rationalism, rationalists, 4, 178, 180–83, 200, 203, 208, 277, 310, 343, 365, 455; *see also* reason
*Rationalism in Europe* (Lecky), 261*n*, 268*n*
Ravenna, Italy, 218, 269
reaction, reactionaries, 314, 319–22, 339, 407
reading, 261
Reading of the Law, Reading of the Torah, 64, 118–19
realism, 360
reason, 167–68, 199–202, 232, 288, 299, 344, 365; *see also* rationalism
Reason, Age of, *see* Age of Reason

Reccared, Visigothic king, 216, 218–19, 226
Reconquistadores, 226
recreational centers, 379
Red Army (of Russia), 142, 322
Red Sea (Reed Sea), 26, 190
redeemers, 36, 141–42
redemption, 4, 142, 289–90, 303
Reed Sea (Red Sea), 26
reform, 322
Reform Jews, 173, 419
Reform Judaism, Reform movement, 308–9, 345–46, 384–88, 390–91
reform orthodoxy, see neo-Orthodoxy
reform, parliamentary, see parliamentary reform
Reformation, the, 11, 180, 204, 215, 220, 223, 231–36, 245, 251, 258, 272, 327–28
reformers, 134
reforms, religious, 55, 133–34
Rehoboam: son of Solomon, 44; succeeds Solomon as king of Judah, 44–45; revolt of the ten Northern tribes of Israel against, 44
Reichstag, Reichstag members, 353, 396
Reiner, Fritz, 384
Reinhardt, Max, 352
Reitlinger, Gerald, 392n
relativity, theory of, 349, 350

relief agencies, public, 379
relief organizations, Jewish, 319, 379
religion, 3, 5, 6, 8, 41, 43, 57–58, 82, 215, 253, 263, 272, 292–93, 299, 327–29, 343, 348–49, 366–67, 375, 384–85
religion, Mosaic, see Judaism
religious conformity, see conformity, religious
religious disputations, see disputations, religious
religious freedom, 11, 45, 73, 81, 219, 229
religious life, 266–67, 385; see also life
religious intolerance, see intolerance
religious services, see worship
Rembrandt van Rijn, 301–2
remission of sins, 95
Remus, co-founder of Rome, 86, 218
Renaissance, 71, 180, 215, 220, 223–24, 231, 234, 256–58, 269, 279, 340, 359
Renaissance, Jewish, 357
Renan, Ernest, 139, 344
Renoir, Pierre, 342, 355
rent, 351
Representatives (of the United States), 375
republic, republican form of government, 87
Republic, French, 311
Responsa, 118, 163, 168, 172, 179, 256

rest, day of, *see* Sabbath
restrictions, restrictive legislation, *see* discrimination
resurrection, 21, 94, 137–38, 141, 152, 277, 289
retail trade, 303, 376, 380
Reuben, Tribe of, 283
Reuchlin, Johann (1455–1522), 223–24, 251, 280
Reuveni, David, 283–85
revelation, 164, 203, 261, 290, 386
revolution, revolutions, 164, 200, 232, 235, 245, 247, 272, 309, 310–11, 314–17, 330, 375, 381, 411–12, 416
Revolution of 1830–1831, 315
Revolution of 1848, 317, 416
Revolution of 1849, 315–16
revolutionaries, revolutionary movements, 315–16, 321, 323
Revolutionary War, American, *see* American Revolution
reward and punishment, 76, 95
Rhine River, 253
Rhineland (Germany), 246, 250
Ricardo, David, 351
Ricci, Gregorio, 350
Rice, Elmer, 382–83
Richard the Lionhearted, 181
Riencourt, Amaury de, *see* de Riencourt, Amaury

Riesser, Gabriel, 353
righteousness, 56, 163
rights, civil, *see* civil rights
rights of man, 216, 331–32; *see also* human rights
rights, social, *see* social rights
Rindfleisch (14th-century German Jew-baiter), 242
Risorgimento (of Italy), 316
ritual, 21, 45, 58, 94, 166, 364, 390, 460; *see also* customs
ritual-murder accusations, 220, 230–31, 240–41, 242–43, 246, 250, 262
"Roaring Twenties," 381
Robespierre, Maximilien François Marie Isidore de, 10, 311, 411–12
Rodgers, Richard, 383
Romains, Jules, 342
Roman Catholic Church, Roman Catholicism, Roman Catholics, 246–47, 248; *see also* Catholic Church
Roman Empire, Romans, Rome: influence of, on history of man, 4; Hellenization of, 5; conquest of Greece by, 45; relations of Jews to, 17; destruction of Etruscan culture, 38; constitutional monarchy of, 41; attitude toward religion, 41; destruction of Temple

Roman Empire (*cont.*)
in Jerusalem, 65; defeat of Jews, 78; rebuff of Antiochus Epiphanes, 78; defense pact with Simon the Maccabee, 81–82; Roman perfidy in downfall of Hasmonean kingdom, 82; appeal for aid by Aristobulus II, 85; description and history of Romans, 86–97; Jewish war against Rome, 95; crucifixion of Jesus by, 95, 231; first Jewish uprising against, 95; later revolt of Jews against, 97–106; education of Josephus, 98; siege of Jerusalem by, 98–102; destruction of Jerusalem by, 101–2; destruction of the Temple by, 101; further Jewish revolt against Romans, 102–3; last Jewish revolt against Romans, under Bar Kochba, 103–5, 115; three Jewish-Roman wars, 105, 147, 151, 410–11, 456; Roman citizenship conferred upon Jews, 106; superiority of Jewish culture to Roman, 106; Roman writers' view of the Jews, 107; Jewish population of Roman Empire, 110; Paul's preaching to, 113; crucifixion a Roman practice, 107; collapse of, 122; domination of Judea by, 131; Herod Antipas appointed ruler of Galilee, 132; source of danger to Jesus, 133; Romans and Jesus, 135, 136–37; execution of James, brother of Jesus, 137; Paul a Roman citizen, 138; Pauline Epistle to Romans, 141; Romans' view of Jews after work of Paul, 142; attitude of Romans toward early Christianity, 141; Christians become masters of Roman Empire, 146; persecution of Christians by, 144–45; religious tolerance of Romans, 145, 195; treatment of Jews by, 146, 175, 215; eastern part of Roman Empire taken by Arcadius, 147; reasons for fall of Roman Empire, 147–48; invasion by Visigoths, 148; sacking of Rome, 149; Rome threatened by Huns, 149; collapse of the Western Roman Empire, 149, 209; Christians seek protection from Romans in the

synagogues, 151; esteem of the Old Testament by, 151; barbarian invasions of, 169; Jews under Roman procurators, 175; immigration of Jews into Western Rome, 190–91; adoption of Judaism by some Romans, 191; work of Paul among pagans of Roman Empire, 191; demise of Roman Empire, 195; various sackings by barbarians of, 218; Jews invited by Theodoric the Great to settle in Rome, 218; relations between Constantinople and Rome, 222; Roman gods, 239; Jewish-Roman soldiers, 250; view of Roman emperors regarding the Germans, 250; Roman civilization, 253; establishment of the first ghetto in Rome (1555), 255; non-existence of capitalism in, 264; Roman law of *obligatio,* 266; oppressive rule of Romans, 289, 453; liberation of Rome by Napoleon, 315; Ernesto Nathan elected mayor of Rome, 316; Roman circuses, 321; challenge to, by the Carthaginians, 325–26; 3rd-century Roman empire, 413; Roman Empire becomes Christian (A.D. 325), 413

Roman law, 33, 74, 266
Romania, Romanians, 305, 309, 378, 380, 398, 406
Romanian Jews, 387
Romanism, 87, 300
Romanovs (of Russia), 317–22
Romantic Revolution, 377
romanticism, romantics, 201–2, 359–60
Romberg, Sigmund, 383
*Rome and Jerusalem* (Hess), 416, 421
Romier, Lucien, 312*n*
Rommel, Erwin, 427
Romulus, co-founder of Rome, 86, 218
Ronciere, Charles de La, 371
Roosevelt, Franklin Delano, 352
Rosenberg, Alfred, 331, 335
Rosenwald (family), 376
Rosenzweig, Franz (1886–1929), 365–66
Roth, Cecil, 257
Rothschild, house of, 353
Rothschild, Salomon, 317
Rousseau, Jean Jacques, 251, 307, 308, 312, 331, 411
Royal Academy of Arts, of Austria, 305
royal ministers, 256
*Rubáiyát* (Omar Khayyám), 201

Rubinstein, Artur, 384
rulers, 310, 314, 392–93; *see also* kings; monarchy
Runciman, Steven, 222*n*
rural life, rural areas, 262–63
Russia, Russians, 3, 9, 48, 59, 105, 148, 202–3, 217, 241, 245–46, 248–50, 259, 263, 287, 304, 309, 317–22, 334, 347, 360–62, 377–78, 380–81, 393, 398, 404, 405, 406–7, 411, 417, 458; *see also* Soviet Russia
Russian Enlightenment, *see* Enlightenment, Russian
Russian Jews, 249–50, 304, 309, 317–20, 322–23, 360–61, 370, 377, 385–86, 406–7, 417, 425, 434, 458
Russian Judaism, 389
Russian Orthodox Church, Russian Orthodoxy, 202–3, 248–49
Russian Revolution (1917), 10, 249, 361–62, 411
Russo-Finnish War, 48
Ruth, Book of, 63

Saadyah Gaon (born in A.D. 882), 208
Sabbatai Zevi (1626–76), 285–86
Sabbatean movement, Sabbateanism, 285–89
Sabbath, 35, 64, 79, 108, 110 136, 172–73, 269, 387
"Sabbath-goys," 269

Saboraim, 170, 173
Sachar, Howard M., 392*n*
sacrifice, 57, 83, 109, 134, 386, 390, 460
sacrifice, human, 38, 47, 240
Sadducees, 83–85, 90, 93–96, 109, 132, 166, 208
sadism, 37, 257
Safed, Palestine, 182
sages, 166, 167
sailors, 256
St. Bartholomew's Day, massacre of (1572), 232
St. Louis, Mo., 375–76
*St. Louis Post-Dispatch,* 383
Saint-Saëns, Charles Camille, 342
saints, 277, 456
Saladin, 181
Salamis, battle of (480 B.C.), 72
salesmen, 380
Salk, Jonas, 383
Salomon, Haym, 374
"Salon Jews," 306–7, 309, 352
salons, Jewish, 306
salvation, 131, 191, 218, 220, 276, 322, 348, 358, 367, 418–19
Samaria: made capital of Kingdom of Israel by Omri, 46; capture of, by Sargon II, 48–49; assigned to Archelaus, 92; revolt of Jews against Rome, 97
Samaritans, 92, 153
Samnite wars, 86
Samuel, rabbi, 168

San Francisco, Calif., 376
Sanhedrin, 39, 62, 74, 91, 94, 103, 135–36, 151, 313
Sanhedrin, the Great (of Napoleon), *see* Great Sanhedrin
Saracens, 169, 223
Sarah (matriarch), 18
Sarah, wife of Sabbatai Zevi, 285–86
Sargon I: Semitic king, 18; founder of the Sumerian-Akkadian kingdom, 18
Sargon II, Assyrian king: captures Samaria, 48–49
Sassanians, Sassanid Empire, 163, 169, 175–76, 190, 194
Satan, 244
satire, 257
Saudi Arabia, 423
Saul, first anointed king of Palestine, 41
Saul of Tarsus (Paul the Apostle), 95, 138–39, 140–42
savior, 286, 289
Savonarola, Girolamo (1498), 204, 232
Saxons, 216
Saxony, Elector of, 251
Scandia, Scandinavia, 217, 232, 406
Schechter, Solomon (1850–1915), 387
Schick, Bela, 342
Schicklgruber, Alois, 395
Schiff (family), 376
Schiller, Friedrich von, 392

schisms, 204, 207–8
Schliemann, Heinrich, 127
Schnabel, Artur, 352
scholars, scholarship, scholastic life, 65, 103, 110, 154, 167–68, 178, 198, 208, 224, 243, 253, 257, 267, 277, 280–81, 303, 306–7, 318, 354–55, 358, 370, 377, 379–80, 382, 419, 453, 456–58, 459
Scholasticism, Scholastics, 234, 278–79, 344
schools, 85, 99, 119, 168, 177–78, 307, 318, 434; *see also* public schools
Schopenhauer, Arthur, 342
Schubert, Franz, 342
Schwarzschild, Karl, 350–51
science, scientists, xi, 3–4, 6, 71, 89, 108, 115, 116, 154, 166, 167, 170, 183, 194, 197–99, 216, 224, 253, 256, 263, 277–81, 299, 308, 341–42, 348–49, 355, 356, 358, 367, 369, 371, 380, 383, 455, 458; *see also* natural science
"science of Judaism," 345
Scotland, 232
scribes, 62
Scripture, Scriptures, 55, 99, 147, 165, 199–200, 207, 230, 276; *see also* Bible; Old Testament
Scripture, canonization of, 54, 112
"Scripturism," 205
Scrolls of the Law, *see* Torah

sculptors, sculpture, 37, 256
sectarianism, 167
sects, Christian, 150, 414
sects, Jewish, 93–95, 132, 138–39, 207–8, 357
secular literature, *see* literature, secular
secular studies, *see* secularism
secularism, 64, 197, 200, 299, 317, 330, 386
securities, 265
seers, 56
Seleucid Empire, Seleucids, Seleucia, 75, 77–80, 81, 84, 163, 175, 190, 431
Seleucus, successor of Alexander the Great, 74
self-government, 74, 77, 120, 174, 182, 218, 246, 249, 426
Semites, Semitic peoples, Semitic world, 17–18, 24, 33, 59, 64
Semitic Arabs, 190
Senate (ancient Israel), 39
Senate (Rome), 87, 100
Senate (U.S.), 39
Senators (U.S.), 375, 383
Seneca, 110
Senior, Abraham, 228
separation of church and state, *see* church and state, separation of
"Separatists" (Pharisees), 83
Sephardic Jews, 252–53, 304
Sephardic Judaism, 252–53
Septuagint, 112, 191
serfdom, serfs, 218, 223, 234, 236, 247, 254, 265, 306, 313, 317–18, 319
sermons, 141, 170, 386
sermons, conversionist, 244
services, religious, *see* worship
Settlement, Pale of, *see* Pale of Settlement
settlements of Jews, *see* emigration; immigration; migrations
Seven Years' War, 303
Severus, Julius, Roman general, 104
sex, 22, 35, 73, 148, 257, 287, 290, 348, 359
Shakespeare, William, 201, 238
Shalmaneser V, Assyrian king, 48
Shamai, 167
Shamai, school of, 167
Shaw, George Bernard, 342
Shaw, Irwin, 382–83
Shechem: crowning of Rehoboam at, 44; transfer of the capital to Samaria, by Omri, 46
Shem, son of Noah, 18
*Shema Yisroel*, 203, 275
Sherman, William T., American general, 104
Sheshbazzar, 61
shipowners, 374
shipping industry, 376
shipyards, 267–68
Shlomo Itzhaki, *see* Rashi
shoemakers, 256, 260
*Shoftim, see* judges
Sholem Aleichem (Shalom Rabinovich) (1859–1916), 363–64

shtetls, shtetl Judaism, 259–63, 357, 361, 363–64, 417, 433

Shubert brothers, 382

*Shulchan Aruch* (Joseph Caro), 182

Shylock (character in *Merchant of Venice*), 238

Sicily, 257, 282

Sidon, Sidonites, 47

Sigismund I, of Poland, 246

Sigismund II, of Poland, 246

Silas, early Christian, 141

Silesians, 305

silk trade, 268

silversmiths, 256

Simon bar Giora, 100*n*

Simon ben Cozeba, *see* Bar Kochba

Simon the Maccabee, 81, 83, 86

sin, sins, 57, 95, 141–42, 200, 221, 269, 322, 335, 348, 364

sin, original, *see* original sin

Sinai, desert and peninsula, 26, 33, 39*n*, 435, 436

Sinclair, Upton, 172

singers, 260

Sinic civilization, 9, 457–58

Six Day War, 438–39, 443

Six Hundred Thirteen Mitzvoth, *see* Mitzvoth, the 613

skepticism, skeptics, 19–20, 165, 199

slaughtering of animals, 171–72

slavery, slaves, slave trade, 23, 24–30, 35, 87, 105, 107–8, 118, 147, 153–54, 193, 196, 352, 374

slaves, ransoming of, *see* ransoming of slaves

Slavic civilization, 9, 320–21, 457–58

"Slavophilism," Slavophiles, 320

Slavs, 216, 320

Smolenskin, Peretz (1842–85), 417, 421

Smyrna, Turkey, 285

social agencies, social bureaus (Jewish), 379

social classes, *see* classes, social

"social contract," 299, 308

*Social Contract, The* (Rousseau), 251, 310, 312

social justice, 293, 347, 384, 460

social legislation, 394

social life, social institutions, social progress, society, 8, 12, 40, 43, 45, 55, 178, 227, 231–38, 253, 268–69, 271, 290, 293, 306, 308, 313–14, 328–30, 346–47, 355, 367, 373, 378–79, 387–88, 418

social reform, 62, 85

social rights, 55

social sciences, 358

socialism, 330, 347, 381, 416–17

"societies" (hevras), *see* hevras

Society for Ethical Culture, 386

sociology, sociologists, 37, 55, 387

Sohm, Rudolf, 143

soil, 8

soldiers, 44–45, 101, 103, 256, 316–17, 376, 406, 407; *see also* military

Solomon: son of David, 41; as a peaceful ruler, 41; builder of the Temple in Jerusalem, 41; as the king of Palestine, 41–44, 52; death of, 44; Rehoboam the son of, 44; documents found in the Temple of, 55; rivalry of, with his brother Adonijah, 85

Sombart, Werner, 263–64, 271, 272–73, 353

"Son of Man," 114*n*

songs, 178

Sonnenfels, Joseph von, *see* von Sonnenfels, Joseph

Sonnino, Sidney, 316

sophistry, 109

Sophocles, 109, 199

Sorbonne, the, 163

soul, 114, 217, 270, 293, 367; *see also* immortality

soul, immortality of, *see* immortality

soup kitchens, 319

South (U.S.), 120, 376

South Africa, 120

South America, 229, 301, 369, 372, 458

South American Jews, 458

Southern Europe, 217, 234

Southern Jews (U.S.), 376

Southern Kingdom, 31

Soutine, Chaim, 342, 356*n*

Soviet Russia, 322, 406–7, 434; *see also* Russia

Spain, Spaniards, 86, 148, 153, 163, 177–78, 182, 194, 196–97, 216, 218–19, 224–29, 236, 252, 277, 282, 299, 300–301, 304, 312, 326, 342*n*, 371–72, 458

Spain, expulsion of the Jews from, 227–29, 231, 236, 253, 257, 268, 299, 301, 371

Spanish Armada, *see* Armada, Spanish

Spanish Church, 227

Spanish Civil War, 361

Spanish Inquisition, *see* Inquisition

Spanish Jews, 226–29, 278, 282, 301, 304, 370, 375

Spanish Judaism, 252–53

Spanish language, 253, 303, 375

Sparta, Greece, 72

Spencer, Herbert, 342

Spengler, Oswald, 9, 52–53, 54, 81, 454–57

spice dealers, spice trade, 256, 268

Spinoza, Baruch (1632–77), 4, 178, 277, 343–45, 349, 355, 416, 460

spirituality, 22, 36, 109, 256

stage, the, 256, 382–83; *see also* theaters

stage directors, 256

Stalin, Joseph, 56, 381, 412

*Star of Redemption, The* (Franz Rosenzweig), 365

state, the, 33–34, 39, 121,

174, 218, 265, 266–67, 272, 299, 308–9, 310–14, 329, 331, 336, 353, 360

"state, Jewish," *see* "Jewish state"

statesmen, 6, 316, 370, 377, 453

steel industry, 376, 378

Stephen, Christian martyr, 139

Stern, Isaac, 384

stock exchange, stock market, 353

Strabo, Greek philosopher and geographer, 75

Straus (family), 376

Straus, Oscar S., 383

Stroop, Jürgen, 404–5

Stuart, Gilbert, 374

study, 65; *see also* learning; scholars; scholarship

*Study of History* (Arnold Toynbee), 9–10

Stuyvesant, Peter, 372

Suez Canal, 421, 436, 443

sugar trade, 268, 372

Sumeria, Sumerians, 18, 33, 190

sun-gods, 29

superman, 333, 335

superstition, 76, 169, 181, 240, 254, 261, 263, 277, 281

Supreme Court (of Italy), 316

Supreme Court (of the United States), 34, 136, 172–73, 383

Supreme Court justices, 352

Sura, 163

surgeons, 256

survival, Jewish, 4–7, 10, 20–21, 52–53, 58, 60–63, 100, 115–16, 117–19, 154–55, 163, 167, 174, 198–99, 203, 265, 276, 292, 308–9, 319, 340–41, 353–55, 368, 386–89, 409, 416, 419, 453–57, 459

Susa, city of Mesopotamia, 17

Süss, Michaele, 274

Sviatoslav, Duke, of Russia, 202

Sweden, Swedes, 194, 217, 248, 249, 406

Switzerland, 232, 342*n*

symbolism, 278

synagogue, the synagogue, 20, 58, 64, 65, 76, 83, 118–19, 134–35, 141, 151, 165, 172–73, 237, 242, 257, 258, 306, 345–46, 375, 386, 388

Synoptic Gospels, 132; *see also* Gospels

Syria, Syrians, 49, 53, 74, 85, 97, 111, 190, 194, 196, 423, 437–38, 442, 446–47

Syriac, 198

"Syriac society," Syriac civilization, 9, 454

Szigeti, Joseph, 352

Szilard, Leo, 351

Tacitus, 102

tailors, 256, 260

Talmud, Talmudic Age, Talmudic code, Talmudism, Talmudists, 6, 72,

Talmud (*cont.*)
103, 118, 136, 138,
163–65, 169–73,
177–83, 203, 205–7,
208–9, 219, 224,
230–31, 237, 240,
242–44, 251, 253, 259,
261, 266, 269–70, 276,
285, 287, 288–89, 292,
344, 355, 357, 362, 366,
385, 453, 460; *see also*
Gemara
Talmud, codification and
codifiers of, 179–83
Talmudic Judaism, 390
tanners, 260
tariffs, 154
Tariq, 194
Tatars, 202, 248
tax collectors, 246
taxation, taxes, 17, 42–43,
74, 77, 88, 92–93, 119,
147, 154, 176, 195, 239,
246, 275, 312, 378
Tchernichovsky, Saul
(1875–1943), 361–62,
434
teachers, 35, 58, 119,
132–33, 380
Temple (of Jerusalem):
Solomon's building of,
41; temple in Bethel
erected as a rival to
the Jerusalem Temple,
46; destruction of, by
Nebuchadrezzar, 51;
documents hidden in,
55; the Temple fixed
by law at Jerusalem,
58; Sheshbazzar's re-
building of, 61; com-
pletion of building of,
by Zerubbabel, 61; de-
struction by the Ro-
mans, 65, 101, 313; side
by side with the syna-
gogue, 65; pagan rites
introduced by Jason,
78; rededication by
the Maccabees, 80; the
Temple favored by the
Sadducees, 83; Sad-
ducees as the pre-
servers of the Temple
cult, 94; Hadrian's
broken promise to the
Jews permitting them
to rebuild the Temple,
103; connection of the
Sadducces with, 109;
Jesus' plan to reform,
133; reformation of
the Temple cult by
Prophets, 134; promise
of Julian the Apostate
to restore the Temple,
151; ritual of, 166
temples, 390
Ten Commandments, 21,
25, 26, 35–36; *see also*
Decalogue
Ten Tribes, Kingdom of
the, 44, 52–53; *see also*
Israel, Kingdom of
Terah: father of Abraham,
18; emigration from
Ur, 18; wanderings
and death of, 19
Terror (French Revolu-
tion), 311
Teutons, 217
theaters, 75, 352, 382–83,
434; *see also* stage, the
Theatre Guild, 382

theocracy, 62

Theodoric the Great (c. A.D. 454–526) 216, 218

Theodosius (died A.D. 395), Roman emperor, 147, 220

Theodosius II, Laws of (A.D. 439), 152

theologians, 10, 178–79, 366

theological seminaries, 251

theology, 56, 109, 111–13, 148, 223–24, 322–23, 366–67, 459

theophany, 37

Thessalonians, 141

Third Estate (peasants), 253

Third Reich (Germany), 392, 395

Thirty Years' War (1618–48), 234, 252, 270, 272, 285

Thot, 30

Thotmose, 30

Tiber River, 255

Tiberius, Roman emperor, 96, 137

Tiglath-Pileser III: becomes king of Assyria, 48; wars of, against the Kingdom of Israel, 48–50

Tillich, Paul, 10, 366

Tilly, Johan Tserclaes, 232–33

Timothy (early Christian), 141

Timurids, 196

Titian (Tiziano Vecellio), 223

Titus, Roman general, 100–101, 105

Titus, Arch of, see Arch of Titus

tobacco, 372

Toledo, Spain, 182, 201

Tolerance, Patent of, see Patent of Tolerance

tolerance, religious, 43, 59, 94, 132–33, 145, 146, 169, 195, 204, 306, 313–14

Tolstoy, Leo, 360

topography, 8

Torah, 33, 94, 104, 114–15, 118–19, 132, 138, 139, 163–69, 172, 179, 197, 203, 205, 206–8, 242, 253, 276, 332, 357, 366, 385–87, 453, 457, 460; see also Five Books of Moses; Law, the; Pentateuch; Reading of the Law; Written Law

Torah, interpreters of, see interpreters

Torah, Reading of the, see Reading of the Law

Torquemada, Thomas de, 227–28

Torres, Luis de, 371

Tosaphot ("additions"), 179

totalitarianism, 200, 330, 382

"tournaments of God and faith," see disputations, religious

Tours, battle of (A.D. 732), 194

town halls, 255–56, 258

towns, 234, 255, 259, 423–24, 434; see also cities; urbanization; villages

Toynbee, Arnold, 9, 54, 81, 455

trade, 43, 46, 59, 227, 235, 246, 265–68, 301–2, 353–54; *see also* commerce

trade unions, 353

trades, 237, 256, 260, 305

tradesmen, traders, 6, 234–35, 246, 254, 265, 370, 374–75, 378

tradition, traditionalism, 361, 386–87

tragedies, Greek, 360

Trajan, Roman emperor (died A.D. 117), 102–3, 143–44

Transjordan, 410, 423; *see also* Jordan

translations, translators, 198, 208, 224, 242, 278, 302–3, 308, 361–62, 425

Transubstantiation, Doctrine of (in Christianity), 241

treason, 120

Treaty of Versailles, 393, 395

Treaty of Westphalia (1648), 235, 252, 304

Treblinka, 403

Trent, Council of (1545–63), 386

tribes, 39, 42–43, 58; *see also* Twelve Tribes

trigonometry, 279

Trinity, Christian, 287

Triple Alliance, 316

triumvirates (in Rome), 88

Trotsky, Leon, 142, 322, 381, 411–12

Troy (Asia Minor), 127

Troyes, France, 178

Troyes, Battle of (A.D. 451), 149

Truman, Harry S., 427–28, 429

Turgenev, Ivan, 360

Turkey, Turks, 19, 182, 190, 194, 196, 222, 229, 247, 248, 283, 285–86, 314, 414–15, 421, 423, 425

Turkish Jews, 434

Turner, J. M. W., 342

Twelve Tribes of Israel, 39, 41; *see also* tribes

Two Tribes, Kingdom of the, 44; *see also* Judah, Kingdom of

Tyre, 47

Uganda, 420

Ukko, Finnish god, 217

Ukraine, 249

Ukrainian Jews, 290–91, 360–61

unbelievers, *see* nonbelievers

unemployment, 43

Union Army (Civil War), 376

United Nations, 410, 428, 433, 440, 448

United States, 34, 35, 39, 42, 89, 153, 171, 220, 357, 368, 369, 372, 375, 377, 381, 384, 390, 436, 458; *see also* America

United States Chamber of Commerce, 272

United States, constitution of, *see* Constitution (of the United States)

United States House of Representatives, *see*

House of Representatives

United States Representatives, *see* Representatives

United States Senate, *see* Senate

United States Senators, *see* Senators

United States Supreme Court, *see* Supreme Court

universalism, universalists, 32, 58, 167, 177, 293, 392, 460

universe, the, 277, 281, 345, 349

universities, 163, 217, 246, 251, 262, 277, 280, 306, 318, 354, 379, 387, 415

Ur, Babylonian city: departure of Abraham from, xii; city of Mesopotamia, 17; departure of Terah from, 19, 27

urbanization, urban life, 43, 255, 263

usurers, usury, 269

utilitarianism, 341

Valens, Roman emperor, 413–14

Valentinian, Roman emperor, 413–14

Vandals, 148–49, 154, 169, 216, 218

van den Ende, Francis, 343

van Eyck, Jan, *see* Eyck, Jan van

Van Gogh, Vincent, 342, 355

Vasco da Gama, 279

Vatican, 397

Venice, Italy, 218, 223, 258, 269, 282

Venus (goddess), 88

Verdi, Giuseppe, 342

vernacular, 179, 346, 388

Verrocchio, Andrea del, 238

Versailles Peace Treaty, 393, 395

Vespasian, Roman general and emperor, 98–100, 456

Vespucci, Amerigo, 371–72

viceroys, 342, 352

Victoria, Queen of England, 352

Vienna, Austria, 268, 305

Vienna, Congress of (1815), 314, 316, 318

Vienna, University of, 251

Vikings, 217–18

villages, 232, 246, 255, 259, 263, 317, 434

villeins, 313

Vilna, Lithuania, 357

Vilna Gaon (Elijah ben Solomon (1720–97), 249, 357–58

Virginia, 374

virginity, 148

virtue, 109–10

Visigoths, 148, 154, 216

Vistula River, 317

Vitovt, Grand Duke of Lithuania, 246

Vladimir, successor to Sviatoslav, Russian duke, 202

vocational schools, 379

Voltaire, François Marie Arouet de, 305, 307, 310, 325, 411

von Eck, Johann Maier, 243
von Sonnenfels, Joseph, 305
vote, voting, 255–56, 321; *see also* franchise

wage-earning class, wages, 265, 351
Wagner, Richard, 342
wagonmakers, 260
Waksman, Selman, 383
Waldseemüller, Martin, 372*n*
Wallenstein, Albrecht Eusebius Wenzel von, 233
Walter, Bruno, 384
"Wandering Jew," 200
war, wars, 38, 41, 44–45, 47–52, 80, 86–90, 91, 93, 95–97, 101–6, 120, 148, 190–91, 272, 303, 321, 376, 381, 413, 428; *see also* civil war
war ministers, *see* ministers of war
War of 1812, 319
*War of the Sons of Light with the Sons of Darkness* (Dead Sea Scrolls), 129
Warburg (family), 376
Warsaw, Poland, 268
Washington, George, 10, 50, 374
Wassermann, August von, 342, 350
Waterloo, Battle of, 314, 315
wealth, 43, 54, 87, 94, 255, 304, 346, 357, 380, 418,

weavers, 256
Weber, Max, 42, 271, 387
Weimar Republic, 394
Weizmann, Chaim, 420*n*, 421–22
West, Western civilization, xii, 3, 7, 11, 45, 108, 150, 163, 177, 194, 219, 221, 237–38, 245–46, 252, 255, 269, 273, 277, 279–80, 300, 304, 308, 322–23, 341, 349, 356–57, 365, 366, 368, 409, 431, 457–58
West (U.S.), 375–76
West Goths, *see* Visigoths
Western Europe, Western Europeans, 89, 148, 177–78, 180, 194, 198, 209, 216–17, 232, 236, 245, 252, 253, 261, 264, 270, 278–79, 299, 315, 329, 341–44, 352, 354, 357, 372, 382, 385
Western Hemisphere, 370
Western Jews, West European Jews, 341, 353–54, 368, 406
Westphalia, Treaty of (1648), 235, 252, 274*n*, 304
white-collar class, 329, 333, 394, 424
White Paper (1939), 427–29
white race, 120, 259, 331
White Russians, 322
Wilde, Oscar, 49
William the Conqueror (1066), 231
William of Ockham, *see* Ockham, William of

William Rufus, English king, 231
William III (William of Orange), 303
Willstätter, Richard, 351
Wilson, Woodrow, 383, 393
Wise, Isaac Mayer (1819–1900), 384
witchcraft, 245
Wittenberg, Germany, 231
Wittgenstein, Ludwig, 350
women: place of, in Mosaic Law, 35–36; pagan, 53; laws forbidding inter-marriage, 152; Jewish men attractive to Christian women as husbands, 154; inter-marriage not forbid-den, 154; treatment of Baghdad women by Mongols, 196; Renais-sance Jewish women, 256; Friedrich Niet-zsche's view of, 332; men and women al-lowed to sit together in synagogues, 346; Arab women given vote in Israel, 434
wool trade, 268
"Word, the," see Logos
Word of God, see Law, the; Torah
work, 172–73, 254, 269
workers, working class, 154, 320, 329, 378, 380, 394, 419; see also labor
World War I, 314, 316, 321, 326, 333, 341, 361, 365, 369, 380–81, 391, 393, 421, 422–23, 425, 433

World War II, 48, 369, 405–8, 416, 427
Worms, Germany, 250
Worms, Diet of (1521), 235
worship, 36, 346
writers, 198–99, 260, 329, 356, 359–68, 380, 382
writing, 24
Written Law, 163; see also Torah
Württemberg, Germany, 274

"Yahveh," 19n
Yeats, William Butler, 342
yellow badge, 220, 230, 237, 262, 334
Yemen, 434
yeomen, 313
yeshivas (academies), 64, 100, 106, 164, 168, 177–78, 180, 182, 201, 267, 386, 459
"YHVH," 19n
yichus, 260
Yiddish language, 5, 112, 357, 359–64, 368, 375, 421–22
Yiddish literature, see liter-ature, Yiddish
Young Italy, 315
Youngstown, Oh., 378
youth, youths, 76, 165, 257, 308, 318, 322, 358, 361, 385, 458
Yugoslavia, Yugoslavs, 393, 399, 407, 429

Zacuto, Abraham, 371
Zadok, high priest, 61n
Zadokite Fragments (Dead Sea Scrolls), 128–29

Zadokite High Priest, 61
Zadokites, 61
Zealots, 83, 93–94, 95–97, 98–99, 100n, 102, 208
Zechariah (biblical book), 62
Zedekiah, last king of Judah: capture of, by the Babylonians, 51
"zero," concept of, 198–99
Zerubbabel, 61
Zimbalist, Efrem, 384
Zion, 413, 419
Zion Mule Corps (World War I), 425
Zionism, Zionists, 61, 121, 167, 200, 357, 360–61, 366, 368, 409, 412–13, 415–21, 425, 433, 453, 459
Zionist Congress, 419
Zipporah: daughter of Jethro, 26; marriage to Moses, 26; saves Moses' life, 30; meeting with Moses, 128
*Zohar* (13th century), 277, 279, 287
Zola, Émile, 339
Zoroaster, 189
Zoroastrianism, 169, 277, 289
Zunz, Leopold (1794–1886), 345–46, 365, 385
Zwingli, Huldreich, 232

# READ THE TOP 20
# SIGNET CLASSICS

1984 BY GEORGE ORWELL

ANIMAL FARM BY GEORGE ORWELL

FRANKENSTEIN BY MARY SHELLEY

THE INFERNO BY DANTE

BEOWULF (BURTON RAFFEL, TRANSLATOR)

HAMLET BY WILLIAM SHAKESPEARE

HEART OF DARKNESS & THE SECRET SHARER
   BY JOSEPH CONRAD

NARRATIVE OF THE LIFE OF FREDERICK DOUGLASS
   BY FREDERICK DOUGLASS

THE SCARLET LETTER BY NATHANIEL HAWTHORNE

NECTAR IN A SIEVE BY KAMALA MARKANDAYA

A TALE OF TWO CITIES BY CHARLES DICKENS

ALICE'S ADVENTURES IN WONDERLAND &
    THROUGH THE LOOKING GLASS BY LEWIS CARROLL

ROMEO AND JULIET BY WILLIAM SHAKESPEARE

ETHAN FROME BY EDITH WHARTON

A MIDSUMMER NIGHT'S DREAM BY WILLIAM SHAKESPEARE

MACBETH BY WILLIAM SHAKESPEARE

OTHELLO BY WILLIAM SHAKESPEARE

THE ADVENTURES OF HUCKLEBERRY FINN BY MARK TWAIN

ONE DAY IN THE LIFE OF IVAN DENISOVICH
   BY ALEXANDER SOLZHENITSYN

JANE EYRE BY CHARLOTTE BRONTË

SIGNETCLASSICS.COM

# Penguin Group (USA) Online

*What will you be reading tomorrow?*

Tom Clancy, Patricia Cornwell, W.E.B. Griffin,
Nora Roberts, William Gibson, Robin Cook,
Brian Jacques, Catherine Coulter, Stephen King,
Dean Koontz, Ken Follett, Clive Cussler,
Eric Jerome Dickey, John Sandford,
Terry McMillan, Sue Monk Kidd, Amy Tan,
John Berendt...

You'll find them all at
**penguin.com**

*Read excerpts and newsletters,
find tour schedules and reading group guides,
and enter contests.*

Subscribe to Penguin Group (USA) newsletters
and get an exclusive inside look
at exciting new titles and the authors you love
long before everyone else does.

**PENGUIN GROUP (USA)**
us.penguingroup.com